Mexico
A Comprehensive Development Agenda
for The New Era

Edited by

Marcelo M. Giugale,

Olivier Lafourcade,

and Vinh H. Nguyen

THE WORLD BANK

WASHINGTON, DC

Contents

Part II
Fiscal Sustainability

Growth and Competitiveness

Poverty and Inequality

A Sustainable Future

Acknowledgments

This volume is the result of a team effort and, as such, it has benefited from an array of invaluable contributions. Our thanks are therefore due to a large number of people. First, the chapters' authors, who have provided not just material of outstanding technical quality but a remarkable commitment to enriching the debate about Mexico. We consider ourselves fortunate to share this book with these principal authors—Oscar Alvarado, Ana-Maria Arriagada, Robert Ayres, Christopher Barham, Adolfo Brizzi, Tania Carrasco, James Cercone, Raffaello Cervigni, Richard Clifford, Vittorio Corbo (Pontificia Universidad Católica de Chile), Maria Correia, Rafael de la Cruz, Jean-Jacques De St. Antoine, Joost Draaisma, Stephen Everhart, Maria Emilia Freire, Gillette Hall, Kristin Hallberg, Jonathan Halpern, Linn Hammergren, Elizabeth Katz, Karin Kemper, Luis Landa, William Maloney, Augusta Molnar, Fernando Montes-Negret, Sheoli Pargal, Sonia Plaza, Mirtha Pokorny, Bertrand Renaud, P.S. Srinivas, Mariana Urbiola, Eduardo Velez Bustillo, Walter Vergara, Steven Webb, and Quentin Wodon. All authors are affiliated with the World Bank Group unless otherwise indicated. Other contributors to individual chapters are recognized in the credits of each specific chapter.

While this book reflects the authors' own views (and not necessarily the views of the World Bank, its Board of Executive Directors or its member countries), its production was institutionally housed at the World Bank. We thus benefited enormously from the general guidance of Guillermo Perry (Chief Economist for the Latin America and Caribbean Region), Ernesto May (Director, Poverty Reduction and Economic Management Division for the Latin America and Caribbean Region), and from the auspices of the office of David de Ferranti (Vice-President for Latin America and the Caribbean Region).

We also recognize the importance of and thank the participants at the workshop held on October 12–13, 2000, in Mexico City. This workshop not only brought together a majority of the authors under one roof for two days of candid discussions, but also included Mexican officials from both the outgoing and incoming federal administrations. We are very grateful to all the Mexican officials present at the workshop and wish to express our special appreciation to: Luis Ernesto Derbez, Carlos Gadsen, Angel Gurria, Rodrigo Morales, Carlos Garcia Moreno, Carlos Noriega, Ricardo Ochoa, Moises Pineda, Cecilia Ramos, and Eduardo Sojo. Their comments, suggestions, and inputs added greatly to this volume.

Finally, we are especially grateful to Michael Geller, who managed the production and support team. At various stages, this team included: Claudia Contreras,

Elizabeth Toxtle, Gabriela Vidals, and Liliana Wiesner who not only assisted in the actual preparation of various chapters but more importantly helped manage the minutiae of this large project; Peggy O'Donnell, who acted as our planning and budget advisor; Diane Stamm, the principal language editor; Lee Morrison, who oversaw the Spanish translation of the Synthesis; Christopher Neal, who led the external relations and press liaison team; Paola Scalabrin and Brenda Mejia, who spearheaded the printing efforts; Richard Creighton and the staff of the Magazine Group, who created the design and layout of this book and its cover; and Mariana Perez at Galería de Arte Mexicano in Mexico City and Heidi Coleman at Visual Artists and Galleries Association in New York who assisted in securing the art of Carlos Mérida for use on the cover of this volume. Our thanks to all of them.

Marcelo M. Giugale, Olivier Lafourcade, and Vinh H. Nguyen
Washington, D.C., and Mexico City
January 2001

Foreword

Mexico's economic achievements in recent times have been remarkable. Six years after a major macroeconomic crisis, the country is now the fastest growing economy in Latin America, an investment grade borrower, and a model of financial and commercial integration. More fundamentally, its poverty head-counts are again descending and its creative social assistance programs are beginning to bear fruit. Mexicans can also point proudly to the watershed July 2000 elections as another step toward the strengthening of a modern state that is not only economically sound but also forward looking and responsive to its citizens. President Fox will be leading a vibrant country—a country striving for genuine accountability, where development can be achieved only by government and citizens working together.

However, as Mexicans well know, development is a long, arduous, and complex process. More than anything else, theirs is a country of contrasts—between rich states and states still struggling with poverty; between thriving urban centers and destitute rural areas; between those members of the economy seeking to compete with OECD countries and the majority of the population for whom the promise of globalization has not yet materialized. In spite of its many achievements, and like most of the Latin America Region, Mexico still faces major economic challenges.

This book reflects the knowledge accumulated through decades of policy dialogue, reflection, and operational work, a knowledge enhanced by learning experiences in many countries. By its nature, the book tends to stretch the boundaries of the possible. In many cases, there will be ample room for debate—be it over policy, strategy, or implementation. But I suspect that this is exactly where the excitement begins, especially because we share with the Mexican authorities an unwavering commitment to poverty alleviation.

The work presented here is organized along five overarching themes. They are Fiscal Sustainability, Growth and Competitiveness, Poverty and Inequality, Sustainable Future, and Good Government. The main messages within each of these themes are captured in their respective thematic chapters, and summarized and brought together into an overall agenda in an opening synthesis chapter. The thematic chapters form Part I of the book. Part II contains 29 sector-specific chapters in which the reader can find more detailed, in-depth discussion of the issues, and recommendations on each topic. All this adds up to a compendium on Mexico's development process, one that acknowledges the multi-faceted, comprehensive nature of that process.

We are extremely grateful for the cooperation and contributions of our many friends in Mexico to this very important endeavor, both directly and through several years of working side by side with us. I would also like to thank the staff who have put this together, especially the three editors.

David De Ferranti
Vice President
Latin America and Caribbean Region
January 2001

Editor Biographies

MARCELO GIUGALE, an Argentine/Italian national, holds a Ph.D and a MSc in Economics from The London School of Economics, and a B.A. in Economics from Universidad Catolica Argentina. After a spell in academia, he joined the World Bank in 1989 as an economist in its financial research department. From 1990 to 1994, he was a Senior Economist in the Middle East Operations Vice-presidency, supervising Egypt's structural adjustment program and leading the Bank's reconstruction work in post-war Lebanon. From 1994 to 1998, Mr. Giugale was a Principal Economist in the Eastern Europe and Central Asia Region, responsible for the Bank's lending and analytical economic work in Lithuania and Kazakhstan. In September 1998, he became the Lead Economist and Sector Leader for the Colombia-Mexico-Venezuela Department, the position he currently holds. He held teaching positions at the London School of Economics and the American University in Cairo, and has published in the areas of applied econometrics, finance, business economics and economic development. In 1999, he led the World Bank team that delivered the US$600 million Decentralization Adjustment Loan for Mexico. Similarly in 2000, he led the World Bank team that delivered the recently-approved US$505 million Adjustment Loan for Estado de México.

OLIVIER LAFOURCADE, a French national, is Director of the Colombia-Mexico-Venezuela Country Management Unit of the World Bank, located in Mexico City. Mr. Lafourcade joined the World Bank in 1973. A graduate of Ecole Nationale Supérieure Agronomique of Rennes (France), and holding MSc and Ph.D degrees in Agricultural Economics from the University of Maryland (U.S.A.), he started a career in the Bank working largely on agriculture and rural development projects in Bolivia, Mexico, Brazil, Cameroon. From 1980 to 1982, he was Personal Assistant to two successive Bank presidents (Robert McNamara and Tom Clausen). He then was responsible for the Bank's agricultural programs for several African countries (Zaire, Rwanda, Burundi) before taking charge of the agricultural program for India. He became Director of the European Office of the World Bank in Paris in 1988. In 1992, he moved back to Washington to become Director of the West Central Africa Department (Benin, Burkina Faso, Cote d'Ivoire, Ghana, Niger, Nigeria and Togo), before taking his current assignment in Mexico in September 1997. Before joining the Bank, Mr. Lafourcade worked in Argentina for two years as a researcher in the Argentine National Agricultural Research Institute.

VINH NGUYEN, a United States national, is the Chief of Staff in the Colombia-Mexico-Venezuela Country Management Unit, helping coordinate and facilitate the various sectoral activities under the department's work program. Since joining the World Bank in 1991, he has spent his time equally between direct operational activities (mostly in the Human Development sector) and fiduciary and administrative areas such as quality enhancement, portfolio management, budget, and office administration. Except for a brief turn in the Europe and Central Asia region, he has been involved mostly with Mexico, Central America and parts of the Caribbean. He has an MBA from George Washington University and a B.A. from Amherst College.

Acronyms

ACs	Aquifer Committees
ADR	American Depository Receipts
AED	Academy for Educational Development
AFORES	Administradoras de Fondos para el Retiro
AIDS	Acquired Immune Deficiency Sindrome
ANAGSA	Aseguradora Nacional Agropecuaria, S. A.
ANDSA	Almacenes Nacionales de Deposito, S. A.
APAZU	Programa de Agua Potable, Alcantarillado y Saneamiento en Zonas Urbanas
APIs	Administraciones Portuarias Integrales
ARE	Aprovechamiento sobre Rendimientos Excedentes
ASA	Aeropuertos y Servicios Auxiliares
ASERCA	Apoyos y Servicios a la Comercialización Agropecuaria
BANCOMEXT	Banco de Comercio Exterior
BANOBRAS	Banco Nacional de Obras y Servicios Públicos, S.N.C.
BANRURAL	Banco Nacional de Credito Rural, S. N. C.
BLT	Build-Lease-Transfer
BORUCONSA	Bodegas Rurales Conasupo, S. A.
BOT	Built, Operate, and Transfer
BP	Basis Points
BPAs	Bonos para la Protección del Ahorro
CAPUFE	Caminos y Puentes Federales
CENAPRED	Centro Nacional para la Prevención de Desastres
CENEVAL	Centro Nacional de Evaluación para la Educación Superior
CETES	Certificados de la Tesorería de la Federación
CFC	Comisión Federal de Competencia
CFE	Comisión Federal de Electricidad
CIDE	Centro de Investigación y Docencia Económica
CIESAS	Centro de Investigación en Estudios Superiores de Antropología Social
CIF	Cost, Insurance and Freight
CIMO	Programa Calidad Integral y Modernización
CIPI	Comisión Intersectorial de Política Industrial
CIT	Corporate Income Tax

CM	Cazzora Magisterial
CNA	Comisión Nacional del Agua
CNBV	Comisión Nacional Bancaria y de Valores
COFETEL	Comisión Federal de Telecomunicaciones
COMPITE	Comité Nacional de Productividad e Innovación Tecnológica
COMPRANET	Sistema Electrónico de Contrataciones Gubernamentales
CONABIO	Comisión Naciaonal para la Biodiversidad
CONACyT	Consejo Nacional de Ciencia y Tecnología
CONAFE	Consejo Nacional de Fomento Educativo
CONALEP	Colegio Nacional de Educación Profesional Técnica
CONANP	Comisión Nacional de Areas Naturales Protegidas
CONAPO	Consejo Nacional de Población
CONASUPO	Compañía Nacional de Subsistencias Populares
CONAZA	Comisón Nacional de Zonas Áridas
CONMUJER	Comisión Nacional de la Mujer
CONOCER	Consejo de Normalización y Certificación de Competencias Laborales
CONSAR	Comisión Nacional del Sistema de Ahorro para el Retiro
CONSNET	Consejo del Sistema Nacional de Educación Técnica
CPI	Corte Penal Internacional
CPP	Costo Porcentual Promedio
CRE	Comisión Reguladora de Energía de los Trabajadores del Estado
CRECE	Centros Regionales de Competitividad Empresarial
DEP	Derecho a la Extracción de Petróleo
DGAC	Dirección General de Aeronáutica Civil
DGCC	Dirección General de Conservación de Carreteras
DGCF	Dirección General de Caminos Federales
DGTTFM	Dirección General de Tarifas, Transporte Ferroviario y Multimodal
DICONSA	Sistema de Distribuidoras Conasupo, S.A. de C.V.
DIF	Sistema Nacional de Desarrollo Integral de la Familia
DIM	Dual Index Mortgage
DSH	Derecho Sobre Hidrocarburos
ECD	Early Childhood Development
EEEP	Encuesta de Evaluación de Educación Premaria
EIA	Encuesta Industrial Anual
EMS	Environmental Management System
ENAMIN	Encuesta Nacional de Micronegocios
ENE	Encuesta Nacional de Empleo
ENESTyC	Encuesta Nacional de Empleo, Salarios, Tecnología y Capacitación
EU	European Union

FAEB	Fondo de Aportaciones para la Educacion Basica y Normal
FAIS	Fondo de Aportaciones para la Infraestructura Social
FAMEVAL	Fondo de Apoyo al Mercado de Valores
FAO	Organización de las Naciones Unidas para la Agricultura y la Administración
FARAC	Fideicomiso de Apoyo al Rescate de Autopistas Concesionadas
FASSA	Fondo de Aportaciones para los Servicios de Salud
FDI	Foreign Direct Investment
FDSM	Fondo de Desarrollo Social Municipal
FINFRA	Fondo de Inversión en Infraestructura
FIRA	Fideicomiso Instituido en Relacion con la Agricultura
FISM	Fondo para la Infraestructura Social Municipal
FNM	Ferrocarriles Nacionales de México
FOBAPROA	Fondo Bancario de Protección al Ahorro
FONAES	Fondo Nacional de Apoyo a Empresas Sociales
FONDEN	Fondo Nacional de Desastres Naturales
FONHAPO	Fideicomiso Fondo Nacional de las Habitaciones Populares
FORTAMUN	Fondo de Aportaciones para el Fortalecimiento de los Municipios
FOVI	Fondo de Operación y Financiamiento Bancario a la Vivienda
FOVISSSTE	Fondo de la Vivienda del Instituto de Seguridad y Servicios Sociales de los Trabajadores del Estado
FSC	Forest Stewardship Council
FUNSALUD	Fundación Mexicana para la Salud
GAAP	General Accepted Accounting Principles
GATT	General Agreement of Trade and Tariffs
GDP	Gross Domestic Product
GEF	Global Environmental Facility
ICEES	Instituto de Crédito Educativo del Estado de Sonora
ID	Irrigation Districts
IDB	Inter American Development Bank
IEPS	Impuesto Especial Sobre Producción y Servicios Aplicado a la Enajenación de Gasolina y Diesel
IICA	Instituto Interamericano de Cooperacion para la Agricultura
ILO	International Labour Organization
ILS	Indigenous Language Speakers
IMF	International Monetary Fund
IMSS	Instituto Mexicano del Seguro Social
IMTA	Instituto Mexicano de Tecnología del Agua
INE	Instituto Nacional de Ecología
INEGI	Instituto Nacional de Estadística, Geografía e Informática

INFONAVIT	Instituto del Fondo Nacional de la Vivienda para los Trabajadores
INI	Instituto Nacional Indigenista
INIFAP	Instituto Nacional de Investigaciones Forestales y Agropecuarias
IPAB	Instituto de Protección al Ahorro Bancario
IPP	Independent Power Producer
IRP	Impuesto a los Rendimientos Petroleros
ISAN	Impuesto Sobre Automóviles Nuevos
ISSSTE	Instituto de Seguridad y Servicios Sociales de los Trabajadores del Estado
LAU	Licencia Ambiental Única
LFC	Luz y Fuerza del Centro
LGEEPA	Ley General de Equilibrio Ecológico y Protección al Ambiente
LICONSA	Leche Industrializada Conasupo, S.A. de C.V.
LPG	Liquid Petroleum Gas
MSME	Micro, small, and medium scale enterprise
NAFIN	Nacional Financiera, S.N.C.
NAFTA	North American Free Trade Agreement
NEP	Nueva Estrategia Programática
NGO	Non-Governmental Organization
NHF	National Health Fund
NPR	Nominal Protection Rate
O&M	Operation and Maintenance
OECD	Organization for Economic Cooperation and Development
OOs	Organismos Operadores
OPEC	Oil Producers Exporting Countries
PAC	Programa de Ampliación de Cobertura
PAED	Programa de Apoyo a Escuelas en Desventaja
PARE	Programa para Abatir el Rezago Educativo
PAREB	Primary Education II Project
PAREB	Programa para Abatir el Rezago en Educación Básica
PAREIB	Programa para Abatir el Rezago en Educación Inicial y Básica
PASAF	Programa de Asistencia Social Alimentaria a Familias
PAYG	Pay-as-you-go
PAZI	Programa de Atención a Zonas Indígenas
PCC	Programa de Consolidación de la Cobertura
PCS	Personal Communication System
PEMEX	Petróleos Mexicanos
PEO	Program Evaluation Office
PEP	PEMEX Exploration and Production

PET	Programa de Empleo Temporal
PIARE	Basic Education Project (IDB-financed)
PICs	Pagarés de Indemnización Carretera
PIDIREGAS	Proyectos de Impacto Diferido en el Registro de Gasto
PILEOT	Proyecto de Iniciativas Locales de Empleo y Ocupación Temporal
PIT	Personal Income Tax
PROBECAT	Programa de Becas de Capacitación para Desempleados
PROCAMPO	Programa de Apoyos Directos al Campo
PROCEDE	Programa de Certificacion de Derechos Ejidales y Titulos de Solares Urbanos
PROCYMAF	Proyecto de Conservación y Manejo Sustentable de Recursos Forestales en México
PRODEFOR	Programa de Desarrollo Forestal
PRODEI	Programa para el Desarrollo de la Educación Inicial
PRODEPLAN	Programa para el Desarrollo de Plantaciones Forestales
PRODER	Programa de Desarrollo Regional
PRODERS	Programa de Desarrollo Regional Sostentable
PROFECO	Procuraduría Federal del Consumidor
PROFEPA	Procuraduría Federal de Protección al Ambiente
PROGRESA	Programa de Educación, Salud y Alimentación
PROMAP	Programa de Modernización de la Administración Pública
PRONAM	Programa Nacional de la Mujer
PRONAP	Programa Nacional para la Actualización Permanente de Maestros de Educación Básica
PRONARE	Programa Nacional de Reforestación
PRONASOL	Programa Nacional de Solidaridad
PROPICE	Programa de Política Industrial y Comercio Exterior
PROSAVI	Programa Especial de Créditos y Subsidios para la Vivienda
PSA	Programa Sectorial Agrario
PSP	Private Sector Participation
RAN	Registro Agrario Nacional
RBCs	River Basin Councils
SAGAR	Secretaría de Agricultura, Ganadería y Desarrollo Rural
SAHR	Secretaría de Agricultura y Recursos Hidráulicos
SAR	Sistema de Ahorro para el Retiro
SAT	Sistema de Administracíon Tributaria
SCT	Secretaría de Comunicaciones y Transporte
SE	Secretaría de Energía
SECODAM	Secretaría de Contraloría y Desarrollo Administrativo
SECOFI	Secretaría de Comercio y Fomento Industrial
SEDESOL	Secretaría de Desarrollo Social
SEMARNAP	Secretaría de Medio Ambiente, Recursos Naturales y Pesca

SEP	Secretaría de Educación Publica
SEP–CONACyT	Subsistema de Desarrollo Tecnológico del Sistema de Centros
SIEFOREs	Sociedades de Inversión Especializada de Fondos para el Retiro
SIEM	Sistema de Información Empresarial Mexicano
SINAP	Sistema Nacional de Areas Protegidas
SINAPROC	Sistema Nacional de Protección Civil
SMEs	Small- and Medium-sized Enterprises
SNC	Sistema Normalización de Competencias Laborales
SNCF	Sistema Nacional de Coordinación Fiscal
SNIM	Sistema Nacional de Información de Mercados
SNTE	Sindicato Nacional de Trabajadores de la Educación
SOEs	State Owned Enterprises
SOFES	Sociedad de Fomento a la Educación Superior
SOFOL	Sociedades Financieras de Objeto Limitado
SP	Social Protection
SRA	Secretaría de la Reforma Agraria
SSA	Secretaría de Salubridad y Asistencia
STPS	Secretaría del Trabajo y Provisión Social
SUF	Subsidio Unico Familiar
TELMEX	Teléfonos de México
TIIE	Tasa de Interés Interbancaria de Equilibrio
TORTIBONO	Subsidio a la Tortilla
UCANP	Comisión Nacional de Areas Naturales Protegidas
UDI	Unidad de Inversión
UMA	Unidades para la conservación y Aprovechamiento de la Vida Silvestre
UNCTAD	United Nations Conference on Trade and Development
UPN	Universidad Pedagógia Nacional
VAT	Value Added Tax

A Comprehensive Development Agenda for The New Era

Synthesis

This Chapter was written by Marcelo M. Giugale.

I. Rationale and Organization

It has been the privilege of the World Bank to provide incoming Presidential Administrations in its client countries with a comprehensive account of its diagnoses and policy recommendations for the sectors that contribute to the client's development path.[1] It is hoped that this practice will be particularly relevant and useful for Mexico today as the next President takes office in December 2000 to lead a nation that is changing rapidly and that faces formidable challenges and opportunities. On its part, the Bank will be entering its sixth decade of continuing partnership with, and assistance to, the Mexican government, something that positions it well to take stock of the country's development progress, needs, and options.

This Chapter presents a synthesis—a summarized overview—of Mexico's forthcoming development agenda, from the Bank's vantage point. It is based on and distills the Thematic Chapters that make up Part I of this compendium. Those Chapters are, in turn, supported by some 30 sector-specific Policy Chapters contained in Part II. The purpose of these papers is not to provide definitive answers to the many policy questions that are likely to occupy Mexican policymakers over the sexenio. Rather, it is to provide an independent analysis of the issues in the sectors the Bank is involved in and a set of feasible options to address them. This book was finalized in November 2000; policy developments that may have taken place after that time are not reflected in this work.

---

1. A similar account, in the form of a collection of Strategy Notes, was delivered in 1994 to the then-incoming Zedillo administration.

II. Core Messages

By most accounts, the Zedillo sexenio has been very successful. After a brutal but brief recession following the December 1994 crisis, Mexico has enjoyed 4 consecutive years of economic growth, averaging 4.9 percent over the period 1995–99 while reducing inflation from 52 percent in 1995 to a projected 9 percent in 2000. In doing so, the country has managed to recover most of the ground it had lost as a result of the crisis, and poverty indicators (which are quick to fall during recession and tend to lag during economic recovery) have recently reversed themselves in an unmistakable manner.

The government has also implemented or started a number of structural reforms, most notably in the financial sector (banking and private pensions), social security, and fiscal decentralization. On the other hand, fiscal constraints, increasing political plurality, and a cautious policy outlook have left important reforms still unattended. National investment has also suffered, as austerity programs reduced public infrastructure investment from over 10 percent of GDP in the early 1980s to less than 2 percent in 1998, without the private sector having the adequate incentives to fully fund current and future gaps. Much, therefore, remains to be done in terms of completing, consolidating, and commencing reforms. The remaining agenda can be summarized in five main messages:

1. Consolidate macroeconomic gains
2. Accelerate growth through enhanced competitiveness
3. Reduce poverty through human capital development
4. Balance growth and poverty reduction with protecting natural resources
5. Achieve all of the above by means of an efficient, accountable, and transparent government.

The "storyline" behind these five themes is relatively simple. First, the macroeconomic gains of the last five years need to be protected and consolidated through continued expenditure discipline, strengthening of the fiscal accounts through a comprehensive fiscal reform, decreasing reliance on oil-based revenues, sound management of public debt (federal and subnational, explicit and contingent, domestic and foreign), and so on.

Second, to meet the demands of not just the natural growth in its labor force but also the imperative of ascending to the status of a First World economy, Mexico needs to globally compete its way onto a higher path of long-term growth. This means (a) establishing a sound financial system to both encourage private investment and protect the population's savings (held in banks, in pensions, or in the capital markets); (b) removing barriers against private capital flows through the gradual liberalization of sectors currently dominated by public or quasi-public monopolies (such as energy and housing) and the enforcement of competition-friendly regulations (especially in fast-moving markets such as telecommunications); (c) undertaking structural reforms in various sectors such as water and transport; and (d) dealing with specific cases of market failures or unintended distortions (especially in the rural sector).

Third, the government needs to attend to the human capital at the base of the development pyramid. The first aspect is to protect vulnerable groups which have largely been left behind; the second, to provide them with the basic inputs with which to increase their productivity (that is, a healthy life and a solid education); the third, to remove labor market distortions and encourage migration from the informal to the formal employment sector; and the fourth, to be sensitive to the specific needs of groups such as the indigenous or, more broadly, women.

Fourth, the country needs to do a better job at protecting its environment in order to ensure that tomorrow can bring the same or better use and enjoyment of natural resources as today. For industrialists, farmers, and consumers alike, this means treating resources such as water as the scarce, dwindling, and therefore valuable commodity it really is. For the rural poor, this means developing policies which would help transform the relationship of man and nature from one of tradeoffs (conservation vs. survival) to one of partnership (sustainable use and economic growth). For the government, this means mainstreaming "green" considerations into the regular activities of line agencies.

Finally, the reforms above can be achieved and sustained only through a new contract between government and citizens which elevates to a level much higher than before standards for both government accountability and civic participation. The government will need to learn to respond swiftly to the growing forces and demands of democratization (that is, to become efficient and accountable), globalization (to have transparent and fair processes to attract additional capital), decentralization (to further devolve power to the lowest levels), and justice (to redress social imbalances and create a level playing field).

Behind these five messages, which serve as the organizing themes of this book, lies a mass of diagnoses and policy recommendations. Implementing those recommendations will prove an overwhelming task for any government, making prioritization critical. Therefore, the analysis presented below carries an implicit structure of priorities. The reader will also have to keep in mind the following limitations. First, there are no singular answers in development. What is contained in these chapters is the result of years of experience of Bank staff in Mexico, augmented by what they have learned elsewhere in the world. As is always the case, there is ample room to strategize—and disagree—about what interventions will work best and, as importantly (if not more so), how. Second, the implicit prioritization and sequencing also lends itself to interpretation, depending on one's perception of relative importance and feasibility (both technical and political).

The World Bank stands ready to assist the new Mexican officials in implementing their policy agenda. With a standing Mexico exposure of some US$11 billion, a project pipeline in a broad range of sectors worth about US$1.5 billion per year, and an annual budget for economic and sector analysis of over US$3 million, the Bank can mobilize resources to support Mexico's efforts in policy design and implementation.

Consolidating Macroeconomic Gains

Sound macroeconomic management is perhaps the most important economic success of the outgoing Administration. After the deep financial crisis of 1994, the macro framework was anchored on (a) a tight and fairly independent monetary policy, (b) a flexible foreign exchange regime, (c) a proactive foreign financing package, and (d) a conservative fiscal stance. This not only took the economy out of its crisis but delivered a respectable rate of growth, single-digit inflation, a viable external balance, and a comfortable debt position, all despite three major international crises that dampened economic prospects worldwide (East Asia 1997, Russia 1998, and Brazil 1999). Foreign direct investment has recovered to US$11 billion annually (and growing) from anemic levels immediately following the 1994 crisis. While much of the turnaround could be attributed to the strength of the U.S. economy, Mexico's recovery is nonetheless remarkable, because the country achieved it with virtually no domestic banking system.

It thus seems sensible to stay the course in macroeconomic policy, with one exception: The fiscal anchor has, in its current form, become unsustainable and will likely jeopardize the macro framework in the medium term. Mexico could usefully reassert its monetary policy (for example, by giving the *Banco de México* an explicit inflation target—with the long-term target of convergence to the inflation rate of its NAFTA partners—and the enhanced independence to pursue it); reemphasize its commitment to a flexible foreign exchange regime; and continue to refrain from heavy foreign borrowing, especially of the short-term kind. Yet, these policies may soon become unfeasible, and less than credible, if a program to strengthen fiscal sustainability is not put in place.

Such a program is also particularly relevant as a tool to mitigate the four main macro risks faced by the Mexican economy: a "hard landing" in the United States, a "hard landing" in international oil prices, a state-level fiscal crisis, and a sudden change in "sentiments" if the market expectations raised by the smooth election process prove exaggerated. In other words, Mexico needs to strengthen its structural fiscal position not just because it is a weakening pillar of its macro framework, but also because this framework may have to withstand major economic turbulence during the coming sexenio.

What needs to be done to achieve fiscal and, hence, macro sustainability? Five policies stand out: First, and foremost, Mexico urgently needs a comprehensive tax reform. The country's non-oil tax revenues amount to approximately 10 percent of GDP, a dismal proportion by international standards (comparable to Haiti's, less than Ecuador's, and about half of Russia's). Many tax reform packages are possible, and different tax arrangements are likely to affect different interest groups. Each package should, however, be judged on five merits: revenue impact, economic efficiency, social equity, administrative simplicity, and political feasibility. On those scores, it appears that a "no privileges and better administration" combination is an attractive option.

More specifically, by removing most of the existing exemptions (be they product, income, region, or taxpayer based) from the VAT, the corporate income tax, and the personal income tax, and implementing a major phased improvement in tax administration, the federal government could raise additional resources approaching 5 percent of GDP within four years, with an immediate impact estimated at over 2.5 percent of GDP.[2] This reform alternative implies using the currently-highest VAT rate (15 percent) on almost all products, including most foods and medicines,[3] which are currently at zero rate, and will require a compensatory transfer to the poorer segments of the population. It also implies doing away with geographically targeted corporate exemptions, with the system of corporate "income consolidation," and with long-exempted sources of personal income (such as capital gains and interest). While removing exemptions from corporate and income taxes may be resisted by their beneficiaries, the fact that the package does not modify the current, progressive rate structure, and does not establish new taxes, makes it easier to convey the removal politically under the mantra that all Mexicans will contribute to the fiscal effort and no individual sector will enjoy "privileges." This is the trend that has been successfully employed in other OECD countries in recent times (for example, Italy).

The removal of exemptions will be a key component of the other pillar of tax reform—a major improvement in tax administration. This can be achieved through a combination of three main factors: enhanced taxpayer services (especially of the information technology type); auditing systems that focus on tax evaders (rather than tax "compliers"); and better incentives, management and working conditions for the staff of the tax collection office (SAT). The potential benefits of a more efficient administration of taxes are large: it is estimated that, even if no reform in the tax code were implemented, improved administration of the existing tax structure would produce an increase in revenue of 0.3 to 0.4 percent of GDP per year over four years. In sum, the "no privileges, better administration" package would eliminate the central peculiarity of Mexico's tax system—that is, it has an unsustainably low actual burden that is perceived as unfairly high by most citizens, who resist it accordingly. (Further details of the suggested tax reform package and of variations of it, are presented in the relevant Policy Chapter in Part II.)

The second area where policy effort is called for in order to ensure fiscal sustainability is oil revenue stabilization. Unlike other oil-exporting countries, Mexico's balance of payments is only partly dependent on oil (which accounts for about a tenth of its total exports); yet, its fiscal accounts are dominated by oil (a third of the total fiscal intake is oil related). This introduces a de facto volatility in the overall fiscal balance that has, on many occasions, derailed macroeconomic performance.

---

2. It should be noted that these estimations are necessarily tentative (because adequate and disaggregated data on tax collection in Mexico is not readily available) and based on partial-equilibrium analysis only.

3. As a transitory measure, exemptions on grains, cereals, vegetables, and legumes could be retained.

The possibility of establishing an oil stabilization fund has been explored by Mexican policymakers, and was formally instituted in the federal budget for 2000 (but has not been implemented). While it represents a move in the right direction, that fund would not in its current form solve the problems that it is supposed to address. A well designed stabilization fund is a fiscal institution that would help to implement countercyclical fiscal policies by tying the hands of both Government and Congress, in order to resist short term political and social pressures to spend right away any potential fiscal surplus in good times, so as to have enough credibility to be able to finance compensatory deficits in bad times. Thus, a well designed stabilization fund can not be altered by an annual budget law and has automatic rules for saving in good times and for retirements in bad times, as is the case with the Chilean Copper stabilization fund or the Colombian Oil stabilization Fund.[4]

While such a fiscal institution is enacted, Mexico would be well advised to implement a tax reform of the kind described earlier; project and budget for low oil-related income; and use any oil revenue that materializes above budgeted amounts to retire public debt, especially foreign, short-term, high-rate debt. This will not only carry a certain return in terms of avoided interest payments (and likely, cheaper interest rates for any debt rollovers), but will also eliminate the potential for the real exchange rate appreciation and disruptions in export–import dynamics that large inflows of foreign currency entail.

The combination of comprehensive tax reform and a properly designed stabilization funds, (or debt-reducing oil revenue stabilization) will directly help address the third main source of fiscal sustainability—management of the public sector's liabilities. The explicit (that is, legally recognized) debt of Mexico's federal government is low (about 25 percent of GDP). Even adding the implicit debt (that is, debt for which the government is factually, though not yet legally, liable; for example, IPAB and FARAC), the total "realized" debt burden is not high by international standards (about 46 percent of GDP, which is below the OECD average). However, Mexico faces an array of public contingent liabilities that, if unattended, can overwhelm its

---

4. These Funds exclude from "current revenues" the income in excess of a pre-determined level, related to a moving average of past prices in the case of Chile and to a moving average of past revenues in the Colombian case, so that such "excess income" in good times cannot be included in the budget laws. Thus, the amounts to be saved in good times are not discretional. Both funds also have limitations on the use of their reserves—they can only be invested in foreign currency or used to prepay debt—and have ceilings on annual retirements in bad times—the Colombian fund has a predetermined rule. More recently, several countries have considered broader "expenditure stabilization funds" that would apply such rules to overall current revenues—instead of just "commodity"-related revenues—recognizing the fact that all revenues tend to have an income elasticity greater than one (revenues/GDP ratios go automatically up in booms and down in busts), so that stabilization of just commodity-related revenues may not be enough. This is the rationale behind provisions for expenditure stabilization rules included in the recent Brazilian and Peruvian Fiscal Responsibility laws.

fiscal position. Three such liabilities are of primary concern: the actuarial imbalance of ISSSTE (the federal public sector pension system), the financially unsustainable operations of INFONAVIT and FOVISSSTE (the public housing fund for private and public sector workers, respectively), and the viability of the 31 state-level pension systems (which were decentralized by the federation in recent times).

Apart from addressing the underlying policies that generate those deficits (specific recommendations in each case are presented in the relevant Policy Chapters in Part II, and are summarized later in this chapter), it is advisable to start making provisions for the payment of those liabilities. The cost of such provisions will be somewhat mitigated by the lower interest rates that the federal government will face in its realized (as opposed to contingent) debt—creditors, especially foreign creditors, already know of the contingent liabilities of the federation and are pricing the ensuing risk into their loans. In parallel to provisioning for contingencies, the new government will be required to take a more holistic approach to public debt management. Several public institutions at both the national and subnational level (notable among them, IPAB) are planning to issue debt over the next few years. While full flow-of-funds calculations are not available, it is safe to expect that the sum of those issues will vastly surpass the absorptive capacity of the domestic market and, thus, crowd out the private sector through much higher interest rates. In particular, the original FOBAPROA 10-year, zero-coupon notes will become due in 2005–07 and will have to be refinanced. This calls for a new institutional mechanism to coordinate and program the borrowing of all public sector entities, perhaps with the technical assistance of the *Banco de México* (the fiscal agent in many of the debt issues).

The fourth weakness in Mexico's fiscal sustainability is the health of its state governments' finances. To be sure, Mexico is not Brazil. Its total subnational debt is worth about 2 percent of GDP, compared to Brazil's 20 percent. Moreover, Mexico's subnational governments are forbidden by constitution from borrowing from foreign creditors or in foreign currency. Yet, a "Minas Gerais" episode, although unlikely, is not unthinkable in Mexico. While the roots of the problem are in the nature of the Mexican decentralization process (addressed later), from the federal point of view the solution rests in imposing hard budget constraints on subnational entities.

Much progress has recently been achieved in this area—on the one hand, the federal budget for 2000 did away with the possibility of discretionary transfers to states (by virtually eliminating *Ramo 23*) and, on the other, the federal government implemented in April 2000 a new regulatory system that links the capital risk weighting, and thus the interest rate, of bank loans to states and municipalities to the borrowers' credit ratings. This has substantially reduced "moral hazard" among subnationals and their lenders, because the perceived probability of federal bailouts all but disappeared.

It is critical for the incoming Administration to maintain these hard budget constraints on states and municipalities, and to make a credible commitment not to bail out states by both renouncing any power for discretionary transfers in its annual budgets and by enforcing the new lending regulations, including on its own development banks (especially BANOBRAS). The immediate effect will be that, when unable to continue borrowing, a number of weaker states will find the incentive to undertake structural adjustments in their fiscal accounts. In those cases, the optimal role for the federation will be to facilitate those adjustments, rather than eliminating the need for them. This will be especially true among "early adjusters," because it will carry a valuable demonstration effect to more reluctant states. As explained later, the need for adjustment will also raise the interest of the subnationals in the unfolding of the decentralization process.

Finally, Mexico's fiscal sustainability will be much enhanced through counter-cyclical overall fiscal policy. Partly because of oil dependency and partly because of the nature of the budget process, the federal government has tended to relax its fiscal stance when growth accelerated, and to restrain it when the economy slowed down. This exacerbated economic cycles, and fueled external imbalances (especially balance-of-payments current account deficits). Apart from the required change in policy attitude, two other initiatives could mitigate the problem—building contingency plans into the federal budget and formalizing three-year budget programs.

In summary, policy efforts to ensure fiscal sustainability are a necessary condition for Mexico to enjoy a stable, conducive, macroeconomic framework. As will become apparent below, those efforts are equally critical for two other objectives at the core of the next Administration's likely agenda: competitiveness-driven growth and human-development-driven poverty reduction.

Accelerating Growth through Enhanced Competitiveness

The incoming President inherits an economy that is growing apace, perhaps as fast as 5 percent or more during 2000. While that growth rate is wholly respectable, Mexico will have to accelerate it by as much as 2 percentage points in the long term, if it is to meet the needs and expectations of its citizens, especially in terms of job creation among the poor. (By some estimates, Mexico requires the creation of 1 million jobs per year only to accommodate new labor market entrants, while it creates about 600,000 at present.) In the past, Mexican governments sought to foster growth through interventions that, in essence, bolstered aggregate domestic demand, the result of which were short-lived growth spurts brought to a halt by balance-of-payment crises. Today, with the country already integrated in, and enjoying the benefits of, the global economy and, in particular NAFTA, long-term growth acceleration will be sustainable only if it is achieved through enhanced competitiveness in foreign markets.

A large array of factors contribute to a country's competitiveness, and policy-making should concentrate on those that, for the country in question, carry the largest marginal enhancement. This section focuses on the three such factors which, at present, most hamper Mexico's competitiveness—a weak financial sector, poor infrastructure, and low productivity in agriculture. It is worth reemphasizing that there are other important, direct and indirect determinants of competitiveness (for example, labor reform and corruption); many of them are treated separately in this chapter (for example, labor as part of human development and corruption as part of governance).

Mexico's financial sector is dominated by its banking industry, the problems of which are well known: the 1994 crisis left a serious stock problem (a "bad loan" portfolio effectively absorbed by the taxpayers, equivalent to just under 20 percent of GDP), and an equally serious flow problem (the debt service faced by IPAB for the foreseeable future). Other factors have affected the performance of the banking sector—among others, weak bank regulation, little incentive for debt repayment, no transparency. As a result, bank lending to the private sector has fallen since 1994 by about 40 percent in real terms, consumer credit by private banks all but disappeared (leaving public banks and funds with a virtual monopoly in, for instance, housing lending), and the productive private sector itself became bifurcated between large, export-oriented corporations that can access foreign finance, and cash-constrained relatively smaller firms catering to the domestic market. The travails of the banking industry also stiffened development in the rest of the financial sector—with few creditworthy agents, little reliable information about them, and the court system clogged with collateral recovery cases, it was difficult for stock, bond, or even insurance markets to develop.

In spite of these formidable problems, progress has recently been made in putting the banking industry back on its feet. Following the creation of IPAB; the gradually phased limits to deposit insurance; the introduction of sounder accounting, valuation and bank capital rules; and the congressional approval of new secured lending and bankruptcy laws, a major consolidation effort through bank mergers and acquisitions is now under way, with encouraging participation by foreign investors. Other nonbank financial institutions were also successfully reformed, including the private pension system in 1997.[5]

This progress points to the core policy priority in the financial area over the coming sexenio—to deepen already-initiated reforms. This will primarily involve the consolidation of currently-fragmented regulatory and supervisory functions, enhanced independence for the ensuing regulatory entity, establishment of the necessary institutions to implement the new secured lending law (like registries), and further strengthening of banks' capital position. This last item highlights the important role of IPAB, since many of the weaker banks are under its technical ownership while others count large amounts of IPAB-related bonds among their assets.

Beyond strengthening the banking industry, the next critical area of pending financial sector reform is that of the public pension system (ISSSTE) and of its links with the public housing fund (INFONAVIT). It will fall into this presidential

---

5. Another subsector which may pose fiscal risks are development banks (BANOBRAS, NAFIN, BANRURAL, and the like). At this time, however, not enough information is available to make a judgment on the soundness of their balance sheets and their lending practices.

sexenio to provide a more reliable source of long-term savings for federal employees by allowing the conversion of their current pension scheme to the same privately administered, capitalized, defined-contribution arrangement used by private workers. This will generate an additional fiscal cost (maybe as much as one percent of GDP per year for two decades). That cost is worth paying, because it may be more than offset by the impact of the new system on both the development of longer-term financial markets and, ultimately, on the economy's rate of long-term growth.

Reforming the public employees' pension system will both facilitate and be facilitated by necessary policy actions in two other financial markets—equity and mortgage. Mexico is already seeing the migration of its blue chip firms to foreign bourses due to delays in tackling issues involved in cross-ownership of financial conglomerates (possibly through regulatory firewalls separating businesses), better protection of minority shareholder rights, enhancement of corporate information disclosure, removal of barriers to listing and delisting, and elimination of trading restrictions for foreigners (among others, NAFIN trust fund requirements). The lack of breath and depth in the capital markets (and the legal restriction against AFORES investing in foreign securities) may force the pension funds to go "down market" and invest in companies with substandard risk. In the mortgage market, roughly a third of all pension contributions are allocated to finance publicly-owned housing funds (INFONAVIT, FOVISSSTE) which, through price subsidization, control three-quarters of the mortgage market, are in effect a barrier to private mortgage development, and nonetheless prove unable to satisfy Mexico's pent-up demand for housing (estimated at 800,000 new housing units, and 6 million units in need of repair). INFONAVIT and FOVISSSTE should be reformed (if not decommissioned), put under common regulation (together with FOVI), stripped of their price subsidies (which, if so decided, should be given openly through the federal budget), and given better origination and servicing standards (similar to FOVI's).

Deepening reforms in the financial sector will contribute much to delivering the second pillar of competitiveness—adequate infrastructure. Yet financing, by itself, will not suffice. Bringing Mexico's infrastructure to an adequate level will also require a major change in the way infrastructure-related sectors are owned and regulated. Over the past two decades, the country rightly sought to substitute private for public infrastructure investment. This suited well the fiscal austerity needs of the time, especially since the 1990s. However, the private sector's response did not materialize as fully as had been expected, and Mexico effectively began to accelerate the rate of depreciation of its capital stock (total public investment fell from over 10 percent of GDP in the early 1980s to about 2 percent today; in the same period, total investment fell from about 25 percent to below 20 percent). Even if it (mistakenly) wished to, the government can no longer afford to fill that rapidly growing infrastructure gap—in the energy sector alone, it is estimated that investment requirements amount to some US$10 billion per year over the next 10 years, that is, roughly the size of the annual federal budget allocation for health. Instead, the solution lies in private funding and better regulation.

The nature of the required funding and regulatory reforms varies across infra-structure-related sectors. The electricity sector needs cost-recovering tariffs (residential customers and agricultural customers pay about a half and a third of the service's cost, respectively, a subsidy equivalent to just under 1 percent of GDP); a new institutional organization breaking up CFE into generation, transmission, and distribution and allowing competition at both ends; and independent, tariff- and standard-setting regulation through a vastly strengthened *Comisión Reguladora de Energía*. This would allow for private participation to contribute to the almost doubling of electricity capacity that the country needs in the next 10 years, an investment outlay estimated at some US$37 billion.

Cost-recovering electricity tariffs and the ensuing elimination of cross-subsidization from the oil sector, a new fiscal regime, and new concession arrangements for exploration and production could provide more conducive incentives for PEMEX, the state-owned oil company, to improve its below-par performance. Equally important, there is no valid reason to maintain PEMEX's monopoly in downstream activities (including refineries).

A complete overhaul is called for in the water sector, not least because, as explained later, Mexico is on the brink of a water crisis. That overhaul will involve collaboration at the three levels of government (federal, state, and municipal) to begin to set tariffs that reflect scarcity, to enforce the payment of those tariffs, and to find a new institutional equilibrium, in the context of decentralization, between the federal CNA, at one end of the spectrum, and local water operators and users, at the other. A new institutional arrangement will also be in order for the federal highway and road systems, especially through the merger of FARAC and CAPUFE, the establishment of a functioning Road Maintenance Fund, and an overall, independent transport sector regulator. These arrangements would allow for the capture of longer-term finance, greater private participation in service delivery (including the completion of railways and airport privatization), and network-based concessions.

In brief, much can be done through policymaking to raise Mexico's infrastructure standards, and to see positive results within the sexenio. Still, closing the country's widening infrastructure gap will require major investments, preliminarily estimated at US$20 billion per year over the next decade. Such an outlay is well beyond the financing capacity of the public sector. It is thus critical to give a new role to the development banks, especially as facilitators for private financing. Rather than acting as a pass-through window for federal government funds (and, in so doing, crowding out private financiers), those banks, and in particular BANOBRAS, could help subnational governments enhance their creditworthiness and pool their risks to access private long-term financing, act as administrators of state-specific federal trust funds meant to attract private participation in infrastructure financing, and provide "second-tier" services in the securitization of state and municipal debt. (Further details on infrastructure reforms are presented in the relevant subsectoral Policy Chapters in Part II.)

Finally, Mexico's competitiveness could be much enhanced by policy efforts to remove the remaining distortions that affect its rural economy. This is the sector where, arguably, the most drastic structural reforms have been carried out over the last decade (GATT- and NAFTA-driven trade liberalization, elimination of price interventions, constitutional reform of land tenure) but where the results have been most disappointing (stagnating growth in agriculture, lack of competitiveness, increased rural poverty) in spite of much public support (PROCAMPO, PROCEDE, *Alianza para el Campo*, CONASUPO, ASERCA, and so forth). It is a crude but telling example of its dismal sector productivity that the rural economy today generates barely 5 percent of Mexico's GDP, but employs a fifth of its labor force. Well-meaning structural reforms appear to have led to little or no structural adjustment, an uncomfortable position to be in for a sector that, under the NAFTA agreement, will be put in open competition with Canada and the United States in 2008. What has gone wrong and what can be done now to correct it?

Many of the problems of Mexico's rural economy are either beyond the control of policymakers or heavily ingrained through decades of mismanagement—low international prices, regional and cultural differences, poorly functioning markets, and a history of nonconducive foreign exchange regimes and of counterproductive government interventions in rural financial markets. However, public policies and public programs can do much to improve the conditions under which the rural sector will operate in the coming years.

First and foremost, policymakers should stay the course in preserving macroeconomic stability and in completing the liberalization of the grain sector (by converting subsidization from marketing support to income support to foster a shift toward higher-value crops). Second, they should focus on reducing transaction costs by investing in basic rural infrastructure, promoting farmer organizations and microenterprises, regional exchanges, and prices and market information flows. Third, they should set up a currently-lacking legal and regulatory framework for the operation (and supervision) of nonbank financial institutions, and promote the development of rural financial intermediaries (including savings and loans, commercial banks, specialized institutions, NGOs, cooperative structures, etc.), complemented by financing from second-tier institutions. Fourth, they should establish an adequate regulatory, grading and inspection system for the development of the warehousing market (following the recent withdrawal of CONASUPO), and food safety and quality norms and standards. And fifth, they should increase the efficiency of public support—disconnecting PROCAMPO's benefits from planting, making *Alianza para el Campo*'s programs more effective as a vehicle to promote diversification and technical assistance, supporting more integrated and productive irrigation strategies, and the like.

Reducing Poverty through Human Capital Development

This paper has so far argued that macroeconomic stability and competitiveness-driven growth should be two core priorities in the agenda of the new Presidential

Administration. Yet, stable growth is not an end in itself. It is in fact a tool, perhaps the most powerful tool, to achieve the ultimate objective of development—poverty reduction. Mexico's poverty (and inequality) statistics and their evolution are the subject of much technical and political debate. In the World Bank's unadjusted estimation, in 1996 roughly two of every three Mexicans were poor, and one in three was extremely poor. These figures statistically confirmed what was already a safe assumption—that the 1994 crisis completely reversed the 10 percentage point reduction in poverty counts that Mexico had painstakingly achieved since 1984. And there lies a key message for the new authorities: macroeconomic stability and growth are *necessary* conditions to fight poverty successfully. They are, however, not sufficient.

Virtually all incoming Presidents made commitments to reduce poverty and launched programs accordingly. Much has been achieved (primary education is nearly universal, basic healthcare now reaches most Mexicans, political consensus exists for quantifiable emphasis on the social sector in the federal budget, and the like). Still, judging by the numbers quoted above, poverty remains rampant. So, short of avoiding macroeconomic turbulence, what can the new administration do to reduce poverty that has not been done before? The answer has to do with the *quality* of the public provision of education, health, social protection, and other human-capital-forming services, and with the way the poor can profit from their human capital when they join the labor market.

Mexico's education system has been, and continues to be, the focus of many quality- and outreach-improvement programs (*Carrera Magisterial*, PRODEI, PARE, *Escuelas Comunitarias*, PAREIB, *Telesecundaria*, and so forth). Many of these programs are achieving their objectives. This provides a good stepping stone from which to start addressing a broader challenge in Mexico's public education—to bring the system to the next level of quality, a level more compatible with the demands of a modernizing economy. The current teacher-centered teaching model, which effectively emphasizes memorization to the detriment of comprehension and was designed for the average student, has to be abandoned in favor of cooperative, student-driven learning by investigation, where the teacher is not the source of knowledge and the custodial controller of the students but, rather, the class facilitator.

This new teaching approach will be reflected in the curriculum (which will have to put more weight on critical thinking and communication); in time-on-task (more time devoted to classroom teaching and less to classroom administration and mechanical repetitions—it is estimated that a Mexican primary school teacher spends less than half of the prescribed 810 classroom hours per year actually teaching); in the school environment (teachers will need to have more say about the type and amount of textbooks, material, and infrastructure that their individual classes get, and the government's near-monopoly in textbook production will need to be eliminated to give room to creative competition); and, most critically, in the nature of the mechanisms for teacher and school accountability (supervisor and parent participation will have to focus less on process and more on actual results, as measured by published student scores in standardized national tests). In all these reforms, the teachers themselves, individually and collectively through their unions, will have to be included as partners. All this amounts to a change in the culture of Mexico's education system, a change that will take time but that can be put well under way during the coming sexenio.

A change in culture is also the key to quality improvement in the health sector. In the past, Mexico used centralized institutions and vertical programs to control infectious diseases and increase prevention and education. This brought about major first-generation successes—lower maternal and infant mortality, higher vaccination rates, and higher life expectancy. These and other factors have, however, changed the country's epidemiological profile, whereby chronic diseases and injuries are becoming the main causes of death and disability, new health threats are emerging (such as AIDS and pollution), and increasingly sophisticated consumers demand advanced-technology medicine. This second-generation reality calls for a change in the government's role—away from command-and-control and toward facilitating private provision, while ensuring universal access to an essential health package.

To fulfill its new role in the health sector, the government will need to put in place new institutional and financing arrangements and a different market structure for health services. The current array of public health institutions (SSA; IMSS; IMSS-Solidaridad; ISSSTE; the health services of PEMEX, the Federal District, the police, the armed forces, and other parastatals), each of which has tended to finance and operate health systems with its own facilities and physicians in a sometimes overlapping way, is not adequate to reduce costs and pool risk. The creation of a National Health Fund (NHF) could do away with those problems—it could gather all mandatory healthcare contributions (and the bulk of federal and state health budgets) and act as a strong purchaser of services on a competitive basis from private and public providers, including managed care organizations. This integration-with-competition formula under an NHF would allow the government, and more specifically its *Secretaría de Salud*, to concentrate on certifying and licensing drugs, setting standards for medical training, regulating healthcare providers, funding and coordinating research, and other externality-capturing activities. Coverage, especially basic health coverage, for the poor would continue and expand under the new scheme both through federal and state government payments into the NHF and through those governments' existing, targeted programs (PAC, PCC, PROGRESA, and the like), which would benefit from the purchasing muscle of the NHF to procure the delivery of their services.

It would make little sense for Mexico, as a country, to invest resources in building human capital through health and education without setting up adequate mechanisms to protect that investment, especially among the poor. While technical assessments are generally missing, the available evidence suggests that the outgoing Administration has made very solid progress in social protection. The task of the incoming Administration is, in essence, to consolidate that progress. This will involve parallel efforts on two fronts—carrying out open, participatory evaluations, and closing gaps in coverage.

Mexico currently spends about 1 percent of GDP on targeted social protection programs. The flagship among those programs is PROGRESA, a direct income transfer arrangement for the rural poor conditional on the consumption of selected education, health, and nutritional services. PROGRESA is one of the few government programs that has been evaluated, and has been found to be extremely successful (especially in reducing infant morbidity, increasing female schooling, and raising attendance to basic health clinics). While fine-tuning is possible, PROGRESA should be maintained and, where possible, expanded. Much less can be said of other programs, which lack thorough evaluation. The general trend in food-related programs (Liconsa, Tortibono, Diconsa, DIF Breakfast, and so forth) has been the right one; means-testing has largely replaced universal subsidization. The same appears to be the case for income-generating interventions (PET, PROBECAT, *Apoyos Productivos*, and so forth). Yet, whether these programs actually reach the intended beneficiaries in an efficient manner and, more important, whether critical gaps in coverage exist, is difficult to say.

Program evaluations will thus be instrumental in undertaking the second leg of consolidation—identifying and closing the gaps in Mexico's social protection coverage. Preliminary age-based analysis of social risk suggests that important gaps do exist: malnutrition and lack of access to preschool among the 0 to 5-year-old poor; low primary school attendance among the 6 to 14-year-olds in isolated rural poor areas (especially indigenous); low secondary school enrollment and high inactivity rates among 15 to 24-year-olds in general; low earnings, under- and unemployment among 25 to 64-year-olds; and scant pension coverage for the elderly poor (65 and above). Much more narrowly focused identification of risk pockets is clearly called for, and should guide further public interventions.

Even though building and protecting human capital is the key to reducing poverty, human capital does not by itself reduce poverty. The poor need to be able to extract income from that capital. The link between human capital formation and actual poverty reduction is provided by the labor market. It is therefore a serious concern that the legal and regulatory framework in which Mexico's labor market operates is, at best, outdated (part of it dates back to 1917) and, at worst, an impediment rather than a tool for workers, especially poor workers, to extract the most out of their human capital. It is not surprising that roughly one in every two Mexican workers does not attend the formal labor market and, of those who remain in informality, about half do so against their will. Nor is it surprising that NAFTA investors resent Mexican labor regulations—they impose a "tax wedge" worth 31 percent of payroll, compared with 12 and 19 percent in Canada and the United States, respectively. Put in economic terms, Mexico's labor laws, regulations, and institutions are meant to allow for real-wage flexibility but not for employment flexibility, something that is usually credited for the country's low formal unemployment rate. Yet, this one-sided flexibility better suits a protected economy where inflation is high and unions are strong, than the integrated, more stable, and participatory Mexico of today.

What needs to be done? The current system of severance payments; collective bargaining and industry-binding contracts (*contratos-ley*); obligatory union memberships *(cláusula de exclusión)*; compulsory profit sharing; restrictions to temporary, fixed-term and apprenticeship contracts; requirements for seniority-based promotions; registration of firm-provided training programs; and liability for subcontractors' employees *(patrón indirecto)*, should all be phased out. As with the minimum wage (currently set well below market-clearing levels), the problem with those systems is not necessarily that they bind firms' decisions. The problem is that their cost is effectively born by Mexican workers in the form of low salaries and fewer job opportunities, in exchange for no obvious benefit. Income security of workers could still be achieved through more portable, incentive-compatible mechanisms (like contributions to individual unemployment accounts). Equally important, social security contributions should be more closely related to the benefits workers get, and perceive they will get, from those contributions. This closer association has partly been pursued in recent years (notably, through the reform in the private sector's pension scheme and in health) and should be furthered (for example, by making INFONAVIT contributions voluntary).

Labor reforms of the kind mentioned above will have a subsidiary benefit—they will directly contribute to the formalization, and later growth, of the mass of micro and small informal enterprises that make up Mexico's "other economy" and that, by some estimates, may account for as much as a quarter of GDP. Indeed, eliminating labor-related rigidities, proceeding with the comprehensive financial sector and infrastructure reforms described earlier and, importantly, rationalizing and decentralizing the 200-odd federally-funded, size-specific support programs will positively alter the trade-off faced by the typical informal entrepreneur—to avoid regulatory costs by remaining small and informal ("under the regulator's radar") or to abide by the regulations in order to expand and reap economies of scale. In other words, the objective is not to promote (that is, increase the number of) micro and small enterprises, but to help them develop (that is, grow into their technologically efficient size).

Finally, it is important to note that improving the quality of the public provision of human-capital-forming services and of the legal and regulatory framework for the labor market will work for the "average" Mexican poor. Yet, large segments among the poor also face group-specific needs that may hamper their chances to benefit from those improvements. Two overlapping such groups are noteworthy—women and indigenous populations. While detailed diagnostics and recommendations with regard to these groups are provided in Part II, it is not difficult to illustrate here the issues involved.

Socially ascribed gender roles have placed women at a clear disadvantage in terms of both health (especially reproductive health), education, labor and, most disturbing, personal safety (a 1995 survey conducted in Monterrey, one of Mexico's most progressive cities, found that almost half of all women were victims of some kind of abuse, and just under a fifth of them were victims of physical and sexual abuse). Similarly, about 1 in 10 Mexicans defines himself or herself as indigenous and holds and responds to, essentially, a different set of economic values, whereby assets (especially land) are nontradable sources of group identity, community benefit is held in higher regard than individual profit maximization, traditional social governance bodies are trusted over those dictated by the country's laws, social organization is based on prestige and civic duty, and the language of preference (and frequently the only language) is not Spanish. Even though these problems are clearly group specific, it is subject to debate whether the solutions should be. It could be argued that gender and cultural sensitivity should be a feature of policymaking across sectors, from taxation and finance to health and education. Building that sensitivity will require government interventions to raise awareness and educate.

Balancing Growth and Poverty Reduction with Protecting Natural Resources

In past decades, Mexico's development was essentially a "mining" process. Energy, water, forests, and the like were depleted to fuel growth, without much consideration for the implied transfer of wealth from future generations or for the costs that depletion was putting on the current generation (through, for instance, health hazards). Since the early 1990s, this attitude has dramatically changed, partly because of Mexico's more active participation in the international arena (NAFTA, OECD, Kyoto Protocol, Basle Convention, and so forth) and partly because of its more participatory democracy at home. An array of sound legal, regulatory, and institutional frameworks were thus put in place, including the National Water Law (1992), the General Law for Ecological Equilibrium and Environmental Protection (1996), the Forestry Law reform (1997), the creation of an environmental ministry (SEMARNAP, in 1994), the formation of the National Commission for Protected Areas (2000), and a recent effort to foster the decentralization of environmental management.

While excellent first steps in the right direction, these reforms are not sufficient to reverse Mexico's environmental degradation. Of the country's 258 aquifers, more than 100 are overdrawn and major water crises are in the making in some states, especially the northern most productive sites. Less than a tenth of the country's wastewater is adequately treated. Only 35 percent of solid waste is disposed of in a sanitary manner. Atmospheric contaminants in many urban centers regularly exceed safe standards. Some 300,000 hectares of Mexican forest disappear every year (the highest rate in Latin America). Biodiversity is declining and the marine and insular ecosystems are under threat from agriculture and tourism. Notwithstanding the caveats of "green" national accounts, it is estimated that the cost of annual environmental degradation is equivalent to about 10 percent of GDP.

It will fall on the new federal government to address such an urgent environmental challenge. The first, and politically most difficult, step is to make prices reflect scarcity by removing, in all sectors, explicit and implicit subsidies on water, energy, and basic grains. The elimination of subsidies should occur at the three levels of government; for example, there is not much point for CNA to properly price water if local municipalities would not transfer to and enforce the payment of those new prices on their final consumers, while seeking ways to pass the ensuing loss back to the federation. Since many of those subsidies are collected by the poor (although not exclusively by the poor), compensatory income support may need to be put in place. Better pricing would, however, carry a large concomitant benefit—it would make environmental investment and preservation a good business for the private sector, both in terms of its own conservation and as a delivery partner in public services (private investment in water is a good example of that possibility).

Second, property rights should be clarified across the spectrum of natural resources (while progress is being made in water and land, less is being made in forests and fisheries). Third, the vicious circle of environmental degradation as a short-term survival tool, in which some poor rural communities are trapped, needs to be exogenously broken; while respecting communal preferences and structures, direct support programs may be needed on a case-by-case basis. Fourth, SEMARNAP should be given power to operate as a "function" across ministries, rather than alongside them in a vertical "silo" basis. This would make possible the continuous environmental evaluation of all government policies and programs (not just SEMARNAP's); that is, it would make possible the so-called "greening" of the Mexican government.

Finally, with few exemptions (for example, irrigation districts), decentralization of the environmental sector is not proceeding apace (in spite of recent efforts by SEMARNAP), even though it is a sector where higher proximity between policy-makers and users would be particularly beneficial. Much of the reason for the limited sector decentralization has to do with the overall fiscal framework faced by states and municipalities, where the definition of responsibilities is still unclear and the incentives for local taxation or application of user charges are weak (the general problems of the decentralization process are addressed later).

Building an Efficient, Accountable, and Transparent Government

The task of putting the Mexican economy on a sustainable, rapid, poverty-reducing, environmentally-balanced growth path will have to be carried out within a new framework for governing. This is because, over the last decade, two formidable forces have fundamentally altered the nature of government in Mexico—globalization and democratization. Commercial and financial integration, and the scrutiny they impose on fiscal accounts and macroeconomic performance, made it all but impossible for Mexican governments to continue substituting for private market-based resource allocation. Should they try, they would be immediately shunned by internationally mobile investors. Similarly, enhanced political competition (especially after 1997) gave a new meaning to the country's federalism. States and municipalities reclaimed their constitutional role in policymaking, thus placing it under the closer scrutiny of local constituencies. In brief, globalization and democratization have made the business of government in Mexico much more accountable to both markets and voters.

This trend toward government accountability is irreversible, and certain to intensify over the coming years. The new President will face an urgent demand for "better government" (broadly understood as a more effective, more efficient and more transparent body of providers of public goods), and will be held accountable for delivering it. Improving the quality of government in Mexico is, however, a multifaceted, multiyear task the full completion of which will likely span over several sexenios. It is therefore imperative for the incoming authorities to focus on a few critical areas where the marginal returns in terms of quality improvement are highest. This paper suggests that three such areas stand out—decentralization, the judicial system, and corruption.

As mentioned, decentralization in Mexico is already under way and progressing rapidly. It has tremendous potential for improving the quality of government services by bringing policymakers and final beneficiaries closer together. It can rightly change the role of the federal government away from pursuing those results that the subnational governments can achieve on their own, and toward capturing nationwide externalities. But decentralization also has the potential to be a destabilizing factor for public finances at all levels and, ultimately, for the country's macroeconomic framework. Worldwide experience suggests that decentralization should not be carried out without a coherent overall strategy and adequate institutional infrastructure at the lower levels of government. Those were, however, the conditions under which decentralization was launched and is being pursued in Mexico. Thus, the core policy challenge in this area is to put the process of decentralization on a sustainable path.

The outgoing government sought to ensure that sustainability by imposing hard budget constraints on states and municipalities. It achieved this by renouncing, in the federal budget for 2000, its own powers to hand out discretionary transfers, and by establishing a regulatory link between capitalization requirements for bank loans to subnationals and these borrowers' independently determined credit ratings. These reforms were the right short-term response and are already bearing fruit—key states, including *Estado de México*, are beginning to articulate structural adjustment efforts. In this respect, the new Administration will be well advised to maintain those hard budget constraints, by continuing to renounce discretionary transfers in the federal budgets and enforcing the new bank regulations (including on its own development banks).

However, in the medium term, subnational fiscal discipline will have to be supplemented with a framework more conducive to decentralization. In particular, the Fiscal Pact that currently delegates most state taxing powers to the federation should be reformed to devolve much of those powers to the subnational governments. With a tax base of their own, states and municipalities would then be able to absorb the other necessary change in Mexico's decentralization framework—a clearer assignment of expenditure responsibilities, not just in terms of actual procurement of good and services, but also in terms of the policy decisions behind that procurement (for example, how much to pay teachers, how many hospitals to maintain open, or which roads to build). Having to pay for their expenditure (and borrowing) decisions out of taxes directly imposed on their local voters would make subnational governments much more disciplined, efficient, and accountable in the management of their fiscal affairs.

It is important to note that the devolution of taxes and the assignment of expenditure responsibilities are much more than technical matters, for they will define the type of federal nation Mexico wants to be. For example, the amendment of the Fiscal Pact to devolve taxes will call for a parallel amendment of the transfer formulas which, in effect, currently carry resources from richer to poorer states and smooth development disparities across regions. Similarly, full decentralization of expenditure responsibilities may or may not be conditional on minimum standards of achievement (say, in education) meant to ensure a certain level of national homogeneity.

The second governance front where the payoffs of reform will be particularly high in terms of improvements in the overall quality of the government function is the judicial system. Although currently void of comprehensive and systematic evaluations, this is an area where consensus seems to exist on the broad diagnosis—the system provides services in insufficient quantity and of poor quality, is not free of corruption, and is not accessible to the nonaffluent. The cause of such weak performance is a combination of outdated substantive and procedural laws, inadequate administrative structures and processes, inadequate human resource management, underfunding and, critically, limited independence from political powers (especially at the state level).

Those shortcomings of the judicial system, and the burden they impose along the whole development spectrum (from lack of credit to corporations to unenforceable land titles), have been the target of many reform efforts (most notably, the constitutional amendments of 1988, 1994, and 1999). The puzzle, and the challenge for further policy design, is that, by and large, those reforms did not produce the expected results. What can the new officials do to make reforms work? First, the many sources of friction between the federal and the 31 state-level judicial systems need to be eliminated (overlapping jurisdictions in commercial cases, abusive use of *amparos*, uncoordinated investigations, and so forth). Second, the independence of state judicial systems, especially from the states' executive branch, should be ensured, something that may call for further constitutional amendments. Third, the focus of reforms should extend beyond the judges, and over the array of other justice sector agents (court administrators, prosecutors, litigators, and so forth) and mechanisms (private arbitration, mediation, conciliation, and the like). More mundanely but equally important, transparent mechanisms for monitoring and evaluating reform implementation should be put in place, both to ensure timely corrective action when needed and to disseminate across states those practices that prove successful.

The third and, perhaps, most conspicuous improvement in the quality of Mexico's government will be a reduction in the incidence of corruption. Regrettably, this is a phenomenon that lacks systematic diagnosis and documentation. Yet, citizen perceptions suffice to illustrate the magnitude of the problem—according to a recent independent survey carried out by Mexican media, only 3 percent of the population think that the government is not corrupt, and one in every three respondents thinks it is "very corrupt." In other words, there is a pent-up demand for transparency.

Addressing the corruption problem in Mexico will be difficult and will take time. It will thus be critical to focus first on key incentive-setting institutions. SECODAM and the *Contaduría Mayor de Hacienda* (the government's internal and external auditors, respectively) need urgent modernization. SECODAM, while advanced in its efforts to streamline government procurement (through COMPRANET), lacks mechanisms to make it accountable to citizens (adequate procedures for handling complaints, a public "scorecard", and so on). The *Contaduría Mayor de Hacienda*, by design or by practice, does not fulfill its prime mandate of verifying public expenditures in a timely manner. These problems with the executive branch's external and internal auditing are, with various degrees, also spread over the 31 state governments.

In parallel with setting up adequate incentives for its auditors, the federal government needs to give adequate incentives to its own employees through the creation of a career civil service where promotion and compensation are market-competitive and performance-based and where official information (records, accounts, decisions) is kept confidential only by specified exception.

Institutions outside government will be equally important in establishing anti-corruption incentives. Three are especially noteworthy: the judicial system (addressed above); the police (which, although not treated here, are critical to break the link between crime and corruption); and the media (whose role in the new, more open Mexico is likely to expand, testing the strength of the legal protection framework for its operation).

III. Conclusion: Putting It All Together

The agenda described in this paper, and substantiated in the two parts of this compendium, is just short of overwhelming. In essence, it advises the new Administration to pursue macroeconomic sustainability as the sine qua non condition; to accelerate long-term growth through the enhancement of competitiveness, rather than short-lived aggregate demand boosts; to seek poverty reduction through human capital formation, rather than temporary handouts; to make poverty-reducing growth an environmentally balanced undertaking, not a mining exercise; and to achieve these goals from the platform of an efficient, accountable, and transparent government.

Implementation will undoubtedly call for prioritization. Choices will have to be made to map out the sequence of policy efforts to be undertaken at each stage. There is no universal answer as to what sequence fits Mexico best, and much will depend on the value the incoming team attaches to various objectives and on its assessment of its own capacity. It would be highly optimistic to think that all, or even a majority, of the reforms described above can be achieved during the next sexenio. Consensus on major reforms can be maddeningly elusive in a participatory democracy, and implementation no less difficult. It is therefore crucial that the new government achieve some early, demonstrable successes in order to build momentum for subsequent efforts.

As in any pluralistic society, success is defined as much by public perception as by actual results. This perception can be influenced by the degree of citizen participation and ownership in the design of policy reforms and by the extent to which short-term costs and long-term benefits are perceived to be shared fairly. For example, a fiscal reform program will succeed—and receive legislative and popular approval—only if the public can be convinced that (a) it is necessary (that is, incremental tax receipts will be used for good causes and not be wasted); (b) it is just (those "punished" are those who have most egregiously avoided their share in the past); (c) it is fair (the burden will be shared in an equitable manner); and (d) it is compassionate (measures are included to protect or compensate the poor). During its first several months, the new Administration will be able to tap into a full reservoir of optimism and good will to engage the entire country in a national dialogue about where it wants to be in six years, and it should be careful not to lose it.

Although challenging, the agenda is feasible. Mexico can marshal the necessary human and material resources to implement it. The country has a unique opportunity to do so—the historic political changes that the 2000 elections brought about opened the door wide for daring and participatory reform. The prize at the end of the sexenio will not be a Mexico free of all its development problems; rather, it will be a Mexico on a fast and sustainable development path—and a better future for all its citizens.

Una Agenda Integral de Desarrollo para La Nueva Era

Síntesis

Este Capítulo fue escrito por Marcelo M. Giugale

I. Fundamento y Organización

El Banco Mundial ha tenido el privilegio de proporcionar a las Administraciones Presidenciales entrantes de sus países clientes un informe completo de su diagnóstico y recomendaciones de políticas para los sectores que contribuyen a la senda de desarrollo del cliente[1]. Se espera que esta práctica sea hoy especialmente pertinente y útil para México, puesto que el próximo Presidente asume el mando en diciembre de 2000 para dirigir una nación en proceso de rápido cambio y que se enfrenta con enormes desafíos y oportunidades. Por su parte, el Banco Mundial ingresará a su sexta década de colaboración y asistencia contínua al gobierno mexicano, lo que lo sitúa en condiciones especialmente favorables para realizar un recuento del progreso, necesidades y opciones del país en materia de desarrollo.

En este capítulo se presenta una síntesis —una visión general resumida— de la próxima agenda de desarrollo de México. Esa síntesis resume y se basa en los Capítulos Temáticos que conforman la Parte I de este libro. A su vez, esas Capítulos están respaldadas por 30 Capítulos de Política para sectores específicos que están contenidas en la Parte II. El propósito de estos documentos no es entregar respuestas definitivas a los diversos aspectos de política que posiblemente deban enfrentar las autoridades mexicanas durante el nuevo sexenio. Su objetivo más bien es proporcionar un análisis independiente sobre los problemas en los sectores en que el Banco participa y un conjunto de opciones factibles para abordarlos. Este libro fue finalizado en Noviembre de 2000. Desde su producción y publicación, pudieran haberse desarrollado algunos cambios de política económica los cuales, naturalmente, no han sido reflejados ni incorporados.

---

1. En 1994, se entregó un informe similar, en forma de un conjunto de Notas de Estrategia, al entonces futuro Gobierno del Presidente Zedillo.

II. Mensajes Básicos

Según la mayoría de los informes disponibles, el sexenio del Presidente Zedillo ha sido muy exitoso. Después de una recesión dura, pero breve, que siguió a la crisis de diciembre de 1994, México ha gozado de cuatro años consecutivos de crecimiento económico, con un promedio anual del 4.9 por ciento durante el período 1995–1999, mientras que la inflación se ha reducido del 52 por ciento en 1995 a un 9 por ciento estimado para el 2000. Así, el país ha logrado recuperar la mayor parte del terreno que había perdido como resultado de la crisis. En cuanto a los indicadores de pobreza (que suben en forma rápida durante una recesión y tienden a quedarse atrás durante las recuperaciones económicas), su reciente mejoramiento es indudable.

El gobierno también ha implementado o iniciado varias reformas estructurales, especialmente en el sector financiero (pensiones bancarias y privadas), seguridad social y descentralización fiscal. Por otra parte, debido a las restricciones fiscales, el aumento de la pluralidad política y una actitud cautelosa en materia de políticas, hay todavía importantes reformas por abordar. La inversión nacional también se ha visto afectada, puesto que los programas de austeridad redujeron la inversión en infraestructura pública del 10 por ciento del PIB a principios de los años ochenta a menos del 2 por ciento en 1998, mientras que el sector privado no cuenta con los incentivos adecuados para financiar por completo las brechas actuales y futuras. Por lo tanto, queda mucho por hacer en lo que se refiere a completar, consolidar e iniciar reformas. El programa de acción por realizar se puede resumir en cinco mensajes principales:

1. Consolidar las ganancias en materia macroeconómica
2. Acelerar el crecimiento a través de una mayor competitividad
3. Reducir la pobreza a través del desarrollo del capital humano
4. Equilibrar el crecimiento y la reducción de la pobreza con la protección de los recursos naturales
5. Lograr todo lo anterior a través de un gobierno eficiente, responsable por sus acciones y transparente.

Los argumentos detrás de esos cinco mensajes son relativamente simples. Primero, se deben proteger y consolidar los logros macroeconómicos de los últimos cinco años mediante una disciplina permanente en materia de gastos, consolidar las cuentas fiscales a través de un programa de reforma fiscal integral, reducir la dependencia de los ingresos provenientes del petróleo, realizar un sólido manejo de la deuda pública (federal y subnacional, explícita y contingente, interna y externa), etc.

Segundo, para satisfacer no sólo las demandas de una fuerza laboral en rápido crecimiento, sino también el imperativo de ascender a la categoría de economía del Primer Mundo, México necesita aumentar su competitividad en el mercado global hasta alcanzar un sendero de crecimiento de largo plazo más elevado. Esto significa (a) establecer un sistema financiero sólido para estimular la inversión privada y proteger los ahorros de la población (ya sea en bancos, fondos de pensión, o mercados de capitales), (b) eliminar las barreras que obstaculizan los flujos de capital privado mediante la liberalización de los sectores actualmente dominados por monopolios públicos o cuasipúblicos (como la energía) y la aplicación de regulaciones favorables para la competencia, (c) emprender reformas estructurales en diversos sectores, como agua y transporte y (d) tratar casos específicos de fallas de mercado o distorsiones no intencionales (en especial en el sector rural).

Tercero, el gobierno necesita prestar atención al capital humano como la base de la pirámide de desarrollo. Para ello primero debe proteger a los grupos vulnerables que en gran medida han sido descuidados; segundo, proporcionarles los insumos básicos para aumentar su productividad (esto es, una vida saludable y una buena educación); tercero, eliminar distorsiones en el mercado laboral y estimular la migración del sector de empleo informal al formal; y cuarto, ser sensible a las necesidades específicas de determinados grupos como los indígenas, o más ampliamente, las mujeres.

Cuarto, el país necesita ser más eficiente en la protección de su medio ambiente, para asegurar que mañana los recursos naturales se puedan utilizar y gozar de la misma forma o mejor que hoy. Para los industriales, agricultores y consumidores por igual, esto significa que los recursos como el agua se deben tratar como el bien escaso, en desaparición y, por consiguiente, costoso que en realidad es. Para los pobres rurales, esto significa elaborar políticas que ayuden a transformar la actual relación de disyuntiva entre el hombre y la naturaleza (de conservación versus supervivencia) en una relación de colaboración (uso y crecimiento económico sostenibles).

Por último, las reformas recién nombradas sólo se pueden lograr y mantener si se establece un nuevo contrato entre el gobierno y los ciudadanos, en el cual los estándares de responsabilidad pública del gobierno y de participación ciudadana se eleven a un nivel mucho mayor que antes. El gobierno deberá responder en forma rápida a las fuerzas y exigencias cada vez mayores de democratización (esto es, llegar a ser más eficiente en su rendición de cuentas), globalización (tener procesos transparentes y justos para atraer capital adicional), descentralización (transferir el poder a los niveles más bajos) y justicia (corregir los desequilibrios sociales y crear un terreno de participación equitativo).

Estos cinco mensajes, que sirven de guía para este capítulo, se basan en un amplio conjunto de diagnósticos y recomendaciones. Implementar estas recomendaciones de política resultará una tarea abrumadora para cualquier gobierno, de modo que la asignación de prioridades será decisiva. Por lo tanto, el análisis que se presenta a continuación contiene una estructura implícita de prioridades. El lector también deberá tener en cuenta las siguientes limitaciones. En primer lugar, no hay una respuesta única en los temas de desarrollo. Lo que estos Capítulos contienen es el resultado de años de experiencia del personal del Banco Mundial en México, enriquecido con lo que se ha aprendido en otras partes del mundo. Como siempre sucede, existe un amplio campo para formular estrategias (y disentir de ellas) acerca de qué intervenciones funcionarán mejor y, lo que es de igual importancia (si no más), cómo. En segundo lugar, la asignación implícita de prioridades y secuencias también se presta a interpretaciones, dependiendo de la percepción del lector acerca de la relativa importancia y factibilidad de la política en cuestión.

El Banco Mundial está preparado para ayudar a las nuevas autoridades mexicanas a implementar su agenda de políticas. La experiencia acumulada en México y a nivel internacional por el Banco en el transcurso de los años puede ser de valor para las autoridades de este país. Dada la actual exposición crediticia en México de unos US$11 mil millones, la tramitación de proyectos por un valor cercano a US$1,5 mil millones anuales en una amplia gama de sectores, y un presupuesto anual para el análisis económico y sectorial de más de US$3 millones, el Banco está en buena posición para movilizar recursos que permitan apoyar los esfuerzos de México en el diseño y aplicación de sus políticas.

Consolidación de las Ganancias Macroeconómicas

La sólida administración macroeconómica quizás es el logro económico más importante de la Administración Zedillo. Después de la profunda crisis financiera de 1994, el marco macroeconómico se basó en (a) una política monetaria restrictiva y claramente independiente, (b) un régimen cambiario flexible, (c) un paquete de financiamiento extranjero proactivo y (d) una posición fiscal conservadora. Esto no sólo hizo salir a la economía de su crisis, sino que le permitió crecer a una tasa respetable y tener una inflación de un solo dígito, un balance externo viable y una posición de deuda cómoda, todo esto a pesar de las tres crisis internacionales que complicaron las perspectivas económicas a nivel mundial (Asia oriental, 1997, Rusia, 1998 y Brasil, 1999). La inversión extranjera directa se recuperó a niveles de US$11 mil millones anuales (y sigue creciendo), a partir de los débiles niveles que siguieron inmediatamente después de la crisis de 1994. Aunque gran parte del cambio se podría atribuir a la fortaleza de la economía estadounidense, la recuperación de México de todas maneras es notable, ya que el país la logró prácticamente sin contar con un sistema bancario interno.

Por lo tanto, parece razonable mantener el curso en la política macroeconómica, con una sola excepción. El ancla fiscal, en su forma actual, se ha vuelto insostenible y probablemente comprometerá el marco macroeconómico en el mediano plazo y mantendrá la reciente tendencia de subinversión pública. México podría reafirmar en forma provechosa su política monetaria (por ejemplo, mediante la asignación de una meta de inflación explícita al Banco de México —con una meta a largo plazo de convergencia a la tasa de inflación de sus socios en el NAFTA— y una mayor independencia para tratar de alcanzarla), recalcar su compromiso con un régimen cambiario flexible y seguir absteniéndose de endeudamientos externos elevados (en especial de corto plazo). Sin embargo, estas políticas pronto podrían volverse impracticables y poco creíbles si no se aplica un programa para fortalecer la sostenibilidad fiscal.

Ese programa también es especialmente pertinente como herramienta para mitigar los cuatro principales riesgos macroeconómicos que enfrenta la economía mexicana: un "aterrizaje brusco" en Estados Unidos, un "aterrizaje brusco" en los precios internacionales del petróleo, una crisis fiscal a nivel de estado, y un cambio repentino en las percepciones si las expectativas de mercado impulsadas por el exitoso proceso eleccionario resultaran ser exageradas. En otras palabras, México necesita fortalecer su posición estructural fiscal no sólo porque es un pilar débil de su marco macroeconómico, sino también porque este marco podría tener que resistir importantes turbulencias económicas durante el próximo sexenio.

¿Qué se necesita hacer para lograr la sostenibilidad fiscal y, por ende, macroeconómica? Hay que destacar cinco políticas: Ante todo, es urgente que México reforme integralmente su sistema tributario. Los ingresos tributarios de México, sin incluir los que corresponden al petróleo, equivalen a menos del 10 por ciento del PIB, una proporción deficiente respecto a los estándares internacionales (comparable a la de Haití, menor a la de Ecuador y cerca de la mitad de la de Rusia). Se pueden aplicar muchos posibles paquetes de reforma tributaria y es probable que las diferentes disposiciones tributarias afecten a distintos grupos de interés. Sin embargo, cada paquete se debería evaluar según cinco méritos: efecto recaudatorio, eficiencia económica, equidad social, simplicidad administrativa y factibilidad política. Según esto, al parecer una opción atractiva es la combinación "ningún privilegio y mejor administración".

En términos más específicos, si se eliminan todas las actuales exenciones (ya sea basadas en productos, tipo de ingreso, región o contribuyente) al IVA, al impuesto sobre la renta de las sociedades y al impuesto sobre la renta de las personas y se implementa un mejoramiento importante y gradual en la administración tributaria, el gobierno federal podría obtener recursos adicionales equivalentes entre el 5 y el 6 por ciento del PIB en cuatro años, con un efecto inmediato de cerca del 3 por ciento del PIB[2]. Esta alternativa de reforma supone aplicar la tasa de IVA más alta existente en este momento (15 por ciento) a todos los productos, incluidos alimentos y medicamentos (que en la actualidad tienen tasa cero) y realizar transferencias compensatorias para los segmentos más pobres de la población. También supone eliminar las exenciones a las sociedades según ubicación geográfica[3], el sistema de "consolidación" de ingresos de las sociedades y las fuentes de ingreso personal libres de impuestos (como las ganancias de capital e intereses). Aunque los beneficiarios de estas exenciones podrían resistirse a su eliminación, el hecho de que el paquete no

---

2. Cabe señalar que estas estimaciones necesariamente son tentativas (debido a que no hay una disponibilidad inmediata de datos adecuados y desagregados sobre la recaudación de impuestos en México) y se basan sólo en un análisis de equilibrio parcial.

3. Se podrían conservar, como medida transitoria, las exenciones sobre granos, cereales, vegetales y legumbres.

modifique la actual estructura de tasas progresivas y no establezca nuevos impuestos permitirá plantear políticamente que con esta eliminación todos los mexicanos contribuirán al esfuerzo fiscal y que ningún sector en particular gozará de "privilegios". Esta es la tendencia empleada con éxito en otros países de la OCDE en los últimos tiempos (por ejemplo, en Italia).

La eliminación de las exenciones será un componente clave del otro pilar de la reforma impositiva, y quizás uno más importante: un mejoramiento importante en la administración tributaria. Esto se puede lograr mediante una combinación de los siguientes tres factores principales: mejoramiento de los servicios a los contribuyentes (en especial, del tipo de tecnología informática); sistemas de auditoría que se centren en los evasores de impuestos (más que en los que "cumplen" con los impuestos) y mejores incentivos, administración y condiciones de trabajo para el personal del servicio de administración tributaria (SAT). Los posibles beneficios de una administración tributaria más eficiente son importantes: se estima que aun sin ninguna reforma al código tributario, una mejor administración de la actual estructura tributaria generaría ingresos adicionales de entre el 0,3 y el 0,4 por ciento al año en cuatro años. En resumen, el paquete "ningún privilegio, mejor administración" eliminaría la particularidad central del sistema tributario de México, esto es, su carga impositiva real insosteniblemente baja, la cual los ciudadanos perciben como injustamente alta y a la cual, en consecuencia, se resisten. (En el Capítulo de Política pertinente de la Parte II, se presentan más detalles del paquete de reformas tributarias sugerido).

La segunda área en que se requiere un esfuerzo de política para asegurar la sostenibilidad fiscal es la estabilización de los ingresos provenientes del petróleo. A diferencia de los demás países exportadores de petróleo, la balanza de pagos de México depende sólo en forma parcial del petróleo (el que representa cerca de un 10 por ciento del total de sus exportaciones); sin embargo, sus cuentas fiscales están dominadas por éste (un tercio del ingreso fiscal total se relaciona con este producto). Esto introduce una volatilidad de facto en el saldo fiscal general, el que en muchas ocasiones ha sido negativo para el desempeño macroeconómico.

Las autoridades responsables han examinado la posibilidad de establecer un fondo de estabilización del petróleo, el cual se instituyó formalmente en el presupuesto federal para el año 2000 (pero no se ha implementado). Aunque representa un paso en la dirección correcta, ese fondo, en su presente forma, no resolverá los problemas para los cuales se constituyó. Un fondo de estabilización adecuadamente diseñado es una institución fiscal que ayuda a implementar políticas fiscales contracíclicas, "atando las manos" del gobierno y del Congreso para que puedan resistir presiones políticas y sociales de corto plazo que pretenden gastar inmediatamente superávits fiscales en tiempos favorables, algo que, a su vez, otorga credibilidad para financiar déficits compensatorios en tiempos desfavorables. De esta forma, un fondo de estabilización adecuadamente diseñado no puede ser modificado en las leyes anuales de presupuesto y tiene reglas automáticas para fomentar el ahorro en buenos tiempos y para efectuar retiros en tiempos malos, como es el caso con el fondo de estabilización del cobre en Chile o el fondo de estabilización petrolera de Colombia[4].

Entretanto se pueda establecer un fondo de estabilización petrolera adecuado, sería conveniente para México proceder a implementar una reforma tributaria del tipo descrito anteriormente; proyectar y presupuestar ingresos bajos relacionados con el petróleo, y usar cualquier ingreso real proveniente de éste por encima de los montos presupuestados para amortizar la deuda pública, especialmente la deuda externa a corto plazo y a altas tasas. Esto no sólo significará cierta retribución en términos de evitar pagos de intereses (y probablemente, tasas de interés más bajas para cualquier renovación de la deuda), sino también eliminará la posibilidad de apreciación del tipo de cambio real y perturbaciones en la dinámica exportaciones-importaciones que implican las grandes entradas de moneda extranjera.

La combinación de una reforma tributaria integral, fondos de estabilización adecuadamente diseñados y la estabilización de los ingresos del petróleo con su aplicación a la reducción de la deuda ayudará a abordar directamente la tercera fuente principal de sostenibilidad fiscal: el manejo de los pasivos del sector público. La deuda explícita (esto es, reconocida legalmente) del gobierno federal de México es baja (cerca del 25 por ciento del PIB). Incluso agregando la deuda implícita (esto es, la deuda a la cual el gobierno está sujeto de hecho, aunque todavía no legalmente, como por ejemplo la deuda del IPAB [Instituto de Protección al Ahorro Bancario] y FARAC [Fideicomiso de Apoyo para el Rescate de Autopistas]), la carga total de la deuda "realizada" no es alta según los estándares internacionales (cerca del 46 por ciento del PIB, lo que está por bajo del promedio de la OCDE). Sin embargo, México enfrenta una serie de pasivos públicos contingentes que, si se descuidan, pueden trastornar su posición fiscal. Existen tres pasivos que son de especial preocupación: el desequilibrio actuarial del ISSSTE (el sistema federal público de pensiones), las

---

4. Estos fondos excluyen del "ingreso corriente" los ingresos por encima de un nivel predeterminado relacionado con el promedio móvil de los precios pasados en el caso de Chile y del promedio móvil de los ingresos pasados en el caso de Colombia, de modo que tales ingresos "excedentes" no pueden ser incluidos en la ley anual de presupuesto. De esta forma, las cantidades que se ahorran en tiempos favorables no son discrecionales. Ambos fondos también tienen restricciones en el uso de sus reservas—éstas solo pueden ser invertidas en moneda extranjera o usadas para pre-pagar deuda—así como "techos" a los retiros anuales en tiempos desfavorables (el fondo Colombiano tiene una regla predeterminada). Más recientemente, algunos países han considerado "fondos de estabilización de egresos" más amplios que aplicarían reglas al ingreso corriente en su totalidad (en lugar de sólo al ingreso relacionado a un producto específico), reconociendo así el hecho que los ingresos totales tienden a exhibir elasticidades con respecto al producto bruto interno mayores que uno (tal que la tasa de ingresos con respecto al PBI sube en épocas de auge económico y baja en depresiones) y por lo tanto la estabilización sólo de los ingresos relacionados a un producto específico puede no ser suficiente. Este es el razonamiento detrás de las reglas para la estabilización del gasto incluidas en las recientes "leyes de responsabilidad fiscal" en Brasil y Perú.

operaciones financieramente no sostenibles de INFONAVIT y FOVISSSTE (los fondos públicos para la vivienda de los trabajadores del sector privado y público, respectivamente) y la viabilidad de los 31 sistemas de pensión a nivel de estado (que hace poco fueron descentralizados por la federación).

Además de abordar las políticas subyacentes que generan esos déficits (en los Capítulos sobre Política pertinentes de la Parte II, se presentan recomendaciones específicas para cada caso y más adelante se resumen en este capítulo), es recomendable comenzar a realizar provisiones para el pago de esos pasivos. El costo de esas provisiones se moderará en cierta forma por las menores tasas de interés que enfrentará el gobierno federal en su deuda realizada (en oposición a la contingente), ya que los acreedores, especialmente los extranjeros, ya saben de los pasivos contingentes de la federación y están fijando el precio de sus préstamos en función del riesgo resultante. Al mismo tiempo que la provisión para contingencias, el nuevo gobierno deberá asumir un enfoque más holístico frente a la administración de la deuda pública. Diversas instituciones públicas a nivel nacional y subnacional (especialmente el IPAB) piensan emitir deuda durante los próximos años. Aunque no se dispone de cálculos completos del flujo de fondos, se puede esperar que la suma de esas emisiones superará ampliamente la capacidad de absorción del mercado interno y, por lo tanto, desplazará al sector privado mediante tasas de interés mucho más altas. Específicamente, los pagarés FOBAPROA no comercializables, sin cupón, y originalmente a 10 años vencerán en julio del 2005 y deberán ser refinanciados. Esto requiere un nuevo mecanismo institucional que coordine y programe el endeudamiento de todas las entidades del sector público, tal vez con la asistencia técnica del *Banco de México* (el agente fiscal de muchas de las emisiones de deuda).

La cuarta debilidad en la sostenibilidad fiscal de México son las finanzas de sus gobiernos estatales. Sin duda, México no es Brasil. Su deuda subnacional total equivale a cerca del 2 por ciento del PIB, en comparación con el 20 por ciento de Brasil. Además, los gobiernos subnacionales de México, según la Constitución, no pueden endeudarse con acreedores externos o en moneda extranjera. Sin embargo, un episodio como el de "Minas Gerais", aunque improbable, no es inconcebible en México. Si bien la raíz del problema se encuentra en la naturaleza del proceso de descentralización de México (que se aborda más adelante), desde el punto de vista federal, la solución reside en imponer restricciones presupuestarias "duras" a las entidades subnacionales.

Recientemente se ha avanzado bastante en esta área: por una parte, en el presupuesto federal para el 2000 se eliminó la posibilidad de hacer transferencias discrecionales a los estados (eliminando virtualmente *Ramo 23*) y, por otra parte, en abril de 2000 el gobierno federal implementó un nuevo sistema regulatorio que vincula los requerimientos de capitalización, y por tanto la tasa de interés de los préstamos bancarios a los estados y municipios, con la calificación de deuda de los prestatarios. Esto ha reducido en forma considerable el "riesgo moral" entre los gobiernos subnacionales y sus prestamistas, porque casi ha desaparecido la percepción de probabilidad de rescates federales.

Es decisivo que la Administración entrante mantenga estas restricciones presupuestarias duras sobre los estados y municipios y que se comprometa a no rescatar a los estados renunciando a toda facultad para realizar transferencias discrecionales en sus presupuestos anuales y aplicando las nuevas regulaciones crediticias, entre ellos a sus propios bancos de desarrollo (en especial, BANOBRAS). El efecto inmediato será que cuando ya no puedan seguir endeudándose, estados más débiles tendrán incentivos para realizar ajustes estructurales en sus cuentas fiscales. En esos casos, el papel óptimo de la federación será facilitar esos ajustes, más que eliminar la necesidad de ellos. Esto será especialmente cierto para los estados que realicen ajustes anticipados, algo que producirá un valioso efecto de ejemplo para los estados más reticentes. Como se explicará más adelante, la necesidad de ajuste también despertará el interés de los gobiernos subnacionales en profundizar el proceso de descentralización.

Por último, la sostenibilidad fiscal de México se fortalecerá con una política fiscal general anticíclica. En parte debido a la dependencia del petróleo y en parte debido a la naturaleza del proceso presupuestario, el gobierno federal ha tenido la tendencia de relajar su posición fiscal cuando el crecimiento se acelera y a restringirla cuando la economía se desacelera. Esto exacerbó los ciclos económicos e incentivó los desequilibrios externos (en especial, los déficits de cuenta corriente de la balanza de pagos). Además del cambio requerido en la actitud en las políticas, otras dos iniciativas podrían mitigar el problema: la incorporación de planes de contingencia al presupuesto federal y la formalización de programas presupuestarios a tres años.

En resumen, los esfuerzos de política para asegurar la sostenibilidad fiscal son una condición necesaria para que México goce de un marco macroeconómico estable y propicio. Como quedará evidente más adelante, estos esfuerzos son igualmente decisivos para otros dos objetivos centrales de la agenda probable de la próxima administración: crecimiento basado en competitividad y reducción de la pobreza a través del desarrollo humano.

Aceleramiento del Crecimiento Mediante una Mayor Competitividad

El Presidente entrante hereda una economía que crece con rapidez, quizás hasta en un 5 por ciento o más durante el año 2000. Aunque esa tasa de crecimiento es enteramente respetable, México tendrá que acelerarla hasta en 2 puntos porcentuales en el largo plazo si quiere satisfacer las necesidades y expectativas de sus ciudadanos, especialmente en términos de creación de empleos entre los pobres. (Según ciertas estimaciones, México requiere la creación de 1 millón de empleos al año, sólo para acomodar a los nuevos trabajadores que se incorporan al mercado laboral, mientras que en la actualidad crea cerca de 600.000). En el pasado, los gobiernos mexicanos intentaron fomentar el crecimiento mediante intervenciones que, en esencia, impulsaban la demanda agregada interna. Con ello se obtenían breves rachas de crecimiento, las que se detenían con las resultantes crisis en la balanza de pagos. Actualmente, dado que el país ya está integrado a la economía global y goza de sus beneficios y especialmente del NAFTA, la aceleración del crecimiento a largo plazo será sostenible sólo si se logra mediante una mayor competitividad en los mercados externos.

La competitividad de un país depende de una amplia serie de factores y la formulación de políticas debe centrarse en aquellos que generan el mayor mejoramiento marginal. Esta sección se centra en los tres factores que en la actualidad más dificultan la competitividad de México: un sector financiero débil, una deficiente infraestructura y una baja productividad de la agricultura. Cabe recalcar que existen otros factores determinantes importantes, tanto directos como indirectos, de la competitividad (por ejemplo, la reforma laboral y la corrupción), muchos de los cuales se tratan por separado en este capítulo (por ejemplo, el trabajo como parte del desarrollo humano y la corrupción como parte de la gobernabilidad).

El sector financiero de México está dominado por su industria bancaria, cuyos problemas son bien conocidos: la crisis de 1994 dejó un serio deterioro de cartera (una cartera de "préstamos incobrables" que tuvieron que absorber los contribuyentes, equivalente a casi un 20 por ciento del PIB) y un problema de flujo igualmente serio (el servicio de la deuda enfrentado por el IPAB en el futuro previsible). Otros factores han afectado el rendimiento del sector bancario: una deficiente regulación bancaria, pocos incentivos para el pago de deuda, falta de transparencia. Como resultado, desde 1994 los préstamos de los bancos al sector privado se han reducido en cerca de un 40 por ciento en términos reales, los créditos al consumidor de los bancos privados casi han desaparecido (dejando a los bancos y fondos públicos virtualmente con un monopolio, por ejemplo, en los préstamos para vivienda), y el mismo sector privado productivo se ha dividido entre grandes empresas orientadas a la exportación que pueden acceder al financiamiento externo y empresas relativamente más pequeñas con restricciones de liquidez que proveen sólo al mercado interno. Las dificultades de la industria bancaria también afectaron el desarrollo en el resto del sector financiero, puesto que dado el escaso número de agentes solventes, la poca información confiable acerca de ellos y el sistema judicial atascado con casos de recuperación de garantías, era difícil lograr el desarrollo de los mercados de acciones, bonos e incluso, seguros.

A pesar de estos enormes problemas, recientemente se ha avanzado en la recuperación de la industria bancaria. Después de la creación del IPAB, la incorporación gradual de límites al seguro de depósitos, la introducción de una contabilidad más sólida, reglas más adecuadas de valoración de activos y capital bancarios, y la aprobación por parte del congreso de nuevas leyes de garantías y quiebras, ahora está en curso un importante esfuerzo de consolidación mediante fusiones y adquisiciones de bancos que estimula la participación de inversionistas extranjeros. Otras instituciones financieras no bancarias también tuvieron reformas exitosas, incluido el sistema privado de pensiones en 1997[5].

---

5. Otro sub-sector que podría presentar riesgos fiscales es el de bancos de desarrollo (incluidos BANOBRAS, NAFIN, BANURAL). Sin embargo, no se dispone actualmente de suficiente información par a formar una opinión sobre la solidez de sus balances o sus préstamos.

Este avance apunta a la prioridad central de las políticas del área financiera en el próximo sexenio: profundizar las reformas ya iniciadas. Esta profundización implicará principalmente la consolidación de las funciones normativas y de supervisión, que en la actualidad se encuentran fragmentadas, una mayor independencia de la entidad reguladora resultante, el establecimiento de las instituciones necesarias para implementar la nueva ley de garantías (como registros) y un mayor fortalecimiento de la posición patrimonial de los bancos. Este último punto pone de relieve el importante papel que cumple el IPAB, puesto que muchos de los bancos más débiles técnicamente están bajo su propiedad, mientras que otros registran entre sus activos grandes cantidades de bonos relacionados con el IPAB.

Además de fortalecer la industria bancaria, otra área decisiva del sector financiero es la reforma del sistema público de pensiones (ISSSTE) y sus vínculos con el fondo público de la vivienda (INFONAVIT). Le corresponderá a este sexenio presidencial proporcionar una fuente más confiable de ahorros a largo plazo a los empleados federales, que permita la conversión de su plan de pensiones actual al mismo esquema de aportes definidos, capitalizado y administrado en forma privada usado por los trabajadores del sector privado. Esto generará un costo fiscal adicional (puede ser de hasta un 1 por ciento del PIB por dos décadas). Vale la pena pagar este costo, puesto que puede ser compensado con creces por el efecto del nuevo sistema en el desarrollo de mercados financieros a más largo plazo y, en definitiva, en la tasa de crecimiento a largo plazo de la economía.

La reforma del sistema de pensiones de los empleados públicos facilitará y será facilitada por las medidas de política necesarias en otros dos mercados financieros: acciones e hipotecas. México ya está presenciando la migración de sus empresas de primera clase a bolsas de valores extranjeras, debido a los retrasos en abordar la cuestión de la propiedad cruzada de conglomerados financieros (posiblemente mediante barreras normativas que separen las empresas) y la necesidad de una mejor protección de los derechos de los accionistas minoritarios, mayores obligaciones de divulgación de la información por parte de las sociedades, la eliminación de obstáculos para la cotización de valores en la bolsa y su retiro de ella y la eliminación de restricciones a transacciones por parte de extranjeros (entre otras, exigencias del fondo fiduciario de NAFIN). La falta de amplitud y profundidad en los mercados de capital (y la restricción legal contra AFORES de invertir en valores extranjeros) obliga a los fondos de pensión a operar en un mercado más reducido e invertir en compañías con riesgo agravado. En el mercado hipotecario, aproximadamente un tercio de todas las aportaciones a las pensiones se destina al financiamiento de fondos públicos para la vivienda (INFONAVIT, FOVISSSTE). Estos, a través del subsidio de los precios, controlan el 75 por ciento del mercado hipotecario y de hecho constituyen una barrera para el desarrollo hipotecario privado, aún cuando resultan incapaces de satisfacer la demanda contenida de México por viviendas (estimada en 800.000 nuevas unidades de vivienda y 6 millones de unidades que requieren reparaciones). Es necesario reformar ambos fondos (si no eliminarlos), someterlos a una misma normativa (junto con FOVI), privarlos de sus subsidios de precios (los cuales, si así se decide, se deberían proporcionar en forma abierta a través del presupuesto federal) y se les debería dar mejores estándares de tramitación y servicio (similar a FOVI). Otro subsector financiero que puede significar una fuente de riesgos fiscales está constituido por los bancos de desarrollo (BANOBRAS, NAFIN, BANRURAL y similares) y otras instituciones financieras no bancarias. Sin embargo, en este momento no existe la suficiente información disponible como para emitir un juicio sobre la solidez de sus balances y sus prácticas crediticias.

La profundización de las reformas en el sector financiero contribuirá en gran medida a proporcionar el segundo pilar de la competitividad: una adecuada infraestructura. Sin embargo, el financiamiento en sí no es suficiente. Para llevar la infraestructura de México a un nivel adecuado, también se requerirá un cambio importante en el sistema de propiedad y de regulación de los sectores relacionados con la infraestructura. Durante las dos últimas décadas, el país acertadamente intentó reemplazar la inversión pública en infraestructura por la privada. Esto se ajustó bien a las necesidades fiscales de austeridad del momento, en especial a partir de los años noventa. Sin embargo, la respuesta del sector privado no se materializó en la medida de lo esperado y, así, México comenzó a acelerar la tasa de depreciación de su capital nacional (la inversión pública total descendió de más del 10 por ciento del PIB a principios de los años ochenta a cerca del 2 por ciento en la actualidad; en el mismo período, la inversión total se redujo de aproximadamente 25 por ciento a menos de 20 por ciento). Aun si lo deseara (equivocadamente), el gobierno ya no tiene la posibilidad de costear esa brecha de infraestructura que crece con rapidez: sólo en el sector energético, se estima que las necesidades de inversión ascienden a US$10 mil millones anuales durante los próximos 10 años, esto es, alrededor del monto de la asignación del presupuesto federal anual para salud. En su lugar, la solución reside en el financiamiento privado y en una mejor regulación.

La naturaleza del financiamiento y las reformas regulatorias requeridas en el área de infraestructura varía según los sectores. El sector eléctrico necesita tarifas que permitan recuperar los costos (los clientes residenciales y los clientes agrícolas pagan cerca de la mitad y un tercio, respectivamente, del costo del servicio, un subsidio que equivale a poco menos del 1 por ciento del PIB); una nueva organización institucional que divida la CFE (Comisión Federal de Electricidad) en generación, transmisión y distribución y permita la competencia en ambos extremos, y un mecanismo más eficiente de determinación de tarifas y estándares mediante el fortalecimiento considerable de la Comisión Reguladora de Energía. Esto permitiría la participación del sector privado en duplicar prácticamente la capacidad eléctrica, algo que el país necesita en los próximos 10 años y que requiere, un gasto en inversión estimado de unos US$37 mil millones.

Tarifas eléctricas que permitan recuperar costos y la consecuente eliminación del subsidio cruzado del sector petrolero, un nuevo régimen fiscal, y nuevos planes de concesión para la explotación y producción podrían proporcionar incentivos más propicios para que PEMEX, la compañía petrolera estatal, mejore su deficiente rendimiento. De igual importancia es que no hay razón válida para mantener el monopolio de PEMEX en las actividades secundarias (incluidas las refinerías).

Se requiere una revisión general en el sector del agua, en gran parte porque, como se explicará más adelante, México está al borde de una crisis hidráulica. Esa revisión significará la colaboración de los tres niveles de gobierno (federal, estatal y municipal) para comenzar a fijar tarifas que reflejen escasez, imponer el pago de esas tarifas, y encontrar un nuevo equilibrio institucional en el marco de la descentralización, entre la CNA (Comisión Nacional del Agua) federal en un extremo del espectro y los operadores y usuarios locales de agua, en el otro. También será conveniente un nuevo plan institucional para los sistemas federales de carreteras y caminos, especialmente mediante la fusión de FARAC y CAPUFE, el establecimiento de un Fondo de Mantenimiento de Caminos que funcione, y un regulador independiente del sector de transportes. Estos planes permitirían la captación de financiamiento a mayor plazo, una participación privada más importante en la prestación de los servicios (como completar la privatización de ferrocarriles y aeropuertos) y concesiones de redes.

En resumen, es mucho lo que se puede hacer a través de la formulación de políticas para elevar los estándares de infraestructura de México y para presenciar resultados positivos en el sexenio. Sin embargo, terminar con la brecha de infraestructura cada vez mayor del país requerirá importantes inversiones, estimadas en forma preliminar en US$20 mil millones al año durante la próxima década. Este gasto está mucho más allá de la capacidad financiera del sector público. Por lo tanto, es decisivo asignarle una nueva función a los bancos de desarrollo, en especial como facilitadores del financiamiento privado. Más que actuar como un medio de transferencia de fondos fiscales federales (lo que desalentaría a los financistas privados), esos bancos, en particular el BANOBRAS, podrían ayudar a los gobiernos subnacionales a aumentar su solvencia y mancomunar sus riesgos para acceder a financiamiento privado a largo plazo, actuar como administradores de fondos fiduciarios federales específicos de los estados destinados a atraer la participación privada en el financiamiento de infraestructura local, y proporcionar servicios secundarios en la bursatilización de la deuda estatal y municipal. (En los Capítulos sobre Política subsectoriales pertinentes de la Parte II, se presentan más detalles sobre las reformas en el área de infraestructura).

Por último, la competitividad de México podría verse incrementada por esfuerzos de política para eliminar las distorsiones restantes que afectan su economía rural, realizando las inversiones necesarias para fomentar la productividad dentro de un marco normativo adecuado. Este es el sector donde posiblemente se han efectuado las reformas estructurales más drásticas durante la última década (liberalización del comercio impulsada por el GATT y el NAFTA, eliminación de intervenciones de precios, reforma constitucional de la tenencia de la tierra), pero donde los resultados han sido más decepcionantes (estancamiento del crecimiento en la agricultura, falta de competitividad, aumento de la pobreza rural), a pesar del importante apoyo público (PROCAMPO, PROCEDE, Alianza para el Campo, CONASUPO, ASERCA, etc.). Un crudo pero revelador ejemplo de la deficiente productividad del sector es que hoy la economía rural genera apenas el 5 por ciento del PIB de Méx-

ico, pero emplea un 20 por ciento de su fuerza laboral. Las reformas bien inten-
cionadas parecen haber generados muy pocos o ningún ajuste estructural, una posición incómoda para un sector que, bajo el acuerdo NAFTA, en el 2008 quedará
expuesto a la competencia abierta con Canadá y Estados Unidos. ¿Qué ha salido mal
y qué se puede hacer para corregirlo?

Muchos de los problemas de la economía rural de México están más allá del control de las autoridades responsables o están profundamente arraigados debido a
décadas de mala administración: bajos precios internacionales, diferencias regionales
y culturales, mercados con funcionamiento deficiente y una historia de regímenes
cambiarios poco propicios y de intervenciones contraproducentes por parte del
gobierno en los mercados financieros rurales. Sin embargo, las políticas y programas
públicos pueden todavía hacer mucho por mejorar las condiciones en las cuales el
sector rural funcionará en los próximos años.

Como aspecto más importante, las autoridades responsables deberían mantener
el curso de la estabilidad macroeconómica y completar la liberalización del sector de
los cereales (permitiendo que el subsidio de apoyo a la comercialización pase a ser un
apoyo a los ingresos para fomentar un cambio hacia cultivos de mayor valor). En
segundo lugar, deberían centrarse en la reducción de los costos de transacción
mediante la inversión en infraestructura rural básica, la promoción de organizaciones y microempresas agrícolas, intercambios regionales, y flujos de información
sobre precios y mercados. En tercer lugar, deberían abordar el deficiente desempeño
del sector financiero rural y de los servicios públicos en general, establecer un marco
legal y regulatorio, el que no existe en la actualidad, para la operación (y supervisión)
de las instituciones financieras no bancarias y promover el desarrollo de los inter-
mediarios financieros rurales (como asociaciones de ahorro y préstamo, bancos comerciales, instituciones especializadas, ONG, estructuras cooperativas, etc.). En
cuarto lugar, deberían establecer un sistema regulatorio de calificación e inspección
adecuado para el desarrollo del mercado de almacenaje (luego del reciente retiro de
CONASUPO), y normas y estándares de seguridad y calidad para los alimentos. Y
en quinto lugar, deberían aumentar la eficiencia del apoyo público mediante la sepa-
ración de los beneficios de PROCAMPO de la siembra, una mayor eficacia de los
programas de Alianza para el Campo como un instrumento para promover la diversificación y asistencia técnica, y el apoyo de estrategias de riego más integrales y productivas, entre otros.

Reducción de la Pobreza Mediante el Desarrollo del Capital Humano

Hasta aquí, en este documento se ha sostenido que la estabilidad macroeconómica y
el crecimiento impulsado por la competitividad deben ser dos prioridades básicas en
la agenda de la nueva Administración Presidencial. Sin embargo, el crecimiento
estable no es un fin en sí mismo. De hecho, es una herramienta, quizás la más
poderosa, para lograr el objetivo final del desarrollo: la reducción de la pobreza. Las
estadísticas de pobreza (y desigualdad) de México y su evolución son motivo de un

amplio debate técnico y político. Según la estimación no ajustada del Banco Mundial, en 1996 aproximadamente dos de cada tres mexicanos eran pobres y uno de tres se encontraba en situación de extrema pobreza. Estas cifras confirman en términos estadísticos lo que ya era un supuesto seguro: que la crisis de 1994 revirtió por completo la reducción de 10 puntos porcentuales en los registros de pobreza que México se había esforzado por alcanzar desde 1984. Esto encierra un mensaje clave para las nuevas autoridades: la estabilidad macroeconómica y el crecimiento son condiciones *necesarias* para luchar con éxito contra la pobreza. Sin embargo, no son suficientes.

Prácticamente todos los Presidentes Mexicanos entrantes se comprometieron a reducir la pobreza y lanzaron programas con ese objetivo. Se han producido grandes logros (la educación primaria es casi universal, la atención de salud básica ahora llega a la mayoría de los mexicanos, existe consenso político en poner un énfasis cuantificable en el sector social dentro del presupuesto federal, etc.). Sin embargo, a juzgar por las cifras antes citadas, la pobreza sigue siendo muy extendida. Así, aparte de evitar la turbulencia macroeconómica, ¿qué puede hacer la nueva administración para reducir la pobreza que no se haya hecho antes? La respuesta se relaciona con la *calidad* de la educación, salud, protección social y otros servicios para la formación del capital humano que entrega el estado, y con la forma en que los pobres pueden aprovechar su capital humano al incorporarse al mercado laboral.

En el sistema educativo mexicano han habido y hay muchos programas de mejoramiento de la calidad y de extensión de la cobertura (*Carrera Magisterial*, PRODEI, PARE, *Escuelas Comunitarias*, PAREIB, *Telesecundaria*, etc.). Muchos de estos programas están logrando sus objetivos. Esto proporciona una buena base desde la cual comenzar a abordar un desafío más amplio en la educación pública mexicana: llevar el sistema al siguiente nivel de calidad, un nivel más compatible con las exigencias de una economía que se moderniza. El modelo actual de enseñanza centrado en los maestros, que en realidad enfatiza la memorización en perjuicio de la comprensión y que fue diseñado para el estudiante promedio, tiene que ser reemplazado por un aprendizaje cooperativo, liderado por el estudiante, que emplee la investigación y en que el maestro no sea la fuente de conocimientos ni el vigilante de los alumnos, sino más bien, el facilitador de la clase.

Este nuevo enfoque de enseñanza se reflejará en el plan de estudios (el cual tendrá que darle más importancia al pensamiento crítico y a la comunicación); en el tiempo real de estudio (más tiempo dedicado al aprendizaje en la sala de clases y menos a la administración de la clase y repeticiones mecánicas, puesto que se estima que un maestro de escuela primaria mexicano emplea menos de la mitad de las 810 horas de clase prescritas por año efectivamente enseñando); en el entorno escolar (los maestros deberán tener más influencia en el tipo y cantidad de libros de texto, material e infraestructura que obtengan sus clases y se deberá eliminar el monopolio que prácticamente posee el gobierno en la producción de textos para permitir una competencia creativa); y en forma más decisiva, en la naturaleza de los mecanismos de rendición de cuentas de los maestros y escuelas (la participación de supervisores y padres se centrará menos en el proceso y más en los resultados reales, medidos con las calificaciones publicadas de los estudiantes en pruebas nacionales estandarizadas). En todas estas reformas, los maestros, en forma individual y colectiva a través de sus sindicatos, deberán incorporarse como colaboradores. Todo esto significa un cambio en la "cultura" del sistema educacional de México, un cambio que tomará tiempo, pero que bien se puede poner en marcha durante el sexenio.

Un cambio en la "cultura" también es la clave para el mejoramiento de la calidad en el sector salud. En el pasado, México se basaba en instituciones centralizadas y programas verticales para controlar las enfermedades infecciosas y aumentar la prevención y la educación sanitaria. Esto produjo importantes éxitos de primera generación: una menor mortalidad materno-infantil, tasas de vacunación más altas, y mayor esperanza de vida. Sin embargo, estos y otros factores han cambiado el perfil epidemiológico del país, con lo que las enfermedades crónicas y las lesiones han pasado a ser las principales causas de muerte e invalidez, han surgido nuevas amenazas para la salud (como el SIDA y la contaminación), y los consumidores son cada vez más sofisticados y exigen una medicina de tecnología avanzada. Esta realidad de segunda generación requiere un cambio en el papel del gobierno, donde en lugar de imponer autoridad y control se dedique más a facilitar el suministro privado, asegurando al mismo tiempo el acceso universal a un paquete de salud básico.

Para cumplir con esta nueva función en el sector salud, el gobierno deberá implementar nuevos planes institucionales y de financiamiento y una estructura de mercado diferente para los servicios de salud. La actual serie de instituciones de salud pública (SSA; IMSS; IMSS-*Solidaridad*; ISSSTE, los servicios de salud de PEMEX, el Distrito Federal, la policía, las fuerzas armadas y otros organismos paraestatales), cada una de las cuales ha tendido a financiar y operar sistemas de salud con sus propios establecimientos y médicos que en ocasiones se superponen, no es adecuada para reducir costos ni distribuir el riesgo. La creación de un Fondo Nacional de Salud podría eliminar esos problemas: permitiría reunir todos los aportes obligatorios para atención de salud (y el conjunto de los presupuestos de salud federal y estatal) y actuar como un poderoso comprador de servicios en forma competitiva a proveedores privados y públicos, incluidas organizaciones de atención regulada. Esta fórmula de integración con competencia bajo un Fondo Nacional de Salud permitiría al gobierno y, más específicamente, a su *Secretaría de Salud*, concentrarse en la certificación y licencia de medicamentos, el establecimiento de estándares para capacitación médica, la regulación de los proveedores de atención de la salud, el financiamiento y coordinación de las actividades de investigación, y otras actividades que capten externalidades. Bajo el nuevo plan seguiría existiendo y se ampliaría la cobertura para los pobres, en especial la cobertura de salud básica, mediante pagos de los gobiernos federal y estatales al Fondo Nacional de Salud y mediante los actuales programas focalizados del gobierno (PAC, PCC, PROGRESA, PIAJA, POR CIENTO y similares), que se beneficiarían de la fuerza compradora del Fondo Nacional de Salud para lograr la entrega de sus servicios.

Sería poco razonable para México, como país, invertir recursos en la creación de capital humano a través de la salud y educación sin establecer los mecanismos adecuados que protejan esa inversión, especialmente entre los pobres. Aunque en general se carece de evaluaciones precisas, las evidencias disponibles sugieren que la Administración saliente ha logrado progresos sólidos en la protección social. En esencia, la tarea de la Administración entrante es consolidar ese progreso. Esto implicará esfuerzos paralelos en dos frentes: realizar evaluaciones abiertas y participativas, y eliminar las brechas de cobertura.

En México actualmente se emplea cerca del 1 por ciento del PIB en programas focalizados de protección social. El programa más representativo entre estos es PROGRESA, un plan de transferencia directa de ingresos a los pobres rurales condicionado en el consumo de servicios seleccionados de educación, salud y nutrición. PROGRESA es uno de los pocos programas de gobierno que ha sido evaluado y ha resultado ser extremadamente exitoso (especialmente en reducir la morbilidad infantil, aumentar la escolaridad femenina y aumentar la asistencia a los consultorios de salud básica). Aunque es posible afinarlo más, PROGRESA debería mantenerse y si es posible, ampliarse. Se puede decir mucho menos acerca de otros programas, los que carecen de una evaluación cuidadosa. La tendencia general en los programas relacionados con alimentación (Liconsa, Tortibono, Diconsa, Desayuno DIF, etc.) ha sido correcta, el subsidio supeditado a los medios de vida ha reemplazado en forma significativa al subsidio universal. Lo mismo parece aplicar a las intervenciones en materia de generación de ingresos (PET, PROBECAT, *Apoyos Productivos*, etc.). Sin embargo, es difícil afirmar si estos programas en realidad llegan a los beneficiarios previstos en forma eficiente y más importante aún, si existen brechas críticas en la cobertura.

Por lo tanto, será decisivo evaluar los programas para emprender la segunda etapa de la consolidación: identificar y eliminar brechas en la cobertura de protección social de México. El análisis preliminar del riesgo social, basado en la edad, sugiere que en efecto existen importantes brechas: desnutrición y falta de acceso a la educación preescolar entre los pobres de 0 a 5 años; baja asistencia a la escuela primaria entre niños de 6 a 14 años en áreas rurales pobres y aisladas (en especial, indígenas); baja matriculación en la escuela secundaria y altas tasas de inactividad entre los 15 y los 24 años en general; bajos ingresos, subempleo y desempleo entre la población de 25 a 64 años; y escasa cobertura de pensiones para los ancianos pobres (65 y más). Claramente se requiere una identificación más exacta de los focos de riesgo, la que deberá ser la base de intervenciones públicas.

Aun cuando crear y proteger el capital humano es la clave para reducir la pobreza, el capital humano en sí mismo no reduce la pobreza. Los pobres deben ser capaces de obtener ingresos de ese capital. El vínculo entre formación de capital humano y reducción real de la pobreza lo proporciona el mercado laboral. Es por este motivo que existe una seria inquietud de que el marco normativo y legal en el cual funciona el mercado laboral de México está obsoleto, en el mejor de los casos (parte de ese marco se remonta a 1917) y, en el peor de los casos, de que es más un impedimento que una herramienta para que los trabajadores, especialmente los trabajadores pobres, obtengan el mayor beneficio de su capital humano. No es de sorprender que aproximadamente uno de cada dos trabajadores mexicanos no pertenezca al mercado laboral formal y que de aquellos que permanecen en la informalidad, cerca de la mitad lo hace contra su voluntad. Tampoco es de sorprender que a los inversionistas del NAFTA les disgusten las regulaciones laborales de México, puesto que esas regulaciones imponen una "cuña impositiva" del 31 por ciento de la nómina, comparada con el 12 por ciento y 19 por ciento de Canadá y Estados Unidos, respectivamente. En términos económicos, las leyes, regulaciones e instituciones laborales mexicanas tienen el objeto de permitir una flexibilidad en los salarios reales, pero no una flexibilidad en el empleo, y la baja tasa de desempleo formal del país por lo general se atribuye a este factor. Sin embargo, esta flexibilidad unilateral se ajusta más a una economía protegida con una elevada inflación y sindicatos fuertes, que al México integrado, más estable y participativo de hoy.

¿Qué se debe hacer? Se debe eliminar el sistema actual de pagos por despido, negociación colectiva y contratos obligatorios para la industria (*contratos-ley*); el ingreso obligatorio a sindicatos (*cláusula de exclusión*); la repartición obligatoria de utilidades; las restricciones a los contratos temporales, de plazo fijo y de aprendizaje; los requisitos de promociones basados en antigüedad; el registro de programas de capacitación proporcionados por las empresas; y las obligaciones por los empleados de subcontratistas (*patrón indirecto*). Al igual que con el salario mínimo (actualmente bajo los niveles de equilibrio de mercado), el problema de esos sistemas no necesariamente es que limitan las decisiones de las empresas. El problema es que su costo en realidad es asumido por los trabajadores mexicanos en forma de salarios más bajos y menos oportunidades de empleo, a cambio de beneficios poco evidentes. La seguridad de los ingresos de los trabajadores se podría lograr con mecanismos más prácticos y más compatibles con los incentivos individuales (como aportes a cuentas individuales de desempleo). También es importante que los aportes a la seguridad social estén más estrechamente relacionados con los beneficios que obtienen los trabajadores, y que estos perciban que obtendrán de tales aportes. En los últimos años, se ha intentado en forma parcial esa asociación más estrecha (especialmente mediante la reforma del plan de pensiones del sector privado y de salud) y debería continuarse (por ejemplo, haciendo que los aportes a INFONAVIT sean voluntarios).

Las reformas laborales del tipo antes mencionado tendrán un beneficio adicional: contribuirán directamente a la formalización y posterior crecimiento del conjunto de microempresas y pequeñas empresas informales que componen la "otra economía" de México y que, según ciertas estimaciones, producen hasta el 25 por ciento del PIB. De hecho, la eliminación de las rigideces relacionadas con el trabajo, las reformas integrales del sector financiero y de infraestructura descritas anteriormente y, lo que es igualmente importante, la racionalización y descentralización de los 200 programas públicos de apoyo a empresas de tamaño específico financiados a nivel federal, alterará en forma positiva la disyuntiva que enfrenta el empresario informal común: evitar los costos que representan las regulaciones al seguir siendo pequeño e informal ("bajo el radar del regulador") o cumplir con las regulaciones para expandirse y obtener economías de escala. En otras palabras, el objetivo no es promover las microempresas y pequeñas empresas (esto es, aumentar su número), sino ayudarlas a desarrollarse (esto es, crecer hasta su tamaño tecnológicamente eficiente).

Por último, cabe señalar que mejorar la calidad de la entrega de los servicios públicos formadores de capital humano y del marco normativo legal del mercado laboral funcionará para el mexicano pobre "promedio". Sin embargo, grandes segmentos entre los pobres también enfrentan necesidades específicas del grupo social al que pertenecen y que pueden dificultar sus posibilidades de beneficiarse de los esfuerzos de política del gobierno. En este sentido cabe mencionar dos grupos que se superponen: las mujeres y las poblaciones indígenas. Aunque en la Parte II se proporcionan recomendaciones y diagnósticos detallados con respecto a estos grupos, no es difícil ilustrar aquí los problemas involucrados.

Las funciones atribuidas socialmente a los géneros han colocado a las mujeres en clara desventaja en términos de salud (en especial, salud reproductiva), educación, trabajo y, lo que es más perturbador aún, seguridad personal (en una encuesta realizada en 1995 en Monterrey, una de las ciudades más progresistas de México, se concluyó que más de la mitad de todas las mujeres son víctimas de alguna clase de maltrato y casi un 20 por ciento de ellas eran víctimas de maltrato y abuso sexual). De forma similar, aproximadamente 1 de cada 10 mexicanos se declaran indígenas y mantienen y responden en esencia a un conjunto diferente de valores económicos, en que los activos (en especial, la tierra) son fuentes no transables de identidad del grupo; el beneficio de la comunidad se considera de mayor importancia que la maximización de las utilidades individuales; se confía en la gobernabilidad social tradicional más que en la dictada por las leyes del país; la organización social se basa en el prestigio y el deber cívico; y el idioma de preferencia (y con frecuencia el único idioma) no es el español. Aun cuando estos problemas claramente son específicos de determinados grupos, todavía hay debate en torno a su adecuada solución. Sin embargo, además de preservar los valores y preferencias sociales, se podría argumentar que la sensibilidad cultural y de género deberían constituir una característica de la formulación de políticas a través de los sectores, desde la tributación y finanzas hasta la salud y educación. Crear esa sensibilidad requerirá intervenciones del gobierno para despertar conciencia y educar.

Equilibrio del Crecimiento y la Reducción de la Pobreza con la Protección de los Recursos Naturales

En las décadas pasadas, el desarrollo de México era esencialmente un proceso de "explotación". Energía, agua, bosques y similares se agotaban para estimular el crecimiento, sin mucha consideración por la transferencia de riquezas en contra de las generaciones futuras que implicaba o por los costos que ese agotamiento significaría para la generación actual (por ejemplo, en riesgos para la salud). Desde principios de los años noventa, esta actitud cambió radicalmente, en parte debido a la participación más activa de México en el terreno internacional (NAFTA, OCDE, Protocolo de Kioto, Convención de Basilea, etc.) y en parte debido a su democracia interna más participativa. Así, se aplicó una serie de sólidos marcos legales, normativos e institucionales, como la Ley Nacional de Aguas (1992), la Ley General para el Equilibrio Ecológico y Protección del Medio Ambiente (1996), la reforma de la Ley Forestal (1997), la creación de un ministerio del medio ambiente (SEMARNAP, en 1994), la formación de la Comisión Nacional para Áreas Protegidas (2000) y un reciente esfuerzo por fomentar la descentralización de la administración del medio ambiente.

Aunque estas reformas constituyen excelentes primeros pasos en la dirección correcta, aún no son suficientes para revertir la degradación ambiental de México. De los 258 acuíferos del país, más de 100 están agotados y se están originando graves crisis de agua en algunos estados, en especial en las zonas más productivas del norte. Menos del 10 por ciento de las aguas servidas del país se trata en forma adecuada. Sólo el 35 por ciento de los residuos sólidos se elimina en forma sanitaria. En muchos centros urbanos, los contaminantes atmosféricos habitualmente exceden los estándares de seguridad. Unas 300.000 hectáreas de bosque mexicano desaparecen cada año (la tasa más alta de América Latina). La biodiversidad está en disminución y los ecosistemas marinos e insulares están amenazados a causa de la agricultura y el turismo. A pesar de los problemas propios de las cuentas nacionales "verdes", se estima con confianza que el costo de la degradación ambiental anual equivale a cerca del 10 por ciento del PIB.

Le corresponde al nuevo gobierno federal abordar este urgente desafío ambiental. El primer paso y el más difícil políticamente es hacer que los precios reflejen la escasez, eliminando en algunos sectores los subsidios explícitos e implícitos al agua, energía y cereales básicos. La eliminación de los subsidios debería producirse en los tres niveles de gobierno; por ejemplo, no existe mucha justificación para que la CNA fije el precio del agua en forma adecuada si los municipios locales no transfieren ni imponen el pago de esos nuevos precios a sus consumidores finales (y al mismo tiempo buscan las formas de traspasar la pérdida nuevamente a la federación). Puesto que muchos de esos subsidios son obtenidos por los pobres (aunque no exclusivamente por ellos), se deberá aplicar un apoyo de ingresos compensatorio. Sin embargo, una fijación de precios más adecuada producirá un beneficio concomitante: hará que la inversión y preservación ambiental sea un buen negocio para el sector privado, tanto en términos de su propia conservación como en la forma de un socio prestador de servicios públicos (la inversión privada en el agua es un buen ejemplo de esa posibilidad).

En segundo lugar, se deben aclarar los derechos de propiedad en el espectro de los recursos naturales (mientras se están obteniendo progresos en el agua y la tierra, estos son menores en el sector forestal y pesquero). En tercer lugar, se debe romper en forma exógena el círculo vicioso de degradación ambiental como herramienta de supervivencia a corto plazo (en la cual están atrapadas algunas comunidades rurales y pobres), respetando al mismo tiempo las preferencias y estructuras comunales; probablemente se necesitarán programas de apoyo caso a caso. En cuarto lugar, se le debe entregar a SEMARNAP la facultad de actuar como una "función" en todos los ministerios, más que al costado de ellos en forma de "silo" vertical. Esto permitiría la evaluación ambiental permanente de todas las políticas y programas de gobierno (no sólo las de SEMARNAP), esto es, permitiría que el gobierno mexicano en su conjunto tenga una actitud más consistente con la protección del medio ambiente.

Por último, con algunas excepciones (por ejemplo, distritos de riego), la descentralización del sector ambiental no se está llevando a cabo con rapidez (a pesar de los recientes esfuerzos por parte de SEMARNAP), aun cuando este es un sector en que la mayor proximidad entre las autoridades responsables y los usuarios sería de particular beneficio. La limitada descentralización del sector se debe en gran parte al marco fiscal general que enfrentan los estados y municipios, en que la definición de responsabilidades aún no está clara y los incentivos a la tributación local y a la aplicación de tarifas a los usuarios son deficientes (los problemas generales del proceso de descentralización se abordan más adelante).

Creación de un Gobierno Eficiente, Responsable y Transparente

La tarea de colocar a la economía mexicana en la senda de un crecimiento rápido y sostenible, que reduzca la pobreza y esté en equilibrio con el medio ambiente, tendrá que realizarse dentro de una nueva manera de gobernar. Esto se debe a que durante la última década, dos poderosas fuerzas alteraron en forma fundamental la naturaleza del gobierno en México: la globalización y la democratización. La integración comercial y financiera y el control que ambos imponen en las cuentas fiscales y el desempeño macroeconómico, hicieron que fuera casi imposible para los gobiernos mexicanos seguir siendo un sustituto de la asignación de recursos basada en el mercado privado. Si trataran de hacerlo, de inmediato serían esquivados por los inversionistas internacionalmente móviles. De igual manera, el aumento de la competencia política (en especial después de 1997) le dio un nuevo significado al federalismo del país. Los estados y municipios exigieron la restitución de su función constitucional en la formulación de políticas, colocando así esa formulación bajo un escrutinio más directo, por parte del electorado local. En resumen, la globalización y la democratización han hecho que las actividades del gobierno en México sean mucho más responsables frente a los mercados y frente a los votantes.

Esta tendencia hacia una responsabilidad pública del gobierno por su gestión es irreversible y seguramente se intensificará en los próximos años. El nuevo Presidente se enfrentará con la exigencia urgente de un "mejor gobierno" (que en términos generales se entiende como un cuerpo de proveedores de bienes públicos más eficaz, más eficiente y más transparente) y se le hará responsable de proporcionarlo. Sin embargo, mejorar la calidad del gobierno en México es una tarea multifacética, de muchos niveles y varios años, cuyo cumplimiento total probablemente se extenderá por varios sexenios. Por consiguiente, es imperativo que las autoridades entrantes se centren en unas pocas áreas críticas, en que los rendimientos marginales en términos de mejoramiento de calidad sean los más altos. En este documento se sugiere que tales áreas de concentración deberían ser tres: la descentralización, el sistema judicial y la corrupción.

Como se mencionó, la descentralización en México ya está en curso y avanza con rapidez. Su potencial de mejorar la calidad de los servicios del gobierno acercando a las autoridades responsables y a los beneficiarios finales es enorme. La descentralización permite eliminar la función del gobierno federal de perseguir aquellos resultados que los gobiernos subnacionales pueden lograr por sí mismos, y dirigirla hacia la captación de externalidades a nivel nacional. Sin embargo, la descentralización también tiene en última instancia la posibilidad de ser un factor de desestabilización para las finanzas públicas en todos los niveles y, para el marco macroeconómico del país. La experiencia mundial indica que la descentralización no se debería realizar sin una estrategia general coherente y sin la adecuada infraestructura institucional en los niveles inferiores de gobierno. Sin embargo, esas fueran las condiciones en las cuales se inició la descentralización y se está intentando en México. Así, el desafío básico de política en esta área es colocar el proceso de descentralización en una senda sostenible.

El gobierno saliente buscó acertadamente asegurar esa sostenibilidad imponiendo restricciones presupuestarias "duras" a los estados y municipios. Lo logró renunciando, en el presupuesto federal para el 2000, a sus propias facultades de realizar transferencias discrecionales y estableciendo una conexión regulatoria entre las exigencias de capitalización para préstamos bancarios a los gobiernos subnacionales y las calificaciones de deuda de estos prestatarios determinadas en forma independiente. Estas reformas fueron la respuesta a corto plazo correcta y ya están dando frutos: los estados claves, como el *Estado de México*, están comenzando a articular sus esfuerzos de ajuste estructural. A este respecto, será recomendable que la nueva Administración mantenga esas duras restricciones presupuestarias, siga renunciando a las transferencias discrecionales en los presupuestos federales, y haga cumplir las nuevas regulaciones bancarias (incluso en sus propios bancos de desarrollo).

Sin embargo, en el mediano plazo, la disciplina fiscal subnacional tendrá que ser complementada con un marco más propicio para la descentralización. En particular, se debe reformar el Pacto Fiscal que actualmente delega la mayor parte de las facultades tributarias a la federación, para que se devuelva gran parte de esas facultades a los gobiernos subnacionales. Con una base tributaria propia, los estados y municipios podrían absorber el otro cambio necesario en el marco de descentralización de México: una asignación más clara de las responsabilidades de gasto, no sólo en términos de adquisición de bienes y servicios, sino también en términos de las decisiones de política que están detrás de esas adquisiciones (por ejemplo, cuánto pagarle a los maestros, cuántos hospitales mantener abiertos o cuántos caminos construir). Al tener que pagar por sus decisiones de gasto (y endeudamiento) con los impuestos aplicados directamente a sus votantes locales, los gobiernos subnacionales serían mucho más disciplinados, eficientes y responsables ante la ciudadanía por el manejo de sus asuntos fiscales.

Es importante señalar que la devolución de los impuestos y la asignación de las responsabilidades de gasto abarcan mucho más que aspectos puramente técnicos, puesto que definirán el tipo de nación federal que México desea ser. Por ejemplo, la enmienda del Pacto Fiscal para devolver impuestos requerirá una enmienda paralela de las fórmulas de transferencia, que en efecto actualmente transfieren recursos de los estados más ricos a los más pobres y moderan las disparidades de desarrollo entre las regiones. De forma similar, la descentralización total de las responsabilidades de gastos puede o no depender de estándares mínimos de logro (digamos, por ejemplo, en educación), con el objeto de asegurar cierto nivel de homogeneidad en toda la nación.

El segundo aspecto de la gobernabilidad en que las retribuciones de las reformas serán especialmente altas en términos de mejoramiento de la calidad de la función pública es el sistema judicial. Aunque actualmente se carece de evaluaciones integrales y sistemáticas, esta es un área en que parece existir consenso sobre el diagnóstico general: el sistema proporciona servicios que son insuficientes en cantidad y calidad, no está libre de corrupción, y no es accesible para las personas que no tienen dinero. La causa de este mal desempeño es una combinación de un derecho procesal y substantivo obsoleto, estructuras y procesos administrativos inadecuados, un inadecuado manejo de los recursos humanos, falta de fondos y, críticamente, una independencia limitada de los poderes políticos (en especial a nivel de estado).

Esas falencias del sistema judicial y la carga que imponen en todo el espectro de desarrollo (desde la falta de crédito a las sociedades hasta los títulos de propiedad imposibles de hacer cumplir) han sido el objeto de muchos esfuerzos de reforma (especialmente las enmiendas constitucionales de 1988, 1994 y 1999). El problema, y el desafío, es que, en su conjunto, esas reformas no generaron los resultados esperados. ¿Qué pueden hacer las nuevas autoridades para que las reformas funcionen? En primer lugar, se deben eliminar las diversas fuentes de fricción entre el sistema judicial federal y los 31 sistemas estatales (superposición de jurisdicciones en casos comerciales, uso abusivo de *amparos*, investigaciones no coordinadas, etc.). En segundo lugar, se debe asegurar la independencia de los sistemas judiciales estatales, en especial con respecto a la rama ejecutiva de los estados, algo que puede requerir enmiendas constitucionales adicionales. En tercer lugar, el campo de las reformas se debe extender más allá de los jueces y cubrir el conjunto de los demás agentes (administradores de tribunales, fiscales, litigantes, etc.) y mecanismos (arbitraje privado, mediación, conciliación, entre otros) del sector judicial. En términos más mundanos, pero igualmente importantes, se deben establecer mecanismos transparentes para vigilar y evaluar la aplicación de la reforma, tanto para garantizar medidas correctivas oportunas cuando sea necesario como para difundir las prácticas que resulten exitosas a través de los estados.

El tercer mejoramiento y quizás el más visible en la calidad del gobierno de México será una reducción en la incidencia de la corrupción. Lamentablemente, este es un fenómeno que carece de documentación y diagnóstico sistemáticos. Sin embargo, las percepciones de los ciudadanos bastan para ilustrar la magnitud del problema: según una reciente encuesta independiente realizada por los medios de comunicación mexicanos, sólo el 3 por ciento de la población piensa que el gobierno no es corrupto y uno de cada tres encuestados piensa que es "muy corrupto". En otras palabras, existe una demanda acumulada por transparencia.

Enfrentar el problema de la corrupción en México será difícil y tomará tiempo. Por lo tanto, será decisivo centrarse en primer lugar en las instituciones clave para la fijación de incentivos. SECODAM y la *Contaduría Mayor de Hacienda* (los auditores internos y externos del gobierno, respectivamente) necesitan una urgente modernización. SECODAM, aunque ha avanzado en sus esfuerzos por modernizar las adquisiciones del gobierno (a través de COMPRANET), carece de los mecanismos para responder ante los ciudadanos (procedimientos adecuados para manejar quejas, una "ficha de evaluación," etc.). La *Contaduría Mayor de Hacienda*, por diseño o por práctica, no cumple con su cometido principal de verificar los gastos públicos en forma oportuna. Estos problemas con la auditoría externa e interna de la rama ejecutiva también existen, con diversos grados de magnitud, en los 31 gobiernos estatales.

Junto con establecer incentivos apropiados para sus auditores, el gobierno federal debe proporcionar los incentivos adecuados a sus propios empleados mediante la creación de un servicio civil de carrera, en el que la promoción y la compensación sean competitivos con el mercado y basados en el desempeño y donde la información (registros, cuentas, decisiones) se mantenga confidencial solo por excepciones especificadas en la ley.

Muchas instituciones fuera del gobierno tendrán importancia en el establecimiento de incentivos contra la corrupción. Cabe mencionar especialmente tres: el sistema judicial (tratado anteriormente); la policía (que, aunque aquí no se ha tratado, es decisiva para romper el vínculo entre crimen y corrupción) y los medios de comunicación (cuyo papel en el México nuevo y más abierto probablemente se amplíe, probando la fortaleza del marco de protección legal para sus operaciones).

III. Conclusión y Recapitulación

La agenda que se describe en este capítulo y que está sustentada en las dos partes de este compendio es poco menos que abrumadora. En esencia, se recomienda a la nueva Administración que busque la sostenibilidad macroeconómica como una condición sine qua non; que acelere el crecimiento a largo plazo mediante una mayor competitividad externa (y no a través de estímulos a la demanda agregada de corto plazo); que intente reducir la pobreza mediante la formación de capital humano (y no a través de donaciones temporales); que haga del crecimiento con reducción de la pobreza una tarea que esté en equilibrio con el medio ambiente (y no un ejercicio de explotación); y que logre estas metas sobre la base de un gobierno eficiente, responsable por su gestión y transparente.

Sin duda, su puesta en práctica requerirá asignar prioridades. Se deberán tomar decisiones para trazar la secuencia de los esfuerzos de política que se emprenderán en cada etapa. No hay respuestas universales con respecto a la secuencia que se ajuste mejor a México y mucho dependerá del valor que le asigne el equipo entrante a los diversos objetivos, y de la evaluación que tenga de su propia capacidad. Sería muy optimista pensar que todas o incluso gran parte de las reformas aquí descritas pueden lograrse durante el próximo sexenio. El consenso con respecto a las principales reformas puede resultar enloquecedoramente esquivo en una democracia participativa, y su implementación, no menos difícil. Por lo tanto, es decisivo que el nuevo gobierno logre algunos éxitos demostrables en una etapa temprana, con el fin de crear el impulso decisivo para los siguientes esfuerzos.

Aunque difícil, la agenda es factible. México puede movilizar los recursos humanos y materiales necesarios para implementarla. El país tiene una oportunidad única para hacerlo: los cambios políticos históricos que originaron las elecciones del año 2000 abrieron las puertas para una reforma emprendedora y participativa. La recompensa al final del sexenio no será un México libre de todos sus problemas de desarrollo, sino más bien un México en una senda de desarrollo rápida y sostenible, y un futuro mejor para todos sus habitantes.

Part 1

1

Fiscal Sustainability

This Thematic Chapter was written by Fernando Montes-Negret, with the valuable input of Stephen B. Everhart and Joost Draisma.

I. Introduction

Public sector deficits and the burden of the public debt have always been at the center of the macroeconomic policy debate in Mexico. The reduction of *explicit* public sector deficits was a cornerstone of the country's macroeconomic policies during the 1990s.

One of the major reasons for concern regarding high and increasing public sector deficits is the fear that sooner or later the government will resort to printing money to finance the deficit (base money creation), and that this monetization of the debt will lead to inflation. A second major reason for concern results from the other two modes of financing public deficits: increased taxation and additional public sector borrowing through bond finance. Increased taxation leads to reduced private investment and consumption. In extremis, bond finance could lead to a debt–deficit spiral in which interest payments on an ever-increasing debt would grow explosively leading to major macroeconomic instability, including crowding out of the private sector, and even to an eventual, total or partial, repudiation of the public debt.

This Thematic Chapter provides, first, a conceptual overview of the solvency constraints faced by governments, and the sustainability of fiscal policies. Second, it focuses on the distinction between explicit and implicit fiscal deficits, realized or contingent, resulting from other realized but unaccounted or yet-to-materialize expenditure pressures. The chapter then focuses on some of the recent trends observed in the Mexican economy, highlighting areas of concern and possible eventual action by the incoming Administration. The accompanying chapters on strategy for fiscal sustainability, public sector debt management, and pension reform provide a more detailed discussion of these respective topics.

II. Government Solvency and Sustainable Debt

The public sector is said to be solvent if its outstanding debt does not exceed the present discounted value of its anticipated future revenues, net of expenditures. For a single period budget this implies that:

$$D^e_{t+1} \cdot \delta_t + D_{t+1} = \delta_{t\text{-}1} \cdot D^e_t (1+I^e_t) (1+d\delta_t) + D_t (1+I_t) - (T_t - G_t) + (H_{t+1} - H_t),$$

where: D^e and D are foreign-and domestic-currency-denominated debts outstanding at the beginning of the period $(t+1)$, respectively; δ is the exchange rate in units of domestic currency per unit of foreign currency, and $d\delta$ is the proportional rate of depreciation of the domestic currency; I^e and I are the foreign and domestic interest rates, respectively; T stands for total net tax collections; G stands for nominal government non-interest expenditures; and H stands for the outstanding base money.

If one rewrites the above equation in terms of GDP ratios, and solves the single period budget identity for the public sector forward over an infinite horizon, it is possible to establish the solvency condition requiring that the outstanding debt be no greater than the present value of planned future primary surpluses plus expected seignorage revenues. Manipulating the above equation and assuming that the interest parity condition is met in the long-run (that is, that there are no deviations between the domestic and international interest rates), the long-run sustainable growth of the debt-over-GDP ratio is given by $(r-g)/(1+g)$, where (r) is the long-run real rate of interest and g is the long-run growth rate of real GDP.[1] In other words, *the dynamics of the debt-to-GDP ratio over the longer run depends on the difference between the real interest rate and the real rate of output growth.* The policy implication of this result is that in the event of a large and widening gap between the real interest rates and the real rate of output growth (i.e.; $r>>g$), the debt-over-GDP ratio could move to an explosive trajectory, unless the primary surplus rises further, to counter this tendency. The threat of an explosive debt-over-GDP ratio is heightened if the starting point for the ratio is very high. If the debt ratio is, for example, 100 percent of GDP, and $r = 8$ percent and $g = 2$ percent, then a stable debt ratio requires the government to generate a primary surplus of no less than 6 percent of GDP per year forever in order to maintain the debt ratio constant at 100 percent of GDP.

Luckily the relative burden of Mexico's measured debt declined from levels close to 120 percent in the mid-1980s to less than 30 by 1993, to rise again modestly after

---

1. A more intuitive explanation of this result comes from the simpler expression of the debt-over-GDP ratio in (t+1): $[D\ (t+1)\ /\ Y\ (t+1)\ ] = [\ Dt\ (1+rt)\ (1+\Pi\ t)\ /\ Yt\ (1+g)\ (1+\Pi t)]$, where r is the real interest rate, g is the real rate of growth of output, and P is the rate of inflation. Eliminating $(1+\Pi t)$ from the numerator and denominator and dividing both sides by (Dt / Yt), we get an expression for the change in the debt over GDP ratio (**d**) as a function of $[(1+r)\ /\ (1+g)]$, or **d = f(r-g)**.

the 1994 crisis. Nonetheless, if the off-balance sheet *Fondo Bancario de Protección al Ahorro* (FOBAPROA) debts inherited by the *Instituto para la Protección del Ahorro Bancario* (IPAB) were to be included as part of the government's domestic debt, it would add another 20 points of GDP. Once other unaccounted liabilities are added, the debt ratio would be significantly higher than the one resulting from including only the explicitly recognized public debt. Moreover, good growth performance in the recent past compares favorably with the prevailing real rate of interest, which has also declined (7 to 8 percent). With a debt-to-GDP ratio of 50 to 60 percent and an *(r-g)* difference of 4 to 5 percent, Mexico would need a primary surplus of 2 to 3 percent of GDP to keep constant the debt-to-GDP ratio. While the debt ratio is not high, the outlook seems less favorable when seen against Mexico's actual tax effort (less than 10 percent of GDP), against which IPAB's unaccounted liabilities are already making a claim for 1 percent of GDP per year for the foreseeable future.

The viability of a current set of policies, or the need for policy reforms, hinge on, among other things, whether the projected path of public sector debt is or is not sustainable. Traditional analyses (Buiter 1983) center on the difference between the long-term expected value of the government's primary surplus (that is, the difference between government spending, excluding debt service, and tax revenues) and the expectation of the required debt service to maintain a constant outstanding public debt-to-GDP ratio.[2]

III. Conceptual Distinctions: Explicit and Implicit (Real or Contingent) Fiscal Deficits

Mexico's explicit fiscal deficits were drastically reduced from 15 percent of GDP in 1987 to 1.24 percent in 1998. However, unaccounted, actual and contingent liabilities, if let unattended, could bring into question the permanence of the fiscal consolidation effort undertaken by the two last Administrations. Among the *unaccounted liabilities* a distinction needs to be made between those which are *actual* liabilities of the public sector, even if for legal or other reasons they are not explicitly reflected in "the books" of the government, and *contingent* liabilities, which are those that have a probabilistic element or an element of uncertainty as to their impact and the timing in which they will be reflected explicitly in "the books" of the government. The first category includes, for example, the liabilities inherited by IPAB from FOBAPROA, which are losses (largely) already realized (that is, there is no real uncertainty as to their nature and size as liabilities of the broadly defined public sector) but which, for legal reasons, are not part of the government's accounts and are not included as part of the country's domestic public debt. The second group includes contingent liabilities, for example, in the unfunded pay-as-you-go

---

2. The measure of sustainability of the set of policies required by the latter is known in the literature as the "permanent primary gap" or the "primary gap."

(PAYG) social security system, and other contingent liabilities which are even more difficult to quantify, such as unlimited bank deposit insurance schemes, public guarantees for private investments, or accelerated depletion in public infrastructure, which are not only contingent on the occurrence of certain events, but which are not, like the latter, even effective liabilities to a third identifiable party.

Proper recognition of those not-clearly-identified or off-balance sheet liabilities of the public sector do not diminish the accomplishments of the authorities who have responded to major imbalances (in 1982, 1986, and 1994) and to external volatility (1998) with decisive actions, tightening fiscal policy (mainly through cuts in public expenditures) and leading to significant primary surpluses. However, remaining unaccounted liabilities need to be examined, quantified, and controlled, given their destabilizing potential once they become explicit liabilities of the government on the public accounts.

IV. Recommendations

As discussed above, a sustainable fiscal policy is expected to generate sufficient net future government revenues to service and amortize the outstanding public debt, even in the presence of unexpected shocks. For this to be possible, we offer the following recommendations.

Fiscal Sustainability

Our findings indicate that Mexico's fiscal policy does not lean against the wind; rather, because its fiscal policy stance is quite strongly pro-cyclical, it leans with the wind. The automatic stabilizers in place are weak, and are further weakened by the tendency of another automatic component of the budget, oil-based revenue, which responds sensitively to exogenous world oil prices, to move pro-cyclically (that is, amplifying the external shock as oil price declines are met with rapid expense cuts). Furthermore, the discretionary component of the budget surplus also tends to move pro-cyclically. The policy implication is that not only is the government not using fiscal policy to dampen economic swings, it is amplifying such swings.

Continued and excessive reliance on oil revenues for as nearly much as one-third of government revenue makes Mexico's fiscal accounts extremely vulnerable to instability in the oil market, consequently, strengthening other areas of the tax system and diversifying government revenues would mollify these concerns and reduce the volatility of government revenue.

In the past, fiscal adjustment has relied excessively on cuts in government investment, particularly capital formation, creating a significant backlog of unattended public, physical and social investments. Public investment in Mexico has fallen from over 12 percent of GDP in 1981 to less than 2 percent in 1998. Clearly this is not sustainable. Estimates of capital requirements for the next 10 years in the energy sector alone approach MXP$1,000 billion in constant 1999 pesos. This equates to approximately MXP$100 billion pesos a year, representing 2.5 percent of current GDP, or the total health or education budgets for a given year.

Public Debt Management

Over the next few years the main challenge faced in public debt management in Mexico will be to refinance a large stock of public debt. Debts inherited by IPAB from FOBAPROA as a result of the 1994–95 banking crisis, and the debts of *Fideicomiso de Apoyo al Rescate de Autopista* (FARAC) from the rescue of toll roads, add MXP$817 billion, or 18 percent of GDP, to the explicit debt stock of the nonfinancial public sector of 28 percent of GDP, bringing the total explicit public debt stock to 46 percent of GDP. The previous adjustments do not include the implicit liabilities of the government in off-budget public investment projects guaranteed by the government with a deferred cost (known as *Proyectos de Impacto Diferido en el Registro del Gasto*, PIDIREGAS), under the two modalities being used (direct and conditional investment projects).

The rapid rise in the "expanded" debt-to-GDP ratio poses two types of challenges for future Administrations. The first challenge is the direct service of these debts per se in view of relatively low fiscal effort. The second challenge, which is major, is to refinance or roll over the outstanding, largely domestic, debts simultaneously with the lengthening of the mostly short-term maturities in a relatively undeveloped domestic capital market. It should be noted that a large portion of the "new" debts (IPAB and FARAC) are held by the domestic banking system and consequently must rely on market conditions for their future rollover. This is particularly important to avoid the negative carryovers that contributed recently to the failure and intervention of a major Mexican bank.[3] The following issues should be addressed:

- Full integration of Mexico's public debt and public debt management within SHCP would be highly desirable. For legal reasons IPAB's and FARAC's debts are being managed independently of the explicit domestic debt of the government (which is managed by the SHCP), although in full coordination with the SHCP and the *Banco de México* as fiscal agent. Nonetheless, the present system results in higher costs (to the extent that there is a small premium on the non-government debt), less transparency, and added difficulties in

---

3. SERFIN's insolvency was finally precipitated by the negative carryover resulting from the bank's funding of the zero-coupon FOBAPROA bonds at rates above those at which the bonds were accruing interest. During the latter years to maturity, the bond yield was equivalent to accruals at the rate of (CETES-1.35), while at the margin SERFIN was borrowing in the interbank market at (TIIE+2 or 3 percentage points). In the words of SERFIN's President, "the medicine ended up killing the patient."

achieving the desired optimal composition with the required flexibility in response to rapidly changing market conditions. Eventually SHCP might consider diversifying the currency composition of these debts if symptoms of saturation are observed in the domestic market or if domestic institutional investors are not prepared to extend the maturity of these debts. In other words, deliberate policy actions might be required to rebalance the largely unplanned and now possibly excessive dependence on the domestic market through an integrated public debt management strategy.

- While at 46 percent the debt-to-GDP ratio in Mexico is well below the average for OECD countries, it is also true that given the significantly smaller size of the Mexican public sector in the economy compared to the average OECD country, the debt service cost represents a much larger part of public expenditures.[4] For this reason two types of broad policies are required: one intended to raise the fiscal effort through a comprehensive tax reform, and another to policies directed at bringing down the level of the explicit and implicit public debts. In the case of IPAB, the proceeds of a rapid sale of bad assets, received in exchange for government bonds, should be used to retire debt.

- A strategy for extending the maturity and duration of Mexico's public debt is particularly important in view of the short-term destabilizing impact of increased volatility and shocks on public finances.

- The international financial institutions can play a significant role in complementing IPAB's efforts to refinance its liabilities with the banking sector by issuing *Bonos para la Proteccion del Ahorro* (BPAs). At the present pace IPAB will not be able to refinance all the bonds maturing between 2000 and 2007; only 44 percent of the bonds maturing from 2000 until 2007 will be refinanced, implying that the amount of BPAs being issued weekly needs to double to meet the 2007 target. Nonetheless, excessive pressure on the domestic market could crowd out the private sector even more, and put additional upward pressure on domestic interest rates.

- An integrated debt management strategy must take into account the absorptive capacity of Mexico's domestic market, while having the flexibility to shift to the international market depending on changing market conditions. At present an already historically high level of 59 percent of total financial savings included in the definition of M4 is kept in domestic public debt instruments. Further diversification of the currency composition of the public debt and increased depth of the domestic capital market would contribute to reducing crowding out of domestic investors.

---

4. The size of the public sector in the economy as measured by the current revenue of the central government in Mexico is about 15 percent of GDP compared to 35 percent average for the OECD countries.

Pension Reform

The combination of the relative growth in the number of elderly Mexican citizens, unrealistic benefits, poor management, and the push for greater efficiency and competitiveness have put the various social security systems under increasing strain.

PRIVATE SECTOR WORKERS' PENSION SYSTEM. The mandatory public pension system for over 14 million affiliated private sector workers was reformed in 1997. All formal, private sector workers are members of the new mandatory, private, individual account, defined contribution system. On average, 17.5 percent of the wages of private sector workers are contributed to their individual pension accounts. Of this amount, 5 percentage points are deposited in workers' individual accounts at INFONAVIT, and 4 percentage points go to IMSS to cover disability and life insurance. The balance is deposited in the individual accounts at the AFORES. Future government reform efforts should continue to be guided by three core objectives: fiscal sustainability, equity, and efficiency. To implement this set of principles the following actions are recommended:

- It is essential to ensure that the unique identification number SUA is sound and able to identify each worker.
- There is a need for improvement in the efficiency of the resource transfer system from the time a worker's contribution is deducted to the moment the funds are credited in his or her individual accounts in the AFORES.
- The severe restrictions that have been placed on the AFORES investment regime need to be relaxed, allowing them to offer multiple *Sociedades de Inversión Especializada de Fondos para el Retiro* (SIEFORES), to expand the maximum percentage authorized for investing in private securities, and to allow investments in foreign assets, thus expanding the choices demanded by different workers with different interests and risk tolerance.
- Efforts should be made to reduce the administrative costs of the system in order to improve equity and efficiency.
- The private pension system supervisory agency (CONSAR) needs to continue to be strengthened, in part by increasing its autonomy and scope of action by including under its jurisdiction voluntary pension plans.
- Major reform—or even closing—of INFONAVIT should be a priority of the new Administration. At the very least, the reforms should include the amendment of its enacting law and its governance structure. These reforms are a priority considering the significant threat that INFONAVIT poses to the overall success of the private pension system by putting at risk 40 percent of the accumulated contributions to workers' pensions, while seriously distorting Mexico's housing and mortgage markets.
- As private pension reform matures, complementary reform of capital markets increases in importance, particularly in order to stimulate the supply of longer-term bonds, housing mortgages, and equities.

- The development of the insurance industry, and in particular of the annuities market, should receive increasing attention.

PENSION SYSTEM FOR FEDERAL GOVERNMENT EMPLOYEES. The *Instituto de Seguridad y Servicios Sociales de los Trabajadores del Estado* (ISSSTE) pension system for 2 million federal government employees is already in a cash flow deficit position (that is, it depends on government transfers to pay pensions), and is actuarially insolvent. Part of the problems result from generous benefits, which allow retiring employees to receive 100 percent of the average salary of the last 12 months, in addition to access to subsidized services, including housing finance through FOVISSSTE. The total implicit debt of the ISSSTE pension system is estimated at 120 percent of 1997 GDP. Reform of this system should be a high priority of the incoming administration.

PENSION SYSTEMS FOR STATE GOVERNMENT EMPLOYEES. Almost all of the 34 pension systems for the 2.5 million state government employees face problems rooted in their PAYG nature, and carry large actuarial deficits. These systems have, on average, a still-favorable dependency ratio of 10 (that is, 10 active workers support a retiree). However, the actuarial projections undertaken for 29 state systems indicate that the dependency ratio will decline to 4.65 workers by 2010, and to 2.15 by 2025. In parallel, pension payments as a percentage of the wage bill are set to increase from 17 percent in 2000 to 26 percent in 2010 to 46 percent in 2025. This trend makes clear the importance of acting now, when conditions are favorable, particularly in view of the large estimated actuarial deficit of about 37 percent of 1997 GDP. Future unfunded claims of this magnitude will pose a serious threat to fiscal sustainability.

PENSION SYSTEM FOR PARASTATAL EMPLOYEES. Not much is know about this segment, which includes over 500,000 workers at large state-owned companies like PEMEX and the military. SHCP should assess the actuarial soundness of these systems and, if necessary, take corrective actions.

EQUITY, POVERTY, AND INCREASED COVERAGE. Low coverage of the contributory social insurance system in Mexico is of particular concern because there is no income transfer program in place for the indigent elderly, leaving the minimum pension guarantee and the social quota—both restricted to participants in the formal pension system—as the only social safety net for old age income security. In the transition, and until the effects of increasing coverage are felt, it may be justified to implement an old age income assistance program for the very poor.

2

Growth and Competitiveness

*This Thematic Chapter was written by Richard Clifford
based on the input of the authors and contributors of the chapters
under this theme.*

The past six years in Mexico have been characterized by economic crisis, recovery, and growth. For Mexico's future development five challenges must be met: (a) maintaining fiscal sustainability; (b) sustaining recent growth through enhanced competitiveness; (c) decreasing poverty and inequality; (d) ensuring an environmentally sustainable future; and (e) fostering good government. This Chapter focuses on the issue of sustaining growth and competitiveness over the next six years, and particularly on three key sectors: the financial sector, infrastructure, and agriculture.

I. Macroeconomic Overview

The stabilization efforts and successes that preceded and have underpinned Mexico's sweeping market-oriented structural reforms since the late 1980s have been anchored in strong fiscal adjustment. Fiscal deficits were drastically reduced (from 15 percent of GDP in 1987 to less than 1 percent at present), allowing for tighter monetary policy and lessened inflationary pressures (over the same period, inflation fell from 160 percent per year to the current single-digit level). This created an environment in which long-needed structural reform could proceed. The sustainability of these reforms and adjustments is thus central to the government's macroeconomic policy and, ultimately, to the country's development future. Despite these achievements, challenges remain in five key areas: (a) GDP recovery is quite uneven across sectors; (b) trade and foreign direct investment appear more concentrated since NAFTA; (c) there is procyclical (or absent) public investment policy; (d) the banking system remains weak; and (e) real wages has yet to recover from the 1995 crisis.

Mexico's recent macro experience is well known and well documented. During the early 1990s the economy grew at a relatively stable pace, averaging over 3 percent per year. The onset of the Tequila crisis led the economy into a severe but short-lived recession. Recovery from this downturn was quick, in part due to the aid package assembled by international organizations and the U.S. government, and in part due to appropriate macroeconomic policy responses to the shock. Since 1995 growth has continued apace, with some sectors far outperforming others (see Table 1). NAFTA is cited as both a cause of the crisis and a factor enhancing the recovery.

One indisputable outcome of NAFTA is the increased reliance on the U.S. economy. Distinguishing between what has happened and what might have happened in the absence of NAFTA is difficult to discern; however, two areas of concern are foreign direct investment (FDI) and exports. FDI has helped alleviate the absence of domestic sources of funding since the 1995 crisis (see Figure 1). In Mexico, FDI growth has been strong, yet the U.S. share has increased dramatically, up from 46 percent in 1994 to 71 percent in 1998, much of it concentrated in the manufacturing sector. Positive effects of FDI flows on growth the are satisfying of financing needs, transfer of new technology, fostering of competitiveness in the economy, and, to a certain extent, higher wages paid in the sectors benefiting from such flows. An onerous negative effect is the volatile nature of FDI, to which Mexico, among other developing economies, has already proven itself vulnerable in this decade.

Exports have also witnessed a marked concentration since the passage of NAFTA, with exports to the U.S. increasing from less than 80 percent before NAFTA to almost 90 percent in 1999 (See Figure 2 next page).

A well-functioning labor market is one of the keys to sustainable economic growth. The labor market in Mexico suffers from the fact that while GDP has recovered strongly since 1995, real wages have not (see Figures 3 and 4). Productivity may be an issue,[1] and an inelastic labor supply, particularly in the unskilled sector, also explains this phenomenon. A major challenge for the incoming administration is to create the conditions for a recovery of the purchasing power of labor earnings.[2]

Another aspect of the labor market that must be confronted is the large and growing informal sector. One explanation for the growth in this sector is that much of the population views the contributions to social security as a burden, not a benefit. The absence of a genuine social safety net makes participation in the formal sector less attractive.

II. The Financial Sector

Overview

The Mexican financial sector is small by international standards. Three factors have affected its development: (a) domestic macroeconomic management, in particular the historical experience with high inflation, and macroeconomic volatility; (b) vul-

---

1. See the recent OECD study by Scarpetta et al. (2000).
2. See also the Labor Market Chapter.

Table 1. GDP: Average Yearly Growth Rates by Sector

	Total	Agric., Cattle Raising, Fishery	Mining Extraction Activities	Mfg Industry	Construction	Electricity, Gas & Water	Dom. Trade, Rest. & Hotels	Transports & Comm.	Financial Services	Other Services
1990	5.07	5.63	3.39	6.77	9.19	2.59	6.21	3.57	4.45	3.15
1991	4.22	2.32	1.04	3.43	4.88	0.39	6.08	3.43	4.70	4.48
1992	3.63	-0.97	1.26	4.16	6.68	3.07	5.30	5.29	4.58	1.52
1993	1.95	3.08	1.84	-0.67	3.02	2.56	0.09	4.03	5.45	3.32
1994	4.42	0.18	2.54	4.07	8.43	4.77	6.78	8.71	5.42	1.26
1995	-6.17	1.83	-2.68	-4.94	-23.46	2.15	-15.53	-4.93	-0.32	-2.32
1996	5.15	3.80	8.11	10.83	9.77	4.58	4.80	8.03	0.57	0.99
1997	6.76	0.16	4.47	9.96	9.28	5.21	10.61	9.93	3.73	3.34
1998	4.80	0.05	3.39	7.42	4.60	4.66	4.22	10.14	3.77	2.61
1999	3.65	3.47	-3.25	4.08	4.46	4.41	4.07	8.81	2.69	1.51
2000	7.90	0.90	3.00	9.40	6.90	7.20	15.00	11.90	4.00	3.20

Note: Yearly growth rates were estimated by obtaining the percent change between yearly GDP. From 1990 to 1998 the calculations were made based on the Presidential Report data. For 1999 yearly GDP was estimated as the average of quarterly GDP reported by INEGI. For 2000 we have data only for the first quarter, thus the growth rates represent the year-on-year change for the first quarter.
Source: Presidential Report and INEGI.

Figure 1. Foreign Direct Investment

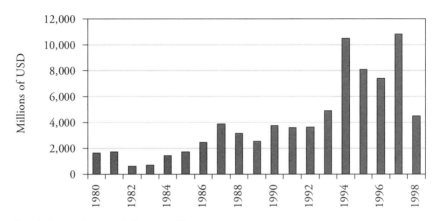

Data before 1994 is not strictly comparable.

FDI Composition 1994

FDI Composition 1998

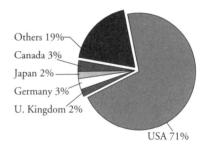

Others 32%
Canada 7%
Japan 6%
Germany 3%
U. Kingdom 6%
USA 46%

Others 19%
Canada 3%
Japan 2%
Germany 3%
U. Kingdom 2%
USA 71%

Source: INEGI

Figure 2. Exports by Region 1990

Exports by Region 1999

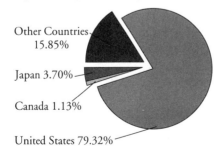

Other Countries 15.85%
Japan 3.70%
Canada 1.13%
United States 79.32%

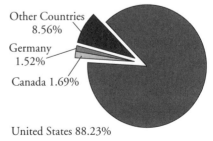

Other Countries 8.56%
Germany 1.52%
Canada 1.69%
United States 88.23%

Figure 3. Evolution of the Minimum Wage

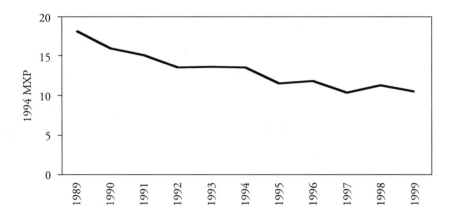

Figure 4. Evolution of Mean Daily Earnings Per Worker, Manufacturing Sector

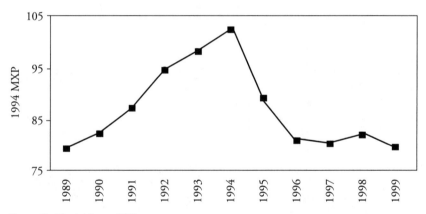

Source: Presidential Report 1999.

nerability to external shocks due to the high levels of correlation between Latin American financial markets; and (c) numerous internal and structural factors—the legacy of directed credit, financial repression, and banking system rescues that are still being paid for, the pervasive influence of the *grupos financieros* and consequent links between banks and nonbanks, and the closely held ownership structure of the domestic corporate sector.

Undoubtedly, the weakness of the banking sector has impeded development. Direct commercial bank financing to the nonbank private sector fell by 73 percent in real terms from December 1994 through June 2000. Similarly, bank liabilities as a proportion of GDP declined from 32 percent in 1994 to 23 percent in June 2000, partially due to the sustained growth in the competing mutual funds industry. In 1999 alone, real growth in portfolio assets was 36 percent.

The banking industry as a whole, hit hard by the 1994–95 crisis, has gone through noticeable improvements in terms of quality of capital, profitability, and risk management practices. Financial information for the banking industry by June 2000 showed signs of improvement. Past-due loans decreased to MXP$57.7 billion from MXP$84.5 billion in 1999, reflecting a decline in the non-performing loan index from 8.9 percent in 1999 to 6.4 percent in June 2000, the lowest level since the new accounting principles were implemented (January 1997). However, these improvements were at the expense of the capitalization index which, adjusted for market risk, declined to 14.3 percent by June 2000 from 16.2 percent in 1999.[3] Operating profits increased substantially, and the industry's coverage ration (substandard loans over loan-loss provisions) rose to 110.8 percent.

The decline in real lending to the private sector has been offset by the other low-risk assets which have become the main components of the industry's balance sheet. By June 2000, portfolio securities (33 percent), direct government loans (9 percent), and interbank lending (one percent) represented 43 percent of total assets. The change of the attitude of banks toward private sector lending has caused a credit crunch in some segments. Increased lending to the government is now channeled through the purchase of securities, rather than by direct lending as occurred during the years of bank nationalization.

The change in the balance sheet composition in favor of less risky assets has also changed the sources of bank profitability. Banks now depend to a great extent on government-issued instruments (Special Cetes, FOBAPRO Bonds, Cetes, Bondes, Udibonos, etc.). Figure 5 shows that by June 2000, 23 percent of total interest earned came from the loans sold to FOBAPROA while interest earned from securities positions represented 32 percent, rising significantly from their 23 percent participation in 1998. In other words, Mexican banks might be going in the same direction as some of the Brazilian banks, functioning more like *casas de bolsa* than traditional deposit-taking and lending institutions.

The challenge for the new Administration is to continue to strengthen and deepen the financial sector in order to increase its participation in the development process. This will require a series of actions to increase its efficiency, improve accessibility, and ensure stability and soundness.

Need for Increased Efficiency

Inefficient financial markets impose an implicit tax on consumers and entrepreneurs, limiting the economy's ability to grow and reduce poverty. Good corporate

---

3. This indicator should be viewed with caution since credit restructuring under the "Punto Final Program" reclassified some nonperforming loans as performing.

Figure 5. Public Investment versus Oil Prices

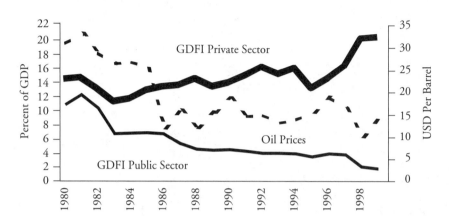

governance, supervision, accounting, auditing reporting and disclosure rules, a sound legal and judicial framework and adequate tax treatment, market depth and liquidity, are the underpinnings of efficient markets. Competition, including strategic investment by foreign financial institutions, provides incentive for modernizing the domestic banking industry. Capital markets add diversity, depth, and liquidity to the financial system and provide a stimulus for competition and increased efficiency in the corporate and banking sectors.

The financial sector has undergone massive changes since the crisis. The banking sector has stabilized and has been consolidated with strong foreign presence. A new bankruptcy law and several amendments to existing laws concerning secured lending were approved by Congress in 1999. Because the fiscal cost of the banking crisis has been quite high (19.3 percent of GDP), the financing of this cost will maintain the dominance of government securities on the domestic debt market for the foreseeable future. The financing needs of IPAB and other government programs will be a continuing factor in the competitive access of other issuers. For the immediate future several initiatives are critical for strengthening and deepening the financial sector.

BANK LENDING. The banks have not yet resumed their intermediation function. Banks are more risk averse, partially due to the adoption of stricter risk management and credit review practices. It is unlikely the passage of the new legislation mentioned above will lead quickly to increased lending. For numerous reasons—better risk management, and tighter credit standards, cited above—the resumption of credit will occur gradually during an extended period. *Banco de México* estimates that if the proportion of bank credit to the private sector increases from its current 11.5 percent of GDP to 21.5 percent, the annual long-run growth of the economy would increase by 0.5 percent per year.

DEBT MARKETS. The greatest challenge facing the further development of Mexico's debt markets at present is the extension of maturities of instruments on issue. In the long term it would be desirable to promote longer-term, fixed-rate paper. The development of a full-fledged government yield curve extending beyond 3–5 years, with a liquid secondary market able to provide a minimum risk benchmark for the pricing of privately issued liabilities, remains to be established. In this regard, enhanced growth in pension funds and mutual and insurance companies is essential. More integrated management of domestic and external debt would be desirable. Finally, further clarification in the legal framework for debt management is needed. At present, the Law on Public Debt is silent on the subject of government guarantees. This is growing increasingly problematic as the volume of domestic debt by quasi-governmental entities such as FOBAPROA/IPAB and FARAC has increased.

EQUITIES MARKETS. As with all segments of its financial markets, the equities market in Mexico was hard hit by the 1994–95 crisis. Despite some recent signs of improvement, many indicators of the market suggest that there has been no fundamental recovery from the downturn. The volatility, shallowness, concentration, poor liquidity, and declining number of participants, both in terms of listed enterprises and market intermediaries, may be attributed to a combination of factors. Market volatility, particularly during the last decade, has been greatly exacerbated by difficulties with domestic macroeconomic management and external shocks, and their impact on the financial system. Corporate governance factors have deterred the development of a broad investor base. In addition, difficulties encountered in the listing process discourage companies from being listed on Mexico's stock exchange, and difficulties in delisting imply that a large number of firms reluctantly linger on the lists of the exchange, continuing to pay membership and other dues, although their float on the exchange is near zero.

INSTITUTIONAL INVESTORS. Each of the institutional investor segments face distinct issues. Mutual funds have a poor public image due to perceived weaknesses in management skills, incentives for financial groups to promote banking products at the expense of mutual fund products, lack of separation of activities between asset management and the other activities of the financial groups, and weak regulation and enforcement. Pension funds face the problem of extremely strict regulation on their activities and their limited investments in instruments other than government debt. Insurance firms are small by international standards and are ill-equipped to offer products such as annuities for which there will be significant demand due to the privatization of the pension system.

Need for Improved Accessibility

The fact that economic growth has been achieved in the absence of commercial bank lending is evidence of both strength and weakness. The productive sector continues to be characterized by a dual structure that seems to have become increasingly differentiated in the wake of trade liberalization and the banking crisis of the 1990s. On the one side is a dynamic export sector made up of internationally competitive firms, including *maquiladoras*, and on the other is a less efficient domestic-market-oriented sector dominated by microenterprises and small- and medium-scale firms. The former, like many globalized corporations, have turned to alternative sources of financing offered through the international capital markets. The latter have been largely shut off from financing. Ensuring their access will open up significant possibilities for growth and poverty reduction.

MICROBUSINESSES. These firms have traditionally been financed by the development banks, particularly NAFIN, through first tier commercial banks. During the crisis, the volume of credit to SMEs declined significantly, and has not recovered. The total amount of loans at the end of March 2000 was still lower by 42 percent in real terms than at the end of 1994.

RURAL FINANCE. Financial markets in most rural areas have remained shallow and segmented, operating in seemingly monopolistic lender–borrower clusters defined by informational advantages and transaction costs. Past government intervention in the sector has also prevented the development of well-functioning and sustainable rural financial markets. By allowing directed credit programs with poor recovery, subsidized rates, and debt forgiveness, not only has government intervention failed to address the needs of small farmers, it has also undermined financial discipline and crowded out private lenders or hindered the development of a self-sustaining cooperative structure based on savings mobilization. On the savings mobilization side, the sector remains shallow and underserved. Lack of confidence in financial institutions and transaction costs seems to explain the pattern of rural household savings. A two-pronged approach may be required: (a) improve the legal, regulatory, and supervisory framework under which the auxiliary credit institutions operate; and (b) develop partnerships between these institutions and community-based saving groups so that the latter may act as "certified agencies" of the former. Eventually the ability to engage in land transactions as envisioned with the constitutional change of 1992 will promote more efficient allocation of land and possibly enhance access to credit, because farmers may use land as collateral.

LOW-INCOME HOUSING FINANCE. Current government policy is to give priority to the provision of home mortgages by public or quasi-public agencies for social interest (that is, higher-income) finished housing. Yet, the majority of Mexicans do not qualify for a home mortgage, and thus must look now to informal and often illegal housing solutions. There is a need to reorient housing policy to (a) provide financing for progressive housing and home improvement; (b) deliver more efficient up-front subsidies and combine them with new savings instruments; (c) expand the supply of serviced urban land; and (d) improve the regulatory framework for real estate development.

Need for Increased Stability and Soundness

As in several countries, the regulatory structure in Mexico reflects, in part, results of past financial crises. SHCP is the main regulator for setting global banking, fiscal, and credit policies. It has broad powers over the Mexican financial system and regulates its structure and operation by issuing policies that govern the activities of the financial groups and its subsidiaries. It is also responsible for licensing financial institutions. The CNBV regulates the banking system, the exchange system, and the auxiliary credit institutions. Significant reforms have been undertaken since the crisis: (a) definition of regulatory capital; (b) credit portfolio classification rules; (c) new accounting and valuation rules; (d) increased transparency and disclosure by requiring commercial banks to disclose in a timely fashion all "troubled" transactions; and (e) the elimination of discretionary regulatory forbearance. Nevertheless, the remaining agenda is also large.

EXCHANGE SYSTEM. Mexico's stock exchange is recognized legally as a self-regulatory organization. However, its role in this regard is limited by the wide-ranging powers of the CNBV, and its activities are largely promotional or informational, and supportive of the regulator. The CNBV should undertake an examination of the relative roles played by the two institutions and consider amending the secrecy provision of the Securities Markets Law so that the exchange could function properly as an SRO, in keeping with best international practices.

BANKING SYSTEM. Despite the measures recently introduced, the fragmentation of supervisory functions and powers between SHCP, the Central Bank, and CNBV must be addressed, since this has debilitated the implementation of prudential policies reflected by frequent conflicts of interest, especially in the phase of problem recognition, intervention, and failure resolution policies of ailing banks following the 1995 crisis. The lack of autonomy of CNBV in exercising the functions of lead supervisor of financial institutions and capital markets might, in the end, compromise its effectiveness by completely subordinating its role to SHCP. Just as a modern financial sector requires an autonomous central bank, it is also important to have autonomous supervisors and regulators overseeing the banking system—both the private banks and the development banks.

HOUSING FINANCE. To the detriment of institutions and consumers, a largely neglected area has been housing finance. The development of a common regulatory and supervisory system for INFONAVIT, FOVI, and FOVISSSTE is urgently needed. These three lenders overlap and compete for the same clientele, but they have different charters, governance structures, and programs. They offer mortgage loans at significantly different prices, and their financial policies and programs differ markedly. This fragmentation is an important impediment to the development of a deep housing finance system.

AUXILIARY CREDIT INSTITUTIONS. There is a wide range of financial institutions that remain largely unregulated. Most of these provide financial services to the poor. Of the variety of financial cooperatives operating in Mexico—savings and loan societies, *cajas de ahorro cajas solidarias*, credit unions—many are confronting severe problems which can be traced to flawed governance rules, an unhealthy dependence on external subsidized funding, inadequate diversification, and weak prudential supervision. In particular, the recent bankruptcy of a number of *cajas de ahorro* has highlighted the need for these unregulated entities to become part of the mainstream regulated institutions, either through the CNBV or through an alternative mechanism of self-regulation. Legislation on this matter, currently under preparation, should be one of the most important short-term priorities of the current Administration.

III. Infrastructure

Infrastructure appears to have been an unwelcome guest at Los Piños for the last six years. As the government focused its efforts on balancing the budget and stabilizing the currency after the 1994–95 crisis, infrastructure investment was stopped in its tracks. As noted above, public investment in Mexico has followed a disturbing trend, apparently guided more by oil prices than by need. Figure 5 illustrates that the correlation between oil prices and gross domestic fixed investment from the public sector is quite strong. This dependency can have negative effects in the long run. First, the procyclical nature of investment (relative to oil price) calls into question the "quality" of infrastructure projects initiated during booms and, second, accommodating fiscal cuts through infrastructure is dangerous because of the effects this may have on other sectors of the economy. Public-infrastructure investment was only 1.9 percent of GDP, down from 4 percent in 1994, 6 percent in 1990, and 12 percent in 1980. Although Figure 5 indicates that the private sector offset much of the decline, there is evidence that public and private investment serve as complements rather than substitutes (see Figure 6 next page).[4]

More important, the services provided by this investment declined significantly as well. The upshot of these developments is that Mexico now faces an important challenge in addressing both a large backlog and an explosive new demand. The estimated requirements in energy alone are on the order of US$10 billion per year for the next 10 years, representing 2.5 percent of current GDP, or the total health or education budget. The challenge is equally pressing for both "national" infrastructure—telecommunications, roads, and energy—and "urban" infrastructure—housing and water. The new administration must not only reverse this decline, but to do so in a way that (a) fosters integration with the U.S.; (b) aids in opening other key markets (for example, the European Union); and (c) addresses regional imbalances.

---

4. World Bank, (1998), *Mexico: Enhancing Factor Productivity Growth, Report 17392-ME.*

Figure 6. Mexico: Public, Private, Total Investment as Percent of GDP

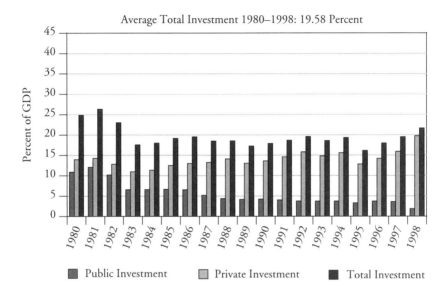

There are also important obstacles to meeting the challenge of improving the coverage and quality of infrastructure services:

- The investment requirement is beyond the financing capacity of the public sector alone. This is especially true given the urgent competing demands for support to critical social programs.
- There is a lack of depth in the domestic capital market. As noted above, the financial sector is relatively small, and debt markets are mainly short term. Additionally, there is some expectation that IPAB issuances may crowd out others.[5] Though there are promising developments, for example, the increasing presence of AFORE, the implication is that only the highest quality issuers will have ready access.
- The new paradigm for development bank financing requires greater differentiation among states and municipalities in terms of creditworthiness. This will likely lead to greater borrowing costs for those states that do not quality as investment grade.
- Mexico has a varied track record on private provision of infrastructure.

The solution lies in a series of mutually reinforcing actions to (a) improve efficiency of services, such that future investment in some entities (for example, municipal water operators) can be financed from internal generation of funds; (b) improve

---

5. See also Domestic Debt Management Chapter.

the financial condition of states, municipalities, and operating entities to assist them in obtaining better credit ratings; (c) sharpen and reorient public financing; and (d) leverage these actions to attract private financing. Doing this will require consolidating and extending the sectoral restructurings of the last decade for both national and urban infrastructure, and developing new financial products and services.

Consolidating and Extending Sectoral Reforms

During the past decade important structural reforms have been introduced in some sectors. While there have been significant gains, much more can and needs to be accomplished. The World Competitiveness Index for 2000, for example, developed by the International Institute of Management Development, ranks Mexico 36th out of 47 large economies. National infrastructure sectors—telecommunications, transport, electricity, oil, and gas—play an important role in sustaining growth and competitiveness. As core upstream sectors, their performance has cascading effects throughout the economy, affecting the cost of doing business.

Telecommunications

Since the late 1980s the Mexican telecommunications sector has undergone a dramatic transformation. TELMEX was privatized in the early 1990s, and in 1995 the Mexican government passed major legislation establishing a new regulatory framework. By 2000 competitors were reasonably successful in mobile wireless telephone service and in domestic and international long distance. Nevertheless, overall sector performance remains deficient. Four years after liberalization, TELMEX remains the dominant carrier, with 75 percent of the long-distance market, 95 percent of its fixed lines, and 80 percent of the mobile market. As a consequence, Mexico has fewer lines per person than most comparable countries in the region. Tariffs for local calls and lines are high. Regulation by COFETEL has been relatively ineffective. A number of legal and regulatory actions are required to address these issues:

- COFETEL needs true independence from SCT.
- COFETEL should be required to follow open decisionmaking processes for regulatory proceedings. Rather than bilateral negotiations, public processes of consultation (for example, public hearings) should be followed.
- An alternative mechanism to the *amparo* system needs to be developed. Resolution of conflicts can be achieved by specialized courts, arbitration, or mediation. Similarly, COFETEL and the CFC need to be able to obtain information relevant to the regulatory process. Companies can now file injunctions against these requests and derail the regulatory process.

Highways

Mexico's road system is the most intensively used transport infrastructure in the century, with 98 percent of domestic passenger traffic and 85 percent of surface freight cargo.[6] The highway network comprises about 96,000 paved roads, about half of which are operated by the federal government and the other half by the states. The network includes 6,500 km of toll roads, most of which were concessioned during 1990–92, and 1,420 km of roads managed by CAPUFE. Most of the former failed during the crisis and are now under the control of the federal government through the FARAC trust fund. The federal network is divided into 10 national axes that connect the most important production and consumption areas in the country, the most relevant tourist locations and all the major urban areas. The average daily traffic flow on the national axis oscillated between 2,000 and 10,000 vehicles.

Road density is about one-half the level of Brazil and one-quarter the level of the U.S. Until the early 1980s, Mexico continued to extend and deepen its road network, but the program was overtaken by the macroeconomic difficulties during that decade. Since that time the only significant additions to the network have been through the toll road program. Today, maintenance and improvement of the main corridors lags behind demand. Many federal roads go directly through central cities, thereby increasing congestion and delays. Bypasses need to be built to improve traffic flows, especially for long-haul and trade-related traffic. Road access to ports and border crossings is inadequate and there is a need to expand bridge capacity to the U.S. The rescued toll roads face similar problems: quality has deteriorated significantly over the past three years as revenues have been channeled to debt service. CAPUFE roads, however, have not faced these problems because they are backed by much stronger traffic volume.

Two operational requirements must be addressed in the near future to ensure that the sector does not become a bottleneck to growth:

- The main initiative for the next decade is to upgrade the federal network, where about 50 percent of the roads are in poor condition. This will require investments of MXP$9 billion over the next 10 years, about three times the current level.
- There is a need to rationalize the toll-road system—FARAC and CAPUFE— to maximize use of existing infrastructure (for example, through cross-subsidies), foster better concession design, increase operating efficiency, and improve planning for future investments.

Railways, Ports, and Airports

Privatization of these key sectors was an important achievement of the Zedillo Administration.[7] In railways, this included a Constitutional amendment and new legislation in 1995, followed by a breakup of FNM and a concessioning of the key lines. Results to date are impressive: (a) transit times have been reduced significantly

---

6. See also the World Bank Report, "Mexico: Facing New Challenges for Public-Private Partnership in Transport."

7. Ibid.

(from the U.S. border to Mexico City now takes 33 hours versus 60 hours in the past); (b) average speed is up by 20 percent; and (c) cargo theft is down on some lines by 80 percent. From the government's standpoint, the benefits have been substantial: (a) proceeds from the sale of about US$2 billion; (b) continued annual operating subsidies of US$360 million have been eliminated; and (c) income taxes of US$30 million have been received from the concessionaires.

Ports have had a similar experience. A new Ports Law was approved in 1993 and was accompanied by major institutional reform in *Puertos Mexicanos*. Though the ports themselves were not privatized, lines of business within the ports were opened to competition. In general, there have been substantial improvements in efficiency, productivity, and quality of service. As an example, in 1993 Veracruz was handling 34 containers per hour per ship, while now it is handling 74 containers. Manzanillo now moves 65 containers, and Altamira has reached the international standard of 50 containers. Tariffs have also decreased.

Airports have followed a similar privatization process: (a) new legislation (1995); (b) a strategic breakup of the airport system into concession packages; and (c) the award of the concessions. Three of the four packages have been awarded in the last two years. The concessions attracted great interest and the prices were well above government expectations. It is still too early to evaluate impact. Separately, a new Mexico City airport is planned that will also be concessioned. No decision has been taken yet on its location, and thus the concessioning is still a long way off.

Finishing the privatization process and ensuring continued benefits from it are the key challenges:

- An independent transport regulator is needed.
- In rail there is a need to concession the remaining short lines, and in airports the final packages (including Mexico City) need to be awarded.
- In ports there is a need to further reduce waiting times and to ensure that publicly financed investments do not distort the competitive balance with private operators (for example, Lazaro Cardenas versus Manzanillo).

Multimodal and Intermodal Transport

Reform efforts to date have demonstrated the significant efficiency gains and cost reductions from increased competition in transport through deregulation and auctions for concessions.[8] These gains are already quite impressive but they only provide a lower bound of what Mexico will be able to achieve in the transport sector. The next wave of reforms will focus on maximizing these gains by allowing better modal choices to ensure a more efficient use of the transport infrastructure. Currently, Mexico's modal distribution is quite standard for Latin America, where logistics costs are about 30 to 40 percent of final sales prices. This is twice the level observed in most OECD countries. A number of steps need to be taken:

---

8. Ibid.

- Legislation to support the development of brokerage markets for freight.
- Improvements in logistics management of transport modes. The gains achieved through port reform in terms of loading and downloading time are undone by long waiting times for truckers and trains in the interior. A prerequisite for this is higher intramodal competition (within the trucking industry) and intermodal competition (between trucks and rail).
- Better public–private partnerships. The government need to facilitate the use of and open access to essential facilities (for example, ports) and the setting up of dry ports and distribution centers.

Electricity

Mexico has built its present economy in part on two pillars of the energy sector: the state-owned companies PEMEX and the CFE. Both have made large contributions to Mexico's development. CFE is among the largest utilities in North America, and together with *Luz y Fuerza del Centro* (LFC, mainly a distribution company), now provide electricity to 95 percent of the population. Mexico's recent success in economic growth and the high level of connections resulted in a 5.2 percent annual growth in electricity demand over the last decade. Another contributory factor to rapid growth in demand has been extensive subsidies. The average tariff charged to residential customers in 1998 covered just 43 percent of costs, and the average tariff for agricultural use covered 31 percent of costs. Industry and services paid almost 95 percent of costs. The implicit subsidies amounted to MXP$31 billion in 1998, an amount almost equal to one-third of oil tax revenues in that year. To meet this demand Mexico has at present a 35,000 MW capacity. Future demand is forecast to grow at 5.8 percent per year until 2010. This would require additional capacity of about 27,000MW. The costs of meeting this demand, including additional transmission and distribution capacity, would amount to MXP$370 billion over the period (MXP$210 billion for generation, MXP$90 billion for transmission, and MXP$70 billion for distribution). In addition, if the present subsidy and tariff levels remain unchanged, the total subsidies required over the period would amount to MXP$365 billion between 2001 and 2010.

Meeting the rapid growth in demand over the next decade will require the mobilization of very substantial financial, technological, and managerial resources. Reforms to sector policy are urgently needed. The key to meeting these goals is the attraction of new participants into the market, who will dedicate substantial capital to the sector without encumbering directly or indirectly the public finances. To ensure that electricity is supplied to consumers at lowest cost, competitive conditions need to be created. The reform agenda must include:

- Dividing CFE vertically into generation, transmission, and distribution.
- Introducing competition in generation and distribution.
- Creating a market in bulk power.
- Introducing an independent system operator and settlement agent.

- Strengthening CRE to allow it to regulate transmission and distribution, define service obligations, and set retail tariffs.
- Redesigning subsidies and moving them on budget.

Oil and Gas

Mexico has large reserves of oil but relatively low production compared to countries such as Canada, Norway, and the United Kingdom. While the oil sector is no longer the principal source of export earning, it continues to make a substantial contribution to the federal budget, accounting for 30 percent of total fiscal revenues over the last decade. A large part of these revenues, however, has been returned to the sector to finance operating expenses and a restricted investment program, to cover the very large electricity subsidies, and to make provision for financial obligations to private sector financiers (for example, PIDEREGAS). The sector's net contribution to the Treasury has been negative, especially if the implicit electricity subsidies are considered. Moreover, the tax regime through which oil rents are obtained and the manner in which they have been managed have had several negative consequences. Taxes are levied on sales revenue, and at a nominal rate of 60 percent are exorbitant by any standard. This leads to early shut-in of wells and discourages investment in field development and in new smaller fields. In addition, the oil tax is applied to consolidated upstream and downstream activities. Since there are no true rents to be obtained in downstream activities, this severely limits the number of downstream projects that could be undertaken profitably on an after-tax basis.

Very substantial investments will be required for the energy sector to maximize its potential contribution to the economy and to efficiently meet the demand for energy supplies. These investments are likely to be on the order of MXP$315 billion over the next 10 years.[9]

The gas subsector faces similar issues. Demand is expected to grow rapidly over the next 10 years, at about 7.5 percent per year until 2007, and then at 11 percent annually through 2010. Meeting this demand will require extensive investment in upstream and downstream aspects of no-associated gas development. The total cost of meeting all demand through 2010 is MXP$252 billion.

These sectors pose a special challenge for the government requiring:

- A new sector policy framework based on (a) expanded production and delivery systems, (b) minimization of net demands of the sector on public finances, (c) a commitment to international levels of efficiency, and (d) measures to mitigate environmental impacts associated with the expansion of the sector.
- An overhaul of the fiscal regime.
- Attracting new investment in upstream activities through concession arrangements in exploration and production.

---

9. See the Energy Chapter for the assumptions underlying this program.

- Meeting the demand for higher-quality fuels by introducing competition in downstream activities. Mexico should adopt international market prices as the basis for ex-refinery prices and should allow the import of products by any party and the entry of new participants in the industry. To create a level playing field the government should also permit Mexican refineries to purchase crude from any source and not restrict the purchase to domestic crude of a specified composition.
- Ensuring nondiscriminatory access to new participants by spinning off infrastructure from PEMEX (that is, transport pipelines, terminals, and storage).
- Developing a phased program of mandated improvement in fuel quality in tandem with improved vehicle specification and power plant emissions and fuel substitution. As part of this, the government should establish an independent body to monitor fuel quality and other issues such as health and safety.

Water and Sanitation

This sector involves federal, state, and municipal governments. It has proven to be one of the most resistant to reform, due in part to the complex relationships between the three levels of government that have led to a culture of free water for consumers that is provided at any cost, which is ultimately borne by the federal government. As a result, the record on performance in urban water and sanitation is poor. Access to water and sanitation, at 94 percent and 80 percent, respectively, is comparable to other countries in the region and with OECD averages, but these figures mask wide regional differences in Mexico, with access most limited in the southern states. While 95 percent of water provided is disinfected, less than 30 percent undergoes potabilization through a water treatment plant, a percentage that falls below that of many Latin American countries. Only about 15 percent of wastewater is treated, and unaccounted-for water among urban operators is high; on average only 40 percent of each liter produced generates revenue for the *Organismo Operador* (OO, the municipal water company). In general, the performance of the OOs has been poor. In practice most operate as decentralized municipal or state entities rather than freestanding and commercially oriented public companies. Efforts at introducing private participation in the sector have failed across the country. Tariffs are inadequate to cover operation and investment needs. On average, tariffs are about MXP$2.5 pesos when MXP$10 is needed. Finally, investment in the sector has declined steadily since the mid 1990s both in real terms and as a percentage of GDP. An estimated MXP$100 billion is needed over the next 10 years to address deferred maintenance, improve quality, and expand coverage.

Actions are required at all three levels of government to:

- Create credible regulation at the federal and state levels. The federal government could oversee regulatory rules that require common application, such as general standards and norms, basic tariff structures, water quality and environmental standards, and private participation issues (for example, concession design). This should be separated from CNA. The states could provide more detailed regulation, for example, on tariffs, and could supervise contracts with private operators.

- Transform the OOs into autonomous utilities.
- Fix the sector's finances by reshaping financial policies and harmonizing programs. Most important, allow tariffs to be set at adequate levels. Federal assistance should be reoriented to provide incentives for local authorities to implement comprehensive reforms needed to improve service quality and sustainability. Federal grants may be needed to assist OOs in bringing tariffs in line with required levels. Federal loans and subsidies should further focus on investments with large externalities, such as wastewater treatment and urban poverty targets.
- Promote private sector participation. There are numerous modalities for private participation. A "one size fits all" approach is inappropriate. To help promote this, technical assistance should be provided for legislation, regulation, policy, and bid and contract design at the state and local levels. Finally, efforts to introduce private participation should be linked to federal financing.

Housing

This is one of the most problematic sectors in Mexico. Demand is on the order of 700,000 to 800,000 units per year, and an estimated 6 million units (one-third of the stock) are in need of improvement or replacement. The investment requirements are enormous—on the order of US$8 billion per year. The housing system is currently geared to provide finished housing for the social interest market (urban workers) through poorly performing public and quasi-public institutions (INFONAVIT and FOVISSSTE). These offer heavily subsidized home mortgages under poor origination and servicing standards. Moreover, they dominate with about a 75 percent market share. INFONAVIT, in particular, operates as an exclusive franchise of some unions and developers, and has largely been unregulated throughout its 28-year history. INFONAVIT and FOVISSSTE cause additional distortions since they are part of the pension system. Their negative returns drag down the overall performance of the pension system. Only FOVI offers market-rate mortgages under acceptable origination and servicing standards. It has a 20 percent market share. Because INFONAVIT and FOVISSSTE are so large and offer below-market mortgages, capital market access is impossible. Thus, the social interest housing system remains dependent on public and quasi-public funding.

A series of fundamental reforms are needed:

- Obtain better sectoral governance through common regulation and supervision of INFONAVIT, FOVISSSTE, and FOVI.
- Strengthen and deepen the primary market by bringing INFONAVIT and FOVISSSTE up to FOVI origination and servicing standards.

- Separate housing subsidies from financing, reduce them from current levels, provide them up front, and combine them with saving schemes.

These reforms are essential because they will permit the government to focus on the real problem in the housing sector: that most Mexicans do not have incomes sufficient to qualify for social interest housing. Yet because of the bias in housing policy, programs in low-income housing are poorly funded and largely left to the states. The result is that most low-income housing is provided informally, and is often illegal and of poor quality. Several reforms are called for:

- Expand housing finance services through the private sector for progressive housing and home improvement.
- Improve property rights, and expand the supply of serviced urban land.
- Provide well-targeted, up-front subsidies and advisory services to consumers.
- Improve the regulatory framework for low-income housing.

Financing Infrastructure Services

The total investment needed to meet the demand for infrastructure services described above over the next decade is on the order of US$20 billion per year. Funding for these services will come from three sources: (a) greater efficiency in operations; (b) more appropriate pricing; and (c) public and private finance. Clearly, given the constraints on public borrowing and the need to devote budgetary resources to the social sector, the greatest challenge for the new administration is to leverage government actions in such a way as to attract the greatest amount of private finance. Four actions are required:

Define and Implement a New Role for Government

Sector governance is critical in the energy sector. The reforms proposed above imply greater competition in the sector. To ensure their success the government must assume several roles. These include establishing a modern legal framework to allow free entry for domestic and foreign investors. Upstream, it would formulate licensing policies; create a stand-alone geophysical mapping agency; establish a modern tax regime; establish criteria for and ensure compliance with health, safety, and environmental standards; and set out and enforce contractual terms for all companies operating in the sector. A similar role needs to be pursued by SCT. It needs to adapt from its role of builder, operator, and provider of services to one of planning, policy-making, and standard setting.

Maintain Current Decentralization Framework

Enforcing a hard budget constraint on the states and encouraging sound fiscal management with the goal of obtaining investment-grade rating is essential. Without this the states (and municipalities) have no hope of accessing the capital market without substantial and expensive credit enhancement.

Change Perception of Private Sector Regarding Infrastructure Investment

The most critical action is effective regulation. This implies substantial reforms in a number of areas: (a) autonomy and independence for COFETEL; (b) autonomy and independence for CNBV; (c) establishment of a new autonomous and independent transport regulator; (d) strengthening CRE to allow it to take on new functions (for example, tariff regulation) in energy; and (e) defining more clearly the role and responsibility of CFC. In this regard also, the quality and credibility of official information needs to be improved. Better contract enforcement and new mechanisms for dispute resolution are also needed. An alternative to the *amparo* must be found. Finally, the government needs to aid states and municipalities in designing concession for private provision of infrastructure.

Develop New Tools for Public Finance and Use Existing Ones Better

In highways two important initiatives are under way that could have an important impact in the sector: (a) the creation of a Road Fund to finance highway maintenance; and (b) the creation of a Highway Finance Authority through the merger of FARAC and CAPUFE to manage the existing roads as a network, and to issue debt to finance new construction. The latter is especially important given the likely reluctance of the private sector to return to highway finance in the near future.

There is also a need to define a new role for BANOBRAS. Rather than act as a pass-through agency for the federal government, it needs to provide incentives for sound fiscal management in the states, and to help them access the capital markets. BANOBRAS should (a) align its products and services to new markets as defined by the decentralization process (for example, credit and non-creditworthy states); (b) develop a concessional window for direct poverty interventions (for example, in water) or in areas with clear externalities (for example, waste water); (c) develop credit-pooling and enhancement tools for states and municipalities accessing the capital markets; and (d) develop a currency swap facility for foreign-currency-financed infrastructure projects.

Social interest housing finance is one area where existing tools need to be improved. As currently constituted, INFONAVIT will forever be a below-market institution, providing home mortgages to a very small number of beneficiaries by destroying the pensions of many others. It will thus subvert all efforts at developing housing markets and pension reform.

IV. Agriculture

The last 10 years have seen sweeping macro and sectoral reforms and major support programs. These have led to the emergence of a largely liberalized, market-oriented, and private-sector-driven rural economy. At the same time, reforms were accompanied by mitigation measures that helped the transition process, for example, the Procampo, *Alianza para el Campo, Solidaridad,* and the municipal infrastructure program embodied in *Ramo 33*. The GATT and NAFTA agreements laid the foundation for progressive exposure to global forces. Finally, the government undertook a major reform of the land tenure system, including a Constitutional amendment in 1992 that permitted *ejido* land transactions, and in order to ensure better security of ownership rights, the government embarked in 1995 on a program of land titling (*Procede*).

The results of these reforms, however, have been modest. Growth has stagnated, the participation of the sector in total GDP has declined from 7.5 percent in 1995 to 4.0 percent in 1999, and employment in agriculture remains high, at about 20 percent of the labor force (see Figure 7). Poverty has increased in the sector in the last decade. The *ejido* sector, with about three-quarters of farm labor and half of the farmland, is under stress, and is increasingly integrating into the nonfarm economy. There are also positive developments. The commercial sector, for example, that competes on international markets, has benefited from the reforms. During the first five years of NAFTA agricultural exports to the U.S. grew by 70 percent, while imports grew by about 60 percent.

Behind this sector performance are a number of structural issues:

RURAL POVERTY. Clearly, low productivity and extreme poverty, especially among indigenous populations, pose special challenges for the government. The high level of risk and the limited options available to poor farmers to cope with income and consumption variability, have induced them into low risk–low reward investment strategies, which limit their economic opportunities and contribute to placing them in a poverty "trap." Some responses to this have been (a) migration to the U.S.; (b) migration to small municipalities in Mexico; and (c) a search for greater off-farm income.

Figure 7. Economic and Agriculture Growth Rates

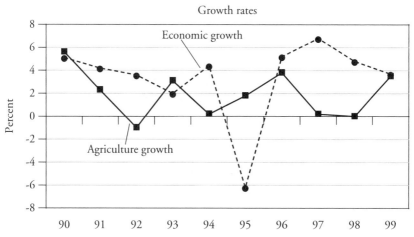

UNFRIENDLY INCENTIVE FRAMEWORK. Throughout the decade Mexican farmers faced declining real prices and unfavorable nominal protection rates on key commodities. The competitive framework also negatively affected farmers—for example, inefficient distribution channels, overvalued exchange rates, and high interest rates. In addition, some government programs may have introduced distortions in other areas of the incentive framework. The phaseout of price support through CONASUPO, for example, was replaced with marketing subsidies through ASERCA.

POORLY FUNCTIONING MARKETS. Mexican producers face a number of difficulties in accessing markets: (a) protectionist policies in industrialized countries; (b) inefficient channels of distribution; and (c) high marketing transaction costs. In particular, storage appears to be a weak element of the marketing chain, with evidence that up to 30 percent of production is lost owing to inadequate transport and storage. The land and labor markets are also undergoing profound change, with more non-farm activities, an aging ejido sector, and the increasing importance of women *ejiditarias*. The expected development of a land market following the constitutional change of 1992 has been slow to materialize. *Ejido* land distribution is still fragmented and the average farm plot is often too small to allow profitable investment opportunities.[10]

Sector Reforms

It is generally admitted that the massive all-subsidy schemes that characterized the government's approach in the past not only were fiscally unsustainable, but also led to a culture of dependency among producers. At the same time some producers compete effectively on international markets. Thus, there are clearly forces for change. The sector has the potential to be a significant economic force and an important source of employment for large segments of the population. The mix of reforms for sustaining growth and competitiveness is a delicate balance between fostering change and integration, while addressing employment and poverty issues.

STAY THE COURSE ON MACRO AND SECTORAL POLICIES. A sound macroeconomic framework, with appropriate stability and exchange rate policies, is critical. The reforms carried out in the past were necessary, and indeed pending reform in basic grains should be completed. Beyond that the subsidy policy should be revisited with an eye to developing less distorting income-support subsidies instead of the current price, input, or marketing support.

STIMULATE PRO-POOR, BROAD-BASED AGRICULTURAL GROWTH. It is also critical to recognize that Mexico will not be able to fully reap the benefits of the macro reforms

---

10. Fifty percent of ejidos has less than 5 hectares, and more than 20 percent of ejiditarios farm three or more plots.

without increased attention to poverty alleviatation in the sector. A pro-poor–pro-growth strategy needs to focus on reducing the productivity gap in sectors with potential for poor smallholders (for example, nontradable commodities, and coffee). A broad effort to reduce transaction costs would also benefit the poor and enhance growth. In addition to the rural finance initiatives described above, investments in rural roads and farmer marketing cooperatives would yield high benefits.

Follow an urban–rural development strategy based on regional development. Current demographic and migration patterns are linking rural and urban areas more closely. Regional development allows better integration of local economies, and a more efficient way of providing services and resolving natural resource and environmental issues.

Foster competition in preparation for the elimination of all agricultural tariffs in 2008 under NAFTA. There is a need to consider more proactively the requirements associated with the diversification into higher-value crops, agro-industrial goods, and the possible shift from surplus crops (white maize) to deficit crops (yellow maize). Contract farming is also a possible avenue for the future. It provides the crucial linkages between input suppliers, credit providers, purchasers, insurance, and farmers. Further expansion, however, will depend on the confidence in the enforcement of contracts and the existence of well-organized producer organizations.

The public sector can foster more efficient markets. The public sector can establish better-integrated price and market information systems, develop appropriate regulatory frameworks and enforcement capacity, develop commodity quality standards, and provide clear rules regarding the amount and timing of duty-free imports of maize and beans.

Government Programs*

PROCAMPO is a well-conceived program with a clear poverty alleviation impact. Its administration could be improved and its multiplier effect enhanced by disconnecting payment from planting, to make it a purely entitlement program. This would lower administrative costs, allow collateralization of the payment right, and offer opportunities to shift from one activity to another. Allowing the farmer to cash out the present value of the 10-year entitlement would greatly improve a producer's investment capacity and bankability. *Alianza para el Campo* could help address the challenges of NAFTA and the equity issues in the sector. This would require greater emphasis on low-income farmers, and promotion of diversification to higher-value crops. A move to a voucher-based system would facilitate consumer choice and stronger channels for inputs and technology. Irrigation programs should be oriented

---

* This topic receives parallel treatment under the Poverty Thematic Chapter, from a slightly different angle.

to supporting yields per unit of water and sustainable management of resources. This will require increased decentralization of water management to local users and further development of water markets. As noted above, grain and energy subsidies need to be eliminated as well. Finally, the social and rural infrastructure funds *(Ramo 33)* offer potential for addressing rural–urban migration and poverty. Their impact can be enhanced by measures to reward good management practices at the local level, intermunicipal coordination to capture economies of scale and avoid wasteful projects, and public–private partnerships.

3

Poverty and Inequality

*This Thematic Chapter was written by Quentin T. Wodon and
Eduardo Velez with the valuable input of Marcelo Giugale
and Adolfo Brizzi.*

I. Introduction

While there are different estimates of poverty in Mexico, there is general agreement that poverty is widespread, and that the reduction of poverty should be a key area of focus for the new Administration. Beyond lack of income, poverty is a complex and multidimensional phenomena which affects many areas of the life of the poor. As a result, a wide range of public policies have been implemented in Mexico, as elsewhere, to reduce poverty and improve the well-being of the population.

It is difficult to organize into a coherent overall strategy the many policies necessary for the reduction of poverty. Substantial progress has been achieved over the last six years in this respect, with the Zedillo Administration relying on both broad-based social policies and targeted programs for the reduction of poverty. In the framework of that Administration (Figure 1), broad-based social expenditures are devoted to social security and healthcare, education, job training, and housing. Targeted programs focus on investing in the human capital of the poor, promoting income and employment opportunities for the poor, and improving the physical infrastructure of poor areas. Importantly, funding for basic education, healthcare for the population without formal coverage, and targeted poverty programs was increased in recent years, despite the fiscal discipline maintained for the budget as a whole.

This Thematic Chapter has two objectives. First, it briefly presents an alternative framework that could be used by the new Administration to prepare its own coherent strategy for poverty reduction. Second, it provides a synthesis of eight background chapters devoted to government programs, social protection, education, health, urban labor markets, rural development, indigenous peoples, and gender.

Figure 1. Broad-based and Targeted Policies

To classify the policies which are necessary for reducing poverty, this Chapter uses the security, opportunity, and empowerment trilogy from the World Bank's *World Development Report 2000* on poverty (Figure 2).

- *Providing security.* The poor suffer from shocks induced by microeconomic events, macroeconomic events, and natural disasters. More broadly, the poor face a number of risks, from malnutrition in the first few years of life to a

Figure 2. An Alternative Framework for Poverty Reduction

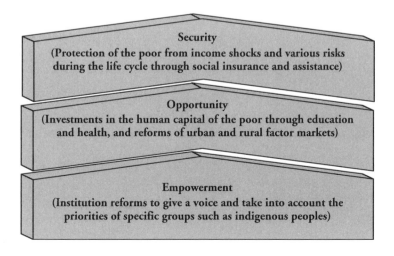

lack of resources at an older age. Public policies can help in providing security for the poor in order to help them deal with shocks and risks. These policies are discussed in the chapters devoted to government programs and social protection.

- *Building opportunity.* Creating better opportunities for the poor requires economic growth and policies designed to ensure that the poor participate in the growth process. The policies necessary to promote economic growth in Mexico are discussed in other chapters. Here, we focus on the policies that can help in ensuring that the poor and the nonpoor benefit from growth.
  - *Human capital (health, education, and nutrition).* The level and quality of public social expenditures for health, education, and nutrition are essential elements for the government to invest in the human capital of all its people, but especially the poor, who cannot afford privately provided services.
  - *Factor markets (urban labor markets and rural development).* Pro-growth reforms in urban and rural factor markets can help in improving earnings and employment opportunities for those who are less skilled, thereby resulting in poverty reduction.
- *Promoting empowerment.* Finally, institutional reforms and special attention to disadvantaged groups such as indigenous peoples are important to give a voice to the poor and take into account their own priorities. Another cross-sectoral area where reforms could be implemented relates to gender issues.

There is an implicit hierarchy in Figure 2 that is worth commenting on. Because policies designed to provide security to the poor tend to be targeted, they immediately come to mind as being essential for a poverty reduction strategy. Yet, while these policies are important, they do not suffice. They represent the tip of the iceberg, because they often help when something has gone wrong—when individuals and families are already in poverty and at serious risk. Moreover, targeted policies tend to rely on redistribution mechanisms, so that they are not the primary engine for growth, without which long-term poverty reduction cannot be achieved. To promote broad-based growth, and to prevent individuals and families from falling into poverty, investments in the human capital of the poor and in reforms to enhance the functioning of factor markets are the key. While investments in human capital tend to have an impact on poverty only in the long run (for example, when healthy and better-educated children reach adulthood), factor market policies may have more immediate beneficial impacts. Finally, empowerment is necessary for enacting policies for opportunity and security. Without empowerment, the poor tend to have little voice in the political economy process, and this often implies that they are not well served. Empowerment also helps in reducing discrimination, which is one cause of exclusion.

Striking a balance between the various policies that must be part of a poverty-reduction strategy is not easy. What is clear, however, is that the success of the next Administration in reducing poverty and improving the well-being of Mexico's population should be monitored over time using a battery of indicators, rather than poverty measures alone. Reducing the share of the population living in poverty or extreme poverty by, say, one-fifth, should be high on the list of targets of the new Administration. Beyond a reduction in poverty and extreme poverty, a reduction in inequality should also be a key objective, simply because people tend to assess their level of well-being not only in comparison to absolute thresholds (as measured by poverty), but also in comparison with others (as measured by inequality).

Beyond monetary indicators of well-being such as poverty and inequality, non-monetary indicators in health (malnutrition, infant mortality, etc.), education (enrollment, assistance, repetition, dropout, etc.), and basic infrastructure services (sewerage, sanitary installation, access to safe water, etc.) matter as well. In some cases, it is feasible to put a monetary value on non-monetary indicators, and this can be useful for the analysis of trade-offs between policies. For example, one can assess the income gains from education and employment, or the value of having access to basic infrastructure services such as electricity, water, and sanitary installations. Yet this will never capture the full cost or benefit of non-monetary indicators. There is an intrinsic value in being well educated or in having a good job that goes beyond the monetary income provided by education and employment. To give a less obvious and more controversial example, there is an intrinsic merit in having public policies that promote better access to culture and art for the poor, even if this does not bring monetary benefits. The poor are not only hungry for food—they are also hungry for creativity, expression, and full participation in the life of society.

Although it is difficult to define what quality services are, it is necessary to focus on delivering quality inputs and programs, and adequate definitions must include outcomes and the value added of the intervention (for example, learning gain, and increased probability of income-earning activities), and that the value added needs to be compared with the cost of the intervention. At this stage it is important for the new Administration to consider cost-effectiveness criteria as a key element to identify programs. An orientation toward outcomes means that priorities in poverty programs and interventions are determined through economic analysis, standard setting, and measurement of the attainment of standards.

Finally, it is necessary to work for maximum efficiency in the allocation and use of resources so as to improve the quality and increase the quantity of inputs to fight poverty. For this it is important to pay attention to policy environment and to institutional strengthening. It is necessary to focus on the federalization process to consolidate it and give local authorities (state, municipal, and community) the incentives to contribute to autonomy and accountability. This does not happens automatically, and it is necessary for the central government to help improve the local capacity by setting standards, supporting inputs known to decrease poverty, adopting flexible strategies for the acquisition and use of inputs, and monitoring performance. The possibility of increasing local and private resources for the expansion of some programs should also be considered, together with more involvement of civil society as part of the monitoring process at the local level.

II. Providing Security

Evaluating Government Programs

Funding for poverty programs has increased (Figures 3 and 4). In 2000, the expenditures for targeted programs will reach MXP$53 billion, an increase in real terms of 20 percent since 1994. Among the MXP$53 billion devoted to targeted poverty

Figure 3. Resources Channeled to Poverty Alleviation Programs
(millions of pesos of 2000)

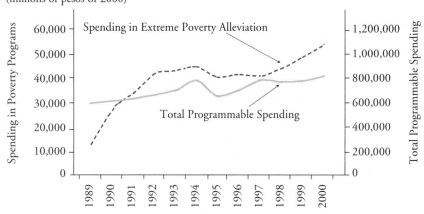

Source: Government of Mexico.

Figure 4. Government Spending for Poverty Alleviation
(2000 pesos in billions)

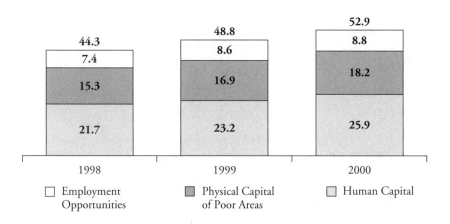

programs, MXP$26 billion are for investments in the human capital of the poor, MXP$9 billion are for income opportunities for the poor, and MXP$18 billion are for investments in the physical capital of poor areas. Together these programs represent 11 percent of social spending, 6 percent of programmable spending, and 1 percent of GDP. Apart from targeted programs, the government is also running large job training programs (discussed below) and agricultural programs (discussed in the section on rural development), which have an impact on the poor.

Investing in Human Capital for the Poor

Human capital programs for the poor include PROGRESA, food subsidies and other programs, compensatory education programs, and basic healthcare programs.

PROGRESA. Begun in 1997, PROGRESA (MXP$9.6 billion) provides integrated support for education, health, and nutrition to poor households living in poor rural areas. Conditional on good attendance, the program provides upper primary and lower secondary school stipends and subsidies for school supplies. It also provides free basic healthcare, health education, a cash transfer for nutrition, and nutritional supplements for pregnant and breast-feeding women and for children under age 5. The program reaches 2.6 million families. Evaluations suggest a 22 percent decrease in morbidity for children below age 2, a 21 percent increase in female enrollment in lower secondary schools, an 18 percent increase in attendance at health clinics, and an increase in schooling of one year among the target population. PROGRESA is a good program with some areas for improvement as follows.

- *Supply-side.* By raising the demand for schooling and healthcare, PROGRESA is generating tensions on the supply side. To avoid these tensions, close coordination with SEP and SSA is needed, and efforts have been made in that direction (for example, the teacher-student ratio in telesecundary, a program for which the demand has increased substantially thanks to PROGRESA, has been kept constant). Still, more generally, there remains an uncertainty as to the relative impact of demand and supply-side programs on improving education and health outcomes among the rural poor.
- *Transfers, targeting, and community participation.* PROGRESA's average income transfer is 253 pesos per month, which represents 22 percent of the beneficiaries' average total income. However, families with many children in school can receive up to 600 pesos per month (less than five percent of beneficiaries fall in that category). The question is whether the program is achieving its objectives at a relatively high cost. The argument for the relatively high stipends is that apart from promoting human development, PROGRESA also provides immediate income support for the alleviation of poverty. The argument is correct, but it could still be valuable to rethink the level of the stipends. The program's targeting is well done overall, but in villages where

most of the population is poor and where the population is highly marginalized, it may be better not to use means-testing to avoid tensions between beneficiaries and nonbeneficiaries. In some areas, the individual-based logic of PROGRESA may not mesh well with traditional communal values. At the same time, not implementing the targeting of the program in small and highly marginalized communities would imply that two families living in different areas but otherwise identical might not be treated in the same way by the program, which could generate fairness issues.

FOOD PROGRAMS. The resources allocated to food subsidies remain twice as large as those allocated to PROGRESA (MXP$16 billion). Two positive changes have been made by the Zedillo Administration. First, the share of targeted (as opposed to universal) food subsidies has increased from 39 percent in 1994 to 95 percent in 2000. Second, the share of subsidies devoted to rural areas has increased from 31 percent to 76 percent, which better corresponds to the country's distribution of poverty. Issues remain however:

- *Food subsidies.* Because they are means-tested, LICONSA (subsidized milk) and TORTIBONO (subsidized tortilla) have larger impacts on poverty and inequality than the former universal subsidy for tortilla. Still, leakage remains high. As for DICONSA (subsidized stores in poor rural areas), few evaluation results are available, but one issue is that the stores tend not to reach the poorest areas.
- *DIF programs.* DIF provides school breakfasts, food support for families with small children, and community kitchens (the agency has a number of other programs, but these are not discussed here). DIF's school breakfasts tend to be better targeted than means-tested food subsidies, and they appear to increase schooling among children aged 8 to 14. Since DIF functions in a more decentralized and community-based way than PROGRESA, with lower-cost interventions, it would be interesting to conduct a comparative cost-benefit–impact analysis of the two programs (while this would not be easy given the fact that the programs are different, it is important to try to establish comparable cost-benefit figures for alternative programs in order to facilitate the establishment of priorities for funding).

COMPENSATORY EDUCATION. Programs such as PROGRESA and DIF's school breakfasts are demand-driven. By contrast, compensatory education programs from CONAFE improve the supply of schooling. A number of programs have been implemented over the years, including PARE and its successors, which provides resources for schools and training for teachers. Preliminary evaluations suggest that while PARE's impact has been positive, the program may have had less impact on indigenous and very poor children than on the rural poor as a whole. Compensatory programs and the role of CONAFE are discussed in more detail in the section of this Chapter devoted to education.

PAC and IMSS-Solidaridad. The *Programa de Ampliación de Cobertura* provides a basic healthcare package of 13 interventions for those who do not have other healthcare coverage in rural areas. Two-thirds of PAC beneficiaries are indigenous. The program is discussed in the health section of this chapter, as is IMSS-Solidaridad.

Promoting Income Opportunities for the Poor

Half the funds for income generation are devoted to the *Programa de Empleo Temporal* (PET). The rest are devoted to a large number of smaller programs. In addition, PROBECAT is functioning as a safety net, even though it is not officially part of targeted programs.

PET. The program provides off-season temporary employment in poor rural areas. It is self-targeted through below-minimum-wage pay. Household data indicate that program participants do need PET more than nonparticipants in that they do not have as much access to occupations providing work all year long. Within participating communities, PET participants are also poorer than nonparticipants. Yet PET does not reach the smallest and most isolated communities of the countryside.

- *Evaluating impacts and assessing needs.* Rough appraisal methods suggest that the cost of generating one peso in additional income for the poor through PET is 3.5 pesos, which is in line with estimates for other countries (this does not take into account the benefits from PET's investments). A more in-depth evaluation, however, is needed to measure PET's impact, assess the demand for the program, and evaluate the role of the various ministries involved.
- *Improving design.* In Argentina's *Trabajar*, among the projects passing a technical feasibility test, funding is allocated according to a points system, rewarding projects which are located in poorer areas, yield larger public benefits, are sponsored by well-regarded groups (local community groups, NGOs, and municipalities), and reduce labor costs further below the minimum wage.

PROBECAT. The access of the poor to training remains both limited (less than 2 percent of those in the poorest decile get training, versus 32 percent among the richest decile) and costly (49 percent of those who get training in the poorest decile pay for their training, versus 25 percent of the rich). PROBECAT's objective has been to provide training and income support to the urban unemployed. But a new evaluation of data gathered in 1994 suggests that the program increases neither wages nor the probability of employment. The program functions (rather well) more as a self-targeted safety net. Some areas still need reviewing:

- *Collecting new data for an evaluation.* New data should be collected for a thorough assessment of the program, in order to evaluate the impact of both its traditional and new modules.

- *A double vocation.* There may be a tension between the dual objectives of training and income supplementation. While the program need not be strong on both at the same time, it could focus on training during periods of expansion, and income supplementation during recessions.

OTHER PROGRAMS. Some programs for the rural poor focus on providing various forms of employment, credit, and other support (for example, *Credito a la Palabra*, FONAES, *Apoyos Productivas* of INI, and *Alianza Para el Campo*). Other programs provide infrastructure and amenities for communities or for selected rural groups, such as migrants (for example, *Jornaleros Agricolas* and CONAZA). All these programs should be evaluated.

Improving the Physical and Social Infrastructure of Poor Areas

Most of the funds in this category (at least 80 percent) are distributed through the decentralized FAIS, but there are some broader issues as well.

FAIS. Funds for new social infrastructure (for example, in education and health) are now distributed through FAIS according to a needs-based formula. This has helped the poorest states increase their share of transfers. The FAIS allocation formula could be improved at the margin, but this would not make a large difference because the various indicators on which the formula is based are highly correlated.

FAEB AND FASSA. More problematic are the decentralized allocations for basic education (FAEB) and health (FASSA), both of which account for three-fourths of *Ramo 33*'s budget. These allocations are not based on need, but on past expenditures and existing costs. Hence, states that are already well endowed continue to receive more funds. Without putting in jeopardy the maintenance and operation of existing infrastructure, alternative ways to disburse these funds should be examined.

MANAGEMENT ISSUES. Mexico's decentralization has taken place so rapidly that local governments have not had time to fully adapt. Management issues remain outstanding. International experience suggests that there may be a risk with devolution, in that local levels of government may feel less favorable toward social spending than federal governments. Federal and civil society controls may help in protecting the poor, but these controls should not prevent innovation at the local level.

DISPERSION AND MIGRATION. Despite valuable initiatives to experiment with programs adapted to small communities (for example, telesecondary for schooling and mobile units for healthcare), access to services and government programs is still lacking in many small villages. Due to the high cost of reaching these villages, difficult choices must be made as to who should be served with which services and programs. A cost-benefit analysis of the existing trade-off is still lacking in Mexico. A good analysis of the costs and benefits of migration for the poor, and of its policy implications, is also lacking.

A priority for the next Administration should be to evaluate government interventions fully, fairly, and publicly. There are two recent examples of progress toward a culture of evaluation and transparency in Mexico. The first example is PROGRESA, which has been evaluated thoroughly and for the most part publicly, with the support of international experts. The second example is the use of transparent poverty formulas for the allocation of FAIS decentralized funds. Beyond these two salient examples, however, other efforts at evaluating programs have been rare, and when available, have not been made public, thereby weakening the democratic debate about what a poverty reduction strategy in Mexico should consist of.

Identifying Key Risks and Gaps in Coverage

In the previous section, the policy framework of the current Administration was used to classify targeted programs for the poor. A number of alternative frameworks could be used, and one of these frameworks relies on the concepts of life cycle, social protection, and risks. The idea is to identify the key risks faced by various age groups, and to recommend best practice policies to deal with these risks. Social protection interventions can then be designed to broaden access to existing social insurance mechanisms and to improve the impact and efficiency of social assistance interventions in favor of the poor. In the case of Mexico, the analysis yields the following risk exposure and policy options (see Table 1):

- *0-to-5-year-olds.* The key risks for the poor are infant (and maternal) mortality, malnutrition, and a lack of access to preschools and Early Child Development (ECD) programs. Best practice interventions include behavior-conditioned transfers and support for ECD services in order to expand supply and ensure affordability.
- *6-to-14-year-olds.* The key risk is the pocket of low primary school attendance among the rural poor. The issue is complex since many of the children not attending school are indigenous and live in isolated communities. Programs focusing on preschools and primary schools, with a bilingual component for indigenous populations, and working through community-based education, can help. In Honduras' PROHECO, the state transfers the funding for the program directly to the community, which is in charge of hiring the teacher. The use of houses, churches, and other buildings greatly reduces infrastructure costs. In Mexico, CONAFE's *Escuelas Comunitarias* is another example.
- *15-to-24-year-olds.* The main risks are low secondary school enrollment among the younger group, high unemployment and inactivity rates (which may lead to violence and crime in urban areas) among the older group, and early pregnancies and deliveries for girls. The best practice policy options include scholarship programs, other return-to-school incentives, and targeted

youth-at-risk programs, complemented by sectoral policies to raise education access and quality. Norms-based training to match industry needs is also an option.

- *25-to-64-year-olds.* The main risks are full-time employment at below-poverty wages, underemployment (as measured by the number of hours worked), and unemployment. Best practice policy options includes social insurance (for example, unemployment insurance) and social assistance (for example, workfare through public works such as Mexico's PET and other targeted income-support mechanisms), combined with macro, labor market, and financial sector policies promoting labor-intensive growth.

- *Over 65.* The main risk is low pension coverage of the elderly poor. Best practice policy options include broadening social security access to include informal sector workers, and combining the contributory pension system with means-tested, noncontributory income transfer for the elderly.

- *General Population.* The main risks are poor quality of housing and lack of access to basic infrastructure services, such as water and sewerage. Best practice policy options (discussed in the chapters devoted to infrastructure) include targeted housing subsidies and programs facilitating access to credit.

- *Special groups.* Special at-risk groups include households living in remote rural villages (many programs do not reach these households) and indigenous peoples, in both urban and rural areas. One of the chapters reviewed in this Thematic Chapter is devoted to indigenous peoples.

According to data provided by the Government, a large number of programs, many of which were introduced in the past 5 years, deal with social protection issues. While the merits of each particular program warrant closer examination, an area of concern is the possible proliferation of programs of varied effectiveness and with overlapping target groups, complex administrative procedures, and cumbersome institutional arrangements. This may signal a dispersion of efforts and a reduced effectiveness of each peso spent on interventions in favor of vulnerable groups. Again, as mentioned previously, a priority for the next Administration should be to evaluate these interventions not only fully and fairly, but also publicly.

III. Building Opportunities

Broad-based social expenditures are allocated chiefly to health, social security, and education. Between 1994 and 2000, the share of programmable spending devoted to the social sectors increased from 52 percent to 62 percent. In education, spending for basic levels (primary and lower secondary) has increased faster than spending for higher levels. In health, spending for the uninsured population has also increased faster than for other categories. All this is good news for the poor, but

Table 1. Managing Social Risk in Mexico: Main Risk Indicators, Size of At-Risk Groups, and Best Practice Policy Responses

Age Group/Main Risk Indicator	Size of Population at Risk* (Number of Poor Uncovered)		Role for Other Programs/Policies	Role for Social Protection (SP) Policy	
	Urban	Rural		Social Insurance	Social Assistance
0–5					
–Malnutrition (0–4)	820,000	990,000	–Nutrition and educational programs	—	–Behavior-conditioned income transfers (PROGRESA)
–Access to ECD (0–4)	2,200,000	3,000,000	–Publicly provided and/or regulated ECD programs and preschool services		–Targeted ECD and community based pre-schools
–Preschool enrollment (age 5)	200,000	300,000			
6–14					
–Primary enrollment	Not at risk	430,000	–Improve primary school access/quality	—	–Behavior-conditioned income transfers PROGRESA)
–Lower second. enrollment	625,000	1,300,000	–Improve secondary school access/quality		–Targeted, community-based schooling services
–Child labor	180,000	515,000	–Distance learning programs		
–Inactivity	160,000	Not at risk			
15–24					
–Upper second. enrollment	1,000,000	1,200,000	–Improve secondary school access/quality	—	–Targeted (need based) scholarships, credit facilities, return-to-school (high-school equivalency) incentive programs
–Unemployment	1,100,000	Not at risk	–Improve university access/quality		
–Inactivity	2,000,000	1,600,000	–Community colleges (terminal degrees, professional/semi-skilled qualifications)		

Table 1. (Continued)

Age Group/Main Risk Indicator	Size of Population at Risk* (Number of Poor Uncovered)		Role for Other Programs/Policies	Role for Social Protection (SP) Policy	
	Urban	Rural		Social Insurance	Social Assistance
25–64			–Labor-intensive growth	–Unemployment insurance	–Workfare (PET)
–Unemployment	460,000	Not at risk	–Financial services development	–Income-risk pooling (crop insurance)	–Targeted income transfers and/or negative income tax
–Full-time employment, below poverty wages	2,800,000	1,600,000	–Training, remedial education		
–Underemployment (hrs)	1,300,000	1,400,000			
65 and Over					
–Low pension coverage	1,000,000	1,250,000	–Financial services development	Social security system	–Targeted income transfers
•General Population					
–Low housing quality	1,600,000 hds.	3,200,000 hds.	–Mortgage facilities –Infrastructure investment		–Targeted housing subsidies
•Special Groups					
–Isolated villages	Not at risk	2,600,000	–Community driven and managed development programs		–Targeted investment in basic infrastructure services
–Indigenous people	No data	11,500,000			

Note: * Preliminary figures for population at risk calculated as the proportion of poor (deciles 1–3 in urban areas, deciles 1–6 in rural areas) in each age category uncovered (subject to revision), based on population estimates by age and risk indicator values by decile group.
Source: Social Protection Policy Chapter.

beyond funding, the next administration will have to address issues of overall coherence and sustainability in health, and issues of quality in education, in order to raise the level of human capital and contribute to poverty reduction.

Poverty reduction cannot be achieved only through targeted and social spending. Poverty reduction results first and foremost from earnings opportunities through the private use of labor and other production factors. The role of the government in labor, credit, and other markets is to ensure that they function adequately (that is, with appropriate incentives) to foster growth and help those who are less well endowed.

Health

Mexico's past progress in health (for example, lower maternal and infant mortality, higher vaccination rates, and higher life expectancy) was achieved through the use of centralized institutions and vertical programs to control infectious diseases and increase prevention and education. Today, however, as in other middle-income countries, the epidemiological profile is changing. Chronic diseases and injuries are becoming the main causes of death and disability, and the country is facing emerging problems such as AIDS and the health effects of pollution. These trends will result in an increase in the demand for specialized healthcare. A better-informed population will also be requesting higher quality services, especially in urban areas. The command-and-control approach that succeeded in reducing infectious diseases is not adapted to the new epidemiological profile. Substantive reforms are therefore needed.

Moving from Fragmentation to Integration

The pillar of Mexico's healthcare system is a mandatory social insurance program funded out of contributions from formal sector employees, employers, and the government. The main institutions are IMSS and ISSSTE, but PEMEX, the *Distrito Federal* government, the police, the metro, and the armed forces also have their own systems. In total, these social insurance organizations cover just over half of the population. Healthcare services for the rest of the population are provided by SSA and IMSS-Solidaridad. In theory, each institution assumes responsibility for a specific population group. In practice, the system leads to duplication among providers and excess capacity. The fragmentation drains resources and prevents improvements in efficiency and quality. Multiple public and private institutions are operating independently, and the creation of the National Health Council has not filled the leadership vacuum. There is a need for competition and at the same time better integration.

HELPING SSA ESTABLISH A NATIONAL POLICY. SSA should lead in setting national health policy, including: (a) establishing a unified system for reporting and statistics; (b) ensuring uniform technological policy with regard to pharmaceutical and medical equipment; (c) certifying and licensing medicines, drugs, equipment, and technology; (d) developing uniform criteria and federal programs for training medical professionals; (e) establishing and enforcing quality standards of medical care; (f) establishing licensing procedures for medical and pharmaceutical activities; (g) financing and coordinating medical research; (h) organizing state sanitary and epidemiological services; and (i) implementing disaster relief. With states now assuming responsibility for implementing health and disease prevention, technical assistance should be provided to the states by the federal government. In addition, while SSA services have been decentralized to states, little progress has been made at the hospital level to improve efficiency, responsiveness to consumers, and quality. Hospital inefficiencies and duplicity between SSA and other public sector institutions will need to be addressed.

REFORMING IMSS AND CREATING A NATIONAL HEALTH FUND (NHF). Traditionally, the government has both financed and operated the health system using its own facilities and physicians, instead of identifying areas of market or public failure and finding ways to address them. The vertical segmentation of health sector institutions and financing creates an inefficient risk-pooling mechanism that inhibits the development of a strong purchasing organization to provide universal access. Separating the provision of services from financing should help resource allocation be responsive to needs as determined by epidemiological and demographic characteristics, rather than ability to pay. To promote the participation of the private sector, the government could increase the pooling of resources under a universal national health fund, which would purchase services from public and private managed care organizations. This new framework would promote greater transparency and competition between public and private providers. In the first two to five years, the NHF would operate as a virtual fund, establishing the overarching framework for financing and purchasing without consolidating financial resources for healthcare services. In the long term, the NHF could merge all mandatory health financing contributions and evolve into a national health insurance fund.

DEALING WITH THE RISKS OF REFORM. Managed care could rapidly attract 10 million people without severe financial implications for IMSS, but two issues would have to be considered with the new system:

- *Cream-skimming.* Financing and regulations should be designed to avoid the incentives under a capitation-based provider reimbursement system or private managed care market to "cream-skim" and offer low-quality care. Payment mechanisms should allow providers to be paid on the basis of output and population covered, and stop-gap loss previsions should help guard providers against catastrophic risks, thereby reducing incentives to avoid high-risk individuals.
- *Sequencing.* In the short term, efforts should focus on developing consistent regulations across all public sector institutions for the purchasing of services from managed care organizations and private providers. This applies to the development of regulations within IMSS to provide the opting-out (*reversión de cuotas*), which allows the insured to leave IMSS and join managed care.

Ensuring Equity

Issues of coverage, capitated payment, and funding priorities must be considered.

COVERAGE IN RURAL AREAS. For the rural poor, PAC and the *Programa de Consolidación de la Cobertura* (PCC) use mobile healthcare units to provide a basic healthcare package of 13 cost-effective interventions. While PCC is a pilot project which does not operate in rural areas, PAC is now a large program. More than 65 percent of PAC beneficiaries are indigenous. PAC also promotes coordination and integration at the local level of other rural programs with a health component, such as PROGRESA, Health Care for Indigenous Zones, Intersectoral Program for Peasant Workers, and Ambulatory Surgery Program. PAC and other programs have reduced the rural uncovered population from over 10 million to 0.5 million, but efforts will have to be made to take care of the remaining gap in coverage within the next few years at a cost of up to US$600 million per year.

COVERAGE IN URBAN AREAS. The IMSS reform to create new publicly subsidized insurance schemes for the informal sector (that is, the Family Insurance and the Voluntary Insurance programs) was designed to allow those employed in the informal sector in urban areas to obtain social security coverage. Efforts to implement the program should continue, within the context of a sustainable financing framework.

CAPITATED PAYMENT. In IMSS, budget decentralization introduced the implementation of a capitated budget system, dividing the country into 139 Medical Area Units. Similar efforts have been made by SSA for the allocation of resources to states under Ramo 33. The capitated budget is adjusted for risk defined by age and sex, making it necessary to improve the capitation formula to incorporate additional variables and provide a greater degree of equity in the allocation of resources based on need and cost of care. The implementation of a capitated payment in IMSS and SSA is an important step in smoothing differences in financing between regions and public institutions. The extension of the capitated financing to other public providers should provide the basis to establish the NHF, which would use homogeneous allocation criteria to transfer funds to managed care organizations.

SUSTAINABILITY AND FUNDING PRIORITIES. The 1995 Social Security Law is expected to help IMSS address the recurrent deficits that existed in healthcare financing by increasing revenues to an estimated 35 percent in 2010. But improving coverage will require additional funding. More generally, Mexico allocates much fewer resources to health than other OECD and Latin American countries. Future increases in healthcare spending should be carefully targeted to increase equality among regions and institutions, and to address the priority health problems of the population. Furthermore, the increasing size of the allocations from general revenues will require contractual relationships in order to establish a direct relationship between public financing and efforts to extend access, increase efficiency, and improve the quality of healthcare services and user satisfaction.

The result of the reform process should be a model in which (a) an essential health package is accessible to all; (b) the role of government is redirected to ensure that the health sector as a whole is structured to provide cost-effective care and to guarantee the provision of public goods; (c) a universal health insurance fund receiving funding from all sources (government contributions, employers and employees, social security institutions) transfers these resources to regulated managed care organizations and health plans on a capitated basis, which is adjusted for risk; (d) the regulated institutions bear the risk of delivering the services, and rules are defined to resolve market failures; (e) the regulated institutions purchase services from public and private providers, which comply with minimum accreditation criteria and standards for service delivery; (f) there is supervisory capacity to ensure that the services are delivered adequately and that the regulations are being complied with; (g) mechanisms are set up to ensure access to services (secondary and tertiary) beyond those defined in the essential health package; and (h) there is a voluntary market for improved quality and service through supplementary, mostly private health insurance.

Education

Except for selected poor rural areas, enrollment in primary education is nearly universal, and progress is being made in ensuring that the children pursue their education through lower secondary school. The challenges facing Mexico in using education policy as a key element for poverty reduction and social equality are to (a) selectively expand at the initial and preschool and higher education levels; (b) improve the quality of education throughout the system; and (c) invest in the skills and education of the labor force to adapt to the rapid economic and technical changes, which demand a human resource policy that aims to create a qualified and flexible labor force that will reinforce the country's economic competitiveness. Training issues for the labor force are discussed separately. Below we focus on quality and equity.

Improving Quality

To improve quality, it will be necessary to deal with (a) teacher training; (b) the curriculum; (c) pedagogical supervision; (d) the school environment; and (e) time spent on task.

TEACHER TRAINING. Teaching qualifications in the classroom are progressively increasing, thanks to a higher proportion of teachers obtaining the *Licenciatura* and benefiting from SEP training programs (for example, *Programa Nacional para la Actualización Permanente de Maestros de Educación Básica*, and *Programa de Actualización del Magisterio*). However, teaching practices are still based on a teacher-centered model emphasizing memorization, to the detriment of comprehension. Mexico's frontal model cannot respond well to diversity of age, interest, ability, and prior experience. Designed for the average student, it has not proved effective in promoting achievement. One exception to the standard model is the child-oriented, participation-based informal method developed by CONAFE.

CURRICULUM. To increase relevance and flexibility, and to take into account people's views on priorities, SEP has introduced topics such as sexual education in primary school, and the study of values, civic life, and ethics (*Formación Cívica y Ética*) in lower secondary school. Improvements in materials and textbooks for mathematics, geography, and Spanish in primary, and Spanish, biology, and physics in lower secondary, have been made. Other efforts designed to improve learning achievement are the reading corner (*Rincones de Lectura*) and the program for writing and reading (*Programa Nacional para el Fortalecimiento de la Lectura y la Escritura en la Educación Básica*). Still, more needs to be done to introduce active learning into the curriculum and to change the role of teachers from that of a source of knowledge and custodial controller of students to that of a facilitator. In this new role, the teacher must ensure that the students understand the instructions and do extra work. The teacher must also counsel students with problems and help all students learn through cooperative learning interaction (group work), using peer teaching to foster a spirit of self-reliance.

PEDAGOGICAL SUPERVISION. The lack of good teacher supervision and administrative oversight result in a lack of feedback for teachers, in teacher absenteeism, and in a chasm between what the curriculum defines and what is actually taught. CONAFE's compensatory programs have tested with some success ways to improve supervision by providing training and incentives to supervisors with the involvement of parents and communities. It is also necessary to use multicultural approaches in order to attend to indigenous groups, and to use the now standard education assessment being applied in most states for quality assurance. Establishing clearer standards (that is, standards of what students should learn at the end of various levels and modalities of education, and standards for teachers and teacher development) will be beneficial not only to monitor quality, but also to facilitate effective decentralization.

QUALITY OF THE SCHOOL ENVIRONMENT. The school environment includes, among other things, the textbooks, the school infrastructure, the teaching material, and the experimental science facilities. Despite a good distribution system (160 million free textbooks for preschool, primary, and lower secondary education in 1999), the quality of the textbooks could be improved, especially in science. Some textbooks have been revised and published in indigenous languages. But the government has kept an important role in textbook production. More competition could have a positive impact on quality.

TIME ON TASK. The actual number of days and hours per day spent by teachers in the classroom is well below the norm in rural and poor urban areas. Out of the 810 hours a teacher is supposed to be in the classroom, less than half may actually be spent teaching in rural areas. Another issue is that too much time is spent on classroom organization and mechanical repetition with little pedagogical value.

Ensuring Equity

A number of programs are being implemented by the government to promote the access to and quality of education for the poor. The main ones are:

EARLY CHILDHOOD DEVELOPMENT. The Initial Education Program (PRODEI), with a per capita cost of about US$50 a year, is a home-based program delivered by community educators who train parents to stimulate their children. The parents' education is developed through periodic group meetings supplemented by home visits. The program promotes the physical, emotional, intellectual, and social development of infants and toddlers, and improves the school-readiness skills of children. There is empirical evidence that the program is effective in increasing returns on primary education. The program also creates job opportunities for young graduates (of primary education) in poor areas. The program also increases women's self-esteem, and provides opportunities for parents to socialize, thereby fostering community development. PRODEI coverage is limited and should be extended.

COMPENSATORY EDUCATION. These programs, operated by CONAFE, a special agency within SEP, reach more than 4 million poor and indigenous children. The first such program was PARE. It focused on physical facilities, books and materials, teacher performance incentives, school management and supervision, and teacher training in the four poorest states. Another program, the CONAFE community schools, relies on specially trained lower secondary graduate volunteers to teach in schools built and maintained by the communities themselves, in return for scholarships to continue their own education. The community schools have been designed to overcome the problem of maintaining and staffing schools in remote areas where it is difficult to attract and retain teachers and where, given the small size of the community, it would not be cost effective to establish regular schools. CONAFE recently launched PAREIB to support a gradual decentralization in the operation of compensatory programs, through a strengthening of the states' institutional capacity and an increased participation of communities and school associations in school management. PAREIB also promotes a better quality of education and increased learning through teacher training, provision of standards for targeted schools, and national evaluation, as a tool to increase accountability at all levels.

CARRERA MAGISTERIAL. This is an innovative program promoting a voluntary "merit pay" system that rewards teacher professional development. The program aims to raise the quality of basic education through teacher professionalization, presence in schools, and better working conditions. The initiative recognizes the important contribution not only of teachers, but also of parents, in providing a good education to children. One component of the program is the training of teachers; another is a merit pay system in which professional staff on a voluntary basis are evaluated and rewarded with salary increases for their performance as classroom teachers, school directors, and supervisors. Although the program's effectiveness and adequacy have yet to be assessed, some preliminary results are good. More training in active pedagogy could be provided as part of the program.

TELESECUNDARIA. The program was created 30 years ago to respond to the needs of rural communities where a regular lower secondary school would not be feasible. It has a single teacher who teaches all disciplines for all three grades. In the 1990s, with the introduction of satellite transmission, enrollment increased to about 1 million students in about 14,000 schools today. Lessons are delivered by means of television programs broadcast on EDUSAT, Mexico's educational broadcast system. Research in the 1970s and more recently in the 1990s shows the cost-effectiveness of the program. Students graduating from *Telesecundaria* get scores in language similar to those of general lower secondary graduating students, in spite of having a more rural background. But the program is still not accessible in the smallest and most remote areas.

TRAINING AND TECHNICAL EDUCATION. The *Sistema Normalizado de Competencias Laborales* (SNC) has provided an objective set of standards, similar to some that already existed in OECD countries, by which to evaluate worker skills and set curriculum for training programs. The *Consejo de Normalización y Certificación de Competencia Laborales*, which was created to oversee the process of establishing the SNC, has also ensured coherence and consistency across competency standards of different occupations by certifying agencies whose main function is to certify that workers have mastered competencies in the standards for occupational clusters.

AFFORDABILITY ISSUES. The main program ensuring affordability for the poor in basic education is PROGRESA, as discussed earlier. Another important policy for affordability is the student loan programs for technical and especially higher education, such as the ones offered by the ICEE and by SOFE, which improve access to education, particularly for academically qualified but financially needy students. At the same time, these programs develop more effective and financially sustainable student loan institutions.

Urban Labor Markets

The urban Mexican labor market shows a great deal of dynamism and is not highly segmented. Unemployment is low and unions are primarily concerned with maintaining employment rather than increasing wages. The low rates of unemployment observed even in periods of crisis reflect the relative ease of adjusting real wages. Downward wage adjustments are also facilitated by the fact that the minimum wage is not binding—in fact, it is so low today as to be irrelevant. From a policy point of view, progress was made over the last *sexenio* in the reforms of both the social security and health systems. Not only were the systems put on a more secure fiscal footing, but contributions were brought more in line with benefits. Still, there are long-term gains to be made by both workers and firms from increasing the flexibility of labor markets and making additional progress in aligning payroll taxes with worker benefits. This should in turn help in reducing the high level of informality.

Increasing Flexibility

While wage flexibility should remain over the medium term, numerous factors, including the fall in inflation, greater openness to trade, and the weakening of labor unions may lead in the future to more frequent labor market adjustments through unemployment. The objective of the next government should be to minimize labor market transaction costs and other barriers to more rapid quantity adjustments by firms, and to better job matches for workers. Three areas for reform stand out.

DISMANTLING EXISTING JOB SECURITY REGULATIONS AND REPLACING THE CURRENT SEVERANCE-PAY SCHEME WITH AN UNEMPLOYMENT SUPPORT SYSTEM. The absence of any system of unemployment insurance and the lack of portability in some pension funds (particularly in the public sector) have led to an excessive emphasis on job stability, very costly severance payments, a system prone to involved litigation, and inadequate protection of workers. This discourages job creation and better job matches, and it inhibits productivity growth. To avoid these problems, the government could institute a system of individualized accounts leading to a *pago a todo evento* that would allow for separations for economic reasons, reduce litigation costs, encourage better voluntary job matches, and maximize incentives to find work. Clearly defined reasons for termination should be established and monitored by independent dispute resolution authorities. However, in order to protect workers who do not have other means of subsistence from more flexibility at the microeconomic level and more openness at the macroeconomic level, workfare programs such as the PET, training programs such as Probecat, and human development programs such as Progresa should be reinforced.

MODERNIZING THE INDUSTRIAL RELATIONS AND COLLECTIVE BARGAINING FRAMEWORK. The current system for collective bargaining is not flexible, is poorly suited to the more competitive global environment, and is not conducive to the more cooperative relations between management and labor that are essential for greater productivity and job satisfaction. The government could eliminate the *contratos-ley*, which are agreements extended to all firms in an industry, regardless of unionization or economic situation (these agreements achieve neither the microeconomic efficiency of decentralized bargaining nor the macroeconomic benefits of centralized bargaining). The *clausula de exclusión*, which mandates union membership for new hires in unionized firms, and the *patrón indirecto* relationship, which raises transaction costs, weaken supplier linkages, and penalize small firms should both be reconsidered. Restrictions on the use of temporary or fixed-term contracts should be eliminated in favor of two-to-four-month *contratos a prueba*, and temporary *contrato por tiempo determinado*, in order to help firms cover increases in business demand. More generally, the government should encourage in the business community and in its own ranks the introduction of flexible job ladders and assignments, and the elimination of rigid provisions on seniority-based promotion, compensation, and training. These provisions inhibit the optimal matching of skills to job, and they impede individual performance and investment in training, since neither the employer nor the worker can fully recover the cost of those investments through higher pay and productivity, or other rewards. Finally, if the minimum wage is to have any relevance, its level should be raised, but not necessarily automatically indexed to inflation, in order to maintain some level of downward mobility in the event of a crisis.

IMPROVING TRAINING. Survey, anecdotal, and statistical evidence suggests that there is a growing demand for skilled labor that is not being met by the existing labor supply. To deal with this mismatch, the government could modify the *Ley de Capacitación* to relax the obligation of firms to register their training programs while maintaining the right to training. If programs such as *Probecat* are to contribute to a better-trained workforce, they should be thoroughly redesigned, given that the evidence suggests a lack of impact on wages and employment (even though the program works well as a safety net). Strictly from a poverty point of view, it is unclear whether programs such as CIMO have large benefits. The government could also consider using vouchers to allow trainees to choose among training modalities provided privately and outside of the firm. Such training could be broken down into part-time modules to enable workers to remain employed. Youth training programs could also be considered, and apprenticeship contracts could be reintroduced into the legislation to facilitate the school-to-work transition, as is done in Germany and Chile (for example, *Chilejoven*).

Aligning Payroll Taxes and Benefits

Informal sector workers are heterogeneous. They can be classified into those who are informal out of choice, and those who would prefer to work in the formal sector. The incidence of poverty is larger in the second group. Indeed, part of those who are informal by choice do so to avoid taxes, that is, they are relatively well-off in the informal sector.

INFORMAL WORKERS BY CHOICE. Workers who choose to be informal tend to be better off, even though some may be poor. The decision to be informal is made possible by the low opportunity cost of self-employment (due to the low productivity of the formal sector), and it is motivated by the weak linkages between payroll contributions and subsequent benefits. When workers value a benefit less than they pay for it, they have the incentive to become informal and to remain uncovered by the social security system. To encourage these workers to join the formal sector, the payroll taxes must be reduced or, equivalently, the benefits for the workers from paying the taxes must be increased. In other words, the objective should be to bring explicit and implicit worker contributions in line with benefits by pursuing the reform of mandated social security contributions. On the tax side, mandated proportional contributions could be substituted with fixed-quota contributions that would entitle the employee to minimum benefits. The planned transition to *cuota única* in the health program could also be pursued, and a competitive rate of return should be ensured for individual accounts. On the benefits side, progress should be made in raising IMSS efficiency and service quality, and in reforming INFONAVIT, whose benefits for Mexican society remain to be demonstrated.

INFORMAL SECTOR WORKERS WHO WOULD PREFER TO BE FORMAL. Roughly 30 percent of informal workers enter the sector involuntary, would prefer to be formal, and earn substantially less than those voluntarily in the sector. Facilitating the transition of this group to the formal sector would reduce the undesirable risks they face, and give them the protections they desire in terms of access to healthcare and other benefits. To this end, the cost of formality for firms should be reduced. Importantly, reducing informality among this group, which has high rates of poverty, would also facilitate the completion of the government's transition from old-style policies, such as food subsidies, to modern, better targeted, and more efficient OECD-type policies. Completely dismantling food subsidies in urban areas today would contribute to higher poverty in the absence of an alternative way to transfer resources to the informal poor. That is, the fact that many of the informal poor in urban areas are out of reach for the Government reduces the choices of policy instruments that can be used to help them.

Ensuring Equity

Aligning the implicit and explicit labor taxes is important to reduce informality and has partly been the justification for the government's promotion of individual retirement accounts, proposals for individual accounts to replace severance-pay and job security mechanisms that prevent firms from firing (the *pago a todo evento* enables the worker to tap into his or her retirement funds when laid off), as well as proposals to make some payroll contributions voluntary when the tax affects all and benefits few (as is the case for INFONAVIT). A possible risk of all these initiatives is that, by definition, they prohibit the use of a key source of government revenues for distributive purposes and for funding anti-poverty programs. As for the possibility of increasing efficiency in the provision of worker benefits, it would reduce the incentives to informality without reducing revenues, and it should therefore receive a high priority as a policy goal.

*Rural Development**

The era of government-led agriculture is over. CONASUPO has been dismantled. Land reform has been enacted and land titling promoted. Agricultural trade restrictions and regulations are being eliminated under NAFTA. The reforms implemented over the last 10 years have led to the emergence of a largely liberalized, market-oriented, and private-sector-driven rural economy. However, while the reforms were necessary to promote future growth, they have not yet reduced poverty. The reforms have neither resolved decades of structural and cultural limitations in the capacity of poor farmers to access production factors and markets, nor addressed the heterogeneity of the rural sector and its regional variations. While helping export-oriented commercial agriculture, the reforms have not prevented stagnation for small-scale producers of domestically consumed and subsistence commodities. As a result, poverty remains widespread, especially in the *ejido*, sector which accounts for three-quarters of Mexico's producers.

Accompanying the Reforms

To contribute to poverty reduction, the agricultural sector will need to generate employment in both the farm and the nonfarm sectors through productivity increases and better access to markets and technology. A number of initiatives from the government could facilitate this:

- *Pro-poor rural growth.* The objective should be to reduce the productivity gap between the agriculture sector and other sectors by investing in technology generation and development that is better tailored to the need of smallholder poor producers (for example, those involved in nontradable commodities and coffee). This touches on a large set of issues including rural roads programs, technical assistance to promote farmer organizations and marketing cooperative structures, better access to capital and land markets, and the provision of matching grants for investments as a temporary measure. Mexico should also strive at pursue better access to other countries' markets and the elimination of export subsidies in developed countries through bilateral and multilateral trade negotiations.
- *Efficient markets.* The objective should be to reduce the transaction costs of doing business. The government could (a) promote better-integrated price and market information systems that build on the mechanisms established by SNIM, CEA, and PROFECO; (b) develop appropriate regulatory frameworks and enforcement capacity aimed at increasing the perception by the private sector that the judicial system works (this is critical in securing transactions for inventory-based financing for agricultural crops, regional

---

*   This topic receives parallel treatment under the Growth and Competitiveness Thematic Chapter, from a slightly different angle.

exchanges, weather and price insurance, nonbank financial institutions, contract farming, collateralization of assets, etc.); (c) facilitate the development of commodity quality standards based on industry participation and needs, and the development of food safety norms; and (d) establish clear rules with regard to the amount and timing of duty-free imports of maize and beans, including an open auction to allocate quotas efficiently.

- *Less distortion through subsidies.* Remaining subsidy mechanisms should be revisited with a view to their modernization to allow for an efficient and competitive intervention of the private sector and functioning markets. Income support subsidies are less distorting, and therefore should be preferred to price, input, or marketing support, an area where the government should refrain from intervening.

- *Regional development plans.* By associating urban centers and rural areas on a continuum of mutually reinforcing activities, regional development plans could help integrate agriculture with off-farm activities, production with marketing, productivity with welfare, and individual interest with ethnically cohesive populations. Regional plans could also help accompany the integration of labor markets through migration and the diversification of the rural sector. Natural resources and environmental issues, including competition for water, energy, and waste management, require that urban growth be addressed from a joint rural–urban perspective. The decentralization process should facilitate establishment of regional development plans rooted in the historic, cultural, economic, and agro-ecological characteristics of the various regions. The Regional Councils established as part of the Marginal Areas Rural Development program include public institutions, producer representatives, and municipalities, and they could serve as models for participation in regional plans.

Improving Rural Programs

Large sector interventions are implemented by SAGAR, including PROCAMPO and *Alianza para el campo,* and programs for irrigation, credit, and infrastructure also affect the poor.

PROCAMPO. The structural reforms adopted in the rural sector were accompanied by mitigation measures that helped the transition process. PROCAMPO is a large cash transfer program for producers of basic crops that was introduced in 1993–94 by SAGAR. The transfers are provided on a per-hectare basis and they will be phased out in 2008. Today, PROCAMPO is distributed to 3 million producers, covering 90 percent of Mexico's cultivated land. According to a World Bank evaluation using 1997 data, PROCAMPO contributed an average of 8 percent toward household income in ejidos, and up to 40 percent in the poorest decile. PROCAMPO also appears to have a multiplier effect, with a transfer of one peso leading to final benefits of two pesos. This multiplier may be Keynesian, whereby higher income leads to higher local consumption, employment, and again income. It may also be due to the producers taking more risks with higher-yielding investments thanks to the security provided by the transfer. Several improvements could be brought to the program:

- Pay the transfer earlier in the crop cycle or announce the amount of payment prior to planting to facilitate the purchase of inputs and to encourage investments by providing a more secure expected income; and facilitate and promote the use by *ejidatarios* of the transfer as a collateral for loans. The possibility should be studied of letting farmers cash the totality (or part) of the income payment over the remaining period of entitlement (10 years) at a discounted rate through banks.
- Change the structure of payments to give higher payments per hectare to farmers cultivating smaller pieces of land (a large proportion of the transfers are captured by large land owners).
- Abandon the requirement to plant in order to transform PROCAMPO into a pure entitlement. This would lower the administrative cost of the annual requalification process, provide more certainty to the producers' income stream, facilitate collateralization, and ease shifts from one activity to another.

ALIANZA PARA EL CAMPO. Alianza was introduced in 1996 to foster agricultural productivity through investments and the provision of support services for a wide range of agricultural subprograms (for example, ferti-irrigation, mechanization, rural equipment, pasture improvement, and kilo for kilo, which provides growers with one kilo of certified seeds for the price of one kilo of normal seeds). *Alianza* is decentralized, with administration and decisionmaking delegated to the states. One million producers participated in *Alianza* in 1997. So far, there is no evidence that *Alianza* contributes significantly to poverty reduction, in part because poor farmers lack resources to provide the counterpart funding necessary for participation in many subprograms, which consist of matching grants. A greater emphasis must be placed on supporting and targeting the program to low-income farmers, thereby avoiding the subsidy being captured by a few providers, deterring entry into the market and establishing rents. Some steps toward improving the program would be to:

- Improve awareness of the program, with an active process of technology generation and diffusion and the program's professionalization (private service providers and counselors could accompany program beneficiaries to promote competitiveness and diversification to higher-value crops).
- Shift toward vouchers to facilitate consumer choice and support the development of private wholesale channels and retail markets for agricultural inputs and technology (allow participants to purchase inputs from local distributors rather than government-certified distributors).
- Improve the economic analysis of the actions being funded, so that the program does not support less risky but lower-value-added crops and behaviors.

- Reduce administrative complexity by having fewer, more encompassing subprograms, with an integrated regional approach limiting overlaps (and internal competition) among subprograms.

IRRIGATION PROGRAMS. The thrust of the next generation of irrigation programs should be to support an integrated approach that improves the efficiency of water resources and promotes their sustainable management. The government should (a) increase the attention given to agricultural competitiveness and promote more efficient cropping patterns; (b) improve institutional efficiency through better coordination among the government institutions responsible for water resources management, irrigation, and agriculture; (c) further development of water markets and decentralize water management to local users (Water Users Associations and River Basin Councils) in the context of hydrographic basins; and (d) help irrigation system improvements through matching grants with Water Users Associations defined according to a sustainable target of consumptive use.

SOCIAL AND RURAL INFRASTRUCTURE. With decentralization, municipalities are receiving substantial federal transfers for social and rural infrastructure, with wide autonomy in the use of the funds. There is a risk of atomization in funding which may limit economies of scale. The federal government also lacks the means to evaluate the use of the funds, and capacity is lacking in small municipalities to manage the funds. To improve the use of the funds, the federal government could provide matching grants to municipalities to reward good management, intermunicipal projects with economies of scale, and investments cofinanced by the private sector or public agencies. An institutional strengthening program should also be established with the participation of the states.

FINANCIAL SERVICES. The government should promote a level playing field among the different actors providing financial services (commercial banks, specialized institutions, NGOs, cooperatives, *cajas populares,* and savings and loans). Technical assistance could be developed for social groups and nonbank intermediaries. There is also a need for a revamped legal and regulatory framework to promote the enforcement of contracts and the use of nontraditional collateral, and to establish an effective supervision system that ensures compliance and promotes savings mobilization.

IV. Empowering Specific Groups

Indigenous Peoples

Despite the existence of a National Indigenous Institute, significant government investment in indigenous areas, advances in the legal recognition of *comunidades agrarias*, and improvement in the enforcement of indigenous land rights, indigenous peoples continue to be overwhelmingly poor, and they perceive widespread and deeply rooted discrimination from mainstream society. To empower indigenous peoples, the government will need to help change perceptions about indigenous peoples in society at large by promoting multiculturalism and strengthening indigenous organizational structures, so that they have a stronger voice in the local and national political arena. The government will also need to find ways to better respect indigenous values when providing social services and programs for poverty reduction.

Changing perceptions in society. A strategy of promoting indigenous development cannot rely only on the promotion of better access to resources and opportunities to earn a reasonable livelihood. It must also build a political space for indigenous peoples to ensure their cultural survival and economic improvement, thereby building a multiethnic society in which "success" can be measured in more diverse ways than at present. Government intervention could be improved in a number of areas:

- *Promoting a multiethnic society.* Developing a healthy society and economy in which 10 percent of the population have different aspirations and values requires a broad view of indigenous peoples issues. Focusing on the problems of indigenous peoples does not help in assessing why solutions to poverty among indigenous groups are so difficult to identify and implement. What is required is an analysis of both the "indigenous" and "non-indigenous" sides of the equation, and initiatives involving both "indigenous" and "non-indigenous" actors in the solution. Experience in other multiethnic countries has shown that discrimination is not necessarily solved when the economic status of the discriminated group improves. To fight persistent discrimination, multiculturalism must be promoted, for example in the education system, as was done in Canada. Strong institutions are needed to do this, and it is unclear whether the National Indigenous Institute has the clout necessary to do more than just promote the integration and acculturation of indigenous peoples into the Mexican mainstream.
- *Building capacity for indigenous governance.* While indigenous institutions have the potential to play a strong development role, their current capacity for mobilizing change is weak. In rural settlements where land continues to underlie indigenous identity, and where traditional systems of governance persist, there is a continuing demand for capacity building on the part of local government and intercommunity organizations. Because many communities have been isolated historically, capacity building is a precondition for the absorption of development resources, and it should be a main focus of government and non-governmental programs. Local leaders need training in fields ranging from accounting and administration to negotiation skills and computer-based information systems. Youths could also be trained as indigenous professionals to

ensure that sectoral interventions (for example, in education and health) are better adapted to indigenous needs (CIESAS and other similar institutes could help in developing culturally sensitive curriculums). When building capacity for joint action among different indigenous communities, it is also important to recognize the long-term process required for collaboration among historically isolated communities to develop in an organic manner.

ADAPTING GOVERNMENT INTERVENTIONS. Many government programs and services do not have the desired impact among indigenous peoples because they are not adapted to their needs and preferences. This can be illustrated with education, health, poverty programs, agricultural programs, and land issues.

- *Education.* The government has been experimenting with a variety of bilingual and mobile education programs to target indigenous populations, including agricultural migrant laborers. Unfortunately, the evidence so far is that many of these programs are not adapted to indigenous needs and are much too centralized in philosophy, control of resources, and staffing. Parents and local governments should have a larger say in how schools are run. Bilingual teachers should be recruited with community oversight to ensure that they are truly committed and understand the local language. Nationally, as already mentioned, the curriculum is still geared to an ideal Mexican mainstream cultural type. It does not routinely include multicultural material that would make education a source of societal evolution for urban and rural residents of varied backgrounds.
- *Health.* Medical services tend not to be tailored to indigenous customs and preferences, with negative results as to the demand for modern healthcare among indigenous peoples. For example, many women deliver their children at home to avoid the culturally inappropriate rules imposed in clinics and hospitals. Moreover, while there are health programs that support indigenous medical systems and the use of medicinal plants, there has been little systematic effort to find ways to integrate the Western and indigenous systems into effective health services delivery systems. Some traditional practitioners are excellent (and there exists a directory of traditional practitioners by ethnic group), but there is little integration of these practitioners into the formal medical network.
- *Poverty programs.* Poverty programs often do not rely on the extended family and community relationships which continue to shape decisionmaking among indigenous groups. The programs tend to promote individualistic exit strategies from poverty at the risk of causing social disruption. The programs also tend to be implemented locally through the creation of parallel committee or delivery structures that compete with traditional organization for influence and human resources while not building long-term capacity. In the case of PROGRESA, for example, a case study of 12 randomly selected commu-

nities suggested that the program has improved the use of schools and clinics and increased disposable income in poor families for food and other necessities. But on the downside, these subsidies have not been spent in the local economy (most cash is spent for goods purchased in the municipal seat, and they have undermined or distorted local governance structures (for example, when targeting is deficient, when no local capacity for service delivery is created, or when communal labor-sharing systems break down because nonbeneficiaries will no longer contribute free labor). A more recent and more representative survey suggests however that 40 percent of the households benefiting from PROGRESA buy their food in their own locality, and one objective of providing cash transfers through PROGRESA has precisely been the development of the local economy.

- *Agricultural programs.* The policy framework within which PROCAMPO was designed included the national fund for productive rural investments from SAGAR. But few indigenous communities have accessed the SAGAR program or have been able to provide the capital match for significant investments, such as expanding access to irrigation, community storage or processing facilities, or creating a significant source of revolving funds. PROCAMPO absorbs a large share of the resources allocated to the rural sector by the government with insufficient leverage of SAGAR and SEDESOL funds, the (sometimes considerable) flow of remittances, or other capital sources. While the program has helped farmers, the individual payments have been used in some cases to maintain unprofitable subsistence production, without opening farm households to fundamental change. For example, when the vocation of communities under subsidy is forestry instead of agriculture, there is a need for incentives that foster alternative livelihood models. Given the nature of common natural resources, most enterprises would require collective action and investment and, therefore, support for organizational capacity building at the community and regional level. Programs based on individual decision-making are ill-equipped for such tasks. There is a need for programs to better promote opportunities that are community based, such as coffee associations, forestry enterprises, organic agriculture, tourism enterprises, marketing of *artesanía*, and cultural-heritage-based employment generation.

- *Land issues.* There are outstanding land tenure issues that have not yet been addressed for indigenous communities and *ejidos*. Successful communities are engaged in active campaigns to buy back lands that were previewing sold off to outsiders and rebuild their consolidated identity or expand the land pool to members. But there are no market-assisted land reform schemes to finance any purchases. Indigenous communities have extensive common lands that are not apt for agriculture, but land regularization programs have provided no support for guaranteeing the status of these lands and protecting them from outside encroachment or illegal extraction (hunting, timber, seasonal agriculture). Indigenous communities also need legal assistance to resolve long-standing boundary conflicts. There is a need to recognize the importance of land and resource rights for indigenous community survival and to promote better natural resource management with indigenous peoples as key actors.

Gender Issues

Different opportunities and obstacles exist for men and women in their pursuit of health, education, livelihood and old-age security. Many women must choose between either working or entering into marriage and caring for children and other household members. This choice is often determined early on. Girls who drop out of school in order to help cook, clean and care for younger siblings are ill-prepared for anything other than domestic work as adults. Girls who stay in school have a better chance of entering the paid labor market, but later in life they will still often have to choose between the labor or marriage market. In contrast, men do not appear to face this dichotomy. However, the fact that men have only one main role, that of provider, means that if they are unable to fulfill that role, they have no other way to affirm their identify and sense of self, which can then lead to destructive behavior such as alcohol abuse and violence, with the latter a growing problem in Mexico.

Institutions, both governmental and market-based, influence gender outcomes. With regard to education, girls in rural areas are more likely to go to high school where the supply of such schools is greater. In the case of child labor, official statistics which ignore girls' work may bias the response of governmental and nongovernmental institutions away from addressing the detrimental effects of domestic work for children. With regard to rural labor markets, some evidence, although not conclusive, suggests that employers may discriminate against female workers. With regard to old-age security, elderly women rely critically on benefits obtained through their status as widows or as dependents from social security institutions with a family orientation. In terms of reproductive roles, health services that focus on maternal and child health tend to exclude men and reinforce traditional female roles.

In 1995, the Zedillo Administration established the National Program for Women (PRONAM) to expand women's participation in development processes and provide equal opportunities for men and women. In 1998, the Government created the National Women's Commission (CONMUJER) to advance legislation, regulations and sectoral programs to benefit women. However, while programs such as PRONAM help in redistributing resources toward women, the root causes of socially ascribed gender roles and other gender issues have received less attention. In some areas, progress has been slow for a number of reasons. First, public sector employees often lack awareness of the importance of gender issues or the knowledge and techniques to address gender in sectoral government programs. Second, organizational weaknesses of public sector agencies limit their capacity to deliver anything beyond the most basic services. Third, CONMUJER and other groups working on gender issues have been unable to provide the required technical support to government agencies.

The challenge of creating greater equality for men and women in Mexico is thus twofold. First, an even playing field needs to be created through legal and institutional reforms. Public sector institutions can play a critical role in creating the opportunities for both women and men to benefit from government programs and reducing discrimination and access constraints. Second, public policies need to address the gender socialization processes that inhibit women and men from taking advantage of those opportunities made available through legal and institutional reforms. Creating equal opportunities for men and women is not enough. Socialization processes affect the roles and identities men and women assume and influence their behavior and choices, which in turn, affect their welfare. Gender roles and identities influence the acquisition of human capital, the opportunities and decisions to participate and advance in the workforce, the negotiating power in the household, and the acquisition and control of assets and economic security in old age. Socialization takes place in the public and private sphere and is influenced by, *inter alia*, the education system, the media and peer groups. Policy and program interventions should therefore focus on these three domains. Interventions should not be limited to women only. Helping to redefine roles, images, and expectations for men is also necessary to achieve long-term gender equality.

4

A Sustainable Future

*This Thematic Chapter was written by Adolfo Brizzi and
Kulsum Ahmed with the valuable input of Masami Kojima,
John A. Dixon, and Kirk Hamilton.*

There are five broad areas which the new Administration must address that are of critical importance to the growth and development of the country. They are: (a) fiscal sustainability; (b) reduction of poverty and inequality; (c) fast, sustainable growth through competitiveness; (d) good governance; and (e) a sustainable future. Indeed, the success of the Administration might be measured by its performance in each of these areas. This Chapter discusses the area of a sustainable future. It is premised on the supposition that the objectives of the other themes cannot successfully be achieved if sustainability is not factored into the development agenda. Accordingly, this Chapter puts forward a number of institutional and policy options to move toward a sustainable future. In conjunction with this Chapter, specific chapters address in detail the areas of water, air quality, solid waste, biodiversity, forestry and land management, and disaster management.

I. Recent Developments

International and Domestic Context

Most of the Mexican development strategy of the 1980s and part of the 1990s was based on the underlying availability of abundant and cheap sources of energy. This led to accelerated industrialization (electricity, oil, gas, chemistry, steel, and manufacturing) and fast expansion of the transport sector. The ensuing pressure on the environment deriving from increased pollution, waste generation, and degradation of natural resources has been significant, and has caused severe damage (see Section II). Such degradation has disproportionately affected an important segment of the rural and urban poor, who have experienced either a dwindling of their resource base or an impact on their health and standard of living.

117

During the 1990s, an important factor played a critical role in changing the attitude of Mexico toward the environment: its new position in the international arena. During that decade, Mexico came to play a much stronger and active role in the discussion of and participation in international treaties and conventions. Key among these are NAFTA with the U.S. and Canada in 1992, and joining the OECD in 1994.[1] In some cases, Mexico has taken a leadership role, such as recently becoming the first OECD member and the largest developing country to ratify the Kyoto Protocol. These international accords, and their binding environmental targets, have acted as a catalyst to push forward the sustainable development agenda, and have been important drivers of a more positive attitude toward the environment, higher standards, and better compliance mechanisms. In addition, Mexico has come to realize, mostly through trade agreements, that sound environmental practices are key elements in determining the country's competitiveness and its ability to expand access to new export markets and to attract foreign investment and tourism.

The domestic context also started to change in the 1990s with respect to the general perception and awareness of environmental issues. During the Zedillo Administration, in particular, three important forces triggered a much stronger visibility of the environment and the realization of the need to address the sustainable development challenge: (a) the deepening of the democratization process, accompanied by an enhanced public debate which has helped establish a more solid environmental constituency; (b) increased decentralization to states and municipalities and enhanced accountability for environmental practices at the local level; and (c) a much stronger political commitment toward environmental issues.

Despite the recognition of the environmental challenge and initial measures taken to address it, progress on this front is recent and needs to be sustained and expanded to show positive impact and results. In particular, the OECD has concluded that no decoupling between environmental pressure and GDP is yet taking place, as is it in most OECD countries.[2] Indicators related to energy, traffic, waste, and natural resources point to the fact that GDP growth is generated through considerable pressure on the environment and unaccounted costs to the society.

The Legal and Institutional Response

During the 1990s considerable progress was made in Mexico on the legal front in the area of the environment. For example,

---

1. Mexico is party to many more international conventions in the area of hazardous materials (Basle Convention); biodiversity (Biodiversity Convention, CITES, Cartagena Protocol on biosafety); the ozone layer (Vienna Convention, Montreal Protocol); climate change (Kyoto Protocol, Clean Development Mechanism); fisheries (FAO compliance agreement); and water (the Hague Ministerial Declaration on water security).
2. Environmental Performance Review, Mexico, OECD, 1998.

- In 1992 the approval of the new National Water Law represented a major step in the modernization of the water sector through the registration of all water users (including dischargers); the promotion of water markets; the establishment of institutional and planning mechanisms for water management at the level of the river basin; and improvement of water monitoring, modeling, and assessment, including better operation of hydraulic infrastructure.
- In 1996, after a year of consultations with representatives from a wide range of society, the *Ley General del Equilibrio Ecológico y Protección al Ambiente* (LGEEPA), was approved. It represented a major reform of the legal environmental framework, through promotion of increased decentralization of environmental management and the participation of civil society in environmental decisionmaking, incorporation of economic instruments into environmental policies, and voluntary practices and mechanisms for environmental compliance.
- In 1997 a major reform to the forestry law was enacted with the objective of strengthening the linkages between the environmental and forestry sectors, better regulating and facilitating participation of the social sector and communities in commercial plantations and in the sustainable use of forestry products, and strengthening the efficiency of the forestry services, including improved enforcement and sanctions.

The capacity for environmental impact assessment has been strengthened considerably over the last few years through the National Institute of Ecology (INE). Of particular note is the progress made in integrating permit delivery through the *Licencia Ambiental Unica* (LAU), which incorporates in a single process the regulatory requirements regarding environmental impact and risk, atmospheric emissions, use of national waters, wastewater discharges, and the management of hazardous waste. It allows the private sector to go to a one-stop window to apply for all environmental permits, thus considerably decreasing the time and paperwork required for such applications.

Environmental modernization has been under way in Mexico for a number of years. Major institutional milestones in this process include the creation of the office of the Federal Attorney General for Environmental Protection (PROFEPA) and INE in 1992, followed by the regrouping of environmental responsibilities under a new Ministry of Environment, Natural Resources and Fisheries (SEMARNAP) in 1994. SEMARNAP brought together the programs and policies of five semi-independent entities: the National Water Commission (CNA), INE, PROFEPA, the National Institute of Fisheries, and the Mexican Institute of Water Technology, in addition to the policies and programs for natural resources, fisheries, soil conservation and restoration, environmental management, and environmental policy planning.

Changes to the LGEEPA in 1996 started a trend toward decentralized environmental management and bringing the environment closer to the final decisionmakers and the end users. This was in line with a more general thrust in Mexico toward increased decentralization, which was consolidated starting in 1998 with the creation of a special line item of the budget for states and municipalities (*Ramo* 33), and in 1999 (change of Article 115 of the Constitution, which gave more antonomy to municipalities) as the government took a considerable step toward increased devolution of responsibilities to municipalities (including for environmental planning and services). Accordingly, SEMARNAP has adopted a new strategy for decentralized environmental management and started to define new approaches consistent with strengthening the capacity of subnational governments, and devising new financial mechanisms for environmental investments at the state level based on cost recovery for environmental services, the polluter-pays principle, and increased fiscal responsibility.

Some Initial Successes and Achievements: Biodiversity and Air Pollution

The 1995–2000 National Development Plan introduced a new vision of Mexico's environmental strategy and sought to define new ways to better integrate environmental protection and economic development. While implementation of the plan will require a sustained implementation effort and commitment beyond 2000 to reap benefits, progress is evident in some areas such as biodiversity and air pollution.

BIODIVERSITY. Although considerable effort is still required to revert to a sustainable path, the government has taken the measure of the challenge and SEMARNAP has been a leader in biodiversity conservation. A comprehensive Biodiversity Conservation Strategy has been finalized, together with the establishment of a more autonomous and permanent institutional setup through the National Council for Protected Areas (CONANP) and the recent National Commission for Protected Areas. In addition, a National System of Protected Areas (SINAP) was put in place, supported by a new financing mechanism (endowment fund), covering 10 areas in the first phase and 15 more being contemplated in a second phase. It will foster sustained long-term flow of funds for the conservation of priority areas. Finally, the government realized the importance of a more proactive approach toward mainstreaming and of better integration of conservation activities with poverty programs, land use planning, rural development, and management of productive landscapes.

AIR POLLUTION. The Air Quality Management Program of the Mexico City Metropolitan Area also deserves special mention as a success story. Substantial reduction in the concentration of critical pollutants, such as lead, CO_2 and SO_2, has been achieved through the implementation of a comprehensive air quality management program, to the benefit of some 20 million people. Recognition of the multisector nature of the issues permitted the pursuit of an integrated strategy which brought together the environment, transport, and energy sectors. It included improved specifications for fuels and generalization of the use of catalytic converters, regulatory reforms for wider coverage of the air monitoring network, better enforcement of vehicle inspection, and reduced emission of volatiles from gas stations. Efforts will need to be sustained to maintain these achievements and address the still important unfinished agenda related to the unhealthy concentration of ozone, fine particles, and further improvement in fuel specification with respect to sulfur.

II. Issues

Environmental Degradation

Severe environmental degradation, resulting in high economic and social costs, continues to pose a serious challenge to the sustainability of Mexican economic growth and quality of life. Reports on the state of the environment in Mexico reveal that:

- Over 100 of Mexico's 258 aquifers are overdrawn, especially in the northern most productive areas, and the pressure on water resources (both quantity and quality) is likely to become the main challenge to Mexico in the medium term, with increasingly recurrent conflicts between agriculture, municipalities, and industries.
- Less than 10 percent of wastewater from municipalities, industry, and agricultural uses is treated, and its discharge into surface waters can have serious public health consequences.
- Only about 35 percent of the solid and hazardous waste generated is disposed of under sanitary conditions.
- Concentrations of some atmospheric contaminants in urban centers frequently exceed acceptable standards.
- Deforestation rates are among the highest in Latin America, with about 300,000 hectares disappearing every year, and posing a real threat to the conservation of the country's vital ecosystems and increasing vulnerability to natural disasters.
- A high percentage of soils are affected by erosion.
- Biodiversity is declining due mostly to endemic pressure from agriculture and livestock.
- The marine and insular ecosystem and coastal zones are threatened by tourism and urban development.
- Natural disasters have been causing tremendous losses in the country, some of which could have been avoided through better environmental practices and prevention.
- Only about 50 percent of small rural households have access to safe water, and 29 percent to sanitation.[3]

---

3. This is reflected in Mexico's under-5 mortality figure of 35 deaths per thousand, compared with 6 deaths per thousand in high-income countries.

Like other countries, Mexico uses the environment in two basic ways: as a source of natural resources and as a receptor and assimilator of waste and pollution. Neither of these uses shows up directly in standard measures of national income. A "greener" measure of net national income would deduct the value of the depletion of natural resources, since this represents a diminution of wealth. Similarly, when pollutants are emitted and human beings and economic assets are exposed to them, the resulting damage should also be deducted from net national income. In addition to yielding truer measures of national income, valuing the depletion and degradation of the environment can also speak to the sustainability of economic development by measuring changes in the national balance sheet. In an effort to value the use of the environment in a national accounting framework, Mexico has published a system of economic and environmental accounts, based on U.N. guidelines, for the years 1988 through 1996.

While there is still considerable debate on the methodology, reliability of information, and sources and standards chosen as reference, the picture that emerges from this analysis is that degradation of the environment is large in Mexico, representing a significant share of GDP. This is true in absolute macroeconomic terms, and in comparison with other OECD countries. This exercise signals to policymakers that there are important trade-offs between the concept of long-term sustainable development and short-term views on growth. Better integration of environmental issues in economywide policy analysis will generate more support for environmental reforms.

Table 1. Sectoral Distribution of Depletion and Degradation, 1996
(millions of pesos and percent of GDP)

Sector	Depletion		Degradation	
Agriculture, forestry, fishing	9,829	0.39%	14,685	0.59%
Minerals	11,129	0.44%	1,897	0.08%
Manufacturing	216	0.01%	8,763	0.35%
Construction	74	0.00%	0	0.00%
Electricity, gas, water	7	0.00%	9,603	0.38%
Commerce, restaurants, hotels	0	0.00%	0	0.00%
Transport, storage & communication	0	0.00%	160,007	6.39%
Finance, real estate, services	1,004	0.04%	41,153	1.64%
Total	22,259	0.89%	236,108	9.43%

Note: On degradation, the value of 9.4 percent of GDP is high by OECD standards. For example, air pollution damages in Europe are estimated to be 2.8 percent in Germany, 4.4 percent in Italy, 3.9 percent in the Netherlands, and 2.0 percent in the UK, compared with at least 6.4 percent in Mexico.
Source: INEGI (1999).

Policies and Incentives

REFLECTING SCARCITY. In the absence of appropriate mechanisms to reflect scarcity, natural resources will be treated as free goods, leading to unsustainable practices. Pricing policies and subsidies are often cited as the main culprits for misallocation and waste of environmental resources. As long as prices convey perverse signals to consumers, or environmental resources are portrayed as public goods, people will tend to internalize the benefits of their use and externalize the cost to society. This can be particularly true in the case of subsidies for water, energy, and some agricultural commodities. Underpricing the extraction costs of water through special energy tariffs, and subsidizing the production of maize can have a triple distortionary effect on the incentive to save water, to shift toward crops of higher value per unit of water used, and to limit expansion of the agricultural frontier through deforestation.

MARKET INSTRUMENTS. Generally, past approaches to environmental policies and incentives have been through regulation and enforcement, without the necessary steps of evaluating the impact of other policies on the environment. This has been costly and of limited efficiency. More recently, information has been accumulating on the possible use of markets for environmental resources as an instrument for their protection. This can take the form of ensuring elimination of distortions caused by subsidies, imposing user fees to increase the cost of using a natural resource (hence internalizing the social cost), imposing taxes on a polluter who has been disposing of wastes into the environment without charges, or establishing new markets in which pollution permits or rights may be traded. The environmental sector remains severely underfunded, and there is almost no incentive for collecting taxes or for recovering costs for environmental services at the state and municipal levels.

PROPERTY RIGHTS. While Mexico has made considerable progress lately in promoting the functioning of markets (notably water and land), the further strengthening of property rights remains an important challenge to address the unregulated open access to resources. This may be the case particularly for forests and fisheries, where providing clear and well-regulated property rights can have a lasting and positive effect on the incentives for better resources management. In the case of forestry, relying on traditional indigenous community conservation practices, and formalizing locally developed management plans, can be powerful instruments in building ownership for conservation. The example of recurring forest fires induced by agricultural practices is a sign of the still perverse incentive existing with respect to the value of the forest and to the opportunities offered for its sustainable use.

THE VICIOUS CIRCLE OF POVERTY AND DEGRADATION. Mexico has a dual economy, with more than 40 million poor people coexisting with a modern consumer society. The well-being of this sizeable population of poor people is disproportionately affected by environmental degradation and by the deteriorating natural resource base upon which their urban and rural livelihoods depend. However, it can be argued that in many cases degradation of the environment is the only way for the poor to survive. This is due to their short-term survival strategies and to the lack of access to markets, basic services, credit, technology, and infrastructure, which limits their opportunities to access a healthier standard of living and to improve agricultural practices. This creates a vicious circle which, given the size of both the degradation and the poverty phenomena, can create dangerous mutually reinforcing links. External factors, such as the occurrence of natural disasters, reveal the magnitude of this causality because (a) environmental degradation tends to exacerbate the negative impact of disasters (floods and erosion deriving from deforestation or illegal settlements); (b) poor people are the most vulnerable to disasters and they represent the bulk of the casualties; and (c) poor people are often the biggest environmental offenders, especially in the case of natural resource use.

THE TRADE-OFFS. It must be recognized that the use of market-based instruments for environmental reforms may be politically costly if they do not lead to short-term, win-win situations. Moreover, some economic reforms cannot succeed if they are not accompanied by a well-thought-through and adequate institutional, regulatory, and enforcement framework. The best approach to avoid environmental damage would be to identify and analyze the most serious economic-environmental linkages, and devise specific complementary mitigating measures. This may be the case specifically when the elimination of subsidies might pose immediate "environment versus poverty" challenges. One could argue, however, that if it is justified for the government to support the most disadvantaged segments of the population in facilitating access to basic goods and services, it is best to do so through nondistortionary targeted income support mechanisms rather than through price support or differentiated tariff structures.

Institutions and Environmental Management

VERTICAL VS. HORIZONTAL SCOPE. While the institutional reorganization of 1994 brought the institutions dealing with environment, natural resources, forestry, and fisheries under one roof, it also resulted in bringing planning, regulatory, enforcement, and productive functions together. This is similar to previous institutional setups, where core environmental functions were combined with sectoral interests ("salubrity," urban development, social development). The current normative and budgetary processes that govern the functioning of line agencies in Mexico also submit SEMARNAP to the strict administrative arrangements of sectoral executing agencies. This has likely restricted the spectrum of action of environmental policies to a sectoral and vertical confinement. Coordination across institutional boundaries has been difficult, because SEMARNAP stands at the same hierarchical level as other more established and powerful ministries. Similarly, a systematic and operational approach to the environmental evaluation of government policies and programs could not really be implemented. It must be recognized, however, that given the limitations inherent in the present setup, SEMARNAP has done wonders in its capacity to "green the government."

ENFORCEMENT EFFECTIVENESS. While consistent with good practice, separation of the normative and enforcement agencies (INE and PROFEPA) may in fact have widened the gap between the two functions: limited institutional coordination may have hampered consistency between what is reasonable and feasible to regulate and to enforce. While progress has been considerable on the legal front, it would appear that a disconnect still exists with the enforcement capacity. Not only are resources clearly insufficient to adequately perform the enforcement function over a country as large as Mexico, but some doubts are cast on the enforceability of legislation that may be too stringent or ambitious, particularly for natural resources. In addition, the use of market-based instruments, public disclosure programs for industries in compliance or below compliance, or those wishing to voluntarily announce their compliance, are still limited, and the LGEEPA should ensure their expansion. The implementation of a more comprehensive set of legal mandates and compliance mechanisms provides significant additional impetus for environmental moderniza-tion in Mexico. The principles underlined by the legal and regulatory arrangements should favor the formation of partnerships among all interested elements of society for the identification, negotiation, and resolution of environmental challenges.

ENVIRONMENTAL DECENTRALIZATION. Despite initial steps encouraged by the LGEEPA, as a new administrative sector in Mexico the environment is still less decentralized than the traditional sectors of health, education, agriculture, and infra-structure. Further decentralization of environmental functions is warranted, together with a better definition of responsibilities among the different levels of Government. Water management is specifically an area where, despite the consider-able progress made in defining an explicit approach to integrated water resources management, it will be difficult to meet the considerable challenges ahead through the current institutional setup. Further decentralization is in order, and a more proactive approach is needed toward empowering river basin and aquifer commit-tees to manage and monitor the use of water. The successful transfer of irrigation districts to water user associations has demonstrated that local stakeholders can improve operation and maintenance considerably. However, it must be noted that decentralization can be a mixed blessing for environmental policies if functions are transferred without the resources to implement them, or without a revision of the sources and mechanisms for financing and for fiscal responsibility at the local level. The fiscal structure does not create any clear incentive to promote local cost recov-ery for environmental services, nor does it encourage industries that use clean tech-nologies or penalize those that pollute. Moreover, fragmentation of responsibility could make it difficult to take environmental action on the scale required, which generally extends beyond the territory of a municipality. Finally, states and municipalities must still adapt and adjust their legal and regulatory mechanisms to a new decentralized context, and need to strengthen their environmental management capacity, an area that SEMARNAP recently has been actively promoting.

PRIVATE SECTOR PARTICIPATION. Private sector participation, if well regulated, can increase service standard, and improve access, quality, and economic effectiveness, and better environmental management. Moreover, in the case of water and sanitation, a "moral hazard" effect against participation of the private sector may be present at the municipal level, because municipalities have been used to being bailed out by the federation when financial problems arose. Hence, public sector water and sewage works are the classic example of a situation where fee collection is low, maintenance is insufficient, and investment is lacking.

III. Options for the Future

Institutional Strengthening

Environmental efficiency in the context of limited resources should be approached from the perspective of identifying the mechanisms, instruments, and policies of greatest leverage and impact, and the most effective ways to integrate the trade-offs between growth and environment in economywide policymaking. Environmental responsibilities fall into two main groups: core environmental functions, and resource-based functions (Figure 1). To be effective, core functions need clout, commitment, and the capacity to exert policy coordination and evaluation between and over the different sectors. Resource-based functions, independent of institutional locations, need to seek integration and influence over sectoral policies through better mainstreaming. The biggest impact for sustainable development may well come through better mainstreaming and linkages with sectoral policies at the federal level, and the implementation of these policies at the decentralized state, regional and municipal levels.

In general, the promotion of an intersectoral approach to environmental policies and the establishment of horizontal coordinating mechanisms are urgently required for identification of priorities, cofinancing, and evaluation of shared responsibilities. The greatest contribution to improved environmental management is likely to come from strengthening of institutions, especially at the local and regional level, while national environmental institutions could focus their intervention on core functions, policy coordination, and national and international areas of public interest.

The decentralization of environmental responsibilities and the definition of a clear distribution of functions among the three levels of government can promote important changes by sharing responsibilities across different stakeholders, such as the private sector and local communities, and bringing the effects of environmental enforcement closer to local users. However, given the underfunding of the sector, it

Figure 1. Environmental Responsibilities

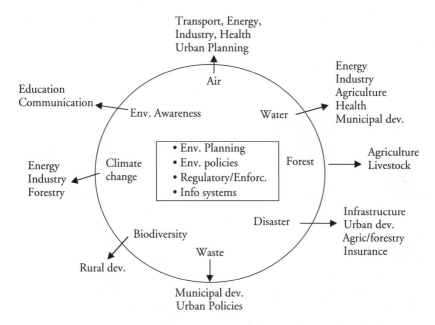

will be critical to broaden the environmental revenue base and to revisit the financing mechanism, including the possibility of retaining, at the local level, new incomes generated through surcharges (gasoline), environmental taxes, and user fees. Increased participation of the private sector can also help in developing new clean technologies and participating in the financing of the sector, but it will require clear pricing signals, adequate incentives, and regulations.

More Clout to Core Functions

ENVIRONMENTAL PLANNING. This remains an essential tool for environmental policymakers at three levels: (a) at the priority-setting level the focus should be on where the biggest impact can be made for the resources available. Green accounting should be pursued to bring greater rigor in policy decisions; (b) at the central level through the establishment of partnerships and agreements with various sectors and the definition of clear indicators against which to gauge performance and evaluate government policies; and (c) at the decentralized level, to maintain a broader approach (particularly when rapid decentralization bear the risk of excessive atomization), and to ensure that land use policies, regional development, environmental infrastructure, and coherent fiscal measures are brought to bear. The government should pursue the effort initiated under the 1995–2000 National Development Plan and continue developing mechanisms for integration and consultation, especially at the regional level.

ENVIRONMENTAL POLICIES. Unless the need to improve the welfare of people is declared a priority, environmental programs are likely to fail. Addressing environmental issues requires, in many cases, that poverty be reduced, especially in rural areas where the link between poverty and environmental degradation is stronger. This will require that those potentially involved in environmental and development programs be more involved in the design stage, and that local knowledge be better incorporated during implementation. The good news is that sound economic policies and poverty alleviation are also good for the environment. Higher incomes and better security over assets will enable the poor to consider longer-range options for resource management, which also gives better returns. Improving land tenure rights and access to financial services not only yields economic gains but also promotes better environmental management. Pricing and taxation are very powerful environmental policy instruments; removal of major price distortions and promotion of market incentives generally will contribute to both economic and environmental management. In this respect, the impact of subsidies on water, energy, and agriculture would need to be reviewed. There is also the need to study and address through targeted programs the immediate consumption and production risks that confront poor households in their capacity to benefit from the reforms or to access alternatives. Further, it is important to examine whether other policy, market, or institutional limitations hinder the potential benefits of proposed reforms.

Global issues and international agreement will probably continue to play an important role in shaping future incentives frameworks, norms, and competitiveness, but also opportunities for business development and employment generation. Mexico should continue to take advantage of globalization and participation in international fora not only as effective drivers for improved environmental management, but also to better defend views of national interest. Tradable emission permits may become an interesting venture to pursue in the future as an efficient instrument for market-driven regulatory measures. Trade and environmental issues in general are likely to become more visible, and Mexico should anticipate future developments because important trade-offs will need to be debated. Environmental protection should not discriminate against trade, especially in cases when standards are different among countries. Helping consumers make informed decisions may be a better way to induce changes, although burdensome labeling requirements could all too easily become protectionist measures. There is a need to develop credible and impartial certification mechanisms and agencies that would establish the incentives for self-regulation by the industry.

REGULATIONS AND ENFORCEMENT. Regulations should be used with discretion and should be assessed against their transaction costs and enforceability. Standards, norms, bans, permits, and quotas will still be necessary to regulate public policies and define the framework within which activities can take place. To this extent, it will be important that the Mexican regulatory functions cover all the sectors that can have a significant impact on or contribution to the sustainability of the development process. However, strict enforcement can be expensive; if regulations are not or cannot be enforced, there is little incentive to obey them. Effective mechanisms for compliance and enforcement should be promoted, particularly voluntary compliance through certification mechanisms in the industry (see Industry and Environment section below), community-driven approaches, and consumer attitudes. Information, sensitization, and communication policies will be key in this respect.

INFORMATION AND COMMUNICATION. These activities are essential to building an environmental constituency and social participation. That is where the pressure for a more prominent sustainable development agenda is going to come from and where the requirements for greater accountability will rest. Meeting the demands of a relatively fast-growing population will only be possible if incentives are provided for all stakeholders, including the different government agencies, water users, the private sector, and civil society, to participate in the management of their resources and in the provision of services. Increased awareness and commitment requires the involvement of professional educators and specialized NGOs. A high level of public participation and demand for improved environmental quality will also be an important determinant of successful institutional mainstreaming.

Mainstreaming

Integration of a sustainable development perspective within the context of sectoral policies and programs has traditionally proved difficult, but is probably one of the areas of higher payoffs. It requires strong political commitment and a level of institutional coordination that goes beyond the usual administrative and budgetary procedures. In addition, greater decentralization of environmental management to the state level provides opportunities to mainstream environmental concerns through the use of appropriate environmental planning tools. Some examples and options follow.

Industry and Environment

Analysis of a survey[4] of 236 Mexican industrial firms found that drivers of good environmental performance were regulatory requirements (over 60 percent), internal policies (over 50 percent), neighbors and local communities (25 percent), NAFTA (35 percent of exporters in sample), customers (20 percent), and chambers of commerce and trade associations (15 percent). On the other hand, external obstacles to environmental improvement were high interest rates, lack of an environmental culture, inconsistency of regulatory requirements, lack of information and

---

4. *Industrial Environmental Management in Mexico: Results of a Survey.* The Lexington Group, 1997. Report to the World Bank and INE on a survey funded by a grant from the Japanese government covering large, medium, and small industrial firms from four potentially polluting sectors throughout Mexico.

regulations, and bureaucracy.[5] Interestingly, the time spent by the industrial facilities covered by this survey (5 percent of total industrial facilities in Mexico) to prepare permit applications was equivalent to a full-time staff of over 3,000 people. Econometric analysis of the survey data indicates that the factor that most strongly differentiated companies with positive environmental performance was the existence of elements of an environmental management system (EMS).[6]

Given the enormous disparity between the environmental management capabilities of large and small companies in Mexico (as the above survey indicates), and the large number of the small-and medium-size enterprises (SMEs) sector, a recent pilot implemented in Guadalajara to help SMEs implement EMSs under the mentorship of their large company clients yielded interesting results.[7] These findings suggested that: (a) EMSs could be implemented by SMEs relatively easily, and with generally more benefits than costs; (b) measurable improvements in environmental and economic performance were observed in the participating SMEs, thus increasing their competitiveness; (c) worker environmental conditions improved; (d) compliance with environmental regulation improved; and (e) the companies' public image improved, and in some cases resulted in attracting new clients.

The survey results point to the importance of (a) rationalizing and simplifying regulations, a process which has been started with the new water standards, but needs to be sustained; (b) continuing with the *Licencia Ambiental Unica* scheme, which has recently been implemented to streamline under one umbrella all environmental licensing requirements at the federal, state, and municipal levels; (c) further enhancing regulatory enforcement through focusing on environmental results rather than paperwork compliance, and more effective use and better alignment of existing public disclosure schemes; and (d) building an environmental culture through education and targeted training. The results of the Guadalajara pilot suggest that (a) SME-targeted technical assistance programs that promote EMSs (regardless of formal certification) can be effective at achieving environmental improvements; and (b) use of client–supplier linkages helps to bridge the gap in capacity between Mexico's so-called dual economy of sophisticated exporters and domestic SMEs. Ideally, such programs should be better integrated into general business promotion initiatives, rather than stand-alone environmental programs. Voluntary and obligatory programs also need to be better aligned, not only those that are government sponsored, such as INE's voluntary *convenios* and PROFEPA's environmental audits, but also with industry initiatives and international standards, such as ISO 14000.

---

5. In addition, internal obstacles included competing corporate priorities, knowledge of technology, senior management commitment, technical assistance and worker interest.
6. Dasgupta, S., H. Hettige, and D. Wheeler. *What Improves Environmental Performance? Evidence from Mexican Industry*. World Bank Development Research Group Working Paper #1877, 1998.
7. *Mexico: The Guadalajara Environmental Management Pilot*, Report No. 18071-ME, The World Bank, September 8, 1998.

Energy and the Environment

Use of energy has a significant impact on the environment. One of the most promi-nent examples is the combustion of liquid fuels in boilers, and stationary and mobile engines. The combustion products include components that are harmful to public health (such as fine particles, ozone precursors, and acid-forming compounds) and greenhouse gases (GHG). Another concern is households and small industries burn-ing biomass, resulting in high levels of fine particles and leading to morbidity and premature mortality. The government has already taken a number of key decisions to meet growing energy demand and at the same time minimize environmental damage. These include (a) expanding the availability of natural gas and promoting its use; and (b) minimizing the flaring of associated gas during crude oil production (thus increasing natural gas production and reduce GHG emissions). The imple-mentation of the decision to expand the use of natural gas, however, faces serious challenges, since domestic natural gas production will not be able to meet demand in the absence of substantial investment in the gas sector.[8]

In the coming decade, energy pricing could and should play a greater role in pro-tecting the environment. Untargeted subsidies, where they exist, lead to misalloca-tion and inefficient use of resources, and strain the government budget. In the energy sector, the most significant source of budget deficit is power tariff subsidies to certain sectors. The government at present is very dependent on fuel taxes as a source of revenue, and is hence reluctant to lower taxes on cleaner fuels. Removal of power tariff subsidies should help the government lower its reliance on fuel taxes for its income, and therefore lower taxes on cleaner fuels such as natural gas. This would not only uphold the "polluter pays" principle, but also help Mexico attract the needed investment in the power sector.

Two key components of air pollution control are (a) switching from fuelwood to gaseous fuels for stationary sources to reduce the emissions of fine particulate mat-ter; (b) and making optimal use of fuel quality–vehicle technology interlinkages for mobile sources. The policy options to encourage fuel switching for stationary sources from fuelwood to LPG or natural gas should be assessed from the point of view of cost-effectiveness, including interfuel pricing and one-off subsidies for LPG cylinder deposits for poorer households. Another important policy option is rural electrification. As for curbing vehicular emissions, a combination of tighter fuel specifications and vehicle emission standards (for both new and in-use vehicles), developing cultural acceptance of regular vehicle maintenance, use of gaseous fuels where appropriate, and measures to remove the most polluting vehicles from the vehicle fleet in major cities should be considered. To support these measures, there is a need to set up an independent monitoring system for fuel quality. At the same

---

8. In the coming decade, demand is forecast to grow at an annual rate of nearly 9 percent. In contrast, domestic production of natural gas in the 1990s grew at an annual rate of 2.5 percent. Therefore substantial domestic investments would be needed to increase domes-tic gas production.

time, the vast investments made to improve fuel quality will not reap the desired benefits if vehicles are not properly maintained. Vehicle maintenance requires that (a) emission inspection systems are effectively run; (b) vehicle registration is accurate and up-to-date; and (c) service and repair facilities with good diagnostic equipment and qualified technicians are readily available.

Agriculture and Environment

Agriculture is one of the sectors where the importance of integrating environmental and economic policies is most obvious. Production-linked support policies, or subsidies directed to reduce agricultural production costs (such as for water extraction or for grain marketing) can lead to excessive pressure being placed on scarce resources (water, forest) and to skewing the incentive against the most optimal and sustainable use of these resources. However, agriculture is also the sector where the trade-offs between poverty and environmental issues are the most difficult to solve in the short term, and may require well-thought-through transitional or mitigation measures.

Generation and dissemination of alternative technologies and approaches to conventional agriculture have a long way to go to demonstrate their viability and prove that they can be financially attractive. It is certainly an area where more attention and public investments are required. Land conservation programs, management agreements through regional development approaches, and initial conversion subsidies to support the shift towards environmentally friendly techniques or organic farming may be considered.

Agricultural and environmental mainstreaming need to be pursued with the full participation of the main actors—the producers—and will require ownership on their part. Producers are well aware of the serious threats that soil erosion, degradation of landscapes, and pollution pose to their standard of living and to the sustainability their activities, but in many cases the lack of access to better alternatives and opportunities, and the weakness of property rights leave no choice but short-term approaches to a survival strategy. This will require the elaboration of more differentiated approaches combining elements of policy, technology, education, and access to alternative options, according to local circumstances.

5

Accountability and the Demand for Quality Government

This Thematic Chapter was written by Marcelo Giugale
with the contribution of Linn A. Hammergren and Robert Ayres.

I. Rationale and Overview

Over the last decade, the role that government can play and is expected to play in Mexico has been radically changed by two formidable and related forces—globalization and democratization.

Commercial and financial integration into world markets (cemented by NAFTA), and the technological revolution which accelerated that integration, made it all but impossible for public policy to continue substituting for market-based resource allocation. Subsidies, protection, and industrial policy, among others, had little or no room in the new fiscal and monetary discipline demanded by internationally mobile domestic and foreign investors. The government's role thus became one of facilitating private decisionmaking (and intervening in those decisions only when public good considerations apply), and doing so in a transparent, accountable manner.

Similarly, Mexico's heightened political competition (especially since 1997, when the party in office lost control of the federal Congress) gave a new meaning to the country's federalism. States and municipalities, some now controlled by opposition parties, reclaimed their constitutional faculties in public policymaking (especially, but imperfectly, on financial and fiscal matters). This put the delivery of government services under the closer scrutiny of local constituencies. The counterpart to decentralization in decisionmaking (incomplete as it may still be) has been the enhanced accountability to voters of all levels of government.

The trend toward more government accountability in Mexico is irreversible, and will be intensified over the coming years. The new Presidential Administration is certain to face an increased demand for quality government services from both markets and voters, and to be penalized for not delivering.

133

Improving the quality of government services is a multifaceted, long-haul task. It is unlikely that comprehensive reform will achieve an optimal level of quality within a single presidential tenure. Even within the tenure, reform efforts will need to focus primarily on critical areas where marginal returns in terms of quality improvements are highest.

This Chapter argues that the three areas that stand out as priority for the new Administration in its efforts to deliver quality government services are decentralization, justice, and corruption. A summary of the background and a diagnosis of the situation in each area is presented below, together with a concrete set of policy recommendations.

II. Decentralization: Assuring the Sustainability of a Process Already in Motion

By constitution, Mexico has been a federation for decades. However, not until actual political competition gathered momentum (especially in the second half of the 1990s) did the country's state and municipal governments exercise their independence. The core consequence of that increasing independence is the speed of the ongoing fiscal decentralization process (an imperfect indication of which is the fact that states currently spend about half as much as the federal government). Decentralization is changing the way public policy is made in Mexico. In virtually all sectors (from education and health to justice and environment), policy initiatives by the federation now require state agreement to be implemented. The very role of the federation has changed—away from results that can be achieved by subnational governments to the capturing of nationwide externalities. Accordingly, the nature of the client for the international donor community is also being transformed.

Decentralization is undoubtedly a beneficial process—the proximity it brings between public service suppliers and their final beneficiaries increases efficiency and reduces costs. However, worldwide experience shows that it can also be a destabilizing undertaking, especially when carried out through across-the-board, abrupt efforts and without a coherent strategy and adequate institutional infrastructure. These were, unfortunately, the conditions under which the initial phase of the decentralization process unfolded in Mexico. Thus, the core policy challenge in this area is to ensure that the process is placed on a sustainable path.

There is no right decentralization model; it is up to each country to define its own form. The spectrum of possible models is wide: from Canada's full legislative federalism, in which the main source of state funds is their own taxes and borrowing, which they can spend with almost complete autonomy, to Germany's administrative federalism, where transfers from the federation are the main source of state income, federal policies guide spending and control borrowing, and federal equalization transfers even out regional disparities. Mexico has yet to define its decentralization model, and the current approach is in effect being dictated by political expediency and sector-specific initiatives.

This lack of an explicit, overall model has led to a series of harmful uncertainties in the relationships between the federal and subnational governments. Three such uncertainties are particularly noteworthy. First, spending responsibilities are not accompanied by decisionmaking power, especially in the areas of education (for example, states are responsible for teachers' salaries but have to follow federally mandated and federally negotiated pay scales), and health (for example, health-related transfers are essentially based on past expenditures rather than current need). Second, mindful of the possibility of politically influencing revenue-sharing formulas, states and municipalities have not developed their own tax bases (these, on average, represent less than a tenth of state income, and about a third of municipal income). With limited room to maneuver on the expenditure side and little incentive to absorb the political cost of taxation, the all-important link between local spending choice and local self-taxation breaks down and weakens the overall purpose of Mexico's decentralization. Finally, and critically, the objectives of the formulas used to calculate transfers remain unclear and, thus, are regularly challenged by subnational governments. The actual working of those formulas seems to suggest that regional equalization and national externalities are the main objectives of the transfer system, but few ex-post evaluation mechanisms exist to confirm whether those objectives are being achieved. In practice, states and municipalities see transfers as a rather unpredictable kind of bulk revenue.

Beyond the above-mentioned problems associated with a lack of overall strategy, Mexico's decentralization has, in general, preceded and outpaced the development of adequate institutional capacity at the subnational level. The transfer of spending responsibilities and a renewed ability to borrow took place independently of the institutional strength of the recipient state and municipalities. Mechanisms for budget planning; execution and evaluation; resolution of conflict among the federal, state, and municipal governments; control and accountability; consensus-building; defining the relations between the Federal District and its neighbors; and civil service training are just some of the institutional underpinnings that are yet to be systematically built into the country's decentralization process (that is, beyond the isolated efforts of exceptionally progressive states).

Fortunately, the Mexican federal authorities are well aware of the need to put decentralization on a sustainable path, not least because they want to prevent subnational fiscal imbalances from jeopardizing the country's macroeconomic framework (as happened in Brazil in early 1999). While the political dynamics of the 2000 presidential elections prevented the drafting of and agreement on an overall decentralization strategy, the federal government sought in late 1999 to bring balance to subnational finances through a single but powerful tool—hard budget constraints.

Those constraints were put in place through two main policies: (a) an explicit renunciation of federal bailouts in the federal budget for the year 2000 (through the elimination of the discretionary *Ramo 26*); and (b) a market-based regulatory system for subnational borrowing that links the capitalization requirements (and, hence, the cost) of bank loans to states and municipalities to their creditworthiness, as publicly established by independent (and, in effect, international) credit-rating agencies. Those two policies have dramatically changed the incentive structure faced by sub-national governments. With little or no expectation of being bailed out, and with interest rates that more closely reflect fiscal discipline, states and municipalities are now committed to strengthening their fiscal and financial positions through, among other things, expenditure rationalizations, payment enforcement, better debt management, planning for contingent liabilities and, critically, additional tax effort (a group of states went as far as calling for the renegotiation of the so-called Fiscal Pact whereby states delegated their taxing powers to the federation). As by products, the new regulatory system has also fostered a virtuous political competition across state (and some municipal) governments to obtain the best credit ratings; driven states in difficulty to seek, rather than postpone, adjustment; and aroused subnational interest in addressing the pending structural issues in decentralization (such as matching spending responsibilities with related policy decision powers).

In this context, it seems clear that decentralization policy in Mexico over the coming years should take a two-pronged approach: recent reforms should be sustained (that is, subnational budget constraints should remain binding) while the pending structural agenda mentioned earlier is addressed. Within this agenda, the priorities are also two. First, the renegotiation of the Fiscal Pact in order to devolve taxing power to the states (and to adjust transfer volumes accordingly) is needed to establish a tighter link between subnational spending (and borrowing) decisions and local tax pressure, subjecting the former to closer accountability by local voters. In addition, renegotiating the Pact will implicitly call for a national debate and position on the role and size of equalization transfers that would, in effect, carry resources from richer to poorer states to even out national disparities. Second, concomitant with tax authority, states and municipalities need a clearer definition of expenditure responsibilities, not so much on the actual procurement of goods and services, but on the policy decisions behind those expenditures (notably in education and health). That definition of responsibilities may still carry minimum standards of achievement (for example, through conditional transfers in favor of universal literacy and vaccination) but, beyond that minimum, the freedom of subnational authorities to set their own objectives and means needs to be decided.

III. Justice: Making Reforms Work

Mexico's judicial framework combines a civil code tradition (shared with all of Latin America) with a less conventional federal organization and certain less usual practices and structures, the results of a unique combination of historical influences. Its performance problems are, however, not atypical. While systematic evidence is scare, enough information exists to suggest that Mexico's judicial system is not delivering an adequate justice service in either quantity or quality, is not free of rent-seeking, and is broadly inaccessible to the poor (the majority of the population).

What causes this lack of adequacy, transparency, and access? Pending more comprehensive analysis, four main factors can be identified: (a) outdated substantive and procedural laws, organization, and administration; (b) poor human resource management; (c) underfunding; and (d) insufficient independence. While legal change has been a perennial favorite of reformers, it is only in the past few decades that the other elements have received attention, first in the dramatic physical expansion of the court systems, beginning in the 1970s, and more recently, in the constitutional reforms of 1988, 1994, and 1999, enhancing the power and independence of the federal judiciary. The latter reforms have also influenced state policies, and both the federal and state courts are beneficiaries of increased funding to support human resource development, technological innovations, and related modernization programs.

Because these more comprehensive reforms are so recent, it may be unfair to evaluate their impact. However, there is some concern as to their ability, even over the longer run, to effect the desired improvements either in real performance or in public confidence in the judicial system. That ability might be enhanced by the adoption of an overarching national strategy with more direct attention to a few critical problem areas. The first of these areas lies in the relationship between the national and 32 local judicial systems, a relationship which arguably has failed to develop in step with the changing needs and capabilities of the parties, and which has consequently given rise to a series of frictions and diseconomies.

The problems start with resources. Compared to the federal system, even the most generously financed state institutions are grossly underfunded, despite handling roughly 80 percent of the total caseload. Resentments caused by this imbalance are compounded by overlapping jurisdictions in commercial cases, where federal law prevails, but original jurisdiction usually lies with the state courts, which thus believe they are unduly burdened and bound by a legal framework they cannot modify. Similarly, the federally implemented writ of *amparo,* introduced to protect constitutionally guaranteed rights and applied by extension to judicial decisions, has become a major source of delays and congestion at both the state and federal levels. And finally, the reservation of certain kinds of cases (for example, drug trafficking) to federal authorities poses problems inasmuch as they are often first brought to the attention of local actors whose incentives or ability to cooperate may be substantially reduced.

A second area requiring more direct attention is the continuing lack of independence of state courts, where political interference is said to be worst. This, combined with financial shortcomings, increases the difficulty of improving the human resource base. It also means that even the most effective reforms are often a top-down imposition, driven by a progressive Governor and Chief Judge, but without the participation from other stakeholders or constituencies which might assure continuity and sustainability. A further consequence is that current reforms rarely have a long range strategy and, in most cases, lack grounding in adequate information and analysis. Not surprisingly, the quality of justice services varies widely across states.

Finally, although the overall goal is an improved justice system, most programs have focused on the courts alone. An effective strategy must recognize the role of other actors and institutions, including those entirely outside the sector. Even as regards purely sectoral performance, it is not only the judges, but also the litigators, police, prosecutors, administrative staff, officials in charge of enforcing judgements, and the public (in their capacity as system users), who determine the quality of output and who thus must be incorporated in any change strategy. However, many of the goals pursued through reform require a still broader focus. For example, the multitude of conflicts generated by a modern or modernizing society cannot reasonably be resolved by the courts, and thus there is an increasing need to rationalize court use and encourage the development of complementary institutions, ranging from alternative dispute resolutions mechanisms to practices and structures which avoid the development of conflicts in the first place. Similarly, a crime prevention strategy extends far beyond the criminal justice system to include improved education, job creation, and other social services. If the results of justice reform are sometimes disappointing, it may be because of unrealistic expectations rather than poor planning and implementation.

Aside from attention to these substantive themes, the development and implementation of a global strategy would also benefit from certain procedural modifications. First, there is a need for better information, at both the federal and state level, on the real problems and their causes. Second, mechanisms for monitoring progress and evaluating results are required to allow mid-course corrections and optimize the benefits of successful innovations. Third, the overall reform strategy will have to strike the right balance between reform (that is, change of the incentive structure faced by system participants) and modernization (that is, improvements that facilitate behaviors within the existing incentive framework).

Within those guidelines, where should the policy efforts of the next Presidential Administration focus? First, even if implementation remains decentralized, national-level discussion of reform needs, strategies, and challenges should be prioritized to ensure that programs address important problems; that where information on their causes and resolution is insufficient, measures (ranging from further diagnostic studies to review of international experience) are taken to remedy that gap; and that all stakeholders have a chance to participate. Second, while this discussion would feature all elements in ongoing reforms, increased attention might be given to such critical themes as measures to rationalize the division of labor between the federal and state justice systems, and legal (and other) changes to enhance judicial independence, especially at the state level. Third, ongoing modernization efforts (especially in streamlining of procedures and upgrading court infrastructure) should be evaluated, and those producing satisfactory results should be supported and publicly held up as a source of demonstration effect across states. As mentioned earlier in this Chapter, the nature of the overall decentralization process unfolding in Mexico will condition the feasibility of sector-specific reforms, and the justice system is no exception to that phenomenon—finding federally coordinated incentives to effect state-level changes will remain a major challenge (as it is in education, health, and infrastructure, and other sectors where decisionmaking has been decentralized).

As it has done in many other countries (several in Latin America), the World Bank can provide Mexico with a broad spectrum of assistance in justice sector reform. Due to political sensitivities, until very recently that assistance had not been requested by Mexico. While Bank interventions have so far been limited (for example, a diagnostic analysis of Executive Proceedings in the Federal District Courts, ad hoc advisory services), the battery of possible support tools is large. It includes lending (both sector adjustment as in Venezuela and investment loans as in Argentina to the federation or states) grants, knowledge management, and consensus building.

Given Mexico's constitutional context and decentralization process, a logical first step for a program of Bank support would be an initially small loan focusing on diagnostic studies; information exchange (both among Mexico's judiciaries and with outside actors); pilot activities, especially at the state level; and the formulation of more comprehensive nationwide reform strategies. In a second stage or follow-up program, the federation would seek to capture the nationwide externalities of an adequate justice system by enacting the legal (and other) reforms within its purview while, at the same time, making World Bank loan funds available on preferential terms to competing states to exact specific judicial reforms.

IV. Corruption: A Broad, Pending Agenda

There is no rigorous, comprehensive diagnosis of how serious corruption in Mexico's public sector really is. Yet, the strength of the corruption *perceived* by citizens and businesses is overwhelming. As an example, a recent national survey conducted by independent media found that only 3 percent of the population believe the government is "not corrupt," while one in every three Mexicans thinks that their government is "very corrupt." Whether this perception is proven wrong or not, there is no question that the next Presidential Administration will face a pent-up demand for transparency, and the success of its tenure will in no small part be judged by its ability to satisfy that demand. This will involve all branches (legislative, executive, judicial) and all levels (federal, state, municipal) of government.

Indirect indications show that corruption is no longer systemic in Mexico, and is becoming somewhat less systematic. Heightened political competition (especially since 1997) has done much to reduce corruption. From more substantive annual discussions of the federal budget to a much closer oversight of SECODAM (the federal administrative control agency), a Congress where no single political party holds majority has made major contributions to public transparency. SECODAM itself has implemented encouraging changes to its financial management and procurement functions—notably, in launching COMPRANET, an open electronic bidding system for public purchases at the federal level. Similarly, the decentralization process described earlier has brought the delivery of public services closer to their beneficiaries and, thus, to their beneficiaries' scrutiny.

However, formidable issues remain in Mexico's fight against corruption. Some of those issues concern SECODAM itself. The agency has made little progress in handling citizens' complaints and conducting social audits. In both cases, clear mechanisms for follow-up, decisionmaking, evaluation, and remedial action are lacking. More broadly, SECODAM could benefit from more direct accountability to the public, because it has no public "scorecard" through which the average citizen can judge its performance.

In spite of its important role, SECODAM is only a small part of Mexico's solution to its corruption problem, and of any policy agenda to solve it. First, the federal executive has no effective external auditor. This role is formally invested on the congressional *Contaduria Mayor de Hacienda* (in contrast to SECODAM, which is the internal auditor), of which verification of public expenditure accounts have been known to lag beyond the expiration of the statute of limitations on abuse of office. Whether recent constitutional reforms to address the weaknesses of the *Contaduría* can succeed is still a question.

Second, the weakness in the internal and external auditing of public spending has potentially been transmitted to the 32 Mexican subnational governments through the decentralization process. As mentioned earlier, states and municipalities were given expenditure responsibilities (worth 3 to 5 percent of GDP) without matching institutional capacity, opening possibilities for corruption that much weaker local agencies (including state congresses) may find difficult to detect and combat.

Third, Mexico still lacks a civil service structure. A related reform that would create a career civil service, install performance-based and results-oriented administrative organization, and, more generally, address the incentive framework faced by average public officials was debated at various points of the Zedillo Administration, but has not materialized. This hampers the possibility of discouraging and detecting corruption among the ranks of the government.

Fourth, with a few exceptions, the role of Mexican civil society in fostering transparent governments has been limited, and is only now emerging (for example, *Transparency Mexicana* was founded only in 1999). NGOs could, however, play a major role in ensuring transparency in one specific area of public expenditure—poverty reduction programs. These programs are allegedly subject to political manipulation and, given the small size and geographical dispersion of the distributed benefits, are difficult to supervise from the top down.

Fifth, while much enhanced over the last decade, freedom of information remains incomplete. While freedom of the press is now widely exercised, the legal framework for the disclosure and dissemination of official government records, accounts, and decisions requires substantial overhaul and amplification.

Sixth, there is undoubtedly a strong link between crime (particularly drug-related) and corruption. At the core of the link is the quality of law enforcement in all regions of the country. This problem, which is not atypical in Latin America, has been shown to carry a tremendous cost in terms of reducing the country's long-term rate of growth, and has already become an impediment to foreign direct investment in Mexico.

Finally, it goes almost without saying that reducing corruption in Mexico necessitates a major overhaul of its judicial system, a matter addressed elsewhere in this volume.

Part II

Fiscal Sustainability

6

Macroeconomic Assessment

This Chapter was written by Vittorio Corbo (Pontificia Universidad Católica de Chile), with the valuable input of Marcelo Giugale and Claudia Sepulveda.

I. Introduction

Recovering from the trauma of the 1994–95 crisis, which destroyed the financial system, paralyzed credit flows, and generated a deep recession, Mexico has, in recent years, made considerable progress in the reordering of its public finances, in stabilizing its economy and in increasing its growth rate. The profile of its foreign debt has also evolved toward the longer term and Mexico has been able to manage the liabilities associated with the rescue of its financial system without suffering an inflationary explosion and/or having to reschedule its foreign debt. These advances are even more significant if it is recalled that, since the second half of 1997 until early 1999, Mexico, as the rest of Latin America, experienced the aftershocks of the crises (East Asia, Russia, Brazil) of the emerging markets in the form of increased costs of and reduced access to external credit.

While stability was being recovered, supported by a severe fiscal adjustment, progress was also made on institutional and policy reforms geared to improve the functioning of markets. Significant progress has also been made in recent years in the targeting of State subsidies on the poorer groups in rural areas and in the decentralization of public spending toward the state and municipal levels.

Among the advances made at the macroeconomic level, programmable State spending declined, from 17.5 percent of GDP in 1994, to an estimated 15.6 percent of GDP in 2000 is noteworthy. Since one percentage point of GDP went to financing the transition costs of the pension reform, the reduction in programmable spending equaled around 3 points of GDP for the six year period. At the same time, annual inflation fell, from the 52 percent peak reached in 1995, to less than 10 percent in 2000 (see Figure 1). Fiscal austerity, which made it possible to orient monetary policy mainly toward achieving a gradual reduction in inflation, aided this

Figure 1. Annual Inflation (Variation: December to December)

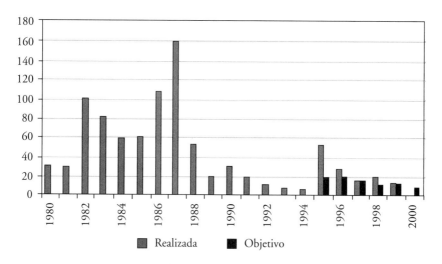

process. Moreover, as inflation and programmable spending as a percentage of GDP fell, the rate of growth of GDP rose. Thus, between 1996 and 2000, the Mexican economy will have achieved an average annual growth rate of around 5 percent (Figure 2).

In spite of those advances, however, much still needs to be done to a sustain growth rates at levels needed to improve general living conditions and reduce the high current levels of poverty. Due to the fragility of public finance (see Chapter on

Figure 2. Annual Growth of Real GDP

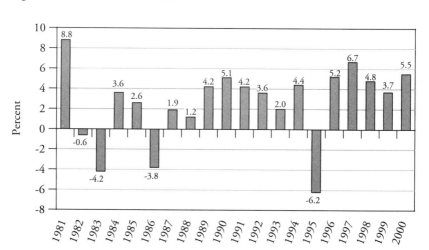

Fiscal Sustainability) and of access to international financial markets, macro-economic and financial stability is not assured.

Given the weight of history, any review of the macroeconomic situation in Mexico must begin with an analysis of its vulnerability to an exchange rate crisis. In this regard, the current situation is different from what prevailed at the end of previous six-year periods: today, Mexico has a flexible exchange rate, whereas previously that rate was rigid. In the current system monetary and fiscal responsibility provides an anchor to inflation and to the evolution of the nominal exchange rate. In this arrangement, domestic and foreign shocks affect exchange rate values, interest rates and, much less significantly, international reserve levels. Although a traditional exchange rate crisis is not possible with the current scheme, abrupt changes in the exchange rate and in interest rates can also have macroeconomic consequences and therefore they need to be monitored. The outgoing administration has been aware of this potential problem and has, therefore, attempted to take precautionary steps to lessen the likelihood of this type of events.

Mexican prospects for long-term growth depend both on the country's capacity to remain stable and avoid crises, and on its ability to make further inroads in the use of market mechanisms for resource allocation and for the production and distribution of goods and services. Policies along these lines lead to increased investment and higher employment, to greater efficiency in the use of those resources, while they contribute to achieving increased factor productivity. In this area Mexico has many opportunities to alter policies to achieve higher and sustainable growth, in particular, lifting the quality of labor, improving education, and creating opportunities for the absorption of the new technologies associated to the revolution in information technology. A strategy that promotes growth also entails ever greater openness to foreign competition. Here Mexico has made substantial progress with the market oriented reforms of the last fifteen years, and with the opening up process associated with NAFTA. There are also many unexplored opportunities in the introduction of competition into the area of non-tradable services: telecommunications, transportation, electricity, gas and water.

The following section reviews the current macroeconomic situation in Mexico from the point of view of its vulnerability to an abrupt adjustment in the expectations of economic agents. The third section examines Mexican macroeconomic sustainability potential for the coming years and the areas in which significant opportunity exists for reforms which would increase potential growth and reduce poverty. The fourth section analyses short-term macroeconomic management issues that will need to be addressed early on by the incoming administration. The following two sections analyze issues related to the choice of an exchange rate system and the implementation of monetary policy. Particularly, the fifth section examines an issue that it is debated in Mexico still today, namely, which exchange rate system is most suitable? The sixth section takes as given the current exchange rate system and asks what the question of what is an adequate nominal anchor for reducing inflation, as well as the related question of how monetary policy should be formulated.

II. Macroeconomic and Financial Vulnerability

Compared to 1994, Mexico's economy in mid 2000 is less vulnerable to external shocks and better supported by domestic policy (Table 1). First, Mexico today has a flexible exchange rate system, in which external pressures appear as changes in the nominal exchange rate and, occasionally, in interest rate hikes, while in 1994 there was a rigid exchange system, the defense of which required high interest rates and/or losses of international reserves. It was the resistance to allow interest rates to increase in 1994, and thus to go against the rules of the game, that resulted in a sharp drop in reserves, and a substantial increase in the outstanding balance of teso-bonos. Those high reserve losses and the high balance of teso-bonos encouraged eventually the speculative attacks on the currency. Perhaps the alternative road of higher interest rates was not followed because higher rates would have lowered output and increased unemployment. In the end, however, the exchange rate crisis degraded the quality of loan portfolios and the strength of the financial system. The combination of severe macroeconomic imbalances, internal (political) shocks, and the maturity and currency mismatch of assets and liabilities created the conditions for the exchange rate crisis.

The difference in the area of high interest rates between a fixed and a flexible exchange rate system is subtler than may appear at first. In the face of a pronounced increase in the market exchange rate, the Bank of Mexico may decide to react by restricting liquidity, raising interest rates in order to avoid the threat to its inflation goals posed by a "too" pronounced adjustment of the exchange rate. If the interest rate levels required to avoid a sharp depreciation of the currency are very high, then, even in flexible exchange rate schemes, interest rates may be so high as to create problems similar to those seen in the defense of rigid exchange rates. In fact, some

Table 1. Indicators of Foreign Vulnerability

Indicators	1994	Projected 2000
Domestic Savings (percent GDP)	14.7	21.7
Current Account (percent GDP)	-7	-3.1
Direct for. Inv./Def. in Current Acct. (percent)	37	73
Exchange Regime	Fixed	Flexible
Net For. Pub. Debt/Exp. (percent)	126.3	54.1
Due date of Short Term for. Pub. Debt (billions of dollars)[a]	33.3	1.6
International Reserves (billions US$)[b]	6.1 (11.4)	32.2
Financial Support Program (billions US$)	—	23.7

Notes:
a. Amort. for 1995 and 2001 (to 15/5/2000). Includes Tesobonos payment dates.
b. To June 16, 2000. The figure for June 1994 is presented in parenthesis.
Source: SHCP and IFS.

analysts believe that, in fear of the inflationary effects of devaluations and in order
to minimize the volatility of the nominal and real exchange rate, Mexico is operating with an exchange system very similar to a fixed exchange rate (Calvo and Reinhart, 2000). However, a more accurate description of what the Bank of Mexico is
doing seems to be that it is softening abrupt changes in the exchange rate adjusting
short-term liquidity, although, generally, it is allowing the exchange rate to move in
function of more fundamental variables. The evolution of the exchange rate in
recent months points in that direction.

    With regard to indicators of macroeconomic strength, the investment rate today
is more than three percentage points higher than it was in 1994, and 88 percent of
that investment is financed by domestic savings, while in 1994, only 68 percent of
the even lower investment rate was financed by domestic savings. Consequently, foreign savings or the deficit in the current account was 7 percent of GDP in 1994,
while it is only around 3.0 percent today (see Figure 3). It can be argued that, with
lower oil prices, savings rates will also be lower and, therefore, once the current price
of oil return to more normal levels, the current accounts deficit will be somewhat
larger. Viewed in terms of the extreme scenario in which, oil prices return to 17 dollars the barrel for the Mexican oil mix, and consumption (private and public) remain
constant, the current account deficit would only increase to around 4,2 percent of
GDP. Moreover, 73 percent of the current account deficit is financed by direct foreign investment, while in 1994, only 37 percent was covered by that type of capital
flow (Table 1, line 4). Thus, the current account deficit is today much less than in
1994 and the financing of the deficit today is much less vulnerable to an abrupt
change in conditions of access to international capital markets. Moreover, Mexican
indicators of the ratio of foreign debt to product, and foreign debt to exports, are
the best in the region (Table 2).

Figure 3. Current Account Balance (percent GDP)

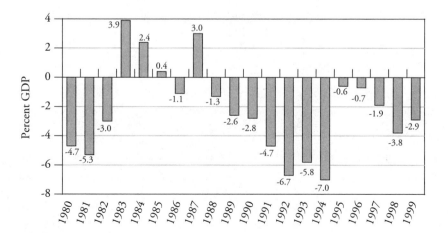

Table 2. Foreign Debt in Regional
Context

Country	As percent of:	
	GDP	*Exports*
Argentina	51.2	521.3
Brazil	41.9	445.2
Chile	50.4	175.1
Colombia	49.6	255.3
Mexico	34.6	112.7
Peru	50.0	367.0
Uruguay	72.5	352.5
Venezuela	31.2	139.6

Source: National Sources and UBSW.

After the Mexican crisis of 1994–1995 and the crises of East Asia, Russia and Brazil, considerable importance has been assigned to the maturity and currency mismatch of the public and private debt (Krugman, 2000). In this area, the situation today is radically different from that which prevailed in 1994. With respect to debt maturity of the public sector, liabilities in foreign currency with less than one year to maturity are today less than two billion dollars, while in 1994, they amounted to 33.3 billion dollars. As a ratio of international reserves, they are today less than 5 percent of the international reserves held while they were 2.9 times those reserves in June 1994 (Table 1, line 7). With respect to currency mismatch the situation is also radically different today. The quasi-fixed exchange rate system of 1994 had encourage taking open positions in foreign currency; however, the current floating exchange rate system put exchange rate risk in the forefront of credit risk assessment.

The level of real exchange rate has attracted the attention of many observers that are looking for early warnings of a potential crisis. If we compare the evolution of the real multilateral exchange rate, computed on the basis of the evolution of consumer prices in Mexico and in its major trading partners (see Figure 4), it can be seen that the real exchange rate in May, 2000, was at a level similar to the one that prevailed in the first half of 1994. The mere observation of the numbers may lead to the conclusion that the real exchange rate is "quite similar," which would mean that Mexico is vulnerable to an abrupt adjustment in that variable. However, it is necessary to consider that this estimate of the real exchange rate, which is based on purchasing power parity, contains no control for the evolution of a series of real factors which affect the evolution of the equilibrium real exchange rate. In fact, in the case of Mexico, it can be argued that, as a result of the pressures imposed by openness to foreign markets and, especially, its entry into NAFTA, important gains in productivity should have occurred. Those gains, when greater than those of its major trading partners, imply a drop in the equilibrium real exchange rate. The significant gains in the terms of trade associated with higher oil prices and the productivity effect on Mexican industry of the expansive cycle in the United States operate in the same direction. Of course, the reversal of those factors will require, at some future moment, a depreciation of the real exchange rate. Moreover, given that Mexico is an exporter of labor intensive products to the United States, it is also relevant to compare the evolution of the real exchange rate measured in terms of unit labor costs, as a measure of prices. Thus, using unit labor costs instead of prices the real exchange rate in May of this year was around 24 percent more depreciated than in the first half of 1994 (Figure 4). Additional evidence that the real exchange rate should not be very far from the equilibrium rate is provided by the evolution of non-oil exports. Thus, the comparison of exports during the mobile trimester ending in May 2000 with those of the same trimester in 1999 reveals that made-in-bond (maquila) exports grew 23.9 percent and other exports—excluding maquila and oil—grew 11.1 percent. Moreover, under the current exchange rate scheme, pressures for real depreciation are converted into an adjustment of the market exchange rate or into higher interest rates (when the Central Bank reacts to exchange rate pressures with more restrictive monetary policy). With an expected inflation for the next twelve months of around 8.5 percent, an international dollar interest rate of 6.8 percent, a country risk of 270 basis points, and supposing that economic agents expect a constant real exchange rate and an international inflation of 2.5 percent, using uncovered interest rate parity, a domestic interest rate of 15.9 percent would be required so that economic agents would be indifferent to whether their assets are in pesos or dollars. The annual interest rate for 28 days CETES has been below that value recently, so that it can be concluded that there is no evidence that the exchange rate has "appreciated so much" that economic agents are expecting a large depreciation of the real exchange rate.

Recent studies of the vulnerability to change in conditions of access to foreign financing (Caballero, 2000) show that Latin American countries, and Mexico specially, have been very vulnerable to the sudden rationing of access to international capital markets, with very high real costs in terms of decreases in output, increased unemployment and, in some cases, even macroeconomic and financial crises. Against this background, Mexico appears to be much more robust in 2000, than in

Figure 4. Real Exchange Rate Indexes (1990=100)

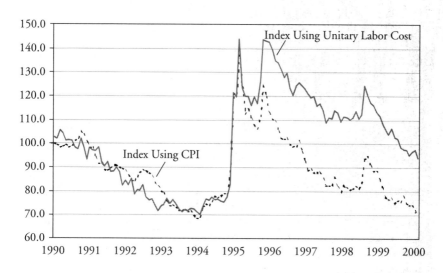

1994. Fully aware of the importance of reducing the threat of sudden rationing of access to international markets—as a result of external or domestic shocks—the outgoing administration has negotiated an emergency line of foreign financing. This financing is much like a line of credit, with international financial institutions, their NAFTA partners, and the Exim-Banks of its major trading partners, mainly United States and Japan.

One of the lessons learned from recent financial crises is that they are more likely when financial systems are weak, and their consequences are also worse in those cases. In that regard, Mexico is also now less vulnerable than in 1994. In recent years, progress has been made in a very expensive and very necessary reconstruction of the financial system; banking regulation and supervision has been improved; and the banking system has been opened to foreign investment. As a result of those changes, Mexico has today a much firmer financial system that is much more integrated into international capital markets.

In summary, and in light of preceding analysis, it is possible to conclude that Mexico today is much less vulnerable to domestic or external shocks.

III. Fiscal Sustainability and Opportunities to Increase Potential Growth

In spite of the relatively positive scenario described above, Mexico is vulnerable on several fronts, which require the immediate attention of the incoming administration. First, although fiscal stability was maintained in the difficult environment generated by the profound crisis of 1995, the fiscal position is still very precarious (see Figure 5). Although the fiscal deficit is on the order of 1 percent of GDP, new public debits (associated with the FOAPROA debt and the State retirement regimes) will generate pressure on public resources in the coming years (see Chapter on Fiscal Sustainability). At the same time, to reestablish macroeconomic stability the government has reduced domestic spending by reducing public investment so drastically (see Figure 5) that the supply of public goods today is probably far below optimum levels. The country faces needs to improve basic infrastructure and the human capital of the poor—especially by improving access to and the quality of education and health services. All this will require increased public spending. Furthermore, government revenue is volatile. More than a third of government revenue comes directly from oil and is vulnerable to world price fluctuations. Therefore, to maintain order in public finance and reduce vulnerability to fluctuations in oil prices, it will be necessary to increase tax revenue and to evaluate more closely the effectiveness of current government expenditures. This means acting on two fronts. First, clear rules must be introduced to include in the budget only the most stable component of oil prices. To this end, a stabilization fund must be created—with clear operational regulations—that will accumulate funds when oil prices are above normal and will disburse funds when oil prices are below normal. Second, with

Figure 5. Public Sector Indicators

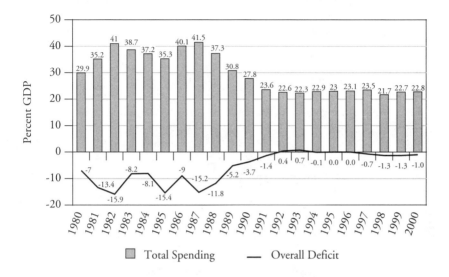

□ Total Spending — Overall Deficit

respect to the overall public sector balance, a public budget must be designed which is balanced when public income is computed on the basis of a long term or "normal" price of oil. Indeed, additional steps should go further and attempt to achieve a fiscal surplus to be invested in market assets that will generate income flows and eventually replace income from oil, which will be lower in the long term—given the nonrenewable nature of oil. Such investments could help to meet the higher social security costs associated with the aging of the population. That public surplus should also reduce dynamically the growth of the public debt.

A recent review of the functioning of primary product stabilization funds (Fasano, 2000), mainly oil and copper, shows mixed results, depending on the objectives, the institutional implementation, and their isolation from political pressures. On one hand, some of the funds have helped to build sizable assets to meet future needs (associated with lower prices of primary products), and, also have helped to enhance the effectiveness of fiscal policy by channeling away from the budget the extra revenues from temporary high prices. In addition, they have been useful in reducing the real appreciation associated with higher export prices, by investing the extra revenues abroad (this is the case of the Norwegian oil fund and the Chilean copper fund). On the other hand, the effectiveness of the funds could be very low if the rules are changed frequently or if the main purposes are changed due to political pressures. This is the case of the stabilization funds implemented in Venezuela and Oman.

A review of Mexico's institutional structure and implementation of the public spending and income systems leads to the conclusion that it is necessary to employ a combination of adjustments of public spending and greater tax pressure. After the considerable cuts in public spending carried out in recent years, reductions can now be achieved mainly through the elimination/consolidation of entities which have similar purposes, and by targeting and rationalizing spending. With regard to government revenue, priority should be given to action centered on improving tax administration and on eliminating tax exemptions and loopholes, which lower the efficiency of the current tax system (see Chapter on Fiscal Reform). It will be especially necessary to progressively eliminate the special regimes currently applied to favored geographical regions and to agriculture and transportation and to create a uniform value added tax (VAT). Differential VAT rates make for inefficient tax administration and create opportunities for evasion and corruption. It is often argued that a VAT on food is strongly regressive, but the most efficient way to give a progressive character to public finance is to focus public spending on the poorest groups. To employ that mechanism, however, it is necessary first to acquire the capacity to collect public funds and, here, a VAT has proven to be a very efficient tax instrument (Engel, Galetovic and Raddatz, 1999).

IV. Fiscal and Monetary Policies: Their Role in Macroeconomic Management

In the short term, Mexico's economy presents symptoms of overheating. Private consumption and investment indicators reveal that domestic demand is growing at a pace far above the rate of growth of capacity output, creating pressure on the current account of the balance of payments and threatening the control of inflation. Evidence of overheating in the economy is provided by the tightness in the market for skilled labor that it is reflected in low unemployment rates for this type of labor and is resulting in upward pressures in skilled wages. The inflationary consequences of the wage dynamics could be a level of inflation above target.

Three factors will be critical in the evolution of aggregate demand over the coming few months. First, improved expectations in the business community, related to the opportunities that open up with the change of government, should increase the dynamism of private investment, especially that driven by foreign investment. Second, the reduction in the unemployment rate and the higher income levels should result in further rises in private consumption acting as another expansive factor. Third, the expected slow-down in the United States should contribute toward a slow-down in the dynamism of exports, acting as a contractionary factor. Rapid growth in the U.S. economy and a very high price of oil the risk of overheating have increased substantially in recent weeks, requiring close collaboration between the outgoing and the incoming administrations to avoid the sharp appreciation that could develop if all the stabilization work is left to monetary policy. Indeed, the only instrument available to the Central Bank to slow down domestic demand and keep inflation under control, is the interest rate. Nevertheless, given the Mexican exchange system, the use of high interest rates to slowdown the economy would result in a nominal and real appreciation. The resulting real appreciation would hurt exports, compounding the effect of the eventual U.S. slowdown. Also, Mexico has to prepare for the moment when a downward adjustment in the price of oil would require a real depreciation. In view of these factors, a fiscal correction is urgently necessary so as to not overload interest rates with the full weight of the adjustment.[1] Thus, both the intertemporal consolidation of the solvency of the fiscal accounts and short-term macroeconomic management demand fiscal contraction. To complete the portrait, it is well known that fiscal corrections are more effective when applied at the beginning of an administration.

The point, in other words, is that the overall macro framework needs to have a more balanced mix between monetary and fiscal policy, with a greater adjustment from the fiscal side. In the short-run, however, given the long lags involved in the implementation of fiscal policy, monetary policy will continue to be the central piece of a stabilization strategy. In this regard, in Mexico there is room today to improve the effectiveness of monetary policy by shifting to the use of a explicit interest rate instrument instead of relying mostly on the short-position of borrowed bank reserves. Given the instability of the demand for money and especially the demand for borrowed reserves (the "corto"), the current system is prone to result in high interest rates and exchange rate volatility. Indeed, most central banks that target inflation have during the 1990s converged in operating procedures and instruments of monetary policy. In the 1970s and 1980s, as financial systems were bank-dominated, the use of reserve requirements and the discount window as monetary control tools was persuasive. In contrast, during the 1990s, liberalizing financial markets and opening the capital accounts have led central banks to rely more on short term interest rate as the main instrument of monetary policy. The use of an explicit short-term interest rate instrument leads to a more extensive use of open market operations to regulate overall liquidity. Now that inflation has declined below ten percent per annum and that Mexico is well on the way toward achieving industrial country's inflation levels, it should consider introducing a more predictable monetary policy in which the short term interest rate is the main instrument.

V. The Choice of an Exchange Rate System[2]

In Mexico many observers call for moving towards a fixed, and credible, exchange rate system. However, one should be careful. The recent series of crises which have

---

1. A similar problem has emerged in the case of New Zealand, see Brash, 2000.
2. After the Asian and Mexican crises, the debate on the most appropriate exchange system has taken a new turn. Currently, the debate is framed more in terms of feasibility than of optimality (See especially Obtsfeld and Rogoff, 1995, Eichengreen, 1999, and Mussa, et al., 2000).

affected developing countries with access to capital markets has reopened the debate on the most appropriate exchange rate regime for a country such as Mexico. It is no coincidence that all countries that suffered severe crises in the 1990s had some sort of fixed exchange rate. Exchange rate systems and the structural characteristics of an economy, particularly with regard to prices and wage flexibility, affect its ability to adjust in the face of shocks. This acquires special relevance because countries are always exposed to real and nominal shocks. Exchange rate systems also affect the volatility of the real exchange rate and the effectiveness of monetary policy, with final effects on the level of output and unemployment.[3]

Fixed exchange rates have the obvious advantage of reducing volatility in the nominal exchange rate, thus contributing to a better inflation outcome and, perhaps, the expansion of foreign trade. They also provide a nominal anchor for the conduct of monetary policy and allow for more efficient adjustments when shocks are nominal. Their main costs are that they make depreciation of the real exchange rate difficult and weaken the effectiveness of monetary policy in the face of pronounced changes in aggregate demand. Thus, when real shocks require real depreciation and prices are rigid—for example, when wages are indexed—an adjustment with a fixed exchange rate, generally, results in a sharp increase in unemployment. Another not insignificant cost of fixed exchange rates is that they facilitate an expansion of foreign indebtedness, as the risk of an exchange rate adjustment is underestimated, which may be very costly in weak financial systems.

In contrast, flexible exchange rates facilitate adjustments of the real exchange rate in situations in which real shocks make those adjustments necessary. They also facilitate the implementation of active monetary policies for purposes of stabilization. Another advantage is that they force agents to internalize the cost of a depreciation of the local currency when they decide to take open foreign currency positions. One significant cost, however, is high volatility in the nominal and real exchange rates.

One of the main lessons to be learned from the recent crises, is that, with free capital movement and high levels of workers remittances, fixed—but adjustable—exchange rates are very vulnerable to speculative attacks. That vulnerability causes both potential conflicts in domestic monetary policy, and distrust in economic agents with regard to the authorities' ability to maintain the fixed parity. That distrust arises when it is believed that the increases in interest rates required to maintain interest rate parity would not be sustained because they will lead to sharp rises in unemployment, an excessive increase in risk to financial loans and/or an increase in the fiscal cost of public debt expressed in domestic currency.

To avoid these problems, the main options are either to establish a credibly fixed exchange rate system or to employ a more flexible one, developing, at the same time,

---

3. Real shocks are changes in the terms of trade, the discovery of a mine, drought, earthquakes, political change with positive or negative impact on aggregate demand and the like; nominal shocks include changes in the international interest rate and sudden changes in the demand for money.

instruments to cover exchange rate risks. In order for any of these systems to function adequately, a solid financial industry and macroeconomic stability must first be achieved. A third option, in certain cases to avoid exchange rate crises, is to introduce controls on capital flows. Given ever lower communications costs and advances in information technology, however, the world is an ever more integrated market, so that control of capital movements is all but impossible to implement and, at best, is only temporarily effective (until the private sector finds ways to avoid it). Therefore, this will not be a real option for a country like Mexico (De Gregorio, Edwards and Valdés, 2000).

Fixed exchange rate systems can be made credible by using a currency board (for example, Hong Kong since 1983 or Argentina since 1991) or replacing domestic currency with that of a large country (for example, Panamá or Ecuador). However, those schemes have certain prerequisites and introduce significant rigidities. First, a country needs sufficient foreign reserves to finance the short-term liabilities of the monetary system or it will not be credible. The financial system must also be sufficiently strong to be able to survive without a lender of last resort. If this is not possible, provision must be made for emergency loans from foreign commercial banks—as is the case in Argentina—or from a financial institution, probably the U.S. Federal Reserve or the European Central Bank. Wage flexibility and labor mobility must also be sufficient to facilitate real exchange rate adjustments, when a change in macroeconomic fundamentals makes a real depreciation necessary. Nevertheless, the discipline inherent in a currency board means that a government must be ready, and must have the political support, to live with the high interest rates (and high unemployment) which are an integral part of an adjustment to a drop in foreign reserves. Moreover, countries which go down this currency board road renounce the use of monetary policy to soften macroeconomic swings. Argentina is paying this cost today, because that country has had to face a situation of economic deceleration caused by the crisis in Brazil without having the option of employing a more expansive monetary policy. This has caused a sharp, protracted recession.

Some believe that, to reduce the cost associated with distrust with regard to the authorities' ability to maintain a currency board, it is necessary to renounce one's domestic currency and adopt that of a larger country with a history of monetary discipline, such as the U.S. dollar. Obviously, abandoning the domestic currency eliminates the risk of a devaluation, but the country also completely renounces the use of monetary policy and/or adjustments of the exchange rate to face real shocks to the economy, with concurrent large costs in terms of the output and unemployment, especially in countries with nominal rigidity. In fact, aware of this, the central banks in the main industrial countries use monetary policy for stabilization purposes.

Thus, in the choice of an exchange rate system—as for most economic problems—solutions are not black or white. Both credibly fixed exchange rate and flexible exchange rates have both costs and benefits, but given that credibly fixed exchange rates tend to link real negative shocks to recessions, they are not to be recommended for countries like Mexico with potential for large shocks relative to the size of their economies. Flexible exchange rates, given the real costs of volatility in the real exchange rate, must be accompanied by mechanisms which provide coverage for exchange risks and commitments to elements of macro policy and intervention which control volatility. Moreover, as a prerequisite, they require a solid and appropriately regulated and supervised financial system, in which exchange risks can be estimated and priced correctly.

In brief, Mexico, with its remaining internal rigidities, exposure to large shocks, and the hard-earned credibility of its central bank (which brought inflation into the single digits) does not need to tie itself to the rigid structure inherent to a currency board or a unilateral dollarization. In this case, a more flexible exchange rate system is preferable. However, in the long run it could be attractive for Mexico to become a member a larger currency area within NAFTA or an eventual FTAA.

VI. Options with Regard to Monetary Policy Regime

As countries move toward more flexible exchange rate regimes, they have to choose an explicit monetary anchor. For a monetary framework succeed in achieving low inflation, it must give the central bank enough independence to focus its monetary policy towards the ultimate objective of low inflation but without using the exchange rate peg as an anchor. The remaining options are a money anchor or an inflation target. We discuss these two systems in turn.

Money Anchor

The effectiveness of a monetary aggregate as a nominal anchor for inflation depends first on the authority and capacity of the central bank to carry out an independent monetary policy aimed at achieving and maintaining low inflation. Also; at a more technical level, the effectiveness of a monetary anchor depends on the stability of the demand for the particular monetary aggregate—M1 or M2 or the monetary base—that it uses as an anchor. The stability of the demand for the monetary aggregate links with and the rate of inflation. Instability of the demand for money presents a problem when there is considerable financial innovation or a sudden change in the rate of inflation.[4]

Inflation Targeting

Given the problems with using an exchange-rate or a monetary anchor, in the last decade some countries have moved to a third type of anchor: inflation targeting.

---

4. For monetary anchors, see Calvo and Vegh, 1999; Bernanke et al., 1999; and Bernanke and Mishkin, 1997. For the election of monetary anchors in Latin America, see Corbo, 1999 and Corbo et al., 1999.

This type of monetary framework was initially introduced by industrial countries with the objective of keeping inflation close to a long-run low inflation level. New Zealand first introduced the system in March 1990. It has since been introduced in Canada (Feb. 1991), United Kingdom (Oct. 1992), Sweden (Jan. 1993), Australia (Sept. 1994), and the European Central Bank (Oct. 1998). A variation of this system—to adjust inflation towards one-digit annual levels and eventually towards a steady-state low level—have been introduced in a series of emerging or semi-industrialized economies, starting with Chile (Sept. 1990) and Israel (March 1991).[5]

In inflation targeting, the target rate of inflation serves the purpose of a monetary anchor, and monetary and fiscal policies are geared toward achieving the inflation target. The attractiveness of this system is that its effectiveness does not require a stable relationship between a monetary aggregate and inflation and, at the same time, it avoids the problems associated with the fixing of the exchange rate. An additional advantage for emerging countries is that the trajectory of the market exchange rate provides important information on the market evaluation of present and future monetary policy, thus playing the same role that nominal yields on long term government paper play in industrial countries (Bernanke et. al., 1999).

A well-defined inflation-targeting framework has four parts (Svensson, 1999 and King, 2000): 1) a public announcement of a strategy of medium-term price stability; 2) an intermediate target for inflation for a period into the future in which monetary policy could affect the inflation level; 3) an institutional commitment to price stability in the form of rules of operations for the mnetary authority; and 4) a clear strategy of how monetary policy is going to operate to bring future inflation close to the announced target. This strategy usually starts from a conditional interval forecast of inflation for the period utilized when setting the target. The strategy also has to include an operational procedure of what the central bank will do when the inflation forecasts are away from the target. The procedures should be transparent and the monetary authorities should be accountable for the objective that has been set.

Once inflation is close to the steady-state target level and given the normal lags in the operation of monetary policy, the inflation target has to be set for a period long enough toward the future such that monetary policy could have a role in determining inflation over time. In practice, central banks announce a target for the next twelve or twenty-four months. Then, they develop a conditional forecast of inflation on the existing monetary policy and a forecast of the relevant exogenous variables-and set a strategy and communicate to the public what they will do when the range forecast for inflation does not include the targeted value.

In this framework, the established inflation target is the ultimate objective of policy, and an inflation forecast, sometimes not made public, is the intermediate objective. Monetary policy, with appropriate fiscal underpinnings, is the main instrument used to pursue the target, which is carried out through the adjustment in the interest rate. In particular, when the conditional inflation forecast is above the inflation

---

5. See Morandé and Schmidt-Hebbel (1999).

target, the level of the intervention interest rate is raised to achieve an increase in real interest rate with the purpose of bringing inflation close to the target. One advantage of inflation targeting is that inflation itself is made the target, committing monetary policy to achieve the set target and thus helping to shape inflation expectations. However, herein also resides its main disadvantage. As inflation depends also on other variables besides monetary policy, the authorities cannot totally control it; and it becomes difficult to evaluate the monetary stance on the basis of the observed path of inflation. Furthermore, as monetary policy works with a substantial lag, to pre-commit an unconditional inflation target—independently of changes in external factors which do affect the inflation rate—and to change monetary policy to bring the inflation rate back to the set target could be costly. In particular, to try to reach the inflation target, when a shock results in an (temporary) increase in the inflation rate, could be costly in terms of a severe slowdown or increased output volatility (Ceccheti, 1998).

To address some of these problems, several options have been proposed. First, to set the inflation target in terms of a range rather than a point estimate. Second, to set a target for core inflation (that is, the inflation index stripped of highly volatile product prices—for example, oil) rather than total observed inflation. Third, to exclude from the price index the effects of changes in indirect taxes and in terms of trade. Fourth, to set the target for period long enough what short-term shocks to the inflation rate do not require a monetary response.

Mexico has been moving lately towards the introduction of a formal inflation target approach, which is spelled out in its new inflation report. To complete the framework the inflation report needs a chapter with inflation projections for the coming two years, based on a clear and objective method. That information is an integral part of the use of an inflation target mechanism, because it provides economic agents with valuable information and enables them to assess the future course of monetary policy.

VII. Conclusions

In recent years, Mexico has made significant progress toward putting its public finances in order, stabilizing its economy and beginning to grow. This same process has changed the profile of its foreign debt toward the longer term and the country has been able to assume the liabilities associated with the rescue of its financial system, without an explosion of inflation and/or having to reprogram its debt. Mexico is also today much less vulnerable to a shock than it was at the end of previous six year periods especially when compared to 1994.

In spite of the relatively positive scenario with regard to the strength of its current macroeconomic situation, it must be noted that Mexico is potentially quite vulnerable on several fronts that require the immediate attention of the incoming administration. First, although fiscal stability has been maintained in the very difficult environment generated by the deep crisis of 1995, the fiscal position is still very precarious. Particularly, there are public liabilities which must be recognized and addressed, an imperative need to increase spending on social sectors and basic infrastructure, and a dangerous dependency on the volatile and now high income from oil. Thus, there are longer-term structural reasons to increase tax revenue, as well as the shorter-term reason that fiscal tightening will help reduce domestic demand without pushing up interest rates or causing currency appreciation.

Finally, with regard to exchange rate systems and in view of the investment in credibility made in recent years, it may be appropriate for Mexico to maintain a flexible exchange rate system, with clearer central bank operational rules. If this scheme is maintained, it will be necessary to establish much clearer rules for central bank performance within a full-fledged inflation target scheme.

References

Bernanke, B., T. Laubach, F. Mishkin and A. Posen. 1999. *Inflation Targeting*, Princeton, NJ: Princeton University Press.

Bernanke, B. and F. Mishkin. 1997. "Inflation Targeting: A New Framework for Monetary Policy?" *Journal of Economic Perspectives* 11, 2, Spring.

Brash, D. 2000. "How Should Monetary Policymakers Respond to the New Challenges of Global Economic Integration?" Paper presented at The Symposium "Global Economic Integration: Opportunities and Challenges" organized by the Federal Reserve Bank of Kansas City, August.

Caballero, R. 2000. "Macroeconomic Volatility in Latin America: A View and Three Case Studies," unpublished paper, MIT (available at http://web.mit.edu/caball/www/).

Calvo, G. and C. Reinhart. 2000. "Fear of Floating," unpublished paper, University of Maryland, May.

Calvo, G. and C. Végh. 1999. "Inflation Stabilization and BOP Crises in Developing Countries," Chapter 24 in *Handbook of Macroeconomics*, J. Taylor and M. Woodford, eds., Vol 1C, Amsterdam: Elsevier Science.

Cechetti, S. 1998. "Policy Rules and Targets: Framing the Central Banker's Problem," *FRBNY Economic Policy Review* 4, 2, June.

Corbo, V. 1999. "Economic Policy Reforms in Latin America," in *Economic Policy Reform: What We Know and What We Need To Know*, Anne O. Krueger, ed., Chicago: University of Chicago Press (forthcoming).

Corbo, V., A. Elberg and J. Tessada. 1999. "Monetary Policy in Latin America: Underpinnings and Procedures," *Cuadernos de Economía* 109, 36, December.

De Gregorio, J., S. Edwards and R. Valdés. 2000. "Controls on Capital Flows: Do They Work?" *NBER Working Paper* 7645, April.

Eichengreen, B. 1999. "Kicking the Habit: Moving from Pegged Rates to a Greater Exchange Rate Flexibility," *Economic Journal*, 109, March.

Engel, E., A. Galetovic and C. Raddatz. 1999. "Taxes and Income Distribution in Chile: Some Unpleasant Redistributive Arithmetic," *Journal of Development Economics* 59, 1, June.

Fasano, U. 2000. "Review of the Experience with Oil Stabilization and Savings Funds in Selected Countries," *IMF Working Paper 00/12*, June.

King, M. 2000. "Monetary Policy: Theory and Practice," *American Economic Review*, May.

Krugman, P. 2000. "Crises: The Price of Globalization?" Paper presented at The Symposium "Global Economic Integration: Opportunities and Challenges" organized by the Federal Reserve Bank of Kansas City, August.

Mussa, M., P. Masson, A. Swoboda, E. Jadresic, P. Mauro and A. Berg. 2000. "Exchange Rate Regimes in an Increasingly Integrated World Economy," *IMF Occasional Paper 193*, August.

Morandé, F. and K. Schmidt-Hebbel. 1999. "The Recent Experience of IT in Developing Economies," paper presented at the IMF Seminar on IT: Policy Considerations and Implications for IMF Conditionalities, Washington, October.

Obstfeld, M. and K. Rogoff. 1995. "The Mirage of Fixed Exchange Rates," *Journal of Economic Perspectives* 9, Fall.

Svensson, L. E. O. 1999. "Inflation Targeting as a Monetary Policy Rule," *Journal of Monetary Economics* 43, 3, June.

7

Fiscal Sustainability

This Chapter was written by Stephen B. Everhart
with the valuable input of Claudia P. Sepulveda, A. Craig Burnside,
Jozef Draaisma, Robert Duval, and Omar Lopez.

I. Background

Brief History of Mexican Fiscal Policy

The stabilization efforts and successes that preceded and have underpinned Mexico's sweeping market-oriented structural reforms since the late 1980s have been anchored in strong fiscal adjustment. Fiscal deficits were drastically reduced (from 15 percent of GDP in 1987 to 1.2 percent in 1998), allowing for tighter monetary policy and lessened inflationary pressures (over the same period, inflation fell from 160 percent per year to the current level of 13 percent). This created an environment in which long-needed structural reform could proceed. The sustainability of those fiscal adjustments is thus central to the government's macroeconomic policy and, ultimately, to the country's development future.

It has become apparent in recent years, however, that potential imbalances may remain behind these positive results that, if unattended, could bring into question the permanence of the heralded adjustments. As part of the "quality" analysis of the Mexican fiscal adjustment, certain issues have been the focus of increasing attention by practitioners and academics. These issues include contingent liabilities in the unfunded, pay-as-you-go social security system (recently partially reformed), unlimited bank deposit insurance schemes, off-balance-sheet financing of public investments, public guarantees for private sector investments, state and municipal borrowing/indebtedness and accelerated depletion in public infrastructure.[1]

---

1. The idea that posted fiscal accounts may not adequately represent the public sector's pressure on an economy's resources, or the "quality" of fiscal adjustments, has been addressed in the literature by, among others, Towe ("Are all Summary Indicators of the Stance of

One should not, however, underestimate the dramatic improvement in the management of the fiscal accounts in recent years, which has led to, inter alia, the narrowing of sovereign bond spreads and the recent upgrade to investment grade of the sovereign debt. Figures 1 and 2 (next page) show the effects of the stabilization programs since 1980 on budget indicators. The Mexican government has run a primary surplus since 1983. After each major economic crisis the government has tightened its fiscal policy as part of the stabilization program. In the two years following the debt crisis of 1982, the primary surplus averaged 4.9 percent of GDP. After the 1986 crisis, the primary surplus rose to 6.5 percent of GDP. Following the December 1994 crisis, tighter fiscal policy yielded primary surpluses averaging 4.5 percent of GDP in 1995–96. Since then, the stance of fiscal policy has been cautious, a prerequisite for macroeconomic stability.

By contrast, Mexico has run an overall budget surplus (*including* interest payments) only three times in the last 19 years. The difference in Figure 2 between the primary and overall deficit is the interest payments on the government domestic and foreign debt (as a percentage of GDP). Thus during the 1980s, the overall deficit was largely explained by interest payments.

Government debt as a percentage of GDP rose steadily between 1980 and 1986 and then fell between 1986 and 1993. With the peso crisis of December 1994, debt to GDP once again increased to the level of the early 1980s, in large part due to the jump in interest rates, but again started to gradually fall by mid-1996 (see Figure 1).

Fiscal Sustainability Defined

The purpose of this Chapter is to discuss whether this change in fiscal policy has been sufficient to ensure the fiscal solvency of the Mexican economy. We have previously attempted to answer this question using a battery of analytical and econometric approaches and by focusing on selected sources of instability that, at the margin (that is, given existing analytical work), appear to be the most critical and urgent from the point of view of future fiscal policy design.[2]

Broadly speaking, a fiscal policy is defined as sustainable if it is expected to generate sufficient net revenues in the future to repay the accumulated debt and interest expenses without an implosion or explosion of the debt.

In other words, the current real value of its liabilities must by definition equal the present value of future primary surpluses (taxes minus non-interest expenditures), or

---

"Fiscal Policy Misleading?", IMF Staff Papers, Vol. 36, No. 4, December 1989), Mackenzie ("The Budgetary Control and Fiscal Impact of Government Contingent Liabilities," IMF Staff Papers, Vol. 38, No. 1, March 1991), and Easterly ("When is Fiscal Adjustment an Illusion?", mimeo, World Bank, April 1998).

2. This work draws heavily on the recently completed green cover study, *Mexico: Fiscal Sustainability,* (two volumes), World Bank Draft Report No. 20236-ME, March 31, 2000.

Figure 1. Mexico Public Net Debt and Primary Deficit (+) as Percent of GDP 1980–98

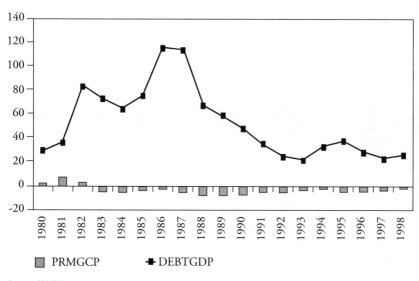

Source: SHCP.

Figure 2. Mexico Overall and Primary Deficit (+) as Percent of GDP 1980–98

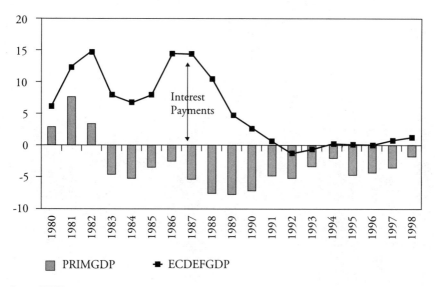

Source: SHCP.

even more simply, any government with outstanding debt must sooner or later run primary surpluses.

II. Issues

Fiscal Policy and Business Cycles

In industrial economies, fiscal policy plays the role of cyclical stabilizer. It is typically desirable for fiscal policy to "lean against the wind," that is, be "counter-cyclical." In other words, it should usually be designed to stimulate output when the economy moves into recession and to be contractionary when an expansion broadens. This is usually accomplished in two ways. The first is by having components in the budget that respond automatically to the business cycle, such as tax revenues (which respond positively) or unemployment benefits (which responds negatively). The second is by using discretionary components in the budget to provide a stimulus during bad times. A counter-cyclical fiscal policy designed in this way leads to larger surpluses during an expansion and, inversely, smaller surpluses or deficits during a recession.

Mexico's fiscal policy does not lean against the wind. World Bank studies[3] show that the reverse is true. The stabilizers in place are weak and are further weakened by the tendency of another automatic component of the budget, oil-based revenue (which responds sensitively to exogenous world oil prices) to move fall during expansions and rise during recessions. Furthermore, the discretionary component of the budget surplus also tends to move in the same manner.

Analysis suggests that an increase in the discretionary surplus of 1 percent of GDP is accompanied by a decline of 0.6 percent of GDP in less than a year. Because in Mexico such increases typically occur during contractions, and these contractions are relatively short-lived (typically less than two years), this implies that discretionary policy exacerbates the cycle.

Mexico's fiscal policy therefore has not played a stabilizing role in the economy. Furthermore, it has not been designed to render itself more sustainable. With procyclical fiscal policy, deficits cause debt to accumulate during economic expansions, but when the economic expansion inevitably ends, this debt suddenly becomes extremely costly. To finance it, the government must either take drastic discretionary fiscal measures, finance the debt by borrowing at high real interest rates, or print money and induce rapid inflation. No matter which action the government takes, the implications are similar: a worsening of the economic downturn.

Another worrisome feature of current fiscal policy is the continued reliance on oil revenues. In recent years oil production's importance to the Mexican economy has varied, fluctuating from almost 14 percent of GDP in 1983, down to 1.7 percent in

---

3. Ibid.

1999. As Figure 3 shows, oil exports as a percentage of total exports have decreased significantly over time, from 80 percent in 1982 to less than 10 percent in 1999.

Although this suggests a relative lessening of the dependency on oil exports, it is important to note that oil *revenues* still represent a significant fraction of public sector revenues (Figure 4).

Figure 3. Composition of Exports

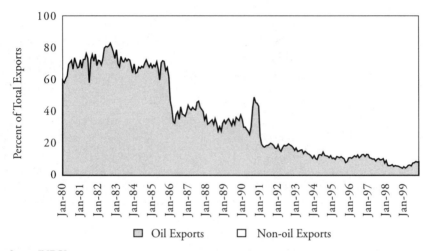

Figure 4. Fiscal Revenues and Oil Dependence

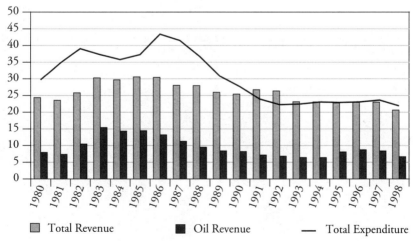

Deficit Reductions and Infrastructure

The fiscal adjustments taking place in the past two decades have substantially reduced government expenditures. One of the components most affected has been real capital expenditure, which fell by 23 percent between the 1980s and the 1990s. In contrast, salaries and wage have declined only about 4.6 percent over the same period.

Figure 5 presents the Mexican budget deficit/public investment relationship. At the beginning of the decade both variables were strongly related, suggesting that the deficit trend was guided by shifts on public investment. While public investment continued to fall steadily by around 2 percent of GDP, primary deficit reduction from 1986 to 1989 doubled that amount, and in 1992 the deficit started to grow again. Contemporaneous correlation between the series is 0.82, suggesting public deficits were cut through reductions in investment.

Figure 6 (below) relates oil prices to public investment for Mexico. This figure shows that Mexican public investment is strongly related to oil prices. Part of the decline in investment may be explained by the privatization process taking place from 1988 to the present, with PEMEX remaining as one of the few state-owned enterprises.

In the past 25 years Mexico's economy has been subjected to a variety of shocks, both internal and external, including sudden increases and declines in world oil prices, changes in U.S. interest rates, economic collapses in Russia and Asia, and bank panic in Mexico. Would changing the provision of certain types of infrastructure can mitigate the effects of such shocks in Mexico?

The study of the first- and second-order impacts of major exogenous shocks (such as changes in the international price of oil or in the nominal exchange rate, or confidence-

Figure 5. Primary Deficit vs. Public Investment (percent of GDP)

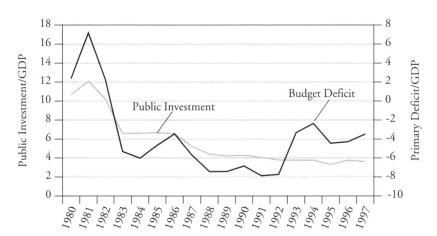

Source: SHCP and IDB–World Bank.

Figure 6. Public Investment vs. Oil Prices

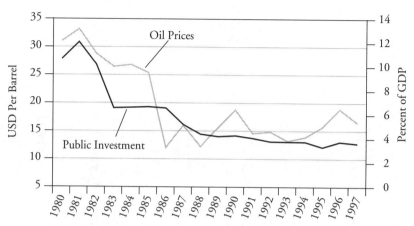

Source: IDB–World Bank and INEGI.

driven contractions in money demand) on Mexico's fiscal accounts, and whether increased provision of infrastructure can reduce the impact of exogenous shocks on the real economy, are questions at the forefront of fiscal policy design in Mexico.

The answer to the last question is a qualified yes. All else being equal, higher stocks of infrastructure will tend to reduce the declines in real income caused by certain types of shocks. This conclusion was reach through a series of numerical exercises based on a general equilibrium model that incorporates various types of estimated Mexican data. World Bank research indicates that given the size of the existing infrastructure stocks, moderate increases in infrastructure *would be welfare improving.* Due to the complexity of the problem and data limitations, precise estimates of the infrastructure gap cannot be given.

Taxation

International Benchmarking

The Mexican government has dramatically reigned in spending over the past two decades, yet there are limits to expenditure cuts. The real problem is revenue. The Mexican tax system has undergone major reforms since 1980. A value added tax (VAT) and indexation to neutralize the effects of inflation were introduced. Personal and corporate income taxes were integrated, ensuring more neutrality between retained and distributed profits. Despite these measures, tax revenues as a percent of GDP have not increased substantially. As Figure 7 illustrates, by regional and international standards, Mexico does not compare favorably as long as there still remains an important need for healthy primary surplus. Clearly, fiscal reform is long overdue.

Figure 7. Tax Revenue as Percent of GDP, Selected Countries 1992–98

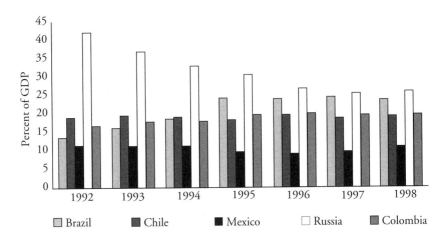

Source: World Development Indicators, World Bank.

There are a number of challenges facing the tax authorities. First, the overly complex tax system creates incentives for noncompliance among private agents. Duplication of tax declarations and poor coordination between collectors' agencies are but two examples of a list of administrative problems. Add to this a large informal sector that contributes only marginally to fiscal revenues and weak law enforcement to motivate possible evaders. Estimates of foregone VAT revenues in the informal sector approach 0.1 percent of GDP.[4]

The VAT system is in need of reform as well. Numerous exemptions exist (for example, zero rate for many domestic transactions) and collection surveillance is weak. As Figure 8 (next page) shows, the VAT contribution is second only to the income tax, followed by production and services taxes.

Estimates of lost revenues due to VAT and income tax evasion are on the order of 5 percent of GDP.[5] Reducing exemptions and stronger surveillance would augment revenues. Undoubtedly, strengthening tax administration would add a few GDP points to the tax coffers.

Contingent Liabilities

One result of the financial crises affecting Asia, Latin America, and other emerging economies over the recent past has been a renewed emphasis on the fiscal risks

---

4. *Centro de Investigación y Docencia Económicas* (CIDE 1999).
5. Two percent for VAT and the rest for income tax (CIDE 1999).

Figure 8. Components of Tax Revenues as Percent of GDP, Mexico 1980–98

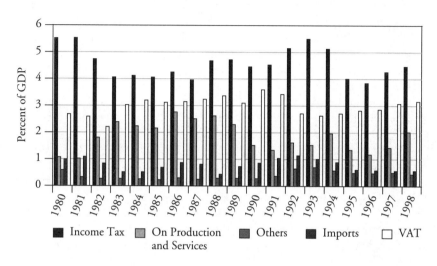

Source: SHCP.

(liabilities) governments face and the means to quantify and mitigate such risks. In general, liabilities can be either contingent or direct. *Contingent liabilities* are defined as "obligations that may or may not come due, depending on whether particular events occur. The probability of their occurrence may be exogenous to government policies (for example, if they are related to natural disasters) or endogenous (for example, if government programs create moral hazard)." In contrast, *direct liabilities* are defined as "obligations whose outcome is predictable."

Delineating further, "*Explicit liabilities* are specific obligations, created by law or contract, that governments must settle. *Implicit liabilities* represent moral obligations or burdens that, although not legally binding, are likely to be borne by governments because of public expectations or political pressures."[6]

For many years, federal government insurance programs were a policy instrument for the Mexican authorities. These programs were primarily concentrated in four areas: government-guaranteed borrowing, infrastructure franchising, unlimited bank deposit insurance, and, more recently, coinsurance of the social security system. Those programs were supposedly justified on the basis of observed market failures (including information-based imperfections in credit markets, high risks in the provision of infrastructure, systemic risk in the banking system in the case of bank failures, and imperfect pooling arrangements in

---

6. Polackova, Hana, "Contingent Government Liabilities: A Hidden Fiscal Risk," *Finance & Development*, March 1999.

the private insurance sector with respect to certain types of insurance). *In effect, before the crisis of 1994, the budgetary implications of these contingent liabilities were largely overlooked.*

Since the crisis, however, it has become clear that the financing requirements to cover the realized losses in these insurance programs have the power to destabilize the government's overall fiscal adjustment efforts. More critically, while the latent fiscal cost of the various insurance programs is widely believed to be large, there is no solid estimate available of the eventual cash outlays that the budget will have to afford, mainly because those programs were not (and, to a certain extent, are still not) considered in the traditional budgetary accounts.

Table 1 presents the most recognized (and highly politicized) contingent liability facing the government, mainly the banking system rescue, *with resolution costs estimated to be on the order of 19.3 percent of GDP*. Of this 18.9 percent, 3.2 percent has already been spent, leaving a government-acknowledged remaining liability of 15.7 percent of GDP.

Since 1998 SHCP has made an effort to report what they recognize as the contingent liabilities of the federal government. Table 2 presents a recent report, reflecting the increasing cost through time.

Public estimation of these liabilities by the government is an important step toward resolution of the problem. However, it must be pointed out that these estimates exclude all subnational debt, subnational pensions, some unrecognized FOBAPROA debt, and some obligations of state-owned enterprises. *World Bank findings suggest the figures above substantially understate the true contingent liabilities facing the government.*

Summary of Empirical Tests of Fiscal Sustainability

Budgets are affected by oil prices, because total revenues quite clearly follow the cycle of oil revenues. In response to this vulnerability to oil prices and the effect of interest rates, the stance of fiscal policy has remained cautious. The latter has been achieved by running consecutive primary (interest exclusive) surpluses since 1983.

This primary surplus has been obtained largely through drastic expenditure cuts. As a fraction of GDP, non-interest expenditures fell from about 25 percent in the

Table 1. Estimate of the Overall Cost of the Financial Rescue, December 1999

	Billions of Pesos	*Percent of GDP*
Debtors aid programs	174.3	3.8
Cost of banking intervention and clean up	579	12.5
Purchase of nonperforming assets	101.8	2.2
Toll roads program	18	0.4
Total	**873.1**	**18.9**

Source: Instituto para la Protección del Ahorro Bancario (IPAB).

Table 2. Contingent Liabilities Recognized by the Federal Government
(billions of pesos)

	Balance Dec. 1998	Balance Dec. 1999	Change from Dec. 1998
FOBAPROA[a]	425.03	395.69	-29.34
FARAC	73.63	90.76	17.13
Credit assistance programs[b]	143.57	165.23	21.66
Development banks	10.08	11.83	1.75
FAMEVAL	4.07	4.80	0.72
Others[c]	5.18	4.37	-0.81
Total[d]	661.56	672.67	11.10

Notes:
a. Includes only the explicitly guaranteed liabilities by the federal government.
b. Includes mainly *Fideicomisos Instituidos en Relación con la Agricultura* (FIRA), *Fondo de Operación y Financiamiento Bancario a la Vivienda* (FOVI), *Fondo para el Desarrollo Comercial* (FIDEC) and FIDELIQ.
c. Includes mainly the *Comisión Federal de Electricidad* (CFE).
d. Preliminary data. Excludes guarantees established in the organic laws of the Development Bank.
Source: SHCP.

1980s to 19 percent in the 1990s, a drop of 23 percent. In contrast, non-oil revenue remained roughly constant at about 16.25 percent of GDP over this period. In particular, the major adjustment in the 1990s came from capital expenditure.

Mexico's public debt relative to GDP fell from 115 percent during 1986–87 to about 26 percent in 1998, due to primary surpluses, a debt management strategy centered on lengthening maturity and reducing interest payments after the peso crisis, and strong GDP growth.

The short- and medium-term projections of fiscal sustainability using an intertemporal approach for the Mexican economy during 1999–2006 show that, with FOBAPROA included, and assuming a discount rate of 5 percent, the government will have to *increase taxes or reduce government spending in the next years approximately between 0.3 and 0.8 percent of GDP*. Note that this calculation includes only part of the contingent liabilities.

The Mexican government has responded to the increase in interest payments on the outstanding debt by running primary surpluses, trying to meet its intertemporal budget constraints through fiscal adjustment instead of inflation or default.

Some caveats are in order. This discussion ignores the asset side of the government's balance sheet due to data shortcomings. This omission can distort our view; the fiscal adjustment can be an illusion if it carried out through asset depletion (for example, oil reserves, which are nonrenewable, or infrastructure). Moreover, the absence of complete information on contingent liabilities (for example, subnational debt and pension liabilities) can favorably bias the results. Thus, the sustainability results should be viewed with caution.

III. Policy Options

Assessment of the Scope of the Problem: Omissions and Benchmarking

Two important contingent liabilities are omitted in the previous analysis due to data limitations: the analysis of the pensions of subnational governmental institutions, and the expected effects on the federal fiscal accounts of the debt restructuring of states and municipalities since the 1995 crisis. Assessing these areas is difficult because of incomplete and inconsistent data; however, these are clearly contingent liabilities at the federal level.

There is sobering evidence on the health of the 32 subnational pension systems (31 states plus the Federal District): *Eleven of these are either in actuarial deficit or will be by 2001.*

There are estimates of the debt stock at the state level only (very limited data exist at the municipal level), where *disturbing trends in both the size and concentration of the debt at the state level are developing: the debt of the Federal District, State of Mexico, and Nuevo León has grown from 37 percent in 1994 to 65 percent of the total outstanding state-level debt in 1998, more than doubling the outstanding subnational debt stock over the period* (see Figure 9 next page).

It is important to note that contingent liabilities are just that—contingent. When Minas Gerais (Brazil's third-largest state) became temporarily insolvent in 1998, not all of the states followed. It is unlikely that every possible contingent liability would come due simultaneously. Furthermore, even with the addition of the government's estimate of the contingent liabilities to the existing explicit stock of debt, Mexico compares favorably to G-7 nations on a debt-to-GDP basis. Table 3 illustrates that even when the estimated contingent liabilities are added to the explicit stock of debt, Mexico would easily qualify for European Union membership, while Figure 10 illustrates that of the G-7 nations, only France would qualify.[7]

Table 3. Mexico Federal Debt
(as a percentage of GDP)

Gross public debt	28.3
Net remaining debt, financial rescue[a]	15.7
FARAC	2.0
Other contingent liabilities[b]	4.0
Total	**50.0**

Notes:
a. IPAB estimates.
b. Includes credit assistance programs, FARAC, Development Banks, FAMEVAL, and CFE.
Source: SHCP, *Informe sobre la Situación Economica, las Finanzas Públicas y la Deuda Pública, Segundo Trimestre 1999.*

---

7. The fiscal criteria under the Maastricht Treaty are set in terms of a general government debt/GDP ratio ceiling of 60 percent and a government financial deficit/GDP ratio ceiling of 3 percent.

Figure 9. Concentration and Growth of Subnational Debt, 1994–98: Selected States

Total subnational debt more than doubled over the period 1994–98; some states witnessed a tenfold increase...

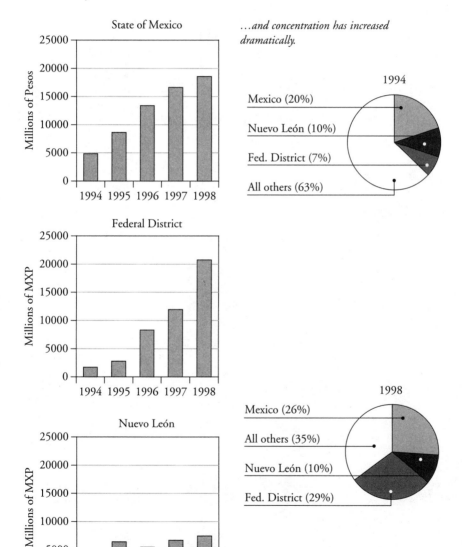

...and concentration has increased dramatically.

Figure 10. Gross Federal Debt as Percent of GDP: International Benchmarks

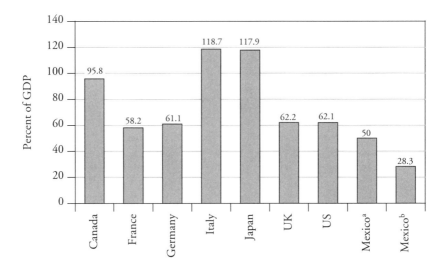

Note: 1998 estimates for G7 countries, December 1999 for Mexico
a. Includes direct and contigent liabilities.
b. Includes only direct liabilities.
Source: October 1999 *IMF World Economic Outlook* for G7 Countries, World Bank staff estimate for Mexico.

IV. Conclusion

The stabilization efforts and successes that preceded and have underpinned Mexico's sweeping market-oriented structural reforms since the late 1980s have set the stage for continued progress. Yet, potential imbalances underlie the positive results posted in Mexico's fiscal accounts—imbalances that, if unattended, could bring into question the permanence of the heralded adjustments.

Excessive reliance on oil revenues to finance current expenditures, and the inability of the government to increase the tax base in spite of repeated reforms, need to be addressed. This is not a sustainable strategy when a large proportion of government revenues are financed by an exhaustible resource.

The slow response to issues around banking, state/municipal borrowing and pension liabilities, as well as accelerated depletion of public infrastructure have been the focus of increasing attention by policymakers and academics as part of the "quality" analysis of the Mexican fiscal adjustment.

Overall, the financial markets have confirmed the favorable econometric findings presented in the Issues section above. Narrowing sovereign bond spreads, a strong peso, and the March 2000 sovereign upgrade by the ratings agencies endorse the measures taken by the authorities.

Addressing the above remaining issues with the same resolve as that shown in managing the debt and fiscal accounts will undoubtedly yield results further endorsed by the financial markets.

References

CIDE. 1999. "Los impuestos en México. Quién y cómo se pagan?" *Programa de Presupuesto y Gasto Público*, CIDE, Mexico.

Polackova, Hana. 1999. "Contingent Government Liabilities: A Hidden Fiscal Risk." *Finance & Development*, March: 46–9.

World Bank. 2000. *Mexico: Fiscal Sustainability* (two volumes), World Bank Draft Report No. 20236-ME, March 31.

8

Challenges and Prospects for Tax Reform

This Chapter was written by Steven B. Webb from the valuable inputs
of Alberto Diaz-Cayeros, Michael Engelshalk, Stephen B. Everhart,
Marcelo M. Giugale, Omar Lopez-Escarpulli, Jorge Martinez-Vazquez,
Charles P. McPherson, Kenneth Messere, Alma Rosa Moreno,
Parthasarathi Shome, and Jaime Vazquez Caro.

I. Background

Over the last ten years it has become clear that Mexico needs greater non-oil tax revenues, sustainable in the long term, in order to provide for more public expenditure in areas such as poverty alleviation, health, education, and infrastructure, as well as to pay for the recent social security reform and banking sector support. In other words, Mexicans are not paying enough taxes to cover the public expenditure that they want. Much of that unwillingness to pay is due to the inefficiency and, critically, corruption with which public resources are perceived to be managed. However, another factor also accounts for a large part of the low tax revenue—a flawed and poorly implemented tax system that allows many firms and individuals to evade paying.

While Mexican tax law has some features that could promote economic efficiency and attract domestic and foreign investment, this report argues that tax collections should be increased through a more effective attack on tax evasion; that the tax system needs to be simpler and fairer through more broadly based value-added tax (VAT), corporate income tax (CIT) and personal income tax (PIT); that relations between the tax administration and taxpayers need improvement; and that subnational governments should take responsibility for a larger share of taxes. (See also Gil Diaz and Thirsk 1997; World Bank, 1989; OECD, 1999; Diaz and McLure 2000). Reducing evasion would not only have a immediate effect on revenues but also improve the fairness of the system, with longer term positive effects on public attitudes toward taxation and the public sector.

II. Level and Structure of Taxation in Mexico

The overall level and structure of taxes in Mexico has changed little over the last two decades (see Table 1). Except for the early 1990s when vigorous enforcement efforts, led by Subsecretario Gil Diaz, temporarily pushed up federal revenues, the revenue from any single tax has not varied by more than one percent of GDP since 1980, and total revenue has not varied more than two percentage points. General government revenues are similar to those in Argentina and Colombia, six or seven percentage points higher than in Peru and Venezuela, and six or seven percentage points lower than in Brazil and Uruguay, although individual taxes, especially the VAT, collect lower GDP shares than most countries, such as Argentina.

Although Mexico's total revenue shares are thus not out of line with similar middle-income countries, the tax revenues shares are lower than most countries and

Table 1. Mexico: General Government Revenues (percent of GDP)

	1980–81	1990–91	1998–99
Total General Government Revenues	17.4	20.4	17.2
Federal Government Tax Revenues	10.8	10.8	10.9
Corporate Income Tax	2.3	2.4	2.6
Personal Income Tax	3.2	2.1	1.9
Value Added Tax	2.6	3.5	3.2
Excises	1.0	1.4	2.1
Import Taxes	1.0	1.0	0.6
Others	0.5	0.4	0.4
Federal Government Non-Tax Revenues	4.5	6.5	3.5
Products, Services	0.3	0.3	0.2
Others	0.2	2.4	0.6
Duties	4.1	3.9	2.6
Of Which			
Hydrocarbon Duties	3.7	3.4	2.2
Other Duties	0.3	0.5	0.4
Social Security (net of Federal contributions)	2.1	2.2	1.9
Subnational Own-Source Revenues		0.9	1.0
Taxes		0.3	0.4
Non-Tax Revenues		0.6	0.6

Source: SHCP and World Bank calculations.

---

1. Revenues of PEMEX are counted separately, within the firm. The derechos on oil are in effect taxes that go to the federal government.

are inconsistent with the OECD-type of standards of living and provision of public services to which Mexico aspires. Federal tax revenues (excluding social security and PEMEX revenues) are only 10 or 11 percent of GDP, and subnational tax revenues are only about 1 percent. Mexico is now at the bottom of the OECD ranking order of tax revenues to GDP, and throughout the eighties and nineties the difference has increased. There is also a growing gap between Mexico's tax to GDP ratio and those of most Latin America countries with a similar per capita GDP.

Oil sector "non-tax" revenues are substantial but widely fluctuating—between 2.1 and 4.5 percent of GDP in the 1990s—and declining on average.[1] Some fluctuations are unavoidable because of international prices, but they could be partially mitigated through a well-designed stabilization fund. In the long-term, the share of oil revenues will inevitably decline if the per capita growth of economy is to close the gap with the rest of the OECD. The gross revenue from oil seems likely to stay roughly constant in real terms and is very unlikely to grow as fast as per capita incomes will need to grow to be catching up upper income countries. Therefore, if Mexico's public sector revenues are to keep up as a share of GDP, much less to grow as a share, then the non-oil revenues—taxes—will have to expand as a share of GDP.

Income taxes—corporate and personal—are the most important revenue source in Mexico, with the corporate income tax holding steady at around 2.5 percent of GDP and personal income taxes declining since 1980 from about three percent of GDP to about two percent. The increase of income-tax revenue should come from widening the base and improving administration, not raising rates. Income taxes are also the most important revenue source in Mexico's main competitor economy—the United States—which allows credit for taxes paid abroad. Thus, Mexico can strengthen its collections without discouraging foreign investment.

Social security for participating private-sector workers has turned into an involuntary personal saving plan, which effectively puts it out of the immediate fiscal concerns, as a revenue source or a liability. This is an important achievement of the 1990s. The remaining challenges are to broaden the coverage of people in the private sector (as part of bringing the informal sector into the formal sector) and to reform the social security (pension) plans for the public sector, both to facilitate labor mobility and to prevent (or reduce) the build up of contingent liabilities of the public sector.

VAT and Excises are the growing portions of Mexico's tax revenue, now up to 3 and 2 percent of GDP, respectively. While many OECD countries have declared their intention to move from income taxes toward consumption taxes, only New Zealand and the United Kingdom have actually done it. Consumption taxes are alleged to have a number of benefits—encouraging saving, fostering exports, and facilitating compliance, but many problems remain in the details, as noted below. The objective of fairness in sharing the tax burden argues against moving toward total reliance on these taxes.

Import taxes are low—less than a percent of GDP—and declining, as in most countries, due to trade liberalization. To the extent that the decline of revenue results from lower rates, because of NAFTA or other reductions in rates, this is good, because increasing international integration improves the prospects for efficient growth.

Sub-national taxes, mainly the state payroll tax and the municipal property tax (*predial*), are very small—less than one percent of GDP. They cover less than 15 percent of the spending done by the sub-national governments, which has increased dramatically in the last decade. Those government may never be able to raise enough revenue to fund all their programs, as long as these include such large "ticket items" as education and health, but they do need to raise more of their own revenue if they are to have proper fiscal incentives and be creditworthy.

The overview provided above suggests that income taxes and value-added taxes have the best potential for growth in Mexico, as does taxation by sub-national governments. Whether sub-national taxation could grow by taking parts of the federal income or value added taxes is a difficult issue discussed later. The next section summarizes the major strengths and weaknesses of each of the major taxes and gives recommendations to improve them.

III. Current Policies and Options in Mexico's Tax Regime

While each tax has its unique issues, two issues are especially noteworthy and common to all the taxes. First, redistribution. Experience in Latin America and elsewhere shows that taxes are a poor tool for redistributing income or wealth. Redistribution is done better through the spending side (transfers to the poor, primary education, health, etc.). Taxes make the whole public sector more progressive when tax policy focuses on efficiently raising revenue.

Second, exemptions and exceptional regimes are the most problematic part of tax policy, leading to evasion, inequity and inefficiency, as well as revenue loss. Exclusions from the bases of the VAT, CIT and PIT, generally in response to the demands of pressure groups, create inequities and economic inefficiencies. They occur in most countries, but have done so excessively in Mexico. Because these measures have an effect similar to that of a budgeted subsidy and they cost the government resources, they are called "tax expenditures." They save some transaction costs by avoiding the overhead expense of passing through the tax collection and budget spending processes. But tax expenditures have serious disadvantages too. They are less transparent politically, easier to pass initially and harder to repeal, as they do not face annual review in the budget process. The incidence of tax expenditures is less clear than with budget expenditures and is usually quite different from the stated intention. While helping sick people, small farmers, or some other group of the poor is usually the rationale, the greatest benefits almost always accrue to high-income individuals who earn and spend the most, because they are subject to the highest tax rate and would otherwise pay the most tax. Thus, eliminating a tax expenditure almost always improves equity as well as reducing evasion and increasing efficiency and revenue. What began as an attempt to bring difficult-to-tax small enterprises and those in certain economic sectors, like agriculture and transport, in to the tax net has degenerated into a complex mix of presumptive and cash-flow taxation, which results in uncertainty and more possibilities for tax evasion than previously existed.[2]

Oil Taxation

Prior to 1994 oil taxation (essentially the taxation of Pemex plus oil products), was negotiated between Pemex and SHCP on the basis of the Government's budget requirements and Pemex's perceived capacity to pay. In 1994 a new system was introduced, designed to explicitly tax Pemex based primarily on profits, while maintaining Government revenues from the sector at levels equivalent to those negotiated in earlier years.

The new system contained transition provisions, in particular the DSH (*Derecho sobre Hidrocarburos*, see below), which allowed Pemex time to prepare its accounts for income taxation and to safeguard the revenue-maintenance requirement. These provisions were to last only one year. Six years later they are still in effect, and Pemex has not yet presented a single tax declaration according to the new regime. The explanation given is that Pemex is still not in a position to provide the data required for income taxation. To date only one corporation within Pemex is providing accounting statements.

The existing system of oil taxation contains the following elements:

- *Income Tax.* The *Impuesto a los Rendimientos Petroleros* (IRP) is an income tax, based on the same elements as Mexico's generally applicable corporate income tax. It is levied at a 35 percent rate on Pemex and each of its subsidiaries. In practice it has no impact because, as noted above, Pemex has yet to come up with the accounting numbers that would enable it to comply.
- *Duty on Oil Extraction.* The *Derecho a la Extraccion de Petroleo* (DEP) is a cash flow tax, levied on total revenues of Pemex Exploration and Production (PEP), Pemex's upstream subsidiary, less total approved expenditures in the year. It consists of three components: *Ordinario* (52.3 percent); *Extraordinario* (25.5 percent); and *Adicional* (1.1 percent). The three components have different beneficiaries. These are, respectively: state governments (based on agreed formulas); the Federal Government; and cities from which oil is exported.
- *Petroleum Products Tax.* The *Impuesto Especial sobre Produccion y Servicios Aplicado a la Enajenacion de Gasolinas y Diesel* (IEPS) is a gasoline and diesel tax levied on consumers. The tax is calculated as the difference between the con-

---

2. This system was advocated as a simplified one by those promoting it as a political compromise. In the end, however, it became a Trojan horse that allowed policymakers to enlarge, year after year, the artificial definitions that have characterized the system in the last decade.

sumer price, fixed on an occasional basis by Government at essentially the same level for all regions of the country, and the producer price equal to Houston spot prices plus transport costs and a quality adjustment. Since Houston spot prices change daily, while Mexico's consumer price remains fixed for much longer periods, the IEPS varies almost daily. Mexico is the only OECD country with an ad valorem rate on petroleum products; the others all have fixed rates per physical unit.

- *Gross Revenue Tax.* The *Derecho sobre Hidrocarburos* (DSH) is levied on Pemex at a 60.8 percent rate on the gross revenues from all of Pemex's operations, upstream and downstream, plus the IEPS. The DSH was designed to have a short life, maintaining Government revenues during the transition to income-based taxation. It remains in effect, however, and is the most important feature of Mexico's oil taxation system. Both the DEP and the IEPS are creditable against the DSH, and whenever their sum is different from the calculated DSH obligation, the DEP is adjusted upwards or downwards to make them equal.
- *Price Cap.* The *Aprovechamiento sobre Rendimientos Excedentes* (ARE) is levied on PEP whenever crude oil export prices exceed the price assumed for annual budget purposes. The ARE rate of 39.2 percent applies to the difference between the budget price and the export price and is additive to the basic 60.8 percent DSH rate, which means that effectively 100 percent of the difference between the export price and the budget price goes to the Government/Hacienda.

At present, Mexico's tax instruments for oil result in investment incentives that are exactly opposite to those for efficient development of the sector. The best tax instrument to promote an optimal allocation of resources would be a profit tax, like the dormant IRP. Under profits-based taxation, a project which shows a positive pre-tax return will show a positive, albeit smaller, post-tax return, thus satisfying the important objective of not discouraging expansion in the underlying activity. Unfortunately, Mexico relies entirely on revenue rather than profits taxes in its upstream oil sector. The profits-based character of the DEP and ISR notwithstanding, the DSH and ARE are the measures actually in effect—both taxes based on gross revenue. Because of the insensitivity of these taxes to profit, production and projects with positive pre-tax margins or returns will not always have positive margins or returns post-tax. The higher the revenue tax, and/or the more modest the pre-tax return, the more likely that outcome becomes, with the result that already established production (flowing oil) is not extended to socially desirable limits or is prematurely abandoned, and investment in desirable new production is not pursued. Economic modeling of Mexico's oil sector shows exactly that outcome.

Many progressive oil producing countries have abandoned the use of revenue taxes. The average effective revenue or royalty tax rate world-wide is now in the 15 to 18 percent range. In sharp contrast, Mexico's 60.8 percent revenue tax is the highest in the world, with the possible exception of Syria. As costs increase on flowing oil, Mexico's aggressive oil-revenue tax begins to take more than 100 percent of pre-tax cash margins, even where these are substantial as in Mexico at today's oil prices. For example, post-tax margins on Norte production and part of Sur appear to be negative, implying that cash operating costs cannot be recovered, let alone prior investment costs. Under normal commercial circumstances, such production would be suspended or abandoned. The DSH and ARE have even more adverse effects on incentives for investment in new projects. Only the very best of the projects will produce post-tax returns on investment above the usually required minimum threshold of 15 percent.

Discouraging as they are, these results are probably an overly favorable portrayal of the impact of Mexico's tax system on its oil industry. They assume the DSH applies at its nominal 60.8 percent rate to upstream revenues. In fact, the effective rate is significantly higher. This is because the 60.8 percent obligation applies to all Pemex revenues, both upstream and downstream. The downstream sector, whether in Mexico or elsewhere is incapable of supporting a revenue tax at this level or any level near to it. At the very best, it might be able to cover a 10 percent tax. This means that, to meet its overall tax obligation, Pemex must be paying an effective tax on its upstream operations well above 60.8 percent of revenues, and a correspondingly higher percentage of pre-tax profits.

What should be done to correct tax distortions in Mexico's oil sector? The tax on the production side of oil, including exports, should be on economic profit and not on gross revenue or output. This means implementing the IRP and dropping the DEPD, DSH and ARE. The rate for the IRP might need adjustment in order to be revenue neutral. Pemex should be required to present proper and audited accounts to facilitate this. A modest royalty, say 10 to 12 percent of revenues, deductible for purposes of the IRP and applicable only to Pemex's upstream operations (PEP), would provide early and dependable income from development and production operations without the severe disincentive effects created by the DSH. The royalty would collect a small percentage of the rents generated by upstream operations before application of an explicit rent tax. Revenues from the IRP would be very sensitive to world oil prices, although perhaps slightly less so than the current regime.

A stabilization fund should be established to assure that short-term price rises, and even medium-term ones, do not lead to unsustainable increases in spending. The tax on domestic consumption of petroleum products, the IEPS, should be made fixed per unit, with the rate adjusted annually for inflation. This would make that part of fiscal revenues much less variable.

Corporate Income (Profit) Tax

The corporate income tax (CIT) is second only to the VAT in revenue importance, bringing in over 2.5 percent of GDP in the late 1990s. It needs to be strengthened both for the sake of its revenue and to facilitate the linkage of the Mexican and US economies. It is also slated to be a key part of oil-sector taxation, as noted above. The CIT has two main regimes: a) the general case, where a rate of 34 percent is applied to corporate income (profit); and b) the simplified cash flow accounting system applicable to agriculture, agro-industry and trucking.[3] With its numerous loopholes and complexities, the CIT system has become hard to enforce and evasion is rampant.

In the general regime, the CIT base is unduly narrow by international standards: The law allows immediate expensing of purchases regardless of inventory changes, and immediate depreciation provisions allowed (until 1999) a substantial deferral of tax payments. During the 1990s a number of new tax expenditures have eroded the base of the CIT. Many of these tax expenditures were the consequence of political pressures and were granted without measuring the revenue losses incurred. Not only do they narrow the tax base, but also provide opportunity for tax avoidance. A good example is the opportunity to misuse the 50 percent tax reductions for the agricultural, livestock, fisheries and forestry sectors. Similarly, the cash-flow tax system for agriculture and trucking has some attractions of simplicity, but it is also much more generous than the general regime, creating opportunities and incentives for evasion, especially in the trucking industry, which is now largely integrated with other sectors of the economy.

Opinions differ on how widely the combined use of the general provisions, the simplified regime, the consolidation of profits and losses, and tax treaty provisions have contributed to tax avoidance. Unquestionably, the provisions are open to abuse and are abused. The situation is particularly bad because of the absence of qualified staff in the tax administration to understand, let alone challenge, what the corporate accountants declare (tax administration is addressed below).

Recommendations on how to improve the CIT are relatively simple. More firms, including all large firms and conglomerates, and trucking and agriculture, should be subject to the general system. The general system itself needs reform, introducing standard depreciation and expensing rules similar to those in the United States, which is the benchmark for most firms in Mexico with international investment opportunities. (The CIT rates in the United States and Mexico are already similar.) This would allow Mexico to take full advantage of international tax treaties, would facilitate compliance by firms, and would make it easier for the SAT to recruit trained tax accountants. Of course, administration and enforcement need strengthening, as elaborated later. As the general system gets simplified enough to be enforceable, should be included, ending their special regimes.

Personal Income Tax

In Mexico, personal income tax (PIT) revenues have declined as a share of GDP over the past two decades. Rates have been reduced and the tax bases narrowed by the

---

3. In addition there is a presumptive deduction of 50 percent in the case of agriculture, cattle raising and forestry, and 60 percent in the case of auto transportation.

introduction of new concessions, such as limited taxation of fringe benefits, which resulted in a more complex and unmanageable PIT. This contrasts with the trend in most other OECD countries, where income tax (PIT plus CIT) revenues have increased during the last two decades because, while rates of both PIT and CIT have been substantially reduced, the tax bases have been widened. Coverage of fringe benefits in the income tax bases is far narrower than most countries, and Mexico is the only OECD country with a fringe benefit subsidy. Mexico is also the only country with a negative income tax for low paid employees that does not take account of the family situation and non-wage income.

Negative income tax schemes in Mexico's PIT cost an estimated 0.5 percent of GDP. The negative income tax for low paid workers and the subsidy for those with little or not fringe benefits greatly complicate the administration of the PIT, without policy justification. The negative income tax credit is alleged to provide aid to the poor employed in the formal sector, but they are far from the poorest members of society. Furthermore, it probably acts more as a subsidy to employers, who are enabled to pay lower wages as a result of the credit. The incidence of the fringe benefit subsidy is also unclear, and is probably regressive. Around 10 percent of the total wages and salaries are not taxed at all because of the special treatment of several benefits given to the employees in addition to their salary and wages.

Of the various possibilities for widening the PIT base, bringing in more fringe benefits[4] into the tax net is the most important in quantitative terms. This could be done either by taxing some benefits presently untaxed, or by adopting the Australian practice of taxing all such benefits in the hands of the employer, or by adopting the Hungarian practice of disallowing such benefits as a deduction against corporate profits.

Once the base is broadened, one possible alternative to the present rate system would be the elimination of negative taxation, a tax schedule with full exemption on the first tax bracket, five intermediate brackets with rate increments larger than at present, and a top marginal rate of 35 percent as in the present Mexican system. It is assumed that individuals would be obliged to include all their income in their statement. Simplification of the personal income tax schedule could help increase revenue. Concentrating personal income taxes on the middle class and on the wealthy would make tax administration much more manageable. Additionally, total revenue should not be directly or significantly affected as a result of the elimination and reduction of taxes in the first income brackets, since the marginal and average rates are quite similar in each relevant bracket.

---

4. Fringe benefits include: motor vehicles, accommodation, low interest loans for housing or other purposes, discounts on goods or services, gifts to employees, education expenses of employee or dependants, contributions to pension or super annuation schemes, medical and dental insurance, life insurance, canteen facilities or meal vouchers, and leisure facilities.

Value-Added Tax

The VAT is currently the largest revenue source for the Government and holds the most potential for increasing revenues. The VAT in Mexico has a standard rate of 15 percent, but as shown in Table 2, it yields only about what would be expected from a rate of 5 percent. This 32 percent effectiveness rate as percentage of statutory rate is far lower than any other OECD country. Italy, where there are also collection problems, at 51 percent effectiveness is the next lowest; the OECD average is around 70 percent.[5] In addition to the most serious problem of evasion, there are four main problems with the VAT policy in Mexico: exemptions that erode the base, a lower rate of 10 percent near the border, a high threshold for firms to have to participate, and enforcement delegated to the states.

To move as far as is politically and technically possible towards a generalized VAT system, as practiced in most other OECD countries, would increase not only VAT revenues but also income tax revenues in the long term, because of the additional accounting information that would become available.

Table 2. Effectiveness of Value-Added Tax Collection, 1997

	Value-Added Tax Revenues in percent of GDP	Standard rate Percent	Effective VAT Rate,[a] percent	Effective VAT rate in percent of standard rate
		A	B	B/A
Japan[b]	1.8	5.0	3.1	89
Germany	6.6	15.0	11.5	77
France	7.9	20.6	14.7	71
Italy[c]	5.7	19.0	9.8	52
United Kingdom	6.9	17.5	10.8	62
Canada[b]	2.5	7.0	4.3	61
Mexico	3.1	15.0	4.7	32
OECD average	6.7	17.7	12.5	73
G7 average	5.3	14.4	9.0	69
EU average	7.3	19.4	14.0	71

Notes:
a. The effective VAT rate is VAT revenues divided by the base (i.e. consumption excluding VAT).
b. Fiscal year basis (Q2/97–Q1/98).
c. The standard VAT rate was raised from 19 to 20 percent on 1 October 1997.
Source: OECD 1999 *Economic Survey of Mexico;* Bank staff calculation.

5. The "Subsecretario de Ingresos," Manuel Ramos Francia, noted that the VAT base is very narrow, because only 55 percent of total consumption is included in the tax base (Reforma, August 21st, 2000).

Extensive zero-rating, including food and medications, reduces the VAT revenues by over 40 percent. The zero rating requires rebating substantial amounts of tax revenues to traders, complicates the system, and opens the way for tax evasion. Ending these zero-rating would increase the burden as a share of income more for the poorer two deciles—about 6.6 percent of income—than for the upper two deciles—about 1.87 percent of income. To address equity concerns, increased income subsidies to the poor through the PROGRESA and other programs should accompany the end of zero rating. This should be fiscally feasible, since over 30 percent of the total implicit subsidy from the zero rating of food and medicines accrues to the two highest income deciles of taxpayers, while only 11 percent of the subsidy accrues to the two lowest income deciles of the population.

The second problem with the VAT is that a rate of only 10 percent, instead of the standard 15 percent, is charged in the border areas. Since the market in the border area is estimated to have around one-tenth of the total market, the lower rate represents a substantial revenue loss. In addition, the present 10 percent rate for border states complicates the system, provides opportunities for tax evasion, and distorts internal competition within Mexico.[6] This measure was designed to protect border merchants against smugglers, but a well-enforced VAT would increase the international competitive position of Mexican producers, including those near the border, because public services in the US are supported mostly with non-VAT-type taxes that cannot be rebated for exports. For these reasons, especially to reduce evasion, the Government should end the differential rate, making it the same throughout Mexico.

The third big problem with Mexico's VAT is the unusually high threshold below which traders can opt out. At 1 million pesos (about US$112,000) the Mexican threshold is much higher than that of other OECD countries, with the exception of Japan.[7] It is clear that, in order to bring more medium size taxpayers into the regular VAT regime, the threshold should be substantially reduced. Enterprises (including those in the agricultural sector) with receipts of 500,000 pesos or even 300,000 pesos, should have to register and pay the VAT. The threshold could drop in phases over two or three years, which would help SAT to cope with the increasing documentation that would result.

The fourth problematic feature of Mexico's VAT is that the states participate in its administration. They are often given responsibility and authority for enforcement (*fiscalización*) and allowed to keep the fines that they collect as a result of their efforts. The logic of this arrangement is that the state authorities know the local situation better and therefore will be better able to identify and prosecute evaders.

---

6. No other OECD country has special low rates for border areas, even though rates of general consumption tax vary considerably between neighboring countries—e.g. Canada/US, Denmark/Germany, and France/Spain.
7. Comparative thresholds for other countries to the nearest thousand US dollars are Japan 270, UK 75, Canada 23, Germany and New Zealand 21, France 14, Portugal 13, Greece 7, Italy 3. (OECD 1999 and T. Dalsgaard and M. Kawagoe, 2000).

And the incentive to the states is the extra revenue they get, which is substantial in some cases. The Federal Government should also benefit as stronger enforcement, with penalties for evasion, makes more firms willing to comply with the regular federal collection. Actual results have not lived up to these expectations. States vary in their interpretation of the tax law and in the vigor of their enforcement, because of varied capacity of local officials, possible corruption, and perhaps even tactics to attract business investment. This creates geographic variation in the effective tax. Also, the reduced federal government involvement in enforcement deprives it of information that would help it to improve and coordinate enforcement efforts not only of the VAT but also of excises and the corporate and personal income taxes. Since direct devolution to states of a share of the VAT is a possible route for reforming the *Pacto Fiscal* in the future, as discussed below, states should continue some involvement in enforcement. But clearly the federal government needs to get more involved in enforcement, at least to assure common standards and to collect and share data. More payment information should be collected to allow better determination of the location of value-adding activity, something that will help improve enforcement of state taxes like the payroll tax, as well as other federal taxes, like corporate income.

Excises

In Mexico the Federal Government collects excise tax on gasoline, tobacco, alcohol, bottled water, and telephone service. Revenue from excises other than gasoline has roughly doubled over the last two decades, exceeding two percent of GDP by the end of the 1990s.

Unlike most places, Mexican excise taxes are levied on an *ad valorem* basis, rather than by physical unit, which is the common practice. Introduction of the *ad valorem* rates in 1980 was regarded as essential to protect excise yields at a time when inflation was high and was increasing rapidly. Nevertheless, *ad valorem* taxation has many defects and now that inflation is relatively low, there is a strong case for following the practice of other OECD countries in basing taxation on physical units, for example, the volume of hydrocarbon oil and the weight of tobacco.[8] Specific taxation of alcoholic beverages according to the strength of the alcohol was already enacted in 1999.

Mexican practice with excise taxes also differs from every other OECD country in applying a VAT-type credit mechanism each time the products are sold, instead of applying a final tax when the goods are imported or leave the domestic factory. The original purpose of this feature was to combat tax evasion. Since a few firms controlled the market from the production to retail stage, they put much of the mark-up at the post-import or post ex-factory stage and thus could reduce the taxable value at the earlier stage. (Taxing by physical volume, not *ad valorem*, would

---

8. Though in the case of cigarettes there is a case for partial ad valorem treatment.

remove any advantage from the VAT type mechanism.) Mexico has recently returned to the standard OECD practice of taxing alcohol at the production or import stage, due to the emergence of many small wholesale and retail producers of alcoholic beverages, but it has not yet done so with the oil and tobacco excises.

The diagnostic described above suggest that excise taxes could be simplified in two main ways. First, *ad valorem* rates need to be converted into rates per unit, with provision for automatic and regular indexation for overall inflation. Second, the VAT-type credits for intermediate sales should be eliminated and taxes should be collected at the production or import stages.

Sub-national Taxes

Sub-national governments in Mexico, as noted earlier, collect very little revenue either as a share of GDP (about 1 percent) or as a share of their own expenditures (about 10 percent). This imbalance is inconsistent with the reality that has emerged in the past ten years: political and constitutional autonomy of the states, opposition control of the federal congress (and of many state congresses), major spending responsibilities in the hands of states, and substantial subnational autonomy to borrow. Redressing that fiscal imbalance is more than a technical tax matter, as it will implicitly define the kind of federal country Mexico wants to be (see Chapter on Decentralization).

Much of the imbalance has a long historical background. The taxes and fees that are the main source of revenue in Mexico are now clearly allocated between levels of government, so that there is virtually no overlap vertically between levels and only minimal tax competition horizontally between states. These are important achievements for making taxes more efficient. This was not always so, as counterproductive tax wars were common in the first half of the 20th century. A series of tax agreements from 1947 to 1980 not only stopped those wars, but centralized taxation much more than in most federations. Although there has been much fiscal decentralization during the last decade, none of it has affected taxation, and taxes remain as centralized as they were twenty years ago.

The constitution does not say much about taxes, only that taxes and fees on natural resources (including oil) are exclusively for the federal government. The law of the *Sistema Nacional de Coordinación Fiscal* (SNCF) was set largely in its present form in 1980 and allocates most of the taxes. Income taxes, excise taxes, and the VAT are exclusively federal, although an agreement delegated to the states the enforcement powers (*fiscalización*) for the VAT and the right to keep the fines they collect. Two other federal taxes, the sales tax for new cars (ISAN) and the annual registration fee (*tenencia*) for cars less than 10 years old are "shared" 100 percent with the states, effectively giving them the right to collect and enforce the taxes. Since they are federal taxes, however, people can pay them in any state they choose, based on convenience, irrespective of location of residence. While the federal government sets the rate of the ISAN, the states treat the *tenencia* as their own tax and set the rate accordingly.

The main source of state revenue for most states is the payroll tax. Most states charge one or two percent (one state charges four percent). States depend on federal transfers for 85 to 95 percent of their revenue. Municipalities depend almost as heavily on transfers. Their main source of own municipal revenue is the property tax (*predial*). They also collect various fees, the most important of which is for water, although this could be counted as a revenue of the water companies.[9]

The centralization of Mexican taxes, as culminated in the SNCF described above, represented a bargain in which the states and municipalities gained a share of 20 percent in most federal revenues—oil royalties, income tax, and VAT, but not import duties. This amounts to almost half of the federal transfers received by states, and these transfers (*participaciones*) are administered by the *Subsecretario de Ingresos* (in SHCP). Most of the rest of federal transfers are earmarked for sectors and not linked to taxes, and the *Subsecretario of Inegresos* administers them, in conjunction with the sectoral ministries.

The allocation of *participaciones* between the states initially followed the distribution of tax revenues that the states relinquished under the 1980 *Pacto Fiscal*, but has become somewhat more progressive. The allocation formula since 1994 distributes 45 percent of the *participaciones* according to the previous year allocation and adjusts it to reward relatively strong tax collection by the state also in the previous year. This encourages states (although not very strongly) to administer taxes better and to foster economic development that expands the tax base. Another 45 percent of the *participaciones* is distributed according to population numbers (the progressive part). The rest is distributed by the inverse of the two other criteria, effectively giving more aid to small poor states.

Of the *participaciones* that come to the state, 20 percent are automatically passed on to the municipalities by a federally determined formula. This formula is very similar to the federal formula for distribution among states, except that 40 percent is linked to the revenue collection in the municipality, 40 percent is proportional to population, and 20 percent provides compensation (to small poor municipalities) that rate low on the other two criteria.

In the past, the federal government would also make extraordinary transfers to states and municipalities (until the late 1990s) or it would do federal investment projects with strongly local benefits. These were often large, larger than the subnational government's own revenue collection, and their allocation was highly political. Also borrowing was usually done with a federal guarantee, which might turn into a federal bailout and effectively a partial grant. So a mayor or governor in need of resources would often try to get more federal money or borrow from soft sources, rather than try to raise more taxes. Indeed the decision to raise local taxes seriously

---

9. The federal district, with some political autonomy since 1997 and with characteristics of both a state and a municipality, collects predial and payroll taxes, raising enough to pay for over half of its outlays. This is far more than other states and demonstrates the untapped potential for revenue raising in at least the more economically advanced states.

was often simultaneous with the decision to break with the party in office at the federal level (Magaloni, Diaz and Weingast 2000). In more recent years, however, the situation has changed dramatically and perhaps permanently. Discretionary federal transfers are no longer available. The allocation of federal investment is mostly disclosed, and is potentially susceptible to congressional oversight and eventually control. New financial regulations have eliminated the federal guarantee of state borrowing and made it harder for banks to lend to uncreditworthy states (Giugale and Webb 2000).

The recent federal government measures—especially ending extraordinary transfers and tightening the regulatory environment for subnational borrowing – give the states more incentive to collect taxes, because now each state's creditworthiness and access to capital depend significantly on raising its own revenue. These federal policies need to continue, but more is needed as well. States and municipalities need technical help to develop their ability to collect taxes, not only with training but also by accessing federal data bases, such as that of social security, which is one of the best.

A growing reaction to the new political and economic context is that many states, typically those with the strongest economic growth and increased need for public services, are demanding more authority to impose taxes. As the motivation and technical capacity of the states are reaching an adequate level, the federal government needs to devolve some tax bases to the states. Some excise taxes are one possibility. A larger step, eventually requiring a revision of the *Pacto Fiscal*, would be sharing a tax like the VAT between the federal and state levels. The sharing could go in stages: first, setting up the reporting and information system to know the location where value added occurs; second, giving the states a fixed percentage of the VAT generated in their state, like 3 percentage points of the 15 percent total rate (with 12 percent still going to the federal level); and third, going to a full piggy-backing where the states can set their own rate for sales within the state, but keeping a 3 percent rate on interstate sales to registered traders, refundable in the receiving state. For more details see McLure 2000 and Diaz and McLure 2000.

For those stages to be feasible, there would need to be some revision of the corresponding administration, making federal-state coordination even closer than at present. Furthermore, if the federal government would no longer put its VAT revenue (say, from the 12 percent federal rate, if 3 percent were given to the states) into the pool for *participaciones*, states with weak tax bases would lose to an unacceptable degree unless there were also a revision of the *participaciones* formula to compensate them. So renegotiating the transfer formulas would go hand-in-hand with renegotiating the allocation of tax bases. Designing such a revision will be technically and politically difficult, but possible (Courchene and Diaz 2000). The reallocation of taxing authority should improve efficiency and motivation for tax effort, generating an increase in total revenue, so that a compensation scheme could make all states and the federal government financially better off than before, even without raising rates.

IV. Administration, Collection and Enforcement

Tax administration is the weakest link between the often sophisticated objectives of Mexican tax policy and the actual tax revenue collected (Gil Diaz 1995). For instance, Mexico collects about 30 percent of potential VAT revenue, compared with about 40 percent in Colombia and Argentina and 50 percent in Chile and Spain (Casanegra, and others 1997). While the VAT is perhaps the most serious area of evasion, the income taxes also fall far short of their potential; total revenues (PIT and CIT) are only 7 percent of corporate profits and less than 5 percent of total wages, salaries and profits. (INEGI and World Bank staff calculations). Existing evidence indicates five key problems: a) evasion is too easy—rarely discovered and even more rarely punished; b) the payment process, even by those willing to pay, is too difficult; c) the tax code is too complex; d) the application of the code by those who administer it is inconsistent across taxpayers and across time; and e) the system collects insufficient information and fails to use it well.

Evasion is the biggest problem with taxes in Mexico, because there is too little effort to stop it. Not enough resources go to enforcement, particularly catching people and firms that have not filed or have not reported all their sales (VAT) or income. Of all the audit actions, only 30 percent lead to increased payment, compared with about 75 in other similar countries, and the most effective type of audit, home visits, are extremely rare, about 0.2 percent of taxpayers (Casanegra and others. 1997, pp. 2, 7). Human and technical resources should thus be shifted from collection to enforcement and be given training in methods of data gathering and investigation. If necessary, more tax auditors should be hired. Furthermore, sanctions are rarely imposed. The government perhaps should eventually stiffen sanctions, but the first priority is to apply strictly the ones existing, even against those with political connections.

While not paying taxes in Mexico is too easy, actually paying them is still too difficult. A well-functioning tax system requires that most people comply voluntarily with it, but in Mexico the payer often finds it difficult to file in a way that meets the rules. The introduction of the Tax Administration Service (SAT) in the late 1990s has brought some improvements, but still not achieved an institutional culture with the objective of customer service. Efforts to make sure that the filed returns are correct and acceptable have too often gone to the extreme of being a barrier to payment. Setting standards for prompt and helpful customer service, and training employees to meet these objectives, is an obvious priority. Establishing a voluntary compliance program, where returns are automatically accepted and then spot checked on a random basis, is another one. Both steps should be complemented by the expansion of the programs of payment at banks and filing and paying by computer.

The complexity of the tax code contributes to the problems with compliance and enforcement. Officials and honest tax payers are often equally unsure of what is required. Evaders take advantage of ambiguities and contradictions to reduce their payment and avoid prosecution. During the 1990s, parts of the tax code originally designed to simplify collection for particular classes of taxpayers became, in practice, open-ended legal constructions that year-after-year have increased the difficulties of tax administration. The code lends itself to tax planning combinations that allow real profits to be transferred to companies eligible for the special regimes. For example, the increase in the allowance for conglomerates to consolidate tax liabilities has also increased the possibilities of tax avoidance through a) using standard consolidation provisions to buy up loss-making enterprises for the sole purpose of reducing or eliminating taxable profits, and b) combining the benefits of consolidation with those of double-tax treaties to reduce tax liability. For example, in 1991 the special cash-flow taxation in the agricultural and transport sectors replaced the previous presumptive taxation, as a way to bring small traders into the tax net. Both presumptive and cash flow taxation have their particular disadvantages, and both enable taxpayers who are subject also to the general regime to arrange their affairs to reduce or eliminate their taxes. Such difficulties indicate that the overall simplification of the tax code, as described in the previous section, especially the elimination of privileges, is critical to improve the quality of tax administration in Mexico.

In terms of consistency of application, Mexico exemplifies to an extreme the adage that "tax administration is tax policy" (Bird and Casanegra 1992). Bureaucrats in the tax administration, even some lower level staff, often have absolute discretion to interpret the law and regulations, thereby determining the effective tax rate and base. The situation encourages corruption among officials under the pretext of misinterpretation. It also has rendered both tax inspectors and taxpayers unsure of what is the proper amount of tax payable. When administration is delegated to the states, as with car taxes and the VAT enforcement, the problem becomes even worse. It is thus imperative to publish national standards for tax implementation and train tax administrators to follow those standards. To assure that tax administration meets national standards, most OECD countries have an independent tribunal to which taxpayers can appeal, and Mexico should follow this example. The independent tribunal generally does not include the tax authorities but rather is composed of professionals with tax expertise—accountants, lawyers, judges, and the like—appointed by the government.

Finally, Mexico's tax administration lacks adequate information and does not use well what it has. Enforcement is weak in part because it does not seek and use information beyond what the filer submits for the tax in question. There is not a unified system of taxpayer numbers, and tax filers are not required to report the tax identification numbers for all persons and firms involved (workers, suppliers, and business customers). Indeed, information reporting requirements were reduced in the 1990s. The electronic data management systems are not all compatible, even within SAT, or capable of sharing data. Tax authorities should therefore increase data-reporting requirements for major transactions, including the identification numbers of all taxpayers whom they pay or by whom they are paid. The computer systems should be fixed to enable efficient sharing of information, including between authorities at different levels. Serious enforcement must use information that is available from other taxes and fees; for example, data from the VAT and automobile registration (*tenencia*) could indicate unreported corporate and personal income; and data from personal and corporate income could reveal property for which no property tax was being paid.

V. Tax Reform Implementation Strategy

The previous sections have identified reforms needed in both the tax regime and its administration. Proper grouping and sequencing will let the reforms work better technically and will make them more feasible politically. A strategic plan for Mexico's tax reform would have three parts.

1. *Improve the tax law* by reducing or eliminating tax expenditures and improving the methods of taxing petroleum and other excises. As in many other countries, but perhaps of more than usual importance in Mexico, taxation is a game of opening, closing and recreating loopholes. Entrenched political forces have, with a few short interruptions, perpetuated many privileges that reflect the structure of power in Mexico. While there might be some chance to close the loopholes piecemeal—overcoming the interest group benefiting from each loophole– special interest groups work best in obscurity, motivated strongly by their narrow interest while the rest of the electorate finds each issue too small to notice. International experience indicates that a comprehensive plan usually has more success—putting together a consensus among most major interests that they will all accept an end to their special treatment. After the general reform, special exemptions may gradually emerge again, but the reversal is rarely total and does not negate the value of the improvement for at least a few years.

2. *Improve administration and reduce evasion* by making compliance easier for those who are paying and making enforcement more thorough for those who are not. This will require better information systems, collecting more information on each payer and potential payer, and linking the information from different tax bases and other sources. It will also require more autonomy and better incentives and working conditions for the tax agency and its staff. An independent tax tribunal to handle appeals should monitor the decisions of the tax agency and ensure the substance and appearance of fairness. Political impetus must come from the top. Some powerful people will have to pay more, and suffer penalties if they do not. If this does not happen, and does not happen visibly, no one will take tax reform seriously. Mexico had a period of more serious enforcement in the early 1990s, showing that it can be done. Making compliance easier and making enforcement more forceful will reinforce each other, and can even lead to a virtuous cycle if social norms change and people who pay exert political pressure to make others pay as well.

3. *Improve the tax effort and authority of sub-national governments.* The last decade has witnessed rapid decentralization of spending authority and transfer of resources from the center. The federal government has little legal authority to monitor the use of these resources or to control directly the amount the states borrow with transfers as collateral. So there are limited opportunities for the federal government to exercise the role of principal over the states as agents, as in a German-type system. The taxpayer-citizens are the other potential principal over the states as agents, and they will only come into this role seriously if the states are allowed to tax more and have to do so in order to fund their programs. In other words, sub-national taxation will strengthen sub-national democracy and accountability.

Some progress is possible immediately in all three areas, but full results in each of them will come sequentially. Improving the tax code first is essential to make substantial progress with compliance and enforcement. Improving policy and administration at the national level will be necessary before substantial devolution of taxes to the sub-national governments can take root, because the most promising ways of devolution would be to share the VAT, PIT, or excises with the states, and eventually to let the states choose what rate they would piggy-back onto the federal tax. This would work only if the corresponding federal tax is working well.

References

Bird, Richard and Milka Casanegra. 1992. *Improving Tax Administration in Developing Countries*, International Monetary Fund. Washington, D.C.

Carey, D., K. Gordon, and P. Thalmann. 1999. "Tax Reform in Switzerland," OECD Economic Department Working Papers, No. 222, pp. 55.

Casanegra de Jantscher, Milka, Paulo dos Santos, Julio Escolano and Patricio Castro. 1997. "Mexico: Fortalecimiento de la Administración Tributaria Federal." Fiscal Affairs Department, International Monetary Fund. Washington, D.C.

Casanegra de Jantscher, Milka, Anthony Pellechio, Julio Escolano, and Paul Bernd Spahn. 1995. *Mexico: Strengthening the Fiscal System for Growth and Stability*, Fiscal Affairs Department, International Monetary Fund. Washington, D.C.

Dalsgaard T. and M. Kawagoe. 2000. "The Tax System in Japan: A Need for Comprehensive Reform," OECD Economic Department Working Papers, No. 231, pp. 87.

Diaz-Cayeros, Alberto and Thomas Courchene. 2000. "Transfers and the Nature of the Mexican Federation," in Giugale and Webb, eds. (see below).

Diaz-Cayeros, Alberto; Beatriz Magaloni and Barry R. Weingast. 2000. "Democratization and the Economy in Mexico: Equilibrium (PRI) Hegemony and its Demise." Stanford University, Processed.

Diaz-Cayerosos, Alberto and Charles McLure, Jr. 2000. "Tax Assignment," in Giugale and Webb, eds. (see below).

Gil Diaz, Francisco. 1995. "Fiscal policy and Tax Administration: The Experience of Mexico," in Tax Administration Reform in Latin America, Inter-American Development Bank, Washington D.C.

Gil Diaz, Francisco and Wayne Thirsk. 1997. "Mexico's Protracted Tax Reform," in Tax Reform in Developing Countries, World Bank, Regions and Sectoral Studies.

Giugale, Marcelo and Steven Webb, eds. 2000. *Achievements and Challenges of Fiscal Decentralization, Lessons from Mexico.* World Bank, Washington, D.C.

INEGI, Instituto Nacional de Estadística, Geográfia, e Informática.

McLure, Charles E., Jr. 2000. "Implementing Subnational Value Added Taxes on Internal Trade: The Compensating VAT (CVAT)," *International Tax and Public Finance* Vol. 7, No. 6 (December): 723–40.

OECD. 1999. *Economic Survey of Mexico*, OECD, Paris.

Varsano, Ricardo. 2000. "Subnational Taxation and the Treatment of Interstate Trade in Brazil: Problems and a Proposed Solution," in Burki and Perry, et al, ed., *Decentralization and Accountability of the Public Sector*, Proceeding of the Annual World Bank Conference on Development in Latin America and the Caribbean 1999. World Bank, Washington, D.C.

World Bank. 1989. *Mexico: Tax Reform for Efficient Growth*, Volume I—Main Report Report No. 8097-ME (November), Washington D.C.

9

Public Debt Management
Stocktaking and Challenges Ahead

This Chapter was written by Joost Draisma and Mariana Urbiola.

I. Introduction

Public debt management has important implications for public finances and macro-economic development in general because the government is often the largest borrower in the economy. In the past rapidly increasing public debt service payments and refinancing requirements contributed to severe financial and economic crises in Mexico. In particular, the experience during the last crisis (1994–95) demonstrated the need for a balanced time profile of amortization. Other important elements identified in a public debt management strategy are the borrowing costs, the development of a domestic capital market and the country's access to international markets. Minimization of long-term borrowing cost is normally the main objective of a public debt management strategy. Fluid access to a broad domestic and international investor base and limiting vulnerability to economic shocks can contribute significantly to this main objective.

The cost of public sector debt servicing largely depends on variables that determine the public debt dynamics, such as fiscal policy and in particular the size of the primary surplus, the amount of outstanding debt, inflation, and economic growth. Though such variables are not completely independent from public debt management, the discussion in this paper will focus on specific debt management issues such as the average maturity and duration of debt; the amortization profile of long-term debt and the use of short-term debt in financing longer-term obligations; the currency denomination of debt, including the choice between foreign versus domestic debt; and the characteristics of the interest rate (fixed, floating, or indexed bonds). This discussion will mainly focus on domestic debt management because of the rapid increase over the past few years of the domestic debt stock and the need to replace or refinance the existing *Instituto de Protección al Ahorro*

Bancario (IPAB) and *Fideicomiso de Apoyo para el Rescate de Autopistas Concesionadas* (FARAC)[1] liabilities.

In order to contribute to an informed discussion on policy options regarding public debt management, this paper will begin by identifying the main characteristics of the stock of outstanding public debt in Mexico. This requires, first of all, a clear definition of the public sector. We will concentrate on the finances, debt, and debt management of the nonfinancial public sector, that is, the federal government and the state-owned enterprises (SOEs) under budgetary control. This definition leaves out the financial public sector, that is, the central bank, development banks, and public sector trust funds, and state and municipal governments. An exception to this basic definition involves two large public sector trust funds, IPAB and FARAC, which are included in a separate analysis due to the widely recognized and significant negative net worth of both trusts and to the special nature of the management of their liabilities, in close coordination with the fiscal and monetary authorities. This definition of the public sector has been chosen for both practical reasons, that is, the availability of information, and conceptual reasons because an integrated public debt management strategy is most likely to be focused on this part of the public sector.

To provide an idea of the size of the issues at stake, the first part of this paper will examine the evolution of the public debt stock, and its composition and management over the past few years. It will rapidly assess the debt liabilities of the nonfinancial public sector, IPAB, and, FARAC; and will review the liabilities contracted largely by state-owned enterprises, such as PEMEX and CFE, to finance their investment programs, the *Proyectos de Impacto Diferido en el Registro del Gasto* (PIDIREGAS). These liabilities are not included in the public debt definition and one generally arranged and agreed to from the beginning of the investment project. Nevertheless, after several years of financing part of the public investments through the modality of PIDIREGAS, the servicing burden is becoming noticeable in public finances and a quick review of the amounts involved is thus warranted. This initial assessment of the size of the public debt issue in Mexico will be concluded with some consideration concerning other public sector liabilities, including contingent liabilities, and the impact these may have on public debt management.

The second part of this paper deals with the possibilities and advantages of the use of inflation-indexed instruments in the management of domestic public debt. The use of additional domestic debt instruments, including the longer maturity and inflation-indexed instruments, is advocated in this paper for both theoretical and practical reasons. The latter is largely due to the substantial increase in the stock of domestic debt after including IPAB and FARAC liabilities, and to the refinancing

---

1. IPAB is the bank deposit insurance agency that inherited a large stock of liabilities from the bailout following the 1995 banking crisis. FARAC is a trust fund through which the public sector has taken over assets and liabilities of illiquid or insolvent private toll road operating companies.

requirements of these liabilities. In particular, it is argued that both the pace and characteristics of the IPAB bonds being issued at present provide IPAB with insufficient resources to start replacing existing liabilities within a reasonable timeframe. The main conclusions are presented in the final section.

II. Public Debt Management: Recent Experience in Mexico

Nonfinancial Public Sector

Although much information on public debt in Mexico is available from different sources, important discrepancies between similar concepts occur, mainly due to differences in coverage of the public sector definition. In this first section, we will review debt figures for the nonfinancial public sector, that is, the federal government and the SOEs under budgetary control, on the basis of information that is sent on a quarterly basis to Congress by SHCP. External debt included in these periodic reports is comprised of external debt contracted or used[2] by the federal government, the SOEs, and development banks, whereas domestic debt refers only to debt contracted by the federal government. External debt reported in the next section refers to the gross external debt used by the federal government and the SOEs under budget control, whereas the domestic debt refers to gross debt payable in local currency contracted by the federal government. The domestic debt definition thus excludes domestic debt contracted by SOEs because no consistent data set is available on such debt.[3]

A few quick observations can be made from the evolution of the ratio of total public debt to GDP over the past decade (Figure 1, next page) and from the breakdown of external and domestic debt-to-GDP respectively.[4] The huge fluctuation of the total ratio of debt to GDP is due partly to a similar fluctuation in the ratio of external debt to GDP, which in turn can be attributed largely to the fluctuation observed in the real exchange rate (Figure 2). Another stylized fact that can be

2. The difference between the entity that contracts and the final user of external credit mainly refers to the role of financial agent that development banks have in the contracting of debt with multilateral agencies such as the World Bank and the Inter-American Development Bank. As the terms of these loans are directly passed on to the federal government (i.e., including the exchange rate risk) the data reported under final user of the credit is taken here. This allows to exclude the external debt contracted by development banks for their own business purposes as development banks are not included under the nonfinancial public sector definition.
3. Data from the annual *Cuenta Pública* de Hacienda indicates that domestic debt contracted by SOEs is a minor amount.
4. Debt to GDP ratios presented here refer to the year-end stock of debt divided by the annual GDP figure for the year and differs from e.g. SHCP data in the *Cuenta Pública* that reports the year-end stock of debt divided by the annualized fourth quarter GDP figure.

observed is the preponderance of external debt in the total public debt. Finally, although slightly more difficult to deduce from Figure 1 alone, the analysis supports the notion of a strategy during the first half of the decade to significantly reduce the (relative) amount of domestic debt, in contrast to the second half of the decade (or

Figure 1. Total, Domestic and External Public Debt, 1989–99
(as a percentage of GDP)

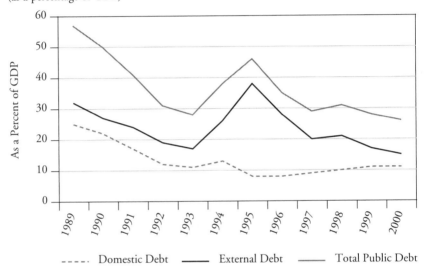

Figure 2. Real Exchange Rate, 1989–99
(Base 1990=100)

at least as of 1996) during which external debt was gradually replaced by domestic debt.

To present a broad idea of the issues related to external debt management of the nonfinancial public sector, it is useful to have an idea of both the main sources of finance composing this debt, and the related maturity. Although this paper focuses largely on domestic debt management issues, a short summary of the composition of external debt is provided to help put those issues into the perspective of overall public debt management. By the end of 1999 the stock of nonfinancial public sector external debt amounted to US$84 billion. A major increase in this stock was observed in 1995 when the refinancing took place of the *Tesobonos*, domestic dollar-indexed debt, initially with U.S. treasury assistance and subsequently with private sources of external finance. Thus the stock of the nonfinancial public sector external debt increased from around US$70 billion during the first half of the 1990s to about US$85 billion during the second half of the decade.

Types of Debt

The stock of external debt can largely be divided into three main types: debt under the 1989–90 commercial bank debt restructuring, now largely denominated in Brady bonds; debt contracted with multilateral organizations such as the World Bank and the Inter-American Development Bank; and debt contracted with private market parties largely through the issuance of bonds on the international capital markets. Differences among these groups are mainly related to the average maturity of each of the groups and the ease with which the debt can be refinanced, particularly under adverse international capital market conditions.

By the end of 1999, restructured debt made up US$30 billion or 35 percent of the total gross external debt stock, with a remaining average maturity of almost 16 years because this debt is composed mainly of Brady bonds (US$23.5 billion) that mature by the end of 2019. Refinancing of this part of the public debt is not an issue, and is done only when favorable international capital market conditions exist to replace Brady bonds with other (cheaper) bonds, liberating the collateral obligations attached to the Brady bonds and by making a capital gain on both the principal and interest component of the collateral effectively reducing the stock of external debt. Debt contracted with multilateral institutions[5] amounts to US$16 billion, or some 19 percent of the total external debt stock. This debt has an average remaining maturity of slightly over five years. Refinancing of these obligations with the same multilateral organizations has been largely possible throughout the 1990s and as a result the stock of debt has stabilized. These refinancing possibilities largely depend on the degree to which agreement on public policies and public investment programs can be reached, and the extent to which the international community wants to maintain use of these institutions as a vehicle to support public policies in middle-income coun-

---

5. Money borrowed from the IMF is channeled to the *Banco de México*, which is not included in the definition of the nonfinancial public sector.

tries. New loans from these institutions typically have an average maturity of 10 to 11 years, and recently a large variety of loans available (repayment schedule, currency choice, and fixed or variable interest rates) have been introduced.

The remaining US$38 billion, or 46 percent of the total external debt stock, is contracted on the international capital markets through bonds and direct loans from commercial banks and others. Refinancing activities are largely concentrated on this part of the total public debt because maturity tends to be shorter, and refinancing conditions largely depend on the conditions prevailing in the international capital markets. Although the average maturity of this kind of debt is approximately six years, a differentiation between a few long-term bonds and the majority of debt contracted in this category shows that the major part, US$33 billion, has an average maturity of four years, whereas a few long-term bonds, amounting to US$5 billion, have a maturity of over 15 years. A careful scheduling of maturities of this part of the external debt stock has reduced the annual amount coming due to only US$ 3–4.5 billion over the next few years.

Debt Maturities

Among the major differences between domestic and external debt, apart from the currency in which each is denominated or payable, is the average maturity of the debt. In the case of Mexico, domestic debt has a much shorter average maturity, requiring much more frequent refinancing through weekly auctions. Even though an important lengthening of the average maturity of domestic debt can be observed over the past few years (Figure 3, next page), the average maturity of the domestic debt is 1.5 years, still far below the average maturity of the external debt described above. Average maturity issues are of importance largely due to the refinancing risk; that is, the risk that market conditions do not allow for refinancing at a reasonable cost.

The substantially shorter average maturity of domestic debt is closely correlated with the risk of domestic currency losing its value; that is, the risk of an unanticipated variation in domestic inflation and, related to this, an unanticipated variation of interest and exchange rates. Increasing the average maturity of domestic debt can thus be obtained only within a more stable macroeconomic environment; that is, a lower risk of unanticipated change in inflation, or through an enhancement of the domestic debt instrument covering the inflation, interest, or exchange rate risk. With the exception of the *Cetes* and *Bonos,* all the other domestic debt instruments available do exactly that. In the case of *Ajusta* and *Udibonos,* the principal is indexed to domestic price inflation, whereas in the case of the *Tesobonos* (used between 1991 and 1995), the principal is indexed to the peso/dollar exchange rate. *Bondes* are variable interest rate instruments, where the interest rate is adjusted every month *(Bondes28),* three months *(Bondes91)* or six months *(Bondes182)* according to the prevailing *Cetes* rate of the corresponding tenor. It has been through the increased use of *Bondes* in particular (Figure 4) that, in addition to an overall more stable macroeconomic environment, has allowed the average maturity of domestic debt to substantially lengthen over the past few years.

Figure 3. Average Maturity, Domestic Public Debt
(in number of days)

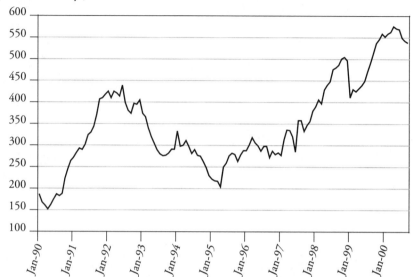

Source: Banco de México.

Figure 4. Composition of Domestic Public Debt Instruments

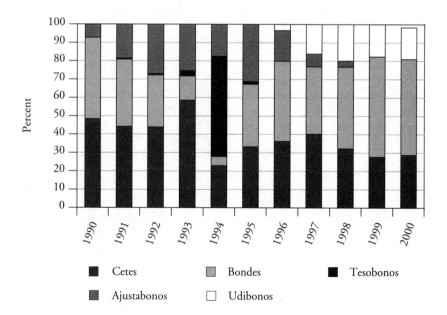

Average maturity provides an indication of how quickly the public debt stock must be refinanced, allowing for newly prevailing market conditions to be reflected in the contractual arrangements, with the risk that market conditions might not allow for an adequate amount of finance available (at a reasonable cost) to rollover the debt stock. Financial duration of debt, an adjusted debt maturity measure, can be used to provide an indication of how quick changes in market conditions have an impact on the cost of public debt, and thus provides an indication on how vulnerable public finances are to a sudden hike in interest rates. After remaining at about 86 days between September 1999 and January 2000, the financial duration of Mexican public debt started to increase, and reached a level of 97 days in March 2000. This implies that a sudden hike in interest rates due to a sudden increase in perceived country risk (for example, contagion from other emerging markets, such as from Russia in August 1998) is, within 90 days, almost fully reflected in the cost of domestic debt servicing.

The introduction of longer-term fixed (nominal) interest bonds (a three-year *Bono* was issued in January 2000, and a five-year *Bono* was issued in May) substantially increases both maturity and duration of the public debt. In addition, important capital market development objectives of extending the yield curve for peso-denominated nominal interest securities are being addressed with these innovations. Every developed debt market is characterized by the government issuance of medium (one to ten years) and long term (ten to thirty years) nominal fixed-rate securities. Without the existence of a well developed and liquid yield curve in this range, a market for corporate bonds and for derivatives cannot develop. In contrast, the successful issuance of a large enough stock of medium and longer-term nominal fixed-rate government bonds can spur the growth of these markets, which in turn deepens the market for government securities in what may become a virtuous circle of financial development.

Government securities are normally issued through weekly auctions held by the *Banco de México*. Since late 1997, quarterly "standard auction" programs with the (minimum) volume of each type of securities to be offered each week, have been announced by SHCP. Initially the intention was to announce semiannual programs, but the volatility experienced in August 1998 forced the authorities to fall back to a quarterly program. The formal announcement of an auction program is generally appreciated by investors because it provides information and some certainty on the future supply of different securities.

It can be observed from the structure of the quarterly auction program (Annex 1) that, in response to the August 1998 volatility, the authorities increased the issue of short-term *Cetes* and of the variable interest *Bonde* instrument. The introduction of a nine-month and a two-year *Bonde* with interest rate adjustment taking place every 28 days (instead of the normal 91 days) helped maintain the maturity structure of government debt. As of the first quarter of 2000, the authorities drastically diminished the amount of *Bondes* issued by SHCP in order to allow IPAB to place *its Bonos de Protección al Ahorro* (BPAs), which have characteristics similar to *Bondes* (see next section). In this regard there may be a problem of too many and too frequent issues, to the detriment of the liquidity of outstanding securities. This has been partly addressed by issuing some type of securities only once every two weeks *(Cetes182)*, once every month *(Cetes364)*, and the newly introduced three and five-year bonds), or once every six weeks (five-year UDI bonds), but more importantly by tapping the same issue more than once as well as the careful matching of maturity dates of newly issued shorter term paper with those of existing, longer term issues.[6] To enhance liquidity in the secondary market for government fixed-rate securities further, market makers were introduced as of October 2000 and which will have to be reappointed every six months based on the activity of each intermediary in the primary and secondary markets. These market makers have the obligation to quote prices both ways on fixed-rate government securities along the curve thereby providing the liquidity paramount to the development of the domestic market.

III. Instituto de Protección al Ahorro Bancario (IPAB)

The systemic solvency and liquidity crisis faced by the Mexican banking system after the 1994–95 financial crisis, and the implicit guarantee provided by the government on all bank liabilities at the time, prompted the government to implement a number of support measures aimed at helping banks, bank debtors, and depositors over the past five years, initially through the then-existing banking deposit insurance agency, FOBAPROA, and subsequently through IPAB, an institution created as a result of the new banking legislation adopted in December 1998. Liabilities passed on from FOBAPROA to IPAB, and those acquired in the meantime by IPAB to complete the full resolution of the problems of the Mexican banking system, are estimated at a total of MXP$722 billion by the end of December 1999 (equivalent to US$76 billion and 15.7 percent of GDP). These liabilities are not included in the figures presented earlier on debt of the nonfinancial public sector. Management and refinancing of these liabilities, although coordinated with SHCP and *Banco de México*, is handled by IPAB.

Given the substantial negative net worth that IPAB represents, which will have to be serviced mainly out of fiscal transfers, and the close coordination between IPAB and SHCP required in the management and refinancing of these liabilities, it would make sense to include IPAB liabilities in the country's public debt

---

6. Even though the quarterly auction program establishes e.g. the issue of a 182-day Cete every two weeks, after an initial auction of a 182-day Cete the auction two weeks later includes a 168-day Cete thereby matching up with the maturity date of the first issue. In addition, the maturity date of these two issues is likely to be the same as that of a 364-day Cete issued 182 days before the first referred 182-day Cete auction thereby increasing the amount of similar paper further. A similar strategy is applied for other longer term issues.

figures.[7] Including IPAB liabilities in public debt figures would notably increase the overall ratio of public debt to GDP for 1999 from 28.3 percent to 44 percent. Though still below the ratio of debt to GDP observed in numerous OECD countries (as, for example, evidenced by the target ratio for countries belonging to the Euro zone, set at a maximum of 60 percent), a ratio of public debt-to-GDP for Mexico of 44 percent can be considered high, particularly because of the relatively small size of the public sector in the economy.

Another impact of including IPAB liabilities in total public debt figures is a shift in the composition of the public debt. In the past public debt consisted of about 65 percent external debt and 35 percent domestic debt (Figure 1). Including IPAB liabilities, which are almost all in domestic currency, would invert these ratios, with 40 percent of total debt contracted abroad or in foreign currency, and 60 percent contracted domestically. A larger participation of domestic debt in total public debt may be desirable because it reduces vulnerability to external shocks and may be supportive of domestic capital market development. However, the often observed higher cost of domestic debt due to exchange rate and inflation risks may be an important drawback of such a rapid change in the composition of public debt. Therefore, all public debt including IPAB liabilities, should be taken into account when considering the issue of an optimal or desirable currency composition of public debt.

Refinancing Issues

By far the most important policy issue related to IPAB liabilities is the refinancing of these obligations. The nature of government interventions in the banking system over the past five years has led to different types of liabilities; that is, liabilities with different maturities, interest rates, and interest payment structures. IPAB has estimated that average interest cost of its liabilities is approximately 120 basis points above the cost of federal government domestic debt. An important part of the liabilities—the notes for the capitalization and loan purchase programs and part of the notes for the financial rehabilitation program—has been contracted at a ten-year bullet maturity, with a full capitalization of the interest obligation also payable in full at maturity. These notes were contracted between 1995 and 1997, with the result that the principal and accrued interest of these liabilities will be due between 2005 and 2007. As this group of liabilities is the one with the longest maturity of all current IPAB debt, refinancing of the total IPAB debt stock between now and the

---

7. Similarly, it can be argued that debt servicing obligations, and in particular interest obligations (payments and accruals), should be included in public finance statistics and the public deficit calculation, thereby substantially raising the posted fiscal deficit. The difference between an augmented fiscal deficit calculated by the IMF for 1999 of 4.8 percent of GDP, compared to the posted fiscal deficit of 1.1 percent, is due largely to the estimated net cost of IPAB and debtor support programs. The posted fiscal deficit measure only includes the annual budget transfers made by the federal government to these programs, whereas the augmented fiscal deficit includes the full nominal interest accrued on IPAB liabilities.

end of 2007 must be arranged. In addition, nontradable IPAB bonds issued make up an important share of the balance sheet of the banking system, and in particular of some individual banks, which would impair their ability to extend more profitable credit to the private sector whenever the demand for bank credit resumes. Refinancing these bonds with tradable instruments would thus allow banks to free some of their assets and increase lending to the private sector.

Since March 2000, IPAB has issued bonds through a program of weekly auctions on the domestic debt market. *Banco de México* acts as financial agent for the IPAB bonds, the BPAs. The BPAs count both with a sovereign guarantee and an alternative payment mechanism, allowing *Banco de México* to automatically charge the Treasury account in case of default by IPAB. Due to these features, the price of the BPAs issued thus far is practically the same as the price of similar federal government bonds. BPAs issued in March have three-year maturities, paying a monthly nominal interest rate which is adjusted according to the prevailing 28-day *Cete* rate. The initial issue involved MXP$1 billion. Subsequently, weekly issues of up to MXP$2 billion have been held. IPAB has announced its intention to issue between MXP$60 and 80 billion this year. In August, IPAB started issuing BPAs with a tenor of five years in an effort to increase the average life of the marketable securities outstanding. It is also planning to start issuing BPAs with quarterly adjustment of interest rates, thereby increasing the financial duration.

A simple debt accounting framework shows that the combination of characteristics of the BPAs and the pace at which they are being issued is far from sufficient to refinance the stock of IPAB liabilities within the required timeframe, that is, before 2007. Under reasonable assumptions regarding fiscal transfers to IPAB, deposit insurance fees, asset recovery, real GDP growth, real interest rates, and inflation, it can be shown that on the basis of an gross annual issue of three-year variable nominal interest-paying BPAs of 1.8 percent of nominal GDP, (that is, the same as the present program of MXP$80 billion over the March to December 2000 period), BPAs would make up only 44 percent of the total IPAB debt stock by 2007 (Annex 2).[8]

Using the same debt accounting framework and assumptions, it can be shown that in order to replace the full amount of existing IPAB liabilities by 2007, the gross issue of three-year nominal interest-paying BPAs should be more than double the present program, to an annual amount of approximately 3.8 percent of GDP. This would be equivalent to the March to December 2000 program of MXP$170 billion,

---

8. This calculation is based on an annual **gross** issue of BPAs equivalent to 1.8 percent of nominal GDP. The same debt accounting framework can be used to show that an annual **net** issue of BPAs of 1.8 percent of nominal GDP would be just enough to refinance all outstanding IPAB liabilities by 2007. A net instead of a gross issue of BPAs by this amount steeply increases the gross issue of BPAs as of 2003 when the first BPAs start to come due. The gross issue initially increases by some 60 percent in 2003 to more than 135 percent in 2007 and would amount more than 4.2 percent of GDP in 2007.

or a weekly issue during 2000 of MXP$3.9 billion. A more rapid build-up of BPAs can also be obtained by lengthening the maturity of the bonds issued, indexing the principal to inflation (that is, the use of UDI bonds by IPAB), and the issue of foreign currency denominated bonds (external debt). IPAB's recent policies aiming at extending average maturity by gradually introducing longer-dated securities (such as the five year BPA), and extending duration by introducing and relying more on securities that fix coupons every three and six months are both steps in the right direction.

A rapid build-up of a tradable IPAB bond stock to replace present IPAB liabilities has the additional advantage of reducing the interest cost of IPAB debt. This is because the present stock has an average interest cost of 120 basis points above the cost of federal government paper, whereas the tradable BPAs issued thus far have a cost similar to the one of federal government paper. In the debt accounting framework presented in Annex 2, this results in a more rapid reduction of the ratio of IPAB debt-to-GDP in the event of a more rapid build-up of BPAs given the same inflow of resources out of fiscal transfers, deposit insurance fees, and asset recovery.

The gradual reduction of the total ratio of IPAB debt to GDP projected in the accounting framework is the result of the inflow of resources from fiscal transfers, deposit insurance fees, and asset recovery sufficient to cover the real interest cost (that is, payments and accruals) of the IPAB debt stock each year. Even though the debt stock remains practically constant in real peso terms, real GDP growth leads to a reduction of the ratio of IPAB debt to GDP.

The strategy of replacing existing IPAB liabilities through the periodic auction of BPAs on the financial market is strongly preferable to one suggested earlier in which through direct negotiations with banks, the existing liabilities are changed for tradable long-term bonds (for example, 30-year UDI bonds). The present strategy adds to transparency and a market-determined price setting, and allows for adjustment of the weekly auction program to conditions in the domestic debt market.

IV. Fideicomiso de Apoyo para el Rescate de Autopistas Concesionadas (FARAC)

Severe liquidity and solvency problems faced by private toll road operating companies after the 1994–95 financial crisis led to a government rescue effort in August 1997 through a trust fund established within BANOBRAS called the *Fideicomiso de Apoyo para el Rescate de Autopistas Concesionadas* (FARAC). As a result of the rescue operation, the trust fund acquired both the assets (the toll roads and the income stream generated by the tolls levied) and the liabilities of the toll road operating companies. Part of the bank debt of the toll road operating companies had already been restructured into long-term UDI-denominated *Pagares* under the different debtors' support program in place before August 1997. As part of the August 1997 rescue operation the (non-UDI) bank debt capitalized the variable interest for three years. As this accrual period will be ending shortly (August 2000) and FARAC's cash flow estimates show a substantial deficit once nominal interest payments on its commercial bank debt will be made, a restructuring effort of FARAC's debt was initiated in November 1999.

FARAC's debt, as guaranteed by the federal government, amounted to MXP$91 billion at the end of 1999.[9] Of this debt, approximately MXP$38 billion is already denominated in long-term UDI-denominated debt. Of the remaining MXP$53 billion, MXP$15 billion held through intervened banks by NAFIN (acting as financial agent for the federal government) will be restructured in subordinated 30-year, zero-coupon, UDI-denominated debt. MXP$14 billion held by BANOBRAS will continue accrue interest and principal at the *Tasa de Interés Interbancaria de Equilibrio* (TIIE) rate until sufficient funds are available to start paying the accruals (in effect subordinated nominal peso-denominated debt). The remaining P$24 billion commercial bank debt is subject to be converted into 30-year UDI-denominated bonds to be issued by BANOBRAS/FARAC over the course of the next two years.

In November 1999, SHCP mandated BANOBRAS to issue through public auction up to 3.5 billion UDIs (MXP$9.6 billion) in 30-year UDI-denominated *Pagares de Indemnizacion Carretera* (PICs), with semiannual interest payments. Nine auctions (in December 1999, and January, February, March, April, May, July, August and September 2000) have raised MXP$7.3 billion.

FARAC has not received any direct fiscal transfers to service its debt, and the policy regarding FARAC envisions eventually servicing and amortizing its debt without budget transfers (referred to as "zero fiscal cost"). Even if the scenario under which this is possible materializes, the strategy involves indirect transfers through channeling part of toll revenues from other parts of the toll road network (for example, the Mexico City–Cuernavaca toll road) to FARAC, possibly deferring maintenance costs, and potentially a complete or partial write-off of the NAFIN and/or BANOBRAS credit. Management of FARAC debt may well be included in the overall public debt management strategy, and not just because of possible direct or indirect fiscal transfers required in the near future. FARAC liabilities are perceived by the market as public debt because of the sovereign guarantee, and the amount of 30-year UDI-denominated bonds to be issued by FARAC seems to be more than saturating that market segment, thereby inhibiting IPAB or the federal government itself from tapping this market. Maintaining both assets and liabilities of FARAC separate from the rest of the public sector accounts may, on the other hand, provide incentives for an adequate asset management focussed on minimizing the fiscal impact of the highway rescue program and more importantly the institutional framework for a direct application of toll road privatization proceeds to the reduction of public liabilities.

---

9. SHCP—*Informe de la Deuda Pública*, 4th quarter 1999.

V. Proyectos de Impacto Diferido en el Registro del Gasto (PIDIREGAS)

As of 1996 modifications to the expenditure and public debt laws allowed for private sector involvement in the execution and financing of highly productive public infrastructure projects under the modality of *Proyectos de Impacto Diferido en el Registro del Gasto* (PIDIREGAS). Part of the public investments in the petroleum and electricity sector have since been implemented through either of the two following schemes:

- Direct investment projects, which are built and financed by the private sector; upon completion ownership is transferred to the public sector in exchange for annuity payments that cover the debt-service cost.
- Conditional investment projects, which are built, financed, owned, and operated by the private sector; the government entity assumes the obligation to purchase the services provided by the project.

Even though the Congress authorizes new projects during the annual budget approval, the impact on the fiscal accounts is shown only when the investments come onstream and the annuities or service payments start to take place. The annuity's amortization component is recorded as public sector investment during the years in which the payments are made, whereas the interest component is recorded as interest expenditure. Services payments are recorded as operating costs at the time when received and paid.

By the end of 1999 the accumulated stock of public investment financed through PIDIREGAS amounted to some MXP\$125 billion (and was projected to increase to MXP\$221.9 billion by the end of 2000), 84 percent of which are of the direct investment type. The majority of private finance for these projects is obtained from external sources. As projects start to come onstream, rapidly increasing annuity payments are required over the next few years. Public debt statistics record only the amortization component of the annuity payment falling due each year, whereas it could be argued that the total direct investment liabilities should be recorded as public debt.

The rapidly increasing payment obligations coming due will clearly be an issue in fiscal management over the next few years, and the total liabilities contracted (both direct investment and service contract obligations entered into) should certainly be taken into account in a fiscal sustainability analysis because they commit part of future public sector revenue. However, the relationship to public debt management is less clear because financing terms have generally been agreed to from the beginning of the project, debt service payments are related to the revenue stream on a project by project basis, and no refinancing of amortization payments is normally envisioned.

VI. Other (Contingent) Liabilities

Other liabilities contingent on some event happening or not, such as pension obligations, are also quite relevant within the framework of a fiscal sustainability analysis, and are therefore relevant for investors to consider when determining the future payment and debt service capacity of the public sector. Only in determining such capacity is there a relation to public debt management because investors in public debt paper will do some analysis regarding payment capacity. However, because outlays on these other (contingent) liabilities are spread out over time, no immediate financing problem, and thus no public debt management issue, arises. For further analysis of the topic, see the separate chapter, Fiscal Sustainability.

VII. Indexation of Domestic Debt Instruments

Economists have long argued that inflation-indexed bonds could reduce government borrowing costs.[10] If the market overestimates future inflation, the government will reduce its borrowing costs by issuing inflation-indexed bonds rather than nominal bonds. Because the government is able to influence inflation through its policies, it may have better information about the future course of inflation, or perhaps has more faith in its commitment to contain it than the public does. The Fisher identity states that the nominal interest rate (i) is the sum of the real rate (r) plus the expected inflation (p_e):

$$i = r + p_e$$

If p_e, which is established in the market, is a biased estimate (too high) of actual future inflation (p^*), then the government would capture the difference $(p_e - p^*)$ by issuing inflation-indexed bonds.

For the debt manager, active management of the debt portfolio by switching between indexed and nominal bonds requires taking a (real) rate view against the market. Wins and losses depend on the ability to outforecast the market. Betting against the market on the future course of inflation implies that the decision to issue indexed bonds is not a long-term commitment. Such behavior may affect market liquidity and require a liquidity premium on indexed bonds. There is another scenario, however, in which indexed bonds may prove cost-effective, and that is where there is a welfare-improving net gain which warrants a long-term commitment to issue inflation-indexed bonds, as a result reducing the liquidity premium. Indexed bonds can be viewed as providing a form of insurance—purchasing power insurance—to investors. Insurance is an option on a contingent outcome, and cannot be worth less than zero. If investors are willing to pay for this insurance, then the issuer should be able to lower the cost of debt. Thus,

---

10. Important parts of this section are taken from Price (1997).

$$i = r + p_e + \delta$$

where a risk premium (δ), based on the variability of inflation, is included in the basic Fisher identity.

Investors are ultimately interested in the real return (r) on their investment. On nominal bonds they receive the nominal rate (i), and thus bear the risk of future inflation $(p_e + \delta)$. On indexed bonds, however, investors receive r with certainty, and the issuer bears the costs of the inflation components p_e and δ, rearranging terms in the above equation. With a straightforward reallocation of risk from one party to another, there is no net gain: government has reduced its borrowing costs by the amount of the risk premium, assuming its expectations of future inflation are correct on average, but has taken on the risk of inflation volatility. If governments are neutral to financial risk, perhaps because they have an infinite planning horizon, because of their size or because they exert some control over the inflation outcome, they may be able to internalize or simply ignore this risk. Borrowing costs would decline by the amount of the inflation risk premium, which has been absorbed by the government issuer. Ex ante cost-saving estimates from issuing inflation-indexed bonds are complicated by the fact that both p_e and δ are unobserved. However, higher inflation may be associated with greater variability in inflation, and therefore with a higher inflation risk premium.

Over the past few years both of the above arguments have been used in several OECD countries to start programs issuing inflation-indexed bonds. In the case of Mexico, an additional argument would be a more rapid replacement of existing, more expensive debt stock of both IPAB and FARAC (parts of which are contracted at above federal government going interest rates, such as TIIE). Because inflation-indexed bonds pay only the real interest rate, as opposed to the nominal interest rate of nonindexed bonds, the outflow of resources that require subsequent refinancing in the case of nonindexed bonds is larger. Clearly, market conditions determine the possibility of issuing inflation-indexed instruments and showed limitations recently as banks and mutual funds have been substituting their holdings of inflation-indexed for nonindexed bonds. The recent emphasis on the development of a market for medium term nominal fixed-rate securities provides another way to increase average maturity and financial duration of domestic public debt and has shown a much stronger secondary market liquidity, critical for the development of domestic debt markets. Careful management of the inflation indexed government debt market, however, is advised in order to maintain this, potential lower cost, type of instrument available in public debt management.

VIII. Absorptive Capacity of the Domestic Debt Market

One of the major challenges facing policymakers over the next few years in the area of public debt management is the refinancing of public debt. This challenge has become more important because, contrary to the past, the major part of the public debt stock is now contracted domestically, and has on average a shorter maturity than external debt. Furthermore, large parts of the domestic debt contracted by IPAB and FARAC through private placements mainly with the domestic banking system, will come due and will require refinancing over the next few years. Refinancing of the debt takes place largely through the issuance of bonds on the domestic money markets. Although some private placements with special segments of the Mexican capital and money market (such as pension funds and insurance companies) may take place, these closely reflect the prices and conditions of the periodic (weekly) auctions of government bonds.

The additional supply of government bonds on the domestic debt market due to the substantial refinancing requirements of IPAB and FARAC, could face a lack of demand due to the unavailability of funds either in specific targeted market segments, or on the domestic market in general (that is, there may be a lack of the availability of financial sector savings). In any case, the additional supply of bonds could drive the price of government bonds down (that is, driving the interest rate or yield up), with a rapid impact on the interest cost of the total domestic debt (due to its short duration), and crowd out credit to the private sector. A careful analysis of the different market segments (including a regularly updated and detailed flow-of-funds model of major market participants or sectors of the economy) is therefore warranted, with some flexibility to adjust the issue strategy according to prevailing market conditions. The present market segmentation on the supply of government bonds between the federal government, IPAB, and FARAC may well lead to a suboptimal issue strategy due mainly to inertia and the lack of flexibility on the part of the three public institutions to adjust in a timely manner to market developments. Consolidation of IPAB and FARAC debt with federal government debt would thus be advisable.

The strategy of IPAB to start issuing BPAs on a weekly basis to gradually refinance and replace existing liabilities is clearly preferable over an earlier suggested strategy of replacing the nontradable FOBAPROA bonds with tradable (30-year UDI) bonds on the basis of direct negotiations with bond-holding banks. In this strategy, the amount of BPAs issued weekly can be adjusted according to prevailing market conditions, and the stock of existing IPAB liabilities is replaced gradually. In the case of direct negotiations, replacement could take place much faster, but the risk exists that banks would like to trade new bonds without sufficient demand for the bonds from other market parties, leading to a sharp drop in prices of these new bonds (and government debt in general) on the secondary market.

At the most aggregate level, a basic flow-of-funds model could make use of the measure of total financial savings held in the domestic economy (that is, savings intermediated through the domestic financial system), such as the broadest definition of money, M4. Over the past decade, the ratio of M4 to GDP in Mexico has been between 40 and 50 percent, and tends to increase at times of (perceived) macroeconomic stability and lower levels of domestic inflation. At the end of 1999 the stock of M4 was MXP$2,239 billion, or 48.4 percent of GDP. The domestic debt stock including, IPAB and FARAC debt amounted to MXP$1,323 billion, or 28.6 percent of GDP, which means that 59 percent of total financial savings M4 was kept in domestic public debt. This historically high level of the ratio of domestic public debt to M4 is similar to the level observed at the end of the previous decade prior to the external debt restructuring, when the cut-off from external credit forced the public sector to finance itself on the domestic market. The level of this ratio observed in 1999 also stands in sharp contrast to the level of 23 percent observed in 1993.

A gradual reduction of this historically high ratio of domestic public debt to M4 should be a target of economic policy and public debt management to assure sufficient absorption capacity of domestic debt refinancing requirements in the near future. The ratio is reduced if the rate of growth of domestic public debt is lower than the rate of growth of M4, and the larger the difference between the two, the sooner the desired reduction of the ratio takes place. Domestic public debt growth depends on fiscal policy and the choice between external and domestic debt in public debt management. Using the constant public debt-to-GDP criterion as a minimum condition for fiscal sustainability, and considering no change in the domestic-versus-external debt composition of total public debt, domestic public debt would increase, at most, at the rate of growth of GDP. Under a stable macro economic environment, however, one would expect M4 to grow at a slightly higher rate than GDP. Other structural policies (for example, reform of the public sector pension system), could further contribute to this financial deepening (that is, an increase of the ratio of M4 to GDP), thereby increasing the pool of resources that can finance the public debt.

If domestic public debt increases at the same rate of growth as GDP, and M4 increases annually at a rate of 2 percentage points above the GDP growth rate, a reduction of the ratio of domestic public debt to M4 of only 6.6 percentage points, from 59 percent at present to 52 percent over a six-year period, is obtained. If, however, the domestic public debt maintains its present level in constant peso terms, GDP grows at an average rate of 5 percent per year, and M4 increases at a rate of 2 percentage points above the GDP growth rate, a reduction of the ratio of domestic public debt to M4 of 19.7 percentage points over a six-year period is obtained, resulting in a decline from the present 59 percent to slightly below 40 percent.

To enhance the absorption capacity of the domestic debt market for the refinancing requirements of the domestic public debt, it is important to obtain two things:

- A growth rate of domestic public debt below the GDP growth rate through fiscal discipline and possibly through a change in the domestic versus external debt composition of total public debt. In this regard, it should be noted that the strategy regarding the composition of public debt in domestic and external debt should be closely coordinated with monetary and exchange rate policies and the prevailing macroeconomic conditions of the country. At present, any additional inflow of resources due to the issuing of additional external public debt would automatically lead to an accumulation of international reserves forcing sterilization of the monetary impact of such reserve accumulation by the central bank (thereby completely off-setting the intended change in composition of the consolidated, i.e. including the central bank, public debt).

- A financial deepening of the economy that is, an increase of the ratio of M4 to GDP through macroeconomic stability and structural reforms that contribute to the channeling of savings through the domestic financial system.

IX. Conclusions

Over the next few years, the main challenge faced by public debt management in Mexico will be to refinance a large public debt stock. Over the past few years the total public debt stock increased substantially as a result of the systemic crisis experienced in the country's financial sector. As already mentioned, by the end of 1999, the debt stock of the nonfinancial public sector, IPAB and FARAC was MXP$2,123 billion, or 46 percent of GDP. This amount does not include PIDIREGAS and contingent liabilities that are likely to be faced by the public sector over the next few years. While an estimate of the size of these liabilities is important for an analysis of the sustainability of the fiscal policies of the country, outlays related to these liabilities are spread out over time and do not require financing by explicit debt issues (such as government bonds).

Even with a very tight fiscal stance and high economic growth that would contribute to a gradual reduction of the ratio of debt to GDP, a major challenge of refinancing the public debt stock remains. This challenge has become more important because, contrary to the recent past, the majority of the public debt stock is now contracted on the domestic debt market, and has on average a shorter maturity. Furthermore, large parts of the domestic debt contracted through IPAB and FARAC have taken place through private placements mainly with the domestic banking system as part of the government's intervention program in the financial sector. Over the next few years these liabilities will come due and require market-determined refinancing.

The Mexican public sector has ample experience in the area of public debt management, making use of a broad range of sophisticated financial instruments. Some of the major issues identified in this paper that require the attention of policymakers are:

- *Full integration of public debt and public debt management within SHCP.* Public debt as identified in this paper is divided between SHCP, IPAB, and FARAC. Even though SHCP plays a strong role as coordinator (in cooperation with the *Banco de México* acting as its financial agent), a full integration and management of public debt by SHCP would increase transparency and allow a more rapid implementation of changes in the desired or optimal composition of debt according to changes in market conditions.

- *Composition of public debt.* The rapid increase of total public debt over the past few years due to public intervention in the country's financial system and in toll road concessions, has changed the composition of public debt from a historic average of about 65 percent contracted through external debt instruments to more than 60 percent of total public debt contracted on the domestic market. Rather than the result of a deliberate public debt strategy weighing respective risks and costs of external and domestic debt issues, the outcome seems largely the result of the mechanism of government intervention necessitated by the bailouts. Reconsidering the optimal composition of public debt between external and domestic debt, given the level of (financial) development of the country, should be part of an integrated public debt management strategy in close coordination with the country's monetary and exchange rate policies.

- *The ratio of debt to output.* Even though at 46 percent the ratio of debt to output for Mexico is well below the target set by, for example, the European Union, the smaller size of the public sector in Mexico (in relation to its GDP) implies that the debt servicing cost makes up a much larger part of public expenditure. Fiscal policies that contribute to bringing down this debt and the debt servicing burden may be well advised, particularly if other contingent liabilities are taken into account.

- *Increasing the maturity and financial duration of domestic debt.* This is an particular, is an important target of a sound, integral, public debt management strategy in order to avoid excess vulnerability of public finances to economic shocks. A stable macroeconomic environment that reduces inflation, interest, and exchange rate risks would provide for the conditions under which the market would accept such an increase of maturity and financial duration at a reasonable cost. Enhancing domestic public debt instruments to cover some of these risks may further contribute to a desired lengthening of maturity and financial duration. In particular a broader use of inflation-indexed instruments should be considered.

- The present pace of issuing IPAB bonds (BPAs) on the domestic debt market is insufficient to refinance the existing IPAB liabilities with the banking system within the required time frame, which is by 2007. Increasing the pace of refinancing these obligations, such that full refinancing with market instruments by 2007 is achieved, will greatly enhance the credibility of the economic program of the Administration, and its public debt management strategy in particular.

- *Absorptive capacity of the domestic financial market.* The consideration of this element has become critical for the management and refinancing needs of the domestic public debt. The increase of domestic public debt over the past few years implies that a historically high level of 59 percent of total financial savings (M4) is kept in domestic public debt instruments. A gradual reduction of this level is desirable to reduce the crowding out of finance to the private sector and the vulnerability of public finances to economic shocks. Decisions on both the composition of public debt (between externally and domestically contracted instruments), and a financial deepening of the economy, may contribute to a reduction of the ratio of public debt to M4, and thereby enhance the absorption capacity of the domestic financial market.

Bibliography

Barro, Robert. 1995. "Optimal Debt Management." National Bureau for Economic Research Working Paper 5327. Cambridge, MA.

Bevilaqua, Alfonso, and Marcio Garcia. 1999. "Debt Management in Brazil: Evaluation of the Real Plan and Challenges Ahead." PUC–Rio. Rio de Janeiro, Brazil.

Kiguel, Miguel. 1998. "Debt Management: Some Reflections Based on Argentina." InterAmerican Development Bank Working Paper 364. Washington, D.C.

Price, Robert. 1997. "The Rationale and Design of Inflation-Indexed Bonds." IMF Working Paper 97/12. Washington, D.C.

Annex 1. Mexico's Domestic Debt: Auction Structure (February 1998–December 2000)
(amounts in million pesos)

	Feb. 1998–June 1998	July 1998–Aug. 1998	Sept. 1998–Dec. 1998	1999 Q1	1999 Q2	1999 Q3	1999 Q4	2000 Q1	2000 Q2	2000 Q3	2000 Q4
CETES											
28 days	800	800	2,500/2,800	2,500	2,500	3,000	3,000	3,000	3,000	4,500	4,500
91 days	1,800	2,300	2,300/3,000	3,000	3,000	3,500	4,000	4,000	4,000	5,000	5,000
182 days	1,800	2,200	—	500	1,000	2,000[a]	2,200[a]	2,500[b]	2,600[a]	2,600[a]	2,600[a]
364 days	1,400	1,500	—	500	600	1,200[a]	1,400[a]	3,500[b]	4,400[b]	4,400[b]	3,500[b]
BONDES											
9 month (28)			2,000/3,500	3,200							
2 years (28)	—	—	—	—	2,400						
3 years (91)	700	1,200	600/800	1,000	1,300	3,000	4,000	800	—	—	—
5 years (182)									600[a]	600[a]	1,700[a]
UDIBONOS (Million of UDIs)											
3 years	200[a]	200[a]	—	—	—	—	—				
5 years	350[a]	200[a]	—	200[a]	250[a]	250[a]	250[a]	1,200[c]	1,200[c]	200[c]	200[c]
10 years	—	—	—	—	—	—	—				
Three year bond	—	—	—	—	—	—	—	800[b]	1,000[b]	1,000[b]	1,000[b]
PIC's	—	—	—	—	—	—	—	1,000[d]	1,000[d]		
Free assignation						1,281		1,000[d]	1,000[d]	1,700[b]	

Notes:
a. These bonds are auctioned every two weeks.
b. These bonds are auctioned every month.
c. These bonds are auctioned every six weeks.
d. These bonds are auctioned every three months.
Source: Banco de México and Secretaría de Hacienda y Crédito Público.

Annex 2. IPAB Debt Accounting Framework
(amounts in billion pesos, unless otherwise specified)

	1999	2000	2001	2002	2003	2004	2005	2006	2007
GDP-real growth		5.0%	5.0%	5.0%	5.0%	5.0%	5.0%	5.0%	5.0%
Inflation		10.0%	8.0%	6.0%	4.0%	4.0%	4.0%	4.0%	4.0%
GDP nominal	4,623	5,339	6,055	6,739	7,359	8,036	8,775	9,583	10,464
Interest rate (real)		6.0%	6.0%	6.0%	6.0%	6.0%	6.0%	6.0%	6.0%
Margin FOBAPROA liabilities		1.2%	1.2%	1.2%	1.2%	1.2%	1.2%	1.2%	1.2%
Cash flows to IPAB									
Fiscal Transfers		34.6	39.2	43.7	47.7	52.1	56.9	62.1	67.8
Fees bank deposits		4.5	5.1	5.7	6.2	6.8	7.4	8.1	8.8
Assets Recovery		20.0	20.0	20.0	20.0	20.0	20.0	20.0	20.0
Issue BPAs		80.0	108.9	121.2	132.3	144.5	157.8	172.3	188.1
Amortization BPAs		0.0	0.0	0.0	80.0	108.9	121.2	132.3	144.5
Net flow BPAs		80.0	108.9	121.2	52.3	35.6	36.6	40.0	43.7
Interest obligations IPAB		130.3	124.4	114.5	101.0	105.5	110.5	116.1	122.3
FOBAPROA liabilities		125.5	106.1	85.1	66.9	67.5	68.9	70.7	72.7
BPAs		4.8	18.2	29.4	34.1	37.9	41.6	45.4	49.6
Stock FOBAPROA liabilities	725.3	716.5	673.0	607.2	596.7	607.5	622.3	639.3	658.8
Stock BPAs	0.0	80.0	188.9	310.0	362.3	398.0	434.6	474.6	518.2
Total IPAB debt stock	725.3	796.5	861.8	917.2	959.1	1005.4	1056.8	1113.8	1177.0

10

Pension Reform

*This Chapter was written by Pulle Subrahmanya Srinivas
and Fernando Montes-Negret.*

I. The Demographic Context to Pension Reform

The demographics of the labor force in Mexico are undergoing profound changes. Mexico's population is aging rapidly. Falling fertility rates, combined with lengthening life expectancy, have increased the portion of the population in old age, and shrunk the number of new entrants into the labor force. The dependency rate—the number of elderly as a percentage of the working-age population—which in 1990 stood at 10.3 percent, rose to 14.3 percent by 2000, and is expected to reach 20.8 percent by the end of the decade (see Figure 1).[1]

This dramatic demographic transition has been accompanied by greater integration of the Mexican economy into world markets. Structural adjustment after the debt crisis in the 1980s, and the need for greater efficiency as Mexico opened its economy to competition from abroad in the 1990s, have forced a steady reallocation of the labor force. In 1999 the working-age population numbered just over 59 million. Of the 42 million who were economically active, 37 million were employed in the private sector, and roughly 4.5 million were either employed by government, served in the armed forces, or worked in public sector enterprises.[2] These figures represent a 40 percent increase in the size of the private sector but only a small contraction in the number of government workers since 1990.[3] Changes in the relative size of different branches of the economy show a clear increase in the number of

---

1. ECLAC: Latin America Population Projections, 1998.
2. The latest data on the size of the public sector are from 1997, but the size remained relatively constant during the 1990s.
3. INEGI-STPS, *Ingreso y Gasto Público en México* 1999.

Figure 1. Mexico's Demographic Outlook, 1990–2035

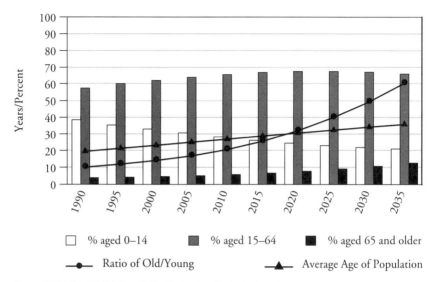

Source: ECLAC (CEPAL), Population Projections for Latin America.

Mexicans employed in small firms and self employed, and a decrease in the number working in large private firms (see Figure 2).[4]

The growth in the number of elderly and the push for greater efficiency and competitiveness, have put the country's labor market institutions—especially its social security systems—under increasing strain. Policymakers have been working to restructure these institutions to accommodate changing demographic, social, and economic trends.

II. The Fiscal Context of Pension Reform

Almost all public social security systems in Mexico are under fiscal strain due to changing demographics, unrealistic benefits, and poor management. Mexico has different old-age income social security systems (hereafter referred to as pension systems) for workers in the public and private sectors, in line with several countries in Latin America. These systems provide income security for old age, severance, disability, and death. Except for the pension system for private sector workers that was recently reformed, almost all other pension systems pose serious fiscal liabilities for

---

4. International Labour Organization (ILO): *Panorama Laboral, America Latina y el Caribe,* No. 6, 1999.

Figure 2. Sector Allocation of Mexican Workers (excluding agricultural workers)

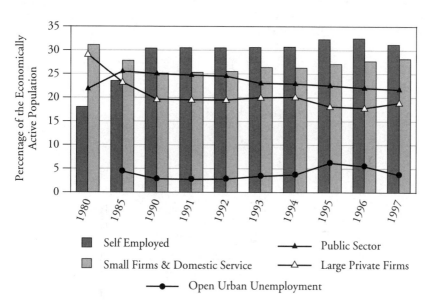

Source: CONSAR.

the government. To the extent that these liabilities are financed through transfers from general revenues, they are passed on to either the current generation of Mexican workers, or to future generations, in the form of debt. Financing public pension liabilities through general taxation has very regressive consequences.

The Mandatory Pension System for Private Sector Workers

The mandatory public pension system for private sector workers was reformed in 1997 (after an initial, failed reform in 1992). The old pay-as-you-go (PAYG), defined benefit pension system was projected to have an implicit debt of 140 percent of GDP in 1994 and was expected to run cash deficits from 2000 onward. Nowadays, all formal, private sector workers are members of the new mandatory, private, individual account, defined contribution system. Over 14 million private sector workers (33 percent of the active labor force) are members of this reformed system. Between 16 and 21 percent (17.5 percent on average) of wages of private sector workers are contributed to workers' individual accounts toward their pension. Of this amount, 5 percent is deposited in the workers' individual accounts at INFONAVIT—a housing fund that provides loans to low-income workers toward their homes—and 4 percent is paid to IMSS—the Mexican Social Security Institute that continues to be responsible for provision of disability and life insurance to workers. The balance amount is deposited in the workers' individual accounts in privately managed pension funds, the AFOREs. The pension income of the private sector workers is a combination of their accumulated assets (contributions plus financial returns) in their individual accounts at the AFOREs and INFONAVIT.

OCCUPATIONAL PENSION SYSTEMS FOR PRIVATE SECTOR WORKERS. Several large private sector employers provide occupational (often voluntary) pension schemes for their workers over and above the state's minimum mandated system. Most of these schemes are defined benefit schemes. CONSAR—the regulator of the AFOREs—is trying to bring these schemes under its regulatory purview. However, they are largely unregulated and their actuarial status is unknown.

Pension System for Federal Government Employees

The ISSSTE pension system for government employees is in cash flow deficit and is actuarially bankrupt. About 2 million federal government employees (and some state government employees) are part of the ISSSTE pension system. In 1998, the Institute made retirement, disability, survivor, and severance payments to over 333,000 beneficiaries. The benefits of the system are generous. Retiring civil servants with at least 30 years of service (28 years of service for women), receive 100 percent of their average salary of the last 12 months. The minimum monthly benefit paid by ISSSTE is MXP$906, and the maximum monthly payment is MXP$9,060. The average retired civil servant is 62 years old and receives retirement benefits for 19 years. In addition to the pension and social insurance benefits seen in other PAYG systems in the region, ISSSTE affiliates enjoy access to a network of health facilities, subsidized pharmacies and retail stores, and housing finance assistance from FOVISSSTE. This system is already in cash deficit, that is, employees' contributions are inadequate to fully pay pensions to retirees, and the government is allocating cash from its budget to make up the difference. This amount was about MXP$1.2 billion in 1997. While complete details of this system in terms of dependency ratios, and other variables, are not available, it is clear that both in cash flow terms and in actuarial terms, under the present scheme of contributions and benefits, this system is a large contingent liability for the government. The total implicit debt of the ISSSTE pension system is estimated to be about 120 percent of 1997 GDP. It is clear that reform of this system is essential in order to avoid continued and large fiscal drains on the federal government.

Pension Systems for State Government Employees

Almost all of the 34 different pension systems for state government employees have problems. These schemes cover almost 2.5 million workers—the majority of whom are teachers—and provide retirement income, disability and life, and survivors' pensions. These pension plans are modeled after the federal ISSSTE regime. Studies done thus far indicate that many of these plans are likely to be under increasing fiscal pressure. Given that most of these systems are unfunded and carry large actuarial deficits, there is a pressing need to undertake comprehensive reform.

Data are available on 29 systems as of the end of 1997.[5] These systems covered about 789,000 workers earning an average salary of about MXP$2,500 per month. Average pensions of about MXP$3,000 per month were being paid to over 80,000 retirees. About 10 active workers support each pensioner (the dependency ratio), with the average pension being 116 percent of the average wage. Actuarial projections undertaken for these 29 systems—using realistic assumptions—indicate that the dependency ratio of these systems will decline to about 4.65 workers per pensioner in 2010, and to about 2.15 workers per pensioner in 2025. Currently, pension payments are about 17 percent of the wage bill in these systems. This ratio is projected to increase to about 26 percent of the wage bill in 2010, and 46 percent in 2025—assuming no changes in benefits. The actuarial pension deficit—the amount that the state governments would have to finance from budgetary resources—is estimated at about 30 percent of 1997 GDP. While different states are in different stages of actuarial deficit and degree to which serious fiscal problems are imminent, it is clear that state-level public pension systems pose a serious threat to future fiscal stability.

Pension System for Employees of Parastatal Enterprises

Few details are available on the pension schemes for employees of enterprises such as PEMEX and the armed forces. It is estimated that there are over 500,000 workers in parastatals that have special pension plans.

III. Status of Reforms

Since the 1994 financial crisis, the overall objective of pension reform of the Mexican government has been to increase the volume of institutional savings and to provide the basis on which domestic savings could be channeled to productive investment with greater efficiency. The government recognized that most pension systems faced expected actuarial and cash deficits, either immediately or in the near term. As a first step, the government articulated a medium-term contractual savings development program for reform of the private sector mandatory pension system aimed at:

- Increasing the equity, efficiency, and sustainability of the old-age security system, gradually leading to greater coverage.
- Implementing a financially viable pension system.

---

5. Detailed data on the pension systems of Chiapas, Distrito Federal, Durango, and Sonora is not available. These systems are estimated to cover a total of about 115,000 workers and 15,000 retirees.

- Limiting the fiscal impact of the current pension system and ensuring transparency of the fiscal costs of transition.
- Enhancing financial market development and reducing volatility by stimulating greater private financial intermediation and increasing the array of financial instruments and contracts available.
- Contributing to enhancing the allocative efficiency of domestic savings and, in the longer term, to raising aggregate savings.

In line with its articulated strategy, the government has implemented a reform of the pension system for private sector workers. The law governing pensions for private sector workers was modified to allow increased efficiencies through private management of a portion of the pension contributions, better alignment of incentives through having benefits being linked more directly to contributions, and reduction of potential fiscal costs through changes in contribution and benefits formulas. It is widely accepted that the Mexican pension reform, as far as its private sector workers are concerned, has been a success in terms of the proportion of the labor force that has affiliated itself to the new system (over 75 percent of workers). Assets under management of AFOREs are over US$10 billion (2.5 percent of GDP). By 2015, total assets under management are expected to exceed US$165 billion. The AFOREs are rapidly becoming the most important institutional investors in Mexico, and the pool of available long-term domestic resources in increasing.

The reform of the private pension system was also the most significant labor market adjustment in the 1990s, and represented a very important step toward increasing efficiency and competitiveness. The new system is better positioned to accommodate demographic shifts and workforce adjustments. By eliminating cross-subsidies to a bloated public health system, tightening the link between contributions and retirement benefits, and cutting the pure-tax component of payroll deductions, the new system reduces the cost of hiring incurred by private employers, discourages early retirement of experienced workers, and increases flexibility and cross-sector mobility in the labor market. However, despite the progress made in reforming social security, Mexico still faces the challenge of integrating the pension regimes for public sector workers into the private system, and extending the reach of formal retirement income security to the large, uncovered sectors of the economy.

IV. The Future Reform Agenda

Despite the impressive achievements in the reform of the private sector pension system, a number of issues remain to be addressed. Several aspects of the reformed pension system need to be improved, and those pension systems that have not yet been touched need to be reformed. The failure of the 1992 reform experiment and the success of the 1997 reform provide useful lessons in the political economy of pension reform.

Going forward, the government's pension reform efforts should be guided by three core principles:

- *Fiscal Sustainability.* This is critical to ensure that the liabilities assumed by the government—implicitly through minimum pension guarantees or the "lifetime switch option," or explicitly through defined benefit schemes for government employees—can be financed without inordinate burden on the state's fiscal situation.
- *Equity.* This is important to ensure that different pension systems for public and private sector workers are equitable across workers and do not pose significant constraints to labor market mobility. As the Mexican economy continues its process of globalization, labor market flexibility will increasingly become a key to its international competitiveness. Artificial barriers to labor mobility through inequitable pension systems will adversely impact labor market flexibility.
- *Efficiency.* The pension systems should be efficient in achieving their fundamental objective—providing a level of benefits to workers commensurate with the risks they have assumed.

Pension Systems for Private Sector Employees

Several aspects of the private pension system need to be fine-tuned to ensure that it is placed on a long-term sustainable path. The existing voluntary pension funds also need to be brought under a regulatory umbrella, their actuarial state assessed, and appropriate remedial steps taken. The major areas of the recently reformed private pension system that need further improvement are:

Asset Collection

This part of the private pension system covers the process by which worker contributions (deducted from their paychecks) are deposited in their individual accounts with the AFOREs for investment.

- One major lesson from the failed SAR92 reform was the critical importance of a system designating a unique identification number for each worker so that contributions continue to go to the same account even if the worker changes jobs. Multiple, unidentifiable accounts were the major cause of the failure of SAR92. It is essential to ensure that the SUA system currently in place for the AFORE system is sound and achieves the objective of identifying each worker uniquely.
- The efficiency of the resource transfer process needs to be improved. At present it takes up to 8 days after the deduction of contributions by employers for the resources to become available to the AFOREs for investment. In the U.S. system, the comparable number of days is less than 3. This is a source of lost

returns to the workers. Improvement in this system will also have substantial externalities in terms of improvement of the payment system as a whole.

Asset Management

This part of the pension system covers the process by which the AFOREs (the fund managers) and the SIEFOREs (the pension funds themselves, which are legally separate from the fund managers) manage worker contributions.

- The severe restrictions that have been placed on the types of investments that can be made by the AFOREs need to be relaxed. At present, assets are largely invested in government bonds with negligible investments in private securities. The rationale was to ensure that the system was not subject to excessive risk in the initial period of its establishment. It is time for the government to recognize that draconian restrictions on investment are counterproductive. They do not allow workers of different ages, wages, and risk tolerances to choose the type of investments they would like to have. Providing a worker with the choice to determine his or her financial future implies and requires relaxing these restrictions. One way of doing so would be to use the provision of the existing law to offer multiple SIEFOREs so that workers could choose the one they want. The present SIEFORE, almost entirely invested in government securities, could continue to be offered as a "safe" alternative, but workers need not be restricted to this one alone. Other SIEFOREs which invest in equities and foreign assets should also be allowed.
- SIEFOREs should be allowed to invest some part of their assets abroad. The pension reform law restricted investments solely to Mexican securities. While this was necessary as part of the political tradeoff made in the reform process, it is important to review this restriction in light of experience with the new system and in light of international evidence that for emerging economies, it is beneficial for some fraction of the pension assets to be invested in international securities. A gradual process of liberalization should be undertaken to ensure that workers can benefit from increased risk-adjusted returns possible through international investments.
- Efforts should be made to reduce the administrative costs of the system. High administrative costs of the AFOREs adversely affect both the efficiency and equity of the system. Workers obtain substantially lower returns net of fees, and poorer workers are proportionately more adversely affected than higher-income workers. While high administrative costs are a feature not unique to Mexico—in fact Mexico has lower administrative costs compared to some other Latin American countries—opportunities for improvements need to be examined.

Regulation and Supervision

CONSAR needs to continue strengthening its institutional capacity and to gear up for a more liberalized investment environment. It has, through its sustained efforts, gained recognition as one of the more effective regulators of a private pension system in Latin America. However, it also needs to be given the mandate to bring the voluntary pension plans under its regulatory ambit. There is some evidence that CONSAR is losing highly qualified staff, which may adversely affect its capabilities. Steps need to be taken to provide a substantial degree of financial autonomy to CONSAR so that it is less subject to political pressures.

Pension Systems for Public Sector Employees

Reform of public sector pension systems is key to the sustainability of fiscal efforts of the government. As described above, all major public sector pension systems pose serious fiscal threats to the Mexican government. It is clear that, given the federal reform of government, the responsibility for reform of the ISSSTE system is entirely in the hands of the federal government, while reform of state-level pension systems is in the hands of the individual states. However, even in a decentralized form of government, unpaid pensions often create enough political pressure to end up being liabilities of the federal government. It is therefore crucial that the federal government consider working with the state governments to reform these systems at an early date. A handful of states account for a major portion of the overall deficit, and it would be useful to begin reform in these states. It is important to note that integration of these systems with that of private sector workers is only one of several options available for reform. Within the framework of fiscal sustainability, equity, and efficiency of pension systems across public and private sectors, alternative schemes need to be examined and appropriate models, selected keeping political expediency in mind.

The generous, unfunded benefits from pension plans administered at the federal, state, and municipal levels and for employees of parastatals are slowing adjustment of the workforce to Mexico's more integrated economy. This is demonstrated by the relatively constant size of the public sector throughout the 1990s. As in Argentina and Brazil, special systems for civil servants are a formidable barrier to reform of public health and education systems, a lingering rigidity in the labor market that hurts competitiveness, and a notorious source of social inequity. Furthermore, pension plans for civil servants are rapidly accumulating liabilities that are endangering the fiscal position of the public sector at the federal and state level and could displace more targeted spending in the social sectors. Reform and integration of civil servant pension plans is an essential for Mexico to make further gains in efficiency and competitiveness.

In designing reforms to the various pension systems, it is critical to ensure that issues such as labor market mobility, equity, and incentive structures are aligned across the systems. A comprehensive view of pensions needs to be taken in order to ensure that moving forward, pension systems do not pose a threat to the competitiveness of the Mexican economy.

INFONAVIT

INFONAVIT poses a major threat to the financial sustainability of the pension system as it generates poor returns on about 40 percent of the pension contributions. If its financial performance continues to be as poor as in the past, the government could be saddled with a substantial fiscal liability as the transition generation workers use their lifetime switch option to opt for a pension under the old system. While there is no explicit government guarantee beyond a small minimum for the workers who joined the new system directly, poor INFONAVIT performance could create political pressures at a future date for government support. Reform to INFONAVIT and improving its financial performance are therefore essential. Reforms to INFONAVIT will also play a major role in improving the functioning of capital markets, quite apart from its role in the pension system.

INFONAVIT also creates a host of other problems, including distortions in the housing and mortgage markets. Given the governance structure of the Institute, reforms to INFONAVIT are challenging, even for a committed government. Past attempts at reform have involved tremendous efforts with substantially smaller accomplishments. The government has recognized the seriousness of the problems of INFONAVIT and recently engineered a series of reforms that should have some positive impact. It is too early to be confident that these reforms will be successful.

INFONAVIT's fundamental problem is one of governance; that is, its Board is equally divided among representatives of the government, labor unions, and real estate developers. Its chief executive is nominated by the President of Mexico, but confirmed by Congress. This structure creates entrenched vested interests, gives the institution an enormous amount of independence from the government, and makes it difficult to implement reform.

From a purely economic perspective, in a modern, globally integrated Mexican economy, it is hard to argue for the continued existence of an institution such as INFONAVIT. The degree to which it achieves its objectives of providing low-cost loans to low-income workers is questionable. In any event, there are alternative institutional designs that could better serve such objectives. Analyses using the limited data available have shown that over half of INFONAVIT loans are substandard in terms of potential repayment. Collection efforts, though strengthened, are still very weak, and information and management systems are poor. Finally, there is substantial anecdotal evidence that the institution is a source of political patronage and has been captured by vested interests.

Before the radical (though possibly first-best) option of closing INFONAVIT can be decided upon, a range of alternatives might be evaluated, all of which will only partially solve the problem. A key recognition of any reform effort should be that INFONAVIT as an institution needs to be gradually marginalized in its operations, if further fiscal costs to the government are to be avoided, and if the sustainability of the pension system is to be improved. One option to achieve this objective is to reduce the share of pension contributions that INFONAVIT receives from 5 percent of wages to a substantially smaller number. The balance should be transferred to the AFOREs along with the rest of the contribution. INFONAVIT could also be forced to invest some portion of its portfolio in government securities, thereby reducing the amount of loss-making loans it makes. The lending instrument and eligibility criteria for INFONAVIT needs to be modified.

Complementary Reforms in Capital Markets

A funded pension system needs a supply of capital market instruments for investment. Since any model that is adopted for public sector workers will inevitably call for a greater degree of funding of pension liabilities, such as the one adopted for the private sector workers' pension system, the government needs to undertake a broad range of complementary capital market reforms to ensure that funded pension systems have adequate securities in which to invest. In addition, an appropriate annuities market needs to be created to ensure that accumulated assets are paid out to retirees in an efficient manner. The government needs to address these complementary aspects of reforms to pension systems to ensure their sustainability. Development of annuities markets also needs to take priority as pensions begin to be paid out of funded systems.

LONG-TERM GOVERNMENT DEBT MARKETS. Mexico's government bond market is poorly developed and provides mostly short-term (less than one-year-duration) bonds. Pension liabilities are typically long term, and the natural asset to hedge such liabilities is a long-duration instrument such as long-term bonds or equities. There is almost no liquidity in long-term instruments. While historically the cause of this underdeveloped state may have been chronic inflation, it is now essential that the government consider development of this market segment.

CORPORATE DEBT MARKET. Development of a sound corporate debt market accompanied by effective rating agencies would provide another vehicle for pension funds. The heavy presence of the banking sector in Mexico's economy has traditionally implied that the level of intermediation has been very high. Most corporate lending has been from banks, which in turn financed these assets from deposits. The presence of institutional pension funds provides a natural alternative source of funds for high-quality corporations to raise funds.

HOUSING MORTGAGE MARKET. Long-term secured housing mortgages are a good investment vehicle for pension funds that have long-term liabilities. The availability of long-term investors should also help stimulate the housing market. However, the quality of the investments depends to a large extent on the availability of appropriate instruments and the efficiency of the mortgage market. Development of an efficient housing mortgage market requires the introduction of new market-based mortgage instruments, transparent and consistent origination standards, presence of a mortgage insurer, and a strong rating industry whose ratings are viewed as objective and reliable.

FINANCIAL INTERMEDIARIES. Credit-rating agencies, custodial services, and third-party performance assessment services (similar to Morningstar and Lipper in the United States) are some of the other players in the overall financial infrastructure that are required for maximizing the economic benefits of a privatized pension system. There currently are three international credit rating agencies operating in Mexico, a central depository that offers partial custodial services, and no independent performance assessment agencies. The government should examine these segments of the financial infrastructure and take appropriate policy actions to assist in their development as part of the overall development of the financial sector.

ANNUITIES MARKET. An essential component of the capital markets that needs close attention along with reform of pension systems is the development of the annuities market. This segment of the insurance industry is likely to grow rapidly as workers purchase annuities using their accumulated pension savings. For most insurance firms, this is a new product with significant impact on capital, investment options, management, and competition. The regulatory capacity of the government will also need to be strengthened to ensure that the industry is sound. All these areas need the significant attention of policymakers.

V. The Social Dimension of Pension Reform: Equity, Poverty, and Coverage

Low coverage of the contributory social insurance system in Mexico is of particular concern. This is because there is no income transfer program in place for the indigent elderly, which leaves the minimum pension guarantee and the social quota—both restricted to participants in the formal pension system—the only safety net for old-age income security. In 1996 only 22 percent of urban and 7 percent of the rural elderly were receiving benefits from the public social security system administered by IMSS. In the same year only 31 percent of workers (41 percent of dependent workers) participated in the national social security system. Proponents of the new AFORE system would point to these low levels of coverage as evidence of the labor market distortions, disincentives, and regressive benefit structure of the public pension system that the AFOREs have replaced.

Recent empirical evidence shows that there is a clear urban bias (Packard and Shinkai 2000) in the probability of being protected by the social security system. There is also a strong positive effect of contracted employment on the probability of being covered, and a negative effect of working in what are often considered "risky" occupations—farming and other manual labor, transit driver, construction vehicle operator, and service sector worker.[6] Unfortunately, little can be said about the effect of self-employment since, as in many countries, the self employed are not asked in most household and labor surveys whether they are covered by the social security system.

Although it is too early to measure the promised improvements in effective coverage expected from the transition to private individual retirement accounts, the critical question that must be posed is whether the AFORE system will correct the failure of the old PAYG system to cover a greater portion of the population. Proponents of funded individual accounts claim that by tightening the link between contributions and retirement benefits, and cutting the pure-tax component of payroll deductions, the new systems increase the incentives to contribute, reduce the cost of hiring incurred by employers, and discourage early retirement of experienced workers. The AFORE system should lead to an increase in coverage if it provides workers incentives to participate, by increasing the returns to invested savings and lowering the costs of participation, especially for workers in small firms and in rural areas.

There are features of the system that should provide incentives to contribute, and that will need to be evaluated in the near future. In the three years since the start of the AFORE system, over 15 million workers in the private sector have opened an individual retirement account. This represents 74.2 percent of potential affiliates (those required to participate under the law), and is more than the total affiliation to the funded systems in Argentina and Chile combined. This last point is particularly important, since the relatively large size of the Mexican market should allow substantial economies of scale in pension fund management to be exploited. The AFORE commissions—that portion of workers' deferred consumption that they will not recover when they retire—are lower than those of their counterparts farther south. Lower AFORE commissions mean that Mexican workers have a greater price incentive to keep contributing into their retirement accounts, which—in concert with returns from investments and the incentives provided by the daily Social Quota cash transfer[7]—should theoretically maintain the system's high levels of effective coverage. As of January 2000, 87.6 percent of AFORE account holders have kept

---

6. Mexican workers in traditionally "informal" industries, where low coverage might be expected—agriculture, construction, and transportation—do not face as strong a negative probability of being covered as their counterparts in other countries in the Latin America and Caribbean region (Packard and Shinkai, 2000).

7. The Social Quota in Mexico is partly an incentive for workers to affiliate with the new system and to keep their contributions up to date and partly a prepaid, invested account supplement toward the minimum pension guarantee. The government deposits MXP$1 per day into the retirement accounts of contributors, indexed to the CPI, estimated to be between 1 and 5.5 percent of the worker's salary, depending on incomes. On average, the social quota will be equivalent to 2.2 percent of wages (Cerda and Grandolini 1998). Pension authorities have yet to report on the impact the social quota has had in terms of new affiliates to the formal pension system.

their contributions up to date—compared to 49 percent of account holders in Argentina, and 52 percent in Chile.[8]

Another important aspect of the system that should be evaluated for its possible impact on the decision to contribute are those features that may indirectly be hurting the new system's credibility, or directly lowering returns to the AFORE accounts. How workers are pooling their contributions is important in examining the incentive structure they face, the sustainability of the system, and the degree to which workers will be protected from falling into poverty when they can no longer work. Figure 3 shows how the 17.5 percent payroll contribution of an average Mexican worker is distributed among the various institutions in the reformed pension system.

The most important thing to notice about this distribution is that about 40 percent of an average worker's mandated retirement savings are going to the subaccount managed by the housing fund institute, INFONAVIT.

From a social perspective, therefore, the government needs to keep in mind the following issues in its future pension reform efforts.

Figure 3. Distribution of Payroll Contributions in a Reformed Pension System

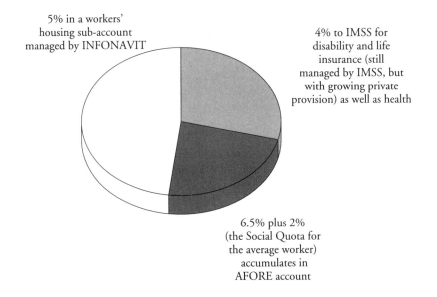

5% in a workers' housing sub-account managed by INFONAVIT

4% to IMSS for disability and life insurance (still managed by IMSS, but with growing private provision) as well as health

6.5% plus 2% (the Social Quota for the average worker) accumulates in AFORE account

---

8. It should be pointed out, however, that since 1997 when workers began to contribute, Mexico has not suffered from the deep economic recessions seen in the Southern Cone that have cast many workers out of covered employment, and constrained the ability of others to maintain retirement contributions up to date. Furthermore, there is some evidence of workers being affiliated more than once—a weakness in Mexico's first attempt at establishing mandatory individual retirement accounts in 1992, and one which could be inflating the affiliation contribution statistics.

- *Coverage of pension systems needs to be closely monitored.* The Mexican system is a potential case study for coverage extension under a multipillar pension model. A more thorough, household-level investigation of participation in the new pension system should be conducted in the next two to three years.
- *The need for noncontributory social assistance for the indigent elderly should be assessed.* There are no old-age income assistance programs in place for the very poor. In the transition period, until the effects of the reform on increasing coverage are felt, such a social assistance transfer may be justified. However, if a noncontributory benefit is introduced, it should be structured to prevent the nonpoor from strategically abusing the minimum benefit provision in the contributory system, and its source of financing should be sustainable and not vulnerable to cyclical budgetary cuts.
- *The design of the reforms of the public pension systems should explicitly address the issues of creating a more flexible labor market and equity across pension systems.* Special pension systems for civil servants constrain labor market efficiency, hinder public sector reform, stoke social inequity, and in Mexico may be crowding out targeted social spending and saddling state and federal government with large unfunded liabilities.

VI. Reform Priorities: A Suggested Plan of Action

It is obvious that the reform agenda is large and that it is necessary to establish priorities to move forward in a realistic manner. One important criterion to use in establishing priorities is the degree of fiscal impact that poorly run pension plans are likely to have. Thus, actuarial assessments are needed of the major public pension systems—state-level systems and ISSSTE. Based on past analyses, INFONAVIT continues to be a high priority for reform. Efforts should focus on those systems most urgently in need of reform. Because pension reform is a highly sensitive political matter, emphasis should be on the two or three issues on which a new administration is willing to spend its political capital in its first two or three years.

One possible course of action is to accord priority to reform of INFONAVIT and public sector systems at both the federal and state level. Fine-tuning of the existing system is important but not critical. Similarly, reform of the parastatal systems and voluntary pension systems could also be taken up in due course.

Growth and Competitiveness

11

Banking Sector

This Chapter was written by Fernando Montes-Negret and Luis F. Landa.

The industrial revolution had to wait for the financial revolution. Although many of the inventions had already been in existence for several decades, they required large commitments of long-term capital which an underdeveloped financial system could not furnish. Only as the British financial system developed further, was the industrial revolution possible.

—*John Hicks*

I. Financial Sector Objectives: Efficiency, Accessibility, and Stability

The role of the financial sector is to support Mexico's broad objectives of fostering economic development and alleviating poverty. Against this backdrop, the objectives of the financial sector itself are anchored in three areas:

EFFICIENCY (GLOBALIZED MARKETS). Inefficient, protected financial markets impose an implicit tax on consumers and entrepreneurs, limiting the economy's ability to grow and reduce poverty. Good corporate governance; supervision, accounting, auditing, reporting, and disclosure rules; a sound legal and judicial framework and adequate tax treatment; and market depth and liquidity, are the underpinnings of efficient financial markets. Competition, including strategic investment by foreign financial institutions, provides incentives for modernizing the domestic banking industry. Capital markets add diversity, depth, and liquidity to the financial system and provide a stimulus for competition and increased efficiency in the corporate and banking sectors.

ACCESSIBILITY (EQUITY). Fostering access for underserved businesses, particularly SMEs and the poor through market-based solutions, enhances growth with equity, limiting government interventions to address genuine market failures.

STABILITY (SOUNDNESS). Ensuring the health of the financial system and preventing crises are necessary to sustain growth and alleviate poverty over the long term. Tightening supervision, promoting better risk management, and encouraging better accounting and disclosure will foster market discipline. Development of markets for longer-term government debt is a prerequisite for developing a robust yield curve and sound financial management practices. Encouraging equity financing helps eliminate excessive leveraging of corporations.

II. The High Cost of Banking Crises

Macroeconomic and financial instability not only disrupt the sector's intermediation role in promoting financial savings and a better allocation of resources, but the huge fiscal cost of crises can set back development and poverty reduction efforts for many years. The cost of crises crowds out social spending and often can lead to explosive debt-over-GDP ratios. Lower growth, worsening unemployment, lower wages, and higher prices for basic commodities all push more people into poverty and worsen the plight of those who were already poor.

By one count, 112 episodes of systemic banking crises have occurred in 93 countries since the late 1970s. On average, governments of developing countries have spent 14.4 percent of GDP to clean up their financial sectors.[1] Some banking crises have cost over 40 percent of GDP. In Latin America, Argentina's and Chile's crises have been the most expensive in terms of GDP (55 percent and 41 percent, respectively). The fiscal cost of Mexico's banking crisis (19.3 percent) roughly matches that of Japan's, which currently stands at 20 percent of GDP.

III. Mexico's Financial Sector Reform

Mexico has been a good example of lopsided financial sector development in two senses. First, Mexico introduced a first generation of reforms which included the rapid deregulation of interest rates and the opening of the capital account, putting less emphasis on building the incentives, the supervisory and regulatory tools, and the financial infrastructure to ensure that intermediaries could perform their functions with safety and soundness. Second, Mexico focused the reform on what was already there—the banking system—and not on developing what was missing—the capital markets. This contributed to firms taking on more short-term bank credit

---

1. According to a survey of 40 crises (Honohan and Klingebel 1999).

and less longer-term debt and equity finance than otherwise. Third, some key pre-conditions for a successful financial liberalization were not in place, particularly strong prudential regulation, supervision and enforcement, and modern and fair legal and judicial frameworks. In summary, the Mexican government's developmental objective was insufficient, at the time, to ensure a smooth transition towards financial liberalization.

As a result of the financial liberalization policies that were implemented in 1989, particularly the abandonment of directed credit, commercial bank resources channeled to the private sector recovered very rapidly. This recovery was further accentuated with the privatization of the banks in 1991–92. From then, and until the 1994 crisis, credit to the private sector grew as much as eight times faster than GDP. During this period, commercial bank credit, as a proportion of GDP, increased from 29 percent in 1992 to 41 percent in 1994.

Having paid premium prices for the privatized banks in 1991–92, the "new bankers" were under considerable pressure to make loans in order to recover their investment.[2] This, combined with an environment of lax banking supervision, led to excessive risk taking that rendered the banking system highly vulnerable to a crisis—as was borne out in 1994–95. In addition, the depth of the non-repayment culture and the dubious ethical behavior of a few of the selected "new bankers," further exacerbated the crisis.

IV. Measures Adopted to Avert a Systemic Collapse of the Banking System

Since the critical year of 1995, macroeconomic instability and inflation have been reduced, partly as a result of better macroeconomic policies and a very favorable external environment, particularly in the U.S. economy. Since then, the Mexican government has implemented a number of support programs that proved instrumental in averting the collapse of the banking system. These programs included:

(i)   A number of bank support programs, including liquidity support to provide banks with foreign currency service their foreign debt in the aftermath of the crisis; actions to recapitalize the banks in exchange for non-performing loans; the intervention and sale of a number of weak domestic banks to foreign investors; and programs to restructure, sell, or liquidate banks intervened because their owners could not provide additional capital to meet the new regulations. These measures were implemented through the Bank Savings Protection Fund (FOBAPROA).

---

2. Banks were overpriced, sold, on average, at 3.5 times their actual value (with prices fluctuating between 2.5 and 5.3 times their actual value), particularly considering the dubious quality of their portfolios and outdated systems.

(ii) Debtor support programs to help families and corporations service and repay their debts.

(iii) Reform Mexico's deficient accounting principles, banking regulations, and supervisory and enforcement practices.

The support programs were effective in avoiding widespread bank failures and deposit runs on banks, while maintaining the course of the tough stabilization program. However, they generated a substantial fiscal cost, estimated at about 19.3 percent of GDP with only a small part of this total cost having been covered by effective fiscal transfers between 1995 and 2000.[3]

One of the most important mechanisms for the removal of bad assets from the banks' balance sheets was the swap of non-performing loans for 10 year nontradable zero-coupon bonds which accrued interest to be paid at maturity. The continuous compounding of interest at high and variable rates, the limited cash contributions from the federal budget, and the negative carryover faced by some banks while financing the accruals in the market, compounded the problem and in some instances worsened the condition of the banks and increased the fiscal cost.[4] The latter being particularly sensitive to *temporary* increases in interest rates which result in *permanent* wealth losses for the federal budget, as the base for compounding future interest on FOBAPROA's zero-coupon bonds increased *permanently*.[5] This is a typical case in which the "least cash solution was not the least cost solution." Figure 1 shows that this indeed became a factor because real interest rates for the benchmark 28-day Cetes rate were substantially higher during 1998–99 compared to 1997.

New banking legislation approved in December 1998 created a new deposit insurance agency, the Institute for the Protection of Bank Savings (IPAB). This law provides a legal framework and a clear timetable to sell the mountain of bad assets acquired by FOBAPROA and to improve incentives in the financial sector, and creates a mechanism for the transparent resolution of undercapitalized and insolvent banks, allowing full participation of foreign investors in existing Mexican banks.

In addition, the regulatory authorities have initiated a profound program of regulatory reforms to strengthen the quantity and especially the quality of the banks' capital, enhance accounting and disclosure standards, eliminate unjustified forbearance, and improve loan classification and provisioning rules. Finally, the government's initiatives for reforms on the Secured Lending and Bankruptcy Laws were approved by Congress in May 2000. When implemented, they will strengthen the loan repayment culture in Mexico and reduce the risks faced by banks in their lending operations.

---

3. Fiscal transfers for the year 2000 will amount to MXP$35 billion.

4. The cost of bank restructuring increased from 8.4 percent of GDP in mid-1997 to 19.3 percent of GDP in 1999, representing three times as much of Mexico's total internal debt.

5. At one point in the third quarter of 1998, the nominal Cetes rate doubled, rising in a short period from about 20 percent to 40 percent. (See Figure 1.)

Figure 1. Real Return on 28-Day Cetes

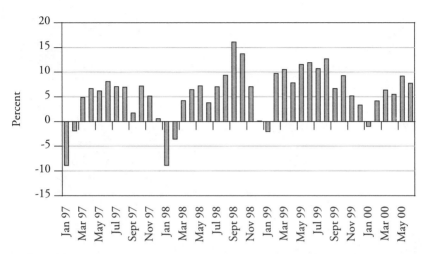

Note: Nominal 28-day Cete rates correspond to the arithmetic average of the monthly primary auctions. Thirty-day equivalent rates were then divided by the corresponding month's annualized inflation rate.
Source: Banco de México.

V. IPAB Bank Recapitalization and Resolution Programs

IPAB was created as a decentralized agency of the federal government with its own legal status, governing body, and equity. One of its main objectives is to manage the different bank support programs aimed at restoring the health of the financial system, which are:

- *Banks in the Capitalization and Loan Portfolio Purchase Program.* This included Banamex, Bancomer, Banorte, BBV, and Bital. The government offered to buy two pesos worth of loan recoveries for each peso of fresh capital injected by shareholders. Banks signed a loss-sharing agreement, by which they had the obligation to pay 25 percent of the residual losses.
- *Banks under the* Saneamiento *Program.* This includes Serfin, Inverlat, Bancrecer, Promex and Atlantico. Serfin and Inverlat have already been sold to Santander and Bank of Nova Scotia (55 percent share ownership) respectively and Promex has been merged with Bancomer. Resolution of Atlantico is still pending.
- *Intervened banks in the final stages of liquidation or resolution.* This includes eight small banks, Anahuac, Capital, Cremi, Interestatal, Obrero, Oriente, Pronorte, and Union, managed by CNBV-appointed administrators, no longer have active deposit-taking operations, but they have been forced to continue funding their remaining liabilities in the interbank market, with the

guarantee of FOBAPROA. Due to the planned removal of the guarantee on interbank liabilities, there is pressure for the liquidation of these banks to be completed by January 2002. This is one of the more expensive and faster growing segments of IPAB's debts.

- *Intervened banks in the process of being sold.* Two other intervened banks, Industrial and Sureste, have some remaining franchise value and may be sold instead of liquidated.

VI. The Regulatory Reform Program

The regulatory reform program consists of a series of reforms intended to improve the health and stability of the banking sector. The announced regulatory reforms are included in Annex I. However, a number of pending regulatory and legal reform issues to which the Mexican authorities are fully committed still remain:

Pending Regulatory Issues and Continuity of Implemented Strategies

The new definition of regulatory capital, effective as of January 2001 and to be fully phased-in by 2003, requires additional capital increases in the banking system. To facilitate this, Mexico now allows new instruments to help the capitalization process, akin to convertible debt instruments that could be well received by the market. The new regulation allow for the use of capital securities to capitalize the banks. Already, increased capital requirements have partially been financed by: (1) Revenue from the divestiture of bank investments in insurance companies and pension funds being reinvested; (2) Capital injections by BBVA to Bancomer; (3) Capital injections by the federal government and BSCH to Serfin, and (4) by reinvesting retained earnings. A notable feature is that, by the end of 2000, some of the larger banks will already be in full compliance with the 2003 capitalization requirements.[6]

- Introduction of early warning and prompt corrective action systems.
- Introduction of new principles and rules for internal controls and management of banks.
- Introduction of new provisioning requirements for repossessed collateral.
- Satisfactory continuation of IPABs asset disposal and recovery program.

Pending Legal Reforms to Improve Incentives to the Financial Sector

INTRODUCTION OF A LIMITED DEPOSIT INSURANCE SYSTEM. IPAB's law requires the phasing in of a limited deposit insurance system. By the end of 2003, the guarantee

---

6. One notable exception is BITAL which, by June 2000, still required approximately US$700 million of fresh capital.

will exclude interbank deposits, and by the end of 2004, it will only cover bank deposits up to a limit of 400,000 UDIs (about US$100,000) per depositor. The elimination of the government guarantee on interbank deposits will be a powerful incentive for banks to improve their solvency in the next two years and for market participants to assist in assessing the risks of the various participants/counterparts in the market.

MODERNIZATION OF THE LEGAL AND JUDICIARY FRAMEWORK. Pending issues in modernizing Mexico's legal infrastructure in which the Bank can make a contribution include:

- *Establishment of legal certainty and the judicial system.* The modernized system must be capable of enforcing contracts between lenders and borrowers at a low cost. For this purpose, two important laws were approved by Congress on May 2000: (a) the Secured Lending Legislation (originally *Ley Federal de Garantías*) and the Bankruptcy Law *(Ley Federal de Concursos Mercantiles)*. The first was not acceptable to Congress in its original form and has been broken down as reforms to various laws, including the Commercial Code. The second law calls for the creation of a new Institute (Instituto Federal de Especialistas de Concursos Mercantiles—IFECOM) in charge of settling disputes between financial institutions and debtors when the latter files for bankruptcy. The Institute would arbitrate, in a first phase, creditor–debtor disputes in an administrative rather than judicial manner, saving judges valuable time. Cases which cannot be resolved under this option would be turned over to the judicial system for final resolution.
- Even though important reforms to the public registries have already been enacted, the process of modernizing operative procedures are still required for the successful implementation of these two key laws. The challenge to achieve efficient results through the court system is enormous and will require significant institutional development, training, and investment.
- *Non-payment Culture.* Debtor willingness to pay, which has been weakened in recent years by the bailout schemes, should be strengthened as a consequence of the regulatory reforms. However, it may not have the full-fledged incentives and conditions to improve if the *Instituto de Especialistas en Concursos Mercantiles* does not perform its function (which is yet to be tested as of year-end 2000) in a transparent, fair, and efficient way.

VII. Supervisory and Regulatory Arrangements

In Mexico, three major agencies share the regulatory/supervisory authority over the banking sector: the SHCP, which retains key regulatory powers given by the Banking Law; Banco de México (BOM) who regulates the money market and foreign exchange operations of commercial banks, sets the minimum entry level of capital and some elements of the banks' capital adequacy ratio, and establishes market risk management practices; and, the CNBV which does most of the traditional off and on-site supervision work, preparing and issuing prudential regulations within its sphere of authority as an "organismo desconcentrado" (a type of decentralized agency) of the SHCP.

The prevailing institutional setup results in excessive concentration of powers and authority on the SHCP. This has resulted in a fragmentation of functions and powers, to some extent debilitating the implementation of prudential policies reflected by conflicts of interests between prudential policy, on the one hand, and fiscal and monetary policies on the other. These conflicts were more apparent in the phase of problem recognition, intervention and failure resolution policies followed since 1995. One consequence was that institutions that should have been subject to take over and prompt corrective actions were left under the control of their initial managers and shareholders for too long exacerbating the associated resolution cost and debilitating financial discipline in the system.

BOM can issue general provisions to regulate banking operations in foreign currency, silver and gold, and also regulates the market and liquidity risks.[7] While BOM acts in principle as the bank of banks, lender of last resort, and clearinghouse regulator, it also determines liquidity and the legal proceedings to perform fund transfers. Moreover, BOM retains a major role in regulating, monitoring and granting regulatory forbearance regarding the banks' capital adequacy ratio.[8]

The SHCP has been put in an odd position of being simultaneously "judge and interested party" in recent instances involving the nationalization and re-privatization of banks; in its dual role as owner and regulator of public development banks; and authority ultimately responsible for adopting sound fiscal policies and resolving the banking crisis. *As it is important to have an autonomous central bank, it is also important to have a less fragmented and more autonomous supervisor and regulator overseeing the financial system and the Mexican capital markets.*

VIII. Financing to the Private Sector

Four out of the six years of President Zedillo's Administration have been spent in the "containment phase" of Mexico's deep banking crisis. In some sense it has been a lost sexenio for the banks, since their role as financial intermediaries has declined dramatically. Direct commercial bank financing to the nonbank private sector has fallen dramatically since the inception of the December 1994 "Tequila Crisis." However,

---

7. Which are important prudential aspects that should belong to the CNBV.
8. This functional oddity fragments the operation of prudential supervision and it is not customarily assigned to central banks in countries where supervision is exercised by a separate agency.

there are recent indications that this trend has possibly bottomed out as several of the larger banks have returned to the mortgage and commercial sector loan markets (Figure 2).

Similarly, bank liabilities as a proportion of GDP declined from 32 percent in 1994 to 23 percent by June 2000,[9] as shown in Figure 3.

The larger companies have been substituting domestic for foreign borrowing in an environment of high domestic rates and a strong peso. The enterprise sector as a whole has been repaying their domestic bank loans, ending with a net creditor position against the domestic banking system. In other words, enterprises are funding, on a net basis (loans minus deposits), the domestic banking system as a group.

The banking industry as a whole, hard hit by the 1994–95 crisis, has gone through noticeable improvements in terms of quantity and quality of capital, profitability and risk management practices. Financial information for the banking industry by June 2000 showed signs of improvement. Past-due loans decreased to MXP$57.7 billion from MXP$84.5 billion in 1999, reflecting a decline in the nonperforming loan index from 8.9 percent in 1999 to 6.4 percent in June 2000, the lowest level since the new accounting principles were implemented (January 1997).

Figure 2. Stock and Flow of Commercial Bank Credit to the Private Sector (in real 1994 pesos)

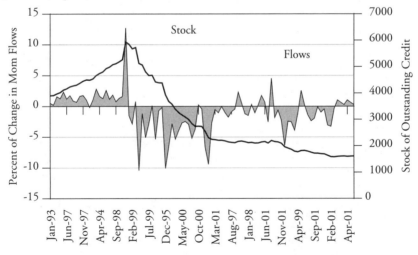

Source: Banco de México.

---

9. Partially due to the sustained growth in the competing mutual fund industry where in 1999 alone, real growth in total assets was a significant 36 percent. Real growth declined by 13 percent through June 2000 due to significant interest rate increases prior to the July 2nd presidential elections.

Figure 3. Commercial Banking System: Total Deposits
(as percent of GDP)

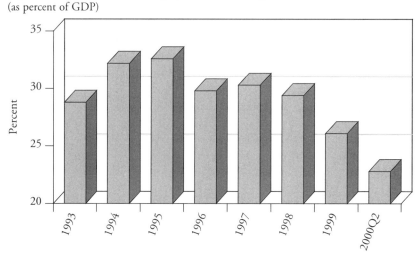

Source: Banco de México.

However, these improvements were at the expense of the capitalization index which, adjusted for market risk, declined to 14.3 percent by June 2000 from 16.2 percent in 1999.[10] Operating profits increased substantially, and the industry's coverage ratio (substandard loans over loan-loss provisions) rose to 110.8 percent.

The improvement of the banks' financial position, however, has not yet resulted in a resumption of their intermediation function in real terms. Since 1994, bank lending has proven to be a bad business and has made banks more risk averse, moving away from their traditional role. Figure 4 shows that the higher-risk-weighted private sector loans continue to decline as a percentage of the industry's total assets (29 percent in June 2000 against 35 percent in 1998). This has been partially due, in addition to the prevailing high real interest rates that curtail demand, to the adoption of stricter risk management practices and client selection criteria, combined with an improved flow of information on repayment performance provided by the credit bureaus. This has made some formerly eligible credit customers no longer creditworthy.

The decline in real lending to the private sector has been offset by the other low-risk assets which have become the main components of the industry's balance sheet. Figure 4 shows that, by June 2000, the securities portfolio (33 percent), government loans (9 percent) and interbank lending (one percent) represented 43 percent of total bank assets. If the FOBAPROA/IPAB bonds are added the percentage rises to 61% of the total. The change in attitude of banks toward private sector lending

---

10. Basically due to the important non-performing loan write-offs by Banamex which is a well received example of "short run pain" in return for "long run gain."

Figure 4. Commercial Banks: Asset Composition

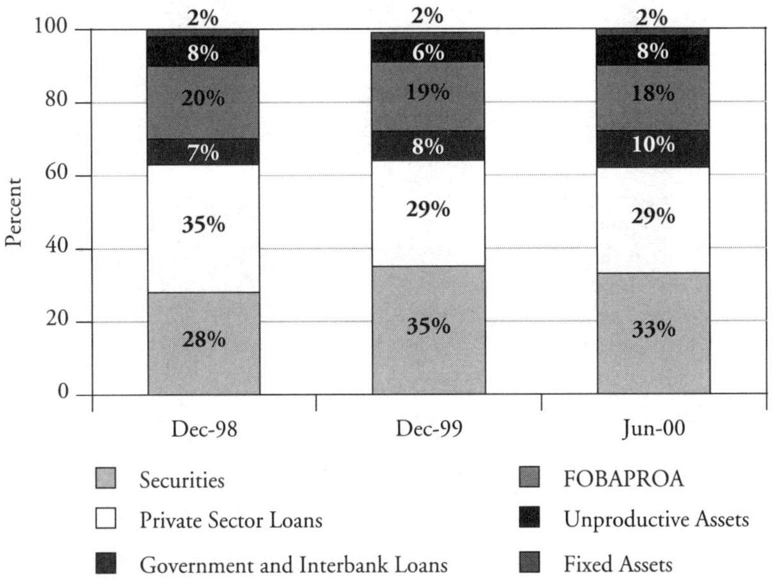

Source: CNBV.

might have caused a credit crunch in some market segments. Increased lending to the government is now channeled through the purchase of securities, rather than by direct lending as occurred during the years the banks were nationalized.

The change in the balance sheet composition in favor of less risky assets has also changed the sources of bank profitability. Banks now depend to a great extent on government-issued instruments (Special Cetes, FOBAPROA Bonds, Cetes, Bondes, Udibonos, etc.). Figure 5 shows that by June 2000, 23 percent of total interest earned came from the loans sold to FOBAPROA. while interest "earned" from securities positions represented 32 percent, rising significantly from their 23 percent participation in 1998. In other words, Mexican banks might be going in the same direction as some of the Brazilian banks, functioning more like *casas de bolsa* than traditional deposit-taking and lending institutions.

Over the last three years, Mexican banks were dependent for about one fourth of their interest revenue on the accruals of the FOBAPROA/IPAB bonds. The collapse of lending was instrumental in the banks not having liquidity problems.

It is unlikely that the expected recovery of lending activities will materialize soon after the approval by Congress of the new secured lending legislation and Bankruptcy Law. Instead, the resumption of credit will gradually occur during a prolonged period as macroeconomic stability settles in and real interest rates decline. In

Figure 5. Commercial Banks: Sources of Interest Income

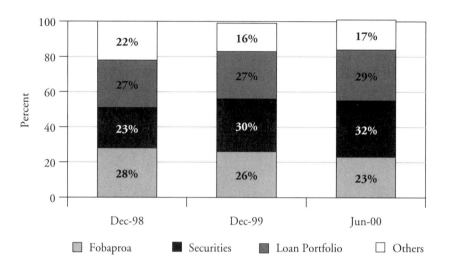

Source: CNBV.

addition, since creditworthy standards have been tightened, many previously eligible firms will no longer meet the new benchmarks. *Banco de México* estimates that if the proportion of bank credit to the private sector increases from its current 11.5 percent of GDP to 21.5 percent of GDP (10 points), the annual long-run growth of the economy would increase by 0.5 percent per year.

The puzzling fact that positive economic growth has been achieved in the absence of commercial bank lending can be explained by the partial substitution effect of alternative funding sources.[11] From December 1994 to December 1999, the stock of non-bank financing and financing from abroad, as a proportion of total financing, increased from 27 percent to 42 percent, as shown in Table 1.

Increased non-bank financing in the consumer, housing and business credit markets has been mostly due to the significant increase in credit channeled by the limited scope financial lending institutions (SOFOLES) which initiated operations in 1994. Outstanding credit from these institutions increased from US$ 31 million in December 1994 to over US$5 billion by June 2000. Other non-bank financial institutions like leasing and factoring companies continue with limited outstanding portfolios which are yet to recover.

In addition to the SOFOLES, the continued importance of business firm financing can also be appreciated from the responses to *Banco de México*'s survey, which

---

11. It should be also noted that one important source of enterprise financing has been the non-repayment of bank loans.

Table 1. Sources of Financing to the Private Sector (percent)

	December 1994	December 1999
Total Financing	100	100
Domestic nonbanks	8	12
Domestic banks	73	59
External financing	19	30
Total Consumer Credit	100	100
Nonbank	4	34
Bank	96	66
Total Housing Credit	100	100
Nonbank	2	8
Bank	98	92
Total Business Credit	100	100
Nonbank	33	48
Bank	67	52

Note: Information only available through December 1999.
Source: Banco de México.

gathers qualitative information from 500 firms of different sizes nationwide. The most important findings of the 2000Q2 survey are that:

- Suppliers' credits continue to be the most widely used source of financing. They represented 61 percent of the sources of financing for small businesses and 50 percent for medium sized enterprises.
- Almost 80 percent of the firms surveyed granted some sort of financing, especially to customers, a common practice among SMEs.
- The survey shows that the most important reasons for businesses not demanding bank credit were high interest rates followed by unwillingness of the banks to lend money and the uncertainty of the prevailing economic situation existent prior to the July presidential elections.

IX. Globalization and the Entry of Foreign Banks

The globalization of the world's financial markets has created a new world environment with new opportunities and risks. Resource flows from developed to emerging countries has increased eight-fold in the last decade. Nonetheless, the increasing globalization has been accompanied by an unprecedented number and severity of banking crises around the world. Globalization implies a freer and significantly more important flow of capital across borders. It also implies an increasing globalization of borrowers represented by the larger and more internationally oriented enterprises in each country which can shop for credit internationally. These factors are really a pair of "scissors" for national banking sectors in emerging countries as they must compete for the top (low margin) segment of corporate borrowers and expand the local market for a second-tier of enterprises.

Globalization in Mexico's financial sector initiated with the NAFTA in 1994. With the relaxation, in two steps, of restrictions allowing foreign investors in Mexico's banking system, international banks increased their market share in total bank assets from about 1.4 percent in 1994 to about 50 percent by mid-2000.[12] Citibank purchased Banca Confia; Santander purchased Banco Mexicano and, more recently, Banca Serfin and it owns 20 percent of Banco Bital;[13] BBVA purchased Banco Mercantil Probursa and Bancomer, which already has the Bank of Montreal as an important shareholder; and Nova Scotia Bank purchased Inverlat. Other banks have shown interest in expanding their operations in Mexico.

Major foreign penetration is still a recent phenomenon, but it is already forcing Mexican banks to increase their efficiency and raise their standards to compete in a globalized market. As shown in Figure 6, the efficiency of the Mexican banking system still lags behind other countries around the world in terms of cost indicators (overhead costs as a percent of total assets).[14]

Figure 6. Overhead Costs as Percent of Total Assets
(period average 1990–97)

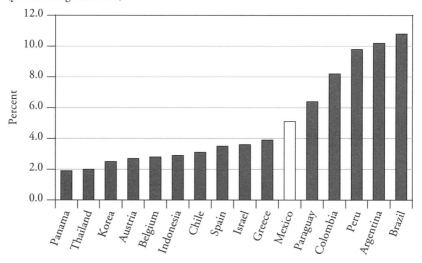

Source: World Bank Financial Sector Databases.

---

12. Includes the purchase of Serfin by Banco Santander and the purchase of Bancomer by BBVA.
13. Which is looking for a partnership with ING Bank.
14. Recently the largest Mexican bank (Banamex) was shedding staff to cut costs and improve its competitive position.

X. IPAB's Liabilities and Funding Requirements

Liabilities inherited by IPAB from FOBAPROA, and those acquired by IPAB directly to complete the full resolution of the problems of the Mexican banking system, were estimated at MXP725 billion by end-December 1999 (equivalent to US$76 billion and 15.7 percent of GDP), with the composition shown in Table 2.

One of the most important tasks faced by IPAB is the refinancing of its outstanding obligations. An important part of the liabilities are the notes issued by FOBAPROA in connection with the Capitalization and Loan Repurchase Program, amounting to MXP$156.6 billion. These notes have a 10-year bullet maturity. Having been issued during 1995–97, their maturities are concentrated in 2005–07.

Table 2. Structure of IPAB Liabilities (Stocks as of December 1999)

Type of Liability	Amount (MXP billion)	Comments
Notes for capitalization and loan purchase program	156.6	Maturity: 10-year bullet. Interest rate: average of Cetes minus 0.21; capitalizes quarterly but payable in full at maturity.
Notes for *Saneamientos*	414.7	
Already Issued	213.5	*For about half of this debt:* Maturity 5 years with periodic amortization. Interest rate: varies among cases; average of TIIE+1, payable quarterly. *For the remainder:* Maturity: Most 10-year bullet, rest 1-year bullet. Interest rate: Cetes, capitalizes quarterly but payable in full at maturity.
Pending	201.2	Maturity, amortization profile, and interest conditions to be determined.
Notes for branch sales	24.3	Varying among cases. Average remaining maturity at 5 years with periodic amortizations. Average interest rate at TIIE, payable periodically.
Guaranteed interbank liabilities including other liabilities and loan loss sharing.	129.8	Very short-term maturities, continuously refinanced. Interest rate: TIIE + spread.
Total	**725.4**	

Source: IPAB.

Another important part are the notes issued in connection with the old *saneamiento* programs, amounting to MXP$213.5 billion, which will mature in 2002[15] (see Figure 7). Because of the sizable amounts due, IPAB has launched a program to issue 3 year and 5 year bonds (BPAs or *Bonos de Proteccion al Ahorro*) which have been well received by the market.

The financing of outflows critically depend on IPAB's sources of income, which are the following:

(i) *Deposit Insurance Premia.* Established at 4 per 1000 pesos on total bank liabilities, to be paid monthly. They represent a small contribution to IPAB's total financing requirements.

(ii) *Asset sale and recovery.* Include the direct sale or administration rights of loan portfolios and the direct sale of tangible assets generating an expected annual cash flow of MXP$20 billion, or twice the size of the expected deposit insurance premia revenues. The law states that IPAB must sell all the assets inherited from FOBAPROA no later than January 20, 2004.

(iii) *Transfers from the federal government.* The funding is determined each year by Congress and represents the largest source of revenue for IPAB. The gov-

Figure 7. FOBAPROA Notes: Debt Service Commitments

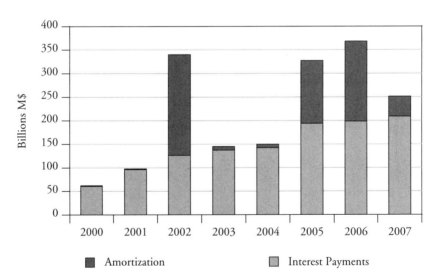

Source: IPAB.

---

15. This amount has been slightly reduced by the recent amortizations of FOBAPROA notes with Citibank-Confia (MXP$24.8 billion) and Serfin (MXP$14.6 billion).

ernment's intention is to transfer a yearly amount equal to at least the real component of IPAB debt net of expected income from asset sale and recovery and deposit insurance premia. The government has indicated its intention to raise the annual transfers above this minimum by keeping it constant at the equivalent of 0.8 percent of GDP per year. This is consistent with Mexico's IMF-supported program, which is designed to accommodate up to the equivalent of 1 percent of GDP in fiscal transfers to IPAB. The latter implies a significant fiscal effort for the foreseeable future, particularly considering the low, overall tax effort in Mexico (10 to 11 percent of GDP).

(iv) *Proceeds from the issuance of* BPAs. In March 2000, IPAB started a program of weekly public auctions of BPAs, which are three-year floating rate notes with coupon payments every 28 days, guaranteed by the federal government. Interest payments are based on the Cetes rate for the same maturity. BPAs are sold below par value (MXP$100.00), with the difference representing the premium that investors will receive on top of 28-day Cetes rates. The federal government has made room for the BPAs by suspending its auctions of 28-day Bondes, which had identical characteristics.

Market investors have received the BPA's with optimism. Initially, premiums paid over the Cetes rate were very similar to those of the now extinct Bondes28. However, pre-electoral market volatility has translated into a demand for higher premium payments (Figure 8). This has made BPAs a more expensive instrument to raise market funds, increasing the pressure for its possible formal assumption as part of Mex-

Figure 8. BPA Premium Costs Over 28-Day Cete Rates

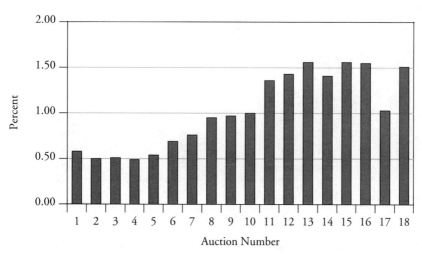

Source: IPAB.

ico's domestic public debt. This would eliminate the uncertainty regarding congressional approval of IPAB's yearly budget allocations. Moreover, it is likely that premium payments over the benchmark 28 day Cetes rate will decline as market volatility settles down.

Agenda for the Future

Putting behind the worst part of the banking crisis, leads to new critical issues related to the efficiency and profitability of the Mexican banking system; regulating competition in the face of the new industrial organization of the sector—in view of the dramatic consolidation that has taken place; the need for continued strengthening and enforceability of the regulatory framework; further movement towards consolidated regulation (which might lead to the merger of the various regulatory bodies, as well as to an enhanced autonomy of the supervising agency); further improvement in the quality of the banks' capital base; and improved access to groups so far largely excluded from formal financing (SMEs)[16] in tandem with the effective implementation of the new secured lending legislation. Other topics certainly include the role of the public banks in view of the international experience which largely points to the poor role of the government as provider of financial services. More punctual and immediate concerns include the following:

IPAB

IPAB's debt management strategy has first aimed at refinancing the most onerous debt, namely, the old notes issued in connection with the *Saneamiento* Program. IPAB's second priority is to refinance the interbank liabilities (guaranteed by IPAB) of banks under the liquidation process, not only because the law established the limit date (January 2002) for the conclusion of these processes, but also because this category of debt is growing at the fastest rate. A third priority would be to refinance the old notes issued in connection with the Capitalization and Loan Purchase Program.

Several risks exist that could jeopardize the sustainability of the bank resolution programs and IPAB's capability to refinance its liabilities.

(i)   The commitment of the officials to transfer, every year, enough resources to IPAB to cover at least the real component of the interest rate on IPAB's debt. These transfers should be explicitly reflected in the annual budget starting with the budget for the year 2001. The risks always will exist of Congressional opposition to the transfer of resources, since it implies a significant fiscal effort, particularly considering the low, overall tax effort in Mexico (10 to 11 percent of GDP).

---

16. The issue of regulating and supervising NBFIs is critical and a new draft law to that effect is under discussions.

(ii) Particularly complex refinancing challenges will be faced by IPAB when the FOBAPROA notes issued in connection with the old recapitalization and loan purchase programs fall due. The solution of intervened banks that are in the final stages of liquidation will also call for the refinancing of sizable interbank liabilities, which must occur by 2002 given the removal of the guarantee on this type of liability.

(iii) There is a risk that IPAB large debt issues associated with the bank recapitalization and resolution process could imply higher and more volatile interest rates than otherwise. The entrance into the market of large amounts of tradable IPAB debt could cause friction, and possibly interest rate volatility, the risk of which can be reduced only by careful debt management planned by IPAB.

(iv) By mid-2000, the proceeds of IPAB's asset and recovery program amounted to MXP$22.5 billion, exceeding the total annual expected amount of MXP$20 billion. Despite the good market signal of IPAB exceeding its target amount, the sustainability of the income generated is far from robust. IPAB has already sold some of its most valuable assets—The Camino Real Hotel chain—for which it received MXP$2.8 billion, and another of its larger assets—Banca Sefin—for which it received MXP$14.6 billion. The remaining assets, possibly with the exception of CINTRA, are less valuable as the ones already sold.

(v)   The anticipated MXP$20 billion of annual flows from the asset sale and recovery endeavors will become highly conditional on the efficiency of delinquent loan recovery by the institutions which purchased the rights for loan collections. So far, the collection rights for the Serfin and Union portfolios have resulted in revenues of MXP$2.7 billion and MXP$0.8 billion, respectively.

Legal

(i)   The Bankruptcy Law *(Ley de Concursos Mercantiles)* calls for the creation of a new Commission in charge of settling disputes between financial institutions and debtors when the latter files for bankruptcy. Needless to say, the challenge to achieve results through the court system is enormous and will require significant institutional development, training, and investments. If the Commission does not perform its functions in an efficient, fair, and transparent way, it will make delay the much needed recovery of credit to the private sector.

(ii) Both the Bankruptcy Law and the Secured Lending Law *(Ley Federal de Garantías)* call for the modernization of the public registries, which must become reliable repositories of records on secured transactions. Once lending secured by movable goods becomes more practicable, lenders will need a rapid method to record pledges, and prospective lenders will need quick access to information about existing liens. Legal reforms alone (enacted

May 2000) are not sufficient to guarantee operative efficiency and modernization of the registries. Inefficient operating procedures are an adverse incentive for credit resumption to the private sector.

Regulatory

(i)   Finally, there are pending regulatory issues that need to be implemented, in particular, the introduction of early warning and prompt corrective action systems. Knowledge of which institutions are the most fragile *a-priori* will allow regulators to act before a potential crisis translates into a fiscal cost.

Annex I
Regulatory Reforms

Changes in the Definition of Regulatory Capital

REDUCTION OF THE WEIGHT OF DEFERRED TAX ASSETS IN TIER 1 CAPITAL. The new rule still allows deferred tax assets to be part of Tier 1 capital, but with a limit equivalent to 20 percent of Tier 1 capital effective January 2003. A timetable is provided to phase in this measure, with a gradual decrease in the limit starting on 1 January 2000, when deferred tax assets are limited to no more than 80 percent of Tier 1 capital, decreasing by 20 percentage points annually until the 20 percent limit is reached.

CONVERTIBLE MANDATORY SUBORDINATE DEBT WILL NO LONGER COUNT AS TIER 1 CAPITAL. Instead these instruments will be included in Tier 2 capital, with no limit. However, existing debentures and cumulative instruments issued in 2000 and 2001 will be included in Tier 1 capital. Any new issues must be part of an integral recapitalization program. Nonobligatory, convertible, subordinated debt is included in Tier 2 capital, as well, with a limit of 50 percent of Tier 1 capital. Noncumulative capital securities will be limited to 15 percent of Tier 1 capital.

DEDUCTION OF ALL EQUITY INVESTMENT IN NONTRADED NONFINANCIAL COMPANIES. The new rule allows them to be fully deducted from Tier 1 capital, in the same way that investments in financial companies are deducted (rather than consolidated). The new capital rule allows for some exceptions, in particular the investments that result from debt capitalization, in order not to undermine debt workouts. The full deductibility of investments in nonfinancial companies from Tier 1 capital will be phased in starting in 2000, when 20 percent of the investments will be deducted. The percentage of deduction will increase to 40 percent in 2001, 60 percent in 2002, and to 100 percent in 2003.

SUBSTITUTION OF SPECIFIC PROVISIONS FOR GENERAL PROVISIONS IN TIER 2 CAPITAL. The reform allows general provisions, up to 1.25 percent of risk-weighted assets, to be counted as Tier 2 capital. In the regulation general provisions are defined as those provisions to cover for losses not linked to a specific loan.

REQUIREMENT TO DISCLOSE THE COMPOSITION OF REGULATORY CAPITAL. The bank will have to disclose, at least once a year, the detailed composition of its capital, distinguishing between Tier 1 and Tier 2 items.

IMPROVEMENT IN THE DEFINITION OF RISK-WEIGHTED ASSETS. The new capital rule introduces guidelines to better define the items that have a capital requirement. It provides guidelines to take into account the risk embedded in derivatives, and establishes that goodwill and other intangible assets are to be deducted from capital. In addition, the value for accounting purposes of assets has to be the same as the value given to them for capital requirements.

New Accounting and Valuation Rules
(CNBV Circular 1343, 10 January 1997)

ACCOUNTING PRACTICES. The modifications involve the improvement of accounting practices toward international standards regarding market valuation of investments. Securities classified in the trading account or as available for sale must be marked to market. Transfers from the trading account or available for sale account to the held to maturity account require CNBV's approval. Losses must be recognized at the time of the transfer. Impairment of securities due to credit risk will be recognized by a valuation reserve for securities created through a charge off to the profit and loss account.

STRENGTHENED VALUATIONS OF FIXED ASSETS. CNBV has issued a new regulation requiring banks to obtain independent appraisals of their fixed assets, both banking premises and other real estate owned or repossessed. Such appraisals would be conducted only once in order to establish an appropriate valuation. If property values are overstated, they will be written down. Thereafter, bank premises will be revalued for inflation; however, foreclosed properties will not be.

CONSISTENCY BETWEEN THE REGULATORY AND FISCAL TREATMENT OF PROVISIONS. The Ministry of Finance plans to enhance the consistency between the regulatory and fiscal treatment of provisions by mid-2000.

ACCOUNTING STANDARDS. The modifications involve the introduction of accounting standards applicable to asset securitization and asset transfers.

Credit Portfolio Classification Rules

CLASSIFICATION RULES FOR CREDIT CARD LOANS (CNBV CIRCULAR 1449, 14 OCTOBER 1999). The new regulation establishes simple and objective classification and provisioning rules based on repayment capacity. This new rule became effective in December 1999.

CLASSIFICATION RULES FOR MORTGAGE LOANS (CNBV CIRCULAR 1460, JANUARY 2000). The new regulation establishes simple and objective classification and provisioning rules based on repayment capacity. The rule became effective as of June 2000.

CLASSIFICATION RULES FOR COMMERCIAL LOANS (CNBV CIRCULAR 1480, 29 SEPTEMBER 2000). The new regulation establishes simple and objective classification and provisioning rules based on repayment capacity. This new rule effective as of January 2000.

Transparency and Disclosure
(CNBV Circular 1448, 14 October 1999)

The *regulation* established the requirement to disclose in a timely fashion "troubled" debt, financial information by business segments, and aggregate information on transactions with related parties.

Regulatory Forbearance
(CNBV Circular 1448, 14 October 1999)

Under the new regulation, forbearance (defined as exceptions to specific existing domestic accounting regulations) could only be granted provided that either systemic issues or individual restructuring plans are in place. In addition, forbearance has to be disclosed in the financial statements, with an assessment of its impact on the financial conditions of the beneficiary banks. Current forbearance has to be ratified by CNBV and disclosed.

12

Micro, Small, and Medium-Scale Enterprises

This Chapter was written by Kristin Hallberg and Sonia Plaza with the valuable input of James C. Hanna.

I. Background

The economy of Mexico is diversified, with the highest proportion of activity in its formal economic structure. Services account for 47.3 percent of GDP, community and social services 22.4 percent, financial services 13.5 percent, and transport and communications 11.4 percent. Industry generates 28.2 percent of GDP, and agriculture 5 percent. The informal sector is large. Although estimates of its size and importance vary widely, it is reasonable to conclude that during 1999 about 15 to 25 percent (depending on the month of the year) of the urban workforce worked, although fewer than 35 hours per week. During the first quarter of 2000, the economy experienced vigorous growth, low unemployment, and an increase in consumption, and GDP grew by 7.9 percent year-on-year in real terms, the highest increase in three years.

Nevertheless, the productive sector continues to be characterized by a dual structure that seems to have become increasingly differentiated in the wake of trade liberalization and the banking crisis of the 1990s. On one side is a dynamic export sector made up of internationally competitive conglomerates including *maquiladoras*; on the other is a less efficient domestic, market-oriented sector, dominated by microenterprises and small- and medium-scale enterprises (MSMEs).[1] The linkages between the export sector and the domestic economy are weak, due partly to the import-processing nature of the maquiladora industry, but also to the concentration of exports among a few large firms and the lack of competitiveness of many MSMEs. In addition, the two groups are financed differently: the first has access to international

---

1. The definition of MSMEs used by INEGI is based on the number of employees: microenterprise = 1 to 15; small, = 16 to 100; medium 101 to 250; large = >250.

sources of finance, and increased its international borrowing during the crisis; the second is more constrained by problems in the domestic banking sector, which reduced its lending to the private sector even during the 1996–99 recovery.

The last National Survey of Microbusinesses in Urban Areas, by INEGI, was done in 1992 (it will be updated in 2000.) Its survey of 9,036 microbusiness owners (those with 6 employees or less, but up to 15 in manufacturing)[2] indicates that microbusinesses tend to have reasonably long operating experience—an average of nearly 7 years for female-headed enterprises and about 9 years for male-headed ones, and that female participation in urban microbusiness was rising (reaching 39 percent of the total in 1992, of which about 33 percent were operated from home). Significantly, however, 67 percent of microbusinesses operated by both sexes had no intention of expanding with new investment, of increasing employees, or of developing new products (versus 21 percent which responded favorably). In response to questions about the main problems they faced, entrepreneurs listed as their principal constraints a lack of clients, excessive competition, low earnings, and lack of economic resources and credit (access and cost).[3]

Though more thorough verification is needed, it is quite probable that the principal growth strategy that many microbusinesses in Mexico need to employ to break out of these constraints consists mainly of developing new markets and upgrading their competitiveness—upgrading product designs, improving quality and operating efficiency, etc. Most are likely to operate within their own local communities, which in general are substantially separate from the mainstream economy. This means that such businesses depend for their production inputs on local retailers and sell mostly to nearby consumers in the area. They sell almost entirely to individual customers (rather than intermediaries like wholesalers, retailers, or other traders) and on spot-cash sales terms rather than on contracts and orders. Likewise, most buy supplies and raw materials from retail firms rather than buying from wholesalers or importing directly.

Mexico has strengthened its position in world trade since 1994. However, the benefits of its trade expansion have not reached MSMEs. Recent World Bank (2000) analysis confirms a clear correlation between exporting and firm-level efficiency (Figure 1). Both exporting and productivity growth are linked with high-performance workplace practices and labor skills, and investments in product quality and modernization are made in anticipation of entry into foreign markets. The productivity benefits of exporting—"learning-by-exporting" effects—grow as the years of exporting experience accumulate. Learning effects are also associated with buyer–supplier relationships through the provision of raw materials, technical assistance, training, and sometimes financing.

2. As recorded in "Gender Earnings Differentials in the Microenterprise Sector: Evidence from Rural and Urban Mexico," by Susana Sanchez, World Bank, June 1998.
3. These conclusions are similar to those in *Mujeres Empresarias en Mexico*, a study prepared by the National Autonomous University of Mexico (UNAM) and the National Foundation for Women Business Owners of the U.S. in 1998.

Figure 1. Export Status by Size, 1993–98

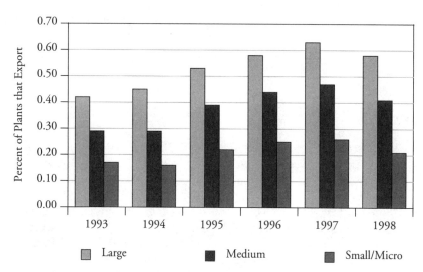

Source: World Bank (2000), from INEGI *Encuesta Industrial Anual* data.

Although greater numbers of Mexican MSMEs became involved in export markets during the 1995–96 crisis, they shifted back to the domestic market in disproportionate numbers when the recession lifted. Larger and foreign-owned firms seem to have a more "permanent" presence in external markets, taking advantage of trade opportunities opened by NAFTA. The reasons for the transitory nature of MSME exporting are not clear, but may be related to financing constraints[4] and the usual list of factors underlying low MSME competitiveness which includes poor labor and management skills, outdated technologies, inadequate product quality and delivery times.

Now that the government has accomplished an impressive set of real sector reforms on the macroeconomic front—liberalization of trade and investment and entry into NAFTA—attention must shift to extending productivity benefits to the "other Mexican private sector." This is mainly a microeconomic agenda, focused on the needs and constraints of MSMEs. It will involve improving the legal and regulatory environment for private sector development, increasing access to financing for MSMEs, and building the "support infrastructure" of nonfinancial services to boost their competitiveness. The MSME agenda is also linked to the government's social objectives (improving income-earning opportunities for the poor and promoting

---

4. Differences in the patterns of financing of small versus large firms and domestic market-oriented versus export-oriented firms are explored in World Bank (1998).

investment in less-developed regions of the country), decentralization objectives (devolving decisionmaking and responsibilities to subnational governments), and public finance objectives (making better use of scarce fiscal resources).

II. Issues

Notwithstanding the wide-ranging economic reforms instituted in the country, Mexican MSMEs will be affected by:

GREATER EXTERNAL COMPETITION. The free-trade agreement between Mexico and the European Union, will enter into force on 1 July 2000. Complete elimination of tariffs will take 10 years (much less time than under the NAFTA provisions). In the short term, EU firms (small and medium firms) seem more prepared to seize the trade creation opportunities of the agreement than Mexican enterprises. However limited international marketing experience, poor quality control and product standardization, and little access to international partners, are likely to impede expansion of MSMEs into European markets. Firms in the country are not ready to face this challenge.[5] European markets demand a different set of export requirements to enter in their markets, such as ISO9000 and ISO 14000. The southern region could take advantage of its closeness to ports to become one of the most attractive production platforms for export-oriented firms. However, the challenge will be to extend the benefits of this liberalization (trade and investment) to MSMEs in a way that these firms can become direct exporters or suppliers of multinational firms selling in Europe.

UNEVEN REGIONAL DEVELOPMENT. The huge differences that exist among the different areas in Mexico in the extent of industrialization and in the divergence of agriculture practices have sharpened the existing divisions. The central region, which includes the Federal District and the state of Mexico, accounts for nearly one-third of GDP, despite the fact that it covers only 1.2 percent of the land area. Monterrey (Nuevo León) and Guadalajara (Jalisco) are the leading industrial cities after the capital. The *maquiladora* industry in the border area has boosted employment. Tijuana in Baja California, and Ciudad Juárez in Chihuahua, have become important *maquiladora* cities. However, most southern states are still exhibiting high levels of extreme poverty. Furthermore, the inadequate transport and communications infrastructure has impeded more balanced regional growth. Certain states, such as Yucatán, have a good infrastructure system; others, such as Campeche, lack electricity and connections for their agroindustry production.

---

5. According to the calculations of Professor Clemente Ruiz of the Economics Department at UNAM, only 3,000 firms will benefit from the trade liberalization with Europe.

DUAL ECONOMY AND CONCENTRATION OF TRADE IN FEW FIRMS. There are highly disparate economies in Mexico, with traditional sectors such as agriculture stagnating, and others, such as services—which now account for 47.3 percent of GDP—growing strongly. Manufacturing is the most important productive sector and the main source of exports (89.4 percent of the total in 1999). Over half of the total, 52.2 percent was produced in *maquiladoras*. Although the country has experienced a boom in trade (double what it was five years ago), the export base has remained rather narrow and concentrated in a few larger firms. According to the president of the National Chamber of the Industry of Transformation (Canacintra), of the 2 million firms in Mexico, only 40,00 are direct or indirect exporters, and only 300 industries have international commercialization capacity.

Furthermore, the Mexican export sector remains very dependent on imports of intermediate and capital goods. Mexican firms supply only 4 percent of inputs to the export sector. This dependence has meant that export growth has increased the import bill. For 1999, Mexico reported an US$895 million trade deficit in December, the highest in 13 months (INEGI data).

POVERTY, INEQUALITY, AND THE ROLE OF MSMES. Mexico is currently among the most unequal countries in the world. Rather than a problem of lack of resources, poverty seems to be an issue of distribution. In this context, the importance of MSMEs in fostering income stability, growth, and employment becomes crucial to alleviating poverty. Thus, a strategy to foster the competitiveness of MSMEs should include support for a decentralized system that would enhance the private delivery of goods and services. Any program should aim to be adapted to local conditions and be responsive to the needs of local enterprises.

It is believed that programs that employ an integrated approach (finance, business development services, commercialization, and improved access to knowledge) will have a greater impact than narrow programs. The country has the human capital, infrastructure, and local initiatives needed to develop a decentralized, integrated, and innovative approach to reach small producers in the most disadvantaged areas. The new strategy could enhance public–private initiatives in which the state's business, government, and community leaders forge a shared vision for the state's economic future, and can take steps to make this vision a reality.

III. Possible Areas of Work

Government Programs that Provide Business Development Services

A recent inventory of federally funded programs in Mexico identified over 200 MSME programs in various Secretariats covering a wide array of services, including export assistance, technology upgrading, provision of information on markets and technologies, technical assistance and consulting services, training of labor and management, and supplier development programs. Many of these programs are new, having been initiated during the current Administration.

Issues[6]

COVERAGE. There is often a discrepancy between the segment of the MSME population for which the program was designed, and the firms that actually use the program. Most federal programs reach larger numbers of small- and medium-scale enterprises than microenterprises. In general the coverage of programs is low, due in part to a lack of information about them on the part of MSMEs, particularly those outside major urban areas.

Duplication. Although there is some duplication of services across programs (for example, in training and basic business advisory services), this does not seem to be a problem relative to the large problem of low coverage.

COST RECOVERY. Although some programs have introduced or plan to introduce methods of recovering costs through client fees, many program managers do not place a high priority on cost recovery, and most clients expect that the state will cover most of the cost of the service. In two-thirds of the programs studied, client fees were zero or less than MXP$15,000.

DECENTRALIZATION. The execution of federal programs is centralized, with little participation of state or municipal institutions, non-government institutions, or the private sector. State and local authorities are rarely included in the identification, design, or implementation of federal programs. However, there are some local programs designed by the state in partnership with the private sector that are working efficiently, such as the *Programa Buenaventura* in Campeche and the similar one in Merida.

PRIVATE PROVISION OF SERVICES. Most federal programs do not use external private service providers. The CRECE program has this objective, but to date most of the services have been provided by CRECE staff. An exception is the COMPITE program, which has developed a market of trained experts. Client surveys indicate that most MSMEs would prefer that BDS programs be private or mixed public-private operations. Another federal program that aims to deliver services through private operators—with some success—is the technology upgrading program in CONACyT. The design of this program included three levels: one level in which the

---

6. The following issues were identified through studies of 12 BDS programs. DFC (1998) and GEA (1998). The programs studied were SIEM, CETRO–CRECE, COMPITE, SSI, and *Agrupamientos Industriales* (SECOFI); *Desarrollo de Proveedores* (SECOFI, NAFIN, and BANCOMEXT); *Capacitación y Asistencia Técnica* (NAFIN); *México Exporta* (BANCOMEXT); FUNTEC (UNDP); and *Sistema de Desarrollo Tecnológico* (SEP–CONACyT).

government plays an important role as a policy adviser and designer of the program; a second level in which a private operator provides the services and assist the training firms; and a third level in which the firms and the consultants they hire interact in a private market to obtain and provide the services.

PROGRAM MANAGEMENT AND EVALUATION. The remuneration of program managers is usually not tied to efficiency improvements and the achievement of program objectives. Internal evaluations of program performance usually depend on program outputs (for example, number of firms served) rather than on program impacts (for example, increased sales and employment).

Internationally, a paradigm shift is emerging in the approach of development agencies to improving small enterprise performance through BDS.[7] There is a shared recognition that traditional interventions by governments and donors have failed to provide quality, affordable BDS to large numbers of MSMEs, and that evidence of sustained impact is scarce. In fact, publicly subsidized services may have crowded out commercially-oriented providers, and led MSMEs to expect continued subsidies. The emerging strategy focuses on developing markets for BDS that are appropriate to and demanded by MSMEs, rather than on direct provision of services by governments and donors. This shifts the focus of public intervention away from the direct provision and subsidies at the level of the BDS transaction to the facilitation of a sustained increase in the demand for and supply of services. Many of the assumptions underlying the change in approach are similar to those that guided the microfinance revolution: that services and delivery mechanisms can be developed that meet the needs of even the lowest-income MSMEs, and can be provided on a commercially sustainable basis.

Recommendations

Both the recent work on federally funded BDS programs and the lessons of international experience suggest that, in order to improve the coverage and quality of nonfinancial services to meet MSME needs, the government should facilitate the growth of a more decentralized, private sector-driven BDS industry. Today, the multitude of training and assistance programs operate largely independently, try to reach their beneficiaries through different means, and lack a monitoring and evaluation mechanism. Shifting the current model into a more decentralized approach suggests the following changes in the role and management of publicly-funded BDS programs:

- Adopting a second-tier "facilitator" role vis-à-vis first-tier BDS providers (that is, leaving provision to private firms, consultants, business associations, universities, nonprofit institutions, and NGOs); this implies a shift away from direct service provision to product development and capacity building of commercially-oriented BDS providers.

7. See, for example, Steel, Tanburn, and Hallberg (2000).

- More businesslike program management, including the use of performance incentives, tighter cost control, and the use of a monitoring and evaluation system as a management tool.
- An explicit goal of financial self-sustainability through gradual increases in cost recovery from client fees, particularly for higher-income MSME clients, and more sophisticated services; new programs should be based on cost recovery.
- A search for lower-cost delivery mechanisms such as information and communication technologies.
- Where possible, privatization of self-sustaining BDS institutions, or the creation of mixed public–private entities.

Being close to the local situation provides better opportunities to design and modify programs according to needs. State and local governments should be involved in the design, implementation, and monitoring of assistance. Some interventions are best organized regionally, for example, with subnational governments coordinating and restructuring existing federal programs in order to come up with regional public-private initiatives. In Mexico, the "champions" of local public––private initiatives have tended to come from the private sector or from state government (for example, the *Transformando Campeche* initiative, and *Chihuahua Siglo XXI*).

Microfinance and SME Finance

As noted above, the dual nature of enterprise financing in Mexico became more pronounced during the crisis of the mid-1990s. On the one hand, large exporters—including the *maquiladoras*—increased their borrowing abroad for both working capital and investment financing. In addition to long-term debt, large companies issued equities abroad, typically in the form of American Depository Receipts (ADRs). On the other hand, smaller and domestic market-oriented firms had less access to international sources of finance. It is difficult to determine whether the different financing patterns of these two groups is due more to size (large versus small) or to market orientation (export versus domestic). Increasingly, however, a small number of SME exporters have been accessing international credit.

SMEs have traditionally been financed by the development banks, particularly NAFIN, through first-tier commercial banks. During the crisis the volume of credit to SMEs declined significantly and remained low even during the subsequent recovery of 1996–97. To compensate for commercial banks' reluctance to lend, the development banks attempted to increase their direct lending to SMEs, but with limited success. This suggests that both demand-side and supply-side factors were behind the decline in enterprise credit during and after the crisis. In fact, the resumption of economic growth after the crisis has been termed the "credit-less recovery." The credit decline has been uninterrupted since the end of 1994. The total amount of loans at the end of March 2000 was still 42 percent lower in real terms than at the end of 1994.[8]

A quarterly survey conducted by the Central Bank since the end of 1998 has shed some light on the way firms have managed within the current credit restrictions. According to the latest data available, in the last quarter of 1999, of the firms surveyed, only 38.2 percent had access to some bank credit. Large firms found it easier to get credit; 61.3 percent of them obtained loans, compared with 38.3 percent of those classified as medium-sized and 28.1 percent of small businesses.

Credit unions serve mostly medium-size enterprises, primarily in rural areas. Between 1994 and 1997 credit unions experienced a sizeable drop in assets and outstanding portfolio (the latter by 60 percent), and arrears soared. A viability assessment carried out in mid-1996 found only 74 of 314 credit unions to be viable.

The smallest firms—microenterprises and small-scale enterprises—have long benefited from nonbank financial institutions such as savings and loan societies. Recent consolidation of these institutions, which fared somewhat better than commercial banks during the recession, has resulted in a core of stronger institutions. Until recently, Mexico has lagged to a number of other Latin American countries in the development of microfinance institutions.

Access to microfinance plays a key role in enabling microbusinesses to reach new markets. However, according to a recent survey by *Acción International*, only 1 percent of microbusinesses have access to such finance in a formal basis. For this to change, the nascent involvement of some of the country's largest microfinance institutions (MFIs) needs to be accelerated. Low-income households can benefit from the increased presence of such institutions, taking advantage of loans for production, consumption, and improved housing. With informal interest rates for loans estimated to range from 10 to 20 percent *per month*, the full cost recovery monthly interest rates of 2 to 3 percent for formal sector MFIs represents an important opportunity for microenterprises to hold on to a greater share of profits.

Recent Reforms to Bankruptcy Legislation and Rules on Loan Collateral

The Mexican Congress passed several pieces of legislation in April 2000: an update of the 57-year-old bankruptcy code, and several laws modifying the rules on credit guarantees. The aim of these reforms is to increase bank lending. Although the laws were needed, there is not much confidence in an immediate credit revival. Firms contend that the rules on loan collateral were issued to formalize already existing practices. The contribution of the new bankruptcy law has been the establishment of two new processes to execute the guarantees, one judicial and one extrajudicial. Both are designed to shorten the process of bank foreclosure when borrowers default on loans. However, given the inefficient judicial system and the still prevalent

---

8. Oxford Analytica Brief, May 10, 2000.

culture of default of payments (since 1995), it will be difficult to see a rapid positive impact on increasing credit to the private sector.

Subsidized credit and debt forgiveness programs should be eliminated to restore financial discipline, especially in rural areas. Doing so would allow established savings and loan societies and emerging microfinance institutions to expand their services to small entrepreneurs and the poor in a sustainable manner. Private commercial banks would also be more likely to provide such services if the lending environment were less distorted.

The regulation and supervision of nonbank financial intermediaries has created some problems related to governance and credibility. For example, the nontradability of voting rights has enabled small groups with negligible equity investments to control some societies. Such control has facilitated collusion with management—a situation conducive to collapses similar to those observed in credit unions. Prudential regulation on portfolio allocation, portfolio quality, reserve requirements, and allocation of net surpluses should be carefully examined.

Recommendations

Government efforts to strengthen microfinance and SME finance should focus on building an enabling environment for better financial contracts and services. These requirements are no different from those which benefit all of Mexico's financial sector. In particular, the authorities should create an effective system of registries, develop faster ways to execute loan guarantees, and foster an efficient legal framework for loan contracts secured with movable property, business receivables, and household durable goods.

Although specialized microfinance institutions are important mechanisms for providing the poor with financial services, they are serving the low end of the microenterprise spectrum. A small portion of their clientele is engaged in activities other than low-skill self-employment. Efforts to increase access to finance by market-oriented microenterprises and SMEs will have to involve institutions working in these sectors—for example, savings and loan societies or commercial banks that are able and willing to innovate and explore new market niches.

Some of the key lessons of the success of microfinance are that sustainable microfinance institutions do not only rely on access to commercially priced credit lines, but also on building management systems to handle rapid growth. Another way to demonstrate how to achieve sustainable microfinance is through the dissemination of best practices. For example:

- Demonstration techniques among a select number of existing microcredit financial intermediaries and NGOs through the provision of training and technical assistance packages and a small credit line managed by a range of large and small microfinance institutions.
- Prudential regulations—share international best practice and conduct studies of the local situation in regulations appropriate to microfinance market devel-

opment (mainly regarding the registration and reporting system, capital adequacy, and loan loss provision requirements).

Monitoring and Evaluation

Recognizing the need for greater coordination across agencies involved in industrial policy, the government established the *Comisión Intersectorial de Política Industrial* (CIPI) in May 1996.[9] The members of CIPI include the Ministers of SECOFI (President), SHCP, SECODAM, SEDESOL, STPS, and SEP, and the *Directors General* of BANCOMEXT, NAFIN, and CONACyT. CIPI meets at least six times a year and provides an important forum for senior officials to share information. However, discussions tend to focus on narrow programmatic issues rather than on policy matters or budgetary issues. Moreover, since the secretariat of CIPI has few staff, it is not able to provide the technical support to the wide range of programs CIPI is supposed to coordinate.

Evaluation

Some of the existing MSME assistance programs (for example, CRECE and CIMO) have established evaluation systems to measure their performance; others have just started to formulate their own systems. However, there is no consistent evaluation methodology that is applied across Ministries, and there is no central repository of information on the performance of these programs. As a result, it is difficult for the government to obtain a comprehensive view of the status of its efforts, hold Ministries responsible for delivering results, and use the information for future planning and budgeting. Better evaluation of the impact of programs on MSME performance would also help individual program managers redesign their programs to meet their objectives.

The government has launched a series of initiatives to reform the planning and budgeting process, and ensure greater accountability for public expenditures. These initiatives include the Programa de Modernización de la Administración Pública (PROMAP) and the Nueva Estrategia Programática (NEP). The basic concept is for agencies to define overall goals in terms of desired outcomes, set specific quality standards for services, develop plans for activities that will lead to the attainment of specified objectives, prepare an appropriate budget, measure actual performance, and report accomplishments. Program evaluation plays a central role in this process. SECODAM has already provided training to agencies in the PROMAP methodology, and has established a unit that focuses solely on evaluation issues.

Recommendations

The government should move as quickly as possible to establish a monitoring mechanism for all its federal programs. An MSME program evaluation system needs to

---

9. For more detail on these issues and recommendations, see Nexus Associates (1998, 1999).

be designed to ensure accountability to the fiscal authorities, transparency, and dissemination of information, while encouraging and assisting program managers to assume direct responsibility for obtaining information to operate programs successfully. Specific recommendations include the following:

- Establish an independent Program Evaluation Office to establish evaluation standards, provide assistance to MSME program managers and evaluation staff, disseminate information on best practices, review and approve evaluation plans, and review and synthesize the results of annual evaluations. This office can be homed under either SECOFI or CIPI. However, taking advantage of the new information technologies, a virtual system can be designed to monitor different programs. This information system can capture all the relevant information from the firms, and all the stakeholders will have access to the same information.
- Establish and monitor indicators of MSME performance.
- Provide information to subnational governments on the results of analysis and on federal MSME programs.
- Require individual MSME programs to conduct evaluations on an ongoing basis as a condition for funding and provide this information to the PEO.

A better system of planning, budgeting, and evaluation of government assistance for MSMEs would allow good projects and programs to be expanded, and those less useful to be discontinued. The structure can also be used to gather inputs from subnational governments and the private sector into the planning and design process, and to establish benchmarks against which to evaluate proposals of state and local authorities.

According to OECD experience, the following recommendations are as a good guide for improving the evaluations of SME policies.[10]

- The evaluation methodology should be designed at the same time as the policy or program so that the necessary data and acceptance by the relevant parties of the evaluation procedures and criteria can be secured.
- Evaluation should be user-oriented, serving the information needs of the different program participants and clients.
- Evaluations should use a combination of methods to satisfy different information needs.
- Evaluation from results must reach the appropriate policymakers and decisionmakers at the right level, and should be encouraged to ensure they will lead to needed improvements.

---

10. Andersson, Thomas. "Policy Design, Implementation and Evaluation—Rationale, Efficiency and Systematic Concerns." For the SME Forum, *Public Policies for SMEs in Europe*, Lisbon, 13–14 April 2000.

References

DFC. 1998. *"Análisis del Diseño y Ejecución de Programas Seleccionados."* BDS Project report for SECOFI and the World Bank, December 18.

Grupo de Economistas y Asociados. 1998. *"Proyecto de Fomento a la Competitividad de las Micro, Pequeñas, y Medianas Empresas en México: Coordinación General del Proyecto."* BDS Project report prepared for SECOFI and the World Bank, January 28.

Hallberg, K. 2000. "A Market-Oriented Strategy for Small- and Medium-Scale Enterprises." Washington, D.C.: IFC Discussion Paper No. 40, February 15.

Nexus Associates. 1998. "Evaluation System for Non-Financial Business Assistance Programs for MSMEs in Mexico." BDS Project report prepared for SECOFI and World Bank, December 8.

Nexus Associates. 1999. "Definition of a Permanent System to Determine the Priority Needs of MSMEs in Mexico." BDS Project Report prepared for SECOFI and the World Bank, June 1.

Steel, W. F., J. Tanburn, and K. Hallberg. 2000. "The Emerging Strategy for Building Business Development Services Markets." In J. Levitsky, (ed.), *Business Development Services: Review of International Experience*. London: Intermediate Technology Publications.

World Bank. 1998. "Mexico: Strengthening Enterprise Finance: Toward Reform of the Legal and Regulatory Foundation of the Financial Infrastructure." Report No. 17733-ME, September 25.

World Bank. 2000. "Export Dynamics and Productivity: Analysis of Mexican Manufacturing in the 1990s." Report No. 19864-ME, February 25.

13

Housing

*This Chapter was written by Richard Clifford, and
Bertrand M. Renaud with the valuable input of Sabino Escobedo
and Thesis Consultores, S.C.*

I. Introduction

The growth of the Mexican economy is now urban based. The quality of the urban stock of housing, therefore, has major economic, social, and environmental impacts on Mexican society. At present the housing sector is at a crossroads: there is an important impetus for reform under way, but at the same time the efficiency of urban investment is constrained by a housing policy that focuses only on the provision of subsidized finance by public entities for finished housing for the benefit of selected urban constituencies. The result is a housing sector that is inefficient by international standards: new mortgage originations have been less than 2.5 percent of GDP in the past five years, about half the level of other middle-income countries. More important, the majority of Mexicans do not have incomes sufficient to participate in even this heavily subsidized housing finance system, and are thus consigned to informal, and often illegal, housing solutions. Therefore, this Chapter focuses on steps to improve social interest housing finance and to provide better housing options to those Mexicans who do not qualify for home mortgages.

II. Characteristics of Supply and Demand

Although there has been significant improvement in the last 40 years, the quality of Mexican housing stock remains a serious problem, and is exacerbated each year by the number of informal housing solutions adopted by people in the low-income market.[1] Improvements are evident in the average size of homes, access to urban services, and the quality of construction materials. Rural areas and the poorer states of the south lag behind significantly in these quality measures. Census data indicate that a large number of homes (in excess of 6 million, about one-third of the existing stock) are in need of replacement or significant upgrading, symptomatic of the large number of informal housing solutions. In addition, there has been a big decline in the availability of rental units. While the share of homes constructed in the formal sector has risen in the last decade, it still represents only about 50 percent of new home construction. The large share of informal sector construction has important implications for urban planning and the cost of providing urban services.

For at least the next decade household growth is likely to be quite strong. Demand for additional housing will be about 700,000 to 800,000 units per year. This is due principally to the structure of the population; even though population growth has slowed significantly in the last 25 years, household formation will continue to grow due to the increase in the population 40 years and older. Fast-growing areas, such as in the north and the State of Mexico, will account for a large share of the demand. The most rapid growth will likely be in medium-sized cities (100,000 to 500,000 inhabitants). Given the decline in the minimum wage over the last 20 years, and the debilitating effect of the 1994–95 crisis on household incomes, most Mexicans are likely to be ineligible for traditional social interest home mortgages. They will likely remain in the progressive and home improvement markets, and at the very low end (for example, PROSAVI) of the new, finished housing market.

III. Institutional and Market Structure

Mexico's current housing finance system dates from the 1970s, when inward looking economic strategies and strong directed credit policies led to the creation of specific institutions established for different market segments and income groups. Since then, Mexico's financial system has remained quite small, and savings mobilization has been weak. Access to housing finance has been dominated by political and administrative processes rather than market driven. Mexican consumers have had little or no choice whatsoever.

The institutions operating the housing finance system are segmented according to markets: (a) low income, attending to people earning less than 3 minimum monthly wages (mmws); (b) social interest, earning 3 to 8 mmws; (c) middle and upper income, earning 9 mmws and above. The Figure 1 below summarizes this highly segmented market in Mexico.

---

1. See also: INEGI data; a report prepared by the Joint Center for Housing Studies, entitled "The State of Mexico's Housing," April 1997; and a report prepared by Thesis Consultores, entitled *"Política Habitacional en México,"* which contains a model of housing supply and demand.

Figure 1. Housing Finance in Mexico

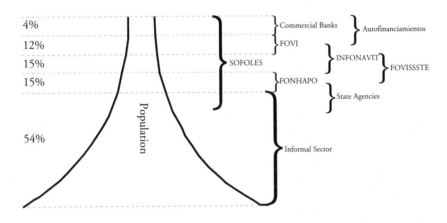

Source: Jose Manuel Agudo.

MIDDLE AND UPPER INCOME HOUSING. The high end of the housing market was funded by the commercial banks until the 1994–95 crisis, when most of their mortgage loans went into default. The banks have yet to reenter the market,[2] thus leaving new and unregulated *autofinanciamientos* as the only participants in the upper income market. There is virtually no lending occurring in this market today.

SOCIAL INTEREST HOUSING. These entities dominate the housing finance system, and rely on public or quasi-public sources of funds.

- INFONAVIT *(Instituto del Fondo Nacional de la Vivienda para los Trabajadores),* with 67 percent of the market, is the largest mortgage lender in Mexico. It is funded itself through a 5 percent payroll tax paid by employers in the formal sector. INFONAVIT acts as a retail mortgage lender and has a notoriously weak origination and servicing record. Since 1994 INFONAVIT has been the second "leg" of the pension system, representing 40 percent of an individual's total pension contribution. A worker's pension payable at retirement is represented by the sum of the accumulated value in his or her pension and INFONAVIT accounts.
- FOVI *(Fondo de Operación y Financiamiento Bancario a la Vivienda)* is a *Banco de México* trust fund that onlends funds to low-income borrowers through

---

2. Some very small commercial bank programs have been recently announced. See also the Financial Sector Policy Chapter for a discussion of the banking sector today in Mexico.

commercial and mortgage banks on a risk-sharing basis. It has about 20 percent of the market. The mortgage banks, known as SOFOLES (*Sociedades Financieras de Objeto Limitado,* or nonbank banks) were approved in 1995 at the height of the crisis. FOVI provides financing in three categories: (a) the Prosavi *(Programa Especial de Credito y Subsidio a la Vivienda)* program targeted at households earning 3 mmws, (b) the "A" program targeted at households earning 4 to 5 mmws, and (c) the "B" program targeted at households earning 6 to 8 mmws.

- FOVISSSTE *(Fondo de la Vivienda del Instituto del Seguro Social al Servicio de los Trabajadores del Estado)* is the other mandated federal program for public employees. It has about 6 percent of the market.
- Some state housing institutes also fund social interest housing.

LOW INCOME HOUSING. At the lowest end of the market—representing about half of the population—informal housing predominates. These are self-built and often illegal settlements. Two federal agencies, FONHAPO (*Fondo Nacional de Habitaciones Populares)* and SEDESOL provide limited resources. FONHAPO is a fund that was initially intended to finance low-income progressive housing programs, but which developed portfolio problems that have severely limited its participation in the sector. SEDESOL operates a small progressive housing scheme. State housing institutes, though also small, focus on low-income housing. Finally, there are numerous private providers of low-income housing finance, which are also quite small.

IV. Recent Performance

The past five years have been characterized by a combination of a major crisis, significant progress, and an important lost opportunity. The economic instability after December 1994 significantly shaped the current state of housing finance in Mexico. High interest rates and declining real wages resulted in severe default problems and a large buildup of negative amortization in all of Mexico's housing finance segments. While the crisis halted new lending and exposed numerous weaknesses in the financial sector, it also provided a strong incentive to address these weaknesses in a more fundamental way. Since 1995 several reforms have been made. They include:

- Continued improvement in the legal structure with respect to foreclosure, with 27 of 32 states (including the D.F.) having an acceptable foreclosure law.
- Passage in 1999 of a new bankruptcy law and several amendments to existing laws to provide for the use of collateral and guarantees in credit contracts (secured lending). Both reforms are considered a breakthrough in financial sector legislation in clarifying creditor property rights in loan contracts, encouraging debtors to honor their obligations, and offering an efficient and expedient mechanism for taking care of illiquid and insolvent debtors.

- Financial sector reform, including changes in commercial banks' definition of
  regulatory capital and credit portfolio classification rules, new accounting and
  valuation rules, increased transparency and disclosure by requiring commercial banks to disclose in a timely fashion all "troubled" transactions, and elimination of discretionary regulatory forbearance.

Institutionally there have been a number of positive developments, and an
important lost opportunity. On a positive note, the SOFOLES performed very successfully during the crisis and, for the most part today, have state-of-the-art origination and servicing systems, and very low delinquency rates (2 percent, on average,
using U.S. GAAP standards). Their market penetration, however, is small, and they
are dependent on FOVI for funding. FOVI itself is embarking on a major reform
aimed at improving its products and services for the primary and secondary markets,
finances, and management. Further, the successful pension reform has led to the
establishment of AFORES, which now have US$13 billion in assets under manage-
ment. As a result, the demand for long-term securities by institutional investors is
now being felt, and the short yield curve appears to be extending. This is a positive
development for the expansion of housing finance, because the f may be expected to
demand high-quality paper from public and private housing lenders.

Most important, there was another unsuccessful attempt at reform of
INFONAVIT. Only modest changes were made in origination and servicing standards, leaving in place a highly subsidized mortgage tied to changes in the minimum
wage, and a delinquency rate of 40 percent percent[3] (under more liberal Mexican
accounting rules). At the same time, changes in the INFONAVIT legislation led to
an increase in the collection of the 5 percent payroll tax, and thus permitted
INFONAVIT to increase its annual production of mortgages from 100,000 to
almost 200,000. As a result INFONAVIT has increased its participation in the new
originations market from 55 percent in 1997 to 67 percent in 1999.

The institutional distribution of new mortgage originations, in number and by
investment amount, and the outstanding low-income mortgage portfolio in Mexico,
are presented in Table 1.

On balance the performance of the housing sector has been poor for many years.
Even before the crisis the housing system did not keep pace with the estimated
demand of 700,000 new housing units per year. In the past five years the housing
sector has produced an average of 195,000 per year, due largely to expanded activities of INFONAVIT, and to a lesser extent of FOVI. The cumulative effect of many
years of shortfalls is an estimated housing "deficit" of 4,000,000 units.[4]

---

3. Unaudited figures released to the press by INFONAVIT indicate that the delinquency rate
   had been reduced to about 25 percent by the end of 1999.
4. Both annual demand and the accumulated deficit are based on (a) survey data from
   INEGI and (b) demographic data. See also the model of housing supply and demand by
   Thesis Consultores.

Table 1. New Mortgage Originations and Outstanding Mortgage Debt

	Total 91–94		Average 91–94		95		96		97		98		99		Total 95–99	
	Amount	%	Amount	%	Amount	%	Amount	%	Amount	%	Amount	%	Amount	%	Amount	%
New Mortgage Originations (Loans)																
INFONAVIT	381,878	57.3	95,470	57.3	96,745	54.4	99,760	61.3	99,231	57.1	108,035	58.3	198,950	71.9	602,721	61.7
FOVI	122,031	18.3	30,508	18.3	51,664	29.0	37,621	23.1	51,297	29.5	60,452	32.6	59,882	21.6	260,916	26.7
FOVISSSTE	162,386	24.4	40,597	24.4	29,529	16.6	25,447	15.6	23,241	13.4	16,712	9.0	18,007	6.5	112,936	11.6
Total	666,295	100.0	166,574	100.0	177,938	100.0	162,828	100.0	173,769	100.0	185,199	100.0	276,839	100.0	976,573	100.0
New Mortgage Originations (MXP$ million)																
INFONAVIT	22,839	71.8	5,710	71.8	8,618	63.9	10,537	63.7	12,121	60.7	14,427	67.6	30,692	76.0	76,395	68.4
FOVI	4,896	15.4	1,224	15.4	2,899	21.5	3,189	19.3	3,508	17.6	4,795	22.5	6,898	17.1	21,289	19.0
FOVISSSTE	4,092	12.9	1,023	12.9	1,315	9.7	1,447	8.7	1,591	8.0	2,114	9.9	2,808	7.0	9,275	8.3
Autofinanciamientos[a]	—	0.0	—	0.0	665	4.9	1,377	8.3	2,752	13.8	—	0.0	—	0.0	4,794	4.3
Total	31,827	100.0	7,957	100.0	13,497	100.0	16,550	100.0	19,972	100.0	21,336	100.0	40,398	100.0	111,753	100.0

	93		94		95		96		97		98		99	
	Amount	%	Amount	%	Amount	%	Amount	%	Amount	%	Amount	%	Amount	%
Mortgage Debt Outstanding (MXP$ million)														
INFONAVIT[b]	25,132	72.5	32,831	71.8	47,517	69.0	60,614	67.1	68,725	63.7	107,620	73.5	138,527	69.4
FOVI	6,973	20.1	9,199	20.1	16,999	24.7	24,934	27.6	34,035	31.5	38,863	26.5	49,531	24.8
FOVISSSTE	2,581	7.4	3,692	8.1	4,356	6.3	4,824	5.3	5,211	4.8	n/a		11,406	5.7
Total	34,686	100.0	45,722	100.0	68,872	100.0	90,372	100.0	107,971	100.0	146,483	100.0	199,464	100.0

Notes:

a. Autofinanciamientos have practically stopped originating mortgage loans after the borrowers with bad credit history in the Credit Bureaus moved to Autofinanciamiento financing and started to default on their loans.

b. INFONAVIT started to create reserves for bad loans starting in 1998 after the restrictions imposed by CNBV.

V. Issues

What explains the poor performance of the housing sector? There are numerous underlying issues: (a) the devastating impact of macroeconomic instability on the financial sector and housing finance; (b) weak sector governance ; (c) the strong bias toward finished housing, leaving insufficient programs and finances to provide progressive housing and other options for low-income families; (d) poor performance of public and housing finance institutions; and (e) poorly designed subsidies that do not effectively leverage scarce public funds.

Macroeconomic Instability

Episodes of macroeconomic instability during the last 30 years have had an important impact on the implementation of housing policy. First, due to the shocks, both the size of the financial sector and the housing finance subsector are quite small relative to GDP. This (combined with poor performance of the public institutions described below) has led to an exclusive dependence on limited public funds and employer taxation programs. Second, the small size of the sector has inhibited the development of the financial infrastructure needed to operate a modern housing finance system, which includes (a) reliable property appraisal and valuation services; (b) efficient, timely and readily available residential real estate market intelligence; and (c) efficient mortgage registry systems. Credit bureaus and rating agencies are already active in the market. While some proactive support by the government will be important, given rapid changes in information technology, Mexico should be able to fill this gap relatively rapidly as its capital market develops.

The 1994–95 crisis also led to the realization that current mortgage designs are inadequate, and can only partially shield lending institutions and households from large macroeconomic risks that they cannot bear. The crisis exposed three problems. First, chronic inflation and volatile real interest rates have made reliance on indexed mortgages inevitable in Mexico. During periods of severe macroeconomic stress, however, so much negative amortization is created that the double index mortgage (DIM) will not pay off in even 30 years.[5] This is particularly true when the stress hits

---

5. The double indexed mortgage (DIM) was developed to make mortgages affordable for borrowers in inflationary economic environments while maintaining a positive value to the mortgagee. It works by amortizing the mortgage balance at a market rate of interest—the "amortization rate"—while basing the borrower payment on a lower "borrower rate." By separating the payment and accrual rates, a loan that is both affordable to the borrower and profitable to the lender can be created. The initial borrower payment is arbitrary and can be set as a payment rate, percentage of required payment, or percent of the initial balance (the most common method in Mexico). After the first period, the payment is adjusted periodically by the cumulative change in an index (for example, minimum wages or price level). The required payment (that is, necessary to amortize the mortgage) is determined by a margin over a market rate index. In Mexico, a variety of indices have

in the first five years of the mortgage. The result is that the financial institutions are left with uncollectable loans that must be written off, foreclosed, or assumed by the government. Second, even when performing reasonably well, the cash flows produced by the DIM are difficult to predict, and this makes securitization of any DIM portfolio extremely difficult. Third, the combination of the DIM design and an inflationary environment also makes the pricing of mortgage insurance extremely difficult, thus posing a major obstacle to the development of a primary mortgage market.

Macroeconomic stability combined with the emergence of new, privately run, long-term institutional investors through pension reforms, however, creates an opportunity to shift risks away from households to professional investors able to manage them better. This opportunity, if properly seized by the government, will also have a major positive impact on the reduction of government contingent liabilities in housing finance and the expansion of the primary market. Over time, it will open the door to the use of simpler mortgage instruments as well.

Sector Governance

The fragmentation of the public programs in social interest housing finance is a longstanding problem in Mexico. The urgency of a serious adjustment has increased further with the completion of the major reforms of the financial systems that have taken place since 1995.[6] The restructuring of the banking sector was essentially completed with the merger of *Bancomer* with BBVA *(Banco Bilbao y Vizcaya)* in June 2000. As already noted, the presence of new pension systems and the AFORES is now being felt in the capital market.

A major task on the agenda of the incoming Administration with respect to the housing sector is the development of a common regulatory and supervisory system for INFONAVIT, FOVI, and FOVISSSTE. Together, these organizations financed 94 percent of the social housing sector in 1999. At present these three public or quasi-public lenders overlap and compete for the same clientele, but they have different charters, governance structures, and programs. They offer mortgage loans at significantly different prices, and their financial policies and practices differ

---

been used, including CETES and CPP. The introduction of this instrument allowed the government to reduce the heavy subsidies in the use of fixed-rate mortgages in the inflationary environment of the early 1980s. Since then, the DIM has been used extensively by the commercial banks and by FOVI, (although the index used by the banks and FOVI are quite different). The DIM performed as expected in the 1980s. The FOVI DIM initially generated significant negative amortization, but began to positively amortize in the beginning of the 7th year and was paid off by the 11th year. The FOVI DIM weathered the 1994–95 crisis better than the commercial bank DIM, due largely to the choice of index. Effectively, all of the commercial bank DIMs "crashed" during the crisis and required significant restructuring.

6. See also the Banking Sector Chapter.

markedly as well. INFONAVIT has traditionally operated outside the purview of the financial sector regulatory body, the CNBV *(Comisión Nacional Bancaria y de Valores)*. In 1997, however, the INFONAVIT Board and CNBV signed an agreement giving CNBV regulatory and supervisory authority. Since then, its regulation has been only marginally effective. For example, the recent audit of INFONAVIT led only to an increased provisioning requirement. The lack of regulation is particularly important given the flow of funds INFONAVIT manages, and its relationship to both the pension system and housing finance systems. In principle FOVI is also subject to CNBV regulation, but in practice it has been regulated and supervised by *Banco de México*. In practice FOVISSSTE is supervised by SHCP.

Further complicating sector governance is the fact that the enabling legislation in some cases is highly restrictive. For example, the design of the INFONAVIT mortgage instrument (using the minimum wage as the price index in the instrument), and certain important servicing standards (maximum percentage of income that can be collected, deferral of payment in the case of loss of employment, loan forgiveness) are described in the legislation. This makes most changes in its procedures and standards extremely difficult as they require new legislation approved by Congress. As a result INFONAVIT has no way of adjusting to changing market conditions.

Finally, corporate governance poses major challenges. INFONAVIT is governed by a self-sustaining board of directors comprised equally of representatives of organized labor, developers, and the executive branch of government. In practice, INFONAVIT has operated as an exclusive franchise of organized labor and developers, who have joined forces to block any attempts at reform. The institution has long been accused of corruption. FOVI has a Technical Committee made up exclusively of line agencies for its governance, and its members act in an uncoordinated fashion and appear to be in disagreement on the implementation of aspects of the FOVI restructuring, particularly as it relates to FOVI's role as a liquidity facility, guarantor, or mortgage conduit. SHCP has exercised control over FOVISSSTE and has effectively reduced lending in recent years.

Bias toward Finished Housing

The Mexican Constitution (Article 123) establishes a worker's right to housing provided by his or her employer. In 1972 the Constitution was amended to establish a *Fondo Nacional de la Vivienda* into which employers would make contributions to benefit individual employees, and thereby comply with their obligations. In the same year INFONAVIT was created to administer this Fund, and to establish and operate a financial system that would permit workers to obtain housing loans.[7]

---

7. *Ley del Instituto del Fondo Nacional de la Vivienda para los Trabajadores,* published in the *Diario Oficial de la Federación* on April 24, 1972. Contrary to what is sometimes asserted, Infonavit has no constitutional protection. Article 123 of the Constitution mentions only the *Fondo Nacional de la Vivienda*.

The creation of INFONAVIT did two things: (a) it effectively disenfranchised from housing finance the millions of Mexican who are not inscribed in INFON-AVIT, and (b) it shifted the focus of housing policy to the provision of home mortgages by the public or quasi-public agencies for finished housing. This focus on financing finished housing has relegated progressive and home improvement, rental, and used housing options to a lesser status, with limited funding and weak institutional support. This, too, has been insufficient to meet demand and has led to the proliferation of informal (low-quality) and often illegal housing options.

The performance of these low-income housing institutions has been very mixed. FONHAPO, which was designed to provide subsidized loans to low-income groups for progressive housing, developed serious portfolio problems, and became a pressure point for well-organized groups in the D.F. who more and more demanded and received highly subsidized finished housing.

Experience in the states has been varied. Some states (for example, Baja California, Guanajuato, and Nuevo León) have adopted innovative approaches to the provision of land, services and credit. Other entities (for example, México and the D.F.) have encountered serious financial and institutional problems that have reduced their interventions to very low levels. The State of Mexico is a good example of the challenges facing states today. Its triple housing challenge is to fill its accumulated housing deficit, provide for the replacement of dilapidated stock, and serve an annual population growth of 265,000. The demographic growth of the state is equivalent to making room for one new city like Guanajuato every year. The State of Mexico must produce some of 80,000 new units per year.

Private lenders offer some hope for an expansion of options for low-income families. The *Caja Popular Mexicana* has moved aggressively into the home improvement market, and has a portfolio of over 40,000 such loans. Other lenders—including NGOs—are important but still small participants. Many have innovative schemes but face difficulties in scaling up their operations. A major gap in this segment, however, is the lack of regulation and supervision of these types of financial institutions providing services to the low-income market.[8]

Poor Performance of Public and Quasi-Public Institutions

Generally poor performance of public and quasi-public institutions has caused a major distortion in the housing market and limit ongoing reform efforts.

At the national level INFONAVIT, FOVISSSTE and FOVI accounted for 94 percent of all mortgage originations in 1999. INFONAVIT, with 67 percent of the market, is the largest and most problematic of the national institutions for several reasons:

---

8. See also the Banking Sector Policy Chapter.

INFONAVIT

INAPPROPRIATE MORTGAGE INSTRUMENT. The INFONAVIT mortgage is a wage-indexed, 360-month mortgage. It is not a DIM as described above. The initial interest rate charged is in the range of 4 to 8 percent and is dependent on the income of the borrower. Both the borrower payment and the loan balance are indexed to the minimum wage, as specified by the government. From a portfolio perspective, the use of the minimum wage to index the loan is problematic because in recent years the minimum wage has lagged behind inflation. Thus, in real terms the mortgage is below market from the time of origination and may continue to be eroded by inflation over time. Additionally, the borrower's payment to income ratio cannot exceed 25 percent at any point during the loan. This implies that if a borrower's income does not maintain parity with increases in the minimum wage, then the rate of negative amortization will increase on the loan, even further increasing the probability of a positive end-of-term balance, thus increasing the cost and lowering the expected yield of the portfolio.

WEAK ORIGINATION AND SERVICING STANDARDS. INFONAVIT operates as a first tier mortgage lender, focusing on the 3 to 4 mmws market. Its origination standards are weak, and characterized by high loan-to-value ratios, large maximum loan amounts relative to income, and a "scoring" system that gives relatively little weight to borrower creditworthiness.[9] By comparison with FOVI, INFONAVIT will lend for a larger house, to a poorer family (usually 3 to 4mmws vs. 5 to 6 mmws), and with lower monthly payments. Similarly, its servicing standards are poor, as evidenced by delinquencies on the order of 40 percent (using the Mexican GAAP definition).

The result is that the INFONAVIT portfolio yields less than a market rate of return. The poor performance of INFONAVIT is important for two reasons. First, it severely distorts the housing finance market due to the combination of size and poor lending practices. This prohibits the development of a larger primary market because private lenders cannot compete with INFONAVIT's lending practices. The sheer size of the below-market INFONAVIT portfolio is also a major impediment to the development of a deep secondary market. Second, with below-market yields INFONAVIT drags down the performance of the pension fund, and will cause workers to opt for the minimum pension guarantee at the time of retirement. Essentially, INFONAVIT, as currently constituted, provides home mortgages to some of its members by destroying the retirement funds of its other members.

FOVI

FOVI has recently embarked on a four-year Strategic Plan, which calls for the origination of 330,000 mortgages, about twice the level of the previous five years. The

---

9. See also Thesis Consultores analysis of the impact of *carreras salariales* on INFONAVIT portfolio.

Plan also calls for ambitious restructuring, aimed at repositioning the institution to access capital markets and thus (a) move away from dependency on official funds, and (b) expand the flow of funds available for social interest housing. Implementation of the Strategic Plan is critical to the government's plans to reform the housing sector. The success of the Plan, however, is in jeopardy due to the overwhelming distortion in the market caused by INFONAVIT. Moreover, implementation involves a series of difficult actions—which are behind schedule—related to FOVI's products and services, risk management systems, and finances:

PRODUCTS AND SERVICES FOR THE PRIMARY MARKET. FOVI currently offers the following:

(i)   A new mortgage product: FOVI has introduced market rate mortgages on the B program (targeted at household earning 6 to 8 mmws) and is scheduled to implement marketrates on the rest of the mortgage products in the next 18 months.
(ii) Improved credit quality: FOVI is introducing an eligibility program for participating institutions to allow FOVI to better manage its own (institutional) credit risk; standardized underwriting, servicing, and reporting procedures; and standards for market agents (for example, appraisers). It is also working with the SOFOLES on a mortgage information system to improve credit risk management and provide a standard origination platform.
(iii) Better channels of distribution: Though FOVI currently funds only the SOFOLES, within the next two to three years the commercial banks, which previously participated actively with FOVI, are expected to return to the market. To strengthen these channels FOVI is preparing a marketing plan to bring more commercial banks into the program and strengthen its ties with the SOFOLES.
(iv) Improved insurance product: Two actions are contemplated: (a) modified DIM to address the systemic risk (that is, positive balance on the mortgage after 30 years) arising from macroeconomic instability. This new product is operating in the market; and (b) a redesign of the current FOVI mortgage insurance product. This critical action is only just getting under way.

SUPPORT FOR SECONDARY MARKET DEVELOPMENT. FOVI will begin to develop the information and risk management systems that will allow it to play a supporting role in what is expected to be a private secondary market (that is, one operating without government guarantees). This work also is only just getting under way.

STRENGTHENED BALANCE SHEET AND DIVERSIFIED SOURCES OF FUNDS. FOVI proposes to (a) add capital through the absorption of another *Banco de México* trust fund (Fidec)—this restructuring is now complete; (b) maintain capital at no less than 10 percent of assets at risk as defined by CNBV—currently FOVI's capital stands at 19 percent; (c) obtain a rating (using U.S. GAAP standards) from an internationally recognized rating agency; and (d) access the capital markets with the issuance of FOVI debt. Work on the latter two items has not yet begun. Given current expectations about continued funding from the government, it is essential that FOVI move quickly to a program of regular issues of FOVI securities.

STRONGER MANAGEMENT. Finally, FOVI will convert from being a manager of public housing programs to a financial institution able to fund itself in the market. This requires a corporate reorganization that (a) strengthens the strategic planning and policy development, credit management, asset liability management, and funding functions—this work is underway; and (b) establishes a second tier of senior management—this work is also under way.

FOVISSSTE

FOVISSSTE faces many of the same problems as INFONAVIT, but its impact has been smaller. It provides subsidized loans to its borrowers through a 30-year indexed rate mortgage. The mortgage is indexed to the minimum wage. FOVISSSTE charges an extra 4 percent premium to its borrowers to service the loans. The loan-to-value ratio is 90 percent. The instrument has a government end-of-term balance guarantee embedded in it. To service the mortgage loans, the government deducts 30 percent of the borrower's monthly payroll and additionally pays FOVISSSTE an extra 5 percent of the borrower's monthly income, as a public sector worker benefit, to amortize the loan.

Poorly Designed Subsidies

Today, almost every mortgage in Mexico contains elements of subsidy. These present several structural problems. First, they form an obstacle to market-based resource mobilization of household savings, particularly through the emerging pension system. Second, they crowd out mortgage supply by market-based lenders. Third, the mixing of subsidies with finance has led to poor targeting of subsidies: the richer the borrower, the larger the loan, and the bigger the subsidy. The subsidies take three different forms: (a) subsidies granted through below-market interest rates on loans offered by the public and quasi-public institutions. These vary across institutions, with FOVI at about 18 percent and INFONAVIT at 36 percent of the mortgage.[10] As noted above, FOVI has begun to address this situation with the shift to market-based lending on the B loans; (b) a contingent subsidy in the form of forgiveness of end-of-term remaining balances. FOVI has begun to require a systemic risk premium to be paid by borrowers. In the case of INFONAVIT these balances are written off against the contribution of other workers; (c) de facto subsidies during loan servicing that result from poor collection practices and lenient payment terms granted on an ad hoc basis. These are widespread in the case of INFONAVIT.

---

10. These are averages. The size of the subsidy varies with the macroeconomic scenario.

VI. A New Housing Policy

The government has already taken important steps toward formulating and implementing a new housing policy[11] aimed at strengthening both low-income and social interest housing by:

- Increasing the resources channeled to the sector, with a market focus oriented toward promoting greater competitiveness and efficiency.
- Increasing the distribution channels for housing finance in order to expand private sources of supply.
- Making credit and origination standards uniform in order to deepen the market.
- Supporting the lower-income segments of the population under a scheme of direct, targeted subsidies, with a transparent assignation.
- Supporting the development of a secondary market, to provide more resources to the sector.

Key Actions

This housing policy represents a radical departure from the past and implies a vastly different government role in the sector. Though the nature of the government role will change very significantly, the government will continue to have a strong presence. It will reduce its role as operator and direct financier and increase its role as policymaker, regulator of markets, and supporter of competitive sectors and industries. Central to the growth and change is a financial system that is much more than a mere conduit of funds, but one that mobilizes and allocates resources and disciplines firms. In continuing to implement this housing policy some key actions are required.

ENSURE THAT HOUSING POLICY IS IMPLEMENTED WITHIN THE APPROPRIATE CONTEXT: MACROECONOMIC STABILITY, SOUND DEVELOPMENT OF THE FINANCIAL SECTOR, CONTINUED PROGRESS ON DECENTRALIZATION AND URBAN POLICY. Such a strategy must integrate housing finance with other key areas: (a) macroeconomic policies, with their direct impact on price stability, the interest rate level, interest rate control policies, and long-term finance; (b) financial policies, in particular the extent to which policies toward long-term savings aim at financing "priority sectors" or financial liberalization policies are in progress; (c) the quality of financial infrastructure already in place (accounting standards, legal framework, regulation, supervision); and (d) the quality of the urban regulatory framework.

---

11. See the Letter of Sector Policy provided as Annex 2 in the World Bank's Project Appraisal Document of February 3, 1999 on the FOVI Restructuring Project.

OBTAIN BETTER SECTORAL GOVERNANCE THROUGH COMMON REGULATION AND SUPERVISION OF INFONAVIT, FOVISSSTE, AND FOVI AND DEVELOP AN INTEGRATED VIEW OF A MODERN HOUSING FINANCE SYSTEM FOR MEXICO. First and foremost, the government will have to reach agreement on what should be the specific present and future public purpose of INFONAVIT, FOVISSSTE, and FOVI. This must be done in the broader context of the housing policy of the government and of its financial development objectives in the areas of contractual savings and mortgage markets. This necessarily includes (a) how best these institutions can contribute to the goal of increased home ownership in Mexico; (b) their efficiency and effectiveness in supporting affordable housing; (c) agreement on a framework for evaluation of their performance; and (d) mechanisms for best leveraging their financial resources. New legislation may be needed.

Given its past performance and highly distorting impact, the first-best solution is to terminate INFONAVIT as they are today, give it a modern charter and transparent governance, and enable it to operate fully within the financial sector. A second-best solution would be to convert INFONAVIT into an AFORE. Similar actions could be taken on FOVISSSTE. Failing this, two things should occur. The payroll tax should be reduced, and a common regulatory and supervisory framework, backed by strong action, should be adopted for INFONAVIT, FOVISSTE, and FOVI. It is very premature to assume that problems would be solved by merging the three institutions. The starting question should be what kind of housing system Mexico wants.

STRENGTHEN AND DEEPEN THE PRIMARY MARKET. It is essential to accelerate and complete FOVI's restructuring from a manager of housing programs to an independent, autonomous financial institution. This will lessen the impact of INFONAVIT in the market. Beyond that, FOVI needs to pursue an active plan of broadening the social interest housing market by developing the PROSAVI, B, and A markets for the informal sector. It should also expand into the used housing and rental housing markets. The INFONAVIT and FOVISSSTE policies, procedures, and products should be brought up to the new FOVI standards, using the FOVI model of strengthening primary market operations. Clearly this is a major challenge and will necessarily involve the following: (a) establishment of a good bank/bad bank system, or some other mechanism to isolate the below-market and nonperforming assets of these institutions; (b) a change in the mortgage product, thus implying new legislation for INFONAVIT; and (c) new origination and servicing standards that will allow these institutions to produce market rate, creditworthy mortgages for the A market.

DEVELOP CAPITAL MARKET ACCESS. Developing capital market access is key to developing a self-sustaining mortgage market that is not dependent on public or quasi-public funds. FOVI must develop access to the capital markets, not only because future government lending is highly unlikely but also, as described above, to finance its expansion into new markets. This is why it is so critical that FOVI assign high priority to the development of funding and asset–liability strategies. In the next 18 months FOVI bond issuance will be a critical test of access for the sector and for FOVI's ability to become a genuine financial institution.

Capital market access will be impossible as long as subsidies are embedded in the mortgage instrument. Subsidies should be separated from finance so that mortgage-related assets can be funded, priced, and possibly traded at market rates.

Mortgage insurance programs should be developed that have the dual aim of lowering credit risk and improving the standardization of mortgage loan products in the primary markets. Ideally, these should be developed by the private sector. Given the track record of the recent past, and the poor quality of information, it is unlikely that a private group will enter the market. Thus the government, through FOVI, will need to pave the way by developing creditworthy, well-serviced, market-rate mortgages supported by the appropriate information systems. Two policy decisions are needed: (a) that the government will not assume 100 percent of the risk, even in the interim period of government provision of mortgage insurance; and (b) that clear "sunset" rules are established for the handover from FOVI to the private sector.

The government should pursue a pilot securitization program, with the goal of using it as a benchmark to reveal the various technical shortcomings that still need to be addressed in the primary market.

RETHINK THE ROLE OF SUBSIDIES, SAVINGS, AND THEIR DELIVERY MECHANISMS. Current subsidies are expensive, poorly channeled, and inhibit market development. A number of actions are required: (a) eliminate subsidies in the B market; (b) reduce subsidies significantly on the A program; (c) provide subsidies on progressive housing and home improvement schemes; and (d) move all housing subsidies up front and combine them with savings schemes.

Most important, it is necessary to unleash the power of savings by low-income groups by (a) removing all obstacles to the implementation of the 43bis program; and (b) developing savings certificates for housing. Savings certificates are especially important to Mexicans outside the INFONAVIT system, who currently have very limited access to savings instruments.

PROVIDE ALTERNATIVES TO INFORMAL HOUSING SOLUTIONS THROUGH IMPROVED DELIVERY OF FINANCIAL AND TECHNICAL SERVICES TO THE URBAN POOR. This poses a special challenge for the federal government, because these informal housing solutions are best influenced at the state and local levels. Finance is national; housing delivery is local. Thus it will be extremely important for the three levels of government to develop a coordinated approach. The benefits of developing successful low-income programs will be major on three fronts:

(i)   From an economic viewpoint, the direct and indirect socioeconomic impacts of quality housing investment in the low-income market segment are very large (the economic multiplier effects of housing investment are large). Surveys shows that housing conditions affect family life so much that households give a higher priority to housing than to education and health. International experience also shows that at least 20 percent of these units are used as places of employment. In other words, progressive housing assets are used for direct income production in addition to the usual multiplier effects experienced in higher segments of the housing market.

(ii) From an infrastructure investment viewpoint, positive (rather than repressive) instruments are needed to avoid the invasion of public lands that will later be very costly to service. Anarchic urbanization is very costly to the nation. The ex-post provision of urban services to irregular settlements is usually three to seven times higher than for a planned urban area. In addition, housing quality is very low. The assets created in illegal, unplanned, and untitled settlements have a very low economic value. In other words, the very poor own housing units of low market value and squat on untitled dead land assets.

(iii) From an environmental and human viewpoint, successful progressive housing programs are also vital to the future of Mexico. Natural disasters are not only more frequent but their impact on human settlements is now much larger than before. The losses from natural disasters in terms of human lives and physical wealth are growing rapidly larger and they concentrate in low-income areas. The reasons are well known: (a) degradation of watersheds and sensitive areas caused by anarchic settlements; (b) violent water runoffs and lack of drainage increase the frequency and scale of floods; and (c) buildings are not earthquake-proof.

Several actions—coordinated at the federal, state, and local levels—are required to expand and to improve housing services for the urban poor, and to avoid chaotic, informal housing solutions.[12]

IMPROVE PROPERTY RIGHTS. Property rights, economic security, and asset formation are tightly related. Secured lending is of strategic significance for the expansion of housing finance across income levels. At the local level there is a very high probability that many states can develop financially self-sufficient property titling and registration systems that are considerably more efficient and more reliable than today. This issue is also closely tied to the sound release of public lands to housing markets and the liquidity of land markets and the eventual disappearance of land invasions. Upgrading registry systems is essential.

EXPAND HOUSING FINANCE SERVICES. The development of private financial services at market rates is central to the future of Mexican cities. This absence or the small

---

12. See the 1992 World Bank Housing Policy Paper *Housing: Enabling Markets to Work.*

scale of operations of such institutions are major constraints to low-income housing because cities are built the way they are financed. The international evidence in this area is overwhelming. For various well-known reasons, state and federal agencies should withdraw from the direct mortgage lending business and support private finance institutions. In addition to supporting the penetration of mortgage lenders down the income scale, there are three major agenda items for the next six years:

(i)   Development of what is becoming known as the microfinance of housing; that is, the provision of loans at unsubsidized rates and shorter maturity than traditional mortgage for home improvement and expansion.[13]

(ii)   Development by the federal government of a sound financing mechanism that aids the flow of private funds into progressive and home-improvement programs. This can be done by introducing FOVI-style auctions for qualifying financial institutions operating progressive housing and home improvement programs. This allows the federal government (perhaps acting together with state governments) to establish operating guidelines and standards (for example, origination, servicing, and capital requirements) for these programs, thus ensuring quality levels. Importantly, such a program will allow these institutions to scale up their existing programs that are operating quite effectively in the poorest areas. Such an initiative, however, would require a strong regulatory and supervisory framework for these institutions.

(iii)   Development of new savings instruments that are well adapted to the volatility of the economy and to the needs of the bottom 60 percent of the state population. Such instruments are under consideration by FOVI in the form of small indexed UDI bonds that families could use for various purposes.

It will be essential that the state authorities abandon old and wasteful special programs and work in close partnership with the mortgage finance industry and the federal regulatory and supervisory authorities to develop sound and open systems.

DEVELOP WELL-TARGETED SUBSIDIES. Many states face severe fiscal constraints for the foreseeable future. To get maximum leverage out of a thin state housing budget and limited federal transfers, present programs must be completely rethought. Similar to social interest housing, a central principle for new action programs will be to separate subsidies from finance.[14] Progress in improving low-income access to housing and affordability can take place in three areas:

---

13. For a recent review and inventory, see Bruce Ferguson, "Mainstreaming the Micro-Finance of Housing," 10 June 2000. Washington, D.C.: Inter-American Development Bank, unpublished paper. BruceF@iadb.org.

14. See Gerardo M. Gonzales Arrieta, "Access to Housing and Direct Subsidies: Lessons from Latin American Experience," *Housing Finance International*, 13(II): 43–53, September 1998.

(i)   In-kind subsidies to lower the price of housing products to bring them in line with the purchasing power of the population groups to be served. There are many steps throughout the real development process where the state—in close partnership with municipalities—can have a positive impact on housing prices. However, in asset-rich, cash-poor states the main feasible in-kind subsidy will be access to land at cost below market.

(ii) Up-front finance subsidies to be combined with market-based mortgage finance. State-level agencies do not have a comparative advantage in designing up-front financial subsidies, either in terms of fiscal resources or of skills and experience. Rather they should work in cooperation with federal financial institutions such as FOVI and the private mortgage finance industry to use the state housing market as a testing ground for viable financial subsidy products. Even then, close attention must be paid to the needs, constraints, and preferences of the beneficiaries.[15]

(iii) Advisory services to consumers. Many countries have learned that low-income families who live in an insecure environment are fearful of the risks associated with access to home ownership. States could become leaders in supporting (not providing) the development of consumer finance and advisory services for mortgage borrowers. It is established by now that in the case of microfinance loans for progressive housing lending, construction advice must be packaged with these shorter and smaller loans to lower risks for both lenders and borrowers.

It is on the supply side of the housing system that states can make the most effective contributions to improving housing conditions in the state—in addition to the fundamental impact of land and property titling and registration already mentioned.

EXPAND THE SUPPLY OF SERVICED URBAN LAND. The constant threat and high cost of land invasions is a reflection of poor access to land for the lower half of state residents. A constructive way for the state to improve housing conditions is to rapidly expand the supply of titled and serviced land; that is, to increase liquidity in the land market.

The operational challenge for the states is to aid the conversion of illiquid land assets into cash resources that can be shared among the initial public land owner, participating municipalities, the developers, and the final users to pay for the servicing of titled urban land and motivate all parties to participate in such operations. The disposal of properly titled and planned land can generate such resources. International experience with land banking over the last three decades, however, has been

---

15. See the recent experience in South Africa in Mary Tomlison, "From Rejection to Resignation: Beneficiaries' Views on the South African Government's New Housing Subsidy System," *Urban Studies* 36(8): 1349–1359, 1999. Mary Tomlison is with the research department of the Banking Council of the RSA.

very poor. Such well-meaning schemes have resulted in continuing state monopolies strangling land supply and a steep acceleration of land prices in the remainder.[16] The challenge to state professionals is to become successful "market makers" who will improve the quality of land supply at low costs.

IMPROVE THE REGULATORY FRAMEWORK FOR REAL ESTATE DEVELOPMENT. Private real estate developers are central to the future of Mexican cities. By now the difference between *contratistas* and *promotores* is well understood. A modern real estate developer is a community builder who sees the opportunities to create housing and other commercial and industrial real projects that will have great value. This work requires the coordination of many professions and products. The legal and regulatory processes at the national and state level can either support or hinder this process. A poor and unpredictable regulatory process raises risk, uncertainty, and the time needed to build housing, which means higher costs for everyone. A weak regulatory framework unnecessarily breeds corruption and distrust, and it lowers housing quality.

REGULATORY REVIEWS SHOULD BE DEVELOPED TO INCLUDE: (a) Streamlining various state and local regulations and practices on all types of housing development projects from high income to low cost; and (b) establishing a special task force to focus on how governments can facilitate sound projects for progressive housing projects and identify what urban planning and regulatory processes will work for this large low-income market segment.

STATES SHOULD ALSO PROMOTION OF COMPETITIVE CONSTRUCTION AND REAL ESTATE INDUSTRIES. States should support the emergence of small-and medium-scale developers and builders who can profitably operate down market. Wherever regulatory costs are high and access to land is difficult, entry barriers are high and only large operators can survive profitability.

Finally, good policies and operations require relevant, accurate, and timely information. State agencies also want to lower their own workload and expand housing supply across the state. This means converting as many of the municipalities and local governments as possible from passive into active partners. Thanks to the development of global information systems and Internet facilities, the provision of advi-

---

16. In Latin America the Brazilian experience with Brasilia and the Venezuelan experience with Ciudad Guyana are also classics. In India, the land supply experience of Bombay and New Delhi contrast greatly with successful results in the state of Tamil Nadu and is well known. In Bombay, the land market has become so distorted and the costs so high that the most a poor family could hope to buy is one square foot or 0.1 square foot. meters of land. In rich and beautiful Sri Lanka, Colombo has now driven half of its population into slums and illegal settlements through a tangle of state land controls that have yet to be unraveled.

sory and information services and interactive systems is well within reach of the state. This should be a very high priority.

VII. Conclusion

The Mexican housing system is at a crossroads. Past poor performance is widely acknowledged. There is an urgent need to address the weaknesses in social interest housing finance in order to strengthen and deepen the market so that the current high levels of public support can be reduced. Doing this will permit the government to focus its resources where they are most needed, that is, low-income housing. This new focus will require the federal government to forge new partnerships with the states, municipalities, the private sector, and civil society. Innovative solutions are being offered by private and NGO lenders, in combination with states and municipalities, in the largest segment of the market—those who do not qualify for a home mortgage. By assimilating and accelerating the whole range of these changes—including the actions described above—the housing sector can make significant progress toward meeting annual demand and addressing the deficit. A goal of providing financing for 6,000,000 homes in the social-interest and low-income housing markets—in the new, used, progressive, home improvement, and rental segments—between 2001 and 2006 is well within reach.

14

Urban Development

*This Chapter was written by Rafael de la Cruz and
Maria Emilia Freire.*

I. Introduction and Background

This Chapter identifies the pillars of a policy agenda for the Mexican urban sector, including the main issues, and the need for an integrated vision that takes into account the linkages between levels of government and public and private sector actors. It also addresses both institutional reform and physical investment.

Mexico is a predominantly urban country. Urban centers account for 75 percent of total population and 85 percent of the country's GDP. Poverty is an increasingly urban phenomenon; with 63 percent of Mexico's poor living in urban areas.[1] According to repeated public statements, local government is the foundation of the country's decentralizing democracy. Thus developments in the urban sector will inevitably influence key aspects of national development—poverty alleviation, economic growth, public finance, and governance.

II. The Challenges in Mexico's Urban Development

Urbanization Trends

The rate of urbanization has grown rapidly in recent years, making Mexico one of the most urbanized countries in Latin America. Four cities—Guadalajara, Mexico City, Monterrey, and Puebla—account for over one-fourth of the country's population. Twenty-one percent of urban dwellers live in medium-size cities of between 100,000 and 499,999 people, and another 21 percent live in cities of 5,000 to 49,999 people (see Tables 1 and 2).

---

1. "World Bank Mexico Country Assistance Strategy, 1999"; 1996 figures.

Table 1. Urban-Rural Population and Crimes in Mexico, 1998

States	Urban Population/ Total	Rural Population/ Total	Urban-Rural Index	Crimes Per Capita/1000	Urban Ranking
Oaxaca	1.54	2.00	0.77	1.36	17
Chiapas	1.74	2.20	0.79	1.24	16
Hidalgo	1.10	1.22	0.90	0.62	21
Zacatecas	0.74	0.73	1.01	1.26	28
Tabasco	1.00	0.92	1.09	1.96	22
Guerrero	1.75	1.45	1.21	0.74	15
San Luis Potosí	1.40	1.02	1.37	1.49	18
Veracruz	4.31	3.08	1.40	1.14	4
Durango	0.96	0.61	1.57	1.24	23
Nayarit	0.62	0.36	1.72	2.87	29
Querétaro	0.88	0.49	1.80	1.67	24
Michoacán	2.74	1.51	1.81	2.27	8
Sinaloa	1.77	0.89	1.99	2.31	14
Guanajuato	3.22	1.61	2.00	1.17	7
Puebla	3.38	1.69	2.00	0.86	6
Campeche	0.50	0.20	2.50	1.39	30
Aguascalientes	0.74	0.21	3.52	1.73	27
Baja California Sur	0.33	0.09	3.67	2.92	32
Yucatán	1.37	0.34	4.03	1.46	19
Chihuahua	2.46	0.61	4.03	2.83	9
Tlaxcala	0.78	0.19	4.11	0.85	25
Quintana Roo	0.62	0.15	4.13	0.99	26
Sonora	1.86	0.42	4.43	2.82	13
Tamaulipas	2.31	0.47	4.91	2.64	10
Jalisco	5.47	1.11	4.93	1.04	3
Colima	0.46	0.08	5.75	2.25	31
México	10.99	1.85	5.94	0.67	1
Morelos	1.36	0.22	6.18	1.50	20
Coahuila	2.10	0.28	7.50	1.24	12
Baja California	2.12	0.20	10.60	3.37	11
Nuevo León	3.62	0.27	13.41	1.03	5
Distrito Federal	9.28	0.03	309.33	1.83	2
Total	73.52	26.50			
Average	2.30	0.83	13.14	1.65	
Median	1.64	0.55	3.01		

Source: Idem.

Table 2. Mexico's Expenditure Assignment

Federal	State	Municipal
• Defense		
• Foreign affairs and economic relations		
• Labor policies		
• Monetary and financial policy		
• Post and telecommunications		
• Education Policies and norms High schools and colleges School construction supervision Textbook production	• Education Financing, implementation, and maintenance High schools and state universities School construction	• Education Minimal role, school maintenance, and some construction
• Health Policies and norms Secondary and tertiary hospitals Capital infrastructure decisions	• Health Primary care for rural population and urban poor Partial financing Epidemiology, preventive care, reproductive health	
• Roads Federal highway construction Financing of rural roads	• Roads State feeder roads Implementation of rural road development Maintenance of secondary federal roads (w/federal funds)	• Roads Local streets
• Police and internal security Transfers to states Federal and border police Special police	• Police and internal security State public order	• Police and internal security Local public order

Table 2. (Continued)

Federal	State	Municipal
• Social assistance/security Funding through *Ramo* 33 and *Ramo* 26	• Social assistance/security Implementation of school lunch program Food assistance to the poor Other programs • Culture and libraries Public libraries	• Social assistance/security Implementing social infrastructure programs
• Parks and recreation Biosphere reserves National parks/ monuments	• Parks and recreation • National parks	• Parks and recreation Local parks
• Public transportation Railways and airports have been privatized Seaports being privatized	• Public transportation Some airports	• Public transportation Local transportation and transit
	• Water sewerage and sanitation Water supply and sewerage	• Water sewerage and sanitation Garbage collection Water supply and sewerage
• Housing National programs for housing development • Agriculture and irrigation Funding for state programs Rural development, forestry	• Housing Some state housing agencies • Agriculture and irrigation Rural development Extension	
• Other infrastructure Financing through *Ramo* 33	• Other infrastructure State infrastructure	• Other infrastructure Cemeteries Slaughterhouses Public markets

Source: Giugale and Webb, pp. 140–42.

Urbanization is occurring at different speeds in different regions. From 1955 to 1995 the population of four states (Baja California, Baja California Sur, Mexico, and Quintana Roo) more than doubled, due primarily to internal migration, while the states of Oaxaca, and Zacatecas, and the Distrito Federal (DF), have lost population. Population growth is greatest among the intermediate-size cities.[2] Mexico City has a special place in the Mexican urban scene. With 17.5 percent of total population, the DF and 16 municipalities of its neighboring State of Mexico account for almost 24 percent of the national GDP. A complex process of urban degradation has led to a decline in Mexico City's downtown population—in the last 30 years the four inner delegaciones have lost 40 percent of their inhabitants—while the city as a whole grew 25 percent.[3]

Migration between urban centers (mostly across states) is a large and increasing proportion of migratory flows in Mexico. Around 40 percent of these are from cities above 100,000 inhabitants. Another 40 percent of internal migration (affecting 3.7 percent of the population) is intrastate and primarily from rural to urban areas. In many large cities, natural population growth is as important as migration in explaining urban growth.[4]

Urbanization trends mirror changes in the growth and locus of economic activity in Mexico. Industries and businesses have been relocating to smaller cities. The border region, port cities such as Lazaro Cardenas and Veracruz, and agro-industry in the north have generated rapid growth and are new poles of attraction for internal migrants. On the other hand, as noted above, the growth of the old urban centers, like Mexico City, has been halted and the urban centers are rapidly deteriorating. The rapid growth of new cities brings challenges as new administrations have to face increasing demands for urban infrastructure and services while trying to cope with ecological and urban rehabilitation needs. Often these nascent administrations are ill-prepared for such tasks.[5] Migration also exacerbates housing shortages. Out-migration from older cities frees up some housing stock, but this is quickly absorbed by natural growth of the current resident population. Moreover, out-migrants are in general the more well-off residents, and as a result the freed housing stock is beyond the affordability range of the lower-income in-migrants.[6]

---

2. Instituto Nacional de Estadística, Geografía e Informática (INEGI), *XI Censo General de Población y Vivienda (1990)*, *Conteo de Población y Vivienda (1995)*, *Resultados preliminares del XII Censo General de Población y Vivienda (2000)*. Mexico: 1990, 1995, 2000.

3. INEGI, *Población de México y sus Entidades Federativas 1895–2000*. Mexico, 2000. http://www.inegi.gob.mx/estadistica/espanol/sociodem/fsociodemografia.html.

4. "Moving Up? Migration and Poverty in Latin America and the Caribbean," World Bank, Washington, D.C., pp. 7–14.

5. Ibid.

6. Ibid., pp. 41–42.

Urban Poverty

Poverty in Mexico is increasingly urban and unequal. About 17 percent of the urban population (13.5 million dwellers) are below the extreme level of poverty. While urban areas generate 80 percent of the country's income, they are also the locus of the highest levels of inequality.[7] It is estimated that one-fourth of the potential poverty reduction from growth is lost due to rising inequality. As of 1996, 36 million poor people lived in urban areas,[8] the majority of whom are concentrated in metropolitan areas and large cities (over 100,000 people).

Between 1994 and 1997, unemployment and the number of people earning less than one minimum wage grew from 10.6 percent to 19 percent of the population in Mexico's largest cities. Urban residents have also experienced declining real incomes and lower returns for low-skill labor. While approximately 31 percent of heads of households in urban areas have not completed primary school, the additional annual return from basic education decreased 65 percent in real terms between 1984 and 1996.[9] The circumstances of the urban poor in big cities and small towns are different. Many small towns are essentially rural and the profile of the poverty in these settlements is more similar to that of the rural poor. Most, though underemployed, are economically active. In contrast, the poor in the dense settlements common in metropolitan areas and large cities are at higher risk. Lack of sanitation has more severe consequences for public health in crowded cities than in small towns; waterborne diseases are the leading cause of infant deaths in these areas. Security also poses a greater risk: crime rates in metropolitan regions, especially Mexico City, are among the highest in the world. In addition, the urban poor experience greater vulnerability to economic instability (compared with rural poor) due to lack of assets. For example, many urban poor do not own their dwelling and must pay rent. These same poor are dependent on cash income, which may decrease in value during economic downturns. Unlike the rural poor, urban poor have no access to subsistence production during periods of unemployment.

Crime and Violence

According to ECLAC, in 1995, Mexico had the sixth-highest rate of homicides in Latin America—19.5 per 1,000 inhabitants, after El Salvador at 117; Colombia at 65; Honduras at 40; Brazil at 30; and Venezuela at 22.[10] Concentrations of popula-

7. R. De la Torre, "La Distribución Factorial del Ingreso en el Nuevo Modelo Económico," as quoted in *Reconstruir las Ciudades para Superar la Pobreza*, Universidad Iberoamericana, Propuesta, Junio 2000.
8. World Bank Mexico Country Assistance Strategy," 1999, World Bank, Washington, D.C.
9. INEGI, *Encuesta nacional de Empleo Urbano*, INEGI, 2000; and R. De la Torre y A. Santana "La Distribución y Educación Superior en México," 1999, as referenced in Universidad Iberoamericana.
10. Arriagada, Irma, and Lorena Godoy, *Seguridad ciudadana y violencia en América Latina: Diagnóstico y políticas en los años noventa,* Santiago de Chile: ECLAC–UN, 1999.

tion and crime are commonly linked worldwide. Figure 1 shows a strong correlation (R^2=90) between state population and crime rates, as expected.[11] Thirteen states have crime rates higher than the national average. Among them are the most urbanized regions of the country (see Table 1).

Land and Housing Situation

Cities are generally unprepared for the wave of primarily poor, unskilled migrants that fuel urbanization. Few urban areas have and enforce land use master plans, urban land use regulations and standards are excessive, and procedures are cumbersome. Lands apt for urban development are limited by complex tenure systems and limited capacity to regularize and provide necessary services. Urban expansion has occurred in large part on land previously used for agriculture under the *ejido* system of communal property. *Ejidal* parcels have provided up to 60 percent of the land necessary for urban growth. While a primary source of land, petitioning for the provision of basic urban services on *ejidal* lands is complicated—local governments can refuse to provide services because *ejidal* lands are designated as rural, or they can refuse to take responsibility because in theory the owner and therefore adjudicator

Figure 1. Mexico: States Population and Crime Rates, 1998

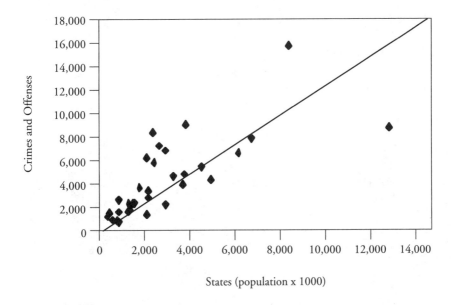

States (population x 1000)

11. INEGI. *Delincuentes sentenciados registrados en los juzgados por principales tipos de delitos segun ambito geografico por ocurrencia, 1998.* http://www.inegi.gob.mx/estadistica/espanol/sociodem/fsociodemografia.html.

of the *ejido* land is the local *ejido* association. Regularization also requires the coordination of all the different levels of government, a lengthy and difficult process. In general, land regulation is too expensive. Illegal settlers pay for access to land plots, they pay again to regularize their land, and finally they pay property taxes, in principle, for services they have never received. The situation is further complicated by a frequent lack of technical infrastructure.[12]

Because Mexican housing policy is focused on the provision of public subsidized finance for finished housing, the majority of Mexico's urban poor do not have incomes sufficient to participate, and resort to informal, often illegal, housing solutions. Low housing quality and declining availability of rental stock exacerbates the situation. Formal sector home construction is expanding rapidly but represents only half of new home construction. The other half is served by informal sector construction. Residents of informal settlements build their houses incrementally, financed by personal savings, informal credit and family–employer assistance.

Over the next 10 years housing demand is expected to remain strong (about 700,000 to 800,000 units per year). Even though population growth has slowed significantly in the last 25 years, household formation will continue to grow due to the increase in the population aged 40 and older. The fastest growth in housing demand will likely be in medium-size cities. On the supply side, the response is likely to be less than adequate, especially for the poor. The economic crisis of 1995 stifled investment in real estate and housing finance, and subsequent reforms aimed at increasing the efficiency of the market and the supply of housing were initiated without an adequate support and targeting for low-income families.

Infrastructure and Services

According to 1997 estimates, urban infrastructure and service deficits are widespread in Mexico. Ten percent of city residents do not have access to safe drinking water, 15 percent do not have access to sanitation services, and roughly one third do not have proper drainage. Access to social services is also weak—16.7 percent of households do not have access to secondary education and 12.5 percent do not have access to a public health clinic.[13] Low-income neighborhoods often suffer from inadequate access to public transport and poor road conditions; consequently, poor households, without employer support for transport, pay a significant percentage of disposable income for mobility. Regional disparities emerge when these figures are desegregated. In urban areas, infrastructure and services are concentrated in formal, higher-income neighborhoods. When services exist, the quality may be low, and it is not uncommon for poor communities to have piped water for only a few hours a day.

---

12. World Bank, "Migration," pp. 44–45.
13. *A Guide to the Global Environment, The Urban Environment, 1996–97*, Universidad Iberoamericana and World Resources.

INEFFICIENT MANAGEMENT AND PRICING POLICIES HAVE LIMITED ACCESS TO BASIC SERVICES. The responsibility for the provision of water, solid waste, transport, housing, and land services at the local level is not clear. Local entities are constrained by limited financial capacity, weak management, an inadequate regulatory framework, and deficiencies in basic equipment and infrastructure. The growing urban populations, poverty, and economic activity are pushing these weak delivery systems to the point of breakdown.

WATER AND SANITATION. Many municipal water companies have good professional capacity; however, decentralization reforms of the late 1980s were incomplete, leading to an unclear and restrictive institutional framework. Most operators are decentralized municipal or state entities, not autonomous, commercial-oriented operators. The lack of transparency and sound policies of the three levels of government on the provision of this service has led to financial instability, dependency on state and federal financial support, underinvestment, and poor targeting of subsidies. To date, participation of private operators has been negligible, and the existing legal and regulatory frameworks discourage moves toward greater private sector participation in the provision of water and sanitation services. In general, the federal government sells bulk water to state governments, then resells water to the municipalities. Very often, the three levels of government charge tariffs to customers well below the level of cost recovery.

FLOOD MANAGEMENT. The most serious impacts of flooding on urban populations stem from damaged houses and the conditions into which these populations are resettled. Low-income residents form the largest proportion of affected urban residents, and for whom floods imply the loss of homes and personal effects due to the weak and substandard construction materials, and the disruption of labor and school activities. Widespread flash flooding in the major cities results in severe economic losses estimated at over US$150 million a year.[14]

URBAN ENVIRONMENTAL SITUATION. Urban areas are affected by lack of proper waste disposal. Per capita generation of urban refuse has grown in step with urbanization. Some 0.7 kilograms to 1.3 kilograms of solid waste is generated per person per day, with an average organic content of about 71 percent. Only 77 percent of solid waste generated in urban areas is collected, and less than 35 percent is disposed of under sanitary conditions. The situation is much worse in smaller cities. In the 100 largest cities, other than the seven metropolitan areas, only 42 percent of solid waste is properly disposed of; in smaller cities this number falls to 4 percent.[15] Solid waste management in Mexico is not a municipal service, but a state government responsibility. In most states, the service is provided free of charge. Poor households and

---

14. Policy Note, "Water Policy," World Bank, Washington, D.C., June 2000.
15. Policy Note, "Solid Waste Management," World Bank, Washington D.C., June 2000.

neighborhoods are disproportionately exposed to the negative health and productivity effects of urban environmental degradation because illegal settlements are often located in risk-prone areas, infrastructure and service deficiencies are highest in poor areas, and slums are usually in closer proximity to sources of pollution.

AIR POLLUTION. While pollutant emissions in Mexico are lower than in many industrialized and LAC countries,[16] most of these emissions are concentrated in the metropolitan areas of Mexico City and Guadalajara. In 1996, the IMECA index reached between 100 and 150 in 91 percent, and 70 percent of the days of the year, respectively.[17] Contamination of the atmosphere is becoming significant in many municipalities, and the transport sector is a major contributor to this problem. Highly polluting diesel bus fleets, with the average age of 15 years or more, are also a significant cause of air pollution.[18]

URBAN TRANSPORT. Key transport goals for cities include improving accessibility for the urban poor and reducing urban congestion and pollution. To adequately address these issues, the responsibilities and capacity of the decentralized public entities and private participation in investment and operation must be increased. The lack of coordination of government agencies with jurisdiction within a metropolitan area limits the ability to set and implement a coherent policy to promote integrated municipal transport services. Moreover, institutionally fractured responsibilities for concession and management of road infrastructure has led to fractured services, weak transport companies, and irrational and unsupervised route operations. The current level of infrastructure and rate of improvement are not keeping pace with the growth in auto ownership and travel. Congestion in urban areas is common, and poor management of the already insufficient road space, especially poor vehicle parking practices and incomplete road signage, contributes significantly to the congestion.

Moreover, the proliferation of informal transport services is affecting the financial viability of the formal and more economically efficient services and contributing to congestion, noise, and other forms of pollution in cities. The poor suffer the most because they live in peri-urban areas where the available public transport services are often badly organized and inadequate in terms of level of service and area served. A large percentage of the urban poor have to make several transfers and take

---

16. In 1996 Mexico carbon dioxide emissions were 3.8 metric tonnes per capita, compared to 20 in the United States, 9.5 in the United Kingdom, 6.2 in France, 3.7 in Argentina, and 1.7 in Brazil.

17. Secretaría de Medio Ambiente Recursos Naturales y Pesca e INEGI, *Estadísticas del Medio Ambiente 1995–1996*. Mexico: 1997. World Bank, *World Development Report 1999/2000*, Washington D.C.: Oxford University Press, 2000. IMECA is an international index which measures a group of air pollutants. A value of 100 and more is considered unhealthy.

18. Mexico Policy Note "Transportation," World Bank, Washington, D.C., June 2000.

hours to reach their destinations. Too often these trips cost more than 20 percent of their income and are made in unsafe buses.

Size Specific Challenges

With over 200,000 localities, urban centers of Mexico include a wide range of cities and accompanying challenges. At the broadest level, Mexican cities can be broken down into the Metropolitan Area of Mexico City, medium-size cities, border cities, tourism centers, and small towns.

- *Metropolitan Mexico City.* While migration to Mexico City has slowed, housing and infrastructure demand continues to grow due to the sheer magnitude of the metropolitan area population. Limited land availability, low density, commercial development, and population pressures are resulting in a substantial shelter deficit for low-income groups. Moreover, investment in low-income center-city neighborhoods has lagged, and the resulting deterioration has been accompanied by increased insecurity and the flight of low-income residents to the periphery. Low-income neighborhoods and slums on the periphery lack basic infrastructure and social services. As low-income populations are increasing segregation into marginal areas of the periphery, longer commuting times limit their access to employment, and decrease the returns to employment as benefits of working hours are diminished by long travel times.
- *Medium-Size Cities.* Rural–urban migration within Mexico is still substantial. During 1970 to 1990 it contributed to an increase in the number of medium-size cities of 100,000 to 1 million inhabitants from 10 to 55. Many of these cities have problems providing sufficient employment and infrastructure for their growing population. The living conditions of urban migrants are often deplorable, and the cost of providing them with access to water, sewerage, and electricity is high.
- *Border Cities.* The northern border of Mexico contains some of the fastest-growing urban centers in the world. Driven by the development of export processing zones, rapid migration to these areas is contributing to phenomenal growth of peri-urban slums along the Mexico–U.S. border. Population growth in these areas averages 7 percent annually, and current efforts to meet the basic housing, infrastructure, and service needs of the slum dwellers have been woefully inadequate. The lack of community infrastructure, and the migratory nature of the slum population, has resulted in a lack of social cohesion and extremely high levels of crime and insecurity in the slums.
- *Tourism Cities.* Tourism cities of Mexico present distinct access problems due to disparities in the type and prices of services provided to tourists and the needs of the local population.
- *Small Towns.* Decentralization in Mexico has been implemented rapidly, and local governments have not had time to adequately prepare themselves for

new responsibilities. This is particularly true in the 2,200 towns with populations between 2,500 and 14,999. The potential detriment of weak local institutions is made worse by the fact that these small towns face some of the largest poverty problems in urban Mexico.

The Institutional Context

Some Mexican cities are well managed and are sources of innovation. Even more encouraging are the growing number of initiatives by small, medium, and large municipalities that have developed models of good practice to tackle urban problems, and the speed with which they are replicated. The focus in this section is on the general decentralization setting, issues faced by less-well-managed municipalities, and the challenges facing municipalities as they seek to upgrade their institutional human resource base.

DECENTRALIZATION. Compared with other Latin American economies, Mexico remains a highly centralized country. Although the three levels of government are democratically elected, the short term of local administrations (only three years) and the prohibition of immediate reelection have grave consequences for the ability of local authorities to effectively manage cities. Most administrative operations of municipalities (contracting third parties for public works, assigning public services provision to private operators, selling public properties, setting tax rates and tariffs) must be submitted to and approved by state legislatures, allowing political bargaining which interferes with local management. Mexico's intergovernmental fiscal relations are based mainly on transfers from the federal government, while subnational taxation powers are severely limited (see Note on Decentralization). In recent years, some federal policies have increased the level of financial resources available to states and municipalities. Although loosely defined, education, health, and social infrastructure have been assigned to states during the last decade. *Ramo* 33, a federal budget transfer mechanism created in 1998, increased substantially the amount of resources given to subnational administrations to manage.

FISCAL ARRANGEMENTS. In 1999, states' own revenues represented 0.8 percent of GDP (mainly payroll tax)—compared with 3.2 percent in Argentina (1994), 9.5 percent in Brazil (1992), and 2.7 percent in Colombia (1990). Net transfers from the federal government to subnational administrations were 5.7 percent of GDP, higher than in countries like Argentina, with a net transfer of 5.2 percent, Brazil with a net transfer of 4.6 percent, and Colombia with a net transfer of 3.7 percent, and not far from average transfers of 5.5 percent in the case of industrialized countries. Mexican municipalities' own revenues were 0.2 percent of GDP (property tax, vehicles, various tariffs), while the larger Latin American economies average 1 percent, and local governments of the most industrialized countries capture 5.5 percent to 7 percent of GDP. Transfers to local governments in Mexico reach 1.2 percent of

GDP, while similar Latin American countries average 1.7 percent, and local governments in industrialized countries receive 2.7 percent to 3.8 percent of GDP. Transfers come from a dozen funds with different formulas, including variables such as population and poverty. On the whole, the system could be less complicated and more transparent.

The net expenditure of Mexico's states is 5.9 percent of GDP (24 percent of total public expenditure), behind only Argentina with 8.9 percent, and Brazil with 7.3 percent. Among the most industrialized countries, state government expenditure reaches levels of 8.4 percent to 12.6 percent of GDP. Municipalities are responsible for 1.35 percent of GDP (5.5 percent out of total public expenditure), behind countries like Brazil with 5.64 percent of GDP, Colombia with 2.52 percent, Chile with 2.76 percent, and Argentina with 2.4 percent. Local governments in industrialized countries are responsible for net expenditure of 8 percent to 10 percent of GDP. Mexico's public sector is fiscally about the same size of comparable LAC economies: total public income is 22.5 percent in Mexico, 25 percent in LAC, and 44 percent in most industrialized economies (see Table 2).[19]

Capacity for Urban Management

The challenges faced by city and town managers are increasingly complex as globalization and pressures to improve productivity affect their economic base. At the same time, low-income groups are increasingly voicing their demands for better services and the environmental impact of their exclusion from basic urban services is a more pressing issue. Public safety issues have also become pressing with rising levels of drug-related and other violence. Mexican cities and towns often lack the overall strategic vision and skills to tackle these problems in an integrated manner, and the upper levels of government lack instruments to assist weak municipalities. Specifically, municipalities suffer from several management problems including (a) poor fiscal management—inadequate expenditure control, lack of prioritization of capital investment, and little incentive to generate own revenues; (b) inadequate administrative infrastructure—for example, poorly maintained municipal databases, including weak basic financial systems (particularly cash flow, capital budgeting, and debt management); and (c) a shortage of skilled staff and a surplus of unskilled employees. These problems are more pressing in smaller towns where skilled people are even scarcer.

---

19. Own calculations based on IMF, *Government Finance Statistics Yearbook*, 1990–99; Secretaría de Hacienda y Crédito Público de México. Estadísticas Financieras del Sector Público: http://www.shcp.gob.mx; M. Giugale and S. Webb, (eds.), *Achievements and Challenges of Fiscal Decentralization. Lessons from Mexico.* Washington: World Bank, 2000; de la Cruz, Rafael, *Descentralización en Perspectiva.* Caracas: IESA, 1998. Special thanks to Alberto Díaz-Cayeros and Enrique Cabrero Mendoza for their contributions and assistance with these calculations.

III. Perspectives and Key Issues

For several decades the Mexican government has given special importance to urban policy. The federal program for 100 cities and the metropolitan areas consolidation program attest to this interest. The decentralization initiatives contained in the 1983 Constitutional amendment strengthened local governments, and in recent years responsibility for the management of urban areas has been increasingly transferred to states and municipalities.

In spite of important developments and a general willingness to formulate a comprehensive strategy,[20] these investments have been made on a case-by-case basis without reference to a strategic framework. This is due partly to a lack of ownership on the part of relevant stakeholders of the different attempts to work out a strategy. As a result, each interest group has being pushing its own agenda in spite of many accords among them on what should be done in terms of urban management. Future urban financial support and technical assistance to Mexico would benefit from the existence of a medium- and long-term programs with objectives shared by key actors in Mexican society. Such programs would need to be based on shared objectives, a clear policy framework, and realistic investment programs with clear mandates and investment responsibilities within a credible financial package.

In developing a strategic program of urban investments in Mexico, the key areas of priority should be:

- Strengthening urban municipal management, finance, and governance.
- Enhancing local economic productivity and competitiveness.
- Improving urban quality of life, with a focus on alleviating urban poverty.
- Catalyzing the accumulated management know-how of public and private institutions to optimize the use of human resources.

Urban Governance and Institutional Design in Mexico

The design of public and private institutions and the relations among them produces a series of incentives that influence institutional effectiveness. It is especially important to study the formal and informal operation and interrelationships of key institutions, and thus better understand the administrative, political, economic, and social dynamics affecting urban development. In Mexico, the key players include the three levels of government, the business community, and civil society. Factors that need to be taken into account include:

- Municipal authorities and state representatives in Mexico are elected for three-year terms and the municipal president (mayor) cannot be reelected. This

---

20. *Mexico Decentralization and Urban Management. Urban Sector Study*, Report No. 8924-ME, World Bank, Washington, D.C., 8 July 1991.

leads to a lack of continuity in policy design and implementation. There is a growing consensus on the need to lengthen municipal terms, but the nature of that reform remains unclear.

- Identification of the key state and municipal functions as they relate to urban development is essential (the 1983 reform of Article 115 of the Constitution established a wide range of municipal duties). It would be important to look at groups of cities by size to determine whether and how well assigned responsibilities have been carried out.

- The role of the private sector in urban development and its interaction with local government is not well understood. Local government–private sector relations are mostly informal, and it is not clear how business investment, contracting out, and other forms of private sector participation are promoting or limiting urban progress.

- Intergovernmental relations can often determine the level of municipal autonomy and, consequently, the success of urban development strategies. Intergovernmental ties tend to be strong where state and local officials represent the same political party, and weak where the governor and mayor are in opposition. It is important to understand the nature of intergovernmental planning, the success of such strategies, and the obstacles that can emerge.

- Municipal administrative autonomy is constantly undercut by state legislative assemblies as they decide on local issues ranging from cadastral values and local public services tariffs to whether municipalities can contract public works, or rent or sell their properties in operations that exceed their period of governance.

- Federal transfers to municipal governments pass through the state governments first, allowing the state considerable control over local decisionmaking. The response of local officials to this situation—from resigned acceptance of their dependent position to greater innovation in raising their own revenue—will shape the future of urban development.

- Participation of civil society in local governance can help reduce the cost of development projects and improve the effectiveness of the public investment. The extent to which citizen participation is producing such benefits—or simply reinforcing existing traditional patron–client ties—needs to be assessed.

- The financial, managerial, and technical capacity of city governments is often weak. Because they cannot adequately provide a public service, for example, urban governments may, through collaborative agreements, cede their authority in this area to the state. Inability to sufficiently recover costs for service delivery, collect property taxes, or manage new resources may also be determining the future of a city's progress.

Enhancing Local Economic Productivity and Competitiveness

City competitiveness will have a major role in Mexico's development perspectives. However, the knowledge of city dynamics and competitiveness is limited, hampering the effectiveness of urban policies. Particular issues to be addressed include:

- *The Case of Border Cities.* Their integration into a global economy and growing job opportunities have been attracting population for more than a decade. Public services and infrastructure will be required to meet the needs of the new residents.
- *The Relation Between Size and Wealth.* Of the seven largest Mexican cities, only Monterrey and Mexico City are among the highest in per capita GDP. The other five cities occupy rank below the 20th place.[21] What explains the relative growth and affluence of Mexican cities? Economies and diseconomies of scale and externalities associated with Mexican city development and expansion need to be better understood in order for policymakers to more effectively influence urban development.
- *The Role of the Private Sector.* Urban development has often been considered the exclusive realm of government action or academic interest. The private sector has rarely been invited to take an active position in the design or preparation of urban plans and strategies. However, private investment has a decisive impact on the formation of cities and urban economic dynamics. There is a clear need to improve our knowledge of what drives urban economic development and to include the productive sector (private and public) in a permanent consultation partnership.

Cities and Poverty Reduction

In Mexican cities, 17 percent of the population live in extreme poverty (below 0.5 minimum wages or, at present 528 pesos per month per household). This population has less access to education, health, waste disposal, water and sanitation, and other urban services. Poor neighborhoods are also more likely to suffer from violence and crime. Larger Mexican cities are characteristically divided into formal zones of high- and medium-income families, and informal zones where low-income groups settle. This situation increases the cost of delivering public services and transportation to informal neighborhoods. Social conflict and crime are frequent in such cities, adding more costs to local governments and private businesses.

Poverty reduction must be achieved in a sustainable manner, beyond classical social programs intended for temporary relief of extreme conditions through the provision of greater and more equal opportunities to the poor. Professional literature and best practices around the world provide some guidance, notably to:

---

21. INEGI, *Producto Interno Bruto medido por entidad federativa, 1993*, México: INEGI, 1994. See also División de Estudios Económicos y Sociales de Banamex, *México Social 1996–1998*, México: 1999.

- Improve access of the poorest populations to good public services, especially education, health, transportation, energy, water, sanitation, public space and safety (most of these being the responsibility of regional and local governments).
- Legalize land tenancy; this will boost the real-estate market and local tax collection.
- Increase access of informal workers to the formal labor market. While difficult, doing so will enhance labor conditions, tax collection, and public service financing.

Learning from Successes and Failures of Urban Management

The study and dissemination of successful urban management experiences might be a valuable tool for helping cities improve their own administrative practices and increase their effectiveness in reducing poverty. A number of interesting cases in Mexico are available as examples of good urban management. Studying the causes of failures of other cases can also be useful to prevent them from recurring. The practices that have shown good results for city development include:

- Innovative strategic plans.
- Innovative techniques to fight crime.
- Managerial training and institutional development of local governments.
- Strengthening municipal fiscal autonomy.
- Community participation in defining municipal budgetary allocation and public services management.
- Public–private partnerships.
- Privatization of public services management.
- Intergovernmental alliances.
- Active cooperation among the same country or different countries' cities.
- Border city alliances.

It is clear that Mexico faces a formidable urban development challenge. While intersectoral experience will be useful, meeting that challenge will call for a participatory rational effort to produce a concerted agenda for public action over the short-, medium-, and long-term. Some general principles should guide that agenda.

IV. Toward an Agenda for Urban Development in Mexico

- *Mexico needs more public–private policy dialogue and consensus building.* Most Mexican political and social actors agree on much of what must be done to improve the quality of life and competitiveness of the cities, but communication among them is not always fluent. A comprehensive policy dialogue on urban development among relevant stakeholders from the public and private sector, including representatives of the three levels of government, the business community, urban specialists, local social activists, and NGOs would greatly help in reaching a broad consensus needed for urban development.

- *Improving the design of the decentralization process and public–private institutional relations would result in better urban development.* The decentralization process is advancing in Mexico and giving local and regional authorities more responsibilities on local issues, although the design of intergovernmental institutions is still not satisfactory. Enhanced governance through an increase of both local and intergovernmental accountability would give communities the means to follow up and evaluate public decisions and would give local and regional officials the tools to improve their performance. Many legitimate relations regarding urban development between the private and public sectors are informal. More institutionalized and transparent interactions would assure broader consensus on urban investments.

- *Urban development is occurring with less public support than necessary.* Given the externalities associated with urban development and city management, public intervention is fully justified from a point of view of equity and efficiency. The economic evolution of Mexican cities is quite unequal. The concentration of GDP in the Metropolitan areas of Mexico City, above its share of population; the accelerated pace of growth of certain cities in the North associated to maquilas; and some cities in the coasts drawn by tourism in contrast to other cities in the center and south that are losing population, have in common the lack of a comprehensive pattern of public investment in basic public services, energy, and transportation. The dynamics of urban economies must be better understood so public investments can be directed in a more efficient way, in partnership with private activities.

- *Good urban management has emerged in Mexico despite institutional, economic, and social obstacles.* Cities can become more competitive by learning from other cities' experiences. The recent development of many urban conglomerates has been characterized by a deep commitment by relevant local stakeholders. Very often this commitment takes the form of a public–private partnership that aligns objectives and means of the society as a whole. Most successful city development strategies show that in spite of adverse environments, visionary leadership, competent management, and citizen participation can achieve great progress. More modest city development projects, such as improving specific public services, defining local investment budgets, consulting the communities, and upgrading deteriorated urban zones, illustrate that a community can advance its city agenda in the midst of difficulties. This is the message that many cities can send and from which many other cities can learn. A city development strategy or other city development projects can be started without waiting for all favorable conditions to be present.

15

Rural Development and Agriculture

*This Chapter was written by Adolfo Brizzi, with the
valuable input of Alberto Valdés.*

I. Recent Developments

Over the past 10 years, Mexico's rural sector has been the subject of sweeping reforms, which have led to the emergence of a largely liberalized, market-oriented, and private-sector-driven rural economy. The government pursued reforms in the areas of prices, markets, and trade liberalization for most crops (maize and beans were initially left out), public investments, privatization, fiscal transfers, and retrenchment of parastatals. Reforms were accompanied by well-thought-through mitigation measures that helped the transition process. The PROCAMPO program permitted a smooth switch from distortionary commodity price subsidies to direct income payments fixed according to the historical (not current) amount of land cultivated for specific crops,[1] and longer on the basis of output. A food security program softened the impact on the poor through targeted tortilla and milk subsidies. The government decided to complete the liberalization effort in the maize sector in 1999 by phasing out the tortilla subsidy and eliminating CONASUPO.

At the same time, the inclusion of the agricultural sector in international trade negotiations through the GATT and NAFTA agreements has created the basis for progressive exposure to global forces and the additional adjustments that will follow. NAFTA (1994) is the first free-trade agreement signed between industrialized countries and a developing country that includes agriculture. Arbitrary and costly trade

---

1. Payments would be fixed amounts per hectare planted in a base period in beans, maize, soybeans, sorghum, wheat, rice, cotton, barley, and sunflower. Later the list of eligible crops was opened up and reforestation was also included. The program has a duration of 15 years. In 1999, PROCAMPO benefited 3.2 million producers, 85 percent of whom had less than 5 hectares, for a total cost of about US$1 billion (0.25 percent of GDP).

restrictions and regulations were eliminated, reduced, or converted into tariff arrangements to be progressively phased to tally by no later than 2008.

Reform of the land tenure system has featured prominently as part of the major achievements in the sector over the past decade. After a long history of land redistribution since the beginning of the 19th century, the 1992 Constitutional amendment and the accompanying change in the regulatory framework permitted *ejido* land transactions for the first time. In addition, to ensure better security of ownership rights, in 1995 the government embarked on a major program of land titling (PROCEDE). The combination of these efforts led the government to recently announce that the agrarian reform era is over.

The objectives of agricultural policy reform were reconfirmed with the implementation in 1996 of the *Alianza para el Campo* program. This far-reaching national program aims at fostering agricultural productivity through productive investments and the provision of support services for a wide range of agricultural subprograms. It should be seen as an important vehicle to accompany the reform process promoting the investments and adjustments required for the sector to face the new environment, fostering its competitiveness, and addressing poverty-oriented rural development issues. The cornerstone of the *Alianza para el Campo* is its decentralized approach and the delegation of administration and decisionmaking to the states.

In parallel to the agriculture sector reform effort, starting at the beginning of the 1990s, a major initiative was undertaken to develop rural areas and fight poverty through the PRONASOL program in SEDESOL, and the implementation of a program of rural and social infrastructure at the municipal level. While this program, and more generically SEDESOL, were seen as the government's flagship initiative for poverty alleviation, this may have acted as a disincentive for other agencies and line ministries to integrate poverty issues into their development agenda. Moreover, the sustainability and effectiveness of the investments promoted in reaching the poor varied greatly, creating the need to reassess targeting and decisionmaking mechanisms. Starting with the last administration, two major changes were implemented to this strategy: (a) an acceleration of the decentralization process to the state level through the *Alianza para el Campo,* including an increasing mainstreaming of social and poverty programs within SAGAR; and (b) the complete devolution in 1998 of the social infrastructure program to the municipal level (with the creation of a new budget line item called *Ramo 33*).

The important reforms carried out during the last decade permitted the establishment of a sound policy framework and fostered efficiency, but the performance of the sector lagged during most of the 1990s, agricultural growth stagnated, and rural poverty increased. It is only in the last two years that indicators have shown an abatement of rural poverty as a result of sustained economic growth since 1996.

A number of studies and comparative analyses have been carried out to assess the underlying reasons for the overall mediocre response of the sector to these sectoral reforms.[2] Among the most important and relevant reasons put forward are: (a) until the end of 1994, Mexico's macroeconomic policies and real exchange rates remained distressingly unfriendly to the sector and to traded commodities, and inflation remained persistently high; (b) low world prices for agricultural commodities; (c) some of the reforms may be considered incomplete (the maize sector was only partially reformed and the financial sector remained largely untouched); (d) by their nature, the reforms did not address the extreme heterogeneity of the rural sector and its regional variations, and market-driven reforms were not likely to have the same impact on small-scale producers of domestically consumed and subsistence commodities as on commercial agriculture; and (e) the reforms did not (and probably could not) resolve decades of structural and cultural limitations in the capacity of small and poor farmers to access production factors and markets.

It is, however, generally admitted that the reforms implemented, though not sufficient, were correct and necessary. If a sound macroeconomic framework can be maintained, the sector is poised for a sustainable enhancement of its productivity and performance. However, a number of second-generation reforms will need to be pursued and constraints removed to respond to the challenge posed by international competition, the need to diversify the productive pattern, and the compelling responsibility to address equity issues in the context of a rural development strategy repositioned in a regional context.

Some Facts

Evidence of the potential of the agricultural sector, in the context of a sound macroeconomic framework, has become increasingly evident over the last several years. After years of erratic behavior, growth in the agricultural sector has been uninterrupted since the third quarter of 1998. However, participation of the sector in total GDP has declined from 7.5 percent in 1995 to about 5 percent in 1999. Moreover, some key agricultural activities, such as basic grain production, have performed less well. Employment in agriculture still remains high, accounting for about 20 percent of the total labor force. The divergence between the participation of agriculture in GDP and the employment share suggests low labor productivity.[3] This productivity gap reveals low returns to primary factors and modest investment levels, but also hides important differences underlying the deep transformation within the rural sector. It is also striking that in terms of growth rates there is almost no correlation between the performance of the economy and the performance of the agricultural sector. The sector, as a whole, appears to be relatively disconnected from the rest of

2. See Agricultural Sector Adjustment Projects I and II, Performance Audit Reports, (Operations Evaluation Department, World Bank, 1996); and Policy Reforms in Agriculture, An Assessment of the Results in Eight Countries, (B. Gardner, University of Maryland, 1996).
3. In the U.S., the main market for Mexico's agricultural imports, agriculture represents 2.2 percent of total employment and generates 2.0 percent of GDP.

the economy: its performance was not significantly affected by the 1994 crisis, nor has it been boosted by the steady growth of the last four years (with the exception of 1999). However, it needs to be noted that if natural disasters were to be factored in, the performance of the sector may well have a different profile. Evidence from other Latin American countries[4] points to a strong long-term causal relationship between agricultural output growth and relative prices and sustained overall rates of growth. More rapid overall growth of the Mexican economy should create more favorable conditions for accelerating agricultural growth.

The commercial sector, competing in the international markets, has largely benefited from the reforms, including the opportunities offered by NAFTA, and responded positively to the 1994 devaluation. The sector's overall external balance is positive due to exports of coffee, fruits, vegetables, and tobacco, but the food balance is negative. Since the implementation of NAFTA in January 1994, the liberalization of the sector has accelerated and most tariffs and subsidies have been eliminated, resulting in an increase of imports and an expansion of the agreed upon import quotas. However, during the first six years of NAFTA, agricultural exports to the U.S. grew by 78 percent, while imports grew by about 60 percent. Mexico has expanded its agricultural exports to the U.S. much more than any other country.[5] Also to be noted is that maize imports largely benefited the livestock and poultry sector and helped make them more competitive. While liberalization has

Figure 1. Growth Rates

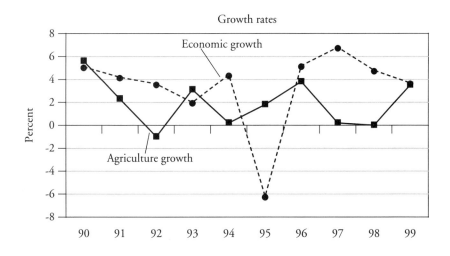

4. *Economía Política de las Intervenciones de Precios Agrícolas en América Latina*, (A. Krueger, M. Schiff, and A. Valdes, ICEG, 1990).
5. El TLCAN en el Sector Agroalimentario Mexicano a Seis Años de su Entrada en Vigor (SAGAR, SECOFI, 2000).

increased the openness of the sector, it remains internally focused and still has great potential for trade expansion because Mexico has one of the lowest rates of agricultural trade to agricultural GDP in Latin America (46 percent in 1996). This is also evidenced by the fact that there was little change in the cropping patterns during the 1990s, with about 50 percent of the cultivated area steadily going to maize.

The response of the rural sector should be differentiated from the response of the commercial sector. The large *ejido* subsector (three-quarters of the farm labor and half of the farmland) is under stress, going through significant adjustments and increasingly integrating into the off-farm economy. It is also the subsector that experiences the highest levels of poverty. The majority of the rural poor are small subsistence farmers, whose income overwhelmingly depends on self-employment in the agricultural sector, with little opportunities for economic alternatives, relatively isolated from labor markets or living in marginal areas. Being indigenous is also closely linked to poverty with four out of five indigenous people being poor. Moreover, poverty is also relatively concentrated in the South of the country where the rate of extreme rural poverty is three times higher than in the North and twice higher than in the Center.

Another large segment of rural poor are the landless agricultural workers in poor rural areas. About 70 percent of total employment in the rural sector does not possess land. In many rural areas these workers are characterized by low education levels, strong dependency on rural wages, and an income of $2 per day in many rural areas. According to a recent World Bank study, both extreme and moderate rural poverty rates may have increased during most of the 1990s, and only after 1996 have they given sign of abating.

II. Key Issues

Rural Poverty

Persistently high poverty rates represent one of the most compelling challenges to the well-being of the rural population. If left unattended, it is an issue that is likely to threaten the social balance of Mexican society by polarizing the economy and the development agenda. The pervasiveness of such high poverty rates, especially among indigenous populations, raises issues of equity, social inclusion, and access to productive factors and assets. It also challenges conventional government programs to find ways to address poverty issues in a more effective fashion, and one consistent with cultural preferences (see Chapter on Indigenous Peoples and Poverty), traditional community practices, local knowledge, and needs. Poverty is also related to exogenous variations in commodity prices of some crops predominant in poor areas, such as coffee. The sharp decline of coffee prices between 1986 and 1993, and again this past year, may have been one of the main elements behind the increase of extreme poverty in the Southeast (especially Chiapas). Chief among the most obvious causes of poverty is the very low level of labor productivity and income, as expressed by the small contribution (5 percent) that a relatively important share of the population (20 percent) makes to GDP. The high level of risk and the limited options available to poor farmers to cope with income and consumption variability have induced them into low risk/low return investment strategies which limit their economic opportunities and contribute to keeping them in a poverty trap. It is imperative to address the large regional differences and diversity existing in the rural sector and the need to design more differentiated policies and programs that incorporate microeconomic aspects, and to pursue second-generation-type reforms.

Over the past decade the *ejido* sector has experienced an increasing integration into off-farm activities and non-farm employment as a consequence of the following factors: (a) a relatively unattractive incentive framework for agriculture (the "push factor" analyzed below); (b) the removal of restrictions on land and labor market participation under the agrarian reform; and (c) large differentials in labor productivity between rural and urban areas. This trend accelerated after the 1994 devaluation, which has made migration to the United States much more attractive. Also, these past five years of sustained economic growth have enhanced the absorptive capacity of the other sectors of the economy (the "pull factor"). In 1997, 60 percent of all households participated in off-farm activities, more than 80 percent had at least one family member residing outside the community, and 45 percent had at least one family member who migrated to the U.S. On average, about 40 percent of the total income of the ejido sector comes from non-farm sources, including remittances.[6] It is to be noted, however, that complete outmigration from the community is relatively rare, and smallholders keep their roots in the region. While posing difficult social constraints and potentially disrupting community organization, this remarkable diversification of income sources represents a very important valve to escape poverty, maintains substantial flow of remittances into rural areas, and smoothens income variations deriving from agricultural cycles, thus providing an important source of informal insurance. These growing connections with the off-farm economy will also eventually have beneficial effects by eroding differential returns to labor and capital across sectors. Migration flows and non-farm employment will probably continue in the years ahead and expand, it should not be resisted but rather better understood and accompanied. It is critical to internalize this pattern of development when discussing options for future rural poverty alleviation policies, and also to flag the relatively little attention devoted to the development of the off-farm rural sector by public programs, despite its importance.

While the increasing integration with the off-farm sector and with the rest of the economy offers opportunities to explore new poverty alleviation strategies, it must be recognized that an agricultural growth strategy, and even more overall economic growth, will remain a critical element of rural poverty alleviation efforts. Such growth will need to be broad-based and capable of generating employment in both the farm and off-farm sectors. The most important contribution to agricultural

---

6. Mexico Ejido Reform: Avenue of Adjustment-Five Years Later, (Louise Cord, World Bank, 1999).

growth will have to originate from the agricultural sector itself, although it may employ a decreasing number of people. This will lead us to examine two key factors in the implementation of an agricultural growth strategy: access to markets and agricultural productivity.

It has to be recognized, however, that a large pool of rural poor will remain relatively untouched by the benefits of growth, new opportunities in commercial agriculture, small-scale intensification or access to non-rural employment. This group is composed of farm workers and small producers in marginal areas with a weak resource-base, typically older and/or indigenous. In these areas, access to output and factor markets, including off-farm opportunities, are limited and as a consequence dependence on primary activities with low productivity (mostly non-tradable) remains predominant. Most of these people are net buyers of food and are exposed to nutritional deficiencies because of their limited purchasing power. They would generally benefit from liberalization measures that would decrease the price of basic commodities and from income support programs or safety nets that would easy the incidence of poverty on their standards of living.

An Unfriendly Incentive Framework

Overall, real prices for key Mexican agricultural commodities declined steadily in the 1990s, with the exception of 1996, when prices rose sharply, reflecting the delayed impact of the devaluation and a marked temporary increase in world market commodity prices (Table 1). This negative trend was compounded by the strong price instability facing Mexican producers, particularly following the devaluation. The existence of an unstable and relatively poor incentive framework facing Mexican agricultural producers is also reflected in an analysis of the nominal protection rates (NPRs) for key crops (Table 2). NPR trend shows that, with few exceptions, agricultural prices were below equivalent international prices between 1992 and 1997.

Table 1. Real Producer Prices for Key Crops (in percent)

	1991	1992	1993	1994	1995	1996	1997	91–94	95–97
Corn	8.6	-6.5	-2.9	-8.3	-22.3	32.3	-22.8	-5.3	5.9
Beans	-14.2	-13.9	-2.4	-10.6	-25.6	39.4	-2.2	-7.7	22.4
Wheat	-0.8	-5.8	-5.2	-4.4	-8.8	26.6	-17.2	-4.6	5.0
Sorghum	-9.3	4.8	-8.0	-11.7	-14.7	46.3	-5.9	-4.5	21.0
Coffee	-10.3	-14.4	2.9	51.2	36.8	-39.4	43.6	18.3	1.5
Tomatoes	-4.1	50.2	-7.1	-2.9	-18.8	-3.8	0.5	18.6	-2.1

Note: Compiled as the annual compounded rate of change in prices for the start and end years. Banco de México producer price series. The prices are deflated by the national producer price index minus the services sector.
Source: Ejido Study.

Table 2. Nominal Protection Rates[a] (in percent)

	1992	1993	1994	1995	1996	1997
Corn	18	16	-15	-34	-45	-23
Beans	-5	-8	-38	-67	-66	n/a
Wheat	-8	-12	-21	-58	-17	-29
Sorghum	-31	-26	-37	-28	-36	-29
Coffee	n/a	18	-52	-34	4	-26
Tomatoes	n/a	15	-26	-67	-63	n/a

Notes:
a. The NPR reflects the difference between nominal producer prices and the equivalent world price at the point of collection. The equivalent world market price is obtained by adjusting the CIF price to reflect the marketing cost (storage, finance, transport, etc.) to bring the imported commodity to the point of collection at the farm level. Unavailability of data did not permit to calculate effective protection rates.
Source: Ejido Study.

It is imperative to address the causes of these negative rates because they represent a major factor underlying slow growth and poverty. This negative incentive framework could reflect a number of factors including:

- *Inefficient marketing channels.* Negative NPRs might signal the presence of uncompetitive agricultural markets and of an implicit taxation deriving from unaccounted marketing margins (see below) and appropriation of rents by traders and agroprocessors.
- *Liberalization.* The removal of trade and exchange rate protection in the early 1990s depressed producer prices.
- *Exchange rate.* The overvalued exchange rate existing before the devaluation facilitated cheap imports and undermined domestic prices; after the devaluation the change in parity did not translate into an equivalent increase in producer prices.
- *Interest rates.* High interest rates raise transaction costs, which lowers domestic farm prices at harvest, due to high financial cost of storage.

While initially designed with the objective of softening and accompanying the transition process, some government programs might have also acted as impediments to the required adjustment process, by introducing distortions in other areas of the incentive framework. For example:

- The market transition following the divestiture of CONASUPO and the privatization of the storage assets has generally proceeded smoothly; however, public policies have not always been consistent, and the pressure has remained strong to maintain price or marketing support schemes for basic grain. Some

US$260 million has been budgeted in 2000 for ASERCA's marketing subsidies (essentially to private transporters and for storage) for fixed volumes of crops in a number of states, representing about 27 percent of the maize producer price in Sinaloa and 35 percent in Chiapas. Although the method of delivering crop subsidies has changed, the share of the maize market affected by subsidies has not decreased from the CONASUPO period.[7] The absence of clear policy signals in this area negatively affect the shifting toward more competitive crops, the involvement of the private sector in the newly emerging storage market, a more competitive transport market, to the development of contract farming arrangements, and to the functioning of a recently created agricultural trade exchange (*Bolsa of Guadalajara*).

- Linking the PROCAMPO payment to actual planting of eligible crops introduced rigidities in the incentive to shift from an eligible crop to a non-eligible crop, and hindered diversification opportunities. The recent opening up to all crops has considerably reduced such distortion.
- The intervention of LICONSA and DICONSA in poor areas, through the subsidization of basic goods consumption, creates differentials with market prices for the same goods, which can promote speculation and stifle the involvement of the private sector.

Poorly Functioning Markets

Output

The capacity to access the market is a key element of an agricultural growth and poverty alleviation strategy. Markets are the mechanism through which an increase of the demand for agricultural products can translate into an expansion of the supply. However, it is commonly known that the demand for basic agricultural products is inelastic with respect to commodity prices and consumer income. This is one of the main reasons why rural areas cannot maintain sustained growth rates unless they can trade with cities, neighboring countries, and the whole world—that is, have access to the biggest possible market. Agricultural protectionist policies around the world, especially in industrialized countries, have done little to generate agricultural growth, as evidenced by the modest 1.8 percent growth of international agricultural trade during 1985–94, compared to 5.8 percent for manufactured products over the same period.[8] Without expanded access to the markets of developed countries and to international markets in general, the agricultural growth required to generate

---

7. CONASUPO's intervention covered about 3.2 million tons of maize in 1997 and 1.6 million tons in 1998. In 1999 ASERCA provided subsidies for about 2.6 million tons. The amount of marketing subsidies has increased in 2000.
8. Agricultural Trade Barriers, Trade Negotiations, and the Interests of Developing Countries, (H. Binswanger and E. Lutz, World Bank, 1999).

employment and reduce poverty cannot happen. Mexico's efforts to integrate agriculture into various international and bilateral trade agreement (NAFTA, EU, Chile) should be encouraged and pursued.

One of the main problems of the sector in Mexico is the inefficiency of distribution channels, and the concentration of power in the hands of very few buyers, whose most important asset is the ability to finance purchase and marketing. The withdrawal of the state from virtually all commodity marketing activities has created a vacuum that has progressively been filled by private intermediaries. In many areas, especially where there is not a sufficient critical mass of production that can promote competition among buyers, or where there is not a sufficient level of producer organization, marketing has organized itself along oligopolistic intermediation and segmentation. Poor areas and domestic marketing channels are the most affected. This is particularly the case for the fruit and vegetable wholesale trade, where 80 percent of the throughput of the *Central de Abasto* of Mexico City (the most important price-setting market for perishables) is in the hands of 6 percent of its traders. The trade in key products such as oranges and avocados is controlled by fewer than 10 traders each, most of whom having fully integrated operation and holding dominant position in the markets of Guadalajara and Monterrey as well.[9] Mexican fruit and vegetable farmers typically gets no more than 35 to 45 percent of the retail price of the product, compared to the 65 to 75 percent obtained by farmers in most Central American countries, or the approximately 50 percent obtained by farmers in more distorted markets, such as in the Dominican Republic. The inefficiency of the domestic marketing system translates into additional transaction costs that stifle the competitiveness of the different commodities and masks their real comparative advantages. Moreover, if markets are not competitive, liberalization will not produce the expected beneficial impact on prices.

Market performance improves with the development of mechanisms that permit businesses to enter into secure transactions involving distance and time (a promise to pay next week for a product received this week). If such transactions cannot be made with a minimum level of confidence, the market fails or may not even exist. This is what happens in poor areas, where contract rights and property rights are poorly defined and enforced, and transactions require immediate payment or exchange. Such rights are critical to developing efficient markets, without which there cannot be growth.

Storage

Storage appears to be a weak link in the marketing chain; it is suggested that 30 percent of production is lost due to inadequate transport and storage. Until recently, government intervention discouraged and crowded out private initiatives for storage and commodity trade financing, particularly for grains. Moreover, guaranteed pur-

---

9. Mexico—Food Marketing Study, (Panos Varangis, Richard Lacroix, Donald Larson, World Bank, 2000).

chases provided little incentive for quality because standards were quite broad and did not reflect the real needs of buyers and consumers. The recent elimination of CONASUPO was accompanied by the privatization of warehouses (ANDSA, BURUCONSA), which has opened up opportunities for the development of private sector mechanisms for inventory financing based on the issuance of Certificates of Deposit *(certificados de depósito)* or Pledged Bonds *(bonos de prenda)*. The storage and inventory-financing sector is still emerging, but its development represents an important step toward the modernization of the grain marketing system, where important efficiency gains are possible. Implementation of a warehouse receipt system carries important benefits for (a) the producer, as an instrument to borrow against inventories and an opportunity to optimize sales by taking advantage of higher prices in the post-harvest season; (b) the processor, as a means of securing their inventories and also borrowing against them; (c) warehousing companies, that can achieve a higher capacity use and improve their business; and (d) banks, as a source of good collateral, highly liquid and easily tradable.

The warehouses *(Almacenes Generales de Depósito)* have also played the role of financial intermediaries for the financing of their inventories. Banks have generally remained absent from this business because of the lack of familiarity with the instrument, liquidity problems, perceived higher risks in lending for agricultural inventories, and uncertainties coming from the government policy on maize. Among the limitations on more effective and wider use of a warehouse receipts system are (a) a deficient legal and regulatory framework, because there are no specific regulations for grain warehouses through a warehouse receipt act, as exist in other countries; (b) inadequate quality and grading standards for grains, particularly maize, and the need for harmonization with the U.S. and Canada in the context of NAFTA; (c) insufficient mechanisms for warehouse inspection and monitoring, and for arbitration in case of discrepancies; and (d) insufficient price information to establish the value of commodities in storage.

Rural Financial Services

This sector is characterized by a legacy of government intervention and subsidies. The cost of government intervention in the rural financial system (essentially through BANRURAL, FIRA, and ANAGSA)[10] during 1983–92 has been estimated at approximately US$28.5 billion, of which 80 percent are associated with subsidized interest rates.[11] Credit organizations *(Uniones de Crédito)* were also promoted to retail in rural areas the subsidized credit provided at the wholesale level by NAFIN and FIRA. By the mid-1990s it was acknowledged that significant costs had resulted in the form of (a) excessive administrative costs and delinquency within public development banks; (b) widespread default induced by a poor loan portfolio and debt-forgiveness programs; (c) worsening income distribution resulting from

---

10. ANAGSA was closed in 1990.
11. The annual average of these costs represented almost 13 percent of GDP.

interest-rate subsidies; and (d) regulatory and sustainability problems with the credit institutions established at the field level.

Past government intervention in this sector has, to a large extent, prevented the development of well-functioning and sustainable rural financial markets. By allowing directed credit programs with poor recovery, subsidized rates, and debt forgiveness, not only has government intervention failed to address the needs of the small farmers, but it has also undermined financial discipline, crowded out private lenders, and hindered the development of self-sustained semi-informal cooperative structures based on savings mobilization. The government has recently started to introduce measures to reduce its exposure by liberalizing interest rates, but had to intervene again at the end of 1999 to bail out BANRURAL.[12] These institutions are shrinking their scope of activities in the search for rural entrepreneurs able to provide collateral, while trying to improve loan recovery performance. A program to build incentives for the private commercial financial sector to increase its presence in rural areas was also initiated in 1996, with little success. The intrinsic weakness of the banking sector, the financial crisis of 1995, and the concomitant controversial FOBABROA rescue package, may have induced commercial banks into even more conservative approaches, possibly worsening the perception of risk widely affecting investments in rural areas.

In this context, financial markets in most of the rural areas have remained shallow and segmented, operating in very localized and "personalized" circumstances with little or no collateral required but at very high costs.[13] In many cases this is aggravated by the repartition of "areas of influence" among few lenders, becoming a source of local monopolies which are very difficult to break. The only sector that somehow managed to survive and proved resilient to financial crisis and government withdrawal is the non-bank savings and loan institutions. While the overall regulatory framework for these institutions is weak and in need of urgent strengthening, their reliance on mobilized deposits to support their loan portfolio protected them from the currency and financial crisis, and they were able to attract new members when the rest of the financial system was shrinking.

Government policies regarding the rural financial sector are in need of reformulation. The lack of access to credit represents one of the major bottlenecks in the development of rural areas because it (a) restricts the economic opportunities of small enterprises, (b) prevents access to the inputs so badly needed to evolve along the technological curve and modernize agriculture, (c) impedes participation of more actors in the marketing business and increased competition, and (d) hampers movements toward more lucrative off-farm activities. Likewise, the paucity of adequate deposit and payment services in rural areas limits the ability of rural households and enterprises to effectively manage their savings and remittances.

---

12. About US$1.1 billion went into the bailout of BANRURAL at the end of 1999.
13. Financial Markets in Rural Areas in Mexico, (Rodrigo Chavez and Suzana Sanchez, World Bank, 1994).

Labor

Labor is the most abundant asset for the rural poor. However, the return to labor for rural households is reduced by their limited education and the high transaction costs of the labor market, which reduces their capacity to access the more lucrative nonagricultural wage market. The lower rates of educational attainment in rural areas reflect both supply factors (availability and quality of schools) and the higher opportunity cost for rural parents to send their children to school (boarding fees, loss of wage income and farm labor). Higher levels of education permit access to activities with higher returns (self-employment, commerce-related wage activities), while the lower levels (or the poorest people) have access to the lowest returns (casual non-agriculture wage labor). There is also evidence of important inefficiencies in terms of high transaction costs related to the remoteness of rural areas, the cyclical requirements of agriculture (limiting employment to certain periods), the suggested gender-based discrimination, the high risks associated with accessing labor markets outside the rural areas, and the lack of information. The functioning of rural labor markets, although little studied, is of critical importance to the future of rural areas and to the capacity of rural households to move out of poverty. Despite the variability of returns, off-farm activities are clearly associated with lower poverty. Together with the increasing integration of the *ejido* sector in the off-farm economy (since 1994, the share of *ejidatarios* involved in off-farm activities rose by 50 percent), two important labor-related trends characterize the *ejido* sector:[13]

THE INCREASING IMPORTANCE OF EJIDATARIAS. In 1970, about 31,000 *ejidatarias* had land rights. It is estimated that at the completion of the PROCEDE titling program, about 500,000 women will have registered as having land *rights (ejidatarias, comuneras and posesionarias)*. This implies an important change in Mexican rural society and will require the adaptation of rural development policies to the needs of female farmers.

THE RAPID AGING OF THE EJIDO POPULATION. The *ejidatarios'* average age is 52, with about half of them over age 50 (Figure 2). The comparison with rural localities of less than 2,500 inhabitants is striking: there, only 15 percent of the people are over age 50 years, and 50 percent are under age 20, as shown in the two age pyramids in Figure 2. This points to the existence of a large, young population in rural localities, most of whom have left the farm, have little possibility of accessing land, and who are in need of economic alternatives. It also raises the question of the viability of the *ejido* sector as full time farming activity in the poorest areas since: i) an aging population is less prone to migration; ii) off-farm employment tends to concentrate in the areas of greatest development and requires a certain level of education; and iii) farm labor productivity declines after a certain age. This special group of population is likely to become increasingly dependent on remittances and possibly welfare or safety net programs.

Figure 2. Age Pyramids

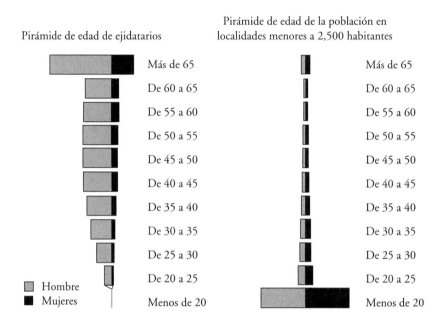

Pirámide de edad de ejidatarios

Pirámide de edad de la población en localidades menores a 2,500 habitantes

	Pirámide de edad de ejidatarios	Pirámide de edad de la población
	Más de 65	Más de 65
	De 60 a 65	De 60 a 65
	De 55 a 60	De 55 a 60
	De 50 a 55	De 50 a 55
	De 45 a 50	De 45 a 50
	De 40 a 45	De 40 a 45
	De 35 a 40	De 35 a 40
	De 30 a 35	De 30 a 35
	De 25 a 30	De 25 a 30
	De 20 a 25	De 20 a 25
	Menos de 20	Menos de 20

Hombre
Mujeres

Source: DEGP, *Procuraduria Agraria,* with RAN and INEGI data.

Land

Land is one of the few assets that poor farmers possess or have the usufruct of. Measures which can formalize and thus enhance security over land ownership or use, are conducive to farmers' capitalization, enhanced opportunities, and less risk-averse attitudes. In this respect, the change of Article 27 of the Constitution in 1992, the implementation of a new regulatory framework authorizing the sale (with community consent), rental, and sharecropping of ejido land, and the subsequent land certification program (PROCEDE 1994),[14] represent major steps in the modernization of the rural sector. However, *ejido* land distribution is still fragmented and the average farm plot is often too small to allow economies of scale and profitable investment opportunities (50 percent of *ejidos* have less than 5 hectares, representing 15 percent of total *ejido* land and an average of 2.8 hectares; moreover, more than 20 percent of *ejidatarios* have their farm split over three or more plots).[15] The development of a land market and the ability to engage in land transactions will eventually promote more efficient allocation of land and possibly enhance access to credit, because farmers could use land as collateral.

14. By January 2000 the land of 70 percent of all *ejidos* had been certified.
15. *Estudios Agrarios* N. 13, *Procuraduria de Agricultura,* (Hector Robles, 1999).

While the sale of land remains relatively rare, since 1992 land rental markets have become more active in the *ejido* sector (in 1997 about 19 percent of the *ejidatarios* were cultivating land they did not own or were renting). However, despite the new legal and institutional framework, most of the land transactions remain informal or not properly recorded. Moreover, very few certified rights have been converted into actual titles. This may be because there is little incentive to possess a PROCEDE title, because it generates few opportunities to access credit, it provides limited perception of additional security, and bears the risk to be submitted to land taxation (*"predial"*). Moreover, the administrative requirements for registration and the possible risk of losing the PROCAMPO payment in case of change of the initial land status, may raise the cost to the farmer of formalizing land transactions. Also, if an extra effort to maintain the PROCEDE cadastre is not made, it risks becoming progressively obsolete. The fact that certification has had little impact on the capacity of farmers to access credit is due to the scarcity of financial service providers in rural areas, and to the fact that *ejido* certificates do not provide the right of seizure (*inembargabilidad*), as does private land. Therefore, the perception of the risks associated with the ability to enforce contracts, and of the functioning of the judicial system, have remained limiting factors.

The Efficiency of Public Goods

There has been much debate about the scope and rationale of the government's role in the agricultural sector, and over the last decade government intervention has diminished considerably. It is generally admitted that the massive all-subsidy schemes that characterized government's largesse in the past, not only were not fiscally sustainable, but induced in producers an attitude of dependency on paternalistic programs. Such an approach has also implicitly maintained the rural sector in a sort of welfare state, limiting opportunities for locally generated initiatives and for productive investments or adjustments. This has changed, but there is still a strong expectation in the field that the government is there to intervene (in input prices, marketing, technical assistance, etc.) and strong farmer organizations, mostly organized along political lines, put the government under constant pressure.

Most of the reforms and the subsequent policies and programs of the agricultural sector have been carried out nationally and homogeneously, with little consideration for the extreme regional diversity and income disparity characterizing the rural sector. This has led to situations where government withdrawal was justified for some segments of the more advanced agricultural producers, while creating important vacuums in poor rural areas. These vacuums were either not filled by private sector intervention, or provided opportunities for local monopolies and rent seeking. Similarly, the elimination of agricultural extension and technical assistance programs in the first half of the decade left a large segment of the small producers unattended. Commercial farmers, however, were more easily able to access required technology information through private providers, suppliers, or crop buyers.

Today, the Government intervenes in the sector through a combination of subsidy instruments that fall in three broad categories: i) "private" (mainly individuals or groups) subsidies, for investment support *(Alianza para el Campo)*, and marketing support for basic grains in some States; ii) income support mostly through cash transfers to individuals (PROCAMPO, PROGRESA, temporary employment); and iii) public programs in basic infrastructure, irrigation, and education. Generally, one would expect that the use of subsidies be directed to the areas of strongest externalities or market failures, and most typically for poverty alleviation purposes. Therefore, it is important to continuously assess the incidence of public programs on the objectives that the society wants to achieve, and the cost of administering them.

THE *ALIANZA PARA EL CAMPO* is a major government effort to try to catch up with years of progressive "decapitalization" of the sector, through a matching-grant approach to finance productive investments. While the use of matching grants could be considered a second-best approach in facilitating access to financing (although a considerable improvement compared to previous all-subsidy programs), it is necessary due to the low performance of rural financial markets in Mexico. Also the generation and provision of technology information is key to the capacity of the sector to adjust to the new environment posed by NAFTA and to the need to maintain some government support to the poorest farmers or where externalities and market failure are strongest. The *Alianza para el Campo* could be an important vehicle to promote and accompany the required adjustments of the sector. However, there is room for improvement in the delivery of the public goods and services. A number of areas are worth mentioning:

(i)   The distribution of individual support is still skewed in favor of medium-size farmers rather than the poorest producers.

(ii)   Technical assistance and extension should strive to enhance productivity rather than merely increase the use of inputs or renew equipment for existing activities. It should also broaden its coverage toward marketing issues and diversification into new crops. This may require a more professional and specialized approach, possibly through private service providers and outsourcing.

(iii) It is important to promote farmer organizations, cooperatives, and microenterprise development as a key step to gain local bargaining power, reduce transaction costs, and enhance the capacity of farmers to access production factors and economies of scale.

(iv) Research efforts have been privatized and decentralized to the state level through Foundations (e.g., PRODUCE), mostly composed of farmer organizations, which determine priorities and direct research programs in a demand-driven way. Although this approach has significantly increased the accountability of research, the public good element related to the need to maintain some strategic research programs of national interest and the need to address technology improvement for small and poor farmers, is to a large extent unaddressed.

(v)   At a time when markets have become so important in the decision-making process of producers, the weakness of an integrated market and price information systems is a major gap in the capacity of the sector to modernize. This is also an area where the public good element not only is openly recognized but could have a large payoff.

(vi)   The increasing integration of agriculture in international trade agreements and globalization has also put a spotlight on the issue of food safety, which deserves more attention in Mexico. This is of great importance to an export promotion strategy because in the future, plant and animal health requirements, quality standards, and sanitary policies, could potentially become the major source of non-tariff barriers and trade conflicts. Measures in this area should cover all food products, including those for the domestic market.

(vii)   The rapid degradation of natural resources, particularly water, soil, and forests (see the Chapters on Water and on Forestry and Land Management) calls for a more proactive role in revisiting the incentives for sustainable management of natural resources at the local level, and the regulatory and enforcement framework. There is also a need to develop agricultural methods for soil conservation and natural resources management in the context of a more integrated approach to watershed management.

Income support programs can have very beneficial effects among the poorest segments of the rural population and can serve both as safety nets and to facilitate access to basic services or investments. Moreover, by focusing on the areas of highest poverty, a less intensive targeting effort may be required for bringing large benefits to the poor at the least cost. By providing a constant stream of income to the beneficiary households, it decreases the likelihood of being below the poverty line but also reduces the risk aversion of the poor and induces them into investment options (PROCAMPO) or into education, health and nutritional programs (PROGRESA) (see the Chapter on Poverty).

Subsidies for marketing support in basic grains may be seen as the most controversial to the extent that they are mostly skewed towards commercial producers in those States that are at a disadvantage (higher production and marketing costs for those commodities) compared to other domestic or external growers. While it is important to examine options for facing the unfavorable pricing situation of these commodities and protect producers' income, it can be argued that substantial public spending is directed towards a relatively small number of beneficiaries to maintain some crops where they are the least competitive, to the detriment of more efficient producers.

The provision of irrigation infrastructure has been an area of heavy government investment. Indeed, the irrigation sector is one of the driving forces behind an

agricultural growth and competitiveness strategy in Mexico. Most federal investments have been in medium- and large-scale irrigation and drainage works in central and northern Mexico by CNA. This was also accompanied by a major and successful program of transfer of the Irrigation Districts to water users associations,
resulting in greatly improved operation and maintenance.[16] One of the major challenges agriculture will face in Mexico in the coming years is the capacity of the sector to become more competitive and diversify away from basic grain production into
higher-value crops or industrially processed products. This shift will be driven
mainly by the irrigated sector in its capacity to increase the economic returns per
unit of "water consumptively used"[17] in the context of increasing scarcity and competition for the use of water. This means that more attention will need to be devoted
to the demand side or the effectiveness of the actual use of water, rather than to the
supply side. A program that focuses only on improving irrigation system efficiencies
may result in no significant increases in yields per unit of water, nor will it necessarily limit consumption to what the resource base can sustain. In this respect, the
present pricing policies and subsidies for water, energy and basic grains, do not send
the right signals that would promote a more efficient allocation of water and higher
productivity (see the Chapter on Water).

PROVIDING BASIC INFRASTRUCTURE SERVICES can have a direct impact on the well-
being of rural families and on the development of rural areas. There is evidence that
the availability of clean water, sewage, electrification, rural roads, telecommunica-
tion, schools, and health centers have a mutual cumulative effect on local growth
and non-agricultural activities. The remarkable diversification of the Mexican rural
sector outside of agriculture, and the importance of off-farm employment, blurs the
difference between the rural and urban sectors. This should lead to a much more
integrated approach to rural development than has been the case in the past, when
public policies have given privileged support to agricultural activities as a way of limiting migration. In this respect, public works in small and medium municipalities
and on rural roads can go a long way in contributing to rural development, creating
an environment conducive to local employment, and reorienting population movements to the benefit of the local economy. Migration movements can represent a
negative externality for the rest of the society by displacing poverty from rural to
urban areas.[18] In addition, from an economic point of view it may be cheaper for
society to invest in rural areas as a way to contain the inflow of uneducated people

---

16. About 94 percent of the total irrigated area under the 81 Irrigation Districts has been
    transferred.
17. "Water consumptively used" (or evapotranspirated, ET) is the water that actually leaves
    the hydrologic system and should be used as reference against which to assess "real" water
    savings, as compared to other types of losses that may return to surface or groundwater
    systems, and are still available.
18. *Como Transformar en Buen Negocio la Inversion en el Campesinado Pobre: Nuevas Perspec-
    tivas de Desarrollo en America Latina*, (A. de Janvry and E. Sadoulet, 2000).

to big cities, than to manage the underlying social problems of expanding cities and the cost of the provision of basic services.[19]

EDUCATION should be seen as a priority for the rural population, and especially education for girls. Better education improves employment opportunities, prepare future migrants to access better jobs, and facilitate their integration to the rest of the economy. In most developing countries, education for women shows among the highest returns especially in terms of reducing infant and maternal mortality and better capacity to sustain and plan the development of the family. Both the demand-side (the opportunity cost of child-labor) and the supply side (the quality of the teachers) should be looked at. Evidence from a number of developed countries shows that a critical factor in reducing income disparities between the urban and rural sector has been a flexible and dynamic labor market, associated with infrastructure and access to education (see the Chapter on Education).

The "Institutionality" of Rural Development

The institutional efficiency of rural development should be seen in the context of two parallel and mutually reenforcing processes that accelerated in Mexico during the last Administration: democratization and decentralization. These processes, by devolving decisionmaking and increasing participation and accountability at the local level, they are altering the respective roles and interrelationships among the different levels of government. Two such moves affecting the rural sector have been the decentralization *(federalización)* of the *Alianza para el Campo* to the state level in 1996, and the decentralization of the Social Infrastructure Fund Program to the municipal level in 1998, through the creation of a new formula-driven budget line item based on poverty indicators (FISM, *Ramo 33*). In addition, the recent reform of Article 115 of the Constitution is likely to increase opportunities and incentives for municipalities to participate in local development through intermunicipal associations to improve the provision of local public services.

The main debate on the institutionality of rural development has centered around the issue of articulating the social demand for services and the institutional supply. On the demand side, it is generally admitted that local development is sustainable only if it is generated through an effective and informed demand by the communities and local administrations, with strong participation of the beneficiaries. Group or community development approaches appear to be effective in permitting better understanding of local priorities and needs, and facilitating more effective participation and ownership in the implementation of rural development programs. However, at present, most of these intervention programs, which usually tend to promote microinvestments, bear the risk of forming a disparate collection of interventions, and may not reach the critical development mass required to attract

---

19. *Pobreza Rural en America Latina y el Caribe* (A. Valdés and T. Wiens, World Bank, 1998).

the private sector, generate buyer competition, facilitate access to markets, and foster the establishment of private support services.

On the supply side, in poor rural areas, where the intervention of the public sector is still predominant, its capacity to organize a response is critical. Such response is subject to vertical coordination, at the different levels of the administration, and horizontal coordination, among sectors. Both types of coordination have proved difficult. Vertical coordination is embodied in a large set of formal agreements and norms between the federation and the states, in the context of various programs. However, there is an increasing challenge deriving from the strong pressure of the states to be more autonomous in the execution of these programs, and the increasing difficulty of the federation to ensure compliance with the numerous established norms. Considerable progress was made in horizontal coordination with the recent initiative of eight ministries to better integrate their efforts in the context of the development of priority regions.[20] However, much remains to be done to ensure consistent approaches among the multiplicities of federal programs operating in rural areas, each one with strict norms and budgets, and in promoting easier access by the beneficiaries. At the same time, municipalities have become very important actors in the ongoing decentralization effort, and increasingly central to rural development strategies. While local capacity still needs to be considerably strengthened, municipalities have been reasonably successful in promoting social and rural infrastructure.

To increase the relevance of community-based development, it is important to look at it in the context of a broader and more integrated territorial approach. Regional development has been embraced by Mexico as an intermunicipal spatial approach that provides socioeconomic, ethnic, and environmental homogeneity at the substate level. This is conducive to better address the sector's strong heterogeneity, significant disparities in income, and its multifunctionality in the context of an ever-increasing diversification out of agriculture. Regional development offers a real opportunity to more effectively link urban and rural policies in a context where agriculture, services, and infrastructure strive to create the conditions for a more integrated approach to local development. It also permits marketing issues to be more effectively addressed, and to more effectively integrate labor markets and pursue economies of scale and private sector development. The establishment of Regional Councils, which include representatives of producers, civil society, public institutions, and municipalities, offers an interesting model to articulate supply and demand for services and better mobilize and coordinate public and private resources for local development needs.[21]

---

20. As part of the *Base de Collaboración Inter-institucional*, the Ministries of SAGAR, SRA, SEDESOL, SEMARNAP, and SCT, subsequently joined by SSA, SEP, and SECOFI, signed an agreement establishing a commitment for an integrated approach to regional development and promoting mechanisms for a more unified approach.
21. See Institutional Coordination for Regional Sustainable Development (Raffaello Cervigni, World Bank, 1999); and the Rural Development in Marginal Areas program (Department of Regional Programs, SAGAR).

There is increasing evidence that institutions can be made more effective if they can operate in the context of a dynamic civil society and developed social capital. This is usually referred to as the density of interactions within and between social groups and associations, which can generate mutual trust, promote self-sustained development, and facilitate the task of public authorities. In this context, while the importance of the large (often politicized) corporate producer organizations (*gremios*) is likely to diminish, the development of public–private partnerships including recognized non-governmental institutions, farmer economic organizations, and local financial intermediation structures, can be seen as an important avenue to enhance accountability of local decentralized authorities and stimulate innovation and joint action. More generally, the availability of human capital, based on access to quality education and information, especially for women, and drawing on the cultural roots and social capital of families and communities, is central to rural development strategy.

III. Options for the Future

The agricultural sector is expected to remain a significant economic force, as both an important source of employment for large segments of the population and of social stability. It counts on a competitive commercial sector that uses modern technology and competes in international markets, and on a largely untapped productive potential, especially in rainfed areas. It will need to foster employment and microenterprise development in rural areas, while simultaneously becoming more fully integrated into the rest of the economy. It will also need to address poverty issues in a more effective way, especially where the benefits of growth do not trickle down and non-farm employment does not represent a viable option.

Mexico should consider a battery of complementary policies and programs as it attempts to meet the challenges facing the agricultural sector, rural development, and poverty. It will be important to address the great heterogeneity of the sector and the different characteristics of its actors. This suggests that a number of policy options towards growth, competitiveness, and poverty alleviation are possible and should be explored.

GOOD MACRO AND SECTORAL POLICIES WILL REMAIN CRITICAL. Despite the mixed performance of the sector over the last decade, the macroeconomic and sectoral reforms that were carried out were right and necessary. However, they were not sufficient to permit a significant improvement in the standard of living of rural dwellers. It is important to recognize that a sound macroeconomic framework— pursuing stability and appropriate exchange rate policies—is critical to the performance of the sector. The government should maintain the course of the policy reforms implemented during the last several years, and complete the reform agenda, in particular in the basic grain sector, where policy signals have to be clear and consistent. Subsidy programs could be revisited with a view to modernize them to allow for efficient and competitive participation of the private sector and thus functioning markets. Income support subsidies are by far the least distorting and most effective, and should be preferred to price, input, or marketing support, an area where the government should refrain from intervening. Mexico should also pursue better access to the markets of other countries and argue for the elimination of export subsidies in developed countries through bilateral and multilateral trade negotiations.

THE ROLE OF THE PUBLIC SECTOR WILL BE KEY IN FOSTERING MORE EFFICIENT MARKETS. Public policies and programs can play a critical role in a number of areas, to promote private sector development and better functioning markets by:

- Establishing better-integrated price and market information systems that build on the mechanisms established by SNIM, CEA, and PROFECO, and by making this information more accessible to all strata of the society (producers, operators, consumers, investors, and policy makers).
- Developing appropriate regulatory frameworks and enforcement capacity aimed at increasing the perception by the private sector that the judicial system works. This element will be critical in all the aspects related to secure transactions for such areas as inventory-based financing for agricultural crops, regional exchanges, weather and price insurance, non-bank financial institutions, contract farming, and collateralization of assets.
- Facilitating the development of commodity quality standards based on industry participation and needs, and the development of food safety norms.
- Establishing clear rules with regard to the amount and timing of duty-free imports of maize and beans, including an open auction to allocate quotas efficiently.

THE NEED TO COMPETE WILL BECOME INCREASINGLY PRESSING. The era of supply-led agriculture is over, and the challenges imposed by NAFTA will become increasingly compelling as elimination of all agricultural tariffs in 2008 looms ever closer. Mexican agriculture is going to be increasingly under the stress of the required adjustment. It will be important to accompany this process through more (not less) public expenditure, but of the kind that does not distort market signals but instead facilitates the adjustment. Government intervention in marketing support does not induce farmers into competitive attitudes because profitability does not need to be farmers' direct concern, and as a consequence it limits the adjustment process. Also, while the argument can be validly made that the level of advancement in other countries is not "symmetrical," it may also be the case that Mexico is trying to compete with the wrong products or with basic commodities when the demand is for transformed food and goods. There is a need to consider more proactively the requirements associated with the need to diversify into higher-value crops, agroindustrial goods, or simply to shift from surplus crops (white maize) to deficit crops (yellow maize).

Global competition and new technologies are promoting new partnerships between different segments of agrobusiness. The industry is integrating fast in the search for economies of scales (this is particularly evident at the two ends of the chain: seeds and supermarkets), while the consumer is becoming more and more informed and demanding. But this is also good news for the farmers because it creates competition in the supply chain and offers more possibilities to circumvent or eliminate intermediaries. Contract farming has been expanding lately in Mexico and is an important development in modernizing agriculture. It provides the crucial linkage between input suppliers, credit providers, purchasers of the crop, insurance, and farmers. It helps farmers reduce risk and facilitates access to capital and technology to young farmers who want to enter the business.[22] However, further expanding contract farming will depend on the confidence in the enforcement of contracts and the existence of well-organized producer associations.

SUSTAINABLE AND BROAD-BASED GROWTH WILL BE A KEY ELEMENT OF A RURAL POVERTY ALLEVIATION STRATEGY. There is considerable evidence demonstrating the positive influence of agricultural growth on poverty alleviation. However, pro-poor growth needs to be broad-based and capable of generating employment in both the farm and the off-farm sectors of rural areas. Such sector growth and employment will need to be generated through factor productivity increases and through better access to markets and technology. Agricultural growth in Mexico has not been sufficiently sustained to contribute to any significant poverty reduction, and has essentially been generated by the export-driven commercial sector. Pro-poor growth will require the implementation of important and effective public programs, to address the externalities facing rural areas, and may need to be more specifically targeted to the poor areas with productive potential. Two main thrusts could drive public programs: (a) reducing the productivity gap by investing in technology generation and development which is more tailored to the needs of poor smallholder; and (b) reducing the transaction costs of doing business in rural areas. This involves a large set of issues including rural roads programs; technical assistance to promote farmer organizations and marketing cooperative structures; better access to capital and land markets; and as a temporary measure, providing matching grants for investments.

PURSUE AN URBAN–RURAL DEVELOPMENT STRATEGY BASED ON REGIONAL DEVELOPMENT. There is an increasingly convincing argument pointing to the need to focus

---

22. There are various types of contract farming. The most basic one is where a buyer, trader, or processor, signs a contract with a farmer committing to purchase a certain amount of crop at or after harvest, but without necessarily committing to a pre-established price. Farmers can, in theory, use this contract to obtain loans from banks or other credit providers. More sophisticated transactions combine credit, inputs, insurance, and technical assistance with a contract to purchase the crop.

development efforts in the context of a territorial approach.[23] The need for a geographic or regional perspective derives from the strengthening of decentralization, democratization, municipal autonomy, and local participation processes, and the demand they generate for more differentiated policies. The definition of this spatial dimension is subject to local circumstances which generally have their roots in the historic, cultural, economic, and agro-ecological characteristics of the region. This approach inevitably associates urban centers and rural areas in the context of a continuum of mutually reinforcing and fully integrated activities. This perspective permits looking at broad-based rural development strategies from a new angle based not only on agriculture but also on off-farm activities, not only on production but also on marketing, not only on productivity but also on income and total welfare, and not only on dispersed groups but also on the existence of ethnically cohesive populations.

Regional development would enhance the ability to view the local economy as an integration of (imperfect) markets and develop or strengthen those activities that can create synergies among urban, rural, and agricultural demands for goods and services. In particular, by rendering rural areas more attractive through the development of local infrastructure and social services, it could go a long way in accompanying the ongoing integration of labor markets (migration) and the diversification of the rural sector outside agriculture. Natural resources and environmental issues, including competition for water, energy sources, and waste management, also require that the growth of towns and cities be addressed from a joint rural and urban perspective. Regional development also implies a way of thinking different from traditional institutional patterns and mandates toward local structures that can effectively develop decentralized ownership and articulate the expression of local priorities and needs. In this respect it would be important to consider the recent experience of the Regional Councils established as part of the Marginal Areas Rural Development program, which include public institutions, producers representatives, and municipalities, with a view to strengthening them.

TACKLING EXTREME POVERTY. It is critical to recognize and understand the pervasive nature of poverty in a number of situations and circumstances. Many Mexicans will not be able to reap the benefits of the progress on the "macro" front, growth or diversification opportunities in the non-farm sector. This includes many of the indigenous people, the elderly, the widows, small-holders in marginal areas without a productive potential, landless workers with US$2 a day, rural dwellers with little opportunities to access factor markets or migrate. Differentiated policies will be needed. Among these we could highlight the impact that safety net programs could have such as public pensions or social security. Also, income support programs could have high pay-offs and reach a large share of the poor. However, their administrative

---

23. See *La Cuestión Urbana en el Desarrollo Rural, Elementos Para una Reformulación de las Políticas*, (A. Shejtman, FAO, 1998); and *El Desarrollo Rural Sostenible en el Marco de una Nueva Lectura de la Ruralidad* (IICA, 1999).

cost should be reduced (PROCAMPO) and their targeting mechanisms should not be to the detriment of traditional solidarity mechanisms within poor communities (PROGRESA). In general, it will be critical to adjust public programs to cultural preferences and community structures especially in indigenous areas. Also, basic infrastructure and education will remain two key elements that can help break the vicious circle that traps the rural poor.

Some Recommendations for the Main Existing Public Programs

PROCAMPO. This is a well-conceived program with a clear poverty alleviation impact and a multiplier effect implying a positive outcome on investment behavior. However, its administration could be improved, together with its multiplier effect. The most important step that could be taken is to disconnect payment with the requirement to plant, and to make it purely an entitlement program. The beneficial effect of this measure would be: (a) it would lower the administrative cost of an otherwise relatively cumbersome and ineffectual annual requalification process; (b) it would provide certainty to the producers' income stream and permit better prospects for the collateralization of the payment right; (c) it would provide more flexibility in making payment at a time when it is most needed by producers; and (d) it would offer more opportunities to shift from one activity to another. The possibility of letting farmers cash the total income payment, or a part of it, over the remaining period of the entitlement (10 years) at a discounted rate *(bursatilización)* through the banking sector would greatly enhance the capacity of producers to invest but its feasibility would need to be carefully studied.

ALIANZA PARA EL CAMPO. This program could make a significant contribution toward addressing the challenges posed by NAFTA, and the compelling equity issues of the sector. However, it would need to be driven by:

- Greater emphasis on supporting and targeting subsidies to low-income farmers, who have greater difficulties accessing private services and markets.
- A stronger focus on the economic analysis and profitability of the actions being supported, because the subsidy element masks the intrinsic value of the activities and could induce, by inertia, risky support for existing crops or behaviors.
- A more active process of technology generation and diffusion, and its "professionalization" through private service providers, so as to accompany subsidies for equipment and promote competitiveness, diversification to higher-value crops, and modernization of the sector.

On the administrative side, the following recommendations could be examined:

- Shift toward an approach based on vouchers, where beneficiaries can redeem the value of the subsidy in the market, thus facilitating consumer choice and supporting the development of private wholesale channels and retail markets

for agricultural inputs and technology. At the very least, community-based programs should allow for direct procurement responsibility by the community.
- Streamline intervention through fewer, more encompassing subprograms, in particular through a more integrated regional approach. This will limit the risks of overlapping (and internal competition) of the many subprograms, each needing separate budget negotiations and norms, and rendering implementation too bureaucracy-dependent.

IRRIGATION. The thrust of the next generation of irrigation programs should be in terms of supporting an integrated approach to sustainable management and use of water resources that improves the efficiency of water use through increasing yields per unit of water used and through conversion to higher value crop. To support these objectives the government should promote: (a) increased attention to agricultural competitiveness and more efficient cropping patterns; (b) institutional efficiency through better coordination between the government institutions responsible for water resources management, irrigation, and agriculture; (c) increased decentralization of water management to local users (water users associations and river basin councils), to better monitor the use of water and regulate and organize its use; (d) the further development of water markets; and (e) modernization of off-farm and on-farm irrigation systems, based on matching grants with water user associations.

SOCIAL AND RURAL INFRASTRUCTURE. The decentralization to municipalities of the social infrastructure fund (FISM) in 1998, through the creation of a federal budget line item called *Ramo 33*, signals a major step in the government decentralization strategy. The resources transferred are very significant (about US$1 billion in 1999) and are distributed according to poverty-driven formulas, with minimum earmarking (basically only establishing a list of eligible categories of works such as water supply, sewage, paving, housing, health centers, schools, and electrification) and no strings attached. While the process has considerably increased the accountability of local governments and their capacity to define local priorities, de facto the federation has no control of or even information on the implementation and effectiveness of the FISM. Municipalities tend to use these resources strictly within their administrative boundaries to the risk of atomization and foregone opportunities to develop economies of scale and intermunicipal projects. In addition, the decentralization of the Fund found small municipalities (the bulk of the beneficiaries) unprepared and lacking technical, planning, and managerial capacity. A meager 2 percent of the Fund can be used for municipal institutional strengthening, with the small municipalities, which are most in need of assistance, receiving insignificant amounts.

Two main types of recommendations can be offered to improve the effectiveness and impact of the Municipal Social Infrastructure Fund through:

- The use of positive incentives to local governments (especially for small municipalities), in the form of "premia" or matching grants for (a) proven good managerial practices, attainment of simple poverty indicators, capacity building, and timely production and disclosure of information; (b) intermunicipal projects in areas with obvious scope for economies of scale, such as the environment, energy, disposal systems, rural roads, school transport, and water treatment; and (c) investments in projects that include cofinancing with the private sector or other federal or state agencies.

- The expansion and improvement of the municipal institutional strengthening program through the establishment of a separate fund, but not as a percentage of what each individual municipality receives under the social infrastructure fund. In addition, state governments should more actively participate in the creation and implementation of capacity building and technical assistance programs for municipalities. This is clearly an area that requires better overall coordination and implementation and knowledge of and access to service providers, and is conducive to considerable economy of scale and quality enhancement.

FINANCIAL SERVICES. Examples of successful reforms of public rural finance institutions exist around the world.[24] The capacity of the government to introduce substantial reforms in the operations of the agricultural development banks will necessarily be driven by political commitment and fiscal pressure. In the meantime, there is still considerable scope for improvement in the sector by:

- Developing a legal and regulatory framework conducive to better enforcement of contracts, more security, and enhancing the use of non-traditional collateral.
- Reforming the legal and regulatory framework for non-bank financial institutions (primarily financial cooperatives, *cajas populares*, and savings and loans institutions), and establishing an effective supervision system that ensures compliance with the new framework.
- Promoting savings mobilization as a basis for access to credit, and as a stable source of funds for rural financial intermediaries.
- Promoting a "level playing field" among the different actors of the real sectors, and minimizing direct government intervention through the revision of the role of the development banks that intervene in the sector.
- Using a wide range of rural financial intermediaries (including commercial banks, specialized financial institutions, NGOs, cooperative savings and loans structures) supported by second-tier institutions that fund sound retail financial intermediaries.
- Financing technical assistance programs, through specialized private service providers, for social groups and for non-bank financial intermediaries, including support for the development of new technologies for delivering financial services.

---

24. ESSD Monograph N.14. Rural Finance: Issues, Design and Best Practices, (J. Yaron, M. Benjamin, and G. Piprek, World Bank, 1997).

16

Federal Transport

This Chapter was written by Mirtha Pokorny,
with the valuable input of Emmanuel A. James.

I. Overview

During the last two decades, Mexico has experienced a profound transformation in terms of redefining the role of the state in the economy, reformulating responsibilities of the federal and local governments, and moving toward a more pluralistic society. These changes, driven in part by the opening up of the economy following the NAFTA agreements, are still evolving. The challenge continues to be to enhance fiscal efficiency while attending to the poorer segments of the economy, all in a framework of difficult choices and increased political competition.

The transport sector mirrors to a great extent the evolution that is taking place at the macro level. After the NAFTA agreement was in place, the government explicitly acknowledged that the country's economic growth critically depended on the development of its external trade and, for growth in this area to be sustained, that transport infrastructure and services would be prioritized. In parallel, the need for fiscal stability called for a retrenching of the public sector, while increasing the efficiency and accountability of those responsibilities the state could not transfer to the private sector.

The changes in the transport sector, for both inter-city and urban transport, are therefore being driven by the rapid advances of the federal government in terms of two key initiatives: greater private sector participation and increasing decentralization of responsibility for the sector to local governments. Given the impressive achievements of these initiatives in the ports and railways subsectors, the focus of the government in the transport sector will now need to be on inter-city and state-level road transport programs, on resolving urban transport bottlenecks, and on establishing an institutional, legal and regulatory framework to enable an optimal public/private mix and the development of intermodal transport.

II. Background

The transport policy, outlined in the *Plan Nacional de Modernización del Sector Transporte* at the beginning of President Ernesto Zedillo's Administration (1995), emphasized three main objectives:

(i)   Increased private sector participation in the provision, operation, and maintenance of transport facilities.
(ii) Deregulation of the sector, retaining only public provision of services not financially attractive to private investors but economically justified.
(iii) Changing SCT's role from operational to normative and promotional functions.

As Mexico enters the new century, much has been accomplished in the areas of privatization and deregulation of transport activities (although the agenda is far from completed), and important inroads are being made in the process of decentralization. Among the main accomplishments are:

- By 1999, the process of privatizing the Mexican railways, which started in 1995, had been mostly completed, and the efforts were successful in achieving its main objectives of promoting competition and ensuring financial sustainability.
- The reform of the country's port system was also highly successful in achieving its objectives of (a) decentralization, granting each port the autonomy to be managed according to its cost and demand conditions; (b) privatization, through the introduction of private operators, and eventually even the selling of the port administration; and (c) liberalization of tariffs and promotion of a competitive environment.
- There has been a substantial deconcentration of road maintenance responsibilities to SCT's regional offices and an increased use of contracted maintenance
- SCT, SCHP, and BANOBRAS have taken decisive steps to restructure the debt of the concessioned roads, an issue that due to its possible fiscal impact dominates the transport sector agenda.

III. Issues

The main issues facing the transport sector are (a) restructuring the road subsector to address its major problem of a growing demand putting strains on an underfinanced, undermaintained, debt-ridden, and deteriorating network; (b) tackling the second-generation reforms to put in place a reliable and transparent interface between the public and private sectors, putting in place a regulatory system that minimizes the uncertainties created by a lack of transparency on what are the rules and how they are going to be applied; and (c) improving accessibility for the urban poor while addressing the problem of urban congestion and pollution. The main stylized facts about these issues follow.

The road network comprises about 42,000 km of federal roads, 62,280 km of state roads, and 160,000 km of rural roads. The system is less dense than in most advanced countries, with 127 km of roads per square km. (The U.S. has 666 km of roads per square km, and Brazil has 228 km per square km.) About 6,500 km of the federal roads are tolled. This tolled system carries more than 80 percent of road traffic.

The tolled network is comprised of (a) the CAPUFE roads, which are mature, high-trafficked roads, well maintained or overmaintained, generating a net revenue of about MXP$3.9 million annually (1998); and (b) the deficit-generating newer FARAC network, consisting of 3,400 km of roads, with a high level of deterioration due to deferred maintenance and a debt overhang partially being covered by the CAPUFE surplus.

The institutional structure for administration of tolled facilities is diffused between FARAC, CAPUFE, SCT, and multiple private and public concessions. An incomplete road network with wide variations in maintenance and pricing standards has evolved.

The toll-setting policy is fragmented, many times based on rigid price escalation formulas that run counter to revenue-maximization objectives and have little or no consideration for the optimal economic use of the existing infrastructure. There are substantial untapped potential savings to be derived from more efficient and technologically advanced toll road management, including outsourcing to the private sector of toll collection and road maintenance. There is a potential for increasing the profitability of the toll road network through investments to increase the connectivity of the system. Additionally, given the limited public investment in the sector, there is a need to restore public and private confidence in financing schemes involving the private sector, which was undermined by the experience of the 1990s.

The Non-Tolled Federal System

The system is over-dimensioned, comprising about 42,000 km of roads, of which about half do not fulfill the functions of a core federal system (that is, connecting main cities or main trade corridors). Previous attempts to decentralize the responsibilities for the non-core network failed because of unreliable funding.

The system is substantially underfunded, both in terms of modernizing and of maintaining the existing infrastructure. About 40 percent of the system is in poor condition, jeopardizing about a third of the network, with a replacement value of about US$8 billion. About 21 percent of the network carries traffic levels above 5,000 vehicles per day on two-lane roads, and 29 percent of the network has capacity problems.

Urban Transport

The current rate of infrastructure improvement and supply increases cannot keep pace with the growth in automobile ownership (now about 12 million vehicles) and in travel demand. Hence, congestion in cities is rather frequent in terms of size of areas affected, though usually of short duration. The inefficient administration of the already inadequate road space, in particular arising from poor vehicle parking practices and incomplete road signage, contributes significantly to the congestion problem.

For freight movements, commercial transport is affected adversely by traffic congestion in central business districts, poorly maintained road surfaces, and inadequate terminal facilities.

The proliferation of informal transport services is affecting the financial viability of the formal and more economically efficient services, and contributing to already problematic levels of congestion, to noise, and to other forms of pollution in cities.

The poor populations suffer the most because they live in peripheral areas and the available public transport services are too often badly organized and inadequate, both in levels of service and in areas served. A large part of the urban poor have to make several transfers and take hours to reach their destinations. Too often these trips cost more than 20 percent of their incomes and are made in unsafe buses.

Contamination of the atmosphere is becoming significant in many municipalities, and the transport sector is a major contributor to this problem. Replacement of the highly polluting diesel bus fleets in many cities would help alleviate this problem. Due to the age of the typical fleet (15 years on average), replacement will become largely unavoidable for many cities during this decade.

Institutional Setting

The current federal network is about twice the size that could be justified on the basis of functionality of a core system. About 20,000 km of roads should be delegated or decentralized to the states. The present revenue-sharing arrangements leave the states in a weak financial position, unable to properly maintain their current state road system, much less take care of an enlarged system due to decentralization.

SCT still needs to adapt to a sector that has experienced a deep transformation, with the privatization of the railways, the decentralization and privatization of ports, and the road concessioning. SCT has yet to change its culture into an institution that oversees policy and regulations, sets norms and standards, oversees integration and harmonization of legislation with trading partners, and makes full use of new technology to encourage trade facilitation and multimodal transport.

Lack of coordination among the several government agencies having jurisdiction within a metropolitan area is also hampering the possibility of taking much-needed action through coherent policies that could promote integral municipal transport services.

IV. Policy Options

Rationalizing The Toll Road System

As the government moves beyond the immediate concerns of managing FARAC's debt, the opportunity arises to undertake a more strategic, long-term view of toll roads and their role in the national transportation framework. Incentives are needed to pursue a potentially difficult reorganization agenda regarding the potential to generate substantial new revenues, improve the use of existing and planned facilities, correct the deterioration of FARAC's infrastructure, and facilitate private investments in new roads. Policy goals that should guide the institutional reassessment include:

MAXIMIZE THE TRANSPORTATION VALUE OF EXISTING INFRASTRUCTURE. Consideration of cross-subsidy mechanisms which permit political, social, and economic policy objectives to be met through transparent pricing actions are recommended as a central component of institutional reform. To the extent that previous tariff policies may have discouraged the very usage that prompted the original decision to build new tolled facilities, a reassessment of the goals and objectives of Mexico's infrastructure finance and transportation planning policies is appropriate. In particular, inflation indexing of toll rates without consideration of other factors is too narrow and inflexible a policy yardstick. A "fuzzy" rate covenant could assist Mexico in resolving toll policy dilemmas.

IMPROVE OPERATING AND MAINTENANCE EFFICIENCY TO PERMIT LOWER TARIFFS OR INCREASE RESOURCES FOR INVESTMENT. There is substantial room to increase the operating, maintenance, and operating efficiency of CAPUFE, thus reducing the burden to road users who are paying higher than necessary tariffs and siphoning potential revenues from needed investments.

ESTABLISH A CLEAR VISION FOR FUTURE INVESTMENTS AND DEVELOPMENT OF THE ROAD NETWORK. The incomplete road network, coupled with the disparity in maintenance and pricing standards brought about by the diffusion of responsibilities among many agencies, points to the need for initiatives to weave the existing pieces into a well-conceived and consistently maintained system. At the same time, requirements for free parallel roads may be undermining the finance and transportation policy objectives the toll network is intended to serve.

EMPOWER EXPERTS TO ESTABLISH TOLL RATES AND MANAGE CONCESSIONS. The knowledge and expertise to establish toll rates and manage concessions currently exists in Mexico, but is diffused among many agencies and private organizations. As part of the reassessment of toll road investment strategy, it is recommended that the government consider granting a strong measure of independence to a professionally staffed public entity to make sensitive tariff decisions and undertake efficiency benchmarking analysis. Tolls across the entire network of CAPUFE, FARAC, and other public securitized facilities should be rationalized on a more economic basis with a goal of increasing public revenues. In addition, implementation of an enhanced planning process focusing on traffic forecasting, engineering analysis, and consideration of environmental impacts should be accomplished before a new round of concessions is considered.

ENHANCE THE SECURITY OF THE FARAC DEBT RESTRUCTURING AND MAKE IT COST TRANSPARENT. Subordination of FARAC obligations on the balance sheets of BANOBRAS and NAFIN should be accomplished transparently. Moral hazard risks assumed by annuity companies purchasing PICs being issued by BANOBRAS to replace FARAC bank debt should be minimized by assuring adequate revenue coverage for eventual repayment of principal.

The government is exploring ways to rationalize the toll road system, including the integration of CAPUFE and FARAC into a "new" entity for managing, operating, and financing Mexico's public toll roads. Most of the required changes can be taken by administrative actions within the existing legal, financial, and administrative framework. Necessary statutory changes can be pursued once the limits of administrative discretion is reached. It is expected that the positive results which can be achieved by the time statutory changes are required will facilitate the process of securing the next level of consensus between the executive and legislative branches. The long-term ideal goal should be the corporatization of the toll road system, with an autonomous agency run on principles of accountability and transparency and subjected to the test of the market, able to leverage its assets through securitization without government guarantees.

Ensuring the Preservation and Modernization of the Non-Tolled Road Network

The systemic problem of unfunded rehabilitation and maintenance is also high on the government's agenda. Efforts are being made to isolate the current and periodic expenditures from the volatility of budget allocation. The government should consider the extension of the basic principles of corporatization of the road network by (a) establishing a road fund based on user fees; and (b) separating the planning and funding functions from maintenance and management. The government is studying the possibility of establishing of a road fund and is looking at different options, such as:

- Whether the road fund should cover only rehabilitation and maintenance of the system or whether it should also finance its expansion.
- Whether the road fund should cover all public roads or be restricted to the federal network, including those in the noncore system that are expected to be transferred to the states.

- Whether sources of funding should be restricted to a surcharge on motor fuels or whether other road user charges should be also considered.
- How the establishment of the fund can and should be used as an opportunity to corporatize highway activities and to improve the technical, managerial, and financial procedures of the state road agencies.

As the government looks into the process of commercialization (bringing roads into the marketplace, putting them on a fee-for-service basis, and managing them like any other business enterprise), it should be kept in mind that roads are a public monopoly, and ownership will remain in public hands for some time to come. Thus, any consideration of commercialization would require complementary reforms in four other important areas:

(i)   Creating ownership by involving road users in management of roads to win public support for more road funding, to control potential monopoly power, and to constrain road spending to what is affordable.
(ii)   Stabilizing road financing by securing a stable and adequate flow of funds.
(iii) Clarifying responsibilities by clearly establishing who is responsible for what (the fund, its possible Board of Directors, SCT, SHCP, etc.).
(iv)   Strengthening management of roads by providing effective systems and procedures, and strengthening managerial accountability.

In the case of Mexico, certain "building blocks" already have been the subject of substantial work and accomplishments, particularly the establishment of methodologies to identify and prioritize maintenance needs. Taking into consideration the change in culture required to establish a sound system of fund governance, the initial fund should concentrate only on the conservation of the federal system, with a second phase to include the conservation of state roads. The government should consider mechanisms for "rewarding" state road maintenance (that is, ex post reimbursement of funds spent on agreed maintenance projects) to obviate possible road fund limitations in the auditing and controlling of expenditures at the state level.

Establish Institutions that Reflect the New Characteristics of the Sector

SCT should carry out an in-depth institutional assessment to develop a blueprint of how and at what pace to change the institution to fulfill its role in a new sector environment. One particularly important item in a sector with a high participation of private provision of services, is to de-link, to the extent possible, the regulatory system from any political influence within SCT. An independent regulatory agency to deal with the railway, port, and airport subsectors should be established on the basis of clear principles of adequate levels of discretionary power to be given to the regulators and of independence and accountability, and of establishing a transition path from being an unit within SCT to a fully independent agency. A consensus should be developed in Mexico on how to structure the regulatory system appropriate for the Mexican cultural and political environment.

As the regulatory system has to gradually evolve to increase its predictability and thus reduce the level of risk and risk premiums charged by the private sector, SCT should seek to build up a cadre of highly professional staff that would allow its transformation into a normative institution that set standards, oversees the regulatory framework, and develops and maintains sector statistics. More important, it must ensure the appropriate interface between the different modes, and the private and the public sector. The development of these "seamless" interfaces is key to the establishment of efficient logistic chains based on intermodalism. Because of its particular geopolitical circumstances, Mexico should take a close look at the experience of the European Union in developing these interfaces. Study tours and roundtables with members of the EU, UNCTAD, and the World Customs Organization can help develop the right program for Mexico.

Improve the Efficiency and Efficacy of Urban Transport

Mexicans live predominantly in urban centers, and an increasing share of the country's GDP is generated in urbanized zones. Enhancing urban transport efficiency thus has a direct impact on the competitiveness, internationally or otherwise, of Mexican productive capacity. To ensure that transportation bottlenecks do not affect production and economic growth, the government should place emphasis on raising the level of efficiency of urban transport to acceptable levels. This will require addressing many issues, and among the key options will be to:

CLARIFY INSTITUTIONAL ROLES AND STRENGTHEN TRANSPORT PLANNING. One of the key areas of focus in successful transport programs is on the development of a comprehensive planning framework, including the professionalization of urban transport by training a critical mass of staff, and the creation or strengthening of planning institutes which were particularly helpful in maintaining momentum during transition periods in administrations.

IMPROVE THE PROVISION AND MANAGEMENT OF PUBLIC TRANSPORT SERVICES. Currently, the states are responsible for concessioning public transit routes, while the municipalities manage the road infrastructure. This has led to fractured services, weak transport companies, and irrational and unsupervised route operations that are not helped by the circuitous side streets which are not well integrated with the main city axes. As decentralization proceeds, management of transport services within its jurisdiction should become a municipal responsibility. In order to permit this, the government needs to accelerate the process of reform of the legal and administrative framework for transport services.

PROMOTE A COMPREHENSIVE BUS FLEET REPLACEMENT PROGRAM. Due to the aging of the fleet and the contamination of the urban environment, most city bus fleets will need to be replaced during this decade. It is essential that this be done at least cost since it is largely the low-income populations who use buses. The government will need to develop a creative program of incentives to encourage the appropriate choices, since the cities will be locked for the next 25 years into whatever technologies and fleet characteristics are chosen by operators.

USE CONCESSIONAL FUNDING TO ADDRESS MORE AGGRESSIVELY THE NEEDS OF POOR COMMUNITIES. Currently, road investments are either financed through nonreimbursable funds (with SCT for the improvement of the inter-city network) or through Banobras loans at Cetes+ rates for municipal projects. No dedicated instrument exists for the financing of road improvements for poor communities which are typically located on the city peripheries and other distant areas of municipalities. Recent World Bank analysis on poverty has identified transport improvements as one of the key triggers of upward mobility for the poor. Addressing the transport needs of poor communities is, however, a national problem that is too large for the municipalities to finance by themselves. Hence, a key improvement step would be to open a "poverty window" that would allow concessional financing for cases where the transport needs of poor communities are well defined.

17

Energy

This Chapter was written by Jonathan Halpern
with the valuable input of Robert Bacon and Charles P. McPherson.

I. Overview

Energy is an essential component of Mexico's well-being. It is crucial to generating growth and employment. Mexico's substantial reserves of oil and gas have the potential to continue to create considerable wealth for Mexican society. Without an adequate and efficient low-cost supply of energy, the economy will not grow at its full potential and improvements in the living standard of the Mexican people will be held back. Access to modern forms of energy is also an important element in reducing poverty. Improved lighting, heating, and motive power can substantially raise the productivity and quality of life of poor households.

Exploitation of Mexico's abundant oil and gas resources should make it possible not only to supply the energy requirements of the country, but also to make a large contribution to the federal budget and the financing of core social services, such as health and education. Given the availability of carbon-based fuels, potential renewable energy resources, and the existence of an extensive transmission and distribution network, it should be possible to provide electricity services at relatively low cost to all Mexicans.

The magnitude of the demands placed on the energy sector over the past decade have been enormous. These demands will grow dramatically as the Mexican economy continues to expand. Moreover, there will be increasing claims on federal funds to expand social services to meet the needs of a young and rapidly growing society. Conservatively estimated, capital requirements for the next 10 years in the energy sector are MXP$1,000 billion in constant 1999 pesos. This equates to approximately MXP$100 billion a year, representing 2.5 percent of current GDP, or the total health or education budgets.

It is neither feasible nor desirable to finance the necessary expansion of the energy sector out of the public purse or through government-backed borrowing. This is

357

especially true given the urgent competing demands for support to critical social and subnational development programs.

Successfully meeting the challenges facing the energy sector will require mobilization of investments on a massive scale. Doing so will require an expansion in the number of actors operating in the sector, and on the government's ability to put in place an appropriate legal, fiscal, and regulatory framework for investment and operations, while simultaneously safeguarding the public interest.

This Chapter discusses key challenges facing the energy sector and policy priorities and options for meeting those challenges. It explores the areas that sector policies need to address, the scope and potential benefits of entry of new participants in the sector, and the structural and regulatory principles for promoting innovation and efficiency to drive down prices, improve services, and attract finance. It also addresses the functions government must undertake, or do better, to achieve the desired investment and efficiency gains without sacrificing important fiscal revenue, and the social and environmental goals the government has established.

II. Current Situation

Mexico has built its present economy in part on two pillars of the energy sector: the state-owned companies PEMEX (*Petróleos Mexicanos*) and CFE *(Comisión Federal de Electricidad)*. Both have made large contributions to Mexico's development. PEMEX is one of the world's largest oil companies; until recently, it contributed about 30 percent of federal tax revenue and thus is a major source of funds for general socioeconomic spending. CFE is among the largest utilities in North America, and together with LFC *(Luz y Fuerza del Centro)* provides electricity to 95 percent of the population.

RECENT POLICIES. Government policy over the past sexenio has emphasized sound macroeconomic management, structural reforms, and modernization of public administration to foster sustained economic growth, reduction of poverty, and improvement in social welfare. In the *hydrocarbon* sector, the principal policies have been:

- Continuing priority to production and export of higher quality crudes.
- Increasing the degree of self-reliance in production of refined products while processing a greater proportion of high-sulfur crude.
- Permitting private participation in some downstream activities such as secondary petrochemicals and natural gas transport and distribution.
- Decelerating the growth in air pollution by upgrading the quality of automotive fuels, expanding availability of natural gas and renewable energy resources in the energy matrix.

For the *electricity* sector, principal policy goals have included:

- Ensuring expansion to maintain service quality and coverage.
- Subsidizing the consumption of large groups to maintain their purchasing power.
- Fostering private participation in construction and financing of new thermal generation capacity.
- Conversion of fuel-oil-fired power plants to comply with Mexican emission standards.
- Mitigating the environmental impact of the combustion of fossil fuels by encouraging adoption of end-use efficiency measures, cogeneration and renewable energy technologies.

More recently, the Mexican government entered into a formal agreement with Saudi Arabia and Venezuela to reduce production in an effort to reverse the decline in world oil prices. This was followed by OPEC-wide action to restrict output, which together with a resumption in global demand dramatically reduced the overhang in world stocks. As a consequence, world petroleum prices have more than doubled over their lows of late 1998. In addition, in early 1999, the Zedillo Administration put forward a proposal for comprehensive restructuring of the power sector, aimed at fostering competition and mobilizing private capital in a manner which does not burden federal finances.

III. Recent Performance

While the energy sector has been successful in providing energy to meet current needs, it has not performed to its full potential and has not been able to make adequate provision for the future. The operations of the state companies (PEMEX, CFE, and LFC) have been constrained by federal budget ceilings, dependence on implicit sovereign guarantees for borrowing and for entering into long-term service agreements (for example, BLTs and IPPs), and are subject to political intervention, particularly when it comes to pricing, tariffs, and execution of investment priorities. Electricity tariffs have generally been held below the cost of service, preventing the sector from recovering costs of operations and investment, leading to gradual but sustained decapitalization. In the hydrocarbon sector, activities to find, produce, and process oil are taxed at among the highest rates in the world, making many otherwise economic activities unprofitable. A growing proportion of oil tax revenues which the reserve base generates has been directed at addressing social and economic needs outside the sector. This has precluded reinvestment of sector revenues sufficient to sustain crude production and improve product quality. At the same time, being insulated from meaningful competition, these enterprises have been characteristically slow to adapt and innovate in response to changing market conditions, technologies, and management practices. Being state-owned, they have also been slow to comply with Mexico's environmental standards in the absence of effective sanctions.

Energy and the Economy

During the last decade the use of energy in Mexico grew at 2.5 percent per year. These are substantial figures but still leave the per capita use well below levels seen in OECD countries. Table 1 gives an indication of the further potential for growth in Mexico's per capita energy use.

In developing countries the consumption of energy grows faster than the economic growth rate, since consumers spend higher proportions of their income on energy-intensive goods as their living standards rise. The Mexican economy is forecast to grow at 4.5 percent per year over the next decade, and this indeed will lead to strong increases in demand for all kinds of energy.

Mexico has large reserves of both oil and gas, as shown in Table 2, but relatively low production compared to countries such as Canada, Norway, and the United Kingdom. There is clearly substantial room to increase production and oil tax revenues without jeopardizing the longer-term future.

Table 1. Index of Energy Consumption Per Capita in 1997

Country	Consumption per capita of Energy (mtoe)
Mexico	1.46
U.S.	8.04
Japan	4.05
OECD Europe	3.39
Non-OECD Europe	2.01

Source: IEA.

While the oil sector is no longer the principal source of export earnings, it continues to make a substantial contribution to the federal budget, accounting, as mentioned earlier, for 30 percent of total fiscal revenues over the past decade. However, because the sector operators are public enterprises, a large part of these revenues have been returned to the sector to finance operating expenses and a restricted investment program, to cover the very large electricity subsidies, and to make provision for financial obligations to private sector financiers under the leveraged lease schemes (for example, PIDIREGAS) and IPP purchase agreements. As a consequence, the

Table 2. Reserves and Production of Certain Oil Producers

| | Oil | | Gas | |
	Reserves billion barrels	Production million barrels/day	Reserves (TCF)	Production (BCF/d)
Canada	6.8	1.8	63	15.7
Norway	11.0	3.1	41	4.9
United Kingdom	5.2	2.6	27	9.6
Mexico	29.0	3.1	30.1	3.9
United States	29.0	7.9	164	52.2

Source: Statistical Review of World Energy; BP-Amoco, 2000.

sector's net contribution to the Treasury has been very modest at best. This has limited the extent to which oil rents could be devoted to financing high-priority social programs and other national goals. In 1998, the oil sector contribution on a net basis to funding public expenditures was MXP$20 billion, after deducting PEMEX investment of MXP$74 billion. Deducting power sector subsidies of MXP$31 billion left a net energy sector deficit of MXP$11 billion. Against this, 1997 total spending on health was MXP$117 billion, and on education MXP$118 billion. In fact, PEMEX investments in 1998 were sharply curtailed, and only partially recovered in 1999. Without the rise in oil prices, the net contribution of the energy sector would well have been more negative.

The tax regime through which oil rents are obtained and the manner in which they have been managed has had several negative consequences. Taxes are levied on sales revenue rather than profits, and are exorbitant by any standard (nominal 60 percent Derecho sobre Hidrocarburos, DSH). This leads to early shut-in of wells and discourages investment in field redevelopment and in new smaller fields, thereby effectively reducing the potential future tax base. In addition, the DSH is applied to the consolidated revenues of PEMEX (that is, upstream and downstream activities). Since there are no true rents to be obtained in downstream activities, this severely limits the number of downstream projects which could be undertaken profitably on an after-tax basis. Moreover, the majority of the tax burden is shifted on to critical E&P activities, leading to effective tax rates well above the nominal 60 percent.

As noted, fiscal revenues continue to be highly dependent on hydrocarbon taxes, and public finances therefore remain vulnerable to changes in world oil prices. In the absence of alternative sources of fiscal revenue (Mexico's ratio of non-oil taxes to GDP at below 10 percent is alarmingly low), the preponderance of the burden of fiscal adjustment to oil price swings and other external shocks has fallen on public expenditures. Current expenditures are difficult to reduce in the short term, so the primary source of fiscal adjustment to external shocks has come from drastic cuts in capital expenditures. Because PEMEX and CFE investments comprise a large share of the capital budget, and given the high priority afforded to social programs, the investment budgets of these enterprises have borne a disproportionate share of such unanticipated cuts. While the effects of such cuts are not felt immediately by consumers, energy development is highly capital intensive, requiring long gestation undertakings which, if deferred or suspended, inevitably leads to escalating costs.

The energy sector finds itself in a vicious circle—reduced budget and borrowing capacity have restricted sector investment. This in turn will limit expansion of production and hence government revenue, thus making it more difficult to fund future financial needs. The government is increasingly forced to choose between the call to spend now on urgent social programs and the need to invest in energy now to maximize value creation from oil production to meet the growing demand for energy and for resources to finance future public spending.

IV. Energy Demand Projections and Supply Requirements

Projections for oil, gas, and electricity demand growth are given in the following sections. These projections are compared to past and projected supply and to the implied investment requirements in order to indicate the magnitude of the challenge that the sector now faces and the tradeoffs to be made. The investment estimates, based on approximations of unit costs, are meant to provide a rough indication of orders of magnitude rather than precise cost projections.

Oil and Oil-Based Products

The historic supply/demand balance for oil is shown in Table 3. The table highlights the growth in oil production and the contribution it makes to exports. Domestic refinery capacity has not increased over the period, despite the increased demand for products. The product slate, however, has changed markedly to meet increasingly stringent product quality requirements. Delays in reconfiguring the domestic refineries to adapt to the phase-out of lead in gasolines in the mid-1990s led to much larger-than-expected imports of blending components and finished gasolines. Imports of oil products are still growing rapidly, particularly gasolines, fuel oil, and LPG. PEMEX is carrying out an extensive refinery revamping program which will, among other things, increase the production of high-octane gasoline and diesel. There have been a number of delays in approval and financing of this program. If PEMEX is able to complete this program by late-2000, Mexico will regain in large part self-sufficiency in gasoline supply, and may even have to contend with a surplus of diesel.

Table 3. Oil Supply/Demand Balance for 1990–98 (thousand barrels/day)

Year	Production of Crude	Supply of Crude to Domestic Refining	Exports of Crude	Net Imports of Refined Products*	Consumption of Products*
1990	2548	1271	1277	-1	1341
1991	2676	1287	1369	44	1403
1992	2668	1265	1368	55	1429
1993	2673	1295	1377	21	1442
1994	2685	1333	1307	79	1553
1995	2617	1267	1305	39	1432
1996	2858	1267	1544	86	1481
1997	3022	1242	1721	206	1569
1998	3067	1276	1719	228	1644
1999	3060	1280	1664	227	n/a

Note: *Products include LPG.
Source: Secretaría de Energía.

The table shows that the entire increase in crude production went into an increase in the exports of crude. At the same time, the increase in the domestic demand for products resulted in an increase in the net imports of products.

It is assumed that it is desirable and technically feasible to at least hold oil production at its likely 2001 peak level of around 3.1 million bdp for the rest of the decade. This level of production would be sufficient to stop exports from declining from their 2001 peak of 1.8 mbd, unless a significant amount of crude is diverted to supplying domestic refineries. Beyond the current refinery revamping program, there do not appear to be plans to expand domestic refining capacity in the foreseeable future. The decision whether to increase domestic refinery production, hence requiring more crude input, would depend on a number of factors, including the extent of liberalization permitted in trade of refined products and sources of crude purchase by domestic refiners.

The costs of undertaking an investment program to sustain this level of production depend on the development costs per barrel. A conservative estimate of the development costs would be US$3.50 a barrel, which implies total capital expenditure of MXP$160 billion (at a current exchange rate of MXP$10 pesos to the dollar). In addition, other needed investment would be on the order of MXP$105 billion in refining, and MXP$50 billion in petrochemicals, so that in total the oil sector would require some MXP$315 billion. That is, it would require, on average, an investment of MXP$31.5 billion a year for 10 years.

If no further investment in exploration and development were to take place after 2000, production would decline from its peak in 2001 to 1.5 million barrels/day by 2010. This would lead to a 40 percent decline in tax revenues and a 50 to 60 percent decline in export earnings if oil prices were to hold relatively constant.

Natural Gas

Mexico has ample gas reserves to supply domestic needs. At present, production is largely associated gas, although there are substantial reserves of nonassociated gas. Over the last decade the production of natural gas grew at an annual rate of 2.5 percent, but there has been a recent acceleration in the use of gas, driven in part by the introduction of gas-fired electricity generation and by the liberalization of gas transport and distribution. This has involved both the introduction of competition and the commitment of Mexican and international private sector capital. The rapid increase in demand, coupled with only modest investment spending on supply, has led to a surge in imports from the United States as local markets have begun to develop.

The demand for gas is expected to grow rapidly over the next 10 years, at about 7.5 percent per year until 2007, and then at 11 percent per year through 2010. The most economic decision would be to meet a high proportion of future demand from domestic production. Maintaining production of associated gas at 1999 levels of crude output would require investments of about MXP$32 billion. This level of output would fall far short of meeting demand, implying massive future dependence on imports. Closing this gap in the absence of significant increases in crude production will require extensive investments in upstream and downstream aspects of nonassociated gas development. The latter is significantly more costly than exploiting associated gas, and is estimated at MXP$220 billion. The total costs of meeting all demand through 2010 would amount to MXP$252 billion. Because the transport system at present has some excess capacity, and distribution has recently been taken over by the private sector, downstream infrastructure costs associated with meeting Mexico's rapidly growing demand for natural gas are excluded from these estimates.

Electricity

Mexico's recent success in economic growth and the high level of connections resulted in a 5.2 percent per year growth rate in electricity demand over the last decade. Another contributory factor to rapid growth in demand has been the extensive subsidies. The average tariff charged to residential customers in 1998 covered just 43 percent of costs, and the average tariff for agricultural use covered 31 percent of costs. Industry and services paid almost 95 percent of costs. These implicit subsidies amounted to MXP$31 billion in 1998, an amount equal to one-third of oil tax revenues in that year.

To meet this demand, Mexico has at present 35,000MW capacity, the preponderance of which is thermal (53 percent), and hydroelectric (28 percent). Future demand is forecast to grow at 5.8 percent per year until 2010. This would require additional capacity of about 27,000MW. The costs of meeting this demand, including additional transmission and distribution capacity, would amount to MXP$370 billion during 2001–10. Of this total, some MXP$210 billion would be needed for generation, MXP$90 billion for transmission, and MXP$70 billion for distribution. Only a small proportion of total estimated transmission investment could unlock a significant amount of existing generation capacity in the south which cannot be otherwise dispatched.

In addition, if the present subsidy and tariff levels remain unchanged, the total subsidies required over the period would amount to a staggering MXP$365 billion over the same period.

Access to electricity service has grown tremendously over the past two decades, with 95 percent Mexicans now connected to the grid. These levels of coverage are among the highest in Latin American and are above the average for OECD countries. Nonetheless, in absolute terms, about 5 million Mexicans still do not have reliable access to electricity. Eighty-five percent of these households are located in rural areas, most of which are far enough from the existing network to make high-cost grid connection unlikely for the foreseeable future. In the mid-1990s, the government made efforts to extend service to these communities with nonconventional renewable solutions under the PRONASOL programs. However, these activities were almost wholly subsidized and executed under public procurement procedures, and have not proven sustainable either financially or in terms of service quality. Consequently, little progress has been made in scaling up such activities. While the financial costs of extending electricity access to household, public service centers, and for productive purposes are quite modest in relation to the sector's overall financing requirements (approximately US$750 million to US$900 million), the development of sustainable decentralized service delivery mechanisms remains a major challenge.

V. Challenges Facing the Sector

Very substantial investments will be required for the energy sector to maximize its potential contribution to the economy and to efficiently meet the demand for energy supplies. As indicated above, funding on the order of MXP$900 billion over the next decade will be needed to meet the majority of projected growth in demand and to make a start in addressing the backlog of deferred investment. If electricity subsidy policies remain unchanged, the total will exceed MXP$1,200 billion. These sums represent a full 2 to 3 percent of GDP per year. Moreover, with GDP growth of 4.5 percent per year and holding the current account deficit at 3.5 percent of GDP, these investment requirements will constitute 10 to 15 percent of the consolidated federal expenditures, and 50 to 60 percent of the federal investment budget, on average, at a projected price for Mexican crude of $20/barrel. Financing them largely through the budget implies massive cuts in other programs already under way, and would sharply restrict the ability to introduce new initiatives to address national priorities.

While the sector's state enterprises have contracted debt to finance a fraction of their investment requirements, the scope for borrowing on the scale required is likewise restricted by governmentwide limits on public sector borrowing required to maintain sound public finances. The policy of maintaining electricity tariffs well below cost, and the high level and poor structure of hydrocarbon taxes, have undermined and will continue to undermine the creditworthiness of the state enterprises, further limiting the ability to take on further debt. The various schemes employed to date for attracting private financing (BLT and IPP) have proven costly and are ultimately unsustainable, because the financing burden with all its attendant risks ultimately rebound to the federation.

Faced with the specter of rapid, sustained growth in demand, it is crucial that energy be produced and supplied as efficiently as possible, something not realized under the prevailing organization of the sector. PEMEX, CFE, and LFC are neither permitted the autonomy to operate along commercial lines nor are subject to adequate arms-length regulatory oversight and competitive pressures to improve efficiency. As a consequence, accountability for performance is weak. As *organismos descentralizados*, they are subject to a myriad of rigid public administration and civil service rules (for example, hiring, salaries, procurement). Revenues are not retained within the enterprise, their budgets being set through the political process, as are prices of key services (for example, electricity tariffs) and episodic debt writeoffs in the case of CFE and LFC. At the same time, they lack transparent, consistent policies for required returns on capital and dividend payments, and they do not face the discipline of capital markets in valuing performance. They do not report financial performance according to GAAP and their financial statements are not made available for public scrutiny. In addition, they do not face the same regulatory controls and sanctions that apply to commercial entities (for example, environmental compliance, quality of service, and enforcement of contracts).

In summary, the status quo cannot be maintained. The sector, as currently organized, will not raise the finance on the required scale, nor can it maximize the productivity of the resources which are available to it.

VI. Policy Priorities and Options

For the energy sector to maximize its contribution to economic and social welfare, policies guiding its development over the next decade should aim to:

- Expand production, delivery systems, and consumption of the nation's energy resources to create efficient growth and employment.
- Minimize net demands of the sector on public finances.
- Reach international levels of efficiency.
- Mitigate environmental impacts associated with the expansion of the energy sector.

Achieving these goals will require the entry of new participants, introducing direct competition where feasible, and providing greater autonomy and accountability for the state enterprises which operate in the sector. Doing so will require significant changes in sector organization and oversight, and in subsidy and taxation policies.

Meeting Investment Needs through Increased Private Sector Participation

Permitting new entry will attract more resources to the sector. New participants to the industry would be willing to commit, at their own risk, substantial amounts of capital if they perceive a credible commitment on the part of the authorities that they will be given the opportunity to earn a fair and predictable return on their investments. This should not imply government implicitly guaranteeing investors' financial obligations as is currently the case in electricity generation and some refinery projects. Experience in a number of OECD and developing countries has demonstrated that new participants will invest large sums in the energy business to the benefit of consumers where changes in sector organization and regulation have permitted clear incentives to continually reduce costs. Moreover, liberalizing entry can enhance the state's capacity to pursue the public interest in the sector through appropriate legislation and regulation, more so than through exclusive public ownership. Recent experience in Mexico with the development of downstream natural gas infrastructure has demonstrated that new participants will indeed enter the Mexican market at their own risk and offer very competitive tariffs when provided with a framework of transparent regulation and juridical certainty.

Entry of the private sector will not, by itself, foster competition. Vertical deintegration of the industry is essential to permit competition in those segments where it is feasible. The government will need to decide which parts of the different energy industries still present a compelling case for maintaining public ownership. Many countries have long permitted extensive changes in ownership throughout the sector and have already reaped substantial benefits, not only in their ability to attract investment for new projects, but also in improved performance of the existing assets. Some of these benefits have been passed on to consumers in terms of lower costs, better performance, and increased access. To the extent that state-owned oil and gas and electricity companies continue to operate in the sector, they should be granted the autonomy to operate in a commercial fashion. They should be taken off budget and permitted to retain revenues in accordance with clear financial principles. The government should establish an initial financial structure for these newly created companies, but thereafter allow each entity the flexibility (within negotiated limits) to raise its own financing. Capital and operating budgets would be set by each entity based on its board's judgement as to how to best create shareholder value. Each state entity should adopt international accounting principles and report regularly and publicly.

A prerequisite for attracting new participants and ensuring vigorous competition is that prices must be allowed to reflect full costs and that there should be a tax structure which permits investors (public and private) to earn a fair return while still capturing a major share of rent from natural resource ownership for the nation. The need for any subsidy should be assessed rather than assumed. To the extent that government deems that subsidies should continue, a clear policy on the social objective and intended beneficiaries of such subsidies would be required. Finally, such targeted subsidies should be financed by the federal budget rather than remaining implicit through setting prices below costs.

Another prerequisite is that potential participants perceive that they will be permitted to operate on the same terms as government-owned incumbents. Ensuring a level playing field and protecting consumers' interests require carefully defined and professionally administered regulation by government. This includes ensuring nondiscriminatory access to bottleneck infrastructure, setting tariffs based on economic principles for those segments of the industry not subject to competition, and restricting potentially anticompetitive activities. Government institutions charged with these and other regulatory responsibilities need to operate transparently and be provided with a high degree of independence from the political authorities to ensure their impartiality.

Whatever the pattern of ownership and sector structure, demand for energy needs to be satisfied with the least possible harm to the environment. This includes ensuring compliance with current legislation and international treaties, establishing policies for the sector on air pollution, encouraging rational use of energy, and promoting development of renewable energy resources. With respect to air pollution, this would encompass development of a phased program of mandated improvements in fuel quality, in tandem with improved vehicle specifications and power plant emission standards and fuel substitution.

The pollutants of principal concern are fine particulate matter and ozone. Most future thermal generation capacity will be combined cycle natural-gas-fired power plants. The principal environmental issue for these plants will be reducing NOx emissions, an ozone precursor. The future environmental policy focus for domestic refineries will be reducing sulfur in gasoline, diesel, and fuel oil. This will pose a very significant challenge to Mexico, with its high-sulfur crudes. The current policy direction appears to target gasoline sulfur first in the beginning of the next decade, followed by diesel sulfur reduction. However, current science indicates that the most damaging pollutant is fine particulate matter, and diesel vehicles are responsible for a much greater proportion of fine particulate matter than gasoline. It would therefore be appropriate to reexamine the cost-effectiveness of targeting gasoline sulfur as a top priority before large-scale investments are undertaken in this area. Greater attention should be directed at measures to reduce pollution from diesel vehicles. A very cost-effective first step in this direction would be to strengthen inspection and maintenance programs for commercial diesel vehicles.

There does not appear to be a concrete plan to reduce the content of sulfur in domestically produced fuel oil, as it would be quite costly given the current and future configuration of the refineries and type of crude processed.

Improving end-use energy efficiency will require continued development of market instruments and regulations (for example, building codes and appliance standards) which reduce per-unit energy consumption, and hence pollution occasioned by energy production. While local efforts to develop renewable energy sources, such as solar energy, biomass, and wind power, have surged in recent years, these resources still constitute a miniscule proportion of energy supply. Geothermal energy is an exception and its contribution has grown significantly in the last decade. The wind resource potential is high in many parts of Mexico, particularly in the Oaxaca region. With the decline in cost of wind turbines and the growth of international operational experience, wind has the potential to contribute to grid supply in the near future. More rapid commercialization of renewable energy resources in Mexico requires a policy framework that provides adequate incentives for private participation, and supports effective institutional arrangements for carrying out a coherent national program.

Deepening Reforms in the Oil and Gas Sectors

There are two key criteria which must be met if Mexico's oil and gas sector is to ful-fill its potential contribution to the economy. First, the country's reserves should generate maximum wealth creation for society, and second, natural gas and oil prod-ucts should be delivered to consumers at the lowest possible cost in order to fuel the growth of the economy.

PEMEX, as it is now situated, is not able to meet these criteria. It is short of funds and burdened by an oppressive tax regime. In addition, the present sector con-figuration does not permit meaningful competition. These factors inhibit PEMEX from operating as efficiently as oil companies operating in the global marketplace. Moreover, the limited form and scope of private participation to date saddles the government with the majority of risk and with virtually all the financing obligations. Taken together, this limits the extent to which Mexico's plentiful hydrocarbon resources contribute to the national welfare.

Oil and Gas Exploration and Production

The upstream E&P sector requires additional investment if Mexico is to exploit its substantial reserves base and maximize state revenues. Private oil companies can be brought in to provide this investment, as well as their technical and managerial expertise. To bring them in on a basis acceptable to Mexico, changes are needed in the legal, regulatory, contractual, and fiscal areas.

The starting point is to decide what is needed to attract such private investors, and there are successful models which can be considered. The use of concession agreements has largely given way to production-sharing agreements, in which the state maintains ownership and control over the resource. Companies entering into a production-shar-ing agreement (PSA) take the exploration risk—if no oil is found it receives nothing. If oil is produced, the government will allow the companies to recover their costs and receive a (small) share of the profits. Governments typically benefit from these arrange-ments primarily because they avoid much of the risk of exploration and development, and capital provided by the companies can have characteristics of an interest-free loan. The details of the contracts can be adjusted to give incentives for efficient field devel-opment, and there are very wide variations found in contracts worldwide to reflect the differing nature of the reserves and aims of the host governments.

All such arrangements start from the position that oil and gas resources remain the property of the state, so that the issues are how to allocate licenses for future development and whether to charge the licensee for existing fields. One option is for PEMEX, with its considerable experience in existing producing fields, to continue to operate them. However, unexploited discoveries, new exploration areas, and pro-ducing fields beyond PEMEX's financial or technical capabilities would be obvious candidates for licensing to private companies. Both new firms and PEMEX should be subject to the same taxation regime. With Mexico's long experience in the sector there should be good opportunities for domestic firms to operate in the sector.

Potential investor interest in Mexico's upstream oil and gas sector, based on substantial low-cost reserves, is very strong. With the proper legal, regulatory, contractual, and fiscal framework, the gains from opening the sector can be expected to be substantial, with corresponding benefit to Mexico's fundamental social and economic goals.

Refining and Marketing

A recent development that will have an enormous impact on the future refining sector in Mexico is the decision taken by the government in the mid-1990s to increase the amount of Maya crude processed to maximize revenues from the sales of sweeter crude on the international market. This strategy appears to be driven by expected growth in the price spread between sweet and heavier sour crude. By doubling the amount of Maya processed domestically, the proportion of sour crude sold on the international market will be reduced. Another important factor appears to be the desire of the government to become largely self-sufficient in the supply of gasoline and other products.

Executing this strategy has required considerable capital investments in the refining sector—in order to handle heavier crude with higher sulfur content—just to meet the current product slate and existing fuel specifications without a marked increase in refining capacity. Moreover, the current investment program for refinery upgrading (through 2006) does not incorporate more demanding fuel quality specifications, the most significant of which is the dramatic reduction in the sulfur content of gasoline and diesel expected in the coming decade. There is a tradeoff between maximizing export revenues from the sales of sweeter crude by unloading as much sour crude as refinery configurations permit on the domestic market on the one hand, and the requirement to dramatically improve fuel quality on the other. It is not clear to what extent PEMEX refineries will be in a position to improve fuel quality and remain competitive with imports, given the current restrictions on sourcing crude supply.

The current trends in industrialized countries calling for sulfur-free gasoline and diesel will make sour crude increasingly unattractive, potentially reducing government revenues in the future. PEMEX has attempted to offload some of the market risk associated with the production and sales of Maya and other Mexican crudes by signing supply contracts with U.S. refiners (presumably offering prices attractive enough to justify refinery reconfiguration to meet low sulfur specifications in the United States by 2004), and embarking on significant capital expenditure programs for Mexican refineries to process more Maya. It is far from clear whether the government could and should manage these risks and continue to remain deeply involved in this low-margin segment of the market.

In order to meet demand while continuing to strive for higher fuel quality to mitigate air pollution, Mexico should introduce greater competition in the downstream petroleum sector by fully adopting international market prices as the basis for ex-refinery prices and allowing the import of products by any party and entry of new participants in the industry. It is particularly important to disengage producers from distributors, so that wholesalers are free to buy refined products from any supplier. To create a level playing field, the government should, over time, also permit Mexican refineries to purchase crude from any source, and not restrict the purchase to domestic crude of specified composition. Such deregulation of the industry can create strong incentives to improve responsiveness and efficiency. The participation of new players should go well beyond the traditional BLT design–construction arrangements if it is to bring in serious capital and marketing expertise.

Petrochemicals is an industry which has all the characteristics of a private sector business. In Mexico, the growth of this sector has been seriously hampered by political constraints. Repeated and futile attempts over several years to begin selling interests in its chemical complexes are due primarily to the terms of the privatization offer—the most significant of which was that the government would continue to retain 51 percent of the shares, thereby denying the strategic investor a controlling stake—widely viewed as inadequate and inappropriate. If conditions were created for effective private sector participation (majority ownership) and competition, this sector would operate within the discipline of the market. Where investment is economically justified, the private sector would provide it, leading to value added and employment. Where not justified, it would not be pursued.

The LPG sector is one where there has been movement toward liberalization. However, distribution and storage still retain oligopolistic elements in terms of industry conduct, and competition needs to be introduced here also. Because of its role in supply to the sector, PEMEX should not be involved in either distribution or storage.

The marketing and distribution of oil products is not a highly technical process. It can be carried out by private investors and, in fact, this is the case almost everywhere for wholesaling, and retailing. To the extent that ownership and control in the refining sector is diversified, it will not be necessary to preclude PEMEX from participating in retail operations.

As the downstream petroleum sector in Mexico becomes deregulated and more players enter the sector, it will be essential to establish an independent body to monitor fuel quality and other regulatory issues such as health and safety. Without a credible independent body which is seen by all to be effectively enforcing existing standards, vehicle manufacturers, for example, may be reluctant to guarantee the performance of pollution control devices. Having multiple distributors and independent operators makes it all the more important to have an effective regulatory agency overseeing fuel quality standards and other regulations. Effective enforcement is a prerequisite for the creation of a level playing field and reaping the efficiency benefits of fostering competitive markets.

Infrastructure

Entry of new participants in production, refining, and marketing will materialize if they are permitted nondiscriminatory access to bottleneck infrastructure: transport pipelines, terminals, and storage. Hence, it is necessary that such infrastructure be in the hands of a properly regulated company, distinct from PEMEX and other participants in each of the production, refining, and marketing subsectors. Otherwise, the interest of potential new investors will be seriously reduced.

These facilities should be reconfigured as separate companies which will provide open access at a reasonable cost. At the outset, this could be done on a cost-plus basis, provided that there is a strong regulator in place to ensure reasonable terms of access. Regulatory formulas exist to encourage the introduction of efficiencies, and these should be applied. Regulations should also provide for adequate and timely additions to capacity, allowing new entrants to construct and operate such facilities.

Natural Gas

Exploration and production of natural gas is the exclusive province of PEMEX. In the future the government should consider granting explicit licenses to PEMEX and to private companies. There is an urgent need to develop natural gas, especially nonassociated gas, particularly as a fuel for power generation. To date, PEMEX has not done so because oil development and production have been afforded higher priority within its limited investment funds.

Demand for both LPG and dry gas will continue to grow very rapidly, necessitating continuing if not growing, reliance on imports to supplement domestic production. Until a competitive market in gas is established, the government would need to articulate a clear policy on which sources of gas should be developed, and which forms of gas are to be given priority in production and which imported.

Recently some efforts have been made to capture associated gas which had previously been vented or flared. Since this is a valuable resource and has positive environmental benefits, care must be taken that future oil production programs make maximum economic use of gas. This can be embedded in the licensing agreements with field operators.

Gas transport should be handled similarly to oil marketing infrastructure. An independent company or companies should undertake this activity. Nondiscriminatory access should be provided at reasonable cost to allow marketing/distribution companies to contract for supplies with domestic or imported suppliers. The government should continue to permit private operators to construct and operate gas pipelines. This should be extended to LPG facilities as well. The government has already achieved much in this area with the establishment of a modern regulatory framework for natural gas transport and distribution.

Marketing/distribution of natural gas is now carried out by independent regional companies. This could continue in the future, although to ensure a level playing field for competition, PEMEX participation in this area of business should be carefully circumscribed.

Government's Roles in the Sector

Adopting the measures outlined above would require commensurate changes to PEMEX's existing structure. The existing subsidiaries should be reconstituted as independent stand-alone enterprises, preferably under company law, to provide them with greater degrees of autonomy and commercial orientation. Opportunities to break these units up further should be explored with a view to creating an environment more conducive to competition among PEMEX units and potential entrants. The principles stated earlier for state companies should apply. An important criterion for this reorganization is that no state entity would be able to dominate to the point of stifling competition.

Beyond addressing governance issues in PEMEX, the government must assume several critically important roles. These include establishing a modern legal framework to allow fair entry for domestic and foreign investors. Upstream, it would formulate licensing policies, create a stand-alone geophysical mapping agency, establish a modern tax system, set and ensure compliance with health, safety, and environment standards, and set out and enforce contractual terms for all companies operating in the sector.

Change in the existing tax system is long overdue. It is regressive, unstable, and overly complex, inhibiting investment in otherwise economic projects and forcing early shut-in of existing wells. The new tax regime should seek to preserve and increase state oil tax revenues, provide clear incentives for PEMEX and other sector participants to invest efficiently in new projects, and maximize economic yield of existing fields on terms comparable to those found elsewhere in the world. Experience in other hydrocarbon countries has demonstrated that under a progressive tax regime, with new entry, the tax base broadens considerably, permitting the state to realize substantial increases in oil tax revenues over time.

Regulation would have to be high quality and independent from government ministries. It must be seen as impartial and transparent. There must be adequate recourse to arbitration and clear dispute resolution mechanisms. The recently established CRE provides a good model. Downstream, the government also faces the need to recast the subsidies and excise tax systems. Restructuring will provide a good opportunity to simplify and streamline.

Finally, the government must ensure that the nation's strategic interests are protected in oil and gas. There is a need for a review of strategic priorities and a clear statement of principles put forth, for example, regarding the desirability of competition, the need for strategic oil stocks, and the degree of dependence on imports to be permitted.

Deepening Reforms in the Power Sector

Meeting the rapid growth of demand for electricity over the next decade will require the mobilization of very substantial financial, technological, and managerial resources. This needs to be done in a manner which ensures that Mexican consumers are provided reliable service at the lowest economic cost, while maintaining sound public finances and mitigating adverse impacts on the environment.

For the sector to realize its potential productivity gains and attract sufficient resources to serve demand at lowest cost over the long term, additional modifications to sector policy are urgently required. The key to meeting these goals is the attraction of new participants into the market, who can dedicate substantial capital to the sector without encumbering, directly or indirectly, public finances. To ensure that electricity is supplied to consumers at the lowest cost, competitive conditions need to be created. This will require a number of buyers and sellers of bulk power. No one agent should be so large as to be able to dominate the market. Creating a competitive market for bulk power will make its value to users transparent, which in turn will foster more efficient patterns of consumption and supply. Achieving these conditions will require substantial restructuring and reorganization.

The existing state company, CFE, should be vertically separated into generation, transmission, and distribution companies. Control of the natural monopoly of transmission and the dispatch function would be separated from buying and selling. Control by a generator or distributor of the bottleneck of transmission would allow them to manipulate it to their advantage, and private capital will not enter, except with guaranteed returns, into a market which is perceived to be biased in favor of incumbent actors, particularly if they are state-owned.

The generating and distribution elements should be separated horizontally to allow several buyers and sellers of bulk power. No individual unit should be large enough to dominate the market, and there should be enough such companies to preclude tacit collusion. These companies should be privatized in a way that maximizes the benefit to consumers rather than to maximize revenues to the state.

The state-owned enterprises that remain would need to be fully commercialized with hard budget constraints so that they are compelled to perform efficiently. Any form of subsidy to the companies would allow them to continue to operate inefficiently, and also would give them an advantage against private sector firms. This lack of a level playing field would act as a disincentive to the entry of private capital.

The new structure should support a system of trading power that allows technological and operating efficiencies to be reflected in prices. The use of long-term contracts of the "take or pay" form are inimicable to this because they do not ensure that the lowest-cost producers would be able to sell their maximum output. The entry of further IPPs into the power sector should be in a framework of the competitive selling of power, because real time competition together with hedging instruments such as "contracts for differences" provide strong incentives for keeping costs low.

Clear rules of operation will need to be specified to organize the market for bulk power. An independent system operator and settlement agent will be needed to establish the merit order and dispatch generation facilities, and facilitate trading and payment. This would ensure that buyers and sellers are treated impartially and transparently, and that transactions are executed according to preset rules.

Regulation of transmission and distribution will be necessary since they are not competitive activities. The form of the regulation will need to be transparent, predictable, and non-discriminatory. Principles regarding planning and finance of transmission investment will need to be articulated to ensure efficient expansion of the system.

Generators should be permitted to sell directly to large final users (large-scale industry initially), while smaller users could purchase from their local distribution company. This arrangement would require that consumer interests be protected through regulation of tariffs and by enforcement of service standards. Tariffs should be designed to encourage efficiency gains and to pass on some of these to consumers, while ensuring that the quality of service improves.

The regulatory agency should be afforded a high degree of autonomy in setting and reviewing tariffs and in defining service obligations. Its dispositions should be applied equally to public and private market participants. Its credibility as an impartial body depends on it not being subject to political interference. In this regard, CRE's powers and governance arrangements should be reviewed.

To allow the generation of electricity at lowest possible cost requires access to different fuel sources under competitive conditions. If generators were prevented from buying from the lowest-cost source, then consumers would not reap the potential benefits that competition between generators could provide. This requirement would mean that the progress in liberalizing trade and transport of natural gas should be deepened and extended to other fuels.

The manner in which power tariffs have been used as an instrument of macroeconomic and social policy has proven counterproductive and has led to the decapitalization of the industry. Tariffs should move to cost-reflective levels to provide incentives to improve service and to foster rational use of the resource. Universal electricity subsidies have led to an unsustainable burden on the budget, and have distorted patterns of consumption leading to the requirement for even more capacity. The focus of government support to society has already shifted from global subsidies for the production of "essential" goods and services, to providing income support only to the poorer members of society. Subsidies to electricity services should thus be redesigned in keeping with this philosophy, and should be borne directly by the budget and not by electricity companies.

Rural electrification is one area where subsidies may well be warranted by virtue of the large gain in welfare that access to electricity provides. While environmentally clean renewable energy technologies are becoming competitive with conventional fossil-fuel-based solutions, the very low incomes of households in off-grid areas pose a major obstacle to establishing sustainable service arrangements without substantial support from the government. The challenge will be to devise institutional solutions to address market failure, target subsidies, attract local businesses to this activity, and provide households with choices. Since it is likely that the majority of the unserved rural population cannot afford the full cost of basic service, their access costs could be subsidized. Such assistance should not be in the form of giveaways because this has proven unsustainable in terms of service, and invariably benefits the privileged minority.

The state would continue to formulate overall policy goals and strategies, and by granting the regulatory authority adequate powers to protect users and to prevent anticompetitive practices, it would retain control of the character and operation of the sector. Environmental policies on air pollution would also be of considerable influence in the electricity sector. These would be implemented by directives with which all market participants would have to comply.

18

Regulatory Environment for Private Sector Participation in Infrastructure

This Chapter was written by Sheoli Pargal,
with the valuable input of J. Luis Guasch.

I. Overview

The World Competitiveness Index 2000, developed by the International Institute of Management Development, ranks Mexico 36th out of 47 large economies analyzed worldwide. As is well recognized, the impact of infrastructure on growth and competitiveness is significant. During the past decade, however, infrastructure performance in Mexico has been mixed: there have been significant gains in some sectors, but much more can and needs to be accomplished. This Chapter focuses on infrastructure regulatory issues related to private participation in infrastructure provision, which is critical to enhancing the competitiveness of the Mexican economy

This Chapter covers regulatory and competitiveness issues in the telecommunications, natural gas, transport, and urban water and sanitation sectors. As these are core upstream infrastructure sectors, poor performance in them has cascading effects throughout the economy, critically affecting the cost of doing business, and thus the country's growth and international competitiveness prospects. The integration of transport modes, for example, has huge implications for production costs—logistics costs in Latin America are typically between 30 and 40 percent of the final sales price of products. This is twice the level observed in most OECD countries.[1] The gains expected from improved multimodal coordination include savings in operational costs (labor and energy), cuts in waiting time, reliability in transshipment and transit, safety, and protection of cargo. Greater efficiency and lower costs in telecommunications, energy, and water supply are likewise passed through to affect economywide competitiveness.

---

1. Guasch and Kogan. "Inventory Levels and Logistics Costs in Latin America." World Bank. 1999.

Investment needs in these sectors are huge, running into billions of dollars per year. In line with the government's policy of liberalization (including opening up the economy to foreign competition, withdrawing from intervention in nonpriority areas, and focusing on the social sectors), and as a reflection of the government's fiscal constraints, the role of the private sector in service provision across most infrastructure sectors has become vital. Attracting private participation in these sectors, especially when it involves the privatization of formerly state-owned monopoly infrastructure, or attracting private investment through concessions for service provision, requires the articulation of a sound regulatory framework and the development of independent and competent institutions to implement it. To date, private sector participation in infrastructure in Mexico has been quite extensive—at least in a relative sense—but has not lived up to its potential. A significant reform agenda remains in legal, regulatory, and procedural aspects, a major weakness in practically all of Mexico infrasctructure sector

To start with, regulation must not become a de facto instrument for re-expropriating the capital investments of private companies, and must encourage efficient investment. At the same time, regulation should seek to facilitate the development of competition or mimic the results of competition. Finally, regulatory policy should be stable, predictable, and timely in order to avoid becoming a source of business uncertainty, which inhibits economically and financially warranted capital investments.

In this context, three themes reoccur in this analysis of private sector participation (PSP) in infrastructure in Mexico. The first is the impact of decentralization on an appropriate delineation of activities and responsibilities at different levels of the government, and on coordination across agencies and levels of government. This is critical in the water sector, but has echoes in the transport subsectors as well, especially where the bundling of concessions has been given an impetus by the decentralization process. The second is the urgent need for clarity on the role of the *Comisión Federal de Competencia* (CFC) and the division of responsibilities between it and the sectoral regulatory bodies. The third theme is the need to develop effective regulation to provide appropriate regulatory tools for regulatory agencies and the general lack of experience in Mexico with autonomous sectoral regulatory entities and the consequent difficulty of orienting them toward regulation rather than promotion and operation.

This Chapter summarizes the policy and regulatory actions still remaining on the agenda. It looks at each of the four sectors mentioned, describes briefly the experience with private sector participation, identifies the institutional and regulatory aspects in which changes are needed and, makes recommendations on possible strategies to be followed.

II. Telecommunications

Background and Diagnostic

Since the late 1980s, the telecommunications sector has undergone a dramatic transformation. During the 1990s, the number of telephone lines in service doubled; the state-owned monopoly telephone company, TELMEX, was privatized; and competition gradually emerged in all elements of the industry. In 1995 the government passed major legislation setting forth its policies and establishing a new regulatory framework. By 2000, competitors were reasonably successful in mobile wireless telephone service and in domestic and international long distance, and had begun to enter fixed-access service in the largest cities.

The privatization of TELMEX and the introduction of competition, first in long distance, then in mobile telephony, and then in fixed-access service, has been a clear achievement. In 1996, 1997, and 1998, the government held successful auctions for electromagnetic frequency assignments for paging, cellular telephones, local microwave distribution, and PCS. Several companies have been reasonably successful in entering wireless telephony, especially mobile service.

However, overall sector performance remains deficient. For example:

- Four years after the liberalization and opening of the telecommunications market in Mexico, TELMEX remains the dominant operator, with 75 percent of the long distance market, 95 percent of its fixed lines, and 80 percent of the mobile market. As a consequence Mexico has fewer telephone lines per person than most comparable countries in the region, despite the fact that it was the second country after Chile to privatize its telephone company. Even Brazil, privatized only two years ago, has more lines per person than Mexico. This is despite vigorous entry and private sector investment in the sector, and with strong competitors (including MCI WorldCom, AT&T, Banamex, and Grupo Alfa).
- Tariffs for local calls and lines remain unacceptably high.
- Regulation has been relatively ineffective and the Federal Telecommunications Commission (COFETEL) is plagued by a myriad of institutional problems and political interference.
- Procedures for decision making back transparency and the agency has been unable to secure relevant information from operators.
- The ease of use and abuse of legal injunctions (*recursos de amparo*)—over 250—by all players has paralyzed sector development and rendered regulation quasi-irrelevant.
- Universal service obligations are still deficient, and there is a lack of strategy for its development.

Important elements of the regulatory system governing the transformation from state-owned monopoly to privatized competition have not worked well. Many major regulatory issues regarding interconnection rules and prices remain unresolved, primarily because the front-line regulatory agency, COFETEL, has not been granted the procedural flexibility and decision-making authority to take decisive, timely action on issues that create significant conflicts among the players in the industry. TELMEX is extremely powerful and does not have a particularly impressive record in investment particularly after 1994. Entrants have had limited success because competition is hampered by slow and ineffective regulation created by limitations on the authority of COFETEL; by an opaque, secretive, and cumbersome regulatory process; and by an inadequate system of oversight in the courts and political branches of the government. As a result, the prospects for continued growth and competitive pricing in many telecommunications services are not good.

In 1990 the newly privatized TELMEX was given a temporary monopoly in domestic and international long-distance telephone service.[2] Thereafter, TELMEX could be subjected to regulation of its prices by the concession-granting agency, SCT, upon a finding by the antitrust authority, CFC, that TELMEX was a dominant carrier. The concession agreement with the newly privatized TELMEX specified that tariff regulation would apply to a basic basket of core services: installation fees, monthly service charges, usage charges for local calling, and prices for domestic and international long-distance calls, with the first two tariffs differentiated between residential and commercial customers. The concession agreement stipulated that the method of tariff regulation would be a price cap for a bundle of these services, and that regulations would seek to encourage efficient expansion of the network, encourage productivity growth, promote competition, and prevent cross-subsidization.

As a practical matter, TELMEX has set prices so that the price cap ceiling has not been reached. The price cap is denominated in U.S. dollars at the official exchange rate, and since the peso crisis, in particular, a gap has emerged between the official exchange rate and purchasing power parity. As a result, TELMEX has been able to increase prices substantially as measured in inflation-adjusted pesos, while the dollar-denominated prices have generally fallen.

Institutional and Regulatory Framework

The present system for regulating communications in Mexico evolved over several years, and was finally put in place only in 1996. The 1995 Federal Telecommunications Law and the 1996 presidential decree that implemented it elaborate the rules and policies regarding the industry, and establish an institutional framework for carrying them out. While the act maintains authority for regulating telecommunications in SCT, the follow-on presidential decree created COFETEL and delegated most day-to-day regulatory functions to this agency.

The regime has several features that prevent effective regulation. The Federal Telecommunications Law retains a system of concessions for all facilities-based carriers that does not differentiate between competitive and monopolized markets. In competitive markets the concession system is unnecessary and forces the agency to use its scarce personnel in unproductive ways.

---

2. In theory, competitors could have entered local service, but none attempted to do so until they were also permitted to enter long distance after 1996 and radio telephony after 1997.

The law included a provision, applicable in the new TELMEX concession, that price regulation for services sold to the public could be imposed only after a carrier was found to be dominant, and further stipulated that firms had to file tariffs with the regulator. As with other sectors, the responsibility for determining whether a carrier is dominant is left to CFC. Interconnection arrangements, including pricing, can be regulated by COFETEL if operators request intervention after failing to negotiate an agreement. The premise of interconnection policy is that interconnection issues should be resolved by the carriers.

COFETEL has not been able to react in a timely and predictable way to the tasks that have been assigned to it. In March 1998, CFC ruled that TELMEX was dominant in five markets, including interconnection. TELMEX owns virtually all fixed access connections, about two-thirds of mobile access connections, and all long-distance facilities outside of the largest cities. Hence, for competition to emerge in local access, domestic long distance, and international, reasonable interconnection arrangements between TELMEX and its competitors are essential. Yet COFETEL has not been able to implement any regulations regarding interconnection, in part because the system of *amparo,* or judicial review, seems to undermine effective implementation of new regulations. Almost every regulation that has been promulgated by COFETEL has been challenged successfully by either TELMEX or its competitors in that the implementation of the regulation has been stayed by an *amparo.* The result is often confusion and disruption.

COFETEL is in some ways a well designed-agency. At the top are four commissioners, who are required to have relevant expertise. The agency appears reasonably well staffed, and because Mexico has a large group of well-educated civil servants, the competence of the agency does not appear to be a problem. Likewise, the 1995 Federal Telecommunications Law provides reasonable policy guidance for the regulator. Price regulation properly is focused on monopolized markets, and regulated prices are to be cost-based and free of cross-subsidy. Moreover, granting to CFC the role of deciding whether a carrier is dominant gives an important function to the competition advocacy agency. However, the new system has some serious gaps.

To begin with, COFETEL is not independent. In most cases, its decisions must be approved by SCT before they are adopted. In addition, COFETEL's commissioners, though appointed to a fixed term, can be removed by the secretary. The continued involvement of SCT in day-to-day decisions vitiates the role that is more natural for SCT, which is policy oversight: to review policy, assess developments, and make proposals for changes in the legislation and decrees that underpin the current system.

In addition, COFETEL's procedures are neither transparent nor open. The agency uses bilateral negotiations to develop regulations, especially with respect to pricing. No other parties, including CFC, have the right to participate in the process. The information that is developed in these negotiations, and the basis for the decisions, are not made public. Moreover, COFETEL lacks the authority to compel information from regulated firms. Because regulations are not explained or supported by public evidence, the underlying policies and procedures of the agency are unclear.

Thus the major policy goals for the sector are to:

(i)   Increase effective competition in telecommunications.

(ii)   Accelerate access and align tariffs with long-term costs.

(iii) Improve regulation, and develop appropriate regulatory standards, accounting and other tools.

(iv) Develop a strategy and implementation of Universal Service Obligation.

Recommendations

The preceding review of the regulatory system suggests several specific policy recommendations that would be likely to improve the performance of the telecommunications sector.

(i)   Grant COFETEL true independence, and strengthen its regulatory capacity. In this regard, SCT should be assigned the responsibility for setting goals for the telecommunications sector, setting standards and norms, and for periodic assessments of the performance of the sector.

(ii)   Require open decisionmaking processes for regulatory proceedings to increase the transparency of the regulatory process. Rather than bilateral negotiations and round tables, public processes of consultation (that is, public hearings, consultative documents, etc.) would be critical in this respect.

(iii) Focus judicial review on whether decisions have a reasonable basis. Since the *amparo* system of injunctions has almost paralyzed the system, an alternative mechanism for the resolution of conflicts needs to be developed, such as specialized courts, arbitration, and mediation.

(iv) Ensure that COFETEL and CFC can obtain relevant information for regulatory processes and antitrust cases, respectively. This will also increase regulatory transparency by ensuring that COFETEL can explain the legal and information bases for its decisions. Currently, companies can file injunctions against information requests of the regulator or the antitrust agency, which is not conducive to creating an environment which encourages entry.

(v)   Enforce the law against such practices as market foreclosure, noncompliance with rules and norms, provision of deficient services by dominant carrier to other operators, non-open access, and bypass. This is the responsibility of both the CFC and COFETEL. Hence CFC should be granted standing on matters related to the competitive effects of decisions.

(vi) Develop an appropriate methodology (complemented with relevant benchmark analysis) for assessing interconnection charges. (For example, a cluster-based cost model has been developed for the Argentine and Peruvian regulators.)

(vii)   Simplify concession requirements for competitive entrants.
(viii) Develop a strategy for universal service.
(ix)   Develop and implement appropriate regulatory standards, accounting and cost models.
(x)   Reconsider sector structure.

III. Natural Gas

Background and Diagnostic

Demand for natural gas in Mexico is projected to increase by 10 percent annually during 2000–07 due to the expansion of private distribution networks, increasing demand for electricity generation, and the entry in force of environmental regulations that require the substitution of natural gas for fuel oil. An industry structure characterized by inefficient production and lack of competition will not be able to meet future demand increases, hence the government's decision to restructure Mexico's natural gas sector.

Reform in natural gas began in 1995 but no decisions have yet been taken on private participation and structural reform in the areas of gas production, oil extraction, and the production of petrochemicals. The reform of the sector allowed for private investment in new gas transportation projects, and in distribution and marketing, but kept the PEMEX monopoly in production and processing. In addition, structural reform of the electricity sector—which has implications for the market for natural gas—has been postponed.

The liberalization of this sector is complex because the natural gas market combines naturally monopolistic with potentially competitive activities. Pipeline transportation and distribution have natural monopoly characteristics and require regulation of price and nonprice behavior. Production is a contestable market, though in Mexico it is still maintained as a state monopoly. Marketing of gas is also contestable but the regulator must make sure that there are no entry barriers to this activity. As a result of existing conditions in 1995, regulation of the price of domestic gas, and development of distribution systems were two specific goals of the reform.

While structural reform in the Mexican energy sector has proceeded slowly, important changes have been introduced to attract private investment in natural gas pipeline transportation, and gas distribution. The regulatory regime now in place provides incentives for firms to invest and operate efficiently, and to bear much of the risks associated with new projects. It also protects captive consumers to a large degree and, more generally, enhances economic welfare.

To date, nineteen distribution permits have been awarded and the distribution infrastructure that previously belonged to PEMEX or CFE has been privatized.

Distributors have made investment commitments of US$868 million and the number of consumers served by distribution franchises is forecast to increase 4 fold between 1995–2004.

Sixteen transport permits have also been granted which carry investment commitments of US$1.1 billion. Substantial additional gas transport capacity will be needed in the next decade, as will interconnections with the US gas transportation system to support the very rapid growth in gas demand in the northern part of the country. While PEMEX's transportation system is projected to grow at an annual rate of 11.0 percent, the increase in pipeline capacity will barely cope with the increase of demand, possibly leading to bottlenecks during peak periods. However, Pemex is by far the dominant actor in transport and marketing and this may continue to discourage private interest in developing gas transport infrastructure. The combined IPP/gas transport projects tendered by CFE can be seen as stop-gap measures to deal with this problem.

At the conclusion of the first phase of investment mobilization and competition *for* the market in distribution, important issues remain. Perhaps the biggest is the evolution of competition *in* the market. The vertical integration of PEMEX in production, transportation and commercialization along with the asymmetry of information between PEMEX and the CFC has hindered regulation and the development of competition in gas marketing—the PEMEX marketing subsidiary has a virtual monopoly on most gas marketing contracts inside Mexico. New regulatory mechanisms are now in place to regulate PEMEX gas marketing activities, but their effectiveness remains to be seen.

Institutional and Regulatory Framework

The main energy regulatory authority, the *Commisión Reguladora de Energía* (CRE), was created in October 1993 and commenced operations in January 1994. It was initially conceived as an advisory body to the Secretaria de Energia (SE) with no financial or operational autonomy, but its mandate was expanded and clarified in tandem with reform measures in the gas sector.

The gas law (Regulatory Law of Constitutional Article 27) was amended in April 1995 to allow private investment in new transportation projects, and in the distribution, storage and commercialization of natural gas. PEMEX was to focus on maintaining its existing large transportation network, and developing exploration and production. The reform also included institutional changes with a view to separating and more clearly defining responsibilities for policy/planning, regulation, and service provision. Previously, the functions of owner, operator and regulator were carried out by PEMEX and the Treasury. The new institutional arrangements included the following:

- The SE's role was strengthened as the rector of the Nation's energy resources, charged with planning and supervision of State firms in the sector.

- The CRE was assigned regulatory authority including permit granting, price and tariff regulation, regulation of access to services, oversight of distribution franchise award processes, and dispute resolution. The CRE in theory has the authority to ensure compliance with regulations.
- PEMEX's role was restricted to operations and it was to disclose previously classified information to the authorities.

An important issue for the sector is the need for co-ordination across government agencies at both the federal level and across sub-national levels, given the existence of varying local regulations in different states and municipalities. CRE, CFE, SEMARNAP, SE, SCT, and the Ministry of Social Development (SEDESOL) are working to establish agreements of coordination with the states and municipalities in order to simplify regulatory procedures, and to foster public awareness regarding the sector.

CRE's formal structure and attributes are designed to achieve technical, operational, and financial independence from the SE.[3] CRE's commissioners are appointed for five years, with staggered, renewable terms to ensure continuity in CRE's policies and independence from the six-year presidential changes. However, since the CRE is an *órgano desconcentrado*, its attributes could potentially be altered radically in Congress without a qualified majority. While this appears unlikely, Cofetel's experience in this regard is not salutary.

Too little time has elapsed to assess the functioning of the CRE, but its decision making is considered transparent. In addition to the appeals mechanism, the CRE is also open to the judicial recourse of the *Amparo* against any penalty or sanction it may impose. However, CRE has not been able to prevent PEMEX from hampering the granting of rights-of-way to private transporters or distributors whose networks would pass close to PEMEX oil pipelines.

Salient aspects of the gas law are as follows.

- PEMEX and private transporters, distributors and operators of storage facilities must obtain permits from the regulatory authority in order to carry out their activities. Permits are issued for thirty years and are renewable. Gas transportation and storage permits are issued under market risk with no exclusivity, for specific capacities and, in the case of transportation, for defined routes.
- Due to the presence of a dominant player (PEMEX), the *Reglamento* permits other market participants some degree of vertical integration, while prohibiting integration between transportation and distribution. Producers, transporters, operators of storage facilities and distributors can buy and sell gas, but must unbundle their services and maintain separate accounting systems for their commercial and service activities in order to prevent cross subsidies.

---

3. The CRE's budget is directly authorized by the Finance Ministry and is independent of the SE budget.

- Imports of natural gas from the United States are freely allowed. Since competition prevails in the North American production market, in theory this should provide some control over PEMEX's pricing and contracting actions.
- Open marketing in the sector. Marketers need no permit to operate, and may carry out commercial transactions, including buying gas, transporting it through the network, and selling it to distributors or to consumers directly connected to the transportation system. In addition, they can sell gas to consumers within a distribution franchise area (i.e. commercial bypass) as well as buy and sell transport pipeline capacity.
- When there is enough capacity access to the natural gas transportation and storage systems must be open in order to create competition. Likewise, distributors must allow commercial by-pass or open access to their distribution network starting from the first day of operation. However, physical by-pass is to be implemented only gradually.

Given the legal monopoly of PEMEX in production the price of domestically produced gas (termed *first-hand-sales* price) is regulated via a price-cap based on the price of gas imported from North America.[4]

Natural-gas distribution in Mexico has "green-field project" characteristics because LPG has traditionally been used for household purposes, and fuel oil for industrial purposes and electricity generation. The natural-gas distribution network consists of temporal regional monopolies in defined geographic zones. Distribution zones are tendered through an open bidding process with the winners being granted exclusive twelve year franchises.

Distribution tariffs are regulated through a price cap based on the "cost of service." Average-revenue regulation is in place during the first five-year regulatory period, in recognition of the high cost and demand shocks likely during the initial phase of build-out and operation of the distribution network. In cases where a single company is the sole supplier within a distribution zone, the government sets the gas *acquisition price*, i.e., the maximum price (resulting from costs of gas purchase, transportation, distribution and storage services) that can be passed through to the final user by the distributor in order to protect captive consumers.

Regulators initially believed that competition in gas marketing would be assured by the contestable nature of this activity. However, the vertical integration of PEMEX in production, transportation and commercialization has proven to be an obstacle to ensuring its compliance with regulations and to the introduction of competition in gas marketing. As a result, the CRE recently issued the directive on first hand sales of natural gas—five years after the liberalization process began.

The new directive requires PEMEX to unbundle its production, transportation, and marketing activities. It also requires that PEMEX not unduly discriminate among consumers, including northern power generation plants that have access to

---

4. This is feasible since Mexico is physically linked to the US natural gas market.

competing supplies (because of proximity to the US market), and southern generators that only have access to PEMEX gas. By requiring similar pricing for first hand
gas sales contracts, competition among power generators will be driven by technical
and financial concerns rather than PEMEX's exercise of market power.

Recommendations

Current policy goals include further liberalization of the sector, including the development of a competitive natural-gas market and the design of a regulatory framework that would create a level playing field in all components of the gas sector that
need to be regulated. Main recommendations are as follows.

(1)   Better definition of the role and functioning of the CRE so that it works as
      a regulator rather than as a promoter of investment in the sector. The capac-
      ity of the regulator to administer the regulatory framework cannot be
      judged yet because the CRE has only just begun to formally regulate the
      conduct of participants. Up till now it has been concerned with issuing per-
      mits, promoting distribution and transportation projects, and incorporat-
      ing PEMEX into the regulatory framework.

(2)   Clarification of the respective responsibilities of the CRE and the *Commi-
      sion Federal de Competencia* (CFC) with respect to development of the nat-
      ural gas sector is urgent since the CRE has yet to establish a relationship
      with the CFC, and the CFC has a mandate to monitor anti-competitive
      behavior.

(3)   Addressing the market power PEMEX wields. Since PEMEX will have the
      monopoly in spot and futures gas sales, the entry of marketing competitors
      is likely to be deterred. The current strategy of electricity generation
      enhancement based on IPPs thus involves a monopsony buyer (CFE) and a
      monopoly supplier (PEMEX). If the government proceeds with wholesale
      restructuring of the power sector, the monopolistic structure of gas market-
      ing in Mexico will prevent the sector from responding with the flexible con-
      tracts that competitive gas markets require. In addition, most industrial
      users and local distribution companies will also be constrained by PEMEX's
      control over supply conditions.

      A priority for the CRE is dealing with PEMEX's discretionary discounts
      on domestic gas prices as well as access to transport services. These are made
      possible by its monopoly in domestic production and its overwhelming
      dominance in transport. The principle instrument currently available to the
      CRE is that of regulating the pricing of contracts by PEMEX. Over the
      longer term, structural reform of the sector will need to be considered,
      including permitting entry of new participants in domestic gas develop-
      ment and production, full legal and financial separation of PEMEX-Gas,
      PEMEX-Transport from the holding company, and more efficient pricing

of competing fuels (electricity and LPG) driven by structural and regulatory reforms in those sectors.

(4)   Encouraging interagency co-ordination between the CRE and the CFC and the Federal Consumer Agency (PROFECO) regarding cross subsidies between industrial and residential consumers.

(5)   Developing new arrangements for risk sharing with experienced private companies in the near term, with associated changes in licensing, taxation and audit policies and practices that will allow Mexico to quickly and economically exploit its natural gas resources and avoid soaring increases in gas imports. Among other issues, these should also address investor perceptions regarding permitting for gas distribution. The data provided by CRE to private entrants in distribution has been deemed unreliable and requirements in practice are different from those in the regulations and norms.

IV. Urban Water and Sanitation

Background and Diagnostic

Water supply and sanitation services in Mexico are under local jurisdiction (municipal or state). While local authorities enjoy a high degree of autonomy in structuring service provision arrangements and in setting service standards and tariffs, they are constrained in undertaking investment in new capacity and in maintenance of systems by very limited borrowing capacity due to lack of own-generated tax revenues, poor water company commercial performance (billing and collection), and a more general lack of municipal creditworthiness. The federal government has made private participation in the water and sanitation sector a principal strategy for improving the performance of municipal water companies. This is reflected in the federal water law and subsidiary regulations, and is a focus of federally funded technical assistance and development bank financing programs, but the experience to date with efforts to attract significant private participation has been mixed.Overall sector performance has also been uneven. Access to water and sanitation of 94 percent and 80 percent, respectively, is relatively high in comparison to Brazil (90/60), Chile (99/89), and the OECD average (95/77). However, these figures mask wide regional differences in Mexico, with access most limited in the southern states. While 95 percent of water provided is disinfected, less than 30 percent undergoes potabilization through a water treatment plant, a percentage that falls below that of many Latin American comparators. Only about 15 percent of wastewater is treated, and unaccounted-for-water among urban water companies is high in comparison with other countries; on average only 40 percent of each liter of water produced generates revenue for the water company.

Investment in the sector has steadily declined since the mid-1990s, both in real terms and as a percentage of GDP. Expert opinion is that close to US$1 billion per year of investment would be required to maintain coverage, cover depreciation of existing assets, and pay for the construction of wastewater treatment facilities. In contrast, investment spending in the water sector was US$265 million in 1998, not even enough to cover depreciation. Average household tariffs were at the lower end relative to comparators in Latin America and the OECD; revenue per connection per year for Mexico is roughly one-quarter that of Brazil and one-third of the OECD average, limiting the capacity of the sector to finance necessary activities. In fact the capacity to take on additional debt is negative, and the sector is not able to finance investment from internally generated resources.

The scope of private participation has been much less than anticipated and has therefore contributed little to improving the performance of urban water supply and sanitation systems. Many private investment contracts have not reached financial closure; those that have, have not mobilized the private investments or achieved the performance results expected and have experienced frequent political intervention.

Since the early 1990s, in parallel with support for public sector operators, a number of municipalities sought to pass on part of their service obligations to private parties through service contracts, BOTs, and concessions in the belief that such arrangements would permit greater efficiency and access to long-term funds. Wastewater treatment plants, financed on a BOT basis, have most often failed to materialize, with only 11 out of 50 projects reaching the operating stage,[5] partly because BOTs, especially for wastewater treatment plants, are difficult to finance and require adequate guarantees, given the current poor financial performance of most *organismos operadores*. Out of more than US$1.5 billion in investment which 68 private contracts were expected to mobilize, commitments for only US$350 million, or 22 percent, have been secured.

The emphasis on risky BOT operations rather than the more financially viable water operations has been worsened by design and procurement flaws, generally the result of overly bureaucratic award processes carried out by unprepared municipalities without proper assistance. There is no program to promote PSP at the federal level. FINFRA, the one instrument to finance PSP processes, has fallen short of expectations with poor incentive design, overbureaucracy and, as of late, lack of funds.

Institutional and Regulatory Framework

The *Comisión Nacional de Agua* (CNA) at the federal level grants water use rights, but municipalities control these rights, and have the legal authority to delegate or concession water service responsibility to third parties, for example by constituting public water companies (*organismos operadores*) or by awarding service contracts and concessions to private parties. Municipalities also have the power to devise governance structures and regulations to guarantee the commercial autonomy of the service entities.

---

5. The remainder were suspended, cancelled, or are under prolonged renegotiation.

ORGANISMOS OPERADORES are delegated only a limited range of responsibilities on behalf of the municipality or group of municipalities: routine operation and maintenance (O&M), billing and collection. They do not own assets, are not generally responsible for planning and undertaking investments, and cannot contract long-term debt. This does not provide incentives for the *organismos operadores* to perform as commercially oriented companies, and has resulted in the poor financial performance of many utilities, which frequently do not cover O&M costs, depreciation, or investment. In addition, the short tenure and politicized governance of the *organismos operadores* work against continuity of policies and programs. The municipal president appoints the *organismo operador* board and general managers, who serve terms at most coterminous with the three-year electoral cycle. CNA estimates that the average term of managers is actually only 1.5 years. The close association with political authorities leads to intervention in the day-to-day management of the water company, resulting in weak accountability for performance and poor incentives to improve service.Several localities do have water companies which perform relatively well (for example, León, Mexicali, Monterrey, Tijuana) but this performance cannot be broadly replicated since good management and performance is due in large part to the leadership and commitment of specific individuals rather than to the presence of a framework of well-articulated policies and institutions.

Because municipalities generate little own revenue, federal and state authorities finance, and can influence investment decisions, at the local level. The design and implementation of federal transfers have a major impact on municipal management, and hence on the manner in which water companies operate. Beyond finance, the federal authorities continue to play a major role in planning, construction, regulation, and oversight of the sector. This concurrence of functions has limited the incentive for local jurisdictions to use available resources efficiently, and to mobilize the finance necessary for improving quality and expanding access to water and sanitation services. Also, apart from the leverage provided by the allocation of federal funds, the federal level has not had as much impact on the sector as it could have had, in terms of regulation as well as technical assistance.

The federal water law, *Ley Nacional de Aguas*, enacted in 1992 and amended in 1994, provides a modern regulatory framework for water resource management. Elements of the law were intended to clarify the responsibilities and powers of different levels of government. However, this was vitiated by the lack of clarity of subnational sectoral and administrative legal frameworks. Nationally, there is no coherent regulatory framework for urban water supply and sanitation.

While most states and municipalities have laws which create public water companies and permit private participation, none have adequate subsidiary legislation (*reglamentación*). In 1996 the federal authorities under the leadership of CNA elaborated a model state water sector law which incorporates elements considered critical for providing clarity and juridical certainty to the local authorities, private operators, and financiers. These include transfer of sector planning from CNA to state water commissions, tariff principles, creation of regulatory entities, water company attributes, concession terms, and arbitration procedures. Many states have since adopted certain elements of the model law, for example those permitting cut-off of service for nonpayment, creation of state water commissions, and granting of concessions to private parties. In contrast, very few have put in place regulations governing concessions and none have established distinct regulatory entities to oversee service provision.

Since most PSP contracts are for a limited range of activities, they do not directly address water company performance problems, which arise from the institutional structure of the sector and poor incentives. In fact the wastewater BOTs may have exacerbated some of the problems of the water companies by placing new financial burdens on them without providing the means to pay for these new obligations. BOTs and concessions require the existence of a well-developed regulatory framework, with credible enforcement and monitoring capacity in place. In the case of comprehensive concessions, like Cancún and Aguascalientes, lack of clarity on policy goals, and hence lack of consistency between goals, investment demands, and tariffs, resulted in constant renegotiation and many concession objectives not being achieved. The lack of a clear policy framework translates into the absence of clear regulatory rules on tariff-setting, quality of service, and sanctions for noncompliance. The result is that political interventions are almost inevitable.

In general there has been a lack of political commitment at different levels of government to see the PSP process through, and an absence of an effective regulatory strategy for concessions, notably the lack of an independent and technically competent regulatory institution to monitor contract compliance and revise contracts where necessary, with often no distinction being made between the operator and the regulator. In many instances the existing water company becomes the de facto regulator—which is the case in all the BOT arrangements to date. This has often led to micromanagement of operations.

Recommendations

(1) Promote the autonomy of operating utilities. Autonomous utilities, with full responsibility for service provision, are key to improving sector performance. This implies autonomous boards, which would elect their managers for periods independent of the municipal or state political cycle. The *organismos operadores* would be fully responsible for true costs, including asset management and depreciation. Municipalities or states would make contractual arrangements with the utilities. In addition, a more arms-length regulatory arrangement needs to be developed and the system needs to be de-politicized by de-linking the operations of the water company from the municipality. This could be achieved by appointing technical experts and business people to the board, for instance, and giving them greater financial and managerial autonomy from the municipality.

(2) Establish a regulatory environment to reduce uncertainty, possibly through a sector management body for policies, norms, and technical assistance. Credible and effective regulation needs to be established at the federal and state levels by reorienting/strengthening general regulatory capacity. In addition, there needs to be an apex organization responsible for the water and sanitation sector in Mexico.

Key to an improvement in the performance of the sector is a reassignment of responsibilities. Municipalities were assigned primary responsibility for water and sanitation services. However, that may not be the appropriate level for such responsibilities because their technical capacity, particularly with regard to planning, policymaking, and regulation, is limited. Another vital requirement is explicit definition of the responsibilities, accountabilities, and governance structures of water companies. Creating regulatory authorities at the state rather than the municipal level has a number of benefits for a federal system as is the case with Mexico. Benefits include ensuring autonomy by maintaining distance from the political authorities, providing access to technical expertise, allowing for yardstick competition, and diminishing the danger of capture by the regulated entity. Regulatory rules that require common application such as general norms and standards, basic tariff structures, water quality and environmental standards, and PSP-related issues (concession terms and award), might require specific federal-level regulations. Sector planning and policy design should also be housed at the federal level since this would promote better integration with water resource management.

The state level could provide more specific regulation, for example, tariff regulation, and some level of control. In addition, given prior delegation from the municipalities, the states could supervise some of the service contracts with private operators. States could also establish technical assistance programs to support municipalities in delegating services, and then supervising the corresponding contracts and promoting informal benchmarking.

Clear policies need to be enunciated at the state level and formalized in law. The regulatory framework must take account of the investment, tariff and financing implications of quality goals or standards, and effective institutions need to be developed to monitor and enforce compliance with regulations. This would reduce the risk for private entrants and thus encourage greater PSP.

(3) Define the role of the federal government in a more coherent fashion, focusing on its role as enabler of reform and policy implementation at lower levels. The federal government needs to change the rules of the game so that its policies, in particular the transfer program, but also its debt and water resource management policies, provide sub-national governments with strong incentives to perform effectively This will also free up state level resources that can be used elsewhere. At the local level, it will be important

to channel both financial resources and substantial technical assistance to reform-minded subnational governments to improve policymaking and regulatory capacity and improve the choice and design of PSP arrangements.

CNA could assist in the development of good regulations by promulgating regulatory guidelines and specifying minimum regulatory requirements in state laws. Federal support could be provided to build capacity in private sector participation arrangements and regulation, information collection, and the exchange of ideas across states. The government could consider establishing a federal regulatory agency, which would have jurisdiction whenever state agencies are not established or are not yet competent to meet minimum federal specifications. In addition, it will be important to concentrate existing water and sanitation areas within CNA into a unit responsible for policies, norms, regulatory guidelines, knowledge and information management, training coordination, and technical assistance. The unit could coordinate investment programs and sector-related agencies, but construction of systems would be decentralized to the state and local levels.

(4) Adjust financial policies and harmonize programs. Mexico needs a consistent and well-targeted financial policy for the sector. Key elements of this would be as follows.

(i)   Reorient federal financial assistance to provide incentives to local authorities to implement the comprehensive reforms needed to improve service quality and sustainability. For instance, lending to municipalities could be tied to the establishment of autonomous utilities.

(ii) Loans and subsidies should help utilities achieve financial viability as they transition to better cost recovery, and should be targeted to the poor. Currently subsidies to the sector are provided in the form of soft loans to water companies and local governments for investment, or direct works by CNA. These subsidies are inefficient because of the poor incentives they create for the water companies to operate efficiently, and because they lack targeting.

(iii) Finance wastewater treatment, which is typically underfunded from a social point of view because of the externalities it generates. By 1996, urban water supply coverage was about 93 percent, while wastewater treatment had reached only 20 percent. Given limited resources, it may be more beneficial to expand sewage collection in densely populated poor areas rather than to enhance sewage treatment, which is cost-effective only after a critical mass of sewage collection coverage is attained. Federal money could be allocated as a grant to local utilities to finance wastewater treatment plants in recognition of the externalities generated by treatment. If a charge were established for wastewater treatment, operators could bid to build treatment plants based on the minimum grant required.

(5) Actively promote private sector participation as a tool to improve efficiency and sustainability of service. Technical Assistance support for legislation, regulation, policy, technical and financing aspects, and bid and contract design should be oriented to municipalities and providers. The federal government could help reduce transaction costs of PSP with models, guidelines, and standardized documentation, and provide information that is currently lacking to local policymakers and regulators. In addition, the federal level could develop financial instruments to attract private investors and operators. In particular, a revitalized FINFRA, focused on commercial returns and playing an active role in investment, could provide rollover bridge financing, subsovereign guarantees and regulatory risk coverage. Above all, the attempt should be to fix tariffs at adequate levels, geared toward self-sustainability and covering depreciation of assets.

V. Transport

Mexico has had significant success securing private participation and investment in the transport sector, including roads, railroads, ports, and airports. However, performance has been uneven, with the road sector having the worst record. In railroads and ports significant efficiency gains have been achieved, but further gains can and should be secured.

An integrated vision and policy for the sector is needed. Modes of transport have been developed without enough attention to their interlinkages and complementarities. Access to facilities (particularly ports) remains deficient, and there is a lack of supporting distribution centers and dry ports to facilitate the smooth movement of goods. A lack of brokerage markets for freight and of overarching insurance legislation across modes, makes the development of effective multimodality difficult. As a result, logistic costs and inventory levels remain high, impacting competitiveness and productivity.

While deregulation of transport has been extensive at the federal level, this has not been matched at the state level, adversely affecting costs and productivity. Sectoral regulation in general remains scattered and weak, needing a significant overhaul both institutionally and at the micro level.

Background, Institutional, and Regulatory Framework

Roads

The federal network (43.7 percent of the total network) is composed mainly of free paved roads, directly managed by SCT. There are also 5,768 km of toll roads under its control. A separate body, CAPUFE *(Caminos y Puentes Federales)*, manages 1,529 km of tolled roads and bridges. Concessions to private sector operators (3,176 km) or to states (1,063 km) make up the remainder of the network.

Mexico has been slow in devolving management of the federal road network to the states. Decentralization has been hindered by a lack of resources at the state level, resistance to transfer of funds from the federal government, lack of technical capacity in the states, and political rivalry between the states and the federal government.

SCT remains an integrated organization that does not separate system funding and planning from maintenance and management. Recently efforts have been launched to expand and improve the quality of construction and maintenance activities, both through private contracting and through more performance-driven internal SCT activities. Within SCT, the responsibility for the federal network is divided between two agencies. The Directorate General of Federal Roads (DGCF) is responsible for upgrading roads and building new infrastructure, while the Directorate General of Road Maintenance (DGCC) is in charge of maintaining the road network. The DGCC is in the process of transforming its role from an operating agency to more of a policymaking and monitoring agency. The DGCC has commenced a program which, if carried out fully, would result in major changes in maintenance contracting, decentralization of functions, and decentralization of highways and roads. In 1996 a national bid was launched to contract out routine maintenance services. Multiyear maintenance contracts were subsequently signed, covering 20,000 km (88 percent of the primary road network).

However, Mexico does not yet have an adequate regulatory system to address issues pertaining to private concessions in the road subsector. Regulatory risk adds to the cost of capital and can compromise the viability of private projects. Regulatory capacity will therefore need to be developed before privatization can begin anew.

Performance of road infrastructure has been disappointing. Over 45 percent of the road network remains in poor condition, as opposed to only 20 percent in Brazil. Maintenance and improvement of main federal corridors lags behind demand, and many federal roads go directly through central cities, thereby increasing congestion and delays. Bypasses need to be built to improve traffic flows, especially for long-haul and trade-related traffic. Road access to ports and border crossings is inadequate and bridge capacity into the United States needs to be expanded. The interregional network is incomplete, while the secondary and rural road network still has many gaps and is often of poor quality. Since the 1980s the only significant additions to the network have been through the toll road program of some 6,500 km.

The private sector experience with the toll road program of the early 1990s has been the major factor in shaping private perspectives on Mexican transport infrastructure investments. The scope and speed of the program, along with its emphasis on domestic construction companies and domestic banks, resulted in extreme financial problems and restructuring of all but 3 of the 27 concessions. Because the initiative was so vast, a majority of banks and the most important construction companies were involved. Lessons from that experience underline the importance of high-quality forecasts and analysis, with independent verification; the need for flexibility in project and concession designs specified by SCT; and the need for faster government action at project inception.

Regulatory risk after the debacle is perceived to be quite high, primarily because of the government's inability to deliver on guarantees or contractually obligated adjustments due to political constraints. Perverse incentive effects are seen in the fact that the highest risk concessionsreceived the best terms in the restructuring, and in the differential treatment of domestic and foreign creditors. In addition, substantial uncertainty remains about regulatory structure and conduct. SCT has not yet shifted its role from operator to regulator, and has applied regulations and laws inconsistently. The internal evolution and reorganization of SCT has lagged developments in the private sector, and there is an impression that the existing regulatory system has been strongly biased toward incumbent operators and may thus be prone to regulatory capture.

Implications for future toll roads

In order to improve the functioning of the road subsector with optimal participation by the private sector:

- Toll roads need to focus on specific "niche" areas. Investments such as the expansion of existing, congested facilities (adding lanes to major arterial roads) that help reduce bottlenecks, as well as targeted bridge investments that serve densely traveled trade corridors are most amenable to tolling. These projects have well-established traffic patterns and tolling histories, so that demand risk is reduced substantially. In addition, they are likely to have substantial political support.
- The government needs to rethink pending toll road concession design, breaking concessions into smaller components and considering delaying some projects. Restructuring the program into smaller pieces would help reduce the financial burden, generate business for more companies, and make sure that the roads with the highest returns are done first.
- Alternative bidding and award mechanisms need to be developed, as well as identifying those segments of the road network where a mix of public and private participation would be possible. Such projects might be bid on the basis of a minimum government equity contribution. As more experience is gained with uneconomic concessions, projects using shadow tolls could be attempted. This would allow the government contribution to be made over time, and could help restore the credibility of public commitments.

Airports and Airlines

AIRPORTS. Most of Mexico's 83 civil airports are operated by *Aeropuertos y Servicios Auxiliares* (ASA), a public corporation created in 1965. Public investment has lagged growth in airport activity due to the country's fiscal constraints. To increase investment and ease its fiscal burden, in 1995 the government decided to offer concessions to the private sector for the operation of the major airports.

The Airports Law that authorized private participation was enacted in December 1995 and the guidelines for private investment were published in February 1998. The process involves the creation of corporate entities in which the government retains majority interest. Each of these will be granted a 50-year concession to operate a specific airport. Concessionaire entities will be grouped under a controlling entity, which will own the shares of capital stock of the concessionaire entities.

Airport activity, while still concentrated in the six major cities, is beginning to decentralize with the expansion of trade and the opening of more international gateways. Since regional packages are more attractive in a decentralized system, this has shaped the design and evolution of the airport concession program.

The airport privatization program was launched in early 1998 with the identification of 35 airports (which handle 97 percent of total passenger movement in the country) to be included in four concession packages. The first package awarded was to the Southeastern Group, which was seen as the most financially attractive since Cancun has a new airport with little investment required and with strong and growing demand. All concession packages are subject to a form of price-cap tariff regulation, with adjustments for inflation.

There is a need to swiftly conclude airport restructuring. This requires decisions on whether concession contracts will be overseen by SCT or by a (proposed) Transport Regulatory Commission; on the timing and procedures for the sale of the 85 percent of airport shares retained by the government; on whether the eventual flotation would enable a private entity to control a majority of the Mexican airport system; and on whether the 15 percent initial stake allowed provides an adequate incentive for performance.

In addition, there is inbuilt uncertainty regarding the process since creating airport packages of diverse characteristics within each group was intended to force an integrated management and implicit cross-subsidization. Although this can be positive from the point of view of risk diversification, private investors probably have a different idea of the business potential of each airport and might have preferred a different ordering. In addition, it is unclear how the government will enforce the cross-subsidies inherent in the packages. It is thus too early to evaluate the results of the airport concessioning process.

AIRLINES. Regulation of civil aviation is the responsibility of SCT, through the *Dirección General de Aeronáutica Civil* (DGAC), which is in charge of authorizing airlines to operate; it is also responsible for technical regulation and safety standards.

Performance of the sector has been improving andinternational issues increasingly affect the operating environment of the domestic industry. Neither Mexicana nor Aeromexico (the main Mexican airlines), operate under focused hub-and-spoke strategies, in which banks of flights connect within short time periods. The advent of an expanded open skies agreement with the United States beginning in 1999 has opened up many new routes as code-sharing gateways, opportunities for which have been quickly seized by U.S. carriers. There is now strong competition from U.S. airlines, which have held a market share of between 55 and 60 percent of international service in recent years. Domestic passengers represent about 68 percent of total passengers carried by Mexican airlines. Cargo operations have grown at a compound annual rate of 14 percent, but Mexican airlines have steadily lost share in this important market, from 59 percent in 1991 to 44 percent in 1997.

After an unsuccessful attempt at deregulation in the early 1990s, the civil aviation sector is currently state-dominated. Through CINTRA, a holding company, the Mexican government holds the majority stake in Aeromexico and Mexicana, Aeromexpress (the largest cargo carrier), the main regional airlines, and associated service providers. CINTRA's holdings (Aeromexico and Mexicana) combined control about 70 percent of the domestic market.

Mexico faces a difficult set of policy options in civil aviation. Huge capital needs, a more competitive international environment, and restrictions on foreign ownership will put severe pressure on Mexican airlines between 2000 and 2005. One alternative is to open up the sector to foreign investment, which is currently restricted to 25 percent of equity. This would help access capital, but is politically difficult to implement. Maintaining the status quo under a single holding company makes raising capital easier than divestiture, but creates potential problems from the viewpoint of competition policy. CFC, the national competition agency, has demanded that CINTRA be broken up to protect consumers and prevent anti-competitive practices. However, SCT has been reluctant to restructure CINTRA since the civil aviation sector is now profitable and competitive for the first time in years.

The decision on forced divestment is important for two reasons. First, it is an important indicator of the independence and power of the competition agency vis-à-vis SCT and powerful private interests. As such, it has implications for competition policy regarding access rules, predation, and ownership structures. Second, the number and financial strength of domestic carriers has a large impact on the financial health of the major airports and the associated packages of concessions. Faced with fleet renewal programs and other investment needs, a swift resolution of the CFC–SCT conflict over CINTRA is important for the volume and type of airline traffic in Mexico. As of October 2000, a decision to split and privatize CINTRA into two operating companies has been made.

Thus, the key issues in the sector from the perspective of private operators are competition policy, the airport concession process, and uncertainty over the ownership structure of airports in the longer term, deriving from the timing and procedures for the sale of the shares that continue in public hands.

Ports

The modernization and reform of Mexican ports started in 1993 with a new Ports Law and the dismantling of the public port agency *Puertos Mexicanos*. The reform consisted of:

- Decentralization, which resulted in the creation of independent Port Administrations (*Administraciones Portuarias Integrales,* APIs) at each port or group of small ports. These are autonomous, self-financing, publicly owned companies that act as landlords.
- Privatization (including the participation of foreign investors) of the operation of terminals and other facilities. Eventually even the administration of the ports is to be privatized.
- Competition between ports and between operators within ports. This was achieved by the liberalization of tariffs and the elimination of cross-subsidies and barriers to entry. Another reform was the liberalization of the labor market, so that wages and work conditions are determined by market forces and firm-level bargaining, rather than collective bargaining.

The concessioning process consisted of three phases: (a) concessions granted by the federal government to the APIs (*Títulos de concesión*); (b) concession contracts signed between APIs and private operators for the use of port assets and the provision of services (*Contratos de cesión parcial*); and (c) privatization of APIs. The federal government, through SCT, acts as port authority, and it is the agency that grants all concessions, licenses, and authorizations.

Between 1990 and 1998, total movement of cargo by Mexican ports increased by 40.5 percent (with a 28 percent rise occurring after the 1995 reform of the port system), passenger traffic doubled, and container traffic tripled, although containerization at 36 percent is still low by international standards. Private participation has induced significant changes in the port industry in terms of investments in infrastructure and improvements in quality of service and tariffs. Total investment in equipment and new terminals was around MXP$6 billion between 1995 and 1998, 62 percent of which was private investment. The number of port workers employed by the public sector has declined, but total port employment by private firms is rising due to an increase in the activity of ports.

Tariffs and prices are now set freely by market forces. Port tariffs, charged by APIs to ships for the use of common infrastructure, are based on price caps derived from port-specific long-run marginal costs. The system as a whole does not require any external subsidy for efficient operation, and the cross-subsidies between ports have been eliminated. The system promotes competition among ports, since APIs can lower their port tariffs to try to attract traffic. The new pricing mechanism has achieved substantial tariff reductions, so that handling costs for containers are now equal to or even lower than at U.S. ports that compete with Mexican ports, such as Los Angeles and Houston.

The net fiscal impact of port reform for the federal government has been highly positive. Since 1995, the system has not only covered its operating costs, but has also contributed to the treasury from the compensation payments received from the APIs for the concession of port assets, and from the taxes that both the APIs and the private concessionaires pay to the government.

Overall, the port concessions seem to be working well, with improved efficiency and financial performance. Emerging issues involve access, pricing of access, and intermodal coordination. Areas for action are:

(1) Reduction of waiting times. While handling and servicing time has been reduced as a consequence of investment in modern equipment and a rise in labor productivity, paperwork and administrative time remain high due to repeated, lengthy, uncoordinated administrative controls on ships and cargo. Recognizing this, the port regulator is considering the privatization of the service of cargo inspection, and the introduction of a degree of automation to reduce ship waiting times and the risk of cargo losses.

(2) Ensuring that regulated tariffs reflect the gains from competition. Using yardstick competition would enable port regulators to avoid micromanaging tariffs in the sector and ensure that tariff revisions reflect potential efficiency gains—but this requires greater capacity than currently exists on the part of the regulator.

Railways

Railroad privatization, starting in 1996, involved the geographical separation of the assets and operations of FNM (the state-owned railroad company controlled by SCT) to set up a number of route-based companies according to preexisting regional divisions, each of which was awarded a 50-year renewable concession title allowing it to operate, exploit, and, if required, build new lines. The second stage of the privatization process was the sale of the 80 percent of the shares of the concessionaire companies owned by the government through a public bidding process.

Concessionaires are free to set their own tariffs in recognition of the extensive competition from trucks and the potential for competition among concessions.[6] To counteract monopoly power over exclusive domains, and to promote effective competition among operators, concessions were designed to share common tracks around major urban and industrial areas (for example, Mexico City and Monterrey) and several ports (Tampico and Veracruz). For these cases, concession titles included detailed mandatory access and connecting rights between concessionaires, with prices to be bilaterally negotiated.

Mexico City's Terminal, *Terminal Ferroviaria Valle de México*, has been privately managed since April 1998. Each of the three main rail operators owns 25 percent of the shares (included in their auction packages), whereas the government retains the remaining 25 percent. For the medium term, the only major rail project in Mexico

---

6. Maximum prices are registered within the DGTTFM, which may intervene if no effective competition exists or if users complain. No subsidies (except for small public service obligations) or other guarantees are granted to overcome potential losses.

will be the Trans-Isthmus railroad in Tehuantepec, which will remain in public hands for possible future development.

The privatization process appears to have worked well, as indicated by the low number and level of disputes and complaints. While it is still too early to carry out a detailed assessment of the impact of PSP on the sector's overall performance, SCT data indicate that the new operators invested more than MXP$3 billion on maintenance of infrastructure and renewal of rolling stock during 1997–98, and it is estimated that another MXP$3.3 billion will have been spent during 1999. In 1998 the total volume of freight handled by the overall rail system in Mexico increased by 21.5 percent from 1997—a record 49,554 million ton-km. As a result of this traffic increase, most productivity and safety indicators have also improved.[7]

The one-shot fiscal impact during 1997-99 of the sale of the main and short lines amounted to more than US$2.3 billion (including savings in the government subsidy).

Remaining issues include the following:

(1) The need to swiftly conclude the process. This means concessioning the remaining short lines; deciding how best to support (through a subsidy from SCT/ SHCP) the provision of passenger train service to the few towns that lack a bus service, as well as commuter services in the Mexico City Metropolitan area; and ensuring that the financial position of the major railroads remains sound.

(2) Encouraging intramodal competition. A detailed scheme for defining access payments is urgently needed, especially as additional trackage and haulage rights are negotiated. A more flexible mechanism for the assignment of these rights wherever necessary is also needed. The slow development of competition among concessionaires is largely related to conflicts over access.

(3) Enhancing intermodal competition. The major obstacle to achieving competition between the rail and trucking industries is the lack of rail-port transfer facilities, particularly for international traffic. Better coordination among different bodies in the federal administration and the enforcement of trucking transport norms is also needed.

(4) Developing a regulatory body and capacity to supervise the transport sector, including the privatized railroad system.A final decision should be taken soon on the proposed regulatory body and its relationship with the SCT in order to limit the risk of regulatory capture that exists as long as regulation is kept within the SCT.

---

7. For example, TFM transit times have been reduced by 36 percent, accuracy is now about 80 percent, and cargo theft has been reduced 80 percent. FerroMex average speed has increased by 20 percent on several routes, and theft has been reduced by 50 percent. Volume at *Terminal Ferroviaria Valle de Mexico* increased by 15 percent between January–May 1999 as compared to the same period in 1998.

Multimodality and Logistics

While the transport system is many faceted, road transport has become the predominant mode in Mexico and for cross-border trade with the United States. Mexico is on its way toward an integration of its transport network—the ports, for example, have improved in turnover time and most performance indicators, including the transfer to trucks. (See Table 1 for a breakdown of Mexico's transport services in international trade.)

In 1995 existing legislation that had not had much success in promoting multimodality in the Mexican transport sector was pared down and improved. Multimodal agents providing integrated intermodal services are no longer regulated, because they are considered to be commissioned traders subject to commercial law. For multimodal terminals, a special permit (ensuring minimal quality) is the sole requirement for entry.

As of 1999, there were 17 multimodal port terminals, 26 railways terminals, and 2 dry ports in Mexico. In addition, 7 new permits for intermodal installations and 2 dry ports have been granted. The only serious problem faced in the door-to-door business is the difficulty of finding insurance coverage because premiums for local operators are high. International operators manage more easily, although they too cannot easily obtain coverage for lost or stolen cargo.

Freight transport (along with passenger transport) still faces the following problems: overlapping of institutional responsibilities between federal and state governments; high costs (due to road tolls, fuel prices, and high interest rates); cartelization; and lack of security.

Remaining issues in logistics integration are:

- Coordination among multimodal agents and authorities needs to be smoother.
- The gains achieved through port reform in terms of loading and downloading time are undone by long waiting times for truckers and trains in the interior. Thus, significant improvements in the logistic management of surface

Table 1. Modal Distribution of Transport Services for Mexico's International Trade

	Freight		Passengers	
	Total (mill. tons)	Percent	Total (mill.)	Percent
Roads	356.5	60.0	2,636.1	98.5
Rail	52.1	8.8	7.2	0.3
Maritime	185.4	31.2	4.7	0.1
Air	0.2	—	29.1	1.1
Total	594.2	100.0	2,677.1	100.0

Source: Primer Informe de Gobierno, 1996.

transport modes and, in particular, a greater user orientation among service providers, is required. A prerequisite for this is higher intramodal competition (within the trucking industry) and intermodal competition (between trucks and rail).

- Legislation and government action are urgently needed to support the development of brokerage markets for freight, and overarching insurance legislation across modes.
- The lack of security for freight movements needs to be addressed.
- The government needs to facilitate the use of and open access to essential facilities (particularly ports), the setting up of dry ports and distribution centers through public private partnerships (when necessary), and the granting of use of public spaces for this activity.

Recommendations

Past financial events have a large impact on the transport sector, since transport is a derived demand, closely linked to economic activity. Keeping in mind the experience of the 1980s and 1990s, the major institutional, regulatory, and policy needs to be addressed by the newly deregulated and partially privatized sectors are as follows.

Institutional

- Across all transport subsectors—roads, rail, airports, and ports—there is a need for greater support for supervision and regulation of the sector in light of the commitments made by the government to private operators, consumers, and taxpayers.
- The biggest challenge is the need for sectoral institutions, in particular the SCT, to adapt to its changing role from a builder, operator, and provider of services to a manager and promoter.
- An independent regulator for the sector needs to be established. Within the government, there is still no clear definition of the regulatory instruments to be made available and of the actual enforcement capacity that a regulator should have.
- It is important to coordinate reforms in a way that generates an integrated transport system. The enactment of a comprehensive insurance law on multimodality is vital.
- A new role for the government in providing financial support to the sector needs to be defined due to the financing difficulties of the postcrisis era.

Regulatory

Regulation and supervision are currently spread over too many entities. Hence the government's decision to move toward an integrated transport regulatory agency. However, major issues remain in the process of creating a new transport regulator, as described below.

- Ensuring sufficient autonomy. As currently proposed, the agency would not be politically autonomous, since it would be housed within the SCT. It would also lack financial autonomy, being financed from the budget rather than from an independent source.
- Clarifying the jurisdiction of the agency and the division of responsibilities between the agency and the competition authority.
- Ensuring an open and transparent regulatory process, by mandating and defining appropriate consulative processes and providing a public justification for agency actions.
- Ensuring that the regulator is able to obtain the necessary information to regulate the sector. There are currently legal restrictions on the use of information collected through the national Statistical Office and most of the cost-accounting data generated through the privatization process.
- Developing clear rules in terms of conflict resolution and for direct interaction with users.
- Deregulating freight transport in all states by leveraging state aid.

Policy

The Mexican crisis of 1995 has had major consequences for project finance for the country's transport infrastructure since it led to extreme uncertainty about traffic levels and revenue-generation capacity. Despite the recent upgrading of Mexico's sovereign rating to investment grade, the risk perceptions of the past have resulted in higher premiums for regulatory and political uncertainty, which are reflected in the cost of capital and the returns private investors seek. Since debt finance is more expensive and of shorter tenure the government faces increased demands to provide access to longer-term financing at concessional rates, through credible guarantees or through direct financial participation. Thus higher levels of equity are now required for projects.

The infrastructure needs in all sectors mean that public finances are insufficient to fund all such projects. Mexico therefore needs to develop new ways to facilitate private investment, to rethink the role of the government in the financing of transport projects, and to develop appropriate financing instruments. Options include:

- Expanding the legal ability of international investors to own majority stakes. This strategy places a premium on continued macroeconomic stability, since most transport revenues are peso-denominated.
- Developing a mix of public investment instruments, ranging from direct investment to guarantees, to stimulate private investment that otherwise would not be made. Rather than direct investment being a substitute for guarantees, it now replaces other sources of portfolio equity. Guarantees could be provided for project volumes or revenues, or for debt service to reduce borrowing costs. While guarantees are helpful in attracting debt capital on better terms, the experience in Mexico has been poor, so guarantees are likely to be extremely expensive in practice.

- Developing an infrastructure fund, perhaps in partnership with an international investment bank. The equity positions acquired by the Mexican government through restructuring companies or through direct investment could be transferred to the fund for subsequent offering to investors. In addition, the government could consider dedicating a portion of its transport revenues to such a fund, which would allow it to raise debt capital like a development bank. Subsequent loans could then be used to establish an earmarked revolving fund.
- Establishing a consortium of a high-quality insurance firm and multilateral institutions to develop insurance products that would be jointly offered. Premium payments could then be made by project sponsors or as part of canons paid to the government.
- Developing a privatized pension system. Over the long term, infrastructure investment will fit well into pension portfolios, fostering a longer maturity domestic capital market.

Poverty and Inequality

19

Reform of the Mexican Healthcare System

*This Chapter was written by James Cercone (Consultant) and
Jean-Jacques de St. Antoine, with the valuable input of
Patricio Marquez and Claudia Macias, and Carmen Hamann,
Thesis Consultores, and Dov Chernichovsky.*

I. Introduction

Each year in Mexico nearly 7.5 million life-years are lost unnecessarily due to a poorly functioning healthcare system. The ill health of the population places a heavy burden on the economy and on the healthcare system. By some estimates, the economic value of mortality among the working age population is over $13 billion annually, or approximately 5 percent of GDP.

By 2006, the burden will be considerably greater unless reforms produce significant improvements in the performance of healthcare system. At the end of the next Administration, as the population increases from just under 100 million to over 107 million, there will be an additional 8 million Mexicans requiring healthcare services. More important, the number of people over 65 years of age will increase by 25 percent to over 5.8 million. The total enrollment in the Mexican Social Security Institute (IMSS) is likely to have passed 60 million people, representing an increase of nearly 30 percent. At current mortality rates, the total number of life years lost is likely to increase by over 30 percent.

To address the emerging paradigm of lifestyle-related diseases, and to deal with existing problems, the healthcare system will have to change. The changes in organization and financing will become paramount to address the changing needs of the population, and to provide greater value-for-money in the health sector. Three factors will be key to achieving the quest for better outcomes in the sector.

- First, the ***challenge of achieving universal access*** need to be met. While important advances have been made to increase access to healthcare services, the challenge of the new century is to create a healthcare system based on universal access and shift the focus from merely providing the needed infrastructure to obtaining the desired outcomes for all.

- Second, the *fragmentation in the system* that underpins the problems of access and efficiency will have to be addressed within each of the public institutions. Duplication among providers drains valuable resources needed to attack the country's health problems, and is a barrier to improving efficiency, equity, and quality.
- Third, the *role of the private sector* will have to be addressed to capture the potential benefits that private providers can offer, while mitigating the risks associated with an unregulated or under-regulated private sector. In other words, health system planners and politicians should look beyond the simple dichotomy of public or private sector to develop stronger public–private healthcare partnerships.

This policy note is the continuation of several years of dialogue between the World Bank and the government of Mexico on health reforms aimed at improving health system performance. The dialogue was initiated around the need to improve access to health services by poor populations, to decentralize the system to improve efficiency and quality, and to provide a regulatory framework for the introduction of managed competition.

The objectives of this policy note are to analyze the challenges facing the Mexican health sector; to inform policymakers and stakeholders about the issues, relevant international experience and policy options; to stimulate discussion and a policy dialogue with policymakers; to promote consensus about the issues, policy and program options, and priorities; and to develop a comprehensive vision and strategy for further reform. While recognizing key health realities and medical issues, the orientation of this report is toward health system finance, organization, and management.

II. Background and Issues

Sector Overview

Mexico's many achievements in the health sector over the past several decades have led to significant improvements in the health status of the population, a broadening of access to basic services, and support of important public health measures. Rising prosperity has brought an increase in life expectancy, reductions in infant mortality, and a decline in the death rate. In 1940, life expectancy at birth was 41 years, in 1998 it was 73 years. Infant mortality has been reduced by over 75 percent, declining from 72 per 1,000 births in 1970 to 16.4 in 1997. Over the last decade, the mortality rate for children under age 5 fell by 37 percent, and mortality from pneumonia and diarrhea fell by more than 65 percent. Vaccine-preventable diseases have declined drastically, with no cases of polio or diphtheria reported since 1993. Between 1980 and 1997, maternal mortality rates were reduced by 45 percent.

Much of the progress in addressing the most pressing health needs of the population has come from the use of centralized institutions and of vertical programs to control infectious diseases and to increase prevention and education. The effectiveness of these programs, and the institutions managing them, is shown in the dramatic decline in infectious disease death rates and acute respiratory infections in children under age 5. Between 1980 and 1997, the infectious disease mortality rate declined from 279 per 100,000 children under age 5 to 33.3, while mortality from acute respiratory disease declined from 235 per 100,000 children under age 5 to 67.

Like in many other middle-income countries, however, the epidemiological profile is changing. Chronic disease and injuries represent the main causes of death and disability, and the country is facing emerging problems such as AIDS and the health effects of environmental pollution. The traditional command-and-control health systems that were so effective at reducing infectious diseases are demonstrating signs of breaking down under the strain of the new epidemiological profile. Indications of this are reflected in the slowdown since 1991 in reductions of general mortality, under-5 mortality, and maternal mortality rates.

In addition to the changing demographic and epidemiological profiles, there are considerable differences in equity of access and outcomes between the northern and southern states, between urban and rural areas, and among social classes. A 1994 study by FUNSALUD, and more recent (1997) SSA data, show just how wide the health gap is:

- Mortality rates from infectious diseases are over three times the national average in Chiapas and in Oaxaca, 2.5 times the national average.
- Infant mortality is twice as high in the five poorest states as in the five richest states.
- Adult mortality in Oaxaca is comparable to that of India, while in Nuevo León it is comparable to that of several European countries.
- The burden of disease is greater in rural areas (6.8 million DALYs[1]) than in urban centers (6.2 million DALYs)—the difference attributable primarily to premature death—even though the population in urban areas is significantly greater than the rural population.
- The children of women living in extreme poverty are 2.5 times more likely to die before the age of 1 than the children of women who are not poor.

The organization and financing of the system will have to evolve to meet these challenges and to provide incentives for financiers and providers to restructure.

---

1. DALY stands for disability-adjusted life year, a measure that combines healthy life years lost because of premature mortality with those lost as a result of disability.

Organization of Healthcare

The major pillar of Mexico's healthcare system is a mandatory social insurance program funded out of contributions from formal sector employees, employers, and government. The main institutions are IMSS and ISSSTE, but PEMEX, the Federal District government, the police, the metro, and the armed forces also have their own systems. In total, social insurance organizations cover just over half of the population. The remainder of the population (called the "open population") receives healthcare services primarily from SSA (and to a small extent by IMSS-Solidaridad). Figure 1 illustrates how the Mexican healthcare system is organized. It shows how the different consumer groups are theoretically distributed among the vertically integrated organizations—each institution assuming responsibility for a specific population, with a specific financing source. As later sections of this paper will show, the vertically integrated nature of the system leads to high levels of duplication among providers, excess capacity, and an inefficient and inequitable distribution of resources.

In practice, however, consumers do not follow the vertically integrated rules of the system (see Figure 2). Several studies show that as many as 25 percent of the insured population of the social security institutes use the private sector when seeking care. In addition, a large percentage of the population has double insurance: social security insurance through their employer and private insurance paid out-of-pocket. On the provider side, while many people have some type of social insurance coverage, or access to SSA services, they prefer private providers.

The predominant role of private providers, financed by out-of-pocket payments, and the overlap between the social insurance institutes and SSA, is at the heart of the problems in the sector. Acknowledging and addressing these issues should be the cornerstone of future reforms.

Financing

Over the past 10 years the Mexican government has made steady progress in increasing health and social security expenditures. Between 1995 and 1999 real federal expenditures to all public institutions providing health services increased by 24 percent, despite reductions in spending in other sectors. Overall, however, public spending remains low. At just over 50 percent of total spending (2.8 percent of GDP), it is likely that public financing will have to increase to meet the demands of a universal healthcare system. Mexico's public spending is less than half of the average spending in European countries that have achieved universal access through national healthcare systems, including most European OECD countries, and Latin American countries such as Costa Rica (Figure 3). In Costa Rica, 80 percent of all healthcare spending—6.5 percent of GDP—comes from the public purse.

Notwithstanding the comparisons with other countries, the resources in the system—public and private—are large and growing. Each year between US$15 billion and US$18 billion is channeled to the sector. Roughly half, US$8 billion, goes to pri-

Figure 1. Overview of the Mexican Healthcare System—The Theory

Mexican Health Care System

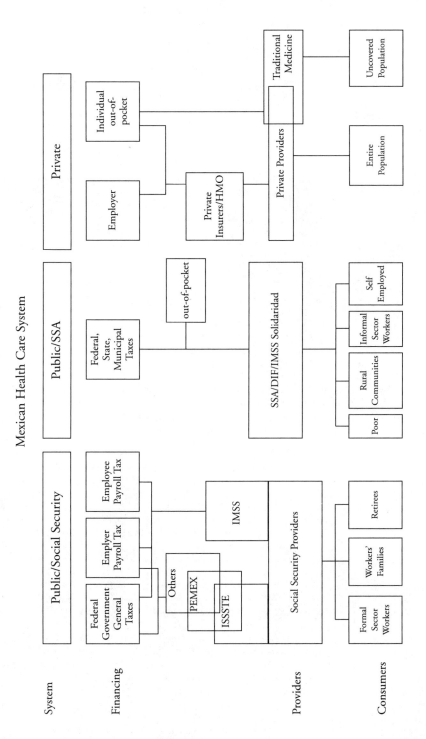

**Figure 2. Schematic View of the Overlapping Functions in the System—
The Practice**

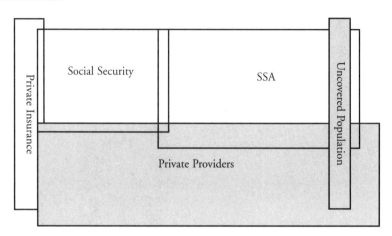

Note: Adapted from Gomez-Dantes (1999). "Prospects of the Mexican Healthcare Reform."
Source: Author's interpretation of original figure by Cerda et al, 1999.

vate sector providers. To develop sustainable economic growth, improve the equitable distribution of resources, and build human capital, it is imperative to obtain the maximum level of health and satisfaction with the resources available (value-for-money).

The distribution of resources and the results obtained vary considerably across institutions and states. While national per capita spending averages between US$180 and US$225, there is considerable variation among public agencies.[2] PEMEX, with a highly sophisticated network of providers, leads all public spending, with a 1999 estimated average spending per insured of over US$500. At the other end of the spectrum, per capita spending for the open population—those who work as part of the informal economy and the unemployed and indigent—varied between US$19 and US$28 per capita. It is also worth noting that those states which are poorest and which have the highest burden of disease receive considerably fewer resources per capita than the national average, thus exacerbating the overall inequity in the system.

For example, in 1995 the northern state of Coahuila spent US$60 of public money per capita on healthcare, while the southern state of Oaxaca spent US$24. In 1995, more than three-quarters of the 2.2 million population of Coahuila were

---

2. There is virtually no consolidated accounting of healthcare expenditures in Mexico and thus total expenditure figures vary among sources. Valiant efforts by FUNSALUD and the government to create national healthcare accounts in 1995 provided insight to the financing of the system; unfortunately, these efforts have not been sustained and 1996 is the latest year of consolidated spending data.

Figure 3. Total Health Expenditure 1998, as percent GDP

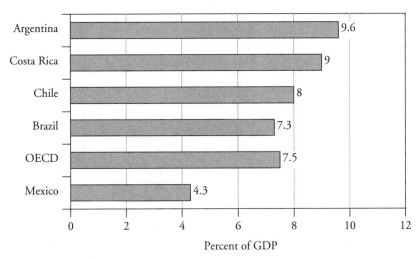

Source: World Bank 2000 WDI Timeseries.

members of the social security system, but less than one-quarter of the 3.4 million residents of Oaxaca were members. Finally, despite the growth of rural facilities, distant parts of the country continue to be underserved compared with national averages. In 1998, Mexico City had 226 hospital beds per 100,000 people, the northern states of Nuevo León and Baja California Sur each had just over 100, while the southern states of Chiapas and Oaxaca each had just 44 hospital beds (Whitaker 1999).

In the future, the tendency will be for overall healthcare costs to increase but this will not resolve the problems of inequity or inefficiency in the system. First, the population is aging and the proportion of the working population aged 16 to 55 and over is increasing. This age group grew from 18 million in 1960 to 59 million in 1998. Moreover, while currently only 4 percent of the population are aged 65 and over, this cohort is growing at an annual rate of 4 percent, compared with the growth rate of 1.5 percent of the total population. Second, the epidemiological profile of the population is shifting to resemble that of developed countries where chronic conditions prevail. In short, it is inevitable that demand for healthcare will rise. Already, the tendency of higher-cost health problems is surfacing. From 1987 to 1997, mortality from cardiovascular problems increased by 62.5 percent. Deaths due to cancer rose from 1 percent of total mortality in 1940 to 11 percent in 1995, and the proportion of deaths due to injury rose from 5 percent to 15 percent during the same period (Whitaker 1999). Third, as the health sector evolves, more sophisticated equipment (such as MRI, CAT scans, and data telecommunications systems) is being routinely used—but at higher cost.

Finally, the population is becoming increasingly informed about health and is demanding better medical services from both public and private providers. As in most countries, it can be expected that as GDP per capita increases, healthcare spending will rise disproportionately. If the public sector does not improve efficiency and quality with the existing financial resources, the private sector will surely play an increasingly important role in the provision of healthcare, through out-of-pocket spending and more accessible insurance programs.

The Private Sector

The private sector in Mexico is also a fragmented and inefficient financier and provider of healthcare. Each year, nearly US$8 billion to US$10 billion is spent on private healthcare. While some of this money is allocated to private insurance and the emerging prepaid managed care organizations (MCOs), most of private healthcare expenditure is accounted for by out-of-pocket payments by individual patients. Between 1995 and 1999, the number of people covered by private insurance has grown by nearly 60 percent. Traditionally, most private healthcare was financed out-of-pocket; however, there is a clear trend to private insurance and managed care plans. The shift to private care underscores the results of a 1994 household survey that shows that many Mexicans, insured and uninsured, seem to prefer private providers over public providers. Respondents to the survey claim that 33 percent of all visits within the last two days were provided by private providers (Figure 4). While private providers may offer better access to healthcare for the population, there is no evidence that the quality is better, or that the providers are more efficient, than the public sec-

Figure 4. Sources of Care (percent)

Provider	1994
Private providers	32.9
IMSS	31.5
SSA	18.4
ISSSTE	6.4
IMSS-Solidaridad	2.8
Others	8.0

Source: FUNSALUD, 1994.

tor. In fact, over 82 percent of all private hospitals have fewer than 10 beds, and only 3 percent have more than 50 beds. With such a relatively small size, and little integration among providers, it is unlikely that private providers can currently take advantage of economies of scale or scope.

An estimated 3.5 million people are covered by some type of private insurance. Those who are insured privately can be divided into two groups: employees within industries which operate under the IMSS' *reversión de cuotas* scheme (described later); and those already covered compulsorily by social security, but who top up their medical benefits with private insurance purchased either individually or through their employers. During the 1980s, insurers began to offer a new product, *gastos médicos mayores* (GMM), which is a classic indemnity policy covering households for hospital treatment only. By 1999 some 2.5 million Mexicans had bought GMM policies. A new model has recently emerged, locally known as *salud integral*, Mexico's own version MCOs. Only a very small percentage of the population has joined in. Total enrollment is estimated at just over 1 million, but it is one of healthcare's fastest-growing areas.

Meeting many of the challenges to developing a universal, national healthcare system will depend on the ability of policymakers to address changes in organization and financing. While there are many micro changes that need to occur for the system to improve value-for-money, there are five overarching issues that need to be overcome. They are: (a) fragmentation and duplication in the system's organizational and financing arrangements; (b) persistent inequality in access and outcomes; (c) increasing dissatisfaction with quality; (d) inefficiency of resource allocation and utilization; and (e) problems in financing the system. The following section analyzes these issues.

Pending Issues

Despite the considerable advances made during the past decade, there is an unfinished agenda in Mexican healthcare system reform. Progress to date has focused on SSA and IMSS, with limited extension of reforms to the other public institutions. Despite early results, reforms still need to be consolidated in these two institutions. The following section analyzes the main issues in the system mainly in terms of overall fragmentation, and outlines how the weaknesses in organization and management directly impact equity, quality, and efficiency.

OVERALL FRAGMENTATION OF THE SYSTEM. The Mexican healthcare system is characterized by a multiplicity of public institutions (several social security institutes, SSA, state institutions, the Federal District, and parastatal regimes) and the private sector operating largely in parallel with very little coordination. While there is some consensus on a vision of what the desired system should look like 10 years from now, it is not clear how the fragmentation can be overcome. To a large extent, the government continues, through individual public institutions, to both finance and operate the system, using its own facilities and physicians. This is not compatible with the public finance principles that the role of government is not to provide, or finance, all clinical care, but to ensure that the health sector as a whole is structured to do so. Under this model this usually means that the government's role is to identify areas of market and public failure (and their consequences) within the health sector, and to find appropriate ways to address them. SSA, which should have the overall role of setting national health policy, governing and regulating the sector to ensure coherence, remains institutionally weak and is but one player among others.

The private sector, which would want to play a larger role, has received mixed signals about how the system will evolve. Over the past few years, SHCP, as a key financier of the sector, has made some attempts to introduce reforms and to improve governance; however, more specific steps need to be taken. The fact that almost no single source exists to provide updated information on healthcare spending is indicative of the fragmentation in the system. The creation of the National Health Council (described later) in 1995 was an attempt at better coordination. However, none of these efforts has resulted in a clear overall leadership. The duplication of institutions and overlapping roles have resulted in significant distortions, reflected by lingering problems of access and equity, dissatisfaction of the population with the quality of services, and significant inefficiencies. Financing schemes exacerbate these problems, and provider payments do not give the right incentives to those who deliver healthcare at the facility level. (See Box 1 for a study of how the state of Coahuila is reducing duplication of services.)

Box 1. Reducing Duplication of Services: Reforms and Innovations in Coahuila

Coahuila's state government has realized that the lack of coordination among public institutions is a major determinant of inefficiency and poor outcomes in terms of health status. To address this problem, in 1998 the local government encouraged the development of a formal agreement to further the coordination among public institutions. This agreement, called the "*Convenio de Coordinación Interinstitucional,*" formalized various cooperation commitments among IMSS, ISSSTE, and SSyDC, dating from 1995.

Some of the measures included in this agreement are: IMSS is allowed to use the external consultation area of the SSyDC General Hospital in Ciudad Acuña during the afternoons; SSyDC and IMSS services complement each other in the municipalities of Allende and Cuatrociénegas; and an analogous arrangement is in force between ISSSTE and SSyDC for the use of facilities in the municipalities of Allende, Morelos, Nava, Piedras Negras, and Viesca.

Aside from the activities of healthcare institutions, 17 municipalities have formed the *Red de Municipio Saludable* to coordinate the implementation of sanitation projects to reduce diseases such as cholera and dengue. Dengue-control activities have been particularly effective in the central and coal-producing regions of the state. In 1998, cholera cases fell to just eight, from 210 in 1997.

Coahuila's *Convenio* is a good start for reducing duplicate coverage, and could well become a point of departure for more complex arrangements, or even for leasing arrangements between public institutions.

CONTINUING INEQUITY. Inequity in access to healthcare services remains a major issue in Mexico as demonstrated below:

(i)   Despite the constitutional universal right to healthcare, *roughly 500,000 people remain without access to healthcare services.* The 10 million Mexicans that lacked access to health care at the beginning of the current administration, plus around 7.6 million born between 1995 and 2000 have been covered with basic health care services. The PAC (Programa de Ampliación de Cobertura) and the PROGRESA (Programa de Educación, Salud y Alimentación) programs have been key in obtaining this achievement. The

500,000 people that remain without access, live in scattered and very small poor rural communities, sometimes with difficult access, and therefore the cost of providing them services under a traditional scheme will be higher than the present average cost.

(ii) *There is a significant difference in spending per capita between different institutions.* PEMEX is by far the largest spender per capita (over US$500 per capita in 1999), whereas the total spent on the open population (those who work as part of the informal economy, such as street vendors and subsistence farmers, or who are unemployed, and have their healthcare paid out of general taxes) varied between only about US$19 and US$28 per capita.

(iii) *There is a significant disparity in spending across geographical regions,* because the open population tends to live in the south, while workers in the formal economy are to be found mostly in the north. Recent efforts by SSA and IMSS to allocate resources according to population will address the problems of inequity only if specific policies are formulated to make the transition to a more equitable financing system, where funds are allocated as a function of health needs rather than the supply of health services.

(iv) Despite the growth in rural facilities, *remote areas of the country continue to be underserved* compared with national averages. In 1998, in the southern states of Chiapas, Hidalgo, and Oaxaca, there was one physician for roughly every 1,150 people, while the northern states had one physician for every 625 people. Differences within states are even more severe. In Chiapas, for example, the five municipalities with the lowest levels of marginality, that is, with better standards of living, had one physician for every 557 inhabitants, whereas municipalities with indigenous populations had one physician for every 3,246 people (Frenk 1998).

(v) Even in existing facilities, *the lack of services in public clinics forces many people to make out-of-pocket payments to obtain healthcare, which in some cases causes considerable hardship.* The 1994 National Health Survey points out that among those with a serious health problem in the past 15 days, 52 percent did not seek care due to financial constraints. The effect on equity and outcomes of this barrier is reflected in higher mortality and morbidity rates among low-income populations.

(vi) The above disparities are associated with *vast differences in health outcomes among regions,* and between urban and rural areas. For example, life expectancy stands at 55 years in rural areas compared to 71 years in urban areas. Rural and urban slum areas exhibit much higher mortality and morbidity rates than non-slum urban areas. The richer northern states have substantially better health indicators than the poorer southern states; for example, infant mortality ranges from under 20 per 1,000 in the northern states to more than 50 per 1,000 in the southern states. Generally speaking, the wealthier segments of Mexico's population have health indicators similar to those found in OECD countries, while poorer segments have indicators closer to those of low-income countries. The data thus suggest that raising the health status of the population in outlying areas has the highest potential to improve the overall health status of the Mexican population.

SATISFACTION AND QUALITY REMAIN A PROBLEM. Despite the significant improvements in medical access and technology, Mexicans crave more and better medicine and are becoming steadily more demanding and critical. Since each of the institutions providing care operates as vertically integrated monopolies, there are few incentives to improve quality and responsiveness to consumers. These problems are borne out in poor clinical quality and increasing dissatisfaction. A study by Bobadilla (1998) demonstrated that a baby born in an SSA hospital was three times more likely to die in its first seven days of life than a baby of the same weight born in an IMSS hospital. While it is possible that the SSA-attended children are predisposed to higher levels of illness, it is clear that the overall quality of the two systems varies considerably with regard to obtaining satisfactory outcomes. Among the insured population of the social security systems, dissatisfaction with the quality of service has led many to seek healthcare outside the institution with which they are affiliated, so they are often "enrolled" in more than one system. This explains the relatively high levels of private spending among small segments of the population.

Dissatisfaction is shown through consumer behavior—turning to the private sector—and through indicators of dissatisfaction voiced by consumers: complaints and user satisfaction surveys. In 1999, the National Medical Arbitration Commission (CONAMED) received nearly 774 official complaints regarding the quality of care. While many of these complaints dealt with ISSSTE, dissatisfaction is common among public institutions. In this first year of operation (1996), CONAMED received 4,000 complaints. A major survey of Mexican public attitudes toward healthcare was carried out in 1994. Fifty-nine percent of Mexicans thought that the current system "has some positive aspects but requires fundamental change." Another 24 percent were less content and thought that "the system works so badly that it needs to be rebuilt completely." Eighty-three percent of the users of SSA services were dissatisfied. Their principal reasons were (a) poor service; (b) lack of resources such as drugs and well-trained personnel; (c) lack of access; and (d) high costs. In addition, the study revealed that quality issues were not limited to the lack of resources, personnel, and technical problems—40 percent of patients felt they were not treated adequately, 61 percent considered services too bureaucratic, and 8 percent did not receive medical treatment when needed.

The *Programa de Ampliación de Cobertura* (PAC) program has demonstrated that it is possible to improve the quality of services. Between 1996 and 1999, the number of users that consider the quality of care to be of "good" or "very good" quality increased from 50 percent to over 65 percent. In general, problems with quality are caused by a number of elements that distort incentives in the system. The main areas that limit quality are:

(i)   *The lack of motivation for doctors.* Paid on a salary basis, doctors have few incentives to work harder or to supply a service that is more satisfactory to patients. Doctors will often give patients drugs or refer them to expensive specialists to keep workloads low. Many public doctors seek additional work to complement public salaries. The number of doctors with more than one job rose from 25 percent in 1986 to 33 percent in 1993, and the percentage may be even higher in 1999. Even after efforts were made to improve work discipline in IMSS clinics and hospitals, the absenteeism rate was still over 22 percent in 1997, meaning that more than 20 percent of all staff is retained to cover potential absences among staff. Absenteeism provokes long waiting lists, dissatisfaction among patients, and problems with quality.

(ii) *A lack of basic production factors: drugs and obsolete equipment limit clinical quality.* Surveys carried out in 1996 by SSA showed that only 18 of the 36 essential drugs were available in surveyed urban and rural clinics. Basic antibiotics, antimalarials, and antituberculosis drugs were lacking in more than 50 percent of these units (Gomez-Dantes 1999). At the same time, a large proportion of IMSS equipment has not been replaced during the last 20 years. Some of it is not working and what works is often obsolete and inefficient. While 1999 surveys show that the availability of essential drugs has increased to 62 percent under the PAC, the lack of drugs to be used on an opportune basis continues to be a detriment to quality healthcare. Finally, there is a bias toward constructing new hospitals rather than replacing and modernizing existing equipment. In 1997, only 1.1 percent of IMSS expenditure went toward buying new equipment or upgrading medical facilities.

(iii) *The shortage of trained people to operate necessary equipment.* According to PAHO, 1998, Mexico had only 98 radiotherapists, or one per 418 cancer patients, compared to one per 274 patients in Argentina. In 1998 Mexico had 30 medical physicists; Brazil had 700. Medical physicists are of vital importance in the area of diagnostic imaging. They are responsible for assuring quality and assimilating new technologies into day-to-day hospital practice. Without their input, machines such as high-energy radiotherapy units and linear accelerators can cause harm to patients.

(iv) *The shortage of trained managers.* There is a vast shortage of trained managers both in the private and public sectors. The current changes in the sector provide more autonomy to local bodies (such as Medical Areas in IMSS), cause the separation of purchasing and provision and the introduction of new forms of provider payments, and introduce the need to master modern techniques of risk estimation, forecasting, financial management, negotiations, contracting, and changes of incentives to personnel. Most Mexican health professionals currently in management positions have received a purely medical training. They need to be retrained and new managers will have to be recruited to make the new healthcare model work.

THERE IS MUCH ROOM FOR EFFICIENCY TO IMPROVE. As costs of healthcare are rising around the world, policymakers are paying increasing attention to ways to improve the efficiency of healthcare systems. In Mexico, much can be done to improve the efficiency of the system.

(i)   *The lack of an effective primary healthcare system contributes to inefficiency and limited effectiveness.* Until recently, there was no functioning primary care system in the social insurance organizations (IMSS, ISSSTE, and others). While SSA has made important advances in strengthening its primary care system and ensuring access to a basic package of essential services, other public sector institutions remain highly dependent on specialists and hospital-based services. The lack of an appropriate gatekeeper function at the primary care level leads many individuals to seek care directly at specialized hospitals. IMSS' own internal studies document large-scale and unnecessary treatment for patients who could have been treated in cheaper primary care facilities. The financial consequences of this are significant.

(ii)   *The proportion of ambulatory surgery remains too small.* Even in the case when a patient has been officially referred to a higher-level facility, much of the surgery is carried out in large, capital-intensive hospitals, which carry high administrative costs and overheads, including expensive equipment. Many procedures (for example, cataract surgery and knee operations) can be performed in ambulatory setups at a fraction of the hospital cost. One private health company estimates that 65 percent of all hospital surgery carried out in Mexico could be performed at ambulatory clinics, where costs are on average one-third lower (Whitaker 1999).

(iii) *Equipment bought is not always the most cost-effective.* Equipment is usually bought in a centralized manner through a competitive tendering system. Close attention is paid to obtaining the lowest price regardless of the efficacy and maintenance costs of alternative equipment that might include higher-priced technologies, but reduce medium-term costs and improve outcomes. Centralized procedures provide economies of scale, but in a large country like Mexico the center may not always identify the needs of local facilities. Some recent decentralized purchasing by IMSS at the regional level has started to address this issue.

(iv)   *Equipment is not used efficiently.* Vertical segmentation among public sector institutions results in hospitals near each other procuring and installing the same equipment instead of sharing facilities. Even the most expensive machinery often stands idle after 3 P.M., the end of the official working day. This is different from the private sector. One company's MRI scanner works 24 hours a day, 365 days a year.

(v)   *Productivity of doctors remains low.* In 1998, the average number of consultations per primary doctor per day was 17.7. In contrast, an European primary doctor will see between 30 and 35 patients per day.

(vi) *Patients cannot select their family doctor.* The OECD countries have
      demonstrated that the ability to select one's family doctor introduces an
      element of competition in the system that allows health managers to sort
      out the better physicians and provide them with appropriate compensa-
      tion. When this choice was introduced in some countries, a surprisingly
      small number of people changed doctors (as low as 2 percent), but the fact
      that a change is possible puts pressure on physicians to provide better
      service. When combined with a compensation scheme that rewards doc-
      tors for improvements in productivity, quality, and patient satisfaction
      (expressed through the selection of the general practitioner), choice aligns
      incentives and potentially leads to better service. IMSS has proposed a
      plan to that effect, and a pilot program is currently under way in the state
      of Tlaxcala.
(vii) *Information management and analysis is poor.* The recent implementation of
      the SSA's management information network (REDSSA) for voice and data
      has allowed for the integration of 32 state agencies and 23 departments.
      The backbone has been established. The challenge still remains to manage
      the system to produce meaningful information at the appropriate level,
      and to incorporate the information into management decisions. There is
      also some evidence that many facilities lack the technological platform
      required. A 1996 PAHO survey showed that only 23 percent of Mexican
      hospitals had computers, and just under half had any sort of systematic
      method of keeping and using paper-based information.
(viii) *There is too much variation in the use of healthcare protocols.* This is a new
      area of analysis in the health sector that attempts to look at the different
      treatment methods used by doctors for the same pathologies, with a view
      to advising on the most cost-effective procedures and drugs. It also applies
      to the organization of care inside health facilities and the establishment of
      critical pathways to improve the flow of patients and make the organiza-
      tion of care more efficient. Both IMSS and SSA have started work in this
      area, where there is much to be gained for Mexico.

THE FINANCING SYSTEM PROVOKES ADDITIONAL INEFFICIENCIES. Four major problems exist. The first results from centralization of decisionmaking on financial matters, which leaves very little room for real management at the facility level. Second,
the vertical segmentation of financing creates duplication in the provider network
and leads to an inefficient allocation of resources. Third, the supply-based financing
system allocates resources for the financing of hospitals on the basis of global historical budgets and payment of a flat salary to doctors, rather than on a population
and output basis. The fourth problem is related to the excessive administrative costs
associated with the centralized system. While decentralization is addressing many of
these issues, more aggressive approaches are required to produce tangible results for
the population.

(i)   *A centralized financing system causes inefficiency.* Until recently, the central-ized financing of equipment and staff has not left much room for hospital managers to organize their care in the most productive way. Good managers could only do the best with what they had. They could not change the mix of inputs. In addition, the budgets have been mostly historical and resource-based (that is, how much equipment and staff a facility already had) rather than based on the size of the population and its epidemiologi-cal profile.

(ii)   Significant progress in this area has been achieved through the sharing of SSA's responsibilities with state governments. Currently, the federal govern-ment has two different ways of assigning funds to the states. The first is through Ramo 33, which includes earmarked funds for health, education, and social development. The second is through decentralized programmed expenditure, established through agreements between the federal and state governments, aiming at strengthening the states' health systems. Today all 32 states control all their health expenditure, while in 1995 they had control of only 21 percent of it. However, considerable effort still needs to be made to help states strengthen their planning and administrative capacities. Apart from SSA and IMSS, all other public institutions remain highly centralized.

(iii) *Vertical segmentation of financing creates an inefficient allocation of resources.* The institutionally fragmented system comprising multiple vertically inte-grated institutions results in considerable overlap in medical infrastructure, personnel, and resources. Duplication of facilities and excess capacity in urban areas is a long-standing problem in Mexico that results in inefficiency and waste. The Armed Forces and PEMEX have considerably more capac-ity than SSA and the Federal District. In 1996, for example, these two insti-tutions had 13.2 and 12.7 operating facilities per 100,000 people, respec-tively, while the SSA and the Federal District had only one-sixth the capacity at 2.6 and 1.9, respectively.

(iv)   *Current provider payment systems do not encourage efficiency.* On a historical basis, how much funding a hospital receives often bears no relationship to its output and needs, and the disparity can be great. IMSS performed an analysis on its hospitals and encountered a few cases where some were receiving as much as twice what they should have received when measured by production, while others received less than 50 percent of the required resources. To remedy this problem, IMSS has started a major program to introduce Diagnostic Related Groupings, or DRGs, to control for varia-tions in hospital activity and case severity. According to this method, the payment for a diagnosis or condition is determined in advance or prospec-tively, according to the expected cost of the condition, rather than retro-spectively, as with other methods. Where this method has been introduced around the world, it has proved to be a powerful incentive to better use financial resources and better manage health facilities.

(v) *The payment of doctors also needs to be reviewed.* On the one hand, the pay and motivation methods for doctors (as is the case for hospitals) needs to be compatible with cost-containment measures. On the other hand, they must provide an adequate remuneration to doctors for their work, and provide incentives to deliver good quality care that ensures client satisfaction. As is often the case, no payment method does it all, and innovative solutions need to be developed. While the Tlaxcala pilot project on choice of doctors is also experimenting with incentives, more work needs to be done to promote productivity at the hospital level and at the central level.

(vi) *Administrative costs may be too high.* One-quarter of all SSA expenses go to administration, a high proportion by international standards. The proportion of administrative costs at IMSS, ISSSTE and other social security insurers is also high at 15 percent. Any exercise to review costs, however, must be carefully conducted: areas with unnecessary bureaucracy and waste must be distinguished from areas that need to be strengthened, particularly management information systems and contracting, where additional investment will be required. Moreover, many of the reforms proposed, namely decentralization and purchasing, are likely to increase administrative expenditures. Trade-offs will have to be made to replace administrative functions that do not provide value added with these new functions that aim to increase efficiency and quality.

III. Health System Reforms to Date

Health sector reforms initiated in the 1980s and continued in the 1990s were aimed at expanding access to and improving the overall quality of healthcare. This was done primarily by: (a) decentralizing SSA services and bringing services to those with no access to care; (b) starting to reform IMSS by introducing major changes in its financing, decentralizing its services, and beginning to introduce incentives for efficiency and quality; (c) improving overall sector coordination; and (d) starting to design better healthcare regulation. Other public institutions, ISSSTE, PEMEX, and the armed forces, have so far been untouched by the reforms. The private sector, small but growing, has a wait-and-see attitude because it is not clear yet to what extent and how the government will promote greater participation of private firms in the sector.

Reforms in SSA

The main thrust of the reforms in SSA has been to promote decentralization and increased access. Starting in the early 1990s, SSA health services were gradually decentralized to the states and coverage extended. Through these changes, resources are transferred to the 32 Mexican states based on a capitated formula (which includes infant mortality and poverty indicators, replacing traditional criteria; i.e. historical budgets and negotiating abilities), and the states assume managerial responsibility for achieving minimum standards of care and increasing coverage. As a result of decentralization(especially under Ramo 33 which was started in 1998), the volume of resources that are managed autonomously by the states increased from 21 percent in 1995 to over 50 percent in 1996 and over 70 percent in 1999. The provision of health services to the open population in the 31 states and the Federal District is now the responsibility of their respective Health Services Secretariats, organized as autonomous public institutions with shared responsibilities with state governments and SSA. In addition to state governments new responsibilities, the Healthy Municipalities Program implemented in 1540 municipalities (around 50 percent of total in the country), involving more than 2 million volunteers integrated in 25,000 health communities, has placed health as a priority in the local government agendas.

As part of the efforts to modernize, the SSA created various areas of sectoral coordination and prevention and control of diseases for the formulation and policy conduction of public health programs. In this context, the implementation of new programs allowed the integration of actions and the strengthening of activities oriented to target populations, such as the Child Health, Reproductive Health, Elderly Health Care and Emergency and Disaster programs. The SSA also started a deep process of updating its legal framework, reforming the General Law of Health in the areas of public health and deregulation. As a result of these reforms, new regulations for health inputs, marketing and services were issued.

In addition to the efforts to decentralize and modernize, SSA has made important advances in extending coverage. Under the development of the PAC, SSA reduced the uncovered population from over 10 million (plus around 7.6 million born between 1995 and 2000) to 500,000. The program provides 13 basic services to populations that previously had no access. SSA officials estimate that the continuation of this program will eliminate the gap in coverage within less than two years. The services provided under this program, while a marked improvement over zero coverage, are limited and should be expanded. The process of *microregionalizacion operativa* started at the municipal and jurisdictional level has been fundamental in the health extension of services and represents an advancement towards the financial synergy between municipalities and health institutions and a start to define the spheres of institutional responsibility (SSA/IMSS-SOL). As a complement to these activities, SSA has also started to implement a continuous quality improvement program to improve the quality of services at lower cost, and to improve managerial development programs. Quality has improved dramatically in those areas where the PAC has been implemented. The challenge is to extend the successful programs to other levels of SSA.

At the SSA hospital level, for example, little progress has been made in improving efficiency, responsiveness to consumers, or quality. Future reforms will have to address the structural inefficiencies that exist among SSA hospitals and the duplication of services and coverage with other public sector institutions.

IMSS Reform

IMSS has introduced a number of reforms in the financing and organization of the system to improve efficiency, equity, and access. Starting with the new Social Security Law that was passed in 1995 and took effect in 1997, IMSS first addressed the recurrent deficits that existed in healthcare financing. The law improved its financing structure and introduced mechanisms to stimulate greater efficiency and better quality. Changes in the financing structure will increase the share of central government spending from under 0.5 percent of public spending to over 2.5 percent in 1997. In terms of IMSS revenues for healthcare, federal financing will increase from 4 percent of IMSS' annual budget to around 35 percent by the year 2010. The government contribution was increased to make IMSS less exposed to fluctuations in real wages and to give Mexicans a better incentive to enter the formal economy.

The so-called "opting-out" option (also named *reversión de cuotas* and *subrogación parcial*) allows people insured by IMSS to leave the healthcare system of the institution and join public or private MCOs, as alternative providers. This right was already held and exerted by the banking sector, a number of industrial companies in the Monterrey area, and the mining industry. These companies, whose employees account for 2 percent of IMSS membership, are permitted to retain on average 71.5 percent of the IMSS health-related premium. In general terms, the opting-out reform was expected to: (a) increase competition and client satisfaction, stimulating greater efficiency and higher quality of care; (b) reduce employment costs and stimulate formal employment; and (c) stimulate two underdeveloped industries, insurance and public and private healthcare provision. However, after the 1995 law, further extension of the opting-out option was not implemented because of the need to introduce regulations to minimize risk selection and protect quality of care, and to ensure a transition for capacity building by the private sector and, at the same time, restructuring and downsizing of inefficient public sector facilities.

On the organizational side, IMSS has started to establish a clear separation between financing and provision of services to promote greater transparency, and to increase autonomy and efficiency in the management of its health services. The rationale behind the separation of provision of services from financing is to enable resource allocation to be more responsive to the community's health needs, determined by its epidemiological and demographic characteristics, rather than its ability to pay. It also makes the system transparent, and creates an even playing field for all institutions involved. The IMSS decentralization process began through the programmed creation of 139 Medical Areas that would each receive a capitated budget adjusted for risk defined by age and sex. Contracts are entered into between IMSS and the delegations (about one per state, but more in the Federal District and some large states) and between the delegations and Medical Areas whereby the Medical Areas undertake to produce certain medical outputs using the funds they receive. It was estimated that about 50 Medical Areas would be in operation by December 1999.

Two other important IMSS reforms have already been described earlier: the introduction of new provider payment systems (DRGs) and the piloting of choice of doctors at the primary level.

Improved Coordination of the Sector

In 1995, a National Health Council (NHC) was established, which included participation of SHCP, SSA, IMSS, other social security institutions, and employers. The NHC is a useful forum for improving coordination of the various players in the sector, and to discuss reform measures and their implementation by public sector institutions. The NHC has been successful in coordinating decentralization in SSA. However, the scope of activities and intersectoral coordination could be increased to better share successful experiences among institutions and to promote a unified framework for reform.

Modernizing Healthcare Regulation

In 1999, a new framework was approved for improving the regulation of private sector managed care plans. This law is a critical first step in modernizing the existing regulation to clarify the rules of the game and ensure level competition in an expanding sector that regularly introduces new innovations in organization and financing. A special department has been established in the National Insurance Commission to issue regulations that balance the objective of protecting consumers in terms of quality of care, risk selection, and ensuring the solvency of providers, while minimizing the additional burden of regulation on private and public institutions.

Undoubtedly these are important reforms which will begin to address the sector issues analyzed earlier. However, more can be done by Mexico to further provide access to healthcare services by the poor, to improve the quality of care, and to contain costs.

IV. Setting the Framework for Reform: Lessons from Abroad

Many of these changes necessary in Mexico's healthcare system are similar to changes implemented in Europe and Latin America. This provides a valuable framework for reform in Mexico and can be integrated to take into account the specific institutional, organizational, and financing systems that form the basis of the Mexican healthcare system. Based on international experience, the two key areas of reform are the financing system and organizational structure.

Financing Options

Universal (and equitable) entitlement to care as stipulated by the 1993 Amendment to the Mexican Constitution implies raising funds on the basis of public finance principles using universal fundraising and allocation mechanisms. That is, funds to finance public entitlement are raised according to payers' means, and are allocated according to care recipients' needs.

While Mexico raises funds for healthcare according to public finance principles, using means-tested, mandatory contributions for medical care by individuals (including through general taxation) and employers, it lacks universality. Each major institution has it own financing system, as discussed in Section II of this Chapter. Future reforms in Mexico can build on the best and most relevant elements in the three general models for the financing of the system: (a) the Beveridge-type system; (b) the social insurance model; and (c) the U.S. system.

THE BEVERIDGE-TYPE SYSTEM. This national health system model is based on universal access to healthcare services through general revenue financing, or a combination of general revenues and social security contributions. Brazil, Canada, the Scandinavian countries, and the U.K. follow some variant of this model. Care is free at the point of service, except for some copayments. Private general practitioners (GPs) are contracted and hospitals are financed with global budgets. The system has the advantage of keeping costs down, but can result in waiting lists. Recent reforms in the U.K. have created a strong purchasing function among decentralized health authorities and budget-holding physician groups to obtain more value-for-money in the healthcare system. Contractual arrangements replace traditional budgetary transfers and *ex ante* regulation. The systems are increasingly focusing on purchasing outcomes, rather than inputs, and driving change through new financing mechanisms that introduce more competition into the system. In the case of Mexico, the institution that broadly follows this model is SSA (although its doctors are public employees).

THE SOCIAL INSURANCE MODEL. This model is followed by Germany and a number of European countries, and to a large extent by Argentina, Chile, and Uruguay. It is based on mandatory insurance contributions of employers and households that are paid directly to sickness funds. In the case of Mexico, IMSS and the other social security institutions are closest to this model. A variation of this model has emerged in Israel, the Netherlands, and Russia. It is based on earmarked mandatory contributions or taxes, but paid into a national or regional public social insurance pool which, in turn, pays to sickness funds and providers. The reforms focus on decentralizing insurance funds to subnational governments, creating competition between insurance funds that operate in parallel, and introducing many of the reform elements associated with the previously mentioned national healthcare system framework, including contracting and changes in provider reimbursement mechanisms.

THE U.S. SYSTEM. Until the 1970s, the U.S. system was largely based on private insurance and the payment of doctors and hospitals on a fee-for-service basis. By 1999, the system had achieved high levels in the quality of care, but about 30 percent of the population remained uninsured, and total expenditure reached 14 percent of GDP. To try to remedy the first problem, the government introduced Medicare (a government-financed program for the elderly) and Medicaid (for the poor). Over time, the pressure to reduce costs increased from private sector employers and led to the creation of a new model of healthcare organization and management, known as health maintenance organizations (HMOs, a version of MCOs). Over the last 20 years, HMOs have helped contain healthcare inflation, mostly through the introduction of capitated payments and "utilization reviews" that encourage providers to cut down on unnecessary care and improve their efficiency. One of the major results was a dramatic reduction in the average length of stay in hospitals. Evidence of good-risk selection by HMOs and complaints from patients about quality of care have led to the introduction of regulation to that effect. The part of the U.S. system that is most relevant to Mexico is Medicare and Medicaid, which are financed out of general revenue but contract their care from the private sector.

It is likely that some variation of the social insurance model currently implemented in, for example, Greece and the Netherlands, would allow Mexico to introduce changes in financing to guarantee universality and, simultaneously, keep the earmarked nature of the funds. This option calls for the establishment of a universal social insurance system in Mexico. This would entail the following institutional and regulatory changes:

- Establishment and operation of a new National Health Fund (NHF) that would, in the short-term, manage the funds of those who "opt into" the system and those who "opt out," and in the long term, become a public health financing institution for the entire system.
- Regulation of the linkage between the federal budget and IMSS health budget, which could be extended to other medical institutions and to a federal health financing system.
- Establishment of a capitation-based universal allocation mechanism.
- Increasing the role of the private sector as an organizer and provider of care and improving the regulations regarding the public-private mix.

The following section highlights some of the organizational changes that are under way and how they might apply to the implementation of health reform in Mexico.

A Converging Framework for Health System Organization

While there are many alternative organizational arrangements in the health sector, policymakers worldwide share many of the same perspectives and themes in the various reform programs because they are responses to common pressures and reflect the possibilities offered by modern management and information systems. A central element of the reforms in Europe, the United States, and other Latin American countries has been the redefinition of the responsibilities of management for the provision of healthcare services. Under prior organizational arrangements, social insurance systems often combined the responsibility for regulating, with a role as "passive" payers for health services and a direct responsibility for providing services. Reformed systems have created a separate role for assessing public need and demand for healthcare, defining and purchasing the healthcare services that can meet the population's demands, and monitoring the cost and quality of the services provided. At the same time, policymakers worldwide are promoting the introduction MCOs at the provider level to balance competitive choice among providers and to introduce controls and incentives to increase efficiency, quality, and consumer satisfaction.

Healthcare systems are increasingly adopting models where an MCO assumes responsibility and accountability for a population's health needs, organizing the provider network to optimize outcomes and control use. The managed care model is based on three important concepts: (a) the market paradigm of microeconomics that highlights the need to separate financing and provision to introduce "market" mechanisms, incorporating individual demands and consumer choice as one of the basic pillars of the healthcare system; (b) the relationship paradigm of systems theory that promotes horizontal system integration and improved coordination among providers. This element also includes the introduction of capitated reimbursement mechanisms and performance-based systems; and (c) the social welfare paradigm that strengthens the role of government to ensure provision of services according to the population's needs and public health interests, including the definition of basic packages of services and efforts to strengthen the regulatory role of Ministries of Health.

Since the early 1990s there has been a clear trend in many middle-income countries toward the creation of "internal markets" in the public sector. The reforms that have been designed in Latin America follow many of the provisions outlined in the reforms in New Zealand, the U.K., and the U.S. transition to HMOs. The reforms are accompanied by reforms of the provider reimbursement mechanisms, and reforms designed to create MCO, to improve the management of service delivery. This trend corresponds to a hybrid solution to the traditional dichotomy between pure public financing, administration, and delivery, and the model of privatization that attempts to introduce greater efficiencies by introducing private insurance on the financing side.

The private sector in Mexico is rapidly advancing toward the development of MCOs. Large insurance companies and smaller companies are introducing MCOs, or *Organizaciones de Administracion de Servicios de Salud (OASIS)*, which provide a solution to the challenge of separating functions and providing patient-focused care. In addition, the IMSS reforms aimed at creating vertically integrated organizations at the local level through the establishment of Medical Areas is a public sector response to the wave of MCOs. Future convergence toward the managed care model will be possible as SSA, ISSSTE, and other public institutions separate finance and purchasing from management of the delivery network. Section V of this Chapter highlights many of the individual steps that should be taken over the short- to medium-term to continue along this path.

V. Policy Recommendations

Mexico's population is large and growing. As its epidemiological profile changes to resemble that of developed countries where chronic conditions prevail, it is inevitable that demand and costs for healthcare will rise. The population is also becoming increasingly informed about health and demanding better medical services from both public and private healthcare providers. Therefore the intention is that in the next round of reform, medical services will be made increasingly available to the poor, the private sector will become a partner to extend coverage and increase the efficiency and quality of services, and the social security system will continue to pursue policies to increase efficiency, cost-effectiveness, and quality of healthcare services (Whitaker 1999). Health policy and the formulation of reform strategies for the new millenium will have to take these factors into account and develop a universal system based on existing institutions and organizational arrangements. This section sets forth the main elements of a reformed healthcare system and then outlines the main actions to be considered in the development of strategies to achieve better performance.

Elements of a Reformed System

The long-term view of the reformed system is based on the consolidation of existing initiatives and the introduction of further changes in the institutional organization of the sector, in the financing schemes used to insure the population and to reimburse providers, and in the organization, management, and delivery systems. To clearly set the path for future development, this section sets forth a schematic overview of the future operation of the Mexican healthcare system.

Healthcare systems worldwide are converging toward a common model based on several guiding principles and the specific cultural and systemic issues that make each system unique. While the specific strategies to implement the reforms will vary over time, there are a number of common principles that should be embraced to strengthen the healthcare system. They are:

- A clear *separation of financing and delivery*, as a key element in the introduction of competition, transparency, and accountability to the health system.
- *Decentralization of managerial responsibility and accountability* from the center to the level at which management can best respond to consumer needs.
- *Development of internal market mechanisms and changes in provider reimbursement* to ensure that resources follow the patients and results, rather than the other way around.

- Greater *accountability to patients* by providing choices to them in terms of providers, and the use of GPs as gatekeepers, or agents, to make purchasing decisions within the system.
- The pursuit of the *highest level of care quality and value with the resources available* in the system.
- The clear definition of a *core package of services* to be guaranteed by all institutions, public and private.
- *Gradual introduction of competition*, both among public providers of healthcare and between public and private providers.
- Assurance of a *high degree of flexibility* to allow for variations in local services in order to respond to specific local needs, to test alternative models of financing and provision, and to change strategies throughout the reform process.

The long-term, end result of the reform process would be a model that aims to achieve universal coverage, under a unified financing framework. The end results of the model, based on the above-mentioned principles, would strengthen the regulatory role of SSA and promote a clear separation of financing and provision, gradually introducing competition among providers and reforming payment mechanisms to better align incentives. The main characteristics of the "ideal system" would include:

(i)   An essential healthcare package is defined and accessible to the entire population, irrespective of the organization providing services.

(ii)   The role of government is redirected to ensure that the health sector as a whole is structured to provide all cost-effective care and to guarantee the provision of public goods.

(iii)   A universal health insurance fund receives resources from all sources (government, employers, and employees), and all social security institutions (ISSSTE, SEDENA, PEMEX, IMSS), and transfers resources to regulated institutions, MCOs, and health plans (including IMSS Medical Areas and private MCOs) on a capitated basis which is adjusted for risk.

(iv)   The regulated institutions bear the risk of delivering the services, and rules are established to resolve market failures.

(v)   The regulated institutions purchase services from public and private providers which comply with minimum accreditation criteria and standards for service delivery.

(vi)   There is adequate supervisory capacity to ensure that the services are delivered adequately, and that the regulations are being complied with.

(vii)   Mechanisms are set up to ensure access to services (secondary and tertiary) beyond those defined in the essential healthcare package.

(viii) There is a voluntary market for improved quality and service through supplementary health insurance.

Figure 5 presents a schematic view of the purchasing and provision functions under the reformed system. Many of the characteristics of the present system are maintained, and additional elements, such as a National Health Fund (NHF) and MCOs, are introduced to improve the functionality of the system. The vertical segmentation of the current system would be eliminated by allowing the population to choose their MCOs and to seek care from the providers that are "contracted" by this MCO to provide healthcare services.

A shared vision of the reformed system will remain a critical element of the reform process. Healthcare systems are evolving toward a situation in which several functions can be distinguished: the steering role of the health authority, financing, insurance/purchasing, and service delivery. In Mexico, the transition from the current vertically segmented model, in which each institution carries out all four of the above-mentioned functions, to the reformed model, in which the functions are clearly separated and institutions are horizontally segmented, is likely to require another decade of reforms.

IMSS and SSA have set the pace for carrying out these reforms at the system level. Efforts in these institutions to separate functions, decentralize and increase management autonomy, and improve resource allocation mechanisms provide important lessons for other public institutions. The following sections outline a series of policy recommendations that will build on these reforms and allow Mexico to steer the course to the reformed system.

Strategic Choices and the Pace of Reform

There is considerable agreement on the need to pursue a universal system based on the main elements outlined in the previous sections. Discussions center on the speed of these reforms and on how to bring about the changes in a complex and fragmented system. Many of the reforms initiated in SSA and IMSS need to be consolidated and deepened to yield their true potential. At the same time, institutions such as ISSSTE and the Armed Forces have yet to initiate structural changes. The many challenges that face policymakers are how to integrate the individual, institutional reforms into sector-wide reforms.

Fast and Flexible ...

While it is difficult to envision rapid and aggressive changes across all institutions, changes in financing and the establishment of nascent MCOs in all public institutions could be achieved over the short-term. Under the most aggressive scenario, starting in 2001 all social insurance healthcare premiums, and all federal contributions that are currently channeled to SSA and to social insurance institutions as subsidies, could be combined into an NHF that would begin to function as a global purchaser of healthcare services. The public sector institutions providing care would have to be reorganized to separate the purchasing function, by creating MCOs, and the provision function, by creating autonomous provider institutions that have to

Figure 5. The Reformed System of Purchasing and Provision

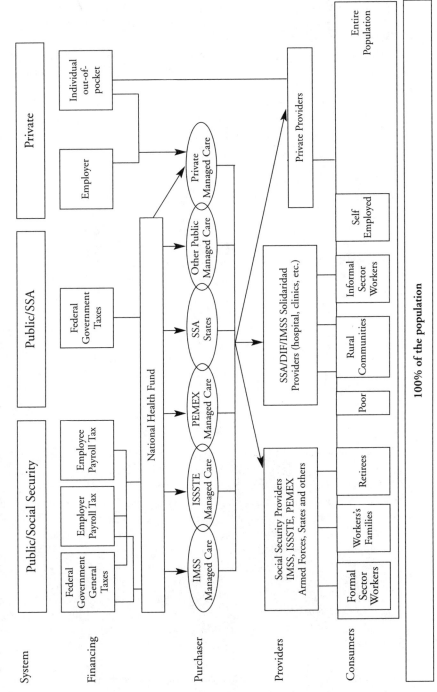

run on a self-financed basis. The NHF would then allocate resources to public and private MCOs based on the population enrolled, a package of services, some risk adjustment factor, and a performance factor.

The vertical segmentation in the system, and the existence of separate laws and regulations for each institution, complicates this situation since individual reforms would have to be carried out in each institution, within a common framework. Typically, when radical reforms of this nature are carried out, flexibility prevails over firmness in order to push through the reforms. The negotiation process in this context could potentially limit the real reforms obtained and significantly distort the results.

...Or Slow and Steady

The other option is to pursue the reforms in a slow and steady framework making persistent and consistent changes across all health institutions. Under this strategy, the decentralization efforts in SSA and the move to separate financing and provision in IMSS and SSA would be extended. At the same time, each social insurance institution would have to begin internal reforms similar to those initiated by SSA and IMSS six years ago. Eventually, many of the elements would be in place and the more profound changes outlined above could be pushed through. To date, this has been the strategy assumed, and is the most likely scenario to work in the future. In this context, the following two sections look at the short- and long-term actions that would need to be taken along the road to reform. The policy options are presented in terms of short-term actions (2001–04) that should be implemented without delay, and medium-to long-term proposals (2005–10) that will extend the gradual implementation of sector reforms.

Short-Term Actions for Health Sector Reform

The short-term actions are related to the consolidation of reform initiatives in IMSS and SSA and the application of these reforms to other public sector institutions. In addition, many of the changes promulgated over the past several years suggest the need to strengthen and reshape the role of SSA, strengthen the regulatory framework, develop improved provider payment mechanisms, and promote the development of management and institutional capacity at all levels of the system. The specific proposals are presented below.

The Role of Government

STRENGTHEN THE ROLE OF SSA IN SETTING NATIONAL HEALTH POLICY. The basic functions of SSA should be focused on establishing national health sector priorities and national health policy, including the establishment of the legal and regulatory framework in pursuit of these objectives. To carry out this function, SSA should continue to strengthen guidelines for: (a) establishing a unified system for reporting and statistics; (b) ensuring uniform technological policy with regard to pharmaceutical and medical equipment; (c) certification and licensing medicines, drugs, equipment, and technology in general; (d) developing uniform criteria and federal programs for training medical professionals as defined by the federal government; (e) establishing and enforcing quality standards of medical care; (f) establishing licensing procedures for medical and pharmaceutical activities; (g) financing and coordinating medical research; (h) organizing state sanitary and epidemiological services; and (i) implementing disaster relief.

Following the progress in decentralization, the states should assume responsibility for implementing public health and disease prevention measures, developing a local network of medical facilities, overseeing quality control of medical care, licensing medical and pharmaceutical activities, and organizing and coordinating work to train healthcare personnel. To this effect, technical assistance should be provided to the states by the central government.

PROMOTE HEALTH EDUCATION. The ongoing changes in the epidemiological profile will require renewed support to health education programs to initiate changes in lifestyle and behavior among the Mexican population. Strong programs to reduce risk factors, such as smoking and diet, complemented with improved control of chronic diseases, including hypertension and diabetes, would have an important impact on the future incidence of the higher-cost chronic diseases that characterize the new epidemiological profile. In addition, efforts by SSA to strengthen health education for communicable diseases among the open population should be consolidated and extended to social security institutions.

INCREASE ACCESS TO THE UNCOVERED POPULATION. Over the past 10 years, the Government has extended coverage of a basic package of services under PAC to an estimated 9 million people that were previously uncovered. Despite these important advances, challenges remain to continue the extension of coverage to an estimated 700,000 people who are still not covered, to consolidate the program, and to include additional services in the basic package. The estimated cost of extending coverage is $600 million per year.

IMSS reforms to create new publicly subsidized insurance schemes for the informal sector, the Family Insurance and the Voluntary Insurance programs, were designed to allow those employed in the informal sector in urban areas to obtain social security coverage. There are considerable opportunities to extend the coverage of social security. Under a system of universal coverage, the entire population would be enrolled in a national health insurance program. To this end, the success of the PAC and the IMSS voluntary insurance schemes offer important opportunities to create mechanisms to increase coverage of formal insurance systems. Efforts to implement these programs should continue, within the context of a sustainable financing framework.

It is likely that the increase in access will require continued increases in overall public sector funding for health. Over the past six years, important steps have been taken to increase public financing for healthcare services. The 1995 reforms of the IMSS law also established an increase in IMSS revenues from general revenues (increasing to an estimated 35 percent in 2010). Despite these increases, Mexico continues to allocate considerably fewer resources to the health of the nation than other OECD and Latin American countries. Future increases in healthcare spending should be carefully targeted to increase equality among regions and institutions and to address the priority health problems of the population. Furthermore, the increasing size of the allocations from general revenues will require the establishment of contractual relationships between SSA and the line institutions. These contractual relationships should also establish a direct relationship between financing and efforts to extend access, increase efficiency, and improve healthcare services quality and user satisfaction.

Strengthen the regulatory framework for managed care. The introduction of a regulatory framework to promote greater transparency and competition between the public and private sector is a key element to ensure the sustainability of the reforms. Initially these reforms could begin in each of the public sector institutions developing purchasing, and eventually the National Health Fund would assume many of the regulations regarding purchasing, in the context of the unified public financing framework. Efforts to strengthen the regulatory environment for introducing managed care should focus on three issues.

The first issue is related to the introduction of financing mechanisms and regulations to avoid the adverse incentives leading to "cream-skimming" and low-quality care that are likely to arise from the introduction of a capitation-based provider reimbursement system, or through the introduction of a private managed care market. Careful attention should be paid to mitigate adverse selection by MCOs by strengthening monitoring and quality-control mechanisms. Payment mechanisms should also be developed to allow providers to be paid on the basis of output and population covered, and to protect against incentives to avoid high-risk individuals by developing stop-gap loss provisions to guard against catastrophic risks.

The second issue is related to the sequence of reforms that are needed to strengthen the regulatory framework. In the short term, efforts should focus on developing consistent regulations across all public sector institutions for the purchasing of services from MCOs and private providers. This recommendation is particularly salient to the development of regulations within IMSS to provide for the opting-out program. In addition, significant progress has been made in developing and negotiating a regulatory framework for private sector health plans operating independently of the public institutions. Finally, the unified financing framework will require a unique regulatory framework to govern the purchase of healthcare services.

The development of institutional capacity to articulate and enforce regulations is the third area where policymakers should focus efforts. At the national level, and in the decentralized agencies of all public institutions, investments should be made in training staff for the new functions, and installing information systems.

Healthcare Financing

PROMOTE THE DEVELOPMENT OF A UNIFIED FINANCING FRAMEWORK TO INCREASE EQUITY AND GRADUALLY INTRODUCE COMPETITION. A critical element of the reformed system will be consolidation of the multiplicity of health sector payers and allocation mechanisms into a common financing framework and, eventually, into a common health insurance fund. The vertical segmentation of health sector institutions and financing creates an inefficient risk-pooling mechanism that inhibits the development of a strong purchasing organization to provide universal access in the context of a national health system.

In the long term, the reformed system would be characterized by the creation of an NHF that could merge all mandatory health financing contributions in the Mexican system, including contributions from general revenues, with those social insurance contributions from all public institutions. As such, the NHF could evolve into a national health insurance fund open to all medical institutions comprising the Mexican healthcare system and purchasing services from all public and non-public MCOs. The creation of a unified financing framework would overcome many of the fundamental shortcomings associated with the vertically segmented financing of health services in Mexico.

Development of the NHF would entail establishment of a clear linkage between the federal budget and the budgets of all health sector institutions to establish guidelines and regulations for universal allocation mechanisms, and to regulate the public-private mix. The first phase of the NHF would operate as a virtual fund, establishing the overarching framework for financing and purchasing without consolidating financial resources for healthcare services. This phase of the reform could last between two to five years and would gradually give way to the management of regulations and financing. As an increasing amount of resources from public institutions are rolled into the NHF, the capacity to articulate a unified population-based purchasing strategy, and to stimulate increased competition among public sector institutions and between the public and private providers, would increase.

IMSS and SSA have begun to take steps to separate functions by consolidating healthcare financing, promoting the development of purchasing capacity, and developing provider reimbursement mechanisms and contracts to improve quality and efficiency among providers. In 1998, IMSS and SSA established internal mechanisms to consolidate health sector funding. The creation of the *Fondo de Seguridad Social para la Salud* (FSSS) and the Fund of Contributions to Health Services (FASSA) in IMSS and SSA, respectively, provides the basis for future implementation of a unified financing framework. Furthermore, the institutional financing contracts, *convenios de fortalecimiento financiero,* also provide a potent instrument to consolidate the contributions of the federal government into the context of the NHF. Over the medium-term these individual efforts could be merged to establish a NHF to provide for a unified financing framework. The extension and expansion of these instruments to other public institutions would further the development of a universal health insurance fund and would promote an increase in choice and competition in the system. These steps would, in turn, increase the quality of service and care and client satisfaction.

INTRODUCE NEW PROVIDER REIMBURSEMENT MECHANISMS. Provider payment mechanisms concern the nature of contracts and financial relationships between payer organizations and providers and between regional administrations and those institutions. Because they provide the incentives guiding provider behavior, reimbursement mechanisms are critical in any healthcare system. Payment mechanisms should be developed to allow providers to be paid on the basis of output and population covered, within the overall budgetary limits in the system.

The introduction of DRGs in IMSS is an important first step to improve the relationship between total resources and output. This system should be extended to other public institutions to develop homogeneous payment mechanisms that will later be used as the basic reimbursement mechanism for the NHF. Short-term efforts should focus on consolidating IMSS reforms to introduce DRGs, and to extend the implementation of the DRG reimbursement mechanism to other public and private sector institutions.

The development of the capitation system for population-based reimbursement is the second key element of the reforms. In IMSS, the budget decentralization introduced the implementation of a capitated budget system dividing the country into 139 Medical Areas. Similar efforts have been made by SSA to introduce a capitated budget formula for the allocation of resources to the states under *Ramo 33*. The capitated budget is adjusted for risk defined by age and sex, making it necessary to improve the capitation formula to incorporate additional variables and provide greater degrees of equity in the allocation of resources based on need and cost of care. Furthermore, it is important to establish a unique formula that increases the equivalence of the IMSS and SSA allocation mechanisms. Further consolidation of the capitated budget will be required over the coming years to take into account variables that reflect expected morbidity and socioeconomic indicators as proxies (González-Pier and Parker 1998). Additional efforts should be made to extend the capitated financing model to other public institutions.

Additional efforts are required to develop performance- and population-based payment systems for general practitioners. Many countries have successfully experimented with capitated payment systems for the reimbursement of general practitioners to increase productivity, promote greater attention to preventive care, and allow for increased consumer choice with regard to the selection of general practitioners.

IMPROVE EQUITY IN HEALTH SECTOR FINANCING. The wide disparity in public financing constitutes one of the more important challenges facing health sector policymakers in Mexico. The implementation of a capitated payment scheme in IMSS and SSA is one of the more important steps taken to smooth differences in financing among regions and among public institutions. The extension of the capitated financing mechanism to other public providers will allow for greater equity among institutions, and will provide the basis to establish a unified health insurance fund—the NHF—which would employ homogeneous allocation criteria to transfer funds to MCOs.

In addition, the extension of coverage to the uncovered population and the consolidation of the PAC program will provide for increasing equity, as the allocation of resources becomes increasingly more progressive.

INCREASE PUBLIC FINANCING OF PRIVATE PROVISION. To date, the public and private sectors have operated parallel provider networks, leading to a duplication of resources and, consequently, an inefficient allocation of resources. The private sector stands poised to address problems of access to services and technology, to increase efficiency, and to provide leadership in the introduction of modern management practices that can later be replicated in the public sector. The efforts by IMSS to create an internal market by separating the management of service provision from the "purchase" of services provide an opportunity to increase the contracting of private providers to ensure adequate levels of health services.

Progress needs to be made in four general areas. First, the private sector can provide, with increasing efficiency and quality, many of the ancillary services, such as cleaning, catering and security services, currently provided directly by healthcare facilities. The subcontracting of these "hotel" services would allow public healthcare facilities to focus their efforts on providing the highest level of medical care, with increasing efficiency.

Second, the private sector can be contracted to provide healthcare services. The increasing population and the changing epidemiological profile have created a significant gap in the availability of healthcare services and technology in the public sector (for example, imaging and general medicine in the northern states). In several areas of the country the private sector offers services that are not provided by the public sector. Expansion of initial efforts to contract services in the private sector would increase overall efficiency and customer satisfaction, and offer significantly greater flexibility to manage the demand for healthcare services.

The third area where private sector providers can collaborate with the public sector is related to the allocation of public financing to private MCOs that assume responsibility for the provision of healthcare services, in a population-based framework. The shift from supply-based financing to demand- or population-based, resource allocation models would create incentives to improve efficiency and promote improvements in user satisfaction and quality. Efforts by all public institutions (including state-level SSAs) to contract selected services should be extended, and improvements should be made in the regulatory and contractual frameworks that govern these relationships with the private sector. A phased approach is needed to build purchasing capacity in the public sector and to ensure the development and application of adequate regulatory instruments. During the first phase, the introduction of contracting could initiate with an increase in the provision of an integrated package of family medicine, similar to the packages currently provided by several private sector MCOs. Hospital services would remain the domain of the public institutions, with the exception of a limited range of services such as childbirth, minor surgery, and dentistry. Over time, this package could be expanded to include a full range of hospital services, generating increased competition between public and private hospitals.

Fourth, public institutions should explore public-private partnerships to strengthen the provider network through the outsourcing of services, development of a model of public concession, or Build, Operate, and Transfer (BOT) and the direct purchase of services from the private sector to guarantee access to high quality services. The model of public-private partnerships has been developed extensively in the United Kingdom. and other Latin American countries, resulting in important improvements in efficiency and quality.

Organization and Delivery

PROMOTE FURTHER MANAGEMENT DECENTRALIZATION. The decentralization of management responsibility and authority is a critical factor in improving the efficiency, quality, and satisfaction of healthcare services. IMSS and SSA have made considerable advances in decentralizing resources and management to the regions, Medical Areas, and state SSAs. However, the decisionmaking process remains heavily centralized. Moreover, little progress has been made in other public sector institutions. International experience suggests that Mexico's health sector would benefit from increased decentralization and greater institutional autonomy.

Following the above, Mexico should introduce more autonomy at the provider level. One area in which to begin would be hospitals. However, caution is required, because it is important to simultaneously improve management capacity at the facility level. Thus, it is recommended that hospital autonomy be introduced gradually. A reasonable pilot scheme would cover one hospital per state. These efforts by the Mexican government should focus on increasing administrative and financial autonomy, creating community-based boards to oversee the operation of public facilities, introducing professional managers, and implementing modern information systems to facilitate management. The gradual introduction of increased institutional autonomy would allow public institutions to balance autonomy with accountability and local responsiveness while improving system coordination.

INITIATE DECENTRALIZATION OF OTHER PUBLIC INSTITUTIONS. The extension of decentralization and institutional autonomy to other public institutions is a critical element in improving the performance of the sector. The decentralization process initiated by SSA and IMSS establishes a coherent framework for other public institutions, such as ISSSTE, to pursue decentralization. The remaining public institutions should be included in the selection process for the creation of autonomous institutions at the state level, and additional resources should be allocated to strengthening the capacity of these institutions to increase the decentralization of financial and management responsibility and accountability.

REHABILITATE EXISTING INFRASTRUCTURE, AND PROVIDE DRUGS, EQUIPMENT, AND CAPITAL IMPROVEMENTS. As mentioned, significant proportions of Mexican facilities contain obsolete equipment or lack essential drugs. To provide better-quality care and to improve access, patient comfort, and satisfaction, changes will be required in the procurement process, and investments in equipment must increase. Many of the purchasing decisions, procurement management, and investments should be made by allowing providers, regions, and states to make their own decisions on what is purchased and where investments are allocated. Nonetheless, these investments should be made following international standards of cost-effectiveness and the design of an equitable mechanism to allocate investments to areas that are under-served. Technology assessment will become increasingly important as more complex and costly equipment becomes available. The establishment of a national entity to oversee choices on technology and cost-effectiveness would be a critical element to allowing greater freedom over the procurement process at the provider level.

TRAIN HUMAN RESOURCES IN BASIC MANAGEMENT SKILLS. Future improvements in efficiency and quality will depend on the development of a cadre of well-trained professional managers in the public and private sectors. Considerable investment is required to strengthen the management capacity of health service administrators in the public and private sectors. IMSS has initiated efforts to train health sector staff in clinical and financial management. Further efforts should focus on extending training programs to other public institutions and to facilitating collaboration between international universities with specialized programs in health services management and Mexican universities and training institutions.

STRENGTHEN THE INSTITUTIONAL CAPACITY OF SSA, IMSS, ISSSTE, AND OTHER PUBLIC INSTITUTIONS. Management of the ongoing reform process requires increasing institutional capacity in the public institutions. Over the past several years, SSA and IMSS have taken important steps to strengthen institutional capacity to manage the reform process and to improve overall institutional efficiency. The continued success of these initial efforts will depend on their expansion to other institutions, the consolidation of technical capacity at IMSS and SSA, and future training investments through short courses, scholarships, and improvements in the in-house capacity of the human resources departments.

Future efforts should also focus on developing institutional capacity to: (a) analyze health expenditures and resource allocation with criteria for equity and cost-effectiveness; (b) promote and implement quality assurance programs across public and private sector institutions; (c) strengthen the capacity to develop and enforce regulations related to the environment, drugs, equipment, and medical devices; (d) strengthen national capabilities for planning, managing, and developing health sector human resources; (e) develop national and subnational capabilities for health technology assessment; and (f) strengthen the capacity for monitoring and evaluating the health sector reform process.

Medium- to Long-Term Policy Options

The majority of the reform initiatives started in the short term (2001–04) should be consolidated over the following five years (2005–10) to ensure sustainability and adaptation to changing market conditions. In addition, many of the reforms related to financing, organization, and delivery would require expanded efforts to obtain the desired results. The policy recommendations for the medium term are presented below.

CONSOLIDATE THE DECENTRALIZATION. The decentralization process of IMSS and SSA will have devolved management responsibility and accountability to the local authorities. Over the short term, it is likely that these reforms will succeed in decentralizing resources to the state level, in the case of SSA, and to the Medical Areas, in the case of IMSS. The consolidation of this decentralization process, however, is likely to require several additional years and continued political support to establish the sufficient management autonomy at these levels, and at the level of public hospitals, to make significant improvements in the services provided. In the case of other public sector institutions that will have started the process later, significant efforts will be required over the medium term to consolidate the changes.

CONTINUE TO ALLOW FOR INCREASED COMPETITION BETWEEN PUBLIC AND PRIVATE PROVIDERS. Over the next few years, it is likely that the separation of financing and provision, improved partnership between the public and private sectors, and the introduction of a contractual framework will facilitate increased competition among and between public and private providers. After this initial period, the reforms should focus on continuing implementation of reimbursement mechanisms, organizational capacity, and the regulatory framework for purchasing.

During this phase of reforms, additional resources would be allocated to the private managed care organizations and to private providers, in the context of the unified financing framework (NHF). The gradual extension of the managed care market, within the framework of the *reversión de cuotas,* could allow for the number of people covered by this scheme to increase to nearly 10 million (Cercone 1997) without severe financial implications for IMSS. Furthermore, the package of services contracted—initially purchasing family medicine in an integrated framework—would be extended to include resources to provide hospital services and to further induce the public institutions to form MCOs of their own that would compete with private MCOs.

INCREASING THE POOLING OF RESOURCES UNDER A UNIVERSAL HEALTH INSURANCE FUND. During the first phase of reforms, the unified financing framework has been designed to include resources from IMSS and, potentially, some resources from ISSSTE. Over the medium term, the proposals would focus on increasingly channeling resources to the NHF and "purchasing" services from public and private

MCOs. Over the next 10 years, it would appear feasible to envision the operation of a universal health insurance fund that consolidates resources available for direct service provision. Resources for regulation, public health, and select activities would still be separated within the budget of the public institutions (SSA, IMSS, PEMEX, ISSSTE, etc.).

INCREASE AUTONOMY TO PROVIDER NETWORKS AND FACILITIES. Medium-term actions would focus on extending the scope of increased provider autonomy to include all public institutions and the majority of all facilities. The rate at which these reforms are implemented will depend on the development of better organizational structures to manage healthcare services, introduction of provider payment mechanisms, and improvements in the institutional capacity of the NHF purchasing function. Management capacity will also play an important role in regulating the scope and velocity with which these reforms are implemented.

VI. Conclusions

The future of health sector reform in Mexico depends on a reform strategy that dynamically adjusts its pace to take advantage of the existing institutional capacity, and the design of instruments and systemic changes to improve efficiency, quality, and user satisfaction. At the same time, policymakers must account for the political economy of reform to balance stakeholders' interests with an appropriate timing and strategy.

Any reform initiatives, fast or slow, should involve stakeholders in the policy debate and reform process. The lack of a clear understanding of the health reform objectives by stakeholders is a potential deterrent to future reform efforts. More effort need to be made by the executive branch of government to involve the Congress, trade unions, insurance companies, private sector providers, and healthcare consumers in the reform process. The provision of information and education campaigns, direct consultation, and the promotion of community-based boards, with stakeholder participation, will be important elements in guaranteeing the reform's success. Specific strategies to address stakeholder concerns should be developed and implemented early in the new Presidential Administration to enrich the reform process and inform stakeholders about the need for reform and its expected benefits.

Policymakers should develop a shared vision of the reformed system. Many healthcare reforms have been limited by divergent views of stakeholders and technicians on the future of their healthcare systems. Improved coordination over the past several years has enabled important progress to be made toward establishing a coherent and cohesive framework for reform; however, the further development of a common vision will be a decisive element regarding the implementation of health system reform.

A key element in developing a coherent reform framework will be the changing role of government. In the future, the government should focus on ensuring that the health system, as a whole, is structured to provide the population with access to cost-effective healthcare services, rather than focusing on directly providing all healthcare services. This will require that the public sector improve coordination of existing institutions and health sector financing, forge partnerships with private sector MCOs, and improve the alignment of incentives at all levels of the system. The changing role of government will be increasingly important in the context of a system that strives to provide universal access and a unified and sustainable financing framework. At the same time, ongoing reforms need to continue in the areas of decentralization, creation of the purchasing function, increasing the role of consumers and the community, reducing inequity in resource allocation, and improving incentives to providers to obtain greater value-for-money.

References

Bobadilla, J.l. 1998. "Quality of Perinatal Medical Care in Mexico City." National Institute of Public Health, Mexico City.

Chernichovsky, D., and D. Chinitz. 1995. "The Political Economy of Health System Reform in Israel," in *Health Economics*, 4: 127–141.

Frenk, J., et al. Economia y Salud. Propuestas para el avance del sistema de salud en Mexico, FUNSALUD, Mexico D.F.

Frenk, J. 1998. "Chiapas: las desigualdades internas." *La Jornada*. January 26: /.

Gomez-Dantes, O. 1999. "Prospects of the Mexican Health Care Reform."

Pan-American Health Organization (PAHO). 1998. Health in *the Americas*. Washington, D.C.

Van de Ven, W.P.M.M. 1995. "Health Care Reforms in the Netherlands" presented at the seminar *Health Care Reform: Learning from International Experience*, Birmingham, U.K., Sept.

20

Education Sector Strategy

This Chapter was written by Eduardo Velez Bustillo with the valuable input of Vicente Paqueo.

I. Background

Mexico is in a period of change. These changes include an increase in political participation, decentralization of decisionmaking, increased participation in the global economy, technological innovation, and a new public–private relationship. All of these changes have the potential to impact the population, positively or negatively. The impact will be negative if the new and improved opportunities are not open to a wide segment of the population, especially the poor.

Convinced of the importance of education, Mexico has set some targets, and has already achieved important goals. They include (a) practically universal primary education; (b) rapid expansion of lower secondary education, with formal educational attainment reaching nearly eight years; and (c) a program to allow every adult access to lifelong learning opportunities. The average schooling level in Mexico increased by roughly one year per decade during 1960–80 (from 2.76 to 4.77 years) and by two years in the decade between 1980–90. In 1999 it was higher than seven years. The acceleration in schooling during the 1980s, in turn, was the product of concerted efforts to increase education coverage: primary school net enrollment rates increased from 91 to 98 percent over this period, yielding virtually complete coverage in the first two grades. In the same period lower secondary net enrollment expanded from 48 to 58 percent, and in the 1990s the government made a significant effort to reach universal coverage in lower secondary (to complete nine years of basic education). The result of these improvements is that the share of workers with less than primary education decreased from almost half of the labor force in 1984 to 36 percent in 1994, while the share of workers with at least a completed secondary education increased from 26 to 39 percent. The increase in the number of average years of schooling and the significant improvement since the 1980s are shown in Figure 1 together with the Table on the next page.

Figure 1. Cross-Country Relation between Education Attainment and GDP

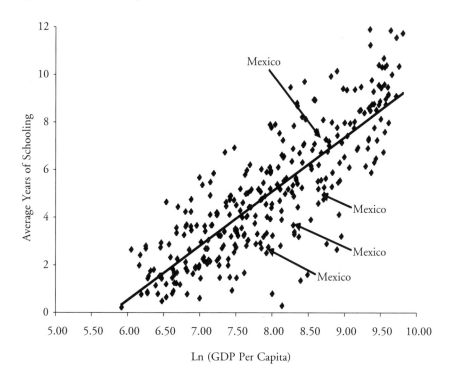

The observations pertaining to Mexico, ordered by date, are as follows:

Year	Average Schooling (Years)	Ln (GDP Per Capita; 1980 US$)
1960	2.76	7.95
1970	3.68	8.29
1980	4.77	8.71
1985	5.20	8.63
1990	6.72	8.67

In each year during the 1990s there was an increase in enrollments by age in primary education (6 to 11 years old; grades 1 to 6), and in lower secondary education (12 to 14 years old; grades 7 to 9), and the gender differences were reduced. In fact, for some years, girls have had a higher enrollment than boys (see the case for 1997 in Table 1). Finally, a better way to see the increase in access to basic education for all is presented in Table 2, which shows the tremendous improvement of average years of schooling by birth cohort, and the equalization by gender.

Table 1. Percent of Children Attending School

Age	1990	1995	1997	1997 Boys	1997 Girls
6	79.5	92.2	93.9	93.8	94.0
7	88.8	96.4	97.1	97.2	97.0
8	91.5	97.1	97.4	97.1	97.6
9	93.1	97.6	97.6	97.5	97.7
10	92.1	96.9	97.4	97.4	97.4
11	91.8	96.1	96.6	97.1	96.1
12	86.6	91.1	90.7	92.2	89.0
13	79.4	84.2	83.7	86.7	80.6
14	69.5	77.0	75.0	78.0	72.0
Total 6–14 years old	85.81	92.15	92.23	93.1	91.4

Source: SEP.

Another important achievement is the trend in the 1990s of an increased allocation of resources to the education sector, moving from 3.3 percent of GDP in 1989
to 5.1 percent in 1999, which helped the country reach quantitative goals. Total
public education spending per student in Mexico increased steadily in the 1990s, in
spite of the increase in total student population. The federal government currently
accounts for 80 percent of total sector spending at a time when private sector spending is decreasing (see Figures 2 and 3).

Table 2. Average Years of Schooling

Age Group	Total Population	Men	Women	Differences b/w Men and Women
15–19	8.10	8.03	8.16	(0.13)
20–24	8.95	9.01	8.89	0.12
25–29	9.00	9.24	8.78	0.46
30–34	8.62	9.00	8.28	0.72
35–39	7.98	8.52	7.48	1.04
40–44	7.11	7.81	6.49	1.32
45–49	6.20	6.82	5.65	1.17
50–54	5.46	6.16	4.78	1.38
55–59	4.39	4.93	3.91	1.02
60–64	3.96	4.54	3.45	1.09
65 and more	3.03	3.33	2.77	0.56
Total nat'l. 15 and older	7.36	7.69	7.06	0.63

Source: SEP/ENIGH. World Bank calculations.

Figure 2. Education Spending per Student

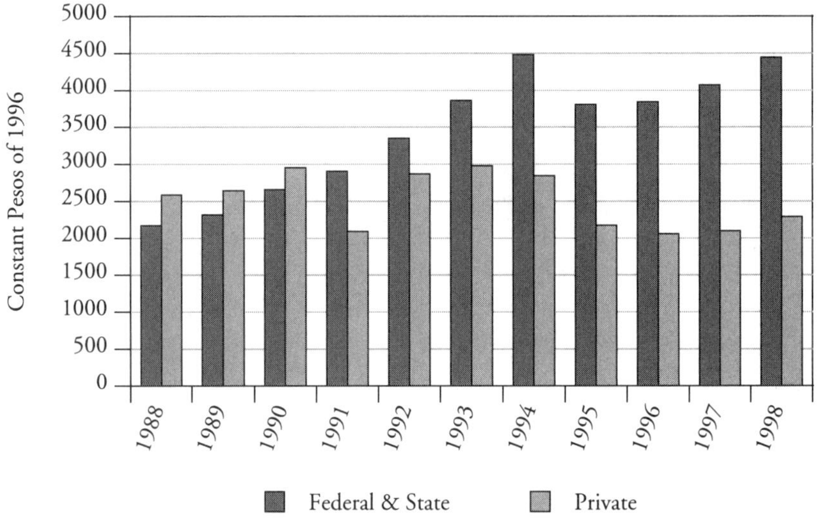

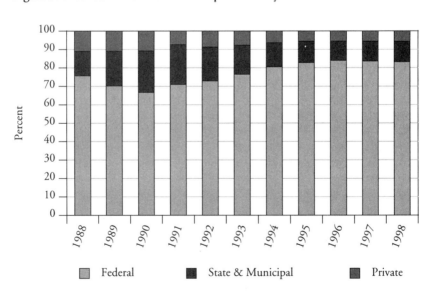

Source: IV Informe de Gobierno, 1998.

Figure 3. Distribution of Education Expenditure by Source

Source: IV Informe de Gobierno, 1998.

An additional achievement is that public expenditure for basic education (primary and lower secondary) has increased from 59 percent in 1996 to about 65 percent in 1999. Public expenditure for upper secondary and higher education levels has been declining, signaling that public spending on education has become more egalitarian in per capita terms. In the early 1980s federal spending per university student was 10 times higher than spending per primary students. Now it is closer to 5 times.

Access is important, but quality is the key. In fact, in spite of all these improvements, problems of quality are pervasive throughout the system. Although important advances have been made in the reduction of primary school repetition and dropout rates, many of the children that complete primary and lower secondary education have not acquired the knowledge and skills specified in the curriculum, or the knowledge and skills to successfully enter the labor force. Some say that this is also valid for upper secondary and higher education graduates.

II. Issues

Coverage

In spite of widening access to education at all levels, including early childhood education for children from birth to age three and preschool for children age four to six, there is still plenty of room for improvements at this level.

EARLY CHILDHOOD DEVELOPMENT (ECD). Mexico is implementing several ECD programs. One of these is a daycare service offered by law as a fringe benefit to working mothers employed in the formal sector, mostly with the public sector, a program handled mainly through the government's Child Development Center *(Centros de Desarrollo Infantil)*. This good quality program is, however, too expensive (about US$1,500 per child per year) to pass a cost-effectiveness criteria. There is also an informal program, the Initial Education Program (PRODEI), with a per capita cost of about US$50 per year which reaches poor Mexican children by educating parents to improve the care of and interaction with their children. It is a home-based program delivered by community educators who train the parents to stimulate their children. Parents' education is the key instrument, and it is developed through periodic group meetings supplemented by home visits. The program promotes the physical, emotional, intellectual, and social developments of infants and toddlers, and improves the school-readiness skills of young children. There is empirical evidence that the program is effective in increasing returns on primary education. It is a way to modify inequalities rooted in poverty and, sometimes, discrimination, by giving children from disadvantaged backgrounds a fair start. It also creates job opportunities for young graduates of primary education in poor areas. An interesting finding has been that it also increases women's self-esteem, and provides opportunities for parents to socialize. It has the additional advantage of having created a way to form captive audiences for programs, such as adult education and health and to foster community development.

PRESCHOOL. Despite the fact that Mexico has one of the highest preschool enrollment rates in Latin America (nearly 75 percent), and that this rate increased by 23.5 percent in the 1990s, one in four states still has a less than 50 percent enrollment rate for 4-year-old children. In spite of some expansion of informal preschool in rural areas, it is precisely in rural areas, where the deficit is highest.

BASIC EDUCATION.[1] With substantial coverage gains in the 1980s and 1990s, primary education is practically universal in Mexico. With the pace of demographic growth, which has been coming down markedly in recent years (the population under age 6 has been decreasing at a rate of 0.5 percent per year, and the population age 6 to 14 has been increasing by only 0.1 percent per year), coverage of primary education is not a problem, except for small pockets in remote areas. Enrollment in lower secondary education has doubled since the 1970s and has been growing at a rate of 3.1 percent per year since 1995. As a result of significant efforts by the current Administration, enrollment has reached more than 60 percent. In 1997, 93 percent of children age 6 to 14 were enrolled in school. However, in spite of an increase in the demand for lower secondary schooling (grades 7 to 9), large numbers still drop out, mostly from the night school programs, which are particularly inefficient.

UPPER SECONDARY. Since the mid-1990s, upper secondary enrollment has also been increasing significantly at 6.3 percent per year. However, in 1998 less than half (47 percent) of youths age 15 to 19 were enrolled in school.

HIGHER EDUCATION. Higher education has also been increasing—at 5.1 percent per year since the mid-1990s—in part because of 38 new technical universities that were created during the period. However, only about 18 percent of people age 20 to 24 are currently enrolled. This is low when compared with economies of similar size and with other LAC countries (in 1994, for example, Argentina had a coverage of 39 percent, Bolivia 23 percent, Chile 27 percent, Costa Rica 29 percent, and Uruguay 30 percent), but the major differences are relative to other OECD countries. The low pace of increase in enrollment increase in higher education is demonstrated by the fact that while in 1980 Mexico had the same higher education enrollment as Korea, today Korea's enrollment is three times higher.

---

1. In Mexico, "basic education" is defined as preschool plus primary education (six years) plus the first three years of (lower) secondary.

Internal Efficiency Indicators

Mexico's primary education terminal efficiency rate rose from 70.1 percent in 1990 to 85.6 percent in 1999. This tremendous improvement is the result of lowering the repetition and dropout rates. The repetition rate in the first grade, for example, declined from 18.5 percent in 1990 to 11.1 percent in 1999. The current dropout rate for primary education is 2.9 percent. It has been declining by 5.2 percent per year since the mid-1990s, in part as a result of the compensatory programs initiated in the poorest states. However, at the state level there are still striking differences in school inefficiencies. States like Chiapas, Guerrero, Oaxaca, Veracruz and Yucatan still have low terminal efficiency in primary schools, at 71.6 percent.

Terminal efficiency in lower secondary schools, 73.2 percent in 1999, is lower than in primary schools. No progress has been observed in this indicator in the last decade, remaining at approximately 74 percent. The dropout rate has remained practically the same—9.5 percent in 1990 and 9.7 percent in 1999. Despite this apparent lack of progress, it is important to note that internal efficiency has not deteriorated in spite of a large increase in enrollment, from 4.1 million students in 1990 to 5.1 million students in 1999. Dropout rates in lower secondary education are not necessarily correlated with poverty and indigenous areas. The states with the highest dropout rates in lower secondary are, in order, Zacatecas, Sonora, Michoacán, Guanajuato, Coahuila, Guerrero and Colima.

Terminal efficiency for upper secondary education has also remained unchanged in the past decade. It was 55.2 percent in 1990 and 55.0 percent in 1999. Although repetition rates have declined during this period, transition rates, around 70 percent, and dropout rates, around 19 percent, have not improved.

In technical education, despite the progress made during the last 20 years, the training system in Mexico still has a way to go to meet the immediate and future requirements of both pre-employment and in-service training. Although there are not comparable internal efficiency indicators, most agree that a critical weakness is the poor preparation of workers for vocational and technical education and training due to the uneven quality of training programs, with no objective measure available to gauge the quality of outputs, and lack of an adequate institutional framework for private sector involvement in the design and provision of training.

Low Levels of Learning Achievement in Education

Educational investment in Mexico has been successful in achieving many quantitative objectives, but the anticipated quality performance levels have yet to be achieved. Several national and international studies indicate that educational achievement in Mexico needs improvement. Although there are excellent schools in Mexico and many students learn enough to progress successfully along the educational levels, scattered empirical evidence shows that a significant proportion of students do not achieve the minimum levels based on curriculum learning expectations.

Since the late 1980s several studies have shown that a majority of students score low in academic performance. A typical case is a study that found that most students scored a grade of 6 or lower on an academic performance scale ranging from 0 to 10. In a study published by SEP,[2] out of a possible score of 100 only those students in the first grade averaged over 50 points. In grades four through six, students' average scores were just above 20. In lower secondary, students did even worse, averaging between 11 and 16 out of 100.

International comparisons put Mexico close to Latin American averages for academic achievement in language and math. In an 11-country study Mexico scored better than Bolivia, the Dominican Republic, Honduras, Paraguay and Venezuela among fourth graders in these two areas. Argentina, Brazil, Chile, Colombia and Cuba attained higher scores than Mexico.

Other studies indicate that there are significant variations in learning achievement by socioeconomic background. As an example, an evaluation of the *Programa de Atención al Resago Educativo*, PARE, produced the results in Table 3. The results indicate that there are significant differences by type of school and that there is significant dispersion of test scores within types of school. It is clear that students in rural schools and indigenous schools have lower achievement. It is interesting to see that the CONAFE "Community Schools" perform as well as the rural, complete, formal schools. The information also shows that there is significant internal dispersion in the scores, indicating that in almost every type of school there are good and bad schools.

Studies conducted by SEP between 1995 and 1998 among primary education students in complete schools, also show that there is a differential in achievement by

Table 3. Test Scores by Type of Primary School; Means and (Standard Deviations)

Type of Primary School	Psycho-motor	Language	Math
Public-State capital	67.1 (19.1)	63.4 (21.2)	78.4 (19.0)
Public-Other urban	67.8 (19.7)	59.9 (22.8)	76.3 (20.3)
Private-State capital	83.6 (17.1)	82.6 (14.6)	91.7 (12.4)
Private-Other urban	79.9 (18.5)	80.9 (15.9)	89.0 (10.9)
Multigrade rural (one teacher)	67.7 (21.0)	47.4 (22.2)	72.4 (21.6)
Multigrade rural (more teachers)	69.6 (19.1)	51.9 (22.6)	71.5 (21.8)
Rural complete	66.3 (21.9)	54.0 (21.7)	74.8 (19.9)
Indigenous school	63.2 (23.4)	50.2 (23.6)	71.8 (22.0)
Community school-CONAFE	68.4 (21.6)	53.7 (25.4)	74.6 (22.7)
Total	67.6 (21.7)	55.1 (24.1)	74.9 (21.3)

Source: PARE survey.

---

2. "*Evaluación De La Educación Prescolar, Primaria Y Secundaria.*" *Dirección General de Evaluación Educativa, SEP, Marzo, 1988.*

states, with some having a larger share of schools classified with low achievement, such as Guerrero, Guanajuato, Michoacán, San Luís Potosí, Tabasco, Tlaxcala, and Zacatecas. In contrast, Baja California, Jalisco, Nuevo León, Tamaulipas, and Veracruz have a larger share of high achievers.

Similar studies for secondary education students also show that there are differences by states, with Coahuila, Guerrero, Michoacán, Tabasco, and Tlaxcala having a larger share of the low achievers, and Aguascalientes, the Federal District, Jalisco and Nuevo León having a larger share of high achievers. In general, low quality is found more frequently in rural, indigenous, and poor areas.

Different tests from the *Consejo del Sistema Nacional de Educación Técnica* (COSNET) and the *Centro Nacional de Evaluación para la Educación Superior* (CENEVAL) systematically show that applicants are poorly prepared for tertiary education. On average the candidates do not obtain the minimum score required, and frequently institutions accept students who failed the tests.

COSNET found that Technical Institutes have three significant problems associated with quality of education: (a) high failure and dropout rates, and as a result, low terminal efficiency; (b) poorly educated teachers; and (c) low academic levels of newly registered students.

Competition in a global economy requires a labor force with stronger skills in mathematics, language, and communication, and more flexibility, creativity, and an ability to work cooperatively. Lower and upper secondary education are critical to the success of nations in this new environment. To compete effectively, Mexico must address the challenge of providing improved access to secondary education, while enhancing its quality and relevance. Six critical areas that the sector has to look at for quality improvement are: (a) increased learning and measurement of achievement; (b) more effective instruction; (c) school and system management reform; (d) use of technology for quality improvement; (e) reassessment of the relationship between secondary schooling and the labor market; and (f) research on "what works."

Why Low Quality?

Low educational quality in Mexico can be due to both school-related factors and broader socioeconomic conditions, such as poverty. Among the school-related factors the more important are: (a) deficiencies in teacher training and/or allocation; (b) weak curriculum implementation, and a curriculum with excessive emphasis on memorization and rote learning; (c) inadequate supervision; (d) school environment; and (e) time on task.

QUALITY OF TEACHERS IN BASIC EDUCATION. Although the proportion of teachers with a *Licenciatura* is increasing—there were 21,597 graduates in 1990 and 39,288 in 1998—and although SEP has made an effort to improve the quality of teachers with pre- and in-service formation and training with programs like the *Programa Nacional para la Actualización Permanente de Maestros de Educación Básica*

(PRONAP), including the *Centros de Maestros*, that has benefited about 500,000 teachers; the *Programa de Actualización del Magisterio*; the work of the *Universidad Pedagógica Nacional* (UPN) with its 16 campuses across the country; and the curriculum reform to the Normal schools (for preschool, primary and lower secondary). However, changes in the school have yet to happen. Teaching practices in the classroom, based on the frontal model (the method widely used by Mexican teachers), has proved to be ineffective in increasing quality of education. A dramatic exception is the informal method developed by CONAFE, which has changed the standard model of education. Unfortunately in Mexico this standard model is still a teacher-centered method that emphasizes memorization, and limits comprehension skills. It does not promote methods that respond easily to diversity of age, interest, ability, and prior experience; it is designed for the average student. CONAFE's model is a good start toward developing a model that is more child-oriented, where learning through active participation is promoted.

QUALITY OF PEDAGOGICAL SUPERVISION IN BASIC AND UPPER SECONDARY EDUCATION. One of the greatest problems facing Mexico's basic education system is the lack of teacher supervision. This applies to both technical–pedagogical supervision and administrative oversight. This results in (a) teachers who receive little or no feedback on their teaching techniques and effectiveness; (b) high teacher absenteeism (see section on Time on Task); and (c) an important disconnect between what the curriculum defines and the actual teaching that goes in the classroom. Weak supervision is due to a lack of funds with which to hire and mobilize supervisors. When supervisors are hired, there are bureaucratic and political problems—selection of supervisors means that they are often elderly, with little disposition to be out in the field supervising teachers; their loyalty is first to the teachers'union, the *Sindicato Nacional de Trabajadores de la Educación* (SNTE), and second to SEP. The compensatory programs have had some success testing ways to improve supervision by providing training and incentives to supervisors. An important factor in the success is the involvement of parents and community in the process.

CURRICULUM. Mexico is moving in a positive direction in producing a more relevant curriculum and making it more flexible, particularly in accommodating people's views on priorities. During the past few years, for example, and after consultations with experts and parents, SEP has been making significant changes in the curriculum, including adding topics such as sex education in primary education, the study of values, civic life, and ethics (*Formación Cívica y Etica*), and educational orientation, mainly in lower secondary. Several improvements in content and in educational materials and textbooks in several subjects, including math, geography, and Spanish in primary, and Spanish, biology, and physics in lower secondary, have been introduced. Several programs specifically designed to improve learning achievement, like the reading corner (*Rincones de Lectura*), of proven effectiveness, and the program in support of writing and reading (*Programa Nacional para el Fortalecimiento de la Lectura y la Escritura en la Educación Básica*) are clear efforts to improve quality of education.

A basic problem, however, is the need to introduce active learning into the curriculum, changing the teachers' traditional role as sources of knowledge (together with the textbooks) and custodial controller of students, to one where they play a role of facilitator, ensuring that written instructions are understood, motivating students to do extra work, counseling students with problems, helping students learn through cooperative learning interaction (group work), using peers to facilitate teaching, and increased self-determination. CONAFE's method is closer to this active learning approach, which also incorporates in a much more practical way local content and community information. It could be improved further, however, by strengthening its student-centered curriculum, by using detailed self-instructional guides, and by establishing a student government body to develop civic and democratic values, stimulate leadership and organizational skills, and involve students in school management. These last curriculum strategies have been developed successfully by the *Nueva Escuela Unitaria* in Guatemala and the *Escola Ativa* in several states in Brazil.

Thus, in spite of curriculum-related improvements, it is necessary to make use of more modern multicultural approaches, and especially to concentrate on indigenous groups, where little has been achieved.

QUALITY OF THE SCHOOL ENVIRONMENT (TEXTBOOKS, SCHOOL INFRASTRUCTURE, TEACHING MATERIAL, AND EXPERIMENTAL SCIENCE FACILITIES). Although Mexico has done a great job producing and distributing textbooks[3] in an efficient way, the quality of textbooks had deteriorated and began to improve only in the 1990s. Revision of textbooks in most subjects, including textbooks in indigenous languages, has been a recent effort which should help to improve quality in the near future. The government has distributed textbooks for free and therefore has kept a near-monopoly on textbook production for primary education. Lack of competition may have had a negative impact on quality. The teaching of science, a subject important to raising students' high-level thinking and to teaching the basic concepts of technology, is an area in need of improvement.

Finally, it is necessary to use the now standard education assessment being applied in most states for systematic standards setting and related quality assurance systems, which establish benchmarking. Establishing clear standards of what students should learn at the end of various levels and modalities of education, and for teacher qualifications and teacher development is something that will be beneficial not only to monitor quality, but also to facilitate effective decentralization.

TIME ON TASK. There are two problems with time on task in Mexico. The first is the actual number of days and hours a day the teacher is present in the school. Anecdotal

---

3. In 1999 Mexico distributed some 160 million free textbooks for preschool, primary, and lower secondary education in a relatively efficient way.

but systematic evidence indicates that this is a serious problem mainly in rural and urban marginal areas. Some researchers have estimated the number of absentee days in rural areas to be half of the prescribed days. Out of the 810 hours a teacher is supposed to spend in the classroom, only between 160 and 450 are really offered, on average, in a rural school. The second problem is that a large amount of time is spent organizing of the group and in mechanical repetition exercises, with little pedagogical value.

Financial Resources

EFFICIENCY IN USE OF RESOURCES. Although federal spending for the education sector has been growing in real terms, and in spite of the above-mentioned trend to support more basic education, a benefit-incidence analysis shows that there is still an unequal distribution of public resources in the education sector. Public spending on education in Mexico clearly benefits the poorest at the basic education level, but it is also true that upper secondary and higher education public spending clearly benefits the higher-income groups. Figures 4 and 5 (next page) compare the cumulative distribution of the various education levels with the distribution of per capita annual total and federal public educational expenditures to show that public expenditure is progressive for primary and lower secondary, and regressive for upper secondary and, especially, higher education. Public education expenditure benefits the rich disproportionately. At the national level, public expenditure seems quite equal, as shown by the fact that the expenditure line lies very close to the 45-degree diagonal.

When disaggregated by region, the benefit-incidence analysis shows that the public expenditure in the Central region of Mexico follows the national pattern. In the South and Tabasco public expenditures tend to be more progressive for primary and lower secondary than for the country as a whole. Even the case of public investing in upper secondary tends to be neutral. For the North public investment in lower secondary, upper secondary, and higher education is more regressive than in the rest of the country.

THE NEED FOR TARGETING IN THE SECTOR. Based on this and other information presented above, it should be a priority to achieve more equity in access to education services targeting the neediest. A relation between poverty and education is evident in Mexico when comparing access to levels of education with poverty levels. All enrollment indicators decline when one moves from the non-poor to the poor. Children from non-poor households enter the school system and enroll for a longer time than those from poorer households. There is a wide education gap between the children of the poor and the children of the rich in terms of the differential enrollment rates at various age levels, and this is true independent of gender, location, or region in the country (Annex A, see tables A.1, A.2 and A.3). The differences are more noticeable at higher levels of education.

To further understand the relation between education and poverty, and given the strong emphasis on poverty alleviation in Mexico, we can see that the probability of

Figure 4. Cumulative Distribution of Total Education Expenditures, 1996 National

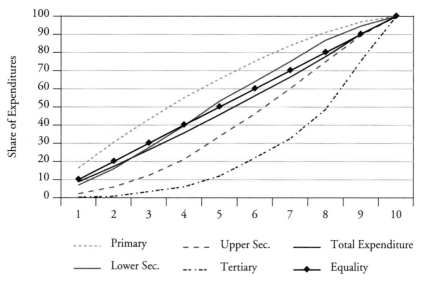

Source: ENIGH 1996 and DGPPyP, SEP.

Figure 5. Cumulative Distribution of Federal Education Expenditures, 1996 National

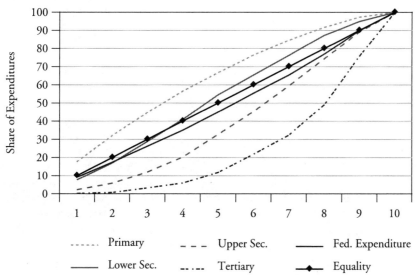

Source: ENIGH 1996 and DGPPyP, SEP.

being a poor household head in Mexico is associated with living in a rural area, being female, and being older. Education exerts a very powerful negative effect on the probability of being poor—every year of additional education decreases by 5 percent the chance of a household being classified as poor (see Annex A, table A.4).

EXTERNAL EFFICIENCY OF PRIMARY, SECONDARY, AND HIGHER EDUCATION. Private returns to education in Mexico are substantive. Those of primary education have steadily fallen over the years from about 40 percent in the 1980s to about 15 percent in the 1990s, as a result of the near-universal coverage of primary education, but they are still significant. Lower and upper secondary have also fallen, but at a lesser speed. They were around 20 percent in the early 1990s. The private returns to university education have fallen and risen with the economic growth of the economy, but are still high. Regarding social returns, the ones for higher education are slightly lower than the ones for primary education (12 percent), and than the ones for lower and upper secondary education (around 15 percent in both cases), but still relatively high at about 11 percent in the early 1990s. Private returns to technical education are also substantive in Mexico, mainly after some minimum threshold of basic general education.

External efficiency indicators show that Mexico has reached a point where the secondary level of education must be expanded, just as the government is trying to do. Indicators also show that primary education quality needs further improvements. After all, and for reasons of positive social externalities, universal primary education of good quality should be an overriding consideration that goes beyond measured (internalized) monetary costs and benefits.

Because there is little room for increased public spending in Mexico, it is necessary to look carefully at the imbalances between investment and recurrent expenditures by, among other things, rationalizing human resources in the sector and analyzing personnel expenditures; and better allocating and using available education resources, including more intensive use of private sector financing and exploration of increased subnational contributions to education.

Institutional Issues

DECENTRALIZATION (CAPACITY OF STATES TO DISCHARGE ADDITIONAL FUNCTIONS, DUPLICATION OF MANAGEMENT STRUCTURES, UNCLEAR ROLES AND RESPONSIBILITIES). One of the most interesting developments in recent years in the education sector in Mexico is the current reforms in basic education that began in 1992 with the decentralization of educational services from the federal to the state level. This fundamental structural change transferred to the state-level secretariats responsibility and budgets for almost 100,000 institutions, and more than 700,000 teachers, facilities, real estate, and materials. The only exception was that the federal government retained temporary responsibility for managing the basic education schools in the Federal District. With decentralization came a number of reforms and initiatives at both federal and state levels, as states experimented with ways to improve their educational systems. These included: (a) a far-reaching curricular reform that wholly reorganized the content and materials for basic education with the focus on providing students with the knowledge and attitudes necessary for a successful life, including the ability and desire for continuous learning; and (b) a vigorous federal government drive to provide diversified teaching and learning materials to primary school teachers and students. Primary school students now have a free textbook for each of the subject areas and primary school teachers have a special text for each of them. Indigenous students have textbooks in their own language for learning and practicing reading and writing up to the fourth grade. Secondary school students in marginal and rural areas now also have access to free textbooks. It is important that national standards be maintained under decentralization.

COMMUNITY AND NGO PARTICIPATION IN PUBLIC EDUCATION. The 1993 General Law of Education mandates the establishing of school-level social participation councils, providing the possibility for parental participation in schools. These councils are repeated at the municipal, state, and central levels. The school-level social participation councils are bodies that represent teachers, parents, graduates, and community authorities, and are chaired by the school principal. The National Social Participation Council was established in September 1999. How the school-level participation councils function in practice remains to be seen.

Although under the Compensatory Programs some communities have been given a limited role in managing some educational inputs, such as teacher or supervisor incentives in remote areas, more concrete actions favoring school autonomy and management still must occur.

USEFULNESS OF EVALUATION SYSTEM. Although Mexico has been a leading country in Latin America to assess academic achievement through tests monitoring how well students learn, the authorities have been very cautious in using the results, questioning the reliability and validity of the information. However, the information is not any worse than the information produced by any other system in the Region. The authorities are not providing timely and accurate information to the public that would increase accountability and transparency of the education system.[4] In addition, in the mid-1990s, SEP started the *Programa de Instalación y Fortalecimiento de las Areas Estatales de Evaluación*, which is a significant step in the right direction to help produce useful information. The idea, which in some cases has been implemented, is to make systematic use of the available information to improve, among others things, the content of teacher training programs. The results from the assessments can be used as feedback for policy design.

---

4. The Clave Unica de Registro de Información, a personal identification number that will allow monitoring the status of each student during his/her years in the education sector. This, indeed, is a significant step to improve information in the sector.

PRIVATE DELIVERY OF EDUCATIONAL SERVICES (NEED TO INCREASE, REGULATE, SUP-PORT, SUPERVISE). In Latin America, Mexico has among the lowest rate of enrollment at all levels in the private sector, for example, less than 1 percent for preschool, about 6 percent for primary education, and 7.2 percent for lower secondary education. Higher education enrollment in the private sector is increasing, reaching about 27 percent today. With the support of the federal government, the *Instituto de Crédito Educativo del Estado de Sonora* (ICEES) and the *Sociedad de Fomento a la Educación Superior* (SOFES) run programs to increase student loan availability for higher education. These efforts, clearly based on demand-side financing criteria, are expected to increase greater equity and quality by improving access to higher education, particularly for academically qualified but financially needy students, and by increasing efficiency of public resources through increased competition in the sector.

III. Government Strategy

Mexico is keenly aware of the competitive environment in which it exists, and of the need to think ahead and keep an eye on the educational advances of its peers and competitors. The government, however, needs to choose a path to competitiveness that is most consistent with the priority of reducing poverty and socioeconomic inequality. This is because the country still faces major problems of poverty and income inequality, a considerable part of which can be attributed to educational inequality.

Therefore, the following education objectives deserve high priority: (a) universal completion of primary and lower secondary education; (b) improvement in the average learning achievement of primary and lower secondary school children; (c) reduction in educational inequality and deficits among the poor, rural, and indigenous population; and, (d) narrowing of the average educational gap between Mexico and its OECD peers.

SEP recognizes the importance of these priorities. This is evident from the *Programa de Desarrollo Educativo 1995-2000* and the *Informes de Labores* of the last several years, which give high priority to the reduction of basic education deficits and inequality. Such policy is consistent with: (a) the promotion of equity and poverty alleviation; (b) the enhancement of the overall competitiveness of Mexican labor through the development of highly trained workers; and (c) the establishment of a solid basis for catching up with OECD peers. The above objectives would engender a bigger pool of students that are better prepared for higher levels of education.

The challenge is how to achieve these goals in the current, changing, more complicated environment. Four points are worth mentioning in this regard. First, the budget is very tight, and the possibilities of increasing it are slim. Second, the government wants to change the way it does business, as reflected in its evolving policy of decentralization and its interest in reforming the methodology of allocating its basic education transfers among the states. Third, the disadvantaged children who are lagging behind in their basic education are dispersed, and are often located in isolated areas. Fourth, demand for post-basic education is projected to rise, as more children finish primary and lower secondary levels, and pressures to meet OECD higher education standards build up.

Another important decision was the creation of *Carrera Magisterial* (CM, Teacher Career Program) to encourage teachers to continue their professional development and to reward excellence and achievement. This professional development support program was created in 1992 as part of the *Acuerdo Nacional para la Modernización de la Educación Básica*. It aims to raise the quality of basic education through teacher professionalization, presence in schools, and working conditions, and represents an effort by the government to provide better support for and recognition of the valuable work of teachers. The program established a system of horizontal promotion for academic staff. This initiative explicitly recognized the critical role of the teacher in the classroom and the importance of parental involvement in the education of their children.

Information and communication technology in both primary and secondary schools has been introduced in Mexico. The *Telesecundaria Program* is a good example of how effectively Mexico has used technology (see Box 1). More and more schools have been connected to the satellite. Schools are being supplied with com-

---

Box 1. The Telesecundaria Program

This program was created 30 years ago to respond to the needs of rural communities where a regular lower secondary school would not be feasible. It is a good example of how Mexico is an innovator in education. It has a single teacher who teaches all disciplines for all three grades. With the introduction of satellite transmission in the 1990s enrollment increased, and today there are about 1 million students in about 14,000 schools. Lessons are delivered by means of television programs broadcast on EDUSAT, Mexico's educational broadcast system. The program puts teachers and students on the screen and provides a context and practical uses for the concepts taught. Extensive use is made of images and video clips to illustrate information and help students.

Research in the 1970s, and more recently in the 1990s, shows the cost-effectiveness of the program. It has a completion rate similar to the general lower education rate (about 79 percent) and much higher than the completion rates of technical and vocational schools. In the area of language *Telesecundaria* graduating students get scores similar to those of general lower secondary, in spite of having a more rural background.

Source: Secondary Education in Latin America and the Caribbean. The Challenge of Growth and Reform, L. Wolff and C.Castro, IDB, Sustainable Development Department Technical Papers, 1999.

puters and connected to a school network that opens many new learning possibilities. This technology is also being applied to in-service teacher training and the initial formation of teachers. All teacher centers and normal schools are connected to the satellite, and many already have connections to the Internet.

Innovative compensatory programs have been developed and implemented to vigorously promote rural education. For example, the government has developed a program (PROGRESA) that seeks to stimulate demand for education among the rural poor. On the supply side, more recent interventions have emphasized a pedagogical and organizational view of the needs of both teachers and whole schools. Furthermore, interesting experiments have been conducted that give more say to the community regarding the functioning of the school. Some compensatory programs have introduced an economic incentive that is paid through the community, giving it an important role in teacher attendance, school functioning, and supervision. Although more studies are needed, this mechanism, in general, has had good results, and is being used extensively.

Networking and partnerships with businesses, employers, and worker associations are important to the improvement of educational opportunities in Mexico. There has been much improvement in the last decade in identifying needed reforms in technical training. Panels of experts at the national and state levels, including curriculum specialists, representatives of the productive sector, and education professionals are among those who have participated. CONALEP, for example, has been transformed from a strictly pre-work, technical training agency into a comprehensive system offering pre-service and on-the-job training, technical assistance, and quality and productivity enhancement to industry. CONALEP has shown that close collaboration between publicly funded training institutions and the private sector is necessary to improve internal efficiency, by improving course content and matching graduate output with employers' needs.

Another positive experience during the 1990s is that of *the Consejo de Normalización y Certificación de Competencia Laborales* (CONOCER) and *the Sistema Normalizado de Competencias Laborales* (SNC). The SNC has provided an objective set of standards, similar to some that already exist in OECD countries, by which to evaluate worker skills and establish curriculum for training programs. CONOCER, which was created to oversee the process of establishing the SNC, has also ensured coherence and consistency across competency standards of different occupations by accrediting agencies whose main function is to certify that workers have mastered competencies in the standards for occupational clusters.

Lessons Learned

Several studies on learning outcomes show that in Mexico, like in most of the world, differences in test scores among children are determined predominantly by their socioeconomic and cultural background. School factors, however, also have a substantive effect. An evaluation of the PARE program (see below for further description of the program) reveals that learning achievement can be increased substantially through appropriately designed and targeted interventions, provided they are reasonably well implemented. When tailored to the needs of disadvantaged children, these interventions can reduce the difference in learning between these children and their more fortunate peers. Data from the PARE survey and analyses based on control and experimental groups illustrate this point.

Relating the cost of these inputs to their marginal effects on test scores, available estimates show that textbooks and other educational materials, along with improvement in physical facilities, have a much higher cost-effectiveness than increased teacher salaries, years of experience, and teacher/pupil ratio.

It appears that a substantial increase in learning achievement is possible for rural and indigenous schools. More specifically, their learning disadvantages could be overcome to a large extent by well-implemented interventions focused on the types of inputs mentioned above. For example, in areas where its design was fully implemented, PARE was able to increase Spanish test scores for the average student by about 42.3 percent for indigenous students, and by 16.5 percent for rural students.

Opportunities for Improvements

Today there are good opportunities to address Mexico's education challenge. Several current public interventions in education are conducive to further educational advancement. These include, the *Carrera Magisterial* program; the compensatory programs for rural and indigenous children like PAREB, PIARE, PAREIB, and PRODEI; CONAFE's programs; PROGRESA's scholarships for the poor; and Telesecundaria's distance education. This list is selective, but all of these programs are related to the issues discussed in this Chapter regarding the dimensions and causes of educational deficits.

The government recognizes that providing educational opportunities for the poor is an important vehicle for achieving equity. Consequently, SEP has developed an education strategy aimed at improving the quality of instruction in the country and ensuring that all children have adequate access to basic education. This strategy is implemented through programs which (a) deliver instructional materials, especially textbooks, to all school children; (b) provide basic school facilities and equipment; and (c) encourage community and parental involvement in the school. To compensate for the specific needs of the poor, a set of programs has also been designed and implemented which targets poor areas and indigenous groups, and attempts to overcome the inequities in the education system.

PARE. The first of these programs was PARE, which was designed as an integrated approach to improving the overall quality of basic education in the four poorest states, with attempts to build on the existing education and culture in traditional communities (which are largely indigenous). PARE assistance focused on improvements in physical facilities, books and materials, teacher performance incentives, school management and supervision, and teacher training. Based on the success of the program, SEP developed further assistance to poorest municipalities and communities in what became the strategy of the compensatory programs. These programs are administered through CONAFE. This agency, while part of SEP, works exclusively with under-served rural, poor, and indigenous communities. The CONAFE community schools have been designed to overcome the problems of maintaining and staffing schools in remote areas, where it is difficult to attract and retain teachers and where, given the small size of the community, it would not be cost-effective to establish regular schools. To overcome this difficulty, specially trained lower secondary graduates volunteer to teach in schools which are built and maintained by the communities themselves in return for scholarships to continue their own education. During the 1996-97 cycle, the compensatory programs covered a total of 4.4 million students in the localities where poverty levels are highest through the distribution of packets of teaching materials, incentives to teachers, and school infrastructure.

PAREIB. SEP, through CONAFE, just recently launched a basic education development project (PAREIB), which can be a useful tool for advancing basic education of the underserved population. PAREIB, designed to promote the government's compensatory education program, supports consolidation of the following policies: (a) a gradual decentralization in the operation of the compensatory programs through strengthening of the states' institutional capacity and an increased participation of communities and school associations in school management; and (b) a better quality of education and increased learning through teacher training, provision of standards for targeted schools, and national evaluation as a tool to increase accountability at all levels.

PROGRESA. This is the government's most recent poverty alleviation initiative, and includes nutrition, health, and education programs. The education component of PROGRESA is aimed at improving attendance and preventing early dropout in the poorest communities in the country. To address the dropout problem, PROGRESA provides educational grants to each child under age 18 who attends school between the third year of primary school and the third year of secondary school. The purpose of the educational assistance is to contribute to the family income and provide an incentive for the child to remain in school. For primary school, at the beginning of the school year, each beneficiary student receives some school materials in communities where CONAFE is not present. Follow-up payments are done bimonthly based on student attendance records. Secondary scholarships can go higher depending on whether the students have books. Scholarships for girls over age 12 are marginally higher because of their higher dropout rate. The scholarship is given at the beginning of the year and represents between 5 and 9 percent of total family income of those in extreme poverty, or the equivalent of 15 percent of the average potential income of children. Experience in Brazil with a similar (although simpler) program *called Bolsa Escola*, suggests that giving poor families cash conditional on their children attending school can be a powerful tool for educational improvement. Comparative evaluation of demand-side and supply-side interventions in terms of cost-effectiveness are needed in Mexico, as in other countries.

PROGRESA is currently targeted at specific regions with the highest levels of marginality in all Mexican states. Although preliminary results of an impact evaluation of the program indicate a good rate of return (around 13 percent), some concerns have been raised regarding the possibilities for corruption in delivering cash transfers, and the duplication in benefits between the some programs and PROGRESA. The first concern can be addressed by revisiting the methodology of beneficiary selection, the second concern by ensuring close coordination between SEP, CONAFE, the SSA, and PROGRESA.

CARRERA MAGISTERIAL (CM). This program, which has several parts, is governed by the *Comisión Nacional Mixta*, which consists of officials of SEP and SNTE. One component of CM is teacher training; another is a merit pay system in which on a voluntary basis professional staff are evaluated and rewarded with salary increases for their performance as classroom teachers, school directors, and supervisors. Clearly, this program is a highly relevant initiative that could provide the basis for further work on the issues of professional development and incentives to improve teacher performance in school. Although its effectiveness and adequacy have yet to be assessed empirically and rigorously, some preliminary results seem to indicate good results. With CM, Mexico is at the forefront of innovation in regard to the development of a voluntary "merit pay" system that rewards the professional development of participating teachers.

EDUCATIONAL DECENTRALIZATION. The most interesting development among the various ongoing initiatives is the unfolding policy of education decentralization. It is the most interesting because it carries both great opportunities and risks. As noted, the policy discussions on decentralization issues are moving toward greater devolution of authority and responsibility to sub-national units. These discussions have begun to open up new ideas on institutional development alternatives and innovations at the federal and state levels. In time, the evolving discussions at the state level could become focused on the empowerment of schools and parents. In fact, under the *Acuerdo Nacional para la Modernización de la Educación Básica*, parents' participation in school affairs is supposed to be a policy, although its implementation has been sporadic.

Decentralization presents the opportunity to rethink the way federal transfers are allocated, and to address the growing interest in the idea of distributing them in a simpler, more transparent manner with less potential for overlap. In particular, interest in a formula-driven allocation and a corresponding accountability framework provides a good opening for more effective alternatives for dealing with equity and efficiency issues. In a country as large as Mexico, the government effort to decentralize is a sound decision that would make the educational system more responsive and agile. It is not, however, a panacea; and improvements in learning and school participation do not automatically flow from it, regardless of its design. In fact, an ill-designed decentralization program can be damaging.

Educational decentralization like those implemented in New Zealand, Victoria (Australia), Minas Gerais (Brazil), and Chile are likely to enhance the performance of the educational system. On the other hand, a decentralized system of finance without an effective compensatory mechanism can be detrimental to children in economically disadvantaged areas. Brazil provides an example of how a poorly designed decentralized structure of education finance had contributed to educational inequality, leading to its recent reform.

Through appropriate policies, the benefits of decentralization can be enjoyed without undermining equity. One of these policies is for the federal government to ensure that, on the whole, disadvantaged states get more resources than others.

But more is needed. Even if interstate inequality in the allocation of federal education transfers were fully resolved, the same degree of inequity within states could persist if they do not effectively use those transfers to improve the education of their disadvantaged children. Without significant improvements within states, not much will be accomplished in reducing learning gaps. An inequality decomposition analysis of *Carrera Magisterial* data shows that 5 percent or less of differences in student test scores are due to interstate variations, suggesting that attempts to equalize resources among states without accompanying changes within states would not significantly reduce student learning inequality.

This observation points to the broader argument that the opportunity to advance education in the foreseeable future very much depends on the extent to which decentralization is able to set in motion improvements in the operating environment of schools and the ability and motivation of teachers in the classroom. Decentralization that simply transfers authority and money from the federal government to the states would have a very limited impact, as has been the case in Argentina. It is notable that much of Chile's remarkable achievements in improving learning outcomes came after its decentralization policy was complemented with implementation of well-designed public school improvement programs that increased material support for disadvantaged schools and strengthened support for professional development of teachers (focus on quality).

Successful decentralization efforts such as those cited above have been effective in improving education because they focused on the school as the "production units." Their administrative and budgetary reforms were designed to ensure that schools and their teachers have the professional competence, authority, resources, and incentives to design and carry out learning and teaching activities that are suitable to the needs of individual students.

It is clear that decentralization to subnational units of government must be seen as only a mere first step toward changing school behavior. Nevertheless, for a large country like Mexico, such a step is crucial. It would be impractical and inefficient for the federal government to bypass subnational governments because there are educational activities that are done best at lower levels. These are activities which the federal government cannot handle efficiently because it is too far away from the problem, and which the schools are not fit to carry out due to economies of scale and conflict of interest (for example, supervision, coordination of location of schools, and ensuring equity among localities within a state).

IV. Options for the Future

Basic Strategies

Despite Mexico's notable educational achievement in the 1990s, much remains to be done. First, data indicate that student learning needs further improvements. This is evident from the low standardized learning achievement test scores of many students. Second, observers have pointed out that what students learn is largely limited to rote memorization, regurgitation of facts, and mechanical application of formulae. Observers also argue that teaching quality needs improvement. Many students are not learning how to think and construct knowledge in school. Third, many students, particularly those in poor, rural, and indigenous communities, continue to be left behind by their more fortunate peers who go to relatively better schools.

The country needs to confront this learning issue. Improving student learning equitably in both the quantitative and qualitative senses is fundamental to the future of Mexico and its ability to fully take advantage of accelerating technological progress and global competition. It is also essential for bringing about greater equity by ensuring that the return to education, which continues to be the most important instrument for poverty alleviation, is kept high.

To meet the above challenge, the states would have to develop their own vision and strategy based on school-level realities. Decentralization reform has given the states the responsibility for the development of their basic education system and opportunities to accommodate national norms, and to try out new ways of ratcheting up the performance of its schools that are consistent with local realities. In this regard, they need to be more aware of the critical issues facing schools and to find solutions that, to ensure sustainability, take into account the views of school stakeholders (students, parents, teachers, principals, supervisors, and state education officials). Without changes in school practices and the way children learn, the expected fruits of decentralization in terms of sustained improvements in student learning will not fully materialize.

Based on these issues, the central education development challenges that Mexico faces are: (a) to selectively expand accessibility at the initial and preschool and higher education levels; (b) to improve the quality of education throughout the system; (c) expand access to education as a key element for reduction of poverty and social inequality; (d) to invest in the skills and education of the labor force to better adapt to rapid economic and technical changes which would reinforce the country's economic competitiveness; and (e) to support the decentralization process at the state level.

In that context, some broad objectives are to:

(i)   Enhance the international competitiveness of Mexico by creating a highly educated and flexible labor force.

(ii)   Address the requirements put forward by the emergence both of an information society and of a knowledge-base economy.

(iii)   Promote equity and poverty reduction.

(iv)   Advance democracy through the broad-based participation of an educated and informed citizenry.

(v)   Build community cohesion, tolerance and social trust in a multicultural environment.

(vi)   Enhance governance in education by modernizing and professionalizing the education administration.

More specific objectives include:

(i)   Increasing lower secondary education enrollment to 75 percent.

(ii)   Encouraging enrollments in cost-effective, demand-designed, technical/vocational education.

(iii)   Increasing higher education participation to levels comparable with countries of similar economic development.

(iv)   Eradicating adult illiteracy and establish the foundations of a life long learning strategy whereby every working adult will periodically engage in deliberate education or training activities.

(v)   Stimulating effective multicultural policies in school education, especially within the context of bilingual education.

(vi)   Improving learning achievement of basic education students.

(vii)   Disseminating IT-supported strategies in basic and secondary schools.

(viii)   Reducing educational inequality by focusing on educational deficits of poor and indigenous populations.

Two Strategic Pathways to Educational Improvement

Within the above-mentioned objectives, various interventions can be classified into supply-side and demand-side measures.

Supply-side Measures

These are interventions directed at the expansion of supply and improvement in the quality of education services. Examples include:

(i)   Federal education transfers to finance public schools and teachers.

(ii) Diversified compensatory programs (for example, PARE and PAREIB) and rural and indigenous programs.
(iii) Strengthening teacher support and professional development.
(iv) Distance education technology *(Telesecundaria)*.
(v) Textbook programs.
(vi) Public education system decentralization.
(vii) Strengthening adult education.

Demand-side Measures

These are interventions that directly reduce the cost of education to the family and change their attitudes. They include:

(i) Providing children and their parents resources for their education (for example, PROGRESA).
(ii) Undertaking mass media campaigns to promote education.
(iii) Student loans for higher education as provided by ICEES and SOFES.

Until recently, almost all government interventions to improve education have been on the supply side. One example is PROGRESA. Public education expenditure on supply-side interven-tions can be effective, but its impact is limited by a number of factors. These include: (a) the nature of the supply and demand constraints limiting learning achievement and educational attainment; (b) the design of intervention and choice of inputs to finance; (c) the quality of implementation; and (d) the institutional context, structure of incentives, and management capacity.

V. An Action Plan

To be useful for actual policymakers, both strategy objectives and demand/supply measures need to be translated into specific, doable policy actions. Table 4 presents a collection of such actions, arranged by each of the key educational issues facing Mexico—access, internal efficiency, quality, finance, external efficiencies, equity, equity, and systemic reform.

Table 4. An Action Plan Matrix

Issue	Policy Objective	Options
I. Access		
a. Limited access to early childhood education (ECD)	a. Ensure that ECD is expanded mainly through informal ways in rural and in poor peri-urban areas	a. Decentralization of education services with central support to states, taking into account regional differences (as in the Compensatory Programs)*
b. Limited access to preschool education by:	b. Target expansion of preschool to areas with low enrollment, including especially indigenous areas	b. Target poor, isolated, and indigenous areas with incentives for preschool teachers*
–geographical region		c. Optimize distance education methodologies*
–urban-rural		d. Promote alternative finance mechanisms like student loans and fellowships for the poor*
c. Need to increase access to lower and upper secondary education	c. Target expansion of lower and upper secondary education	e. Strengthen/improve PROGRESA
d. Need to increase access to higher education	d. Increase opportunities for expansion of tertiary education	
II. Internal Efficiency		
a. Limited terminal efficiency in basic education	a. Improve quality of basic education and upper secondary education	a. Focus on learning*
b. Low terminal efficiency in upper secondary	b. Establish clear ways to measure internal efficiency indicators in technical and higher education	b. Introduce active teaching methods and child-oriented education*
		c. Strengthen community participation*
		d. Undertake mass media campaigns to promote education at all levels*
III. Quality		
a. Low achievement in basic education and variations by region and urban-rural and indigenous areas	a. Improve quality of primary and secondary education	a. Focus on learning*
b. Irrelevance of the assessment system and lack of national standards	b. Ensure that assessment system contributes to quality teaching and the learning process by providing opportune	b. Introduce active-teaching methods (mainly in science) and child-oriented education*
		c. Improve quality of textbooks*
		d. Design a bilingual education model

Table 4. (Continued)

Issue	Policy Objective	Options
c. Limited access to textbook and educational material at basic education in some rural areas d. Curriculum deficiencies—traditional pedagogical model at basic education	feedback to teachers and parents, and to monitor national standards c. Identify and implement cost-effective educational inputs	(All these could be delivered as part of the Compensatory Programs) c. Use tests to establish benchmarks for future tracking of achievement trends and link results to teacher training* d. Improve access to textbooks and learning materials in isolated areas* e. Increase instructional time devoted to core subjects and supervised homework* f. Evaluate the Carrera Magisterial program and introduce ways to improve teaching within the classroom* g. Conduct cost-effective studies*
IV. Finance a. State and private education spending stagnated or declined	a. Maintain a minimum level of spending per student by type of school b. Encourage growth of private schools at all levels	a. Encourage state financial support by (*pari passu*) arrangements* b. Review regulatory framework for private schools and simplify regulations, remove barrier to entry, especially for technical/higher* c. Keep the targeted voucher system to benefit poor students (e.g., PROGRESA, fellowships for upper secondary, etc.), and study its financial sustainability/expansion d. Support alternative financial mechanism for higher education*

Table 4. (Continued)

Issue	Policy Objective	Options
V. External Efficiency a. Rate of returns remains high for all education levels, but declining real salaries	a. Maintain levels of government expenditures b. Identify study programs conducive to employment (PMETYC)	a. Support skill development* b. Focus on private and informal sector, based on demand-driven programs* c. Encourage on-the-job training*
VI. Equity a. Benefit-incidence analysis shows that: *tertiary education consumes a relatively high proportion of public expenditures while the basis of cost recovery is higher at this level *public spending at tertiary level favors the wealthy and enrollment is very low and not equitable *primary education investment is considerable and public spending is pro-poor, but because of the large discrepancies between quality of education determined by type of school, government spending is neither equitable nor effective in targeting the poorest	a. Introduce cost recovery and/or fellowship programs for technical/higher education b. Target additional support to poorest students (in rural and poor peri-urban areas) in basic and upper secondary education	a. Design cost recovery criteria and design system to support low-income students (student loans and fellowships)* b. To maintain high levels of enrollment and school quality, the federal government should keep subsidies like PROGRESA and the Compensatory Programs, not only in rural but also in poor peri-urban areas

Table 4. (Continued)

Issue	Policy Objective	Options
VII. Systemic Reform a. Governance and decentralization b. Support development of standards and assessment	a. Rationalize decentralization, in particular human resources in states where the systems (federal and state) have not been homogenized b. Support management information system in the Secretaries (SEP and STPS) and at the state level c. Monitor university proliferation d. Deregulate education sector	a. Support preparation of state Education Strategies* b. Optimize human resources use* c. To the extent that fee-charging private institutions are already in the areas for which there is demand, it would make sense that the public training institutions be rigorously evaluated* d. Strengthen the education management information system (EMIS) at the central and state levels for monitoring and evaluation purposes. Need to promote the idea of the federal government as the facilitator of educational expansion and quality of education* f. Increase knowledge of evaluation and assessments, even supporting efforts for international comparisons* g. Need to improve capacity-building in weaker local authorities* h. Provide incentives for increased schooling and training opportunities, especially if privately provided, but maintain standards and keep promoting accreditation mechanisms

Note: *Measures which, if implemented, have very little incidence in the budget.

Annex A – Statistical Tables

Table A.1. Total and Public Enrollment by Poverty Level, Gender, and Education Level (Percent)

Poverty Level	Male		Female		Total	
	All	Public	All	Public	All	Public
Primary (6–11 years old)						
Extreme	93.5	93.5	93.2	93.2	93.3	93.3
Moderate	95.7	95.7	96.4	96.4	96.0	96.0
Non-poor	96.1	95.5	96.2	96.0	96.1	95.7
Total	94.8	94.6	95.0	94.8	94.9	94.7
Lower Secondary (12–14 years old)						
Extreme	38.7	38.6	37.0	36.6	37.9	37.6
Moderate	65.1	64.9	64.7	64.9	64.8	64.9
Non-Poor	78.1	77.2	80.2	80.4	79.1	78.8
Total	58.4	57.3	58.4	57.6	58.4	57.4
Upper Secondary (15–17 years old)						
Extreme	14.4	13.1	14.5	12.6	14.5	12.9
Moderate	37.4	35.4	34.4	31.4	36.0	33.5
Non-poor	53.4	47.2	62.9	53.7	58.0	50.1
Total	35.1	31.1	37.9	31.4	36.4	31.2
University (18–24 years old)						
Extreme	1.7	1.7	1.9	1.4	1.85	1.6
Moderate	6.7	6.2	6.1	5.8	6.4	5.9
Non-poor	23.8	17.4	20.2	14.9	22.0	16.1
Total	13.3	9.8	10.8	8.2	12.0	8.9

Source: World Bank calculations based on ENIGH, 1996.

Table A.2. Total and Public Enrollment by Poverty Level, Location, and
Education Level (Percent)

Poverty Level	Urban		Rural		Total	
	All	Public	All	Public	All	Public
Primary (6–11 years old)						
Extreme	93.2	93.2	93.5	93.5	93.3	93.3
Moderate	96.4	96.4	94.6	94.6	96.0	96.0
Non-poor	96.1	95.7	96.4	96.3	96.1	95.7
Total	95.4	95.2	93.9	93.9	94.9	94.7
Lower Secondary (12–14 years old)						
Extreme	49.1	48.9	29.0	28.8	37.9	37.6
Moderate	68.7	68.8	51.0	51.2	64.8	64.9
Non-Poor	81.4	81.3	59.5	59.8	79.1	78.8
Total	68.5	67.7	36.8	36.6	58.4	57.4
Upper Secondary (15–17 years old)						
Extreme	23.5	21.4	6.9	5.9	14.5	12.9
Moderate	39.6	36.8	22.2	21.7	36.0	33.5
Non-poor	61.7	54.0	24.5	21.8	58.0	50.1
Total	45.7	39.8	12.8	11.7	36.4	31.2
University (18–24 years old)						
Extreme	3.4	2.9	0.4	0.4	1.8	1.6
Moderate	7.4	7.0	2.3	2.2	6.4	5.9
Non-poor	24.0	17.6	5.9	5.4	22.0	16.1
Total	15.3	11.5	2.0	1.8	12.0	8.9

Source: World Bank calculations based on ENIGH, 1996.

Table A.3. Total and Public Enrollment by Poverty Level, Region, and
Education Level (Percent)

| | North | | Center | | South | | Mexico. D.F. | | Total | |
Poverty Level	All	Public	All	Public	All	Public	All	Public	All	Public
Primary (6–11 years old)										
Extreme	96.7	96.7	93.5	93.4	92.3	92.3	89.5	89.5	93.3	93.3
Moderate	95.7	95.7	96.3	96.2	96.0	96.0	95.8	95.8	96.0	96.0
Non-poor	97.1	97.0	95.7	94.9	95.7	94.9	95.5	95.7	96.1	95.7
Total	96.5	96.5	94.9	94.6	93.7	93.5	94.8	94.7	94.9	94.7
Lower Secondary (12–14 years old)										
Extreme	44.0	43.5	40.5	40.2	30.5	30.5	58.5	58.5	37.9	37.6
Moderate	66.1	65.7	65.3	65.3	56.1	56.2	76.5	77.8	64.8	64.9
Non-poor	83.1	83.7	75.9	74.1	77.9	80.6	81.1	78.7	79.1	78.8
Total	67.9	67.3	57.5	53.6	45.5	45.3	76.9	76.1	58.4	57.4
Upper Secondary (15–17 years old)										
Extreme	15.7	15.2	13.4	10.7	14.9	14.4	20.5	20.5	14.5	12.9
Moderate	29.0	26.8	33.7	31.2	44.2	40.5	45.8	46.0	36.0	33.5
Non-poor	49.5	43.5	61.2	51.4	66.0	62.0	60.5	51.8	58.0	50.1
Total	36.5	32.2	34.5	28.2	34.1	30.5	51.6	46.0	36.4	31.2
University (18–24 years old)										
Extreme	2.8	2.8	1.3	1.1	1.6	1.2	7.3	7.3	1.8	1.6
Moderate	5.3	4.6	5.6	5.1	7.3	6.8	11.0	11.5	6.4	5.9
Non-poor	19.9	16.1	21.1	14.6	17.5	14.1	22.0	22.0	22.0	16.1
Total	13.6	11.0	10.4	7.4	7.5	6.1	17.5	17.5	12.0	8.0

Source: World Bank calculations based on ENIGH, 1996.

Table A.4. Explaining the Probability of Being a Poor Household Head:
Logit Model

Variable	Logit Coefficient	Independent Variable Mean	Partial Derivative (percent)
Urban	-0.847	0.65	-15.00
Male	-1/051	0.86	-18.00
Age	0.018	44.0	0.32
Years of Schooling	-0.262	5.0	-4.64
Constant	0.333		
-2 log likelihood	4714		

Note: All coefficients are statistically significant at the 1 percent level or better. Mean dependent
variable = 23.1 percent. N= 4362. Data are from the late 1980s.

21

Social Protection

This Chapter was written by Gillette H. Hall and Ana-Maria Arriagada with the valuable input of Evelyne Rodriguez Ortega, Debora Schlam, Indermit S. Gill, Eduardo Velez Bustillo, Gladys Lopez-Acevedo, Christina Alquinta, Anna Maria Sant'Anna, Quentin T. Wodon, Claudia Contreras, Ximena B. Traa-Valarezo, Carmen Hamann and Monica Tinajero.

I. Introduction—Managing Social Risk in Mexico

The purpose of this Social Protection (SP) Chapter is to (a) identify key social risks faced by the Mexican population, and estimate the size of current at-risk populations; (b) examine and assess the effectiveness of Mexico's current SP strategy in addressing these risks, drawing on a detailed review of existing social insurance and social assistance programs; and, (c) identify best practice options for improving the coverage and effectiveness of social protection policies to address the needs of the population at-risk. The Chapter draws on national household survey data and poverty studies to estimate the size of at-risk groups, and detailed information on the universe of federal social protection programs (beneficiaries, budget, targeting mechanisms, etc.) compiled by the *Secretaria de Hacienda y Crédito Público (SHCP)*.

Table 1 draws together basic findings from the chapter, including the main indicators of social risk by age group, the estimated size of the population at risk (number of poor in risk category uncovered by social protection programs), and best practice strategies for addressing the needs of these at-risk groups, setting social protection policies (shaded area of the table) apart from the broader context of macroeconomic policies and sectoral programs, which are discussed in detail in other chapters.

Section II of this Chapter provides a detailed assessment of risk categories, analyzing leading indicators of risk by decile groupings in rural and urban areas. This section also examines the incidence and coverage of current SP programs targeted to these risks where such data are available. Section III provides an overview of Mexico's current Social Protection strategy, assessing social insurance (contributory) and targeted social assistance (non-contributory) programs according to costs, coverage of the at-risk population, and type of service or benefit provided. Section IV discusses best practice options, based on both Mexican and international experience,

Table 1. Managing Social Risk in Mexico: Main Risk Indicators, Size of At-Risk Groups, and Best Practice Policy Responses

| Age Group/Main Risk Indicator | Size of Population at Risk* (Number of Poor Uncovered) | | Role for Other Programs/Policies | Role for Social Protection (SP) Policy | |
	Urban	Rural		Social Insurance	Social Assistance
0–5					
–Malnutrition (0–4)	820,000	990,000	–Nutrition and educational programs	—	–Behavior-conditioned income transfers (PROGRESA)
–Access to ECD (0–4)	2,200,000	3,000,000	–Publicly provided and/or regulated ECD programs and preschool services		–Targeted ECD and community based pre-schools
–Preschool enrollment (age 5)	200,000	300,000			
6–14					
–Primary enrollment	Not at risk	430,000	–Improve primary school access/quality	—	–Behavior-conditioned income transfers PROGRESA
–Lower secondary enrollment	625,000	1,300,000	–Improve secondary school access/quality		–Targeted, community-based schooling services
–Child labor	180,000	515,000	–Distance learning programs		
–Inactivity	160,000	Not at risk			
15–24					
–Upper secondary enrollment	1,000,000	1,200,000	–Improve secondary school access/quality	—	–Targeted (need based) scholarships, credit facilities, return-to-school (high-school equivalency) incentive programs
–Unemployment	1,100,000	Not at risk	–Improve university access/quality		
–Inactivity	2,000,000	1,600,000	–Community colleges (terminal degrees, professional/semi-skilled qualifications)		

Table 1. (Continued)

Age Group/Main Risk Indicator	Size of Population at Risk* (Number of Poor Uncovered) Urban	Rural	Role for Other Programs/Policies	Role for Social Protection (SP) Policy Social Insurance	Social Assistance
25–64					
–Unemployment	460,000	Not at risk	–Labor-intensive growth	–Unemployment insurance	–Workfare (PET)
–Full-time employment, below poverty wages	2,800,000	1,600,000	–Financial services development	–Income-risk pooling (crop insurance)	–Targeted income transfers and/or negative income tax
–Underemployment (hrs)	1,300,000	1,400,000	–Training, remedial education		
65 and Over					
–Low pension coverage	1,000,000	1,250,000	–Financial services development	Social security system	–Targeted income transfers
General Population					
–Low housing quality	1,600,000 hds.	3,200,000 hds.	–Mortgage facilities –Infrastructure investment		–Targeted housing subsidies
Special Groups					
–Isolated villages	Not at risk	2,600,000	–Community driven and managed development programs		–Targeted investment in basic infrastructure services
–Indigenous people	No data	11,500,000			

Note: * Preliminary figures for population at risk calculated as the proportion of poor (deciles 1–3 in urban areas, deciles 1–6 in rural areas) in each age category uncovered (subject to revision), based on population estimates by age (Annex I) and risk indicator values by decile group (Table 2).

along with cost estimates, for enhancing SP interventions in each major category of risk; Section V concludes by discussing costs and trade-offs, policy priorities, as well as design, institutional and implementation issues, and analytical next steps.

II. Identification and Characteristics of Mexico's Key At-Risk Groups

Table 2a presents an analysis of social risk in Mexico by age group, presenting risk indicator values by geographic region and income level (decile groupings). The analysis draws on social risk theory to identify the main risks across the life cycle, then draws on the available household survey information for Mexico (INEGI 1996) to calculate leading indicators of risk for the poorest 10 percent, poorest 30 percent, and poorest 60 percent (rural only) of the population compared to the population average ("all"). The life-cycle approach is supplemented by the identification of other key groups at risk, where that risk stems from characteristics (geographic, ethnic, etc.) that cut across the life cycle. These special groups and their risk indicators are presented in the follow-on Table 2b. Highlighted areas in the table signal prominent at-risk groups. Summarizing this analysis, the main at-risk groups identified are as follows:[1]

- *0 to 5 year olds*: poor Early Child Development (ECD), including malnutrition (30 percent of all children in rural areas) and low/delayed cognitive development, and low pre-school attendance among the poor (71 percent in urban areas, 62 percent in rural areas).
- *6 to 14 year olds*: a pocket of low primary school enrollment rates (85 percent) among rural (largely indigenous) children in the poorest decile; widespread low enrollment rates for lower secondary school (37 percent among the general population).
- *15 to 24 year olds*: low rates of upper secondary school enrollment, particularly among the rural poor (7 percent); relatively high unemployment (29 percent) and high inactivity rates (over 30 percent) among the urban poor.
- *25 to 64 year olds*: full-time employment at below poverty wages (68 percent of the poor urban workforce), part-time employment (46 percent of the rural poor), and urban unemployment which is highest among males in the poorest decile (6.5 percent).
- *Over 65*: low pension coverage of the elderly poor (7 percent in urban areas, 0.2 percent in rural areas).

---

1. For details on statistics cited above, see table 2a which provides risk indicator values by decile groupings and urban-rural breakdowns. For the purposes of this chapter, deciles 1–3 (poorest 30 percent of the population) in urban areas and deciles 1–6 (poorest 60 percent of the population) in rural areas are categorized as "poor").

Table 2a. Mexico: Leading Indicators of Social Risk by Age, Region, and Income Group, 1996
(Bolded areas signal prominent at-risk groups)

Population Group/ Main Risk	Leading Risk Indicators	Indicator Value, Urban Area			Indicator Value, Rural Area			
		Poorest 10 percent	Poorest 30 percent	All	Poorest 10 percent	Poorest 30 percent	Poorest 60 percent	All
Ages 0–5: Stunted development	• Chronic Malnutrition (stunting)			11				30
	• ECD coverage			n.a.				n.a.
	• Preschool attendance (age 5 only)	53	71	82	44	52	62	66
Ages 6–14 Low human capital development	• Primary school enrollment (ages 6–11)	92	94	95	86	91	93	94
	• Age-for-grade* (ages 6–11)	1.07	1.04	1.01	1.13	1.12	1.10	1.08
	• Lower secondary school enrollment (ages 12–14)	41	55	68	24	24	29	37
	• Age-for-grade (ages 12–14)	1.19	1.13	1.07	1.36	1.37	1.31	1.24
	• Child employment (ages 12–14)	**16**	**13**	9	**40**	**30**	**28**	26
Violence/crime	• Inactivity—neither work nor attend school (ages 12–14)	21	12	7	9	14	14	13
Ages 15–24 Low human capital development	• Upper secondary enrollment (ages 15–17)	19	29	46	6	6	7	13
Low income	• University enrollment (ages 18–24)	2	4	15	0.7	0.2	0.9	2
	• Unemployment (ages 15–24) male	24	23	13	4.4	3.2	5.2	4.9
	female	12	12	10	0	6.9	5.3	5.2

(continues on next page)

Table 2a. (Continued)
(Bolded areas signal prominent at-risk groups)

Population Group/ Main Risk	Leading Risk Indicators	Indicator Value, Urban Area			Indicator Value, Rural Area			
		Poorest 10 percent	Poorest 30 percent	All	Poorest 10 percent	Poorest 30 percent	Poorest 60 percent	All
Violence/crime	• Inactivity (ages 15–17)	37	28	18	**31**	**30**	29	27
	• Inactivity (ages 18–24)	49	43	28	**29**	**36**	36	35
Ages 25–64 Low income	• Unemployment: male	**6.5**	**4.9**	3.2	**0.6**	**0.9**	1.5	1.5
	female	**3.5**	**2.8**	1.8	**0.0**	**1.5**	0.8	0.6
	• Part-time job (as of all employed)	37	32	26	**52**	**50**	46	42
	• No education or incomplete primary (low skills) (ages 25–40)	49	36	17	**70**	**68**	61	49
	• No education or incomplete primary (low skills) (ages 41–64)	78	69	42	**93**	**90**	90	85
Ages 65+ Low income	• Receives pension	2	7	22	**0**	**0.1**	0.2	7
General population Low-quality housing	• No piped water	18	15	7	**55**	**53**	48	38
	• No piped sewerage	50	37	18	**96**	**93**	89	79
	• No electricity	5	3	0.9	**29**	**24**	20	14

Note: * Age-for-grade is calculated as [age—grade + 1]/6, such that an individual in the appropriate grade for age will have an age-for-grade equal to 1, whereas an individual in a lower grade than appropriate for his or her age will have an age-for-grade greater than 1.

Sources: INEGI household survey, 1996; Encuesta Nacional de Nutrición, 1999.

Table 2b. Mexico: Leading Indicators of Social Risk, Specific Population Groups

Population Group	Leading Risk Indicators	Indicator Value, Urban Area	Indicator Value, Rural Area
Isolated rural villages (population 100 or less, total 2.6 million people)	• Lack of access to basic infrastructure, social services • High dependency ratio (large proportion of children and elderly relative to working-age population)	Not applicable	—Without access to: electricity (59 percent), sewerage (90 percent), primary school (40 percent), secondary school (100 percent), health mobile unit (30 percent), access to temporary employment program (94 percent), free tortilla (99 percent), etc. —These villages represent 2.9 percent of total population, but 3.3 percent of youth (0–14) and 3.4 percent of elderly (over 65). vs. 2.6 percent of working age population (25–64).
Indigenous (total population 11,500,000 people, of which 80 percent (9,200,000) among the extreme poor, and 1 million monolingual)	• Systematically higher poverty rates and lower social development indicators	(all indicators for indigenous are given in next column—data do not allow rural/urban breakdown)	—Illiteracy rates, age 15 and over: 49 percent (women), 27.8 percent (men). In communities with over 70 percent indigenous populations (total pop. 4,000,000), 28 percent of children do not attend school, most living in communities with 100 or fewer inhabitants. Over 1 million school-age children speak indigenous language, 250,000 of which are monolingual. Only 38 percent of schools in indigenous communities offer all 6 grades of primary education.

Sources: Psacharopoulos and Patrinos (1994), INI (1997), World Bank (1999), Government of Mexico/World Bank (2000).

- *General population*: poor quality housing, particularly lack of basic infrastructure services (48 percent of the rural poor without piped water, and 89 percent without sewerage access).
- *Other special at-risk groups* include isolated rural villages and the indigenous, for whom the above indicators are systematically worse (see table 2b).

Table 3 looks at risk from an alternative perspective, assessing the coverage and incidence of programs targeted to key social risks by geographic region and income decile groups, where such data exist (INEGI 1996).[2] Results, though preliminary, indicate low coverage of certain targeted programs (such as scholarships for lower and upper secondary school) relative to the proportion of the population at risk (as indicated in Table 3). Further, some social assistance programs display a regressive incidence pattern (training programs, food programs and housing credit) along with access to social insurance which is also regressive (pensions, social security), as indicated by the highlighted sections of the table. Finally, while some programs have higher coverage rates among the urban poor, such as training, and food programs, other programs have surprisingly higher incidence in rural areas, such as scholarships. Given the number of new initiatives and changes to programs after 1996, it is important to revise these coverage and incidence estimates as soon as updated survey data (ENIGH 1998) become available for analysis, before drawing specific policy implications from these estimates.

III. Mexico's Social Protection Strategy

Mexico's SP strategy is nested within a broader framework of macroeconomic policy aiming to achieve broad-based economic growth and fiscal sustainability, combined with sectoral reforms to improve access to and quality of basic social services. Within this context, SP programs are designed to complement the above policies with (a) *social insurance* (contributory) mechanisms which pool social risks across population groups (i.e. public pensions, health insurance), and (b) targeted *social assistance* interventions (non-contributory) which transfer resources (in-kind, cash, or services) to particular at-risk groups. Total federal SP spending in 2000 is 223.9 billion pesos (US$24 billion), of which social insurance represents 76 percent and targeted social assistance 24 percent (Table 4). Total SP spending amounts to 44 percent of all federal social development expenditures, 27 percent of total federal expenditures, and 4.3 percent of GDP (social insurance represents 3.2 percent of GDP

---

2. While INEGI provides the only nationally representative data set allowing program coverage and incidence to be analyzed across deciles of the entire population, the validity of these results is likely to be less precise than that drawn from individual program assessments. Data are also old (1996) and thus do not reflect any changes in coverage rates that result from new initiatives.

Table 3. Coverage and Incidence of Social Programs Targeted to Key Social Risks, by Region and Income Decile Groups, Mexico, 1996

(Bolded areas indicate regressive program incidence pattern)

Population Group/ Main Risk	Program Coverage	Indicator Value, Urban Area			Indicator Value, Rural Area			
		Poorest 10 percent	Poorest 30 percent	All	Poorest 10 percent	Poorest 30 percent	Poorest 60 percent	All
Ages 0–5: Stunted development	• Family receives Progresa transfers	n.a						
	• ECD coverage	n.a.						
Ages 6–14 Low human capital development	• Receives scholarship to attend school (6–11)	2.8%	2.0%	2.0%	3.1%	3.4%	3.9%	4.1%
Violence/crime	• Receives scholarship to attend school (12–14)	1.6%	1.7%	2.2%	3.4%	5.6%	5.0%	4.5%
Ages 15–24 Low human capital development	• Receives scholarship to attend school (ages 15–17)	3.6%	1.5%	3.6%	1.9%	1.3%	1.3%	1.3%
Low income	• Receives scholarship to attend school (ages 18–24)	0%	5.6%	5.0%	0%	0%	3.3%	2.8%

(continues on next page)

Table 3. (Continued)

(Bolded areas indicate regressive program incidence pattern)

Population Group. Main Risk	Program Coverage	Indicator Value, Urban Area			Indicator Value, Rural Area			
		Poorest 10 percent	Poorest 30 percent	All	Poorest 10 percent	Poorest 30 percent	Poorest 60 percent	All
Ages 25–64								
Low income	• Has attended training program	0%	2%	12%	0%	0%	0.2%	2%
	• Has access to social security system	9%	19%	43%	0.2%	0.9%	3%	11%
	• Receives 'ayuda alimentaria o dispensa'	1.6%	4%	12%	0%	0.1%	0.7%	3%
Ages 65+								
Low income	• Receives pension	2%	7%	22%	0%	0.1%	0.2%	7%
General population								
Low-quality housing Low access to savings/ credit facilities	• Access to housing credit	0.7%	4%	16%	0%	0.1%	0.4%	

Source: INEGI household survey, 1996. Subject to revision.

Table 4. Federal Social Protection Programs in Mexico

Type of Program	Number of Programs	Budget 2000 (million pesos)	Percent of total Budget	Major Beneficiaries
1. Social Insurance	4	**170,539.0**	**76.1**	
-Social Security	3	158,687.0	70.8	-Formal sector employees
-Negative Income Tax	1	11,760.0	5.2	-Formal sector employees
2. Sectoral Social Assistance	29	**15,861.9**	**7.1**	
-Education	18	6,622.8	3.0	-Poor, low educated
-Health	5	4,740.7	2.1	-Rural poor
-Housing credit	2	3,779.6	1.7	-Public sector employees
-Other	4	718.8	0.3	-Various vulnerable groups
3. Income Transfers and Subsidies	7	**14,765.2**	**6.6**	
-Progresa (conditioned income T)	1	9,635.0	4.3	-Rural poor
-Food Programs	6	5,130.2	2.3	-Poor
4. Income Generation	54	**15,531.8**	**6.9**	
-Temporary Employment	1	3,997.7	1.8	-Poor unemployed
-Labor Training	2	1,683.9	0.7	-Low income
-Rural Development	51	9,850.2	4.4	-Rural communities
5. Social Infrastructure	5	2,250.1	1.0	-Communities with low access to basic infrastructure
6. Natural Disaster Protection	1	4,839.9	2.2	-Communities hit by natural disasters
7. Other	5	202.8	.09	-Poor communities
Total	105	223,990.7	100	

Note: Category "Other" includes institutional strengthening, community development, etc.
Source: SHCP.

while targeted social assistance represents 1.1 percent). In terms of international comparisons, SP spending in Mexico is relatively low—in the LAC region SP spending ranges from 0.7 percent of GDP in Haiti to 8.7 percent in Chile; for North America and Western Europe these figures are 11.2 percent and 12.4 percent of GDP respectively.[3]

Social Insurance

Mexico's social insurance strategy includes two main types of interventions: social security (Instituto Mexicano de Seguro Social—IMSS, and Instituto de Seguridad Social al Servicio de los Trabajadores del Estado—ISSSTE), and a negative income tax (Impuesto Sobre la Renta Negativo). SOCIAL SECURITY (IMSS and ISSSTE) absorbs the bulk of total federal SP expenditures (71.4 percent in 2000). The main weakness of social security in Mexico, historically, has been the fact that eligibility is restricted to formal sector employees. *"Derecho habientes"* or those who have access to the social security system through their own employment or that of a family member, represent less than half of the Mexican population (42 percent), and are largely middle and upper income families. Coverage among the poor is low (just 5 percent of those in the poorest income decile are *derecho habientes*), and is well under half even among the middle class (30 percent of those in decile 5 are *derecho habientes*) according to SCHP estimates. The social security system is also very costly to operate; programs are not fully funded by contributions, and thus require substantial subsidies from general federal revenues—IMSS alone requires federal transfers of $66.3 billion pesos annually (30 percent of *total* federal SP spending, and 1.3 percent of GDP—more than the total spent on all targeted social assistance).[4]

Reforms initiated in the past administration are positive, in that they have begun to broaden coverage of the social insurance system (both pensions and health insurance), including allowing informal sector workers to participate.[5] However, these initiatives appear to be expanding coverage of the system only slowly. Of the total 16.2 million informal sector workers, only 8,724 have subscribed voluntarily under the expanded options of the pension program since their inception in 1997 (about 25 percent of whom are in Mexico D.F.). Coverage under voluntary inscription to the public health insurance system has expanded more rapidly, with 211,798 indi-

3. World Bank, Social Protection Tool Kit, preliminary draft, 2000. Figures are for central government spending on "social security and welfare," defined as social insurance and social assistance or safety-net programs. Expenditure levels may not be exactly comparable across countries due to differing definitions of social welfare and the composition of programs included therein.

4. SHCP, 2000. A significant proportion of this transfer represents liabilities assumed by the federal government as a result of pension reform (see the Pension Reform Chapter).

5. Details on the implementation of these reforms are discussed in the Pension and Health Sector Chapters, respectively.

viduals (representing 618,680 total family members) subscribing. And the IMSS program for agricultural workers (*Seguridad Social para Jornaleros Agricolas*) has expanded its coverage from 184,500 people in 1994 to over 2 million in 2000.

The NEGATIVE INCOME TAX PROGRAM is intended as a transfer to low income workers, but in its current form operates as a tax subsidy to employers. For formal sector employees earning 1–3 minimum wages, the federal government provides a sliding-scale transfer to the employer (an offset to tax liabilities), which is then passed on to the employee, as a 'negative tax' of between 0 (3 minimum wages) and 285 (1 minimum wage) pesos per month. Since eligibility is again restricted to formal sector employees, though intended to reduce low-income risk, this program currently has negligible impact among the poorest deciles. And since one must be employed to obtain the benefit, the program does not address income risk arising from unemployment. There are also questions regarding the degree of compliance—lack of appropriate controls such that employers might apply for the tax reduction without passing the rebate on to employees. The program costs an estimated 11.8 billion pesos per year to operate (5.3 percent of total SP spending, and equal in value to 23 percent of all targeted social assistance spending), more than the total budget for PROGRESA—one of the government's flagship programs (see below). The program is thus a prime candidate for reform, as it absorbs a sizeable amount of resources without reaching intended beneficiaries or addressing key-risks.

Social Assistance

Mexico's other social protection interventions, broadly classified as targeted social assistance in that they are not contributory but involve unilateral transfers of resources to at-risk groups, have a total budget of 52 billion pesos (24 percent of total SP spending, 1.2 percent of GDP). Program categories include sectoral social assistance programs (education, health, housing), income transfers and subsidies (PROGRESA and food programs), income generation programs (temporary employment, labor training, and rural development), social infrastructure, natural disaster protection, and a small category of other programs targeted to individual vulnerable groups.

SECTORAL SOCIAL ASSISTANCE IN HEALTH, EDUCATION AND HOUSING PROGRAMS (15.8 billion pesos) absorbs 6.8 percent of total SP spending, and 30 percent of targeted social assistance spending. Benefits are by and large directed to key at-risk groups; there are 18 education programs directed to poor and low-education individuals in various age categories, and 5 health programs (including the PAC, award-winning project that extends health care to isolated rural areas). The housing subsidy program, FOVISSTE (3.8 billion pesos), is a notable exception, as only public sector employees are eligible for benefits (18,300 loans in 2000); this program is hence a prime candidate for reform of eligibility criteria and targeting in order to improve the risk-reducing impact of these resources. The creation in 1998 of the *Programa de Ahorro y Subsidios para la Vivienda Progresiva,* providing housing credit to urban families in extreme poverty, is a highly positive initiative, however the budget (695 million pesos) and number of families served (32,400 in 2000) remain small relative to the size of the urban population with low housing quality (1.6 million households). Further, the program does not currently serve rural areas, where the size of the at-risk population is far greater (3.2 million households).

INCOME TRANSFERS AND SUBSIDIES (14.8 billion pesos) absorb 28 percent of targeted social assistance spending. The largest program in this category is PROGRESA (9.6 billion pesos), a conditioned income-transfer program targeted to rural areas, and one of the government's most notable initiatives. In 2000 the program served 2.6 million families, implying coverage of over half of all families in rural areas, with income transfers conditioned on school attendance and/or use of health care facilities, and for purchase of basic foods. In addition, 6 food programs (5.1 billion pesos) are in operation. These food programs seem to have overlapping target groups (the extreme poor) and objectives, both with PROGRESA (meeting basic nutritional needs) and among the food programs themselves (3 programs provide a basic food basket and others provide basic commodities such as milk and tortillas), such that there are likely to be significant opportunities for reform by streamlining objectives and consolidating programs.

EMPLOYMENT AND INCOME GENERATION PROGRAMS (15.5 billion pesos) absorb another 28 percent of targeted social assistance spending. These programs include the *Programa de Empleo Temporal—PET,* a temporary employment program (4 billion) which generated 1 million short-term jobs in 2000; 2 labor training programs (1.7 billion), providing training to approximately 600,000 workers,[6] and 51 rural development programs (9.8 billion). It is programs in this last category which seem to present the most potential and need for reform—the budget is spread thinly across a multitude of programs, providing differing and at times competing services (training, agricultural assistance, etc.). Further, one program, *Apoyo a la Comercialization,* absorbs one third of all resources in this category (over 3 billion pesos) yet seems to be directed to mid-size farmers as opposed to the poorest, small farmers.[7] A systematic review of these programs vis-à-vis the needs of target groups (particularly for credit, micro-financing, and savings facilities), followed by development of a coherent strategy by a single coordinating body, is likely to produce significant gains in impact and efficiency in this area of intervention.

---

6. Excluding CIMO, for which the number of beneficiaries was unavailable at the time of writing this report.
7. Note that *Apoyo a la Comercialización* is not always considered a social program, nor always included in calculations of total social expenditures; therefore there is some debate as to whether it should be considered in this discussion of social protection programs.

SOCIAL INFRASTRUCTURE PROGRAMS targeted to at-risk groups (2.2 billion pesos) absorb just 4 percent of targeted social assistance resources. This category includes 5 programs, the largest of which are the rural roads program (901 million pesos), and the potable water program (867 million pesos) which extended water services to an estimated 80,000 families in marginalized urban and rural areas in 2000. Two additional programs target resources for investment in basic infrastructure specifically to indigenous communities, but have relatively few resources allocated to them (142 million pesos) relative to the size of the at-risk population (2.6 million people living in rural villages of 100 or less inhabitants), and the level of need for water, basic sanitation, etc. (see Table 3.b) The one new initiative in this area, the rural telephone program (337 million pesos), does not adequately address the lack of basic infrastructure services, and in any event targets resources to communities of over 100 inhabitants.

Finally, the NATURAL DISASTER FUND (4.8 billion pesos) is a very positive new initiative, setting aside a pool of resources for disaster relief which enhances the nation's safety-net with improved capacity for crisis management. The fund appears to be well-coordinated with existing programs, for example, it is designed to operate in coordinated fashion with the PET, so that reconstruction and disaster relief will also generate temporary employment. Thus, the fund is designed to both provide emergency employment (through PET) as well as reconstruction of infrastructure and housing in disaster areas.

Social Protection in Mexico: Issues, Options and Costs

Best Practice Policy Options for Addressing Key Risks

Addressing the main areas of social risk in Mexico depends on a broad context of policies including a macroeconomic framework which facilitates labor-intensive growth, and sectoral policies which broaden access to basic services (health, education, financial services, etc.) to currently underserved and hence vulnerable groups. Within this context, best practice SP interventions by the government can complement this framework with appropriate social insurance and social assistance programs designed to reduce key social risks where insurance markets fail, and where self-protection mechanisms are out of reach of the most vulnerable sectors of the population. This section highlights identifies best practice options for addressing 7 key areas of risk currently prevailing in Mexico (summarized in Table 5), and where possible provides costs estimates for implementing these options. It identifies both existing programs in Mexico which demonstrate best practice characteristics yet fail to cover the at-risk population, and are thus candidates for expansion, and supplements these findings with further best practice options from international experience. Cost estimates draw on: (a) 1996 ENIGH survey data for estimating the size of the at-risk population; (b) data from SHCP on coverage of current programs, used where possible to adjust

Table 5. SP Strategy & Major Social Risks: Seven Key Problems and Best Practice Options

Problem	Diagnosis	Best Practice Policy Options
1. Low preschool and ECD Program coverage	Public services not widely available, private services cost-prohibitive for the poor.	Mexico's exemplary ECD education services for parents (PRODEI) and community-based pre-school services (CONAFE) illustrate best-practice techniques, but offer insufficient coverage and should be expanded.
2. Pocket of low primary school attendance in rural areas	In rural areas, 15 percent of 6–14 year-olds in the poorest income decile (largely indigenous) do not attend school.	Community-based rural schooling (CONAFE), combined with scholarships and training for indigenous students to become teachers, bilingual education, distance learning and mobile education units.
3. Low secondary school enrollment rates	Opportunity cost of schooling, poor quality, and low access yield high youth employment in rural areas and "inactivity" in urban areas.	Expand demand-side subsidies (for example PROGRESA scholarships) complemented by increased access and quality of secondary schooling; special education programs to bring dropouts back into education system, and high-school equivalency programs.

Table 5. (Continued)

Problem	Diagnosis	Best Practice Policy Options
4. Low earnings among the poor, working-age population	Low education/skill levels yield higher unemployment and underemployment among the poor; but majority of poor (over 60 percent) are employed full time at below poverty wages. Current negative income tax program excludes poorest (informal sector).	Self-targeted workfare program for the poor unemployed (Mexico's PET), complemented by targeted income-support (reformed negative income tax is an option) for poor working families, within macroeconomic and labor market framework promoting labor-intensive growth, along with financial services for the poor.
5. Low access to pension (income support) among the elderly poor	Pension system only recently open to informal sector; current access to pensions regressive with extremely low (0.2 percent) incidence among rural poor.	Expanded options for informal sector participation in public and/or private contributory pension plans, complemented by targeted noncontributory pension system for elderly poor.
6. Low housing quality among the poor	Restricted or access to savings and borrowing mechanisms for the poor, existing public subsidies largely targeted to middle class (public sector employees).	Targeted subsidies to finance small-scale home improvements, complemented by expanded financial services (mortgages) and basic infrastructure networks serving poor areas.
7. Concentration of indigenous people among the chronically poor, and in isolated rural villages	Geographic and social isolation, low access to basic infrastructure, few public interventions specifically designed to foster local control or driven by indigenous cultural norms.	Targeted investment to reduce basic infrastructural deficiencies of these communities (i.e. water), combined with specific, community-driven and managed development programs (see Indigenous Peoples Chapter).

1996 estimates of the size of the uncovered population downwards to account for increased coverage of the at-risk population due to SP initiatives undertaken by the government after 1996;[8] (c) current SP program costs, per beneficiary (including administrative costs) in Mexico (various sources including SHCP and World Bank).

Expanding Access to Early Child Development Programs (ECD)

ECD services targeted to young children may be the most effective intervention for breaking the intergenerational transmission of vulnerability by enhancing learning ability, schooling, and hence earnings potential. Widespread international evidence shows that providing targeted nutrition support and preschool education services to children 0 to 5 consistently leads to improved child nutrition and health, higher school enrollment rates, and better performance on aptitude tests. Further, these results are most apparent in children from poor families as compared to the non-poor. By increasing early abilities, preschool programs increase both the prospective earnings potential from a given year of schooling and the prospective earnings benefits of additional schooling (Young 1996).

Survey data do not allow access to ECD services to be estimated in Mexico, however the limited number of existing programs clearly indicates low access, especially in rural areas. Best practice models for ECD service provision emphasize several features. First, parental involvement (in program design, in service provision, and providing parent training as part of ECD services) is an essential component of successful ECD interventions. Second, especially in countries where fiscal resources and local infrastructure are insufficient to support the universal provision of basic services, collaboration with local groups and NGOs (both national and international) as service providers has proven to be an effective approach to widening service provision, especially to poor and isolated communities. Third, most national governments share the cost of early child intervention programs with subnational governments and program beneficiaries (who either pay a user fee, pay caregivers' honoraria, or do volunteer work at the care center). Finally, television and radio programs have been used in innovative ways to enhance ECD services by offering training programs for care providers and supplementing the local curriculum with ingenious learning programs for children, and to extend these ECD support services to remote areas.[9] Mexico's PRODEI (Programa de Educación Inicial) includes several of these features, focusing on teaching parents techniques for social and motor development among young children. This program is a clear target for expansion in order to raise ECD coverage. The program currently covers 580,000 children at a cost of 540 pesos per child per year. The total size of the target population (poor

---

8. Estimates of the size of the current at-risk (uncovered) population can be made with greater precision by drawing on the 1998 ENIGH survey data, once these become available for analysis.

9. See Young (1996) for further information on the above options, including case studies of programs currently being implemented in a range of countries.

children ages 0–4) is roughly 5.2 million; thus, estimating the number of currently uncovered at 4.6 million, the cost of expanding PRODEI to cover the existing gap is 2.5 billion pesos.

For pre-school, the estimated coverage gap in 1996 was 500,000 poor children (age 5). The CONAFE program (see below), now provides coverage to 125,000 rural children at an estimated cost of 3,510 pesos per child. Assuming a similar cost structure in urban as well as rural areas, CONAFE could be expanded to cover the remaining estimated gap (375,000 children) an at annual cost of 1.3 billion pesos.

Eliminating the Pocket of Low Primary School Enrollment in Rural Areas

While access to primary education is close to universal in Mexico, a small but significant pocket of relatively low attendance rates (85 percent) prevails among the poorest 10 percent of the rural population. The total number of poor children age 6–14 in rural areas not attending primary school was estimated at 430,000 in 1996.[10] The problem is concentrated among children in small, indigenous communities of 100 or fewer inhabitants, where 28 percent of primary-school-aged children do not attend school, and where one-quarter of school-age children are monolingual indigenous language speakers. Mexico's CONAFE program exhibits best-practice characteristics of community-based rural schooling: it is demand-driven, fosters high parental and community involvement, applies active pedagogical models, and allows for learning in students' own (indigenous) languages. The program currently covers 160,000 children, and has achieved systematically positive results as demonstrated by test-scores showing systematically higher achievements scores for students as compared to a control group in traditional schools. Estimating the remaining coverage gap at 270,000 children, closing this gap, at current costs of 3,735 pesos per student per year, would cost 1 billion pesos. Scholarship programs, with a particular focus on top indigenous students graduating from primary and secondary school in order to continue their education and become teachers, would also help close existing gaps in completion rates and over time would help raise the supply of rural schooling and quality of teachers (only 38 percent of primary schools in indigenous communities offer all grades 1 through 6). Distance learning, such as educational radio programs created by indigenous teachers and offered in both Spanish and local indigenous languages, might also help bridge the educational gap in isolated areas. Reliable cost estimates for both of these programs are not currently available.

Improving Access to Secondary Schooling

Secondary school enrollment rates are low, on average, even in lower secondary school (68 percent in urban areas, 37 percent in rural areas), signaling a significant problem in transitioning students from primary to secondary schooling. The prob-

---

10. It should be noted that while access is nearly universal, primary school quality is a significant issue which is addressed in the Education Sector Chapter.

lem is markedly worse among the poor, with an enrollment rate of 41 percent among the urban poor, and 24 percent among the rural poor.

Raising secondary school access and quality, a sectoral responsibility, is the first step. In terms of social assistance programs, raising the demand for secondary schooling through scholarships targeted to poor students is a viable option. Coverage of existing scholarship programs was extremely low in 1996, especially among the poor (less than 3 percent in both rural and urban areas; see Table 3). PROGRESA, introduced in 1997, offers income-transfers for families conditioned on school attendance: 257.5 pesos per month for lower secondary and 300 pesos per month for upper secondary school. Estimating coverage gaps at 1.9 million for lower secondary and 2.2 million for upper secondary, and using PROGRESA per-child cost estimates, covering the existing gap would cost 5.9 billion pesos for lower secondary and 7.9 billion pesos for upper secondary.[11]

Reducing the prevailing high rates of inactivity will likely require complementary sectoral programs that enhance secondary school curricula and teacher quality. To address over-age students who have dropped out of school, intensive education programs to bring students back into the secondary school system can be employed. In addition, community college systems, such as those operating successfully in the United States, offering high-school equivalency programs in the evenings along with 1-to-2-year terminal degrees in technical fields such as nursing and computing, can provide a successful model.

Addressing the Problem of Low Earnings Among the Working-Age Population

The problem of low earnings among the working-age population (age 25 to 64) in Mexico is driven by a range of factors including unemployment, part-time work, and low pay (full-time work at below-poverty wages). Of the three determinants of low earnings, unemployment is the least common, as seen in Table 2a; average unemployment rates are strikingly low (1.5 percent), while the rural poor have even lower unemployment rates than average (0.6 percent). Urban rates among the poor are slightly higher than the average (6.5 percent), but are still very low. Part-time employment explains a far greater proportion of low earnings among the poor, with 37 percent of the urban poor and 52 percent of the rural poor working less than full time. And, with the remainder of the employed poor in full-time employment, low wages (i.e. wages that are insufficient so as to keep a fully-employed person and his/her dependents out of poverty) is obviously a substantial driving force behind poverty in Mexico.

The medium- to long-term solution for low earnings among the poor lies in a macroeconomic framework that promotes labor-intensive growth, so as to bring about wage increases among the working poor. A probable drag on the positive wage effects of such growth is the low human capital (in terms of level of formal education) of Mexico's workforce, particularly among the poor. Furthermore, in Mexico

---

11. PROGRESA has probably reduced this gap, however at the time of writing precise coverage data by school level were not available.

low human capital is not confined to older workers; in the poorest decile, 49 percent of those aged 25 to 40 have less-than-complete primary schooling in urban areas, and in rural areas this figure rises to 70 percent. Thus the problem plagues not only Mexico's current workers, but will persist as these young and relatively uneducated workers remain in the workforce for the next 25 to 40 years. Training and supplemental education programs are the one identified option for addressing this issue. However, international evidence shows that the impact of training programs on long-run employment and wage prospects is at best mixed (Dar and Tzannatos 1999). Recent evaluations of Mexico's training programs indicate that while some of them, such as PROBECAT, are well targeted and hence function well in providing income transfers to the poor, they do less well at providing successfully for future employment at higher wage levels (De Ferranti et al. 2000). Given ambivalent evaluation results, it is difficult to determine whether these programs should be considered for expansion without further assessment. However, for reference purposes, current costs of Mexico's training programs are approximately 2,300 pesos per person, and they cover a relatively small number of people (600,000) relative to the size of the at-risk population. Development of financial markets accessible to poor regions and neighborhoods is also an essential component of the medium-to-long-term strategy for reducing the income vulnerability of the poorest. Financial markets can facilitate small business development and self-insurance mechanisms to help working families accumulate savings that can be used to smooth consumption during crises.

Short-term solutions include workfare programs for the unemployed, and targeted income transfers to poor families. Workfare programs, such as Mexico's *PET*, provide several advantages for crisis relief: (a) they are self-targeted (only those willing to work at low wages doing manual labor participate), and hence given sufficient funding can expand during crises yet contract naturally as conditions improve; and (b) they generate valuable social infrastructure (though this element raises program costs substantially). Program costs are currently substantial, at 3,800 pesos per temporary job created per year. PET currently creates about 1 million jobs per year, having expanded from 660,000 in 1995. The estimated size of total unemployed poor population in 1996 was 460,000, which suggests that the program (if well targeted and if the absolute size of the poor unemployed population has not risen significantly) has expanded to cover the prevailing gap (whether this is in fact so can be determined once 1998 survey data can be used to estimate a more current figure for the poor unemployed).

Transfer programs such as Mexico's PROGRESA can complement workfare by providing supplemental income for poor working families, as can a well-functioning negative income tax (i.e. one well targeted to the poorest income deciles)[12] Mexico's

---

12. A negative income tax relies on a well-functioning and broad-based tax system, but can efficiently provide an automatic subsidy to families whose income falls below a certain target level, with benefits tapering off as income rises.

current negative income tax program, which reaches only the formal sector (thus excluding the bulk of families in the poorest deciles) and operates as an implicit subsidy to employers while absorbing a substantial amount of SP spending (11 billion pesos) is a prime target for reform. Estimating the number of working poor (ages 25–64 and employed full time at below poverty wages) at 4.4 million, providing an income transfer valued at the median benefit under the current negative income tax program (142.5 pesos per month) would cost 7.5 billion pesos (less than the amount currently spent on the negative income tax program).[13]

Increasing Access to Old-age Pensions

There are two main objectives inherent in public efforts to reduce the vulnerability of the elderly poor: (a) to care for the current stock of elderly poor who did not have access in the past to contributory social insurance; and (b) to reduce the future flow of current workers into that category. Options for achieving the first objective are fairly limited and include income and in-kind transfers targeted to the elderly poor. Best practice options for achieving the second, more long-term objective include a combination of instruments to facilitate the acquisition of old-age insurance among the poor, including broadening access to both public insurance (public pension plans) and self-insurance (private savings) mechanisms.

Mexico has already taken several positive steps in pension reform which lay the groundwork for extending pension access to the previously excluded. These steps include moving to a system of individual accounts with broader access to the informal sector,[14] and instituting a matching grant system *(cuota social)* in which the government supplements contributions made into the system to encourage workers to enroll and make regular contributions to the plan, and to subsidize benefit levels once retired.[15] A further initiative (SUF) is designed to facilitate small business participation in the plan, by providing small firms with an information package on enrolling employees in the plan, calculating contribution levels, etc. However, as noted above, progress in actually expanding coverage of social insurance to the previously uninsured (particularly the informal sector) has been slow. An important next step is to examine why take-up of these new initiatives has been so low, followed by adjustment to reforms in order to facilitate wider participation.

---

13. Note that this estimate excludes administrative costs, for which no estimates are currently available. Coverage could also include lower age groups among the working poor (18–24 year olds) or a higher benefit, all of which would imply higher costs.

14. The reform allows any informal sector worker whose employer complies with current labor tax legislation, and self-employed workers who meet the same criteria, to participate in the public pension scheme.

15. The government makes daily deposits of a flat-rate, inflation-indexed subsidy to the individual accounts of all workers participating in the national pension plan, which, together with returns earned from investment should ensure that lower income workers are able to qualify for the minimum pension guarantee.

Financial sector development is perhaps the most fundamental requirement for enhanced coverage in the rural sector (and to marginalized urban populations). Augmenting access to local banks would provide a facility for making contributions to the public pension system, for receiving benefits (either from the pension plan or from a targeted income-support program for the elderly poor), and would enhance self-insurance options (savings). However extending coverage will require a commitment by the government to dedicate resources to this endeavor; offering the existing cuota social to the estimated 8.8 million workers currently working in the informal sector would imply an estimated cost of 6.9 billion pesos per year, for the old-age pension plan alone.[16] Yet it would not provide an immediate solution to the current uncovered elderly poor, numbering 1 million in urban areas and over 1.25 million in rural areas. For these groups, as stated above, an income transfer program (non-contributory pension) is the only known option. Recently developed targeting mechanisms (such as for PROGRESA) might facilitate delivery of these transfers without undue administrative costs. Covering the existing gap of elderly poor, totaling 2.2 million, with a transfer of 100 pesos per month (approximately one third of the value of the current extreme poverty line), would cost 2.7 billion pesos per year.

Raising Access to Basic Infrastructure Services and Housing Quality

Housing quality is still low in Mexico, particularly among the rural poor, where 55 percent have no piped water, 96 percent no piped sewerage, and 29 percent have no electricity. A significant proportion of the urban poor also live without access to water (18 percent) and sewerage (50 percent). Expanding basic infrastructure services to service poor areas is the starting point to addressing these gaps, complemented by financial sector instruments to facilitate mortgages and small-scale loans for home improvement. Housing subsidies well targeted to poor households can complement these lending facilities. While Mexico currently operates a well-funded housing credit program (FOVISSTE), it is not well-targeted to the poor and does not reach rural areas, and is thus a target for reform particularly in terms of facilitating access among the poor. Mexico's housing subsidy program *(PASVP)* is underfunded relative to housing needs among the poor, and could be expanded. At current costs of 2,383 pesos per family covered, covering the estimated 4.8 million poor at-risk households would cost approximately 11 billion pesos. Drawing on Chile's highly successful targeted subsidy for housing purchases, home improvements, and initial connections to water, sewerage, and electricity services for lessons learned and as input to designing the program's expansion is also an option to be considered for raising progam effectiveness.

Water is perhaps the most basic infrastructural need that is currently unmet for one particular at-risk group: the isolated (largely indigenous) communities in rural areas. The uncovered population is estimated at roughly half of the population in these communities, such that there are approximately 1.3 million people currently

---

16. El Financiero, 10-23-2000.

without access to potable water. SHCP estimates costs ranging from 1,900 pesos per person to a maximum of 20,000 pesos per person to install water service in isolated rural areas.[17] Taking a mid-range estimate of water service installation at 10,000 per person, total costs to cover the remaining unserved population can be very roughly estimated at 13 billion pesos.[18]

Addressing Social Risk Among Indigenous People

Looking at the facts, it is clear that extreme vulnerability in Mexico is largely synonymous with being indigenous. For each age and type of risk, the indigenous population exhibits heightened degrees of social risk. Thus, successfully reducing social risk in Mexico depends in large part on developing risk-reduction techniques that successfully meet the needs of the indigenous population. Each of the programs above thus needs to be carefully considered as to whether special modifications, or indeed alternative programs, are needed to appropriately reduce risk among the indigenous population. More detailed evidence and experience on developing such programs is available in the Indigenous Peoples Chapter, but a general review of best practice evidence suggests that in some cases, it is possible to *adapt* existing best practice options under each risk category to suit indigenous communities, but in other cases *entirely different models* of programs and interventions are required (see Indigenous Peoples Chapter). Community-based programs, run by indigenous community members and supported with federal, state, and municipal funding, seem to exhibit higher rates of success. In addition, successful programs for indigenous peoples tend to cost more than those for the non-indigenous because of their relatively small scale, the higher cost of reaching isolated areas, and the fact that they require substantially greater training components (not only for indigenous people, but for those non-indigenous government or program representatives who must learn to work within the indigenous context). In terms of what to avoid, it seems clear that any program that creates parallel government structures alongside preexisting indigenous governance mechanisms is likely to fail; the key is to work with those existing governance structures (which in practice is difficult because they are not incorporated into "mainstream" elements of government, such as state and municipal organizations). With these generalities as a point of departure, further work has to be done on developing precise options for addressing indigenous social risk in each of the key risk categories.

---

17. The upper bound cost of 20,000 pesos per person reflects costs in extremely remote areas (serving 1 or 2 households).
18. Note also that under current policy, the federal government provides only half of the financing of water installation, the other half being provided by the municipality. While in theory this would halve the above cost estimate, poor municipalities may not have sufficient resources to pay the counterpart funding, which may explain the lack of service extension into these areas to date. Therefore in order to provide service to these areas, the federal government may have to absorb the full cost of service provision.

IV. Looking Ahead: Enhancing Social Protection Policy in Mexico

Costs and Trade-offs

Summarizing the above analysis, implementing and/or expanding selected SP programs that address key risks in each of the 7 areas identified above would require, as a preliminary and rough estimate, 60 billion pesos in additional resources (Table 6).[19] This amount represents 27 percent of total SP spending (223.9 billion pesos), 7.4 percent of total federal expenditures (809 billion), and 1.1 percent of GDP (5,238 billion) in 2000. The results provide a broad-brush indication of the of the current level of resources dedicated to SP interventions vs. that which might be required to address key risks, as well as the costs, trade-offs and fiscal implications implicit in implementing policy initiatives in each category of risk.[20] Identifying priorities among the options for reform is a major task facing the incoming government.

Defining Priorities

Among the range of at-risk groups identified in Section I above, it is helpful to begin by establishing a set of priorities, both in terms of the groups to whom policies should be directed first (given limited resources), and the types of social insurance and social assistance interventions that are likely to be most effective at addressing the identified risks, based on both Mexican and international experience.

In terms of prioritizing at-risk groups, breaking the intergenerational transmission of risk suggests a primary focus on SP programs directed at children and youth, such that today's SP interventions not only transfer resources to poor sectors of the population, but reduce their future risk and therefore the need for government intervention in the long-run. Within other age categories, where it is harder to identify a risk group that merits attention over another, reforms might prioritize redesign of certain existing programs so that they better direct resources to the poorest segments of the population first. Focusing reform efforts on programs that meet this criteria while absorbing a relatively high share of SP resources (negative income tax, housing credits) is likely to have the greatest positive risk-reduction impact; reforms might entail improved targeting systems in some cases, while in others will require entire revamping of program design (particularly, eligibility criteria). Finally, there are some cases where it is possible to identify existing programs which address a high-priority risk group, and experience and evaluations indicate are successful, but which

---

19. These estimates are subject to revision, given incomplete data on current program coverage, use of 1996 risk indicators to assess size of at-risk groups, and in some cases very rough estimates of per-person program costs.
20. It is interesting to note, for example, that the current federal subsidy IMSS alone (66 billion pesos) exceeds the amount of additional resources required to implement major policy reforms in each of the 7 key areas.

Table 6. Cost of Implementing SP Initiatives in Seven Major Categories of Risk

Problem	Size of population at-risk (coverage gap)	SP policy initiative	Annual cost per person (pesos)	Estimated cost to cover gap (million pesos)
1. Low ECD and pre-school coverage	ECD: 4.6 million poor children ages 0–4; Pre-school: 375,000 poor children age 5	Expand ECD services (PRONEI) to all poor children 0–4; Expand *CONAFE* preschool coverage to all poor children age 5	540 3,510	2,500 1,300
2. Pocket of low primary school attendance in rural areas	270,000 rural poor children ages 6–12 not attending primary school	Expand *CONAFE* primary-school coverage to all poor	3,735	1,000
3. Low secondary school enrollment rates	1,900,000 poor youth ages 12–14 not attending lower secondary; 2,200,000 poor youth ages 15–18 not attending upper sec.	Offer secondary scholarships (*PROGRESA?*) to non-attending youth ages 12–14 (lower sec.), and to youth ages 15–18 (upper sec.)	3,090 3,600	5,900 7,900
4. Low earnings among the working poor	4,400,000 poor ages 25–64, employed full time	Expand/reform negative income tax (*ISR negativo*) to cover all fully-employed working poor ages 25–64	1,710	7,500

Table 6. (Continued)

Problem	Size of population at-risk (coverage gap)	SP policy initiative	Annual cost per person (pesos)	Estimated cost to cover gap (million pesos)
5. Low access to pension (income support) among elderly poor	2,250,000 elderly poor (over age 64) 8,800,000 current workers w/o access to social security 4,800,000 households	Provide minimum old-age pension to all current elderly poor	1,200	2,600
		Expand access to social security pension system to all informal sector workers	780	6,900
6. Low housing quality among the poor	1,300,000 people in remote villages without access to water	Offer subsidized housing credits to all poor households with low housing quality (PASVP)	2,383 per family	11,500
7. Remote villages with low access to basic infrastructure		Install potable water service in all isolated communities currently without water	10,000 per person (avg.)	13,000
Total Annual Cost of Implementing the Above SP Interventions				**60,100**

currently provide coverage to a narrow or incomplete segment of the poor at-risk population (i.e. PRODEI, CONAFE); focusing resources on expanding such programs is likely to yield high and immediate pay-offs in terms of social risk reduction.

Some general points can be made in terms of prioritizing types of social insurance and social assistance interventions, drawing on international evidence: (a) OECD experience shows that, in general, social insurance programs are more successful at reducing poverty than social assistance programs;[21] however, given that expanding social insurance coverage is a medium-term proposition, because such expansion requires financial sector development as well as mechanisms for incorporating the informal sector into the social insurance system, social assistance programs may play a temporarily larger role in developing countries; (b) innovative social assistance interventions such as PROGRESA, that combine short-term objectives (income support) with long-term objectives (human capital accumulation) are likely to be highly cost-effective, smoothing consumption in the current period while at the same time reducing future exposure to risk; (c) programs that exhibit ease of implementation, transparency of objectives and target groups, and simplicity in design are preferable over programs with complex implementation procedures; (d) programs that easily expand during crises and diminish operations as conditions improve are highly desirable (such as self-targeted workfare), because having such programs permanently in place implies permanent preparedness for crises; (e) programs that are desirable to have in place over the long run, or are easy to disband politically when no longer serving a socially desirable purpose, are preferable to programs that remain in place over the longer term largely because they are politically difficult to disband; and (f) programs that create as few disincentives to productive activity as possible are preferable to programs that alleviate poverty in the short run, but create dependence on public programs over the long run. Here the recent experience of the US in revamping existing welfare policies in order to reduce disincentives to productive activity, provides a recent and interesting case study.

Design, Institutional, and Implementation Issues

Successfully implementing SP policies that can effectively address the main social risks outlined above also depends on consideration of a broader range of design, institutional, and implementation issues. In terms of overall program design and implementation, the preceding analysis suggests that improving coverage and minimizing regressive targeting structures and leakage of intended benefits to the non-

---

21. An analysis of the anti-poverty effectiveness of safety nets in 8 rich nations (1967–present) shows that universal and social insurance transfers have by far the largest impact on poverty, resulting in between 75 to 80 percent of the total poverty reduction derived from SP interventions. Social assistance programs play a relatively small role, though they are important for certain target groups such as families with children and single-parent households (Smeeding and Ross 1999).

poor are important goals. Means-tested targeting in urban areas is particularly important, given the lower poverty rates in these areas, and thus the greater likelihood that benefits will reach unintended beneficiaries. Developing a definitive urban poverty reduction strategy is a challenge that faces the incoming Administration, with a particular focus on instituting effective targeting of benefits. Improving program impact evaluation for major interventions, along the lines of the recent independent evaluation of PROGRESA, and including measures of cost-effectiveness, are also important.

The major institutional issues that arise in the Mexican context are the many agencies involved in SP program implementation at all levels of government, and the uneven effects of decentralization given vastly differing state and municipal capacity for effective program implementation. A clearer definition of division of labor between federal, state, and local levels of government, and a focus on identifying areas of duplication and dispersion of efforts, would significantly enhance efficiency and hence reduce program costs. Training and more intensive support for state and municipal governments with lower capacity levels for implementation would be useful in supporting decentralization efforts.

Other Emerging Issues—Next Analytical Steps

Several emerging issues in SP can be identified for further analytical work in the Mexican context. First, effective crisis management techniques need to be developed, along the lines of FONDEN, including building counter-cyclical funding patterns into social spending and, in particular, into social assistance programs targeted to the most vulnerable groups. Second, building exit strategies into existing programs is needed so that as vulnerability is reduced, beneficiaries automatically "graduate" from program eligibility. Third, forward vision will greatly enhance SP planning, with an emphasis on the dynamics of population change, such as the implications of the aging of the Mexican population, the growing urban workforce as a result of urbanization, and the persistence of small and isolated communities with high dependency ratios. Fourth, being watchful for the emergence of new at-risk groups, such as rising inactivity and crime rates among urban youth, and developing appropriate new interventions and approaches for risk reduction, will be an essential element of successful SP policy. Addressing each of the above issues merits further in-depth work, as does the search for local and international best practice options to guide the way in providing for a sound approach to SP in Mexico for current and future generations.

Finally, the analysis in this paper relies on 1996 survey data for estimates of the size of at-risk groups. The size of these groups is likely to have changed since that time given a) changing economic conditions, in particular poverty levels; b) population growth and/or changes in population structure; c) new program implementation. Some of these factors may have worked to increase the size of at-risk groups (population growth, rising poverty levels through 1998?), while other may have reduced their size (new programs introduced after 1996, for example PROGRESA). The analysis presented here can be strengthened by drawing on 1998 ENIGH household survey data as soon as it is available, as well as by conducting a more rigorous analysis of program costs, in order to generate updated and reliable cost estimates for alternative SP initiatives considered for implementation. This analytical work will vastly enhance the results presented here, and should be conducted as soon as possible in order to provide the most sound basis possible for upcoming SP policy decisions facing the incoming administration.

Bibliography

Carr, Margaret, Helen May, and Val Podmore. 2000. *National Curriculum, Assessment and Evaluation Implementing Te Whaariki for the Before Fives in Aotearoa-New Zealand.* World Bank, Washington D.C.

Dar, Amit, and Zafiris Tzannatos. 1999. *Active Labor Market Programs: A Review of the Evidence from Evaluations.* SP Discussion paper No. 9901. World Bank, Washington, D.C.

De Ferranti, David, et al. 2000. *Securing Our Future in a Global Economy.* Latin American and Carribean Series: Viewpoints. World Bank, Washington, D.C.

Government of Mexico and World Bank. 2000. *National Indigenous Peoples of Mexico.* (mimeo).

INI (Instituto Nacional Indigenista). 1997. *Encuesta Nacional de Empleo en Zonas Indigenas.* Federal District, Mexico.

Psacharopoulos, George, and Harry Patrinos. 1994. *Indigenous People and Poverty in Latin America: An Empirical Analysis.* World Bank, Washington, D.C.

SHCP (Secretaria de Hacienda y Crédito Público). Various years. *Exposición de Motivos e Iniciativa de Decreto. Tomo 1: Proyecto de Presupuesto de Egresos de la Federación para el Ejercicio Fiscal.* Federal District, Mexico.

Smeeding, T., and K. Ross, 1999. *Social Protection for the Poor in the Developed World: The Evidence from the Luxembourg Income Study.* Social Protection and Poverty Conference Proceedings. Inter-American Development Bank, Washington, D.C.

Young, Mary E. 1996. *Early Child Development: Investing in the Future.* Directions in Development Series. World Bank, Washington, D.C.

Annex I

Annex Table 1. Mexico: Estimated Population by Age Group and Geographic Area, 2000

Age Group	Urban	Rural	Total
0–4	7.5 %	3.3%	10.8%
	7,479,965	3,298,083	10,778,048
5–14	15.5%	6.8%	22.4%
	15,461,958	6,817,520	22,279,478
15–24	15.5%	4.8%	20.3%
	15,434,276	4,820,680	20,254,956
25–64	31.8%	9.9%	41.7%
	31,622,094	9,876,717	41,498,811
Over 65	3.4%	1.4%	4.8%
	3,373,067	1,397,891	4,770,958
All population	73.7%	26.3%	100%
	73,371,361	26,210,890	99,582,251

Source: Author's calculations based on *CONAPO, 1998. Proyecciones de la poblacion de Mexico 1996–2050. Consejo Nacional de la Población.* Mexico, DF.

Annex II

SP Programs in Mexico: Design, Coverage and Budget Data
This 50 page annex is not included as an attachment to this document, but is available upon request.

22

Labor Markets

This Chapter was written by William F. Maloney
with the valuable input of
Gladys Lopez-Acevedo and Ana Revenga.

I. Context for Reform

A well-functioning labor market can contribute to a dynamic of sustained labor-demanding economic growth by encouraging savings, investment in human capital, international competitiveness, and an output mix and technology choice that favor labor demand. An appropriate labor policy framework would:

- Stimulate employment growth in the formal sector.
- Provide a favorable environment for investments in human and physical capita.
- Promote the movement of workers from less to more productive activities and the productivity of labor within individual sectors.
- Avoid interventions and biases that reduce the demand for labor.
- Ensure social equity and is seen as legitimate by labor.

The Mexican labor market does not appear excessively rigid and there is little evidence of wage rigidities—minimum wages are not binding (see Annex III) and unions seem primarily concerned with maintaining employment rather than fixing wages.[1] Arguably, the fact that unemployment has remained so low in Mexico, even in times of crisis, reflects the relative ease of adjusting real wages.

The very large informal sector, accounting for close to 50 percent of the workforce, probably reflects the low opportunity costs of self-employment due to low formal sector productivity, and the weak linkages between contributions and ben-

---

1. See Maloney and Ribeiro (1999) in Maloney (1999), "Mexican Labor Markets: New Views on Integration and Flexibility, World Bank."

efits in the formal sector, rather than segmentation as customarily imagined. There is a very high degree of turnover much of it voluntary, and dramatic flows of workers between both formal and informal sectors. Figure 1 suggests that, once adjusted for demographic and other variables, Mexico shows neither a high degree of informality (a measure of segmentation) or low turnover, (a common measure of flexibility). To the degree that there is segmentation and involuntary informality, it is likely to emerge endogenously: in an economy with a weak education system, firms pay "efficiency" (above-market-clearing) wages to retain the workers they have trained. This suggests that conventional concerns with reducing wage rigidities should probably not be the primary focus of Mexico's labor market reform.

However, Mexico needs to continue to modify its labor law with four goals in mind:

- Minimizing transaction costs and other barriers to more rapid adjustments by firms and good job matches for workers.
- Bringing explicit and implicit labor costs in line with their value to workers. When workers value a benefit less than they pay for it, they have the incentive to become informal and to remain uncovered by the social security system.
- Increasing investments in human capital. Public investments in education and training have positive impacts on equity and poverty, reduce skills bottlenecks, and may reduce the need for firms to pay efficiency wages.

Figure 1. Mexico: Labor Market Flexibility

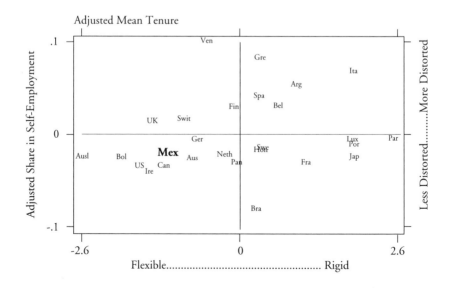

- Maintaining wage flexibility over the medium term. Numerous factors, including the fall in inflation, greater openness to trade, and the weakening of labor unions may lead to more frequent labor market adjustments through unemployment in the future.[2]

It is essential to emphasize that in many of the priority areas, there are net gains to be made by both workers and firms in overhauling an inefficient system: both would unequivocally benefit from restructuring the severance pay system and from improving and expanding worker training. Reform of the industrial relations and collective bargaining framework involves altering some legal structures dating to 1917. But if placed in the context of modernizing the workplace, enhancing the technical proficiency and productivity of the worker, and thus, in the medium term, his or her compensation, common ground is more likely to be found and support generated for a coherent package of far-reaching reforms.

II. Policy Issues and Options

The System of Benefits Provision is Costly, Distorts Labor Allocation, Diminishes Competitiveness, and Poorly Serves Workers

The present system of mandated nonwage payments has several deficiencies:

- *Distorted labor supply decisions and poor benefits delivery.* High mandated benefits and contributions introduce a large "wedge" between the cost of labor to the employer and the total compensation received by the employee. Table 1 lists the components of nonwage labor costs in Mexico, all of which represent a tax on payroll.[3] This total "wedge" of 31 percent is moderately high even by OECD standards. The comparable wedge in the United States is 19 percent, in Canada 12 percent, and in the U.K. 14.5 percent. Only in

Table 1. Tax Wedge on Payroll

IVCM	9.5%
Medical	9%
SAR	2%
Work-related risks	2.5%
INFONAVIT	5%
Local labor taxes	2–3%
Total wedge	31.0%

Note: Daycare (1 percent) has now been rolled into IVCM (*prestaciones sociales*).

---

2. For a complete discussion about trends in employment risk in Mexico see Maloney (2000), *Income Risk and Household Coping Strategies in Mexico*, World Bank.
3. Not included are nonwage costs implied by other mandated benefits, such as paid vacation, annual bonuses, vacation bonuses, and profit sharing.

OECD countries such as Spain (33.2 percent), France (38.9 percent), and Italy (37.8 percent) is the wedge similar. Chile, at a similar level of development, has a wedge of 21 percent, although Argentina has a wedge of close to 60 percent, and Colombia 59 percent.

Over the long term in an environment with flexible wages, much of the incidence of these taxes is passed down to workers as lower wages. However, many of these payments are perceived by workers as a pure tax, since the link between contributions and benefits is weak, and the quality of services delivered is poor (only 3 percent of those with a choice voluntarily joined IMSS schemes), and is cited by informal sector workers and entrepreneurs as a reason to avoid becoming formal.[4] Simulations of the impact of a 1 percent reduction in pure taxes on formal workers yields an almost equivalent rise in the share of the workforce in formal employment.[5]

- *Sizable efficiency losses.* To the extent that there is substantial duplication of social security instruments, and given that there appear to be large transaction costs involved in the monitoring of contributions and delivery of services, the system results in large efficiency losses. A large fraction of resources are wasted due to inefficiencies within the institutions: administrative expenses account for 20 percent of expenditures at IMSS, and almost 30 percent at ISSSTE. Again, to the degree that inefficiency drives a wedge between what workers pay and the benefits received, it discourages participation in these programs.

- *Reduced labor demand in the formal sector.* In the presence of wage rigidities, high payroll taxes increase the cost of labor and reduce competitiveness and formal employment below its optimal level in the formal sector. At present, there is little evidence of wage rigidities—minimum wages are not binding and unions seem primarily concerned with maintaining employment. However, over the long term this may not be the case.

Policy Options

The Mexican government has, over the last six years, made great progress, particularly in the area of social security reform. Not only was an underfunded system put on more solid fiscal footing, but by creating a fully funded system of individual accounts, the link between contributions and benefits should encourage private sector workers to stay or become formal. Nonetheless, there remain numerous areas where further progress could be made:

---

4. See Liviatan and van Wijnbergen, (1994), p. 44; Maloney (1999); and Roberts (1989).
5. Krebs and Maloney (1998), "Quitting and Labor Turnover," in Maloney (1999), *Mexican Labor Markets: New Views on Integration and Flexibility*, World Bank.

CONTINUE REFORMS OF THE STRUCTURE OF MANDATED SOCIAL SECURITY CONTRI-
BUTIONS. This would include:

- Make contributions voluntary for certain components (such as housing benefits) that benefit few workers yet tax all. Shift the funding base for others that
are still justifiably mandatory (for example, daycare) from highly distortionary
payroll taxes to less distortionary direct taxes (that is, fund from general tax
revenues).
- Where possible, substitute mandated proportional contributions with fixed-
quota contributions that would entitle the employee to minimum benefits
while allowing additional voluntary contributions and encouraging the development of private schemes (for example, old-age retirement and medical
benefits).
- An important innovation was introduced in the 1997 reforms of the health
insurance system. Mexico moved away from a system financed by contributions keyed to the worker's salary (12.5 percent), yet provided benefits that
were largely independent of income. This mismatch of the two encouraged
evasion among those contributing more than expected benefits. The reforms
sharply reduced the proportionality of the contributions, and over the next 10
years the system is envisioned to converge essentially to a fixed quota. This
plan should be supported.[6] In addition, emphasis should continue on individual accounts, given that they more tightly link worker contributions to
individual benefits.[7] Where such accounts now exist, a competitive rate of
return should be ensured.

CONTINUE INCREASES IN IMSS RESOURCE EFFICIENCY AND IMPROVE IMSS SERVICE
QUALITY. The last sexenio has seen improvements in IVCM, medical, and SAR quality. Quality and efficiency increases shrink the share of the wedge going to transaction costs.

Large Mandated Severance Payments Reduce Labor Mobility, Impair Resource Reallocation, Increase Labor Costs, and Discourage Job Creation

The absence of any system of unemployment insurance and the lack of portability
in some pension funds (particularly in the public sector) has led to an excessive
emphasis on job stability, very costly severance payments, and a system prone to

---

6. Davila and Guijarro (1999), *"Evolución y Reforma del Sistema de Salud en México."*
7. If workers feel they can get rates of return superior to those offered by the individual
accounts (perhaps through investment in a small business) or if their rate of time preference differs substantially from the rate of return, there will still be incentives to become
informal.

involved litigation. Mexican unions, in fact, appear more concerned with maintaining employment than affecting wages.[8]

Further, the reforms of the last decade may possibly leave workers more exposed to spells of unemployment in the future. The fall in inflation has made it more difficult to respond to aggregate shocks by reducing real wages by holding nominal wages fixed.[9] Liberalization has plausibly led to an increase in labor demand elasticities, leading to greater shocks to the labor market for a given aggregate shock.[10] Further, although overall workers are not facing a higher probability of becoming unemployed, there is some evidence that sectors more open to trade experience higher risks of involuntary separation.[11]

Both labor and firms have a common interest in replacing the severance pay system and unemployment support system and expanding the portable pension system. The current system has had the following adverse effects:

- *An excessive emphasis on employment stability.* This is reflected both in the legal framework, which heavily protects employment and mandates generous severance pay (see Annex I) and in the importance given to corporatist bargaining mechanisms such as the *Pacto.* The latter have allowed for substantial real-wage flexibility in exchange for preserving employment, which has helped dampen short-term social costs of adjustment, but could have detrimental medium-term effects by deterring necessary productivity-enhancing labor shedding.
- *Increased labor costs and reduced employment.* High mandated severance payments represent a substantial addition to the cost of labor: compensation is a function of last salary and years of service and is extremely generous, amounting to four months salary per year of service in the case of "unjust" dismissals. The only other OECD countries that mandate equally large severance compensation are Spain and Italy—both countries that suffer from

8. Maloney and Ribeiro (1998), "Efficiency Wage and Union Effects in Labor Demand and Wage Structure in Mexico." In Maloney (1999), *Mexican Labor Markets: New Views on Integration and Flexibility,* World Bank.

9. Galindo and Maloney (2000) show that a fall in inflation increases the "wage Okun coefficient"(how much a 1 percent fall in output drives down aggregate wages) and increases the "unemployment Okun coefficient." In Maloney (2000), *Income Risk and Household Coping Strategies in Mexico,* World Bank.

10. Fajnzylber and Maloney (2000), "Labor Demand and Trade Reform in Latin America," in Maloney (2000), *Income Risk and Household Coping Strategies in Mexico,* World Bank.

11. Arango and Maloney (2000), "Reform and Income Insecurity in Mexico," in Maloney (2000), *Income Risk and Household Coping Strategies in Mexico,* World Bank.

extremely rigid labor markets (for recent labor market reforms in Spain, see Annex II).[12]

- *High costs of litigation and increased uncertainty.* In contracting labor, firms must incorporate the likely labor costs and legal fees in the case of a dismissal. The accompanying uncertainty and managerial distraction can lead to substantially lower labor demand and reduced employment levels.[13] Further, labor lawyers typically charge between 30 to 40 percent of what the worker would obtain through indemnization. Due to the long duration of cases, the majority of suits end in private settlements.[14]

- *Deficient worker protection.* Severance payments are often demanded exactly at the moment when a firm is least able to honor its obligations, leading to increased stress on weak firms and uncertainty for the worker about the firm's ability to pay. In practice, most severance packages are renegotiated and the worker gets substantially less that the amount mandated by law. Further, the cap of two monthly minimum wages on the payment of 20 days per year has greatly reduced the value of seniority-linked pay.

- *Impaired resource reallocation.* The implied costs of dismissal cause firms to shed less labor in a downturn than if dismissal were costless. Workers for their part are reluctant to investigate more productive employment opportunities, or retire, because of the loss of seniority-related benefits. Should they choose to leave, they are more likely to seek to be fired than to quit.[15] These distortions hamper the necessary reallocation of labor between firms and sectors.

---

12. On the basis of the average manufacturing wage for a typical worker with 10 years of seniority, and the assumption that 10 percent of the manufacturing workforce has to be dismissed each year, the annual cost of labor dismissals is about 32 percent of the total payroll. (Actual costs may be substantially lower, since many firms negotiate severance compensation with the dismissed employee outside the labor courts.) Assuming a moderate wage elasticity of demand for labor of around 0.3, this would translate into a 10 percent reduction in formal-sector employment. Evidence from the introduction of job security protection in Colombia, India, and Zimbabwe shows that the main effect of such legislation is to decrease employment levels (see Fallon and Lucas, *World Bank Economic Review*, September 1991; and Kugler 1999). Evidence from the OECD reveals similar effects (see Lazear, *Quarterly Journal of Economics*, 1990).

13. The rise in the number of wrongful dismissal cases that have challenged the "fire at will system" in the U.S. has led to a 2 to 5 percent decrease in employment despite payments that amount only to US$10 per employee. The subsidiary effects on costs thus appear to be very large, on the order of 10 percent of labor costs at a labor demand elasticity of .3. Dertouzos and Karoly (1992).

14. Davila (1997).

15. Dismissal can imply up to 122 days of salary per year of service in severance compensation; quitting entitles the employee to payment of only 12 days of salary per year of service.

- *Barriers to growth and expansion of small firms.* The proportionally higher transaction costs of dismissals, and the difficulty of financial provisioning for dismissals given poor access to capital markets, may put a greater burden of severance payments on small- and medium-sized firms. This may discourage smaller firms from hiring new workers in good times, or only contracting temporary workers, because of the inability to reallocate internally or shed workers in a downturn. The higher implied turnover may lead to less investment in training. Dismissal costs may also discourage small informal firms from growing and becoming "formal."

Policy Options

DISMANTLE EXISTING JOB SECURITY REGULATIONS AND REPLACE THE CURRENT SEVERANCE-PAY SCHEME WITH AN UNEMPLOYMENT SUPPORT SYSTEM. OECD experience clearly demonstrates the need to design unemployment insurance schemes very carefully—analyzing experiences elsewhere and the needs and characteristics of the Mexican situation—to minimize problems of perverse incentives, and ensure its efficient and sound financial management. Fundamentally there is a trade-off. The more risks are pooled across the population, the more the worker faces a disincentive to prevent being laid off or to find work.

A system of individualized accounts that would lead to a *pago a todo evento*, similar to that discussed in Chile (see Box 1, next page),[16] can be designed that would not discourage voluntary separations, but would allow separations for economic reasons, and would reduce litigation and maximize incentives to find work.[17] Further, if structured as a continuation of wage (slow disbursement) rather than a lump sum, it may better facilitate "smoothing" of consumption and discourage entry into informality.[18] In practice, however unions may see such a "no-fault" severance scheme as leaving workers vulnerable to firing for political reasons. Some distinction between "justifiable" and "unjustifiable" terminations will probably be necessary. Further, some link to seniority may be necessary to counteract the moral hazard problem of workers quitting frequently to collect benefits, and also to acknowledge the earnings loss associated with the nontransferability of accumulated firm-specific human capital.[19]

---

16. See Rene Cortazar, *Political Laboral en El Chile Democratico*, (1993).
17. For example, the present 20 days per month could be reduced to 10, but then raised to 15 if the separation is voluntary.
18. In the presence of credit market imperfections, workers who desire to open their own businesses may rely on a lump-sum severance payment to cover start-up costs. See Aroca and Maloney (1998), "Self-Employment Decisions," in Maloney (1999) *Mexican Labor Markets: New Views on Integration and Flexibility*, IBRD.
19. See Kletzer (1989), Topel (1992), and for Chile, Balmaceda (1992).

Box 1. A Possible Unemployment Insurance Program for Mexico

Establish a category of dismissals for "economic necessity", which receives the standard severance package. This might constitute an expansion of the present category of legitimate dismissals due to technological progress. If labor courts find the dismissal to be for reasons other than true economic necessity, the worker is entitled to 20 percent above the standard package. The relatively low spread between a "justified" and "unjustified" termination reduces incentives to litigate, but does provide a check on abuses by employers of the "economic necessity" category. Dismissals for objectionable behavior pay nothing. The present Chilean system makes very clear how much is to be paid under each contingency. This reduces the discretion of the judiciary process and the uncertainty for both parties.

The standard termination package would offer an up-front payment of one month's salary for each year of work, with a limit of 3 months. For each year after, half a month's salary would be put into a private account associated with the SAR (the AFP in the Chilean case) and could be drawn on no matter why the worker leaves. This eliminates the disincentive for workers seeking more productive employment because they would lose seniority-related benefits, and eliminates the incentive to seek to be fired rather than resign. It also guarantees that the benefits will actually exist should the firm go bankrupt because the firm is paying the insurance premiums when it is healthy, and not when it is financially strapped, as is currently the case. Because the account constitutes part of the worker's wealth, there is a strong incentive to job search.

After the base payments, the worker terminated for economic reasons receives 50 percent of his average salary over the last 12 months for up to four months, financed by a 4 percent monthly payment, half by the firm, half by the worker, and health benefits. If this payment falls below the minimum wage, the state pays the difference.

The *pago a todo evento* is still fundamentally a self-insurance scheme: risks are not pooled over the population and workers absorb the full burden of becoming unemployed. Arguably, the nature of unemployment shocks in the formal sector—relatively infrequent but with large impact on household welfare—dictates true insurance where risks are pooled. However, given the need for continued fiscal discipline and the as-yet poorly understood moral hazard problems, a more general unemployment insurance program is probably not advisable at this time.

RETHINK SYSTEMS OF INCOME SUPPORT TO INFORMAL WORKERS. The system described above serves exclusively workers in the formal sector who would contribute to individual accounts. However, panel household survey data suggest that up to 75 percent of those unemployed originated *in informal jobs*, suggesting that the sector may require some income protection mechanisms and that it should not be considered an adequate safety net.[20]

Workfare programs, such as the Temporary Employment Program (PET) that provides off-season temporary employment in marginalized rural areas, may be extendable to urban areas should unemployment become a problem, as has been done in Argentina, Chile, and Colombia. Attention should be paid, however, to maximizing the transfer to households.[21] Training programs such as PROBECAT also serve as income support, with higher transfer rates than workfare programs. Increasing transfers through PROGRESA during crises also may prove an effective way of transferring income.[22]

ENSURE THAT ARBITRATION AND DISPUTE RESOLUTION RESPONSIBILITIES ARE HANDLED BY AN INDEPENDENT ENTITY. The perception of independence and objectivity, crucial to the acceptance of final decisions by the involved parties, would be reinforced by allocating conflict resolution responsibilities to a separate agency. Establishing a clearly defined set of reasons for termination would ensure that all parties are aware of legitimate and illegitimate reasons for termination.

Insufficient Human Capital Accumulation

Survey, anecdotal, and statistical evidence suggest that there is a growing demand for skilled labor that is not being met by supply.[23] The combination of rising relative wages and shifting labor force composition suggests that, as in much of the OECD

---

20. See Arango and Maloney (2000), "Unemployment Dynamics in Mexico," in Maloney (2000), *Income Risk and Household Coping Strategies in Mexico*, World Bank.
21. Wodon estimates that it costs 3.5 pesos to generate 1 peso in income for the poor, or roughly a 30 percent transfer rate. While better than the Argentine experience with TRABAJAR (20 percent), this is still below that for training or conditional transfer programs. See Wodon (1999), "Government Programs and Poverty in Mexico." World Bank.
22. For a more complete discussion of the design of emergency programs see Maloney (2000), "How Should We think about Emergency Programs," in Maloney (2000), *Income Risk and Household Coping Strategies in Mexico,* World Bank.
23. Survey evidence gathered under the Private Sector Assessment exercise (see World Bank, *Country Economic Memorandum,* 1994) showed that scarcity of qualified labor is perceived among small- and medium-sized enterprises as an important constraint to growth. Conversations with businesspeople and representatives of the chambers of commerce yield a similar impression. Statistical evidence tends to support this claim. Lopez-Acevedo and Salinas found increasing returns to higher education, and Feliciano (1994) and Revenga (1994) found that the wage differential between skilled and unskilled workers has increased significantly in Mexico since the mid-1980s. Revenga (1994) also found that the skill composition of employment in manufacturing has moved toward demanding a higher proportion of skilled workers, particularly in industries that have become most open to international competition.

and in other middle-income countries such as Chile, the relative demand for skilled versus unskilled workers has shifted to favor the former. Table 2 suggests that there are increasing returns to higher education across the liberalization period. Country evidence suggests that a mix of trade and technological factors is driving the increase in demand for skilled workers.

When rising demand for skills is not met by supply, the result is a persistent shortage of skilled labor and constrained growth. It also forces firms to pay above-market-clearing wages in order to retain workers they train, and may cause segmentation in the workforce.[24] On the supply side, the problems can be traced to:

- Low educational attainment.
- Antiquated and unresponsive training; the vocational and technical training system is not providing new entrants with appropriate skills.
- Insufficient investment in post-school, on-the-job training. In addition to inadequate vocational education, there is insufficient on-the-job training on the part of firms and workers. On-the-job training is often associated with a propensity to introduce innovation and, thus, with productivity growth.[25]

Table 2. Marginal Value of Education by Level

	1988	1992	1996	1997
Quantile	0.50	0.50	0.50	0.50
Primary complete	1.16	1.13	1.15	1.17
Lower-Secondary Comp	1.14	1.15	1.15	1.14
Upper-Secondary Comp	1.23	1.30	1.31	1.31
University Complete	1.44	1.66	1.80	1.80

Source: Lopez-Acevedo and Salinas (2000), World Bank.

---

24. Interviews with Mexican entrepreneurs in the 1992 *Encuesta Nacional de Empleo, Salarios, Tecnología y Capacitación* (ENESTYC) support this view. Roughly 30 percent stated that the resignation of recently trained workers was a problem. This is almost certainly an understatement for two reasons. First, "recently" may not capture the relevant period of return on the investment in the worker. Second, if the firm is already paying the optimal efficiency wage to prevent workers from leaving, it will not report excessive turnover as a problem. (see Maloney and Ribeiro 1999, "Efficiency Wage and Union Effects in Labor Deamnd and Wage Structure in Mexico: An Application of Quantile Analysis," in Maloney (1999), *Mexican Labor Markets, New Views on Integration and Flexibility*, World Bank.

25. Direct evidence on the proportion of workers receiving training reinforces this impression. In 1988, only 15 to 20 percent of workers employed in large- and medium-sized Mexican firms, and 10 percent and 5 percent, respectively, of those employed in small- and micro-sized firms, reported receiving any form of training. In contrast, 38 percent of U.S. workers report receiving some training in their current jobs.

- Inadequate information flows; there is little sharing of information on job opportunities and skill requirements among regions and sectors.

Policy Options

Several programs designed to encourage training and retraining of unskilled workers have been implemented in the past few years (CIMO and PROBECAT). Preliminary evaluations suggest that these programs, to date of limited coverage, have enjoyed only limited success.[26] The following policies are proposed to augment efforts to train or retrain unskilled workers:

- *Modify the Ley de Capacitación while maintaining the right to training.* Replace the requirement that firms register their training programs with the government with a less bureaucratically burdensome random spot check system.
- *Consider greater emphasis on technical education.* Figure 2 suggests that technical education substantially augments the hourly earnings of workers with secondary education.[27]
- *Promote private sector training.* The most recent studies suggest that, as with mid-career training programs elsewhere, PROBECAT has not been especially effective at either raising wages or shortening the unemployment spell. The training period may be too short to impart valuable skills, or it may be that PROBECAT's safety-net function conflicts with its training role.[28] Mexico should examine more demand-driven, private-sector-provided programs such as in Chile. This may include using vouchers to allow potential trainees the choice among privately provided training modalities. Emphasis should be placed on flexible programs that can be broken down into modules, and which permit training while working.
- *Reform the system of vocational training to ease the transition from school to work.* Youth unemployment remains high in Mexico and may be partly due to a mismatch of skills provided by the public education system and those demanded by industry. The Chilean program of CHILEJOVEN has been proven effective and may be worth emulating.
- *Reintroduce the apprenticeship contract as a way to facilitate market entry for school leavers.* Ideally, such contracts would be designed to contain a minimum training component and would optimally allow for apprenticeship wages to be set below occupational minimum-wage levels. However, abuses of a previous apprenticeship program make this a sensitive issue.

---

26. For an evaluation of the effectiveness of the PROBECAT program, see Revenga, Riboud, and Tan, *World Bank Economic Review*, May 1994.
27. See Lopez Acevedo and Salinas (2000), "The Evolution and Structure of the Rates of Return to Education in Mexico (1987–97): An Application of Quantile Regression."
28. See Wodon (1999), "Mexico Poverty Assessment."

Figure 2. Conditional Median Real Hourly Earnings

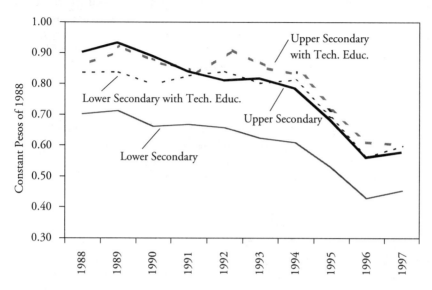

Source: Lopez-Acevedo and Salinas (2000), World Bank.

The Industrial Relations and Collective Bargaining Framework Needs to Be Reviewed and Modernized

The current system of industrial relations and collective bargaining has it roots and underlying philosophy in social relations and production techniques of the early part of this century. As such, it is inflexible, poorly suited to the more competitive global environment, and not conducive to the more cooperative relations between management and labor that are essential for greater productivity and job satisfaction.

Policy Options

AIM TO ACHIEVE A SYSTEM THAT COMBINES FIRM-LEVEL, DECENTRALIZED BARGAINING WITH NATIONWIDE COORDINATION AND SYNCHRONIZATION.[29] One of the great successes of the Mexican reform program has been the degree of collaboration and cooperation achieved among unions, business representatives, and government during macroeconomic stabilization. The challenges of competing in an increasingly open economy, however, may require a more flexible, decentralized system of bargaining in which bargaining occurs primarily at the level of the firm. Such a

---

29. Similar to, for example, the Japanese model, which combines firm-level unions and bargaining, with a highly coordinated and synchronized collective bargaining process.

system allows firms the maximum flexibility to adapt contract negotiations to their financial situations and avoids situations in which firms in economic difficulty are forced to pay wages negotiated at the national, sectoral, or state level. It also allows greater flexibility in the development of firm-specific measures of eliciting effort and encouraging productivity. There has already been substantial decentralization as recent *Pactos* have focused more on productivity-enhancing programs and less on wage agreements, while competitive pressures have induced more firm-level bargaining.

DISCARD A NUMBER OF OBSOLETE LEGAL STRUCTURES AND PROVISIONS GOVERNING COLLECTIVE BARGAINING. The legal framework governing individual and collective labor relations can be traced back to the Constitution of 1917 and the Federal Labor Law of 1930 (revised in 1970). This legislation is ill suited to the needs of a rapidly changing economy that competes in increasingly open world markets, and in which the service sector is quickly gaining in importance. For example, firms in several sectors are still bound by *contratos-ley*, or agreements that are extended to all firms in an industry, regardless of unionization or economic situation; these agreements achieve neither the microeconomic efficiency of decentralized bargaining nor the macroeconomic benefits of centralized bargaining. Legal clauses such as the *clausula de exclusion*, which mandates union membership for new hires in unionized firms, should be reconsidered and possibly eliminated.

ENCOURAGE INTRODUCTION OF MORE FLEXIBLE JOB LADDERS AND ASSIGNMENTS. Eliminate provisions on seniority-based promotion, compensation, and training.[30] Rigid seniority-based schemes impede the reward of individual performance and investment in training since neither employer nor worker can fully recover its benefits.

MOVE TOWARD MORE COOPERATIVE WORK RELATIONS WITHIN THE FIRM. At present, union influence over matters such as training decisions, promotions, and decisions to introduce new technologies tends to reduce the ability of firms to restructure jobs, change production patterns, and adapt to shifting market conditions. As suggested in the last *Pacto*, increased competition in the global market requires a more cooperative relationship that involves workers more in the issues of productivity and quality, gives them a broader overview of the functioning of the organization, and encourages worker input, but which leaves the firm flexible to meet competitive challenges.

---

30. The labor law explicitly states that vacancies in the firm's job ladder will be filled by workers employed in the category immediately below, provided they "prove aptitude" for the job. Increased competition from abroad has led to a decline in seniority-based promotion and compensation, although they remain widespread and prevail in collective-bargaining agreements. An informal survey of export firms, for example, revealed that in 43 percent of them, promotion is based exclusively on seniority. See Hernandez-Laos (1991).

REFORM THE PROFIT-SHARING SYSTEM. The constitution requires that firms distribute an unspecified percentage (currently 10 percent) of taxable profits. Profit sharing in theory can serve several purposes: adding flexibility in labor compensation, thereby permitting greater stability in the quantity of labor employed, serving as an incentive mechanism in tandem with cooperative management-worker efforts to boost productivity, and diffuse risk. If the link between greater job stability and flexibility in bonuses is made explicit, workers might accept a truly flexible 10 percent of *profits*. This would, in effect, cost firms the same as at present, but would make wage payments more flexible. This may become more useful as inflation makes real-wage adjustments more difficult.

RESTRUCTURE THE MINIMUM-WAGE SYSTEM. The minimum wage has fallen so much in real terms that, at least for those laboring in the formal sector, it is minimally binding and thus may not be serving its purpose (see Annex III).[31] Standardizing the minimum wage by the mean wage, Mexico (.34) is far below the average for Europe (~.45), but is above Argentina (.26), Bolivia (.22), Brazil (.24), and Uruguay (.19), and at the same level as Chile (.34). A minimum wage reform package that would ensure simplicity, flexibility, and compliance, and minimize potential anti-employment effects would:

- Merge the existing structure of three regional minimum wages into a single minimum wage. This has been a longstanding request of labor unions.
- Eliminate minimum wages for professional workers and keep it only for entry-level jobs.
- Gradually reduce or eliminate the role of the minimum wage as a reference index for other economic variables such as social security brackets and severance payments.

ELIMINATE THE "INDIRECT PATRON" RELATIONSHIP. This clause makes firms responsible for the employer obligations of workers employed by their subcontractors. While on the surface protecting workers, this rule causes firms to change providers frequently to avoid being considered the indirect patron; raises business costs by forcing firms to thoroughly investigate the solvency of their subcontractors; creates unnecessary vertical integration in firms to avoid the risk of opportunistic providers; and discriminates against small providers who may be assumed not to have the resources to comply with labor obligations.

ELIMINATE RESTRICTIONS ON THE USE OF TEMPORARY OR FIXED-TERM CONTRACTS. Such contracts provide firms with needed flexibility in hiring and dismissals. Consider the establishment of a *Contrato a Prueba* that would last between two and four

---

31. In 1988, fewer than 3 percent of formal-sector workers received less than the minimum wage, compared with 16 percent of individuals working in the informal sector.

months. Extend the *Contrato por Tiempo Determinado* to cover temporary increases in business demand.

RETURN TO PREVIOUS SYSTEM OF NEGOTIATING WAGES EVERY TWO YEARS INSTEAD OF EVERY YEAR. The move toward annual negotiations was prompted by the erosion in real wages in the high-inflation period. This is no longer a problem.

The Urban Informal Sector Needs Policies to Stimulate Growth and Encourage Formalization

In the Mexican economy a modern urban sector coexists with more traditional informal urban and rural sectors. The urban informal sector employs about 40 percent of the workforce, produces 25 to 38 percent of GDP, and accounts for about 55 percent of the poor and extremely poor. Average compensation is slightly higher among the informal self-employed and slightly lower among the informal salaried. Roughly 70 percent of informal workers are informal by choice and cite greater flexibility and higher returns as the reason for entering the sector.[32] However, by definition, they are not covered by basic medical or pension funds, which may lead both to private hardship and public burdens late in the life cycle. Even if the labor force were to expand at a historically low rate of 2 percent per year, the informal will not be absorbed through growth alone.[33] Policies that seek to expand employment and increase productivity in the informal sector are needed.

---

32. When asked why they operated in the informal sector, 30 percent responded that they were unable to find alternate work, but 20 percent said they earned higher wages (informal owners can earn substantially more than salaried workers), 30 percent enjoyed the greater independence and more flexible hours, 5 percent operated in the informal sector for reasons of tradition. Maloney (1999), "Does Informality Imply segmentation in Urban labor Markets? Evidence form Sectoral transitions in Mexico," *World Bank Economic Review*. See also Cunningham and Maloney (2000), "Heterogeneity Among Mexico's Micro-enterprises: An Application of Factor and Cluster Analysis," *Economic Development and Cultural Change*, forthcoming. Many respondents objected to mandatory welfare contributions in the formal sector since the services were poor. For a complete view of interaction of two sectors, see Maloney (1999), *Mexican Labor Markets: New Views on Integration and Flexibility*, IBRD.
33. Consider the following: assume that capital and labor shares in production are roughly equal, and that output and capital grow at 4 percent a year over the next six years. With total factor productivity growth of 2 percent a year, there would be no net growth of employment. If output were to grow more rapidly, at 6 percent a year, net employment would increase by 2 percent a year—barely enough to absorb the flow of new entrants, much less to allow those already in the informal sector to move into the formal sector.

Policy Options

REDUCE THE WEDGE BETWEEN THE IMPLICIT COST OF FORMAL SECTOR LABOR AND THE MARKET-CLEARING WAGE. However, roughly 30 percent report being unable to find salaried jobs. This seems unlikely to be due to binding minimum-wage laws or other rigidities and inefficiencies, and rather may reflect efficiency wage considerations.[34]

REDUCE THE COSTS, FINANCIAL AND OTHERWISE, OF REGISTRATION. Registration costs are about average for Latin America, although the process takes a year compared to 1 to 3 months in Brazil, Chile, and Uruguay. Expand and review the operations of facilities for one-stop registration.[35]

REDUCE THE HIGH COSTS OF BEING FORMAL. Ongoing regulatory costs are thought to comprise 24 percent of total costs for microenterprises. One study found labor obligations to be those most often evaded, partly because, when fully complied with, they account for 50 to 60 percent of annual profits (as opposed to 17 to 30 percent for Chile).[36] In general, firms comply with some regulations and not others.[37, 38] Two barriers to formality need immediate attention.

- Redesign social security programs for the informal sector. Some informal entrepreneurs cited avoidance of IMSS as a reason to be informal.[39]

---

34. See Krebs and Maloney (1998), "Quitting and Labor Turnover"; and Maloney and Ribeiro (1998), "Efficiency Wage and Union Effects in labor Demand and Wage Structure in Mexico," both in Maloney (1999), *Mexican Labor Markets: New Views on Integration and Flexibility*, World Bank.
35. In 1994 there was only one *Ventanilla Unica de Gestion* that provides one-stop registration for all of Mexico City. Only .5 percent were served by the current *ventanilla*, the majority of whose clients are between 15 to 100 workers.
36. Elizondo (1992) and Lagos (1992).
37. See Levenson and Maloney (1998), "The Informal Sector, Firm Dynamics and Institutional Participation," in Maloney (1999) *Mexican Labor Markets: New Views on Integration and Flexibility*, World Bank.
38. This has led in some cases to subcontracting from formal firms to the informal sector. Separate studies suggest that 24 percent of large firms in Guadalajara and 75 percent of all firms in Mexico City subcontracted work to the informal sector. In the latter study, 79 percent of the firms cited "reduction in costs" as the principal reason for subcontracting, and the "flexibility in shedding labor" as also important. Smaller firms suggested that subcontracting allowed them to stay small and thereby avoid labor conflicts (firms under 20 employees need not unionize), as well as avoid sophisticated accounting systems. See Roberts (1989) and Beneria (1989). The *Secretaria de Trabajo y Prevision Social* argues that the level of integration is relatively small and that only 2.6 percent of enterprises work as subcontractors, 60 percent of these in textiles or leather work. "El Sector Informal en Mexico,"(1993).
39. Mesa-Lagos (1989), and Ozorio de Almeida et al. (1994).

- While tax levels are not thought to be burdensome, the system needs to be simplified.[40]

IMPLEMENT POLICIES TO RAISE THE PRODUCTIVITY OF THE FORMAL SECTOR. This would involve:

- Review and expand systems for extending credit to microenterprises.[41] Good results have been achieved using NGOs as intermediaries or working through Empresas de Solidaridad where entrepreneurs individually or collectively present business plans which, if approved, receive funding and technical assistance.
- Expand training in microenterprises through CIMO, should careful evaluations justify it. Entrepreneurs find very valuable the diagnostic analysis of firm operations conducted by CIMO before training programs are begun.[42]

---

40. SHCP estimated that to take a tax deduction for exempt benefits, a company with three employees would have to put together 805 pieces of data and carry out 200 steps. The requirements that tax deductions for expenses be backed by invoices favors enterprises with access to fax and photocopy machines. Ozorio de Almeida et al.
41. The current method of channeling NAFIN resources, largely through commercial banks, has led to only 18 percent reaching firms of under 15 workers. This is partly due to the usual structural constraints: high transaction costs of extending and monitoring small loans and the lack of collateral.
42. The urban formal and informal sectors are also linked through labor training at different phases in a worker's life cycle. In Guadalajara, 67 percent of workers presently employed in firms of more than 100 workers began in firms with less than 20. Smaller, informal firms may thus provide a de facto apprenticeship system where a lower wage is received during training. At the other end of the life cycle, about 80 percent of informal enterprise owners and self-employed were previously salaried in the formal sector (Ozorio de Almeida et al.).

Annex I—The Mexican System of Employment Protection

Existing Arrangements

Mexican labor legislation has a long tradition of employment protection, as reflected in the job security provisions first set forth in Article 123 of the Mexican Constitution (1917) and then expanded in the Federal Labor Law (*Ley Federal del Trabajo*, LFT) of 1931.[43]

Employment protection in Mexico encompasses three elements: (a) advance notice requirements in case of dismissal, (b) mandated severance compensation linked to involuntary separations, and (c) legal procedures to protect workers dismissed "without cause."

With respect to element (a), the LFT establishes that the employer must notify the employee one month in advance, in writing, of the dismissal and the reasons for it. The failure to do so automatically qualifies a dismissal as "unjust" or "without cause," and entitles the worker to the compensation established by the law for "unjust" dismissals.

With respect to elements (b) and (c), the LFT establishes that, with the exception of temporary workers and those hired to fulfill a specific assignment, the relationship between employer and employee is a permanent one. For a worker to be legally dismissed, the employer must prove that the employee committed certain unacceptable behavior, such as stealing, unauthorized absence from work, and drunkenness. Even in these cases, the worker can appeal to the labor courts, and he or she can be awarded the constitutional right to be reinstated, in addition to the restitution of all wages not paid during the hearing period. Alternatively, a worker who is found to have been illegally fired can choose not to return to his or her job and opt instead for a payment of three months' salary, plus wages due since the date of dismissal. Note that the legal treatment of dismissal on economic grounds (redundancy) is the same as for arbitrary dismissals (with the exception of dismissal for "technological change" reasons, see below).

Workers who are legally dismissed are entitled to severance compensation equal to three months' salary, plus 20 days per year of service (with a cap of two monthly minimum wages per year of service), plus 12 days per year of work in the case of workers with 15 or more years of seniority. If the dismissal occurs because of "technological change," the law establishes that the firm will have to pay four months' salary instead of three, plus the 20 days and 12 days of seniority-based severance payments.

Workers who quit or who are voluntarily separated from employment are entitled to a separation payment equal to 12 days' salary per year of service, provided they have fulfilled 15 years of service or more. However, if they quit because of "unjust behavior" on the part of the employer, as defined in the law, they are entitled to the same compensation as under a legal dismissal.

---

43. Amended in 1970.

There are no legal restrictions on temporary or fixed-term contracts, although the penalties associated with dismissal of fixed-term employees are, in some cases, larger than the severance payments mandated for regular workers.

In practice, firms appear to enjoy more flexibility in reducing labor without incurring large severance costs than strict interpretation of the law suggests. Increasingly, firms have come to rely on those categories of labor that can be legally dismissed without significant costs, namely temporary workers and nonunionized white-collar workers *(personal de confianza)*. In addition, collective bargaining agreements appear to be evolving to include provisions that allow firms to reduce their workforce after previous negotiation with the unions. Third, hiring labor through a subsidiary firm (subcontracting), a practice that allows firms to reduce dismissal costs, has also become common. Information collected by Hernandez-Laos (1991) on a sample of enterprises indicates that during the 1980s the proportion of nonunionized white-collar workers in total employment increased from 26.2 percent to 32.1 percent. Similarly, the proportion of workers on temporary contracts increased from 15.0 percent in 1986 to 17.3 percent in 1989. Thus, a sizable proportion of the workforce is covered by contracts that involve no severance payments.

Implications

Mandated severance payments can have important distortionary effects on the hiring and firing, compensation, and training decisions of firms and workers. The most immediate effect is to increase the cost of labor, since employers must take into account the firm's implied liability in the case of a dismissal. This increase in the cost of labor will tend to lower labor demand, and hence reduce employment levels.

Estimated costs of labor dismissals can be substantial, but actual costs may be lower because many firms appear to settle disputes with dismissed employees outside the labor courts. Unfortunately, there are no numbers on what firms actually pay out as severance compensation.

The dynamic effects of firing restrictions are more complex. In a downturn a firm will shed less labor than it would if dismissal were costless, whereas in an upturn it will refrain from hiring as much as it would in the absence of firing costs. In either case, the law limits the firm's ability to adjust employment, affects the cost of labor relative to other inputs, and affects the cost of employees relative to hours. On balance, most empirical evidence suggests that the net effect on employment creation will be negative.[44]

Firing restrictions will also have obvious negative implications for labor mobility and will hamper necessary reallocation of workers between sectors. Moreover, to the extent that such restrictions represent an additional labor cost, they will reduce the international competitiveness of Mexican producers.

---

44. See, for example, Alba-Ramirez (1991); Bentolila and Dolado (1994); Jimeno and Toharia (1992); Fallon and Lucas (1991); and Lazear (1990).

Annex II—Recent Labor Market Reforms in Spain

Employment Contracts

1. Reintroduced the apprenticeship contract. Requirements:
   - Until 25 years of age.
   - Restrictions on maximum proportion of workers to be hired under this contract.
   - Contract duration: minimum six months, maximum three years.
   - Wage: at least 70 percent (80 percent and 90 percent in successive years) of the national wage.
   - Reduction in social security contributions.
   - Employer must provide at least 15 percent of working hours as training.
2. Reformed part-time contract. Already existed. Main changes:
   - Number of working hours can be computed yearly instead of weekly
   - Reduction in nonwage labor costs.
3. Fixed-term contracts without justification (the so-called *contrato temporal de fomento del empleo*):
   - Fixed-term contracts expiring in 1994 can be extended for 18 months. (The contracts expiring in 1993 were also allowed to be extended by one year).
   - In the future, this contract can be used only in specific employment promotion programs and is restricted to the hiring of long-term unemployed by small firms.

Firing Costs

1. Legal severance payment levels have not been modified.
2. Administrative approval is only required for collective dismissals (firings) caused by economic, technological, or demand reasons affecting at least 10 workers in firms with less than 100 workers, 10 percent of workers in firms with 100 to 300 workers, and more than 30 workers in firms with more than 300 workers, in a period of 90 days. Administrative costs and the resolution period are also reduced.
3. Economic reasons can now be alleged to "fairly" fire workers. "Fair" dismissals imply severance payments of 20 days' wages per year of seniority (with a maximum of 12 months' wages). "Unfair" dismissals imply severance payments of 45 days' wages per year of seniority (with a maximum of 46 months' wages). Labor courts decide whether a dismissal is fair or unfair. In practice, fired permanent workers always sue the employer in order to get a labor court resolution. In most cases, labor court resolution is not needed because employers and fired workers reach an agreement, usually consisting of severance payments higher than those for fair dismissals. Labor court resolutions usually favor workers.

Functional and Geographical Mobility

1. Restrictions on worker classification (the so-called *Ordenanzas Laborales*) are to be abolished at the end of 1994. Collective bargaining agreements must provide new regulations in this regard.
2. Working hours can be computed on a yearly basis, so that an irregular distribution of working time through the year is feasible. Restrictions on the maximum daily working hours remain.
3. Overtime pay and premium pay for nighttime working hours established by the law have been abolished. Wage remuneration for special working hours should be established by collective bargaining. Overtime hours can be compensated by vacation time instead of higher wages (this was not feasible before).
4. Administrative approval for modification of substantial employment conditions (geographic and functional mobility) is no longer required, but labor court controls remain, and worker representatives must be consulted. In case of disagreement, the labor administration can delay such modification for a maximum of one year.

Unemployment Benefits

1. Unemployment benefits are no longer exempted from the income tax.
2. Unemployed workers must pay a fraction of their social security contributions. Previously, the public employment agency was in charge and paid the total amount of unemployed workers' social security contributions.

Collective Bargaining

The conditions under which firm-level agreements can establish employment conditions below those established by sectoral agreements must be specified in the sectoral agreement. If a firm agrees with its workers in this respect, then the firm-level agreement is feasible. In case of disagreement between the firm and its workers, the bargaining unit at the sectoral level settles matters.

Active Employment Policies

1. Private employment agencies (without a "profit motivation") are no longer illegal.
2. Private firms can hire workers and provide them to other firms on a temporary basis.

Annex III—The Minimum Wage

Presumably governments mandate minimum wages either on equity grounds, to compress the distribution of earnings, or on efficiency grounds, to address situations in which employers may have a natural monopsony and information superior to that of workers. If a government is going to legislate a minimum wage, it is essential to set it at the appropriate level and in a manner that ensures the greatest degree of flexibility. Yet there is an inherent problem in mandating a minimum wage: if it is too high, it has strong anti-employment effects and tends to hurt precisely those it was intended to help; if it is too low (that is, substantially below market-clearing levels), it has no effect on the distribution of earnings and risks becoming irrelevant.

The minimum wage also serves an important role as a reference price, in that many other economic variables are indexed to it. For example, social security brackets are expressed as a function of the minimum wage. Similarly, severance payments are capped also in reference to the minimum wage. Moreover, in the last *Pacto*, negotiated increases for the minimum wage acted as de facto floors for subsequent negotiation of other wage levels. Because of this role as a reference index, it is essential that the minimum wage not fluctuate widely or increase too rapidly in real terms.

Is the Minimum Wage Binding in Mexico?

Raw comparisons of the real minimum wage across countries are of limited use. From the perspective of both improving equity and minimizing labor market distortions, what is of interest is the level of the minimum wage relative to the distribution of remuneration in the individual country. To argue that the minimum wage in Brazil is "too low" because it is a fraction of that in Argentina is irrelevant if overall labor productivity differs by similar magnitudes.

As a first cut at international comparison, Annex Figure 1 ranks various Latin American and OECD countries by the minimum wage standardized by the mean wage (SMW). Latin America spans the range with Argentina, Bolivia, Brazil, Chile, Mexico, and Uruguay with the lowest values, and El Salvador, Paraguay, and Venezuela with among the highest.

For two reasons, while informative, standardizing by the first moment is not sufficient to tell us whether the minimum wage is binding. First the number of workers affected will depend on the higher moments of the distribution as well: more disperse endowments of human capital (variance) or a particularly large fraction of poorly endowed workers (skewness) would lead to more workers being affected by a given SMW. Second, if the minimum wage is not enforced, very high SMWs are irrelevant. A graphic approach, however, can reliably reveal how the distribution is distorted. The first panel of Annex Figure 2 shows kernel estimates of the density function, with a vertical line to mark the location of the

Annex Figure 1. Minimum Wage/Mean Wage in OECD Countries and Latin America

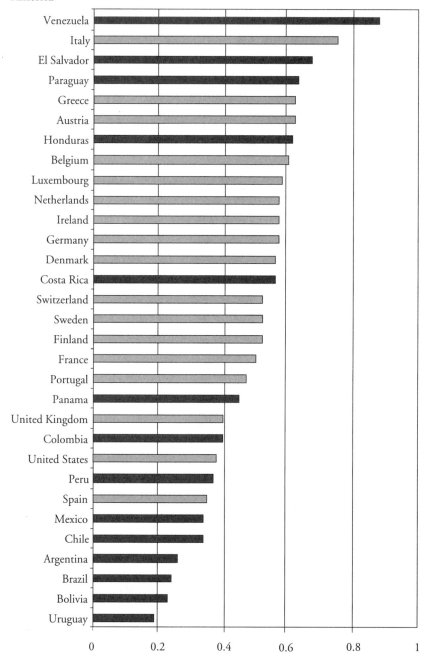

Annex Figure 2a. Distribution of Wages from Formal and Informal Workers

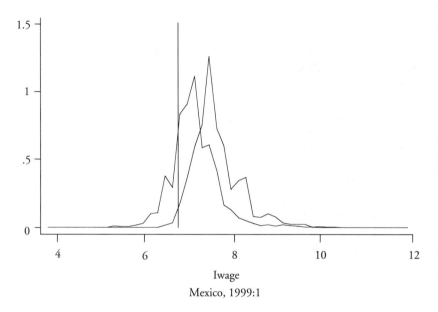

Iwage

Mexico, 1999:1

Annex Figure 2b. Cumulative Distribution of Wages from Formal and Informal Workers

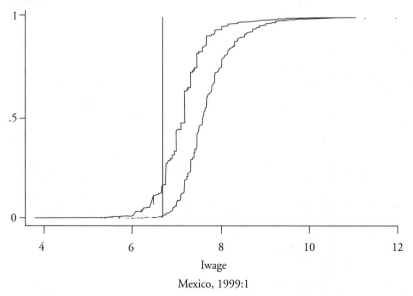

Iwage

Mexico, 1999:1

minimum wage.[45] This has the advantage of giving a clearer idea of the shape of the distribution, but it is sensitive to the bandwidth chosen to smooth. The second panel shows the cumulative distributions of wages. These requires no judgments about bandwidths, and the vertical "cliffs" indicate where the minimum wage, or multiples, may be influencing. Both the formal and informal wage distributions are plotted in light and dark lines, respectively.[46] In both figures, a "piling up" of the probability mass around the minimum wage suggests that the policy has, in effect, forced a change in the distribution.

Both panels suggest that, in the formal sector, the minimum wage is not strongly binding, although in the informal sector it is. This may reflect a "lighthouse" effect where what informal workers consider to be the "fair" wage is indexed off the minimum.

---

45. See DiNardo, Fortin, and Lemieux (1996) for a thorough treatment of kernel density estimation, and Velez and Santamaria (1999) for an application of the CDF to Colombia.
46. Informal sector is defined in each country either by whether a salaried worker is unaffiliated with social security systems, or works in very small firms (around six or less).

23

Indigenous Peoples and Poverty

*This Chapter was written by Augusta Molnar and Tania Carrasco
with the valuable input of Adolfo Brizzi.*

The high incidence of poverty among indigenous peoples in Mexico is due to structural, economic, and social factors, all of which must be directly addressed if there is to be a major change in the future development of these peoples. There is a strong persistence of indigenous social and cultural organization, including local systems of governance and a continued interest in coordinating development efforts through these structures. While these governance systems historically served a function of cultural survival—assisting communities in maintaining self-sufficiency, protecting land and property rights, filtering out integrationist influences, and presenting a palatable image to outsiders—they are adapting to a more secure environment by channeling community efforts and resources toward self-development and self-mobilization.

Urban indigenous peoples are developing distinct organizational networks which adapt traditional structures. Successful models are emerging in rural communities, combining investment in group enterprises with individual household investment to create alternatives to the current system of low agricultural productivity and high rates of outmigration. Where there are important natural resources, these models can be solutions to Mexico's problem of environmental degradation. Current poverty alleviation strategies need to be reviewed in light of this indigenous reality to support a more appropriate exit strategy.

I. Current Developments

Demography

There are 156,557 settlements in 803 municipalities with more than 30 percent indigenous population, and 6,300 of the country's 30,000 *ejidos* and *comunidades agrarias* have more than 30 percent indigenous population.[1] The percentage of the Mexican population speaking an indigenous language or self-identified as indigenous peoples has stabilized at about 10 percent over the past decade, for a total of 10.6 million people in 1997 (as measured by the category "members over 5 years of age of households headed by indigenous language speakers (ILS)"). This is in sharp contrast to earlier census statistics that showed a steady decline between 1930 and 1990 from 14 to 8 percent of the total population.

Moreover, the rate of growth of some groups of the indigenous population is higher than the nation's (2.1 percent per year), such as is the case with the *mixtecos (5.2), nahuatl (3.8), mazateco* (4.0) *and mixe* (3.5). The main reason for this growth is due to the improved prenatal and postnatal care given to these communities by the institutional health system. In turn, the change in the demographic picture seems to rest on two factors: (a) new criteria used in the 1995 interim Population and Housing census to include members of households headed by ILS, and actual speakers; and (b) a re-identification of indigenous peoples as culturally distinct, which appears to be strengthening with a new shift in the patterns of urbanization and rural–urban linkages.

Poverty Rates

For nearly five centuries in Mexico, indigenous peoples suffered destruction, decimation, discrimination, and marginalization. In the last decade of the 20th century, indigenous peoples' issues began to be addressed more directly through the United Nations and other international organizations. There has been increasing recognition of indigenous issues and problems of exclusion and underdevelopment. This changing climate allows for a more open discussion of these issues with the Mexican government which, internally, is fully aware of the issues and problems of indigenous peoples.

With this new openness, a range of statistical information has been produced on the situation of indigenous peoples and their current trends. In terms of poverty and marginality indicators, according to 1990 census data, 96 percent of indigenous peoples live in municipalities with marginality rankings of high and very high, with 4 percent of these in very high marginality (INI, Arnulfo Embriz, coordinator, *Indicadores socioeconómicos de los pueblos indígenas de México*, 1993). While reliable figures do not exist nationally, extrapolations by researchers in INI and CONAPO, along with case study data, estimate that one-quarter to one-third of Mexico's poor are indigenous, and that indigenous peoples make up about 33 percent of the extreme poor.

---

1. Nahmad, S. and Tania Carrasco. National Profile. *Perfiles Indígenas de Mexico (Indigenous Profiles of Mexico),* National Indigenist Institute (INI) and Centro for Graduate Studies in Social Anthropology (CIESAS), Web address: www.unam.mx/ciesas.

Migration

Migration patterns have dramatically reshaped the location and livelihood strategies of indigenous peoples. Indigenous migration increased in the 1940s with the development of an urban, industrialized economy, and the subsequent attraction of indigenous labor from marginal agricultural areas to industrial cities and the commercial agricultural regions of Mexico and the United States. Migration has continued, with an increase in the urban-to-urban type. There has been continued migration of indigenous populations from the southern states to the northeast, and from surrounding rural areas to the traditional *mestizo*-dominated market centers, such as San Cristóbal de las Casas and Oaxaca. The concentration of indigenous population is increasing not only in rural areas, but also in urban or peri-urban municipalities. Mexico City has the largest population of indigenous people in Mexico. In Yucatán state, 40 percent of the indigenous population is urban, and San Cristóbal de las Casas is becoming an indigenous rather than a *mestizo* city. In 1980, 10 percent of the total indigenous population lived in areas other than their region of origin, not counting international migrants.

Temporary migration is an important part of current indigenous livelihood strategies to counter the declining returns from increasingly poor soils in rainfed areas—93.8 percent of indigenous *ejido* and community lands are nonirrigated. Remittances are important resources for family subsistence, expenditures on social and religious events, and education. The value of international postal orders to Oaxaca was more than US$2 billion in 1992 alone, an amount that exceeds the state's annual budget. But remittances have not generally led to significant productive investment in improved agriculture or new off-farm enterprises due to traditional barriers that indigenous peoples face in accessing markets and political spheres of influence.

In addition, temporary migration deprives households of the labor needed to produce higher-value crops. It distorts and disrupts household and community relations and interactions and limits access to services, including regular education for migrant children. In the long term, this migratory phenomenon tends to result in increased dependency on external sources for the livelihood of the community and in the relative stagnation of indigenous communities.

The Rural Economy

Rural indigenous peoples reside in a wide range of ecological niches, many of which are both remote and fragile. Some ethnic groups arrive to their initial niche as exiles from their traditional territories, and then move to new localities as their population increases. One product of colonization programs, such as the movement of Tzertales and Choles to the rainforest (Lacandona) and the influx of migrant refugees from Guatemala have attracted some indigenous populations to tropical and subtropical areas outside their traditional ecological niche, where they do not have the indigenous knowledge to apply traditional agricultural practices.

The economic subsistence base of the typical indigenous community is an area for production of such crops as maize, bean, squash, and pepper, (known as the *milpa*). While productivity of the main crops grown in such areas is low in rainfed areas, there is a wide diversity of products which are grown or collected in these niches, and many of the traditional indigenous areas are the source of very diverse native cultivars, found in cultivated fields and in the wild. More than 100 food, medicinal, fiber, and other household materials are grown in the Huasteca agricultural system or collected in and around the fields (Janice Alcorn has documented 185 plants, 85 of which are medicinal, in Huasteca gardens),[2] and more than 60 species are raised in Totonaca gardens. Agriculture and gathering is supplemented by small livestock rearing, hunting, fishing, artesanal production, and cash crops where viable, including coffee, sugarcane, wheat, tobacco, vanilla, and citrus.

Indigenous Peoples and Biodiversity

There is a strong overlap between indigenous communities and *ejidos* and high biodiversity areas, including official protected areas. Excluding the protection forest category (which can allow controlled log extraction), 40 of the 124 reserved protected areas (40 percent) either border or include municipalities with more than 30 percent indigenous population.[3] The new generation of protected areas management initiatives include indigenous peoples in an increasingly integral role in the protected areas strategy, although the balance of control and design choices still rests with the ecological specialists, not the indigenous communities. Of particular interest to ecologists are the links between indigenous peoples and arid areas. Indigenous groups like the Tarahumara or Huichol have adapted their survival strategies to occupy marginal arid lands over long periods, while preserving a high diversity of original cultivars and creating diverse human-managed systems. In parallel with the revitalization of cultural identity is the growing movement of indigenous peoples to accept decisionmaking roles in protected areas management and to contribute to new models of conservation.

Creating the conditions for sustainable management is challenging in both the traditional areas of indigenous settlement and in the recently colonized areas around biodiverse resources. Demographic pressures and the limited amount of productive land per family combine with illegal or poorly organized logging activities to form serious threats to the maintenance of biodiversity. Well-intentioned agricultural development programs have promoted economic progress through the introduction of models of livestock rearing and cropping technologies that ignore traditional practices and that create no synergy with the surrounding natural resource base and biodiversity. These trends put indigenous communities in danger of losing a variety

2. Alcorn, Janice 1984. "An Economic Analysis of Huastec Mayan Forest Management" *Advances in Economic Botany* 7:63–77.
3. Op cit., National Profile.

of traditional knowledge and natural resource management practices that are, in fact, important options for future conservation.

Indigenous Rural Identity

The indigenous agricultural system is surprisingly resilient. Despite the introduction of new crops and productive practices, and strong linkage to markets (although through intermediaries), indigenous communities retain a traditional social organization based on maize agriculture. A kingpin of this culture is the concept of the land as a sacred good rather than a material good to be possessed or exchanged. The cultivation of the maize plot is both an economic and a magical–religious act without which production is inconceivable. Land acts as the pillar that maintains the cohesion of the kin group and related extended families forming the community. Land provides individual families with security, the community with group cohesion, and the society with cultural continuity. This cultural identity is not stagnant, however. For example, in the indigenous Huasteca, even after individual land redistribution to disenfranchised farm workers in the 1970s, some indigenous beneficiaries provided with individual titles informally re-created "communal" organizational structure. Throughout indigenous regions and urban neighborhoods of Mexico, traditional social and political institutions interact with government and civil society structures to maintain a discrete identity, while permitting evolution toward a changing future.

Communal Systems of Governance

The internal social organization which distinguishes indigenous communities is based on an economy of prestige and social responsibility. Indigenous systems of governance persist to a broad degree in agrarian communities and indigenous *ejidos*, legitimated by the Articles 4 and 27 of the National Constitution, both modifed in 1992. The governing bodies are officials appointed by the General Assembly (adult representatives of all households in the community) who assume a series of positions of responsibility (*cargos*) for tasks which are required by the community. Adult males rotate through this series of positions, "graduating" at the end to become a community elder, serving as a senior advisor to the community. Positions are honorary, and community members living abroad or elsewhere in Mexico can be called back temporarily to assume a position if appointed. This governance system includes religious tasks, coordination of civic activities, maintaining internal systems of law and order, and administering community enterprises.

The system usually functions in parallel to formal local government, which can cause conflicts in situations where municipal authorities make decisions that contradict those of traditional authorities. In states where municipalities include large numbers of localities, the indigenous governance may be the only authority with whom residents have real contact, since few government programs may reach outlying localities, even with the recent decentralization of municipal funds. In northern states, the disconnect can occur between *ejido* and indigenous authorities and with municipalities. In *ejidos* with mixed indigenous and non-indigenous settlements, indigenous localities falling within *ejido* boundaries may never have been formally included as voting *ejidatarios*, leaving entire groups with no representation.

In 1998, in response to federal legal reforms, Oaxaca passed a specific state law to regulate the Article 4 and 27 rights at state level. This law and its regulations gives communities the option of selecting a formal political representation system (by majority elections) or the *usos y costumbres* traditional system with selection by an assembly of the municipal authority, which serves, as in the case of a *cargo*, for one year without pay. Under this system, leaders can return for up to three terms, although the expense of holding this position are high and most step down after one or two years. All policy decisions are referred back to the assembly, which meets once a month or more, so that the local government officials are seen as the executors of community decisions. Currently 412 of the 570 municipalities in Oaxaca are governed by "usos y costumbres."[4] The reforms to Article 27 of The Constitution and the PROCEDE program of *ejido* and community regularization have encouraged the formalization of the *usos y costumbres* through written codification of the "communal statutes" into the National Agrarian Registry (RAN), including agreements *(actas)* on land and resource use and zoning and internal policing systems. This provides a publicly available documentation of decisions that may differ from those mandated in national, state, or local law.

Transition

The political and economic outlook of indigenous communities and *ejidos* is in transition, covering a wide spectrum of situations. Historical and continued discrimination by the larger society creates pressures for indigenous peoples to turn inward for cultural survival, creating centers of refuge with self-governing structures that buffer outside interventions, while still linking to markets, government programs, outside employment, and to a limited extent, private capital. Successful communities in areas with rich natural resources (southern and central forests, northern coastal fisheries, coffee-growing areas of central and southern Mexico) have been able to combine individual household investment with communal enterprises, drawing on the common decisionmaking structure of traditional governance to develop a community business plan. These experiences are in the minority but clearly demonstrate the potential of the traditional organization to act as a bridge to facilitate the transition to a modern setting. During 1993–99, communities in the Chinanteca in Oaxaca implemented and maintained 472 community projects without external support.[5]

---

4. Gonzalez, Alvaro, State Profile of Oaxaca. *Perfiles Indigenas de México.*
5. Op cit., State Profile of Oaxaca.

Creating Political Space

The major problem of indigenous peoples, both in traditional rural settings and in urban indigenous neighborhoods in the cities, has been to create the linking social capital that provides them political clout and access to resources and services on their own terms. The literature on indigenous peoples is filled with cases in which government programs have failed to enable the development of indigenous regions. This isbecause of the individualistic approach for channeling subsidies and inputs, the failure to adapt health and education to indigenous needs and cultural preferences, and the creation of responsibility systems that bypass and compete with organic governance structures at the community and regional levels. Government statistics show high levels of school enrollment for indigenous children. However other studies show much higher levels of failure—to complete primary school among young adults 18 to 24 and failure of educational programs to build children's self-esteem. There is also a high incidence of those illnesses characteristic of poverty, with limited decentralization or cultural adaptation of healthcare services and installations. Road and irrigation infrastructure is sparse in indigenous rural areas, a situation created in part by the decline in government spending, dating from the economic crisis of 1982.

Alliances with political parties and labor unions was a strategy in the past to create political space vis-à-vis local elites and government, but given the very different agendas of these mainstream institutions, the result was internal factionalism which weakened the traditional structures without bringing positive change. Since the 1970s, when indigenous revitalization and self-realization movements emerged, there has been a proliferation and evolution of political and social organizations that are culturally based, to create upward and outward linkages that maintain cultural identities. A number of states additional to Oaxaca, such as Puebla, are in the process of preparing laws and regulations related to the state constitution regarding indigenous rights.[6] A number of communities have taken control of their municipalities as a result of the changes in the legal framework nationally and in Oaxaca. There are also successful examples of social and labor organizations, such as coffee marketing associations, timber processing and marketing associations, and a parent- and indigenous teacher-managed educational program in the Mixe region.

Indigenous Life in Urban Settings

The massive migration of indigenous peoples to cities, combined with the expansion of urban areas to encompass formerly rural settlements, has led to a changing pattern of indigenous settlement, without significantly reducing the number of individuals self-identified as indigenous. There are five types of scenarios in Mexican

---

6. Facilitating the dialogue on these laws has been an explicit agenda item of INI during this administration.

cities: (a) indigenous peoples in industrial cities, where the older immigrants were employed in the petroleum or manufacturing sectors and newer jobs are concentrated in the service industry; (b) traditionally *mestizo* magnet centers which now have majority indigenous populations, encompassing both rich and poor indigenous households; (c) metropolitan cities, where a multiplicity of ethnicities are found and there is vast under-reporting of the presence of indigenous peoples; (d) border cities, which are a stopping-off place for migration to the North or elsewhere in Mexico; and (e) urban centers created around tourism, where large numbers of poorly paid indigenous migrants provide services to the tourist industry and related sectors.

In all these cases, discrimination or self-perceived discrimination seems to be high, and speaking a native language other than Spanish closes opportunities. Access to housing, education, and employment tends to be limited, and more asset creation unstable. On the other hand, there are well-to-do indigenous city dwellers with self-identification to their culture and, sometimes, community of origin. Rural–urban linkages are strong and the flow of resources between them is extensive. However, there tend to be separate spaces for indigenous lifestyles and mainstream lifestyles, with the influx of indigenous peoples failing to create a multiethnic society, despite the Mexican pride for the country's multicultural past and popular revolution.

Educational and Health Indicators

The indicators for educational attainment are disproportionately low for indigenous children, particularly in rural areas. General statistics from the National Educational Advisory Council (CONAFE) show that in 1990–91, repetition rates for first grade were 32 percent. In addition, 38 percent of children completing primary school do not continue due to lack of available locations or the inability of schools to accommodate their work needs.[7] The fact that this has an indigenous dimension comes out clearly in state-level profiles. INI's figures nationally show that 28 percent of children in municipalities with more than 70 percent ILS do not attend school. School quality is also a problem. Thirty-six percent of bilingual schools are actually taught monolingually. Only 38 percent of schools in indigenous areas teach all six grades, and 31 percent of indigenous area schools have only one teacher for the first four grades. In Campeche, illiteracy for the state as a whole is 13.8 percent compared to 10 percent nationally, while in municipalities with 70 percent ILS, it is 36 percent. Teachers in primary schools in the Yacasay municipality noted that there was a 50 percent dropout rate and a 15 percent repetition rate, which was not uncommon for other municipalities studied in 1999.[8] Health indicators are also low. Indigenous municipalities have three times the incidence of death from intestinal infections, and the ten main causes of death are intestinal infections or respiratory illnesses. By comparison, the five main causes of death for the general population are all noninfectious.

---

7. Op cit., National Profile.
8. Mario Humberto Ruz, 1999, *Perfil Indigena del Estado de Campeche.*

II. Issues for Indigenous Development

Problems

Development that leads to positive change for indigenous communities and *ejidos* in the rural setting and for urban dwellers must address the key issues that question the wisdom of the current policy and legal framework. The essential challenge is how to channel government support to indigenous interests and organizational structures, rather than in parallel to them. Part of the problem is one of design, and part is a problem of conceptualization of the problem. Indigenous development is not simply a problem of generalized "poverty" or an inability to access information, resources, and opportunities to earn a reasonable livelihood. It is a problem of conflicting models and insufficient space for culturally consistent development to occur.

This conflict in development models and world views is part and parcel of the problem of systematic exclusion of indigenous peoples from the mainstream Mexican cultural, social, and political life. Poverty programs combine "safety nets"—temporary subsidy supports to ensure that poor populations can weather difficult economic cycles without fundamental loss of human capital or future potential—with longer-term programs for human capital formation (education and health care) aimed at providing tools for exiting poverty permanently. The missing element in this is the building of political space for indigenous peoples to pursue opportunities that permit their cultural survival and their economic improvement, and building a multiethnic society in which "success" can be measured in more diverse ways than at present.

The challenges can be divided into: (a) full adaptation of indigenous governance and organizational capacity to modern conditions; (b) poverty programs that do not fitindigenous peoples' interests and needs; (c) a lack of movement toward a multiethnic society and lack of institutional frameworks at the state and national levels; (d) the lost opportunity to tailor health and education to indigenous reality; and (e) reaching migrant agricultural workers and marginal urban dwellers.

Indigenous Governance and Organizational Capacity

One key issue is the development in support of indigenous governance structures and indigenous organizations. In rural settlements where land continues to underlie indigenous identity and where traditional systems of governance persist, there is a continuing demand for capacity building of local government and intercommunity organizations so that they can shape and implement the development plans of their members. The potential capacity of indigenous institutions overall—both community-level governance structures and intercommunity organizations and political movements—to play a strong development role is very high.

Current capacity for mobilizing change, however, is weak. This is due to factionalism created by political party organization, lack of organizational and modern administrative skills, poor information flow, loss of potential leaders, (that is, loss of educated youth to outmigration, and land boundary conflicts that absorb resources and human energy), and a lack of social capital formation that links the community to political power and resources. Historical isolation of communities is slow to break down, and in a few regions where communities were encouraged to cooperate, more often they isolated themselves from outside pressures and competed with neighboring communities for political space and resources. Capacity building is an important precondition for the positive absorption of development resources, and should be a main focus of government and non-governmental programs, as should be respecting the interests of the indigenous groups concerned, and recognizing the long-term process required for collaboration between communities to develop in an organic manner, when the historical relationship has been deliberate isolation.

Lack of "Fit" of Poverty Programs with Indigenous Interests and Needs

The conceptual framework that has been used to develop the package of "poverty" programs that is financed through a federal fiscal allocation channeled at the state and municipal levels, is based on a model of "social safety nets," where the lack of productive investment and human capital formation is seen as a transitional problem in the process of developing a more open and effective market economy. In addition, there is no concrete projection of the end goal of the transition. The final product tends to be seen not as a healthy adaptation of indigenous values and lifestyle to a modernizing society, where extended family and community relationships continue to shape decisionmaking, but as a shift to an individualistic, profit-maximizing strategy.

PROGRESA

PROGRESA, which targets the "poorest of the poor" with regular cash subsidies to women and children in return for increased use of education and health services, the DIF school breakfast program, and *Jornaleras Agrícolas,* are all geared to infuse targeted resources into the economy and increase access to and demand for services that improve human capital. Generally these programs have positive impacts, but the fundamental issues that limit their effectiveness potential with indigenous people are: (a) the "transitional" philosophy whereby cash transfers or improved access to existing categories of services will be only needed until the economy grows to provide other "exit strategies" from poverty; (b) the individualistic targeting of these subsidies, independently of the community structure, and ignoring the social disruption caused by PROGRESA failing to target all eligible community members; and (c) the creation of parallel committee or delivery structures for these programs and municipal development funds that compete with traditional organization while not building long-term capacity at the local level. [9]

---

9. CIESAS y PROGRESA. 1998. *Alivio a la Pobreza: Análisis de Programa de Educación, Salud, y Alimentación dentro de la Política Social,* Memoria del Seminario, Mexico.

A 1999 case study of 12 randomly selected communities receiving PROGRESA payments, for example, shows that the program has positively improved the use of schools and clinics, provided women beneficiaries a solidarity group, and increased disposable income in poor families for food and other necessities.[10] On the downside, these subsidies may not have resulted in a stimulus to improved services. The increased demand for these services by PROGRESA beneficiaries should be accompanied by an equivalent promotion of the effectiveness of health and educational services for the women and children trying to access them. In addition, the individualistic philosophy of targeting the subsidies may undermine or distort local governance structures (when beneficiaries are left out and when no local capacity for service delivery is created, or when communal labor-sharing systems break down because non-beneficiaries will no longer contribute free labor).

Rural Support

The effectiveness of a large rural program may also be worth exploring further, namely PROCAMPO and *Alianza para el Campo*. In the case of PROCAMPO, providing income support in the form of fixed cash payments to subsistence producers on the basis of the historical (not current) amount of land cultivated has had a positive poverty-alleviating impact. It permitted to switch from commodity price subsidies which did not reach farmers not producing for the market, with a much more equitable and non distortionary support scheme. However, if the program is designed as a transitional support to farmers (15 years), to facilitate adjustments after the agricultural reforms carried out at the beginning of the 1990s, there should be a more proactive poverty-alleviating and diversification strategy, helping farmers shift toward more productive cropping strategies and long-term alternatives.[11] Complementary programs like the *Alianza para el Campo* could be seen an important vehicle to provide the investment support and technical assistance required for increasing productivity or helping farmers to find off-farm sources of long-term employment. However, care should be taken to avoid a situation where individual payments would be used as working capital to maintain unprofitable subsistence production, without opening farm households to fundamental change. Where the fundamental vocation of indigenous communities is forestry, not agriculture, there is a need for incentives and subsidies to foster alternative livelihood models. Given the nature of such common natural resources, most enterprises would require collective action and investment and, therefore, support to organizational capacity building at the community and regional level.

Complementarity

There is not enough complementarity among the different programs operating in rural areas such as PROCAMPO, *Alianza para el Campo*, PROCEDE (the land cer-

---

10. Ibid.
11. World Bank, Mexico 1998 Ejido Reform: Avenues of Adjustment—Five Years Later, Green Cover.

tification program), and SEDESOL (*Crédito a la Palabra* or INI's programs). The requirement to provide the capital match for investments under *Alianza* may have created a limitation for poor indigenous communities. More attention is also needed in *Alianza* to technical inputs that reflect a full understanding of the dynamics of indigenous farming systems and the opportunities to blend traditional and alternative systems, while encouraging farm investments that fit the risk profile of indigenous household or communities. Better institutional coordination is required for more effective use of funds from SAGAR, SEDESOL, SEMARNAP, and municipalities, and to leverage the (sometimes considerable) flow of remittances or other capital sources. A welcome step is the way some well-organized communities or producer organizations have begun to mobilize PROCAMPO payments for more systematic investment.

Tenure

In terms of PROCEDE, there are still many outstanding land tenure issues that have not been addressed for indigenous communities and *ejidos*. A large number of politically active indigenous communities and *ejidos* have not entered into or completed the PROCEDE process, due to concerns that their collective interests are not going to be endorsed by the regularization. In addition, successful communities are engaged in active campaigns to buy back lands that have been sold off to outsiders and to rebuild their consolidated identity or expand the land pool to members. There are no market-assisted land reform programs to finance any purchases. Indigenous communities have extensive common lands that are not apt for agriculture, but land regularization programs have provided no support for assisting communities to guarantee the status of these lands to protect them from outside encroachment or illegal extraction (hunting, timber, seasonal agriculture) or to enable them to invest in the protection, recuperation, or productive use of these lands.

Multiethnic Society and an Institutional Framework

Developing a healthy society and economy in which 10 percent of the population have different aspirations and values, and many of whom live in poverty, requires a broader view of indigenous peoples issues. As has occurred in the switch from "women in development" models to "gender concerns," there is a need for a new paradigm in development policy. Simply focusing on the problems of indigenous peoples and their special needs and interests avoids analysis of the reasons of *why* solutions to poverty of indigenous regions and neighborhoods are so hard to identify and implement. What is required is an analysis of both the indigenous and nonindigenous sides of the equation, and initiatives involving both indigenous and nonindigenous actors in the solution.

Recent work (http://www.unam.mx/ciesas) on indigenous country profiles shows progress with respect to the formal recognition of cultural rights of indigenous people, as expressed in 1992 in Article 4 of the Mexican Constitution. However, important development gaps still exist in the majority of indigenous areas, despite the considerable resources directed by the government through various programs in the 1970s and 1980s. Discrimination (real or perceived) is still a factor that puts indigenous people at a disadvantage in managing and accessing programs and resources, as does the limited infrastructure and remoteness that prevails in these regions. Experience in other multiethnic countries has shown that discrimination is not an easily solved problem which disappears as the economic status of the discriminated group improves. A one-sided approach to ethnicity—special strategies for separate ethnicities—can be one element of a solution, but is not the full solution, unless initiatives are undertaken that open spaces in the mainstream society for multiculturalism. Societies with solidly distinct ethnic minorities which have promoted multiculturalism successfully (such as Canada) introduced multiculturalism into the overall educational system for both the indigenous and non-indigenous population. This provided information exchange and social debate on the basis of "ethnic" and "non-ethnic" identity and values, and allowed "non-indigenous" and "non-ethnic" actors to negotiate new societal relationships.

The possibility of a new paradigm of attention to indigenous peoples raises questions regarding the governmental institutional framework in which initiatives should take place. The National Indigenoust Institute (INI) was originally created as an advisory body to provide expert advice to policymakers and a window of political voice to indigenous peoples. However, INI was created with the assumption that the goal of its efforts would be the full integration and acculturation of indigenous peoples into the Mexican mainstream. While INI historically did create an important political space in past eras, it has become a minor player in overall policymaking and government development action in the face of new indigenous movements, national economic reforms, and the opening of the economy to regional and global markets and information. INI currently is neither meeting the growing demands of an indigenous population, nor having the desired impact on the mainstream policies and programs of federal ministries, state governments, and decentralized development.

Health and Education Services

The Mexican government has been experimenting with a variety of programs in bilingual and mobile education to target a differentiated indigenous population, including agricultural migrant laborers. The evidence so far is that these programs are not adequate to the needs and are much too centralized in philosophy, control of resources, and staffing, and are poor in quality of delivery. Overall educational curriculum is still geared to an ideal Mexican mainstream cultural type, and does not routinely include multicultural material that would make education a source of societal evolution for urban and rural residents of varied backgrounds and aspirations. Female children are disproportionately dropping out of school due to migration to and within urban areas and to work as agricultural labor, to labor and family demands, and to a lack of relevance of the curriculum to their future needs.

Health services are also not providing the range of needed services. There are health programs that support indigenous medical systems and use of medicinal plants, but there has been little systematic effort to find ways to integrate the Western and indigenous systems into effective health services delivery systems. While there are excellent traditional practitioners (and a directory of traditional practitioners by ethnic group), there is little integration of these practitioners into the formal medical network. There are estimated to be one traditional practitioner (healers, midwives, bonesetters, and herbalists) for every 500 to 1,500 inhabitants according to a 1984 study conducted by IMSS-Coplamar.[12] In many regions medical services are not tailored to indigenous customs and preferences, with the result that many women deliver their children at home to avoid the culturally inappropriate rules imposed in clinics and hospitals.

Migrant, Urban, and Indigenous Groups in Arid Lands

In addition to the problems that affect indigenous peoples generically, there are specific problems that affect those populations living outside of the reach of services and social and physical infrastructure. These groups have a greater problem with human justice since they lack secure rights over property and assets, and there are physical, psychological, and administrative barriers to their access to basic services. More programs are being developed to deal with the migrant worker populations in agriculturally rich regions. Very little has been initiated for the recent urban migrant populations who, increasingly, are entering the labor market with only low-paying employment opportunities and simply transferring rural poverty to the cities. For these people, many barriers exist to accessing decent housing, services, and educational facilities. While some of the migration is due to lack of attention to rural development, significant migration will continue regardless of strengthening of the rural economy. Some positive initiatives by the government could help these migrants establish themselves more effectively and increase their opportunities.

Dispersed, small ethnic groups that inhabit the arid lands of the central and northern states are another underserved population. Land tenure and legal rights are a major problem, as are the very different cultural values held by mainstream society and these groups. Where these groups share resources with *mestizos*, such as forests and fishing resources, they are historically both excluded and exploited.

III. Options for the Future

The overarching recommendation for furthering the development of indigenous peoples in Mexico is more technical and financial support for capacity building for indigenous organizations at all levels. More specifically, there are seven important

---

12. Op cit., National Profile.

areas where intervention can help create the conditions for indigenous self-development and an exit from poverty. These are and recommended actions are:

1. *Support capacity building of indigenous institutions and networks and indigenous professionals.*
   - Train local governments and local leaders in accounting, administrative, organizational, and negotiation skills.
   - Promote youth as indigenous professionals, linking these opportunities in the educational field to the sectoral programs.
   - Use specialized institutes to train professionals in culturally sensitive planning and rural development (a diploma course out of Oaxaca planned a standard curriculum).
   - Transfer computer-based knowledge management and information systems to local organizations for self-development planning and problem analysis (forestry communities and indigenous development organizations are acquiring and using GIS-based data sets and internet access to plan).
   - Support community-to-community horizontal learning.
2. *Vastly improve education and health services through more tailored siting, staffing, and design, and hand over more control of services to indigenous communities and neighborhoods.*
   - Schools should be managed more locally by parents and local governments and should have improved bilingual curriculum for bilingual empowerment.
   - Recruit bilingual teachers, preferably with community input, who are truly committed and who understand the local language; in-service training is needed.
   - Gradually introduce a new national general curriculum that would be an empowerment and multi-cultural model and introduce adult diversity awareness training and dialogue.
3. *Adapt decentralization and improved regional planning mechanisms to meet indigenous community and urban neighborhood needs.*
   - Coordinate programs and financing at state and regional levels as a new model and a positive step for Mexico. However, if indigenous peoples are to participate and benefit, there must be a specific advisory groups of indigenous peoples and decentralized planning through local governance structures, and municipal structures that ensure that indigenous community needs and interests are channeled upward.
   - Revise criteria and delivery mechanisms of the targeted poverty programs to work through community delivery mechanisms rather than through parallel structures, allowing communities to devise accountability structures that do not require new committees or institutions to function.
   - Allow more flexible matching of community initiatives, particularly in regions like Chiapas and Oaxaca where many community projects are designed, financed, and executed by the communities and ejidos themselves.

4. *Create programs to support more secure land and resource tenure and better land markets.*
   - Provide legal assistance to indigenous communities to resolve long-standing boundary conflicts and outstanding disputes.
   - Seek mechanisms to strengthen land markets so that indigenous communities can consolidate territories.
   - Recognize the importance of land and resource rights for community survival and development, and promote development options that are consistent with these rights.

5. *Create more culturally appropriate programs for temporary agricultural migrants, and more programs to increase opportunities for urban migrants to establish themselves successfully in the place where they permanently migrate to.*
   - Continue delivery of health and educational services to migrant agricultural workers that fit their patterns of movement.
   - Provide legal aid and legal information so that both urban and rural migrants, are aware of their rights and the services that they should be able to access.
   - Provide specialized services in urban areas that meet the cultural and linguistic preferences for effective service delivery, incorporating and training more indigenous professionals.

6. *Promote better natural resource management with indigenous peoples as key actors.*
   - Devolve natural resource management to communities as a main strategy for environmental and natural resource management.
   - Foster opportunities that are community based, such as coffee associations, forestry enterprises, organic agriculture, tourism enterprises, marketing of *artesanía*, and cultural-heritage-based employment generation.
   - Provide opportunities for more fundamental participation in protected areas (PA) models and community conservation and reserves.

7. *Address need for information and policy research.*
   - Provide better disaggregated statistics.
   - Analyze urban trends.
   - Collect and analyze successful models and strategies of well-off indigenous peoples.

24

The Economics of Gender in Mexico: Work, Family, State, and Market

This Chapter was written by Maria Correia and Elizabeth Katz (consultant).

I. Introduction

At the beginning of the 21st century, as Mexico undergoes significant demographic, social, and economic changes, the distinct roles of women and men in the Mexican economy are rapidly changing. In both urban and rural areas, large numbers of young Mexican women are entering the labor force, and as girls' education reaches parity with that of boys', this trend will likely intensify. However, women continue to face unique constraints on their economic activities—constraints that are largely related to their roles and responsibilities in the household.

This Chapter examines gender differences in the Mexican economy over the course of the life cycle. It focuses on the labor market, and includes a brief discussion of education and child labor, adult urban and rural labor force participation, and the situation of elderly Mexican men and women as a result of labor decisions made over their lifetime. The chapter is based on a series of technical papers on gender in Mexico which are currently being compiled into a book.[1] The papers—which examine the situations of both women and men as distinct groups and in relationship to one another—draw on national labor market statistics, specialized regional household surveys, and firm-level data.

The technical papers identify a strong relationship between work and family. Especially for women, the tradeoffs between marriage, children, and unpaid domestic labor on one hand, and formal education, paid labor force participation, and independent financial security on the other, are central features of their survival strategies. Even as children, girls' domestic responsibilities—whether paid or unpaid—detract from their educational attainment and future earnings potential.

---

1. Katz and Correia (forthcoming).

Girls who "specialize" in housework, forsaking human capital acquisition either in the form of schooling or skilled labor market experience, are more likely to become dependent on the marriage market for economic resources. Wives in both urban and rural areas have much weaker labor force attachment than single women—even when the latter are responsible for the care of young children. As women age, those who have dedicated their lives to their families become even more dependent on them for income and shelter, while those who take a more labor-market-oriented path may be better able to provide for themselves. While it is unclear at what point in their lives many Mexican women are segregated into being either "workers" or "wives," men do not appear to face this same dichotomy—in exchange for providing the principal source of economic support for their families, they are allowed to be both workers *and* husbands.[2]

A second strong theme is that institutions matter for gender outcomes. Whether these institutions are based in the market or the state, it is clear that demographic and household-level phenomena alone do not determine how women and men fare in terms of human capital formation, labor market participation, and old age security. With regard to education, girls in rural areas are more likely to go to high school where the supply of such schools is greater, implying that parents are responsive to government efforts to improve accessibility. In the case of child labor, official statistics which render girls' work relatively invisible may bias the response of governmental and non-governmental institutions away from addressing the detrimental effects of home-based domestic work for children. At a macroeconomic level, gender-differentiated responses to growth, recession, industrialization, and trade are visible, such as the entry of urban wives into the labor market during times of economic downturn, and the effect of changing industrial structure on the gender composition of the *maquiladora* workforce. There is also some evidence—always difficult to pin down empirically, and always controversial—that employers in both the rural labor market and in the *maquiladora* sector do not treat men and women equally with respect to employment opportunities. Also affecting the rural sector is the male bias inherent in the PROCAMPO income support program and the PROCEDE land titling initiative, which are targeted toward male heads of household. As a final example of the role of institutions, an important source of income and healthcare for elderly women is the benefits obtained in their status as widows or dependents, which suggests that many Mexican social security institutions are oriented toward providing for family members, regardless of their labor force histories.

---

2. It is important to note that expectations associated with being 'male' or 'female' limit *both* men's and women's opportunities, their choices and ultimately their well-being. Male gender issues are those associated with unmet societal expectations of being the breadearner, which can lead to alcoholism, depression and risky behavior. There are also important issues of male exclusion in reproductive health and childcare which are only now beginning to be addressed in countries such as Mexico. A discussion of these issues, however, goes beyond the scope of this chapter.

The Chapter is organized around the theme of the life cycle. It is prefaced with a short section on general gender indicators for Mexico, and then begins with the experience of Mexican girls and boys in the educational system and child labor market, continuing with an analysis of the adult labor market (which is divided between urban and rural, with separate discussions on the *maquiladora* and microenterprise sectors and the effect of household factors on labor supply), and followed by a discussion on gender differences among the elderly. It ends with conclusions and policy recommendations.

Gender Demographic and Economic Indicators for Mexico[3]

In Mexico, women outlive men by an average of six years, and both women and men enter their first marriage in their early 20s. Mexico's total fertility rate of just under three children per woman is about average for the Latin America region, and approximately 65 percent of childbearing-age married women (and/or their husbands) are estimated to be using some form of contraception. Female labor force participation is estimated to be about half that of male participation—37 percent of Mexican women are either employed or looking for work, compared to 79 percent of men. In terms of sectoral distribution, men are more heavily concentrated in agriculture and industry, while almost 70 percent of the female workforce are employed in the service sector. Finally, the Duncan Index of segregation, which measures the percentage of workers that would have to change jobs in order to achieve perfectly balanced gender representation across sectors or occupations, stands at approximately 40 percent.[4]

Gender Differences in Educational Attainment and Achievement

Over the last four decades important progress has been made in improving educational attainment in Mexico. The average number of years of schooling attained has doubled, and gender differences in education have been substantially reduced. Given its level of GDP, however, Mexico still lags behind other Latin American countries in terms of education. Furthermore, large differences in educational attainment between rural and urban areas remain—differences which are clearly related to economic status.

Based on their empirical analysis of the 1995 National Survey of the Population and Housing Count, Parker and Pederzini (forthcoming), find that the gender gap in education has fallen substantially over the last 30 years; overall, girls and boys below age 20 do not display significant differences in educational attainment, as

---

3. Sources: GENDERSTATS; *World Development Indicators 2000*; INEGI; CONAPO.
4. The Duncan Index of segregation is the percentage of female or male workers who would have to change jobs in order for the occupational or sectoral distribution of the two groups to be the same—in other words, for men and women to be equally represented across occupations or sectors.

measured by years of schooling completed. Nevertheless, the existing educational difficulties of children appear to differ substantially by gender. By age 12 girls begin to attend school less than boys (presumably due to higher dropout). This is consistent with fewer girls going on to secondary school after finishing primary school. In spite of these trends, a gender gap in years of completed schooling by age does not show up between boys and girls until after age 20. The reason for this is that while boys attend school more after age 20, they are more likely to repeat grades and fall behind in school. Men are still more likely to enroll in college than women. According to their analysis, gender differences in the determinants of school attendance and attainment among 12 to 15 year olds are as follow:

- *Parents' Level of Education.* In both urban and rural areas, parental education levels are a key determinant of educational attendance and attainment. For girls' attendance the mothers' education has a larger positive impact. The education level of the father, in contrast, has a larger impact on boys' school attendance than that of the mother. Moreover, the size of the impact is much greater in rural than in urban areas, indicating that parental education levels make a greater difference to children's education in rural areas. In the case of school attainment, the impact of the mother's education level is greater than the impact of father's education level for both girls and boys. Both in urban and rural areas, the gender gap is generally larger with lower educational levels of parents, particularly that of the mother, indicating that family background is not just an important determinant of overall schooling levels, but of reducing the education gender gap.
- *Family Income Level.* In both urban and rural areas, family income has an important positive impact on children's schooling but the size of the impact is larger for boys than for girls (by about 30 percent in urban areas). A larger impact of family income on boys' education is consistent with an interpretation that boys' education is more responsive than girls'. In other words, increases in family income are more likely to be spent on boys' education, whereas decreases in family income are more likely to hurt boys' education than girls. The magnitude of the impact is much larger in rural than in urban areas.
- *Absence of the Father.* In urban areas the father's absence from the household has an important negative impact on the probability of both male and female children attending school. The magnitude of the impact is similar for boys and girls. Nevertheless, this negative impact is much larger in rural areas than in urban areas, and in rural areas, the father's absence from the household has a negative effect twice as large for boys as for girls. In the case of school achievement, absent fathers tend to increase the schooling gap in urban areas but only for boys; in rural areas the schooling gap increases for both girls and boys, with a greater impact on boys than on girls.
- *Presence of Disabled Individuals.* The presence of disabled individuals is negatively and significantly related to the probability of school attendance but only

in the case of boys. This suggests that boys substitute for family disabled workers in the labor force, thereby reducing the probability that they attend school. As with the results for school attendance, the presence of disabled individuals affects the probability of only boys falling behind in school.

- *Presence of Small Children in the Family.* Small children in the family, on the other hand have a larger negative effect on school attendance for girls than for boys, although it is significant for both. This may reflect the possibility that older daughters have additional domestic and childcare responsibilities that are incompatible with school attendance. For older brothers, younger brothers and sisters may increase the probability of entering the labor force. In the case of siblings one's age or older, the evidence indicates that this negatively affects the attendance of girls only. Small children in the household are likely to increase the extent to which children fall behind in school, and once again, the effects are greater on girls. In both samples, older siblings have a positive and strong impact on the probability of falling behind in school, providing support for the "dilution" of the family resources argument.

- *Supply of Secondary Schools.* The supply of secondary schools is positively and significantly related to the probability of school attendance for both boys and girls only in rural areas, with a larger impact for girls.

The Gender Differentiated Impact of Child Labor and School Dropout on Returns to Human Capital

Child and youth labor force participation has both long- and short-term consequences for individual, family, and social welfare, potentially hindering school performance and harming the health and psychological well-being of children. Based on retrospective survey data for Mexico, Knaul (forthcoming) examines the long-term impacts of child labor and school dropout, in terms of labor market returns later in life. Her findings are as follows:

- A penalty exists for dropping out of school and working early in life. While positive returns to early labor market experience do exist, these depend on continued progression through the school system. The earlier children drop out of school and enter the labor force the greater the penalty they pay in terms of adult earning capacity. Those who only work and never attend school accumulate the least education and marketable experience and have less earning capacity.

- At every level of schooling and early employment, girls pay a greater penalty than boys for not continuing in school or for working while in school. One possible explanation is the "nature" of the work boys and girls do. The types of early employment that boys engage in (industrial, services, etc.) may be more complementary to the occupations they choose later in life. Thus, early work experience counts as real experience. Girls, however, tend to be concentrated in activities in which there is little accumulated experience and low complementarity with education (domestic work). Thus, the returns to their "experience" are low because the "experience" they gain early on has lower value in the labor market.

Gender Issues in Workforce Participation and Self-Employment

As previously noted female labor force participation is estimated to be about half that of male participation, with the participation of both having risen over the past 25 years—from 33.1 percent in 1973 to 36.9 percent in 1998 for women, and from 74.6 percent to 78.7 percent for men. This disparity exists even thought human capital levels of the employed are about equal for men and women. Occupational segregation has decreased and the female–male gender earnings ratio fell from 0.792 to .780 from 1987 and 1993 (Brown, Pagán, and Rodríguez 1999, cited in Pagán and Sánchez, forthcoming a). Furthermore, self-employment rates are about the same for men and women.

Using the 1994 Survey of Rural Entrepreneurs and Financial Services, Pagán and Sánchez (forthcoming a.) analyze the role of gender-specific factors with a view to explaining male–female differences in employment and the incidence of self-employment in both urban and rural Mexico. Their findings were as follows:

- Education, age, and household headship are all positively related to employment. However, the presence of very small children in the household reduces the workforce participation of *single females* but not *single males*. For *married men,* only age, indigenous background, and household headship are positively related to employment. For *married women*, education, age, household headship, household size (a measures of wealth) and residence in Puebla are all positively related to workforce participation. However, the number of working individuals in the household, and dwelling ownership, are negatively related to the likelihood of employment. Moreover, the availability of employment opportunities in the service-related tertiary sector seems to significantly increase employment opportunities for married women.
- The size of the labor market—as reflected by the number of inhabitants in the locality of residence—increases female labor force participation either because of greater job opportunities or because women perceive more opportunities in larger communities and, thus, seek and find employment in these localities. In contrast, men in larger localities are less likely to be working than in smaller localities.
- For married women, secondary and postsecondary education increases the chances that they are in the salaried sector, perhaps because more experienced, more educated Mexican women are less discriminated against.
- Only about 35.66 percent of single women are employed compared to 79.18 percent of single men. If the bivariate probit model estimates for single males

are used to predict the employment rate of single females, the employment rate of women would increase to 75.76 percent. Most of the employment differential—99.03 percent—is explained by gender differences in individual responses to employment and only 0.97 percent is explained by male–female differences in personal characteristics.

- The gender gap between married men and women is much larger; 93.36 percent of married men are employed but only 20.66 percent of married women are employed. The predicted employment rate for married women is 88.60 percent, which suggests that when compared to their male counterparts married women face more barriers to employment than single women. This finding is partly a result of specialization of labor and tasks within the household. However, it is also consistent with the idea that the accumulation of skills differ by gender from an early age within the life cycle, and the male–female differences in acquired experience obtained at a young age.

- Self-employment rates are 19.41 percent for single males and 25.80 percent for females; yet, if the bivariate probit estimates were used to predict the incidence of female self-employment, this would decrease to 15.44 percent. Thus women are probably concentrated in self-employment due to barriers to entry into salaried jobs and to household structure. Married women have a lower incidence of self-employment than married men (38.07 versus 33.58 percent). Nonetheless, the predicted self-employment rate of married women is 15.82 percent, which implies that married women are relatively over-represented in this sector. Self-employment might be a relatively more attractive choice for women because it offers easy entry into the labor force and a flexible work schedule, and allows women to mix domestic and reproductive work. Women could also be disproportionately represented in self-employment because of lower barriers or because of labor market discrimination in the wage and salary sector.

Household Effects on Labor Force Participation

The sex of an individual is considered to be a primary explanatory variable of differential labor supply patterns between men and women. Moreover men and women are assumed to behave in a homogeneous manner. Cunningham (forthcoming) uses the Mexican urban employment survey (ENEU) to identify: (a) whether sex or household gender role is the primary determinant of labor force participation patterns in response to a change in the household's income needs; and (b) how adult men and women with distinct roles in the household use the labor market as a safety net during periods of economic uncertainty. A summary of her findings is as follows:

- Labor patterns appear to be more similar for those with the same household role that for those who are of the same sex. Gender does affect labor market entry decisions but indirectly through constraints imposed by household members, rather than directly, since women who do not have spouses or children to care for behave more similarly to men than they do to married women. In fact, women without a spouse or children are more likely than any other group to be in the higher-paying, inflexible formal sector jobs, bringing into question whether employers discriminate based on sex or based on household role.

- Married women have labor force entry and exit patterns that are distinct from other groups of women. They are very responsive to homecare needs and the presence (or absence) of labor income from other household members. While unmarried women are the primary breadwinners, married women are often the social safety net to catch the household when the primary breadwinner cannot fully satisfy the household's needs.

- Household composition matters. It is the household situation that requires married women not work when they do have a partner but, to join the labor force when they become the primary breadwinner. Furthermore, the presence of children seems to diminish the labor supply of wives, but not single mothers, so we cannot conclude that children alone lead to lower labor supply. Instead, the sole breadwinning responsibility of the single mother is likely to lead to other childcare arrangements that are a substitute for a "stay-at-home mom."

- Wives in particular use the informal entrepreneurship sector as insurance or as a response to real decreases in household income. That is, for women entry to informal entrepreneurship is countercyclical, in contrast to Maloney (1997), who finds that for men, it is procyclical. For both men and women, contract work is a form of insurance when the economy slows down.

- Household composition affects sector of choice. Flexible informal sector jobs do seem to be more feasible for women with young children, perhaps because the nature of the work, hours, and location allow mothers to care for their children while also participating in the labor force. More rigid formal sector jobs do not allow this.

The Maquiladora Sector

Changes in the types of industries comprising the *maquiladora* sector and the increasing attractiveness of the sector for men have lead to a recomposition of the *maquila* labor force. Even though more women than men continue to work in the sector, from 1975 to 1998, women's share of employment fell from 78 percent to 57 percent between 1975 and 1998. And not only do women make up an increasingly smaller percentage of the *maquiladora* workforce, but they are also disproportionately concentrated in those industries with the lowest wages and benefits (such as textiles and apparel). Even within particular *maquiladora* industries, women consistently earn less than men, on average. Fleck (forthcoming) analyzes different data sources with the objective of identifying the major shifts within the *maquila* industry over time and better understand these trends. Her findings are as follows:

- Although the employment share of women is falling—a growing demand persists for both men and women workers. This demand flattens as the value of the peso rises, but historically has spiked after devaluations. Real hourly earnings have fallen over time, but not as quickly as the real minimum wage, and *maquila* manufacturing has become relatively more attractive than other manufacturing work over the 18 years analyzed. The wage convergence between national manufacturing and *maquila* manufacturing provides a partial explanation for men's increased participation in *maquila* work. The expansion of male employment has primarily been in tool assembly and transportation equipment, the latter being a small, technical, and male-concentrated industry and the latter being a large and growing sector run by multinational firms.
- Women's recent increased participation in *maquila* work is due in part to married women being employed in this sector. Labor force growth of men was lower than that of women, but their growth in *maquila* employment was nearly double that of women. Labor demand among *maquiladora* plants has drawn more men into *maquila* employment because the growing participation rate of women still has not kept up with job growth in Mexico.
- An interindustry wage gap exists among *maquila* industries; greater shares of women's and nonborder employment and capital intensity are negatively correlated with real hourly wages, while plant size is positively correlated with wages. Hourly earnings are lowest in food and apparel, both majority female industries. The best paid workers are in the predominantly male machines and tool assembly industries, and in the transportation equipment industry, which has both the largest plant size of all industries and the majority of its production along the border. A wage gap between men and women line workers is evident for all industries, although insufficient detail is available to determine the basis for this inequality.

Gender Differentials in Microenterprise Earnings

Female-owned small businesses in rural and urban areas represent 26 to 44 percent of all of firms in Mexico; nonetheless, women earn 36 to 50 percent of what their male counterparts earn. Using the 1994 Survey of Rural Entrepreneurs and Financial Services and the 1992 National Survey of Urban Microenterprises, Pagán and Sánchez (forthcoming b.) examine male-female differences in earnings in rural and urban microenterprises, focusing on the size of operations, returns to productive factors, and economic sectors of enterprises. Their finding suggest the following:

- Differences in productive factors (years in operation, number of hours worked,[5] number of workers, capital endowments, place of operation, registration and

---

5. Available for urban areas only.

voluntary entry into the sector) and personal characteristics (marital status, years of education, ethnicity[6] and potential labor market experience[7]) are more important in explaining the gender earnings gap in rural than in urban areas. Among urban microenterprises, about 35 percent of the earnings gap is explained by differences in personal characteristics, whereas in the rural areas studied, this component explains almost 42 percent of the overall gap.

- Male-female differences in returns to factors (explanatory variables) explain 62 percent of the earnings gap in urban areas and 59 percent in rural areas. Among urban microenterprises, this component fluctuates from a low of 60 percent to a high of 68 percent. In rural areas examined, the service sector has the largest size of this component—about 68 percent. The magnitude of this component illustrates that unobservable factors—such as discrimination, competition, entrepreneurial ability, credit supply constraints, differential attitudes toward risk, and women's reproductive and domestic responsibilities—are responsible for a large share of the gender earnings gap.

- In all, the empirical results indicate that gender earnings differentials in the microenterprise sector are largely due to the fact that men's microenterprises are bigger than women's in each economic sector, and have differential constraints to profitability. Gender differences in sectoral distribution account for a small share of the gender gap in both rural and urban areas.

Gender, Generation, and Off-Farm Employment on the Mexican Ejido

Since the 1930s, most rural Mexicans have had access to their most important productive resource—land—mediated by membership in the *ejido*. Traditionally, *ejidatarios* have combined the cultivation of basic grain crops with small-scale commercial agriculture and seasonal migration to generate their income. Beginning in 1992, with the reform of Article 27 of the Mexican Constitution and the launching of the national *Ejido* Titling Program (PROCEDE), the *ejido* sector has been undergoing a process of privatization, in which parcels that were previously held in individual usufruct, and some common property resources, are being converted into privately held land. Simultaneously, the agricultural sector as a whole has been significantly affected by the lifting of price and credit subsidies, and by the passage of the North American Free Trade Agreement (NAFTA), which has threatened small-scale basic grains producers by allowing for the importation of cheap grains from the United States and Canada. Taken together, these changes have prompted *ejidatarios* to make necessary adjustments in their livelihood strategies, including the expansion of off-farm employment.

Using the *Encuesta a Ejidatarios y Comuneros 1997*, Katz (forthcoming) examines the intersection of the transformation of the *ejido* sector and shifts in the gender composition of the Mexican workforce to understand the determinants of off-farm

---

6. For rural areas only.
7. Defined as age minus years of education plus six.

employment for *ejido* residents and the degree to which these determinants differ by gender and generation. Her main finding is that intrahousehold labor allocation—and in particular, the deployment of household members to off-farm employment—is differentially responsive to individual and household characteristics, depending on members' gender and generation. Perhaps most important, her analysis reveals the ways in which gender-specific sources of farm-based income—which are themselves part of the adjustment patterns of households—have distinct impacts on the off-farm labor supply behavior of different household members. Her specific results are as follows:

- Opportunities to earn wage income, and the availability of jobs in sectors other than agriculture, are quite unevenly distributed among the major rural regions of Mexico. This has implications for the gender composition of employment insofar as labor market competition and sectoral allocation (which may comprise both discrimination by employers and sectoral preferences by potential workers) differentially affect the ability of men and women to obtain off-farm jobs. Estimated coefficients on the education variable suggest that women are more likely to obtain skilled or semiskilled jobs, while men are filling unskilled positions.
- While women's overall labor force participation rates remain low in *ejido* communities, the younger generation is beginning to catch up with their male counterparts—actually significantly exceeding their duration of off-farm employment in a given year. However, since the majority of these women are still single, it is unclear whether they will continue to work once they marry and form households of their own—in other words, whether the high off-farm employment rates of daughters represent a truly generational or a short-term life cycle phenomenon.
- A relationship exists between farm-based assets and income and the decision to participate in the wage labor market. All household members are less likely to work off-farm—and to work for shorter time periods—if they have relatively large livestock holdings. However, this inverse relationship is especially strong for male household heads, which is also the only group whose off-farm employment patterns are altered by the receipt of PROCAMPO payments. Together, these findings suggest the existence of some degree of private appropriation of farm-based income and assets among the *ejido* population, which in turn influences the labor supply decisions of daughters.

The Welfare of Male and Female Elderly

The age structure of the Mexican population has undergone important transformations in the last two decades as a result of demographic and epidemiological changes. The elderly population (aged 65 and older) is proportionately larger than it has ever been (4.3 million people, 4.5 percent of the population in 1997) and will continue to grow as fertility rates decrease.

According to Parker and Wong (forthcoming), no evidence exists to support the hypothesis that women have lower living standards and higher poverty rates in Mexico; elderly women exhibit living standards similar to elderly men, and this is true for both urban and rural areas. Compared to other age groups, the elderly show consumption levels similar to children, but lower than working-age adults. Both elderly men and women exhibit heterogeneity as a group; the oldest old (those above age 70) appear to be the poorest group overall.

In Mexico, having access to modern healthcare is largely associated with benefits received through formal employment. Women have had low labor market participation throughout their lives, in particular those who are currently aged 60 and older, and given the tendency of women to outlive their husbands and spend the last years of their lives in widowhood, it seems that women would be particularly at risk of living without the benefits of modern healthcare.

The findings on healthcare coverage indicate, however, that women seem to be as protected as men at all ages. The age group with the least protection is the youngest, and the most protected is the elderly. These results could be largely due to two factors: (a) the social security and health systems that extend protection to the dependents of workers and widows of former beneficiaries of the systems; and (b), the informal familial support toward the elderly. These two factors are consistent with a scheme in which women receive protection in old age as remuneration for the social contributions they have made toward the survival and productivity of the domestic units over their lifetimes. All members have benefited from these contributions, and it seems that the unwritten social contract to care for Mexican women and men is being upheld. This paradox of healthcare among women is largely due to the pro-family orientation of the institutions in Mexico that provide employer-driven healthcare benefits to employees, and have historically extended the benefits to the dependents of the employee. Women are largely covered through their status as spouses or as mothers of adult children. Thus the Mexican healthcare system, which tends to protect workers and their families, seems to be protecting women and men.

Regarding pension at old age, only a small minority of men aged 60 and older, and even fewer women, receive any kind of pension. Of these, the majority of the men's pensions are due to retirement, while only one third of the women's pensions are of the retirement type, and two-thirds receive widowhood pensions. When women's pension coverage through their current spouse is considered, men and women are about equally covered by a pension. Thus it seems again that, to the very limited extent that the system of pensions is covering women, this is largely because of their status as spouses or widows.

Although there is no evidence that elderly females are worse off than elderly males regarding living standards, women in old age are more dependent than men on the informal income support of others—thus making women more vulnerable albeit not less poor. Women's dependency is due to a variety of reasons, including the fact that elderly women tend to have worked less in formal labor markets, and therefore are less likely to have contributed to a pension system. Families with female elderly tend to receive more income transfers from individuals outside the household, which in some sense helps compensate for the lower income that elderly females contribute to the household. These transfers may be unstable sources of income and therefore may increase the likelihood of suffering income fluctuations. This may in turn pose high risks of living in poverty for elderly women in the future. Moreover, since most women outlive their spouses, they are more likely to live in extended family arrangements in old age, which again makes them dependent on adult children provide them with food and shelter. When they do receive a pension or healthcare coverage, it is almost always as a dependent.

Taken in sum, the combined results on living standards, healthcare coverage, and pension coverage seem to indicate that marriage may have been an effective long-term strategy toward old-age security for Mexican women in the current elderly cohorts. In exchange for the care and services provided by women to the members of their domestic units throughout their life, our results seem to indicate that women seem to be receiving protection equal to their male counterparts in old age.

II. Conclusions

Three major themes emerge from the technical papers cited:

- *Gender and Life Cycle.* The role of gender in influencing economic activities and outcomes varies across the life cycle. Beginning with school-age children, girls (almost 15 percent of whom report domestic labor as their primary activity) are forced to leave school or combine domestic work with their education, while boys (over 50 percent of whom have entered the labor force by age 15) exhibit higher repetition rates due to their income-generating responsibilities. These patterns are especially strong among poor households and in rural areas. As adults, women are subject to a higher earnings penalty for having combined work and study as children, which may be due to the nature of the occupational concentration of girls and women in domestic services, the skills of which are not valued in other sectors of the economy.

- Despite their often low earnings, young, single women in sectors as different as the rural *ejidos* and border *maquiladora* factories are entering the workforce in record numbers. Married women generally exhibit low labor force participation rates and formal sector work experience; evidence suggests that gender-specific responsibilities for housework and childcare constrain their economic activity. Married men, meanwhile, are more likely to work when they have young children, and to use older children and other household members as sources of unpaid labor for income-generating activities. Finally, gender differences among elderly Mexicans are largely manifest in the greater reliance of women on family support in old age.

- *Marriage Market and Labor Market.* Key to gender analysis of the Mexican economy is understanding the complex interaction between household formation, age-and gender-specific household roles, and labor force participation. By taking a life cycle perspective, the chapter suggests that women, more so than men, are "tracked" at different stages toward specialization in either domestic or market labor. For example, girls who drop out of school in order to help cook, clean, and look after their younger siblings are often ill-prepared as adults for anything but domestic work. Girls who manage to stay in school have a better chance of entering the paid labor market, which must then be balanced against marriage and childbearing, as long as Mexican women continue to have major responsibility for household work. The choice between building up labor market "assets" and family "assets" is keenly felt by elderly Mexicans—most of whom are women—who rely either on formal employment-linked pensions and medical care, or on their children for support in old age.

- *Region, Generation, and Gender.* Significant differences in gender roles and gender disparities exist across urban and rural Mexico, and across the younger and older generations of Mexican women and men. For example, gender disparities in secondary school attendance are significantly larger, and the domestic labor responsibilities of girls are significantly greater, in rural compared to urban areas. Likewise, while national data indicate higher earnings profiles for women than for men, decomposition analysis of a rural sample suggests that women's labor force participation would increase from 28.5 percent to 85.1 percent if they faced same returns to endowments as men, and gender differences in productive characteristics are more important in explaining microenterprise-based gender earnings differentials in rural than in urban settings. Generational differences, meanwhile, are especially apparent in the rural *ejido* sector, where young men and women are more highly educated than their parents and therefore more able to pursue diversified income-generation strategies, including significant participation in off-farm employment and migration.

III. Policy Recommendations

This Chapter makes three broad gender policy recommendations: **first,** interventions targeted at children and young adults—when critical human capital investment decisions are being made—are likely to have positive lifelong consequences for enhancing gender equity. While Mexico has made great strides in achieving gender parity in primary education, too many girls—especially girls from poor, rural families—are dropping out of school to perform paid or unpaid domestic labor. Public support for school- and community-based childcare, together with family income support programs tied to school attendance, such as PROGRESA, have the potential to provide young women with a broader range of labor market options than currently. In the case of boys, who are more likely to drop out or fall behind in school due to early (nondomestic) labor force entry, programs to improve the income-generating capacity of other adult household members could help alleviate the pressure on school-age boys to work.

Second, gender policy must recognize the interaction between the marriage and labor markets that fundamentally shapes the economic activities of Mexican women and men. While it is the case in all countries that married women have lower formal labor market participation rates than their single counterparts, the combination of Mexican family gender roles that assign girls and women primary responsibility for unpaid domestic labor, and structural features of the Mexican labor market that make it difficult for married women to find and keep jobs, creates additional barriers for women who may want to be active in both family life and the paid labor market. There is broad scope for public policy to address these barriers, including: (a) socialization of the most time-consuming domestic tasks (such as childcare); (b) communications campaigns to encourage greater male participation in home-based work; (c) labor market regulation to prevent employer discrimination against married women; and (d) incentives to private employers to offer "family-friendly" work environments (such as flexible work schedules and workplace-based childcare).

Third, public sector institutions should play a leading role in recognizing the gender-specific needs of the beneficiaries of government programs. For example,

- public schools and universities could develop innovative programs to keep girls and young women in school and prevent boys from falling behind and dropping out of school;
- the education system could systematically remove gender stereotypes from textbooks and educational materials and train teachers on the negative effects of gender stereotypes and gender socialization processes;
- child welfare agencies could target the "invisible" home-based domestic work of girls, publicly-financed job training and employment generation schemes could tailor their programs to enhance the skills of working women and accommodate the needs of working wives and mothers (e.g. job-matching services, short-term income-generating opportunities, etc.);
- public credit programs such as *Empresas de Solidaridad* could tailor their services to meet the needs of and counter the constraints faced by both female and male entrepreneurs;
- rural income support programs like PROCAMPO could broaden their definition of beneficiaries to include family members of male ejidatarios;
- joint titling in the name of both husband and wife in the case of PROCEDE would help alleviate problems associated with a lack of property rights for women, including dispossesion and capital market access;
- agencies such as the Desarrollo Integral de la Familia (DIF) could re-orient their programs to include men in family and children's development initiatives; and

- social security and healthcare coverage for the elderly should continue the policy of caring for dependent elderly women.

References

Katz, Elizabeth. Forthcoming. *Gender, Generation, and Off-Farm Employment.* In Gender and the Mexican Economy (Katz, E. and M. Correia, editors, forthcoming). Washington D.C.: World Bank.

Knaul, Felicia Marie. Forthcoming. *Gender Differentials in the Impact of Child Labor and School Dropout on Returns to Human Capital in Mexico.* In Gender and the Mexican Economy (Katz, E. and M. Correia, editors, forthcoming). Washington D.C.: World Bank.

Cunningham, Wendy. Forthcoming. *Breadwinner Versus Caregiver: Labor Force Participation and Sectoral Choice over the Mexican Business Cycle.* In Gender and the Mexican Economy (Katz, E. and M. Correia, editors, forthcoming). Washington D.C.: World Bank.

Fleck, Susan. Forthcoming. *A Gender Perspective on Maquila Employment and Wages in Mexico.* In Gender and the Mexican Economy (Katz, Elizabeth and Maria Correia, editors, forthcoming). Washington D.C.: World Bank.

Maloney, William. 1997. *The Structure of Labor Markets in Developing Countries: Time Series Evidence on Competing Views.* Policy Research Working Paper No. 1940. Washington, D.C.: World Bank.

Pagán, José A. and Susana M. Sánchez. Forthcoming (a). *Gender Issues in Workforce Participation and Self-Emploment in Rural and Urban Mexico.* In Gender and the Mexican Economy (Katz, Elizabeth and Maria Correia, editors, forthcoming). Washington D.C.: World Bank.

Pagán, José A. and Susana M. Sánchez. Forthcoming (b). *Explaining Gender Differences in Earnings in the Microenterprise Sector.* In Gender and the Mexican Economy (Katz, Elizabeth and Maria Correia, editors, forthcoming). Washington D.C.: World Bank.

Parker, Susan Wendy and Carla Pederzini. Forthcoming. *Gender Differences in Mexico.* In Gender and the Mexican Economy (Katz, Elizabeth and Maria Correia, editors, forthcoming). Washington D.C.: World Bank.

Parker, Susan Wendy, and Rebeca Wong. Forthcoming. *Welfare of Male and Female Elderly in Mexico: A Comparison.* In Gender and the Mexican Economy (Katz, Elizabeth and Maria Correia, editors, forthcoming). Washington D.C.: World Bank.

25

Government Programs and Poverty

This Chapter was written by Quentin Wodon
with the valuable input of Gladys Lopez-Acevedo.

I. Introduction and Overview: Ten Strategic Questions

The strategy of the Zedillo Administration for the reduction of poverty relied on both broad-based social expenditures and targeted poverty programs (Figures 1 and 2). Broad-based social expenditures are devoted to the areas of social security and health-care, education, job training, and housing. Targeted poverty programs focus on investing in the human capital of the poor, promoting income and employment opportunities for the poor, and improving the physical infrastructure of poor areas. Public funding for targeted programs has increased much faster over the last dozen years than the programmable budget (Figure 3). Within targeted spending (MXP$53 billion in 2000), half of the funds are devoted to human capital, a third to physical infrastructure, and the rest to income opportunities (Figure 4). This Chapter is based on the poverty assessment for Mexico completed by the World Bank.[1] It evaluates the impact of government programs and policies on poverty. After summarizing the key findings through 10 strategic questions, the Chapter reviews broad-based social expenditure and government programs targeted to the poor.

II. Key Findings

1. Do The Poor Benefit From Broad-Based Expenditures In Health, Education, Training, And Housing? The poor do benefit from these broad-based public expen-

---

1. Especially the Executive Summary and Chapters 2 to 5 in "Government Programs and Poverty in Mexico," Report No. 19214-ME, World Bank, Washington, D.C., 1999, 2 volumes. The report contains a detailed bibliography which is not reproduced here.

Figure 1. Broad-based and Targeted Policies

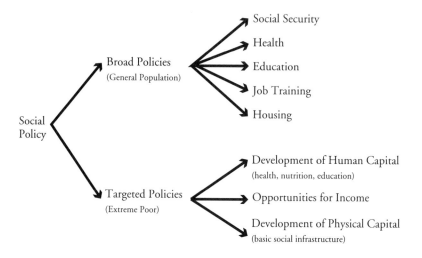

Source: Budget of the government of Mexico (federal level).

Figure 2. Targeted Policies by Group

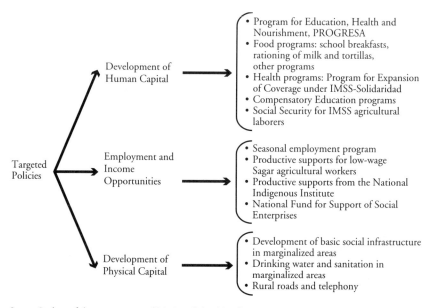

Source: Budget of the government of Mexico (federal level).

Figure 3. Resources Channeled by Poverty Alleviation Programs

(millions of pesos of 2000)

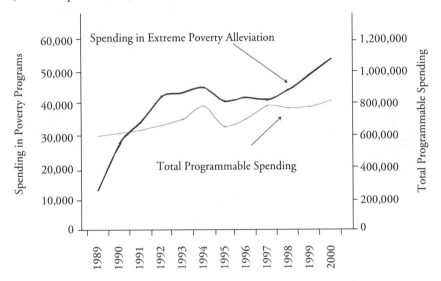

Figure 4. Government Spending for Poverty Alleviation

(2000 pesos in billions)

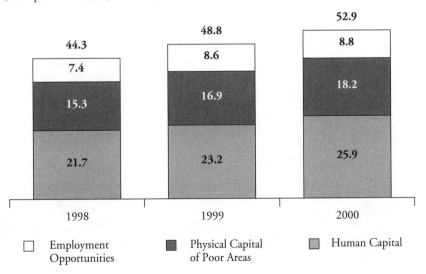

Source: Government of Mexico (1999).

ditures, but not enough. Incidence analysis demonstrates a highly unequal distribution of upper secondary and university education. Beyond formal basic education, the access of the poor to training remains limited. Those working in the informal sector (almost half the population) lack health insurance, and until recently 10 million people did not have access to healthcare. In low-income housing, there is evidence of leakage to the nonpoor of programs in principle devoted to low-wage workers. The increase in social spending observed in the last 10 years will be good news for the poor only to the extent that they are better able to benefit from these expenditures.

2. Are There Other Broad-Based Expenditures Where Adjustments Would Help to Serve the Poor? While the government considers broad-based expenditures in health, education, training, and housing to be part of its strategy for the alleviation of poverty, it does not include in this strategy a number of other large programs which have, or could have, an impact on poverty. PROCEDE may be beneficial for the communities adopting it. This is also the case of the agriculture programs PROCAMPO and Alianza para el Campo. This Chapter indicates that PROCAMPO may have a larger impact on poverty than Alianza para el Campo, but additional work is needed to evaluate Alianza para el Cambio's subprograms using better data. PROCAMPO payments would have an even greater impact if payments were progressive, so that those having less land would receive more support per hectare. The point is that a comprehensive strategy for the alleviation of poverty cannot rest solely on a small number of targeted programs. It is important to make sure that, wherever feasible, the design of these programs are adapted so that their impact on the poor is magnified, even though the programs are not specifically targeted to the poor. (Of course, in helping the poor to benefit from the programs, it must be ensured that no conflicts arise with the objectives of the programs.)

3. Is PROGRESA Functioning Well? PROGRESA provides integrated support at the household level for education, health, and nutrition. An in-depth evaluation of the program has been implemented by PROGRESA staff together with the International Food Policy Research Institute, IFPRI. Overall the program is well thought out and innovative. Yet, in a number of areas, it may be worthwhile to think of potential adjustments in the program. PROGRESA's targeting system may not have always been successful in identifying the needy. Its use of cash grants is appropriate, but the level of the grants may be high. PROGRESA is succeeding in raising the demand for schooling and healthcare, but this generates tensions on the supply side (steps have been taken to improve the coordination with supply-side initiatives). PROGRESA is apparently empowering women in rural areas, but more time is needed to judge its impact. Community participation, including in the selection of program beneficiaries, could be promoted more vigorously. Rather than considering the program's current mix as ideal, PROGRESA staff may want to test how similar or better results could be achieved at lower costs. Finally, in operational terms, progress can be made to increase the efficiency of the program, for example through better supervision, the integration of the various data bases created by the program, the potential use of the banking system for the payment of the stipends, etc.

4. Was It Right to Reorganize Food Subsidies? While the now-defunct generalized subsidy on tortilla did reduce inequality, especially in urban areas, and while it did reduce inequality more than subsidies on utilities such as water and electricity, it created distortions. It was also costly, it did not help the poor in the long term, and it was biased toward urban areas. The decision to phase out this subsidy was appropriate. Should means-tested food subsidies be cut as well? This is a more difficult question because the LICONSA (subsidized milk) and TORTIBONO (means-tested tortilla subsidy) programs have larger impacts on poverty and inequality than generalized subsidies. Still, despite their potential impact on nutrition, it remains true that subsidies may not yield long-term benefits for the poor comparable to the benefits provided by PROGRESA (or DIF's school breakfasts), which apparently helps in keeping children in school. More generally, given the wide array of food and cash programs in Mexico, it would be important in further work to provide cost-benefit analyses of the performance of the various programs, which would go beyond the impact evaluations provided in this Chapter. For this, the results of survey-based impact evaluations should be combined with detailed administrative records on costs and outreach.

5. Do Compensatory Education Programs Increase the Quality of Basic Education for the Poor? While PROGRESA and DIF's school breakfasts increase the demand for schooling, compensatory education programs aim at improving the quality and the supply of schooling. PARE was until recently one of the main programs providing resources for schools and training for teachers. While PARE's overall impact on test scores in sixth grade was found to be positive, the program did not improve the test scores of the poorest indigenous children. Within nonindigenous rural schools, the impact was also found to be positive, but lower for the poorest of the poor. In urban areas, the impact was negative. Some of these results have to be considered with caution due to the limits of the data available for evaluating PARE. Still, while supply-side interventions can have substantial effects on the learning achievement of children in poor areas, greater attention needs to be paid to the poorest and the indigenous so that they too may benefit.

6. Is the Temporary Employment Program (PET) Cost-Effective in Transferring Income to the Poor? PET provides off-season temporary employment in marginalized rural areas. Because the wage is below the minimum wage, the program is self-targeted. Household data indicate that program participants do need PET more than nonparticipants because they do not have access to occupations providing work all year long. Within participating communities, PET participants were also found to be poorer than nonparticipants. Yet there are indications that PET may not reach the smallest and most isolated rural communities. Rough appraisal methods indicate that the cost of generating 1 peso of additional income for the poor through PET is about 3.5 pesos (this does not take into account the benefits from PET's infrastructure works). Overall, PET is a necessary program that helps the rural poor, but its design could be improved by learning from other experiences. In Argentina, for example, *Trabajar's* recent reform increased community participation and funding. Local community groups present projects for selection by *Trabajar* staff. After checking for technical feasibility, the projects are selected on a points basis, with more points awarded to projects that are located in poorer areas and that yield larger public benefits, benefit from well-regarded sponsoring groups, and reduce labor costs below the minimum wage.

7. Do Small Rural Communities Have Access to Social Infrastructure? If Not, What Can Be Done? This Chapter shows that access to governmental services (such as telesecondary) and programs (such as DIF's school breakfast) improve the human capital of the poor by increasing the probability that children remain in school. Unfortunately, households living in poor rural areas still lack access to basic social infrastructure. Many communities with less than 20 households do not have electricity, health, and education services. The smaller the community, the smaller the likelihood of benefiting from government programs as well. This does not imply that government services and programs should be implemented everywhere. Due to the high cost of reaching small rural communities, hard choices must be made as to which communities to serve with which services and programs. A detailed cost-benefit analysis of the tradeoffs should be conducted, taking into account the impact of government interventions on mobility and migration. Work should also be done on the impact of migration on poverty.

8. What Can Be Done to Ensure That the Decentralization Process Is *Pro-poor?* Funds for new social infrastructure (FAIS) are now distributed according to a need based formula. This has helped the poorest states increase their share of transfers. The FAIS allocation formula could be improved in theory, but this would probably not make a large difference because the various indicators on which the formula is based are highly correlated. More problematic are the allocations for basic education (FAEB) and health (FASSA), both of which account for three fourths of *Ramo 33*'s budget. These allocations are not based on need, but on past expenditures and existing costs. Hence states that are already well endowed continue to receive more funds. Without putting in jeopardy the maintenance and operation of existing infrastructure, alternative ways to disburse these funds should be examined. At another level, Mexico's decentralization took place so rapidly that local governments have not had time to fully adapt, and number of management and administrative issues remain outstanding. The provision of training to local governments should alleviate these concerns. Finally, international experience suggests that there may be a risk with devolution, in that local levels of government may reduce social spending in order to compete for (or simply please) wealthier residents. Federal and civil society controls may be needed to prevent this and to protect the poor, but these controls should not prevent innovation at the local level.

9. Has the Government Improved the Design of Its Strategy for the Alleviation of Poverty? The government has made some progress in the design of its strategy for the alleviation of poverty, which was very much needed after the 1995 crisis. As explained earlier, the decision to cut generalized food subsidies was correct. Although reforms could be undertaken for improving each of the government's programs, and although more work could be conducted to optimize the relative weights of the programs in the budget, the three-pronged strategy of the government (investments in human capital, providing income and employment opportunities, and investments in poor areas) is fundamentally sound. Moreover, a culture of evaluation of the programs is progressively being developed, as exemplified by the large-scale evaluation of PROGRESA undertaken by IFPRI, to be completed in 2000. Another example of the culture of evaluation taking shape is the publication of the rules of operation of 135 programs in the *Diario Oficial de la Federación*. Further gains could be achieved by evaluating programs in a consistent cost-benefit framework, and by streamlining programs that do not have a clear comparative advantage.

10. What Is Still Missing from the Government's Strategy for the Alleviation of Poverty? Two things: First, there may not yet be a clear blueprint for urban areas similar to the one being implemented in rural areas. Following the phasing out of generalized food subsidies and the implementation of PROGRESA, rural areas are now benefiting from 75 percent of all expenditures targeted to the extreme poor. Given the comparative levels of extreme poverty in urban and rural areas as measured in the surveys, the pro-rural bias of targeted programs for poverty is sound. Still, in urban areas, even though the government is implementing new programs, more is needed to have a clear vision of what has to be done for the extreme poor. Second, at the national level, despite substantial progress in defining a strategy for poverty reduction, there may not yet be a clear understanding of how broad-based and targeted interventions may build on each other so that the whole is greater than the sum of the parts.

The objective of the Bank Report on which this Chapter is based was limited to providing elements for an evaluation of selected programs used by the government for poverty reduction. Further work will be needed to ensure that all these programs feed into a coherent strategy. The following areas for further work have been identified as potential inputs for an overall poverty reduction strategy: (a) geographic dispersion in rural areas, basic infrastructure, and the impact of migration on poverty; (b) evaluation of microcredit programs in rural areas; (c) more detailed evaluation of the PET program; (d) more detailed evaluation of PROBECAT to improve the training component; and (e) poverty in urban areas, including the reform of social security.

III. Broad-Based Public Expenditures and Poverty

Within broad-based public expenditures, social and agricultural expenditures are among the most important for the poor. Expenditures for education, health, social security, job training, and housing are part of the government's strategy for the reduction of poverty. In 2000 social expenditures[2] will account for 9.6 percent of GDP and 61 percent of its programmable expenditures, compared to 6 percent and 36 percent, respectively, in 1990. As a result, over the last sexenio (between 1994 and 2000), despite a fall in real terms of programmable spending of 5.3 percent, social spending per capita increased by 12.8 percent. About US$500 is now spent in social expenditures per capita. This is almost a third of the resources needed for a family of four to avoid being in extreme poverty. Apart from social expenditures, spending by other Ministries also matter for the poor. The programs of SAGAR are especially important given the high incidence of poverty in rural areas. This section analyzes whether broad-based social expenditures benefit the poor, and evaluates the impact on poverty of broad-based agricultural expenditures.

Access of the Poor to Broad-Based Social Public Expenditures Remains Limited

Education

In addition to improving access to upper secondary and higher levels of education, improving basic education is a priority for the poor. As indicated in Figure 5 (next page), which provides concentration curves for public school enrollment in 1996, the access of the poor to upper secondary and university education remains limited, compared to primary and lower secondary schooling (both of which are mandatory, the latter since 1983). For the poor, apart from access to higher levels of education, improving the quality of primary education and access to lower secondary education, which together form the basic education track, are priorities. Interventions on both the demand and supply side will be needed for this (see Section IV of this Chapter, Investments in the Human Capital of the Poor). Some resources allocated to universities could benefit the poor more if they were reallocated to improving the quality of basic education (and also encouraging access in marginalized rural areas.)

Early Child Development (ECD) programs targeted to the poor tend to be effective in helping poor children succeed later in school. There is an international body of evidence suggesting that ECD programs (preschool combined with nutrition support) can be effective in avoiding malnutrition and in helping children learn. As noted in the Education Chapter, Mexico's Initial Education Program (PRODEI),

---

2. Education, health, and social security represent almost 90 percent of total social expenditures. Education and healthcare (together with social security) each represent more than 40 percent of total social expenditures. Spending on labor, rural and urban development, and food and social assistance make up the rest.

Figure 5. Concentration Curves for Enrollment by Education Level, 1996, Public Schools

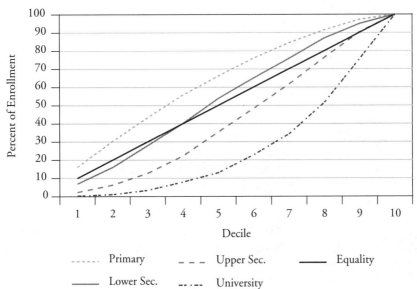

Source: World Bank Staff estimates.

with a per capita cost of about MXP50 per year, is a home-based program delivered by community educators who train parents to stimulate their children. The parents' education is developed through periodic group meetings supplemented by home visits. The program promotes the physical, emotional, intellectual, and social development of infants and toddlers, and improves the school-readiness skills of children. There is empirical evidence that the program is effective in increasing returns on primary education. The program also creates job opportunities for young graduates (of primary education) in poor areas. The program also increases women's self-esteem, and provides opportunities for parents to socialize, thereby fostering community development. PRODEI's coverage should be extended.

Mexico has increased enrollment and reduced dropout and repetition rates in primary schools. The government provides primary education to 14.5 million children, 95 percent of whom are enrolled in mainstream general primary education. The official age of entry into primary school is 6, and this level of schooling should be completed within 6 years. Due to latecomers and repetition, however, the target population goes from ages 6 to 14. The percentage of all children aged 6 to 14 enrolled in primary school increased between the 1990 Census and the 1995 *Conteo*. The increase in primary school enrollment has been especially strong for the indigenous population (an additional 170,000 students, or 30 percent) and for 6 year-olds, which suggests a better ability to attract children early on. However, the fact that enrollment rates are higher for 7 to 11 year-olds indicates persistent problems related to latecomers and repetition rates. The number of schools and teachers has increased faster than the number of students. While this is good for quality improvements, it also induces higher costs. Mexico has also made progress in terminal efficiency (ratio of the number of children completing sixth grade to new enrollments in first grade 6 years earlier), with an 11-percentage-point gain in 5 years. The increase in terminal efficiency is due to improvements in both dropout and repetition rates, which decreased for all grades. On average, dropouts decreased from 4.6 percent to 3.0 percent from 1991–92 to 1995–96, whereas repetition rates were reduced from 9.8 percent to 7.8 percent. Overall, the number of children completing primary school each year has increased by more than 200,000. Still, while completion rates for primary education have reached 85 percent or more overall, they are much lower for the poorest deciles of the population.

While progress has also been achieved in secondary schools, access is far from universal. The lower secondary cycle lasts three years and is intended for age group 12 to 16. Today, 4.3 million students participate. Progress in the 1990s is demonstrated by the following indicators: (a) enrollment has risen by 14.8 percent, translating into an additional 600,000 students; (b) as for primary schools, the number of schools and to a lesser extent the number of teachers has increased faster than the number of students (plus 26.9 percent for schools and 17.5 percent for teachers); and (c) although still low, the enrollment rate in the age group 13 to 15 has gained 7 percentage points, reaching 75.4 percent in the 1996–97 school year. On the other hand, terminal efficiency rates have not improved beyond 75 percent and the average dropout rate was 8.9 percent in 1997–98, which is much higher than the dropout rate for primary education (2.9 percent), and only half a point lower than the 9.5 percent dropout rate for secondary school in 1990–91.

Similarly, the repetition rate for lower secondary education has remained stable, compared to a decrease for primary school. Factors both internal and external to the school system are affecting the performance of lower secondary schools. Internally, there may be a shortage of well-trained teachers, with a higher percentage of teachers lacking appropriate training at the lower secondary than at the primary level. Externally, the need for children to work, especially among the poorest families, may contribute to generating high student absenteeism and poor test scores, which leads to increased repetition.

Beyond formal basic education, the access of the poor to job training remains limited. According to information from the ENE–ENECE 1997, the poor lack access to training programs. As indicated in Figure 6, the distribution of training courses is as unequal as that of income. While the distribution of training hours is less unequal, it is still biased toward the better off. Among the poorest 10 percent of the population, only 1.45 percent have participated in a training course in the last three years. Among richest 10 percent, the participation rate is 32 percent. Public training is distributed more equally than private training, but it still favors the

Figure 6. Distribution of Income, Training Courses, and Hours of Training

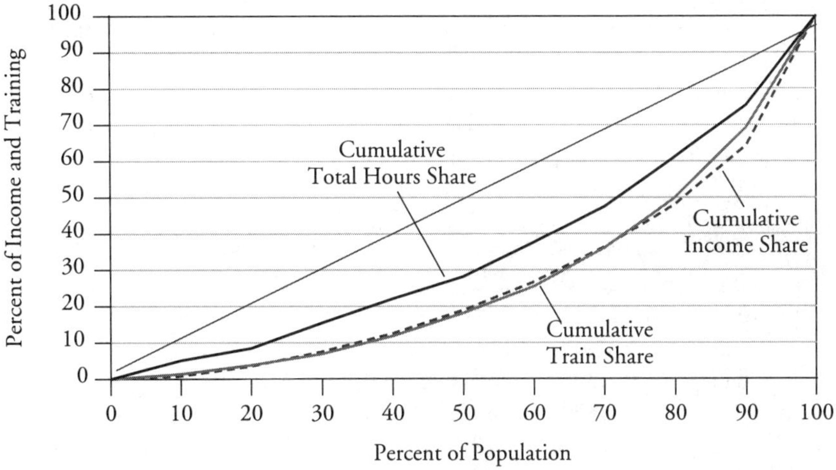

Source: World Bank Staff estimates.

upper deciles. Moreover, while 49 percent of those in the poorest decile who get training pay some or all of the cost of their training, only 25 percent of the rich pay for their training. This is due to the fact that many of the poorest are unemployed and cannot benefit from employer training. In the poorest decile, of all those who get training, only one in six gets training on the employer's premises, compared to more than half in outside institutions. Among the wealthiest decile, 60 percent of those getting training receive it at their firm, and only one third take training at another institution.

Health

Despite progress in health, half the population remains uninsured and one tenth is without access to healthcare. Infant mortality decreased in the 1990s, immunization among children has become nearly universal, and some gains have been achieved in maternal mortality. Life expectancy has increased from 66.8 years in 1980 to 71.7 years in 1996. However, despite such progress, and while the population engaged in the formal labor market benefits from health insurance through IMSS and ISSSTE, the informal sector (43 million adults and children) remains largely uninsured. Until recently, within the informal sector, 60 percent of the population relied on services provided by the SSA, 16 percent relied on IMSS-Solidaridad, and 24 percent had almost no access to healthcare and needs to be covered.

- *IMSS-Solidaridad.* Begun in 1973, IMSS-Solidaridad extends Social Security health coverage to segments of the population that are unable to pay into the social security system. The goals are to improve the access to, and quality of, medical attention for the poor. The program emphasizes reproductive health, nutrition, and sanitation. The mobilization of local communities is an integral part of the program. A general assembly, a health committee, and groups of volunteers are convened locally to help implement the program. As of 1996, the program served about 10 million people in 1,225 municipalities, and it had built 3,540 clinics and 67 hospitals in marginalized areas.

- *PAC.* PAC (*Programa de Ampliación de Cobertura*) provides basic healthcare to those living in marginalized and remote rural areas in coordination with PROGRESA (which is discussed in Section IV of this Chapter). PAC is expected to provide health services to 8 million people by 2000.

Social security reform was enacted in 1997 to ensure the continued financial and institutional viability of IMSS in the face of the challenges posed by a growing and aging population. While the expansion of the economy and the reform of social security should help provide insurance to a larger share of the population, reaching in a cost-effective manner those who fall outside of the system, particularly those living in remote areas, will be a challenge, given the overall increase in the cost of healthcare.

For the rural poor, the priority is access to a basic package of preventive and curative healthcare. Extreme poverty brings with it a high level of mortality and morbidity. In rural areas, the infant mortality rate among the poor is more than twice that among the nonpoor. The participation rates among the poor in family planning and prenatal care are low. While 72 percent of poor rural women say they do not want another pregnancy, less than 56 percent use any sort of birth control. Once pregnant, 1 in 6 poor women in rural areas do not receive any prenatal care. Many factors account for these problems, including lack of access to quality care, unhealthy living conditions, malnutrition, lack of a culture of preventive health, absence of social security benefits, and geographic dispersion. To help the poor, programs such as PAC put the priority on providing a package of basic care. For PAC, this includes the following elements: accident prevention and emergency care; basic sanitation; diarrhea control; family planning; treatment of parasitic diseases; health information, communication, and education; immunization; prenatal and delivery care; prevention and control of hypertension and diabetes mellitus; prevention and control of tuberculosis, nutrition surveillance; treatment of upper respiratory tract infections; and prevention and control of cervical cancer. This type of basic care package emphasizes prevention, but curative services are also being tested and developed, including mobile surgery units.

Housing

Social interest housing programs are not efficient, and they are not accessible to the very poor. Apart from new and small pilot programs, the contribution of the government to the social interest housing sector consists of two agencies facilitating ownership: FOVISSSTE for public sector workers, and INFONAVIT for private sector workers (FOVI is also active in the sector). The management difficulties encountered by these agencies have been documented (also see the Chapter on Housing). In addition, the problem for the very poor is that they are not eligible for mortgages, and therefore cannot benefit from the programs. Moreover, while these housing programs are in principle targeted to low-wage workers, leakage is high. For example, according to 1996 INGEI data, information is available on beneficiaries from INFONAVIT in the six-month period preceding the survey. The mean quarterly household income of beneficiary households was MXP$16,200, versus MXP$10,500 nationally. While the sample size for beneficiaries on which this comparison is made is very small, this confirms that housing programs are not well targeted to low-wage workers.

Social Security

In urban areas, social security reform helped reduce the amount of taxes paid by the poorer segment of the formal sector. While the government has implemented a number of new programs to help the rural poor (these are discussed below and in subsequent sections), there is a feeling that less is done for the urban poor than for the rural poor—at least, there is a perception that the strategy for poverty reduction is less advanced in urban compared to rural areas. Still, one of the positive consequences of social security reform, and more specifically of the *Seguro de Enfermedad y Maternidad*, has been the reduction in the contributions paid by low-income workers. For workers earning up to three minimum wages, the reduction in contributions represents an increase in net earnings of 2.6 percent. A question that remains is how to make such benefits available to informal workers.

Not All Agricultural Programs Benefit the Rural Poor in the Same Way

The government of Mexico has been liberalizing the rural economy. Until the late 1980s, the government played a dominant role in production and marketing decisions in agriculture, especially in the *ejido* sector. The government granted land and water resources to *ejidos*. The community's members, or *ejidatarios*, had usufruct rights over the land they cultivated, but were not allowed to enter sale, rental, or sharecropping contracts. They were prohibited from hiring wage labor, and absences from the *ejido* could lead to the loss of land rights. By the early 1990s, the *ejido* sector accounted for half of Mexico's farmland and three quarters of the nation's producers. It provided a critical instrument for the government to implement its production and marketing policies for the agricultural sector. With the reforms that began in the late 1980s, the relationship between the *ejidos* and the state underwent a dramatic change. Restrictions on the sale and rental of *ejido* land and on the hiring of labor were lifted. The state no longer told the *ejidatarios* what to grow and how to market their output. At the same time, the government no longer provided widespread technical assistance, input and output subsidies, or marketing channels. It could be that the poor have been hurt in the short term by the termination of government support programs for farmers following the liberalization of Mexican agriculture agreed to as part of NAFTA. Yet this is far from certain, since programs such as input and credit subsidies tended to favor large farmers, and since lower agricultural prices may have helped the poorest, who are also net consumers of maize and other crops. Moreover, rather than talking of a reduction in government support to rural areas, it is more precise to talk of a change in the type of support provided, with the implementation of new programs such as PROCAMPO and *Alianza*.

PROCAMPO

PROCAMPO, a cash transfer program facilitating the transition to a rural market economy, reduces poverty among beneficiaries, and it may have a multiplier effect on income. Since 1993–94, under the management of the SAGAR, PROCAMPO has provided cash transfers to eligible agricultural producers of basic crops. The transfers are provided on a per-hectare basis and will be phased out in 2008. In the 1997 fall–winter season, PROCAMPO's transfers totaled MXP$7.5 billion and were distributed to 3 million producers, covering 90 percent of Mexico's cultivated land. According to data from a SRA/World Bank panel survey of households living in the *ejido* sector, the average payment per producer in 1997 was MXP$2,516 (for an average of 5.2 hectares), and 84 percent of all *ejidatarios* participated. Despite a decrease over time in the value of the transfers, the program reduces poverty and inequality (details on PROCAMPO's rules of operations are available in the *Diario Oficial de la Federación*).

- *Impact on Poverty.* According to the 1997 SRA/World Bank survey, PROCAMPO contributed an average of 8 percent toward the *ejidatarios'* household income across all income deciles, and up to 40 percent in the poorest decile. It should be no surprise, therefore, that controlling for other household characteristics, participation in PROCAMPO reduced the probability of being poor. More interesting is the fact that using the panel structure of the survey, PROCAMPO appears to have a multiplier effect over time, in that a transfer of 1 peso leads to benefits of 2 pesos. This multiplier may, but need not be, Keynesian (higher income leads to higher consumption, which generates employment and more income). It may also be due to the possibility for producers to take more risks with higher-yielding investments thanks to the security provided by the transfer. Using other surveys, PROCAMPO has also been shown to reduce income inequality, but not to a very large extent, due to the high transfers received by large land owners.
- *Areas for Improvement.* To increase the impact of the program, the government could: (a) pay the transfers earlier in the crop cycle, or at least announce the amount of payment prior to planting, to facilitate the purchase of inputs and to encourage investments among producers by providing a more secure expected income; (b) allow *ejidatarios* to use part of their payment as a collateral for loans; and (c) simplify the eligibility criteria, and promote better

awareness of these criteria, especially among the indigenous population. Progress has recently been made on recommendations (a) and (b). In addition, a larger impact on inequality and poverty could be achieved by reallocating funds so that the amount received per hectare becomes a decreasing function of the number of hectares cultivated. This may not be the main priority right now, but it could be considered in the future.

Alianza para el Campo

Alianza had not reduced poverty by 1997, but this may be because more time is needed to realize benefits. *Alianza* was introduced in 1996 to provide matching grants to agricultural producers to boost investments. It is the third-largest program managed by SAGAR and accounts for 10 percent of the Ministry's expenditures. The main subprograms are ferti-irrigation; mechanization; rural equipment; pasture improvement; and kilo-for-kilo, which provides growers with 1 kilo of certified seeds for the price of 1 kilo of normal seeds. *Alianza* is decentralized, with cofinancing required from state governments and beneficiary producers. While the cofinancing requirements vary by subprogram, producers tend to contribute an average of 50 percent, the federal government 32 percent, and the state governments 19 percent. In 1997 1 million producers participated in *Alianza*. Of these, two thirds were private producers, 11 percent (120,000) were *ejidatarios*, and 22 percent (241,000) were *comuneros*.

- *Impact on Poverty.* Using the 1997 SRA/World Bank *ejido* survey, *Alianza* was not found to have a significant impact on poverty among *ejidatario* households. This may be because poor *ejidatarios* lack resources to provide the counterpart funding necessary for participation, and thus tend to participate in the subprograms where counterpart funding requirements (but probably also program outcomes) are lower—such as the kilo-for-kilo program. But it may also be because the data collected in 1997 could not yet reflect the benefits of investments made in 1996. It must also be noted that the *ejido* survey is not representative of all the beneficiaries of the program. Finally, it could be that some subprograms of Alianza are more poverty reducing than others (this could be the case of Alianza subprograms for low-income producers which are part of the targeted programs considered by the government in its overall strategy for poverty reduction).
- *Areas for Improvement.* To increase the impact of the program, the government could: (a) improve its dissemination in the *ejido* sector so that a larger proportion of *ejidatarios* are aware of the program, understand its objectives, and are clear on how to access the resources; (b) eliminate the requirements for group participation (which may be difficult for the poorest) in some subprograms; and (c) allow the *ejidatarios* to purchase their own inputs directly from local distributors (rather than government-certified distributors), even if this implies that the purchase price may (but need not) at first be higher.

PROCEDE

PROCEDE may have a positive impact on social capital, thereby reducing poverty. It is the land titling program which was created in 1992 to implement the revised Article 27 of the Constitution and the Agrarian Laws approved earlier that year. According to official data, as of December 1997, 79 percent of the *ejidos* were participating in PROCEDE and 59 percent had received *ejidatario* certificates and house titles. The program was expected to have three main benefits. First, it would encourage investment in *ejido* land because farmers gained greater land security. Second, the reforms would increase the supply of credit, because farmers could use their land as collateral for loans. Third, the ability to engage in rental and sale transactions would promote a more efficient allocation of land among producers. A fourth, unanticipated positive outcome of PROCEDE is that it may have helped at the margin to increase social cohesion and decrease land disputes in the *ejido*, thereby contributing to social capital, which itself has been shown to help in reducing poverty. In the SRA/World Bank 1997 survey, *ejidatarios* were asked whether PROCEDE has had an impact on a number of issues. Two thirds of the respondents replied that PROCEDE did not affect such things as land tenure conflicts, social cohesion, access to credit, migration, land markets, and land investment decisions. However, when PROCEDE was cited as having an impact (by one third of the respondents), those thinking it had a positive impact outnumbered those thinking it had a negative impact. It is in this sense that PROCEDE can be said to have had a positive impact on social capital. In turn, social capital was found to have facilitated the adoption of PROCEDE in the *ejidos*.

Agricultural Programs and the Indigenous Populations

The indigenous differ from the nonindigenous in their attitude toward government programs. Indigenous populations in Mexico make up 10 percent of the population (10 million people), and a much larger share of the poor. In rural areas, they are concentrated in *ejidos* and other traditional communities. Government policy toward the indigenous populations has historically promoted integration rather than an alternative model of development, and indigenous communities have not always responded positively to the government's interventions. A comparison of the attitudes of the indigenous population toward PROCEDE, PROCAMPO, and *Alianza* confirms the existence of an indigenous specificity. Being indigenous or not was found to have more influence on the attitude toward government programs than other household characteristics, such as being poor or not. For example, controlling for these other household characteristics, the indigenous were found to be less likely to be in favor of PROCEDE and *Dominio Pleno* (which refers to the full privatization of the land) than the nonindigenous, not because they fear losing their land, but because of the potentially negative impact of the program on the community. Yet, at the same time, where PROCEDE has been implemented, the indigenous have judged its impact on the community more favorably than the nonindigenous, underscoring the fact that when an indigenous community takes the decision to go for land titling, it tends to be based on wide agreement within the community. The analysis of indigenous attitudes also suggests that the lack of knowledge about PROCAMPO and *Alianza* was more a reason for not participating in the programs among the indigenous population than among the nonindigenous. This suggests that the government should make a deliberate attempt at better informing the indigenous population about its programs and their requirements, a finding measured in the *ejido* survey but likely to be valid in other policy areas as well.

Because the indigenous populations are among the poorest, additional work on how to help them emerge from poverty should be conducted. For example, in the report on which this Chapter is based, the evaluation of government programs in agriculture did not have the information available to analyze structural issues related to different needs or interests among indigenous populations with communal or *ejido* tenure, where traditional governance and values persist. In addition, while this Chapter does compare the impact of education programs such as PARE on school performance among indigenous and nonindigenous populations (in Section IV), it does not discuss the evidence available in both the developed and developing world that bilingual education can be viewed as much more than teaching in two languages. Bilingual education can be, in the case of marginalized peoples, a curriculum aimed at building skills, self-esteem, self-empowerment, parental involvement, and adaptive learning. In healthcare, work could be done on the use and effectiveness of indigenous medicinal treatments, and on whether programs such as PROGRESA and PAC should take into account indigenous medicinal practices. The data available for this Chapter also provided little information about a number of other indigenous initiatives, such as informal credit systems, that may create a synergy with particular types of government interventions (such as the *Fondos Regionales Indigenas*), and thereby improve the impact of government programs. The fact that some government programs are not building on such synergies is one of the main criticisms of government planning put forth by the indigenous leadership.

IV. Investments in the Human Capital of the Poor

Mexico has put in place targeted programs for investing in the human capital of the poor. There is ample evidence that programs benefiting the education, health, and nutrition of children have long-term positive impacts on their well-being. Hence governments around the world have implemented programs dealing with these issues. Mexico's originality is that it is trying to build on the linkages between education, health, and nutrition. This is taking place mainly through PROGRESA, Mexico's new flagship program for the reduction of poverty. Apart from PROGRESA, Mexico currently has three other groups of programs dealing, respectively, with food (subsidies and school breakfasts), compensatory education, and healthcare for the uninsured. The funding levels for 1998 and 1999 (in 2000 pesos) for these four categories of programs are provided in Figure 7.

Figure 7. Spending for Human Capital, 1998–2000

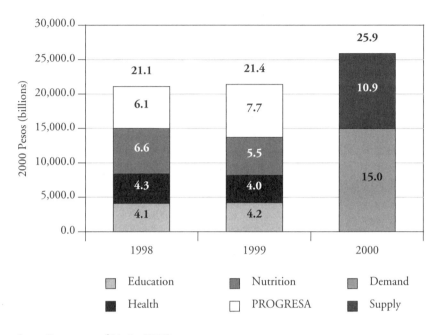

Source: Government of Mexico (1999).

For 2000, the funding is presented in a different format, according to whether the programs are demand or supply side. The demand-side programs include the education component of PROGRESA, *Niños de Solidaridad* (The *Estimulos a la Educación Básica* component of FAIS), the school breakfast programs of DIF, the nutrition component of PROGRESA, the means-tested subsidized milk program (Liconsa), and the means-tested tortilla program (*Abasto de Tortilla de Fidelist*). The programs on the supply side include, for health, PAC, IMSS-Solidaridad, the health component of PROGRESA, the social assistance of INI, and the social security program for agricultural laborers. For education, the supply-side programs include the CONAFE programs, the *Albergues Indígenas* of INI, and the telesecondary program. For nutrition, the supply-side program includes the DICONSA stores. This section analyzes PROGRESA, including a review of preliminary evaluation results; evaluates both food subsidies and school breakfasts, and compares them; and describes compensatory education and evaluates the impact of PARE.

PROGRESA

PROGRESA's share of funds has increased, while funding for food assistance has decreased. Real expenditures for human capital programs are rising, in large part due to the implementation of PROGRESA in 1997. By the end of that year, the program was under way in 12,000 localities and 500 municipalities in 13 states, providing benefits to 400,000 families. Today, the program covers 2.6 million families, which represents 4 out of every 5 families in extreme poverty in rural areas, and 14 percent of Mexico's population. PROGRESA's share of funds devoted to human capital is increasing.

The share of funds devoted to the other programs is decreasing, with the largest drop affecting nutrition (especially food subsidies; these subsidies could however be considered as income transfers to the extent that evidence is lacking regarding their impact on nutrition). This is a deliberate and appropriate choice made to favor programs which are better targeted and which involve co-responsibility on the part of beneficiaries. One issue is that programs such as PROGRESA do not reach the smallest and remotest communities, so that part of the rural population does not benefit from the reform of the programs implemented in the last sexenio.

PROGRESA Has Sound Features, but There May Be Areas for Improvement

PROGRESA aims to improve education, health, and nutrition among the rural poor, and to build on positive linkages between them. Preliminary evaluation results are encouraging. Education has a positive impact on health. In Mexico, infant mortality rates are twice as high among households with illiterate mothers as among households with mothers having at least 7 years of basic education. In turn, good health and nutrition have positive effects on education, if only because they improve a child's learning ability. PROGRESA provides integrated support at the household level for education, health, and nutrition, with the hope that the impact of the program as a whole will be larger than that of its parts. The preliminary results of an evaluation conducted by PROGRESA staff with the support of IFPRI are encouraging. The morbidity among children between ages 0 and 2 has diminished by 22 percent. The female enrollment rate in secondary-level schools has increased by 21 percent. The attendance at health clinics has increased by 18 percent. Overall, school attendance has increased by 1 year, which could translated in the future into an increase of lifetime earnings of up to 12 percent. These results alone would make the program cost-effective.

PROGRESA's targeting mechanism is basically sound, but some questions remain. PROGRESA uses a three-stage targeting mechanism. First, using census data, poor rural localities are selected on the basis of their level of marginalization. Because local access to education and health services is required for participation, some highly isolated localities are excluded. The second stage consists of selecting eligible families within participating communities. For this, PROGRESA collects data on all households living in participating communities. A multivariate discriminant analysis is used to classify households as poor or nonpoor. The analysis takes into account not only income, but also other indicators. Families classified as nonpoor cannot participate in the program. The third stage consists of checking the selection of the program beneficiaries within the community: local communities have the opportunity to review the targeting proposed by PROGRESA, and to suggest a second visit by PROGRESA staff if they believe that some poor families should be reclassified as nonpoor or vice versa. While the targeting mechanism used by PROGRESA is basically sound, a few issues remain:

- *Community Involvement.* There is some evidence that PROGRESA's targeting system is not always successful in identifying the needy. It is of course impossible to achieve perfect targeting and, overall, PROGRESA does a good job at selecting beneficiaries. The third step in the targeting procedure could help in going beyond the statistical correlation between observable signs of income status (house materials for example) and well-being in order to select beneficiaries. Yet, while community-based knowledge exists about who are the most needy, the classification of poor or nonpoor households remains solely based on the prediction made bt PROGRESA staff on the basis of the results of the field survey. One of the reasons why the targeting process is centralized has to do with the desire to avoid political interference in the choice of beneficiaries, and to achieve fairness nationally. Nevertheless, more thought may be needed to assess the role of communities in targeting, not as a primary selection mechanism, but as a useful complement.
- *Need for Targeting in Very Poor Communities.* Another question relates to the very need for targeting in some of the poorest rural communities. The higher the proportion of the poor in a community, the less the need to target within that community, especially if targeting is costly not so much in terms of administration (the administrative cost is low, at MXP$170 per household at most), but rather in terms of social cohesion. PROGRESA has increased the percentage of households receiving benefits in participating communities, with three out of four households now receiving support. In some communities, the percentage is higher. In these communities, rather than leaving a few families without access to the program, it may be better to grant it to all in order to avoid conflicts. This choice has been recommended by IFPRI in Honduras, where it is advising on the redesign of PRAF, a program similar to PROGRESA. However, one problem with the idea of not targeting the program in small and highly marginalized localities is that two households living in different localities but otherwise similar would be treated differently, which raises issues of fairness.

PROGRESA's use of cash grants is appropriate, but the level of the grants is relatively high. PROGRESA provides cash grants in return for parents sending their children to school and using health facilities. The use of cash grants is in principle appropriate because it avoids utility losses associated with in-kind support. The program also provides valuable incentives through its requirements. Yet more work is needed to assess whether the program's cost-effectiveness is optimal. In 1999, the educational grants ranged from MXP$70 per child in third grade of primary school to MXP$255 per child in the third year of secondary school (the grants are the same for boys and girls in primary school, but they are slightly higher for girls than for boys in secondary school). Families can have several children benefiting from the cash grants up to a maximum cumulative amount of MXP$525 per month (see Figure 8). The children also receive a lump-sum payment per year for schooling material (MXP$45 in primary school and MXP$170 in secondary school). Finally, the families receive both monthly cash grants of MXP$105 to help them meet their nutritional requirements, and food supplements free of charge. While on average families receive about MXP$250 (22 percent of their income), they can receive up to MXP$600 per month depending on the number and age of the children.

While the grants may represent a premium over the wages children would earn if they were working, international experience suggests that grants below the prevailing child labor wage may be sufficient to keep children in school because parents value schooling in itself (for altruistic reasons or future intergenerational transfers). To justify the high level of the PROGRESA grants, it could be argued that the grants should provide not only schooling incentives, but also improve the families' overall level of income and quality of life. The question, however, is whether there may be more cost-effective ways to reach this objective. Another argument for the relatively high level of the PROGRESA grants has to do with opportunity costs for participating in the program not directly related to child labor. In some isolated communities it takes time for parents to go to the office where the PROGRESA allowances are paid. These and other transaction costs may make it necessary to provide higher

Figure 8. Monthly Cash Transfers from PROGRESA

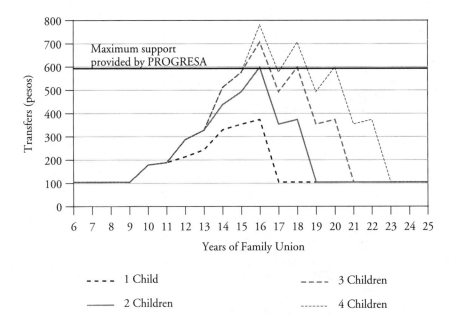

payments to induce participation, but again, more work may be needed to establish optimal benefit levels.

PROGRESA is succeeding in raising school enrollment and the demand for healthcare, but this generates tensions on the supply side. According to data from PROGRESA, school enrollment has increased substantially. Critics argue, however, that while PROGRESA is increasing enrollment, the quality of education is suffering as a result of this increase. Some schools may have found themselves ill-prepared to handle the larger student body. The larger issue in terms of the quality of the education provided relates to the impact of PROGRESA on educational achievement, and ultimately on future earnings. To assess such long-term benefits in a robust way, it may be necessary to follow cohorts of PROGRESA students well into the next decades. As for schooling, the demand for healthcare has increased, but a number of problems remain. At least at the beginning some clinics have had a hard time handling the extra work generated by the program. There is anecdotal evidence that some beneficiaries have had to wait for long periods, and the examinations performed by physicians have not always been thorough due to time constraints placed on them. Some beneficiaries who had to travel for several hours to reach a clinic were told they would not be able to see a doctor and had to return at a later date. Some health centers have been running out of medicine.

PROGRESA may also be encountering resistance to family planning in some indigenous communities. Here, the larger issue is how receptive beneficiaries are to PROGRESA's intended message of preventive self-care, and how attentive health staff are to the social context in which they operate. Steps have been taken to coordinate PROGRESA's action with that of SEP and SSA, but more may be needed to optimize demand- and supply-side interventions and assess the relative impact of both. In Honduras, for example, where IFPRI is building on its experience with PROGRESA in order to advise PRAF staff on how to improve their program, it was decided to evaluate the relative impact of demand-side and supply-side interventions by testing four combinations of programs: demand-side only, supply-side only, no intervention, and both interventions.

Food Programs

Mexico maintains food subsidies for milk and tortilla, and a network of public stores. The three government programs providing food subsidies are LICONSA (milk), Fidelist, and DICONSA (stores in poor rural areas). Their total cost in 1998 was MXP$6.1 billion.

- *Milk.* For the past 15 years, LICONSA (*Leche Industrializada Conasupo*) has been producing milk for Mexico's poor. Qualifying families can purchase from 8 to 24 liters of milk per week at a discount of roughly 25 percent off the market price. To qualify, families must earn less than two minimum wages and have children under age 12. The ration of milk is determined by the number of children under age 12 (8 liters for families with one or two children, 12 liters for families with three children, and 24 liters for families with 4 children or more). About 5.1 million children benefit from the subsidies.

- *Fidelist.* The tortilla program administered by Fidelist is accessible to families earning less than two minimum wages. These families are eligible to receive 1 kilogram of subsidized tortilla per day. Participants use a bar-coded card which is scanned at participating *tortillerias.* The owner of the *tortilleria* is later reimbursed for the cost of the subsidized tortillas he or she has distributed.
- *Public Stores.* DICONSA (*Distribuidora Comercial Conasupo*) is a public network of small stores providing basic products such as rice and toilet paper to marginalized rural communities. Goods are sold at low prices, yielding an average savings of 16.5 percent for beneficiary households. A central feature of the program is community participation through local Rural Committees of Supply. The program operates in 2,300 municipalities, with 23,468 points of sales. In 1997 it sold 1.6 million tons of products, bringing its sales total for that year to MXP$5.7 billion.

Means-tested food subsidies are more effective than other subsidies in reducing inequality and improving welfare. An analysis of the impact on inequality and social welfare of subsidies shows that the long-anticipated phasing out of the general subsidy on tortilla in the first few months of 1999 was warranted because means-tested food subsidies are more inequality-reducing and less price distorting.

- *Food Subsidies are Better than Nonfood Subsidies.* For many years the government provided general subsidies on tortilla. Part of the rationale was that since

Table 1. Coverage of Food Subsidies, 1998

LICONSA	
Points of sale for LICONSA milk (number of dairies)	11,052
Beneficiary municipalities	1,912
Beneficiaries (in thousands)	5,100
DICONSA	
Points of sale for DICONSA (stores)	23,468
Target beneficiary population (thousands)	33,798
Value of distributed volume (millions of pesos)	6,630
Subsidized tortilla	
Kilograms of tortilla distributed per day (thousands)	1,512
Localities attended	1,024
Affiliated tortillerias	13,973

Source: Government of Mexico.

tortilla represented a larger share of the consumption of the poor, the subsidy was to some extent self-targeted. It is true that the tortilla subsidy reduced inequality, especially in urban areas, and much more so than subsidies for utilities such as water and electricity. However, the tortilla subsidy generated price distortions and was costly. Furthermore, it was significantly less effective in reducing inequality than a similar generalized subsidy would have been on corn flour, for example.

- *Within Food Subsidies, Means-Tested Subsidies are Better than Generalized Subsidies.* Using the 1996 INEGI and the 1997 ENCASEH surveys, it has been shown that the marginal reduction in inequality in consumption achieved with the generalized tortilla subsidy does not come close to the reduction achieved with the means-tested subsidies provided by LICONSA and the means-tested tortilla program.
- *Within Means-Tested Food Subsidies, LICONSA and the means-tested Tortilla Program Have Similar Impacts.* In rural areas, LICONSA has a larger marginal impact on inequality, but the means-tested tortilla program is more inequality reducing in urban areas and nationally. Overall, the two programs have similar impacts, but the cost of implementing the means-tested tortilla program is lower than that of implementing LICONSA.

The government also provides school breakfasts, food support, and community kitchens through three food programs administered by DIF (*Desarollo Integral de la Familia*):

- *School Breakfasts.* By end of 1998, DIF's school breakfasts were distributed in more than 2,400 municipalities. From 1995 to 1998, the number of breakfasts distributed daily more than doubled from 1.9 million to 4.4 million. While higher priority is now being given to hot breakfasts (Figure 9), whether this represents a good use of resources needs to be assessed because hot breakfasts imply higher costs, which need not translate into higher learning gains or nutritional impacts. The federal government pays 63 percent of the program's cost, and the rest is covered by states and municipalities. Through local committees, 400,000 mothers participate each day in the preparation of the breakfasts, which is a plus in terms of community involvement, but which also represents an opportunity cost in terms of time for the families involved. While the program had an urban bias in the past, today the rural southern states receive a higher share of the breakfasts.
- *Food Support.* DIF's PASAF (*Programa de Asistencia Social Alimentaria a Familias*) provides monthly in-kind food support for families with children under age 5 or pregnant women. By the end of 1998 the program served 1.4 million families in 1,633 municipalities. Of these, 10 percent were indigenous families and 30 percent lived in areas of high marginalization.

Figure 9. Coverage and Type of School Breakfast

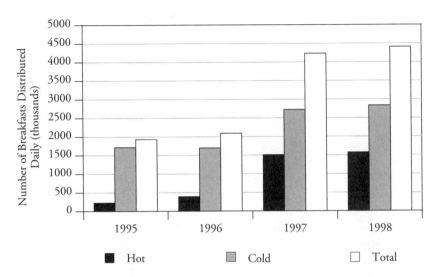

Source: DIF.

- *Community Kitchen.* DIF supports community kitchens by providing equipment and part of the cost of food with the idea that, in addition to benefiting nutrition, these interventions will contribute to the social fabric of the communities and serve as anchors for other education and health interventions. By end 1998, 6,067 kitchens were operating in 1,159 municipalities serving 520,000 beneficiaries.

To some extent, DIF's school breakfasts and *Niños de Solidaridad* improve school enrollment and reduce child labor in rural areas. The aim of the government's food programs is to improve nutrition for the poor, and thereby to build their human capital. While the impact of food programs on nutritional outcomes and learning performance cannot be measured with the data at hand, other criteria such as the impact on school enrollment and child labor can be used to assess how the programs build human capital.

- *Impact of DIF's School Breakfasts.* While food subsidies are unlikely to have strong impacts on school enrollment and child labor, DIF's school breakfasts may have an impact because they are provided in schools. If the benefit of a school breakfast is assimilated to a reduction in the price (opportunity cost) of going to school, economic theory predicts that school breakfasts will increase school enrollment, while the impact on child labor is uncertain due to substitution with leisure. In empirical work based on the 1997 ENCASEH survey, DIF's school breakfasts were found to have a larger impact on schooling than on child labor, as expected.

- *Impact of Niños de Solidaridad.* This program, whose name was recently changed to *Estimulos a la Educación Básica*, is run by SEDESOL. It gives grants to children who complete the first three years of their elementary education in the hope of providing them with an incentive to complete their primary education. Between 1995 and 1997, 857,000 children were awarded scholarships. An analysis similar to that performed for DIF's school breakfast also indicates some impact on schooling and child labor, but not in a systematic way.

DIF's programs and *Niños de Solidaridad* tend to be better targeted than food subsidies. Table 2 provides measures of the targeting effectiveness of food programs using the 1997 ENCASEH. Although there may be underreporting in the survey as to who benefits from the programs, and although the results may be sensitive to the choice of the poverty line, DIF and *Niños de Solidaridad* are clearly better targeted to the poor than means-tested food subsidies, in large part because the means-tested tortilla program and LICONSA are mainly available in urban areas where the incidence of poverty is lower. The same applies to DICONSA (not shown in the table), whose stores are not available in some of the poorest rural communities. Overall, the placement of food programs is apparently driven not only by income considerations, but also by (ease of) supply considerations.

- *DIF, Niños de Solidaridad, and PROGRESA Provide Incentives, While Food Subsidies Do Not, or at Least Do Not to the Same Extent.* Parents must send their children to school if they want to benefit from school-based programs, while they have no such obligation in order to benefit from food subsidies. Of course, there is no guarantee that by increasing school attendance, school-based programs actually increase the human capital of the poor. Beyond the immediate benefit of the programs, parents must buy into the importance of schooling and help their children at home. The schools must also be of sufficient quality for the children to be able to learn. But at least programs with built-in positive incentives, such as DIF, *Niños*, and PROGRESA, hold the promise of bringing long-term changes for the poor. This is less the case with food subsidies. Thus, the strategy of the government to progressively decrease food subsidies is sound.
- *Better Programs Could Be Implemented in Urban Areas if Food Subsidies Were Reduced.* A risk in scaling back food subsidies further is that urban areas may suffer. As noted in the introduction, the current split of the targeted expenditures for the reduction of poverty between urban and rural areas is adequate. Yet cutting food subsidies, which are mostly urban based, could tilt the balance too much in favor of rural areas. Thus the ideal would be to reorient food subsidies toward urban programs which yield benefits similar to what PROGRESA is achieving in rural areas.

Table 2. Targeting Performance of Food Programs (DIF programs and food subsidies)

	National			Urban			Rural		
	All	Poor	Non Poor	All	Poor	Non Poor	All	Poor	Non Poor
Participation Rates (percent of individuals in the group receiving the program)									
DIF food support	2.6	5.5	1.5	1.1	1.5	1.0	7.0	8.5	4.6
DIF school breakfasts	8.7	14.3	6.0	5.8	7.4	5.4	16.1	19.4	9.7
Niños de Solidaridad	3.8	6.5	2.5	2.2	3.8	1.8	7.8	8.4	6.5
Subsidized tortilla	6.7	6.3	6.8	8.3	11.8	7.6	2.2	2.1	2.4
LICONSA	8.5	7.4	8.9	10.4	12.2	10.1	2.7	3.6	1.5
Share of Participants (percent of beneficiary individuals in each group)									
DIF food support		57.1	42.9	32.0	20.9	79.5	68.0	79.8	28.7
DIF school breakfasts		54.2	45.8	47.1	25.2	74.8	52.9	79.9	20.1
Niños de Solidaridad		56.4	43.6	41.3	34.5	65.5	58.7	71.9	28.1
Subsidized tortilla		25.9	74.1	91.6	22.5	78.1	8.4	60.7	39.5
LICONSA		23.9	76.1	91.8	19.2	81.1	8.2	91.0	22.5

Source: World Bank staff estimates.

- *Further Cost-Benefit Analyses Should Be Conducted for Food Programs.* To better assess the performance of various programs, detailed cost-benefit analyses should be prepared by combining survey-based impact evaluations of food programs with administrative records on costs and outreach. More information is also needed about the relative costs and efficiency of cash transfers, food subsidies, food stamps, and direct food handouts, and on the ability of food markets to function well.

Compensatory Education

While PROGRESA is demand driven, compensatory education seeks to improve the quality and supply of schooling. The geographic dispersion of marginalized rural areas presents obstacles for educators and families. Teachers usually teach in a single classroom with children of all ages. Children must travel vast distances to reach their schools, creating logistical problems for their families. The quality of educational materials and instruction provided to children is commonly substandard. In many cases, education beyond sixth grade simply does not exist. Not surprisingly, the academic achievement of these children falls below national averages. The following programs have been implemented to deal with this (Figure 10):

- *PARE.* Initiated during the 1991–92 school year, PARE's *(Programa para Abatir el Rezago Educativo)* objective is to improve regular, rural, and indigenous primary education in the states of Chiapas, Guerrero, Hidalgo, and Oaxaca. A four-year program, PARE provides schools with improved materials

Figure 10. Compensatory Education Programs

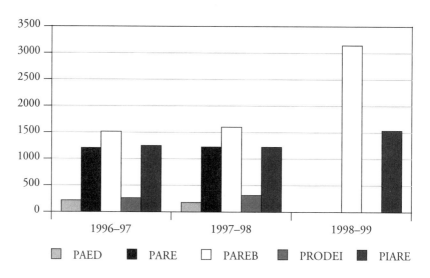

such as textbooks. It also provides financial incentives for teachers, for example to assist in a regular way to classes and to provide support to the children outside of the classroom. PARE has improved education facilities through the construction and repair of schools and the creation of libraries. The program had 1.2 million beneficiaries in 1997.

- *PAREB.* Based on the experiences of PARE, PAREB *(Programa para Abatir el Rezago en Educación Básica)* began in 1994 and continued through the 1998–99 school year in 10 states: Campeche, Durango, Guanajato, Jalisco, Michoacán, Puebla, San Luis Potosí, Tabasco, Veracruz, Yucatán.

- *PIARE.* The *Programa Integral para Abatir el Rezago Educativo* was initiated in 1995 and will be continued through 2000. The program supports preschool, elementary school, and adult education programs in selected communities. It had 1.2 million beneficiaries in 23 states in 1997.

- *PRODEI.* Undertaken in 1981, PRODEI *(Programa para el Desarrollo de la Educación Inicial)* works with parents of children under age 4 to improve child rearing and cognitive development to facilitate the transition to primary education. In 1997 the program had 313,000 beneficiaries in 10 states.

- *PAED.* The *Programa de Apoyo a Escuelas en Desventaja*, was created in 1992 to address the needs of schools not supported by PARE, PAREB, and PIARE. The program provides supplies and furniture to schools in Aguascalientes, Baja California, Baja California Sur, Morelos, Nuevo León, Tamaulipas, and Tlaxcala. It had 178,500 beneficiaries in 1997. Beginning with the 1998–99 school year, the program will be replaced by PIARE in these regions.

The positive impact of PARE is weaker for the poorest of the poor and for indigenous children. Previous analyses have shown that on the whole PARE has had a positive impact on student test scores. But what is the impact of the program on the poorest of the poor? Additional analysis of the PARE panel data was undertaken to answer this question. Four results were obtained. First, controlling for other child, household, and school characteristics, participation at the school level in PARE did not significantly improve the test score in Spanish (in sixth grade) of the poorest children of the indigenous group, while the program had positive impacts on less-poor indigenous children. Second, in the sample of nonindigenous rural schools, PARE improved the learning achievement of both very poor and less-poor children, although the former benefited slightly less than the later. Third, taking both indigenous and regular rural schools together, it would appear that the poorest children increased their Spanish test scores by only half of the gain achieved by less-poor children. Fourth, in the urban sample the PARE interventions appeared to have significantly negative effects on Spanish test scores for both the very poor and the poor. The negative impact (in absolute value) was larger among the poorest students. It is difficult to explain this negative impact in urban areas, but it should be noted that the PARE program did not pay much attention to urban schools, except toward the end of the life of the program. In addition, the fact that PARE did not improve much the Spanish skills of very poor and indigenous children may be due to factors such as poor nutrition and health status among these groups. It would be interesting to test whether programs such as PROGRESA achieve better results. Overall, the conclusion of the analysis is that while supply-side interventions can boost the learning achievement of children, special attention and more resources may need to be devoted to the poorest of poor children.

V. Income Opportunities for the Poor

Government-run programs focus on employment generation in rural areas and training in urban areas. With the liberalization of the Mexican economy, the labor market is undergoing transformation. In urban areas, the requirements for skills are rising and the labor force needs training. In rural areas, temporary employment programs are needed to maintain income opportunities during seasonal slowdowns. Credit and training are also needed to help the rural population make the transition to the nonfarm sector. Finally, while employment opportunities must be created for adults, there is a need to reduce child labor and increase schooling. This section is devoted to selected employment issues. It appraises the targeting and cost-effectiveness of PET; briefly describes the other employment and credit programs targeted to the poor; and discusses PROBECAT, the training program for the unemployed mainly in urban areas.

Programa de Empleo Temporal

This program provides off-season temporary employment below minimum wage in marginalized rural areas. PET provides short-term employment on public projects in marginalized rural areas. Employment is for up to 88 working days at 90 percent of the minimum wage. In 2000, PET's budget will be MXP$4.8 billion, more than half of the budget devoted to income opportunities for the poor. In total, close to 100 million workdays and 1 million jobs will be created.

Apart from benefiting participants through the provision of an income during periods of high unemployment or underemployment, PET benefits communities by building infrastructure and responding to local needs. Projects are labor intensive. Examples include irrigating land, paving roads, clearing land, improving housing, and installing water and sewerage systems. PET has national coverage, but a large share of funds is spent in the Southern states, which are poorer. Separate PET programs are administered in these areas by the Ministry of Social Development (SEDESOL, 47 percent of total funds), the Ministry of Transport and Communications (SCT, 33 percent), the Ministry of Agriculture (SAGAR, 17 percent), and the Ministry of the Environment (SEMARNAP, 3 percent) (Figure 11).

Program participants need PET more than nonparticipants, and they are poorer. Data on PET participants are available in the 1997 ENCASEH survey for margin-

Figure 11. Government Spending for Income Employment, 2000 Pesos

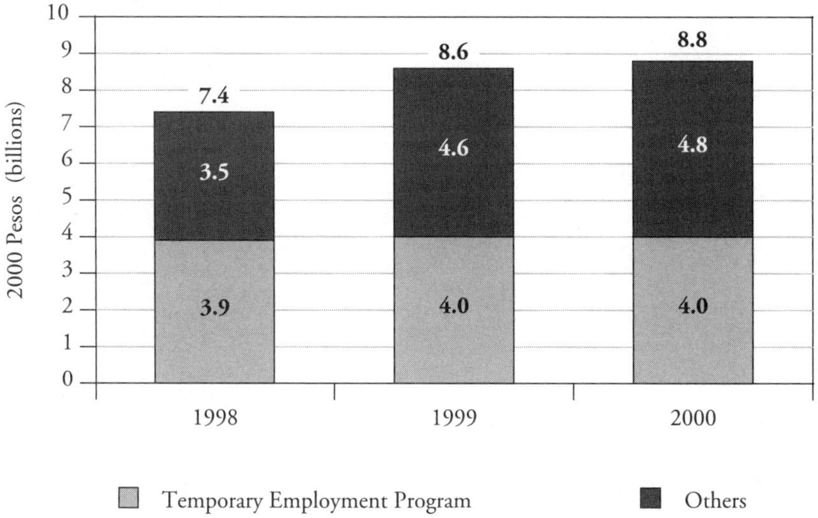

Source: Government of Mexico.

alized rural areas (which are those targeted by the program). A few summary indicators for participants and nonparticipants are given in Table 3. According to the monthly income of the household head, participants are poorer than nonparticipants (with nonparticipants themselves poorer than the national average, since the survey was conducted in poor areas). But if one uses literacy or assets as proxies for well-being, participants are better off than nonparticipants. Participants are less likely to be indigenous and agricultural laborers. A striking difference between participants and nonparticipants is, as expected, that participants need temporary jobs more than nonparticipants because they do not benefit as often from an occupation that keeps them employed all year long. This is either because they are involved in seasonal work or because they work on a solicitation basis. PET thus helps alleviate underemployment, which is its goal.

PET may not reach the smallest and most isolated rural communities. The community-level data of the 1997 ENCASEH for marginalized rural areas also enable us to compare the characteristics of the communities benefiting from PET with those which do not benefit (10.8 percent of 6,886 sampled communities benefit). On average, PET communities are almost twice as large (575 inhabitants versus 344) as non-PET communities. PET communities have better access to electricity (74 percent versus 60 percent), public phones (33 percent versus 19 percent), preschools (81 percent versus 67 percent), primary schools (89 percent versus 82 percent), and telesecondary schools (22 percent versus 11 percent). Thus, the pro-

Table 3. Characteristics of PET Participants

	Participants	
	Yes	No
Household Characteristics		
Household size	5.4	5.2
Age of household head	46.8	44.6
Indigenous language for head	40.1%	48.4%
Literacy for head	76.0%	61.7%
Principal Occupation of Head		
Agricultural laborer	33.5%	44.5%
Work in Principal Occupation		
From time to time	14.0%	8.4%
A few months per year	29.8%	19.1%
All year long	56.3%	72.5%
Reason Why Not All Year Long		
Seasonal-type work	68.6%	81.3%
Work only when solicited	21.2%	13.9%
Assets		
House owner	97.3%	93.3%
Land owner	83.5%	65.0%
Monthly Income of Head		
Household income	578	628
Per capita income	128	153

Source: World Bank staff estimates.

gram may not reach the smallest, most isolated, and in all likelihood poorest, communities. While part of this targeting problem may be due to the higher costs of reaching smaller communities, part may also be due to the lack of bargaining power of small communities in obtaining funds from program administrators at the state level.

The cost of generating 1 peso in additional income for the poor through PET is about 3.5 pesos, but this does not take into account the benefits from the work done by PET workers. As indicated in Box 1, rough appraisal methods are available to assess the cost-effectiveness of employment programs such as PET. While these methods do not replace detailed econometric analysis (for which better data on PET would have to be collected), they provide an order of magnitude of the benefits of the program. The measure of cost-effectiveness used is the share of total program costs which reaches the poor through PET's wages. This share is a function of four

---

Box 1. A Simple Framework for Measuring the Cost-Effectiveness of Public Works

Assume that without public works, an individual has a probability F^* to find employment at market wage W^*. Expected earnings are F^*W^*. With public works, the individual earns the public works wage W. If the individual can continue to search for private or self-employment while participating in public works, with probability F of finding such employment, the expected wage with public works is $FW^*+(1-F)W$. The net wage benefit from the program for the worker is $NWB = (1-F)W - (F^* - F)W^*$. If the worker gets unemployment benefits or a subsistence allowance S, the wage benefit is reduced to $NWB = (1-F)W - (F^* - F)W^* - (1-F^*)S$. If the program costs G to the government per worker employed, a measure of cost-effectiveness is the share of public expenditures transferred to workers as wage gain NWB/G. This measure can be decomposed as follows:

$$\frac{NWB}{G} = \frac{C}{G} \frac{(W+L)}{C} \frac{W}{(W+L)} \frac{NWB}{W}$$

$$\begin{array}{cccc} / & | & \backslash & \backslash \\ \textit{budget} & \textit{wage} & \textit{targeting} & \textit{proportionate} \\ \textit{leverage} & \textit{share} & \textit{performance} & \textit{wage gain} \end{array}$$

The determinants of cost-effectiveness are (a) the leverage ratio C/G, where C is the total cost per worker including community funding; (b) the wage share $(W+L)/C$, where W stands for wages paid to the poor and L stands for wages paid for the nonpoor resulting in leakage; (c) the targeting performance $W/(W+L)$, which is the percentage of wages reaching the poor; and (d) the proportionate wage gain NWB/W. This model can be extended to take into account the benefits of the infrastructure built by public works.

---

parameters: the proportionate wage gain, the targeting performance, the wage share, and the budget leverage.

- *Proportionate Wage Gain.* If having a PET job does not increase the probability of finding another job, which is realistic in poor rural areas, then the proportionate wage gain in the absence of unemployment benefits is one minus the probability of working outside of PET. According to Table 3, half the PET participants have occupations that enable them to work all year long. If they can indeed work on their own or find another job, the proportionate wage gain could be about 0.5, corresponding to those participants who cannot work all year long (0.5 was also the proportionate wage gain observed for Argentina's public employment program *Trabajar* before changes were implemented in the program).

- *Targeting Performance.* In poor rural areas, PET households are poorer than nonparticipating households in terms of income, but they tend to have better human and physical capital. Overall, one could say that participants are similar to nonparticipants within marginalized areas. In this case, the poverty rate within marginalized rural areas, which may reach up to 80 percent, is an appropriate measure of targeting performance, given that the program is precisely targeted to these areas.

- *Wage Share.* Multiplying the number of workdays to be created in 1999 by PET by the wage rate (90 percent of the minimum wage of geographic zone C, which corresponds to MXP$26.70 per day in January 1999), one gets a total wage bill of MXP$2.5 billion. The total budget allocated to PET for 1999 was MXP3.6 billion, which results in a wage share of close to 70 percent.

- *Budget Leverage.* The program is almost entirely financed by the federal government (even though project selection is often at the state or local level). Hence the budget leverage is equal to 1.

COST-EFFECTIVENESS. Given the above (very rough) hypotheses, the overall cost-effectiveness of the program is 0.28. Thus, it would take slightly more than 3.5 pesos of federal funds to generate 1 peso in additional income for the poor through PET. This figure is higher than that of employment programs in India, but lower than what is observed in Argentina, at least before changes were made in *Trabajar*. Note, however, that in the above estimate, the benefits of the public works themselves have not been taken into account, and they can be big. If good survey data were collected on *Trabajar* participants, more precise estimates of the cost-effectiveness of the program could be obtained.

Mexico could learn from experiences abroad to increase community participation and funding. Several useful lessons for PET can be learned from the reform of *Trabajar*. In Argentina, the difficulties of 1996–97, during which unemployment reached 40 percent in the poorest population decile of Greater Buenos Aires, provided an impetus to improve *Trabajar* (adding 300,000 participants from May 1997 to October 1998). While keeping the self-targeting feature of the program (as in Mexico, minimum wages ensure participation by the poor), the focus of the reform was placed on increasing community participation and funding in the choice of the projects to be financed.

Trabajar now works in collaboration with local community groups, NGOs, and municipalities which present projects for selection (some community participation is also observed in Mexico). While *Trabajar* covers the cost of labor, local sponsoring groups cover nonwage costs. Projects must first be approved for technical feasibility. Next, they are selected on a points basis. More points are awarded to projects that are located in poorer areas, that yield larger public benefits, that benefit from well-regarded sponsoring community groups or NGOs, and that reduce labor costs below the minimum wage. These new features have improved targeting both at the geographic and individual level. Apart from increasing cost-effectiveness at the federal level, the involvement of local groups has also improved the quality of monitoring and feedback. All problems have not been solved, however. There remains evidence of political influence in the choice of participants, and of gender discrimination (few women are selected in some areas). Local groups are not always well positioned to contribute to nonwage costs, and the provision of jobs takes precedence over the projects' quality in some areas.

Other Employment Programs for the Poor

Apart from PET, the government operates several smaller employment programs targeting poor areas. The other half of federal funds devoted to employment and income opportunities for the poor is allocated to smaller programs providing credit or infrastructure. Some of these programs are as follows:

- *Jornaleros Agrícolas.* This program's goal is to improve the living conditions of migrant farm workers. It promotes collaboration between public and private (producer) organizations to achieve these goals. In 1998 the program funded 13,650 projects in 14 states and 248 *municipios,* helping 682,000 workers. Of all projects, 23 percent were for housing improvements; 22 percent for culture, recreation, and education; 18 percent for help with legal problems; and the rest (27 percent) for nutrition, employment, training, and health. In 1999 the program expanded coverage into Jalisco.
- *Fondos Regionales Indígenas (Apoyos Productivas del INI).* These regional indigenous funds encourage productive initiatives from local indigenous groups in their place of origin. It is hoped these initiatives will become self-financing in the long term. Earnings from the initiatives are reinvested in the regional fund. Seventy-two percent of beneficiaries have been in Chiapas, Guerrero, Oaxcaca, San Luis Potosí, and Veracruz. In 1995, 146 regional funds were established. This increased slightly in 1997 to 151. During 1995–97, 8,701 projects received some support and benefited 865,000 indigenous people.
- *FONAES.* The *Fondo National de Apoyo a Empresas Sociales* provides support to small firms and other organizations that help develop the local economy, and provide services in both rural and urbanizing areas (*barrios populares*). Funds are used as risk capital, to act as a credit guarantee, and to encourage productive investment and technological development, training is also provided. During 1995–97, 10,343 organizations received funding and 35,571 jobs were created. In 1998, 2,107 new groups received support. About 80 percent of the projects tend to survive.
- *Crédito a la Palabra.* This program was established in 1990 to supply credit for farmers excluded from commercial credit because of their perceived lack

of productive potential and collateral. Farmers are supplied with no-interest credit to finance the crop of their choice for up to 3 hectares. Credit is obtained through a local committee, which petitions for funds. Loans are repaid into a local social fund, which is administered by the municipal government. During 1990–94, loans were for MXP$300 per hectare. In 1995 they were fixed at MXP$400, and today they are worth MXP$500 per hectare. The loans may be insufficient to fund technological development or innovation, and therefore they may simply support subsistence cultivation. The area financed has decreased from 2 million hectares in 1990 to 1.2 million hectares in 1998. A large part of the funds go to the southern states.

- *CONAZA.* The *Comisión Nacional de las Zonas Áridas* targets semi-arid and arid areas with projects for productive growth and investments in local infrastructure. Funds from *Ramo 26* are available through this program, which benefited 354 communities in 1998. Funding was allocated to 88 projects which covered 870 hectares. Projects covered a range of needs. For example, 38 projects have provided and maintained drinking water or sewerage systems.

The impact of these programs on the farm and nonfarm economy should be evaluated; however, due to lack of data it is not possible to do so. Such an evaluation should focus on impacts not only at the household level, but also at the local level within the context of the nonfarm economy becoming increasingly important for survival and social mobility. According to data from the SAR/World Bank 1997 survey of the *ejido* sector, the probability of being poor is reduced by access to employment in the nonfarm sector. Income mobility has increased for households with members who found employment in commerce and other nonagricultural sectors. This interacts with both individual variables such as education and gender, and local variables such as access to labor markets through better roads. Human capital is key for gaining earnings from the nonfarm sector. Yet it is not enough, especially for women. Higher employment rates for men cannot be explained by differences in human capital. Structural factors such as labor market demand, household demographics, and employment practices are at play. This suggests that policies focusing exclusively on human capital will have a limited impact on reducing gender inequity and poverty, which provides a role for employment programs to fill part of the gap.

Training Programs

The two largest training programs are CIMO for the employed, and PROBECAT for the unemployed. While training programs are not officially part of the government's strategy for the reduction of poverty, they are worth discussing here because their goal is to increase human capital and facilitate the adaptation of the labor force to the ongoing restructuring of the economy. There are two main programs:

- *CIMO.* Since 1988, CIMO *(Programa Calidad Integral y Modernización)* has provided technical assistance and financial support to training and productivity programs that take place within small and medium-sized businesses. The program funds projects that increase the businesses' productivity and enable them to expand their workforce, develop their human capital, and improve their working conditions. In 1997 there were 550,000 beneficiaries. While the number of beneficiaries did not rise above the previous year's level, it was a significant increase over the 1995 level of 368,000.
- *PROBECAT.* The *Programa de Becas de Capacitación para Desempleados* was implemented in 1986 as a response to the growth in unemployment that followed the 1982 debt crisis and the subsequent structural adjustment policies. By 1986 almost 20 percent of the workforce (5 million people) were unemployed or seriously underemployed. PROBECAT was designed to combat this mismatch between worker skills and firm requirements while simultaneously helping workers weather economic shocks. Given that PROBECAT targets the unemployed, it is more likely than CIMO to benefit the poor.

There are three main training modalities in PROBECAT. School-based, in-service, and PILEOT. Table 4 provides an overview of the three main training modalities in PROBECAT. The program began by providing school-based training. Later, to better match workers' skills with local employer needs, an in-service modality was created whereby firms provide training to participants who receive their minimum-wage stipend through PROBECAT. On completion of the training, 70 percent of the trainees are guaranteed employment with the local trainer. Finally, in response to the economic crisis of 1994–95, PILEOT *(Programa de Iniciativas Locales de Empleo y Ocupación Temporal)* was initiated in 1995 to reach the economically disadvantaged in marginalized areas. Thirty percent of PILEOT's beneficiaries are rural, compared to 9 percent for the school-based module and 4 percent for the in-service module. PILEOT targets individuals who are self-employed or occupied in community-based initiatives. Participants must have basic literacy and numeracy skills and be unemployed or underemployed. The number of program participants has increased from 100,000 per year in the first years to 581,000 in 2000. Today PILEOT is the largest module, covering more than half the participants; the school-based module is the next largest; and the in-service module is the smallest.

The training gains from participation in PROBECAT may have been overestimated in past evaluations. Two previous evaluations of PROBECAT have been performed using data from 1992 and 1994 participants cohorts. These evaluations, which where completed before the start of PILEOT, suggested that the program had a positive impact on wages and that it reduced the time needed to find employment. Thus, the benefits of the programs for participants surpassed its costs to the government. In both evaluations, the analysis relied on a quasi-experiment by comparing a treatment group (the PROBECAT trainees) with a control group (the urban unemployed). However, a reexamination of the more recent study using the same

Table 4. Modalities of PROBECAT's Main Training Modules

	School-Based Training	In-Service Training	Pilot
Eligibility Rules	Unemployed candidate registered with SES, aged 16 to 55, having completed primary school and having at least 3 months of experience	Unemployed, registered with SES, aged 18 to 55, having completed primary school (this can be waived by firm). No prior experience required.	Unemployed aiming at self-employment, aged 16 to 55, literate, no upper secondary schooling. Special module for community activities
Training Provider	Training schools/centers	Participating firms	Training centers/instructors
Training Duration	1 to 6 months	1 to 3 months	1 to 3 months
Benefits Received	Training, minimum wage, transportation costs, health insurance under IMSS	Training, minimum wage, transportation costs, health insurance under IMSS	Same, plus a set of tools for self-employment module
Training Costs	PROBECAT program	Firm (cost of instructors, equipment, and materials)	PROBECAT program
Training Content	Set by training provider with little customization	Set by firm. Mostly hands-on training	Set by the training provider with customization
Placement	Required to register with SES. No placement	Firms required to employ 70 percent of the trainees	No particular follow up

Source: STPS.

data but with alternative econometric methods suggests that the gains from PROBECAT may have been overestimated. In this reexamination, the program does not appear to have much impact on either employment or wages.

The weak impact of PROBECAT is not unlike that of other training programs in OECD countries. The disappointing results of PROBECAT in terms of raising wages and employment are not surprising. Most retraining programs in OECD countries have been found to be of limited impact. When programs were found to have an impact in the short term, this impact was also found to vanish after a few years. As for PROBECAT, the results observed with the in-service modality in terms of employment at the end of the program need not imply large net gains. It could well be that without the wage subsidy provided by the government, participating firms would have hired the same workers (this is referred to as a deadweight loss in the literature) or other workers (substitution effect). It may even be that the firms which benefited from the wage subsidies became more competitive, and thereby displaced workers in other firms not benefiting from the subsidies (displacement effect). In some OECD countries, the combined impact of deadweight losses, substitution, and displacement has been shown to wipe out up to 90 percent of the effects of training and subsidy programs for the unemployed. While this does not mean that PROBECAT should be terminated, it suggests that rigorous cost-benefit analysis be applied to the program.

There may be a tension between the safety net and training components of PROBECAT. One reason why PROBECAT has a limited impact on employment and wages may be that the duration of training provided is too short (typically two months) to provide skills valuable in the long term. PROBECAT may function rather as a (well-targeted) safety-net program providing temporary relief for the unemployed, with a self-targeting mechanism not unlike that of PET, since participants receive only the minimum wage. If this were the case, there would be a tension between the objectives of training and income supplementation, since the means to achieve both are not necessarily the same. It is probably better to choose one goal or the other, rather than trying to meet both goals with a single program. On the other hand, even if PROBECAT were to better serve as a training program during good times, it could still easily be transformed into a self-targeted and relatively cost-effective safety net during recessions.

VI. Investments in the Physical Capital of Poor Areas

The government's third and last group of programs for the poor deals with the social infrastructure of poor areas. The government programs reviewed in the last two sections are implemented primarily at the household level (PET is an exception in that it affects both households and communities, the latter through public works). But the standard of living of households is not determined only by household characteristics; it also depends on the characteristics of the areas in which households live.

The last group of poverty programs aims at improving the social infrastructure of poor communities. The problems confronted in rural and urban areas are different. In rural areas, there is a lack of basic social infrastructure such as schools and health centers. In urban areas, basic social services are more accessible, but migration creates settlements in which housing conditions are deplorable. In addition, due to the decentralization process, the funds for investments in the physical capital of marginalized areas are now provided by the federal entity to states, and then from states to municipalities, which are ultimately accountable for their use. A new range of issues related to decentralization emerges in the management of these programs. Taking this into account, this section analyzes the infrastructure needs of the urban and rural poor areas, and considers the decentralization process and its allocation formulas for funds.

Most of the funding for investments in poor areas is disbursed through the decentralized FAIS. FAIS, the *Fondo de Aportaciones para la Infraestructura Social*, which provides federal funding to improve the basic social infrastructure of marginalized areas. The fund covers investments in both urban and rural areas for clean water, sewerage, drainage, urbanization, electricity, basic education infrastructure, basic health infrastructure, rural roads, and rural productive infrastructure. Of a total of MXP$18.2 billion allocated to the physical capital of poor areas in 2000, MXP$14.9 billion (82 percent) will be distributed through FAIS (Figure 12). Most other programs for infrastructure in poor areas deal with water and sanitation (through CNA), and rural ways and telephony (through SCT).

Figure 12. Expenditure in Physical Capital in Poor Areas, 1998 and 1999

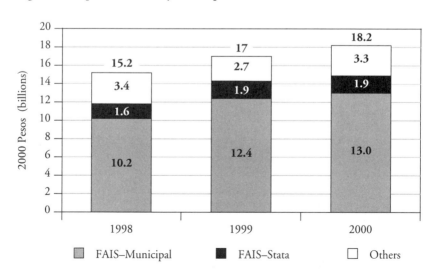

Inadequate Access to Basic Social Infrastructure

The geographic effects on well-being provide a rationale for policies for poor areas. In Mexico, there are large differences in standards of living between states, and between municipalities within states. These differences could be due to differences in the characteristics of the households living in various areas, such as education and occupation. They could also be due, however, to the characteristics of the areas themselves, such as infrastructure. More precisely, the characteristics of an area can have both direct and indirect geographic effects on the well-being of its inhabitants.

- *Direct Effects.* By direct effects, it is meant that statistically significant geographic determinants of income or consumption are observed even after controlling for a wide range of households characteristics. Differences between areas in the returns to household characteristics can also be observed. These direct geographic effects may be due to many causes, including climate, access to markets, demand for labor, and industry concentration. Neoclassical theory predicts that migration should reduce the size of these effects, but the effects can persist for a long time.
- *Indirect Effects.* Apart from direct effects, there may also be indirect geographic effects in that location may affect household endowments (such as education) and opportunities (such as occupational choice), which themselves affect standards of living. For example, the availability of schools may affect education levels, which are themselves a key household determinant of income.

According to estimates based on the INEGI surveys, there are indeed both direct and indirect geographic effects at the state level on standards of living in Mexico. For example, one can provide measures of mean per capita income by state without and with controls for a wide range of household characteristics. This yields geographic effects which are relatively stable over time and coherent with observed migration. This provides some rationale for investing in the physical capital and social infrastructure of poor areas, since area characteristics do matter for poverty reduction. This is true in both urban and rural areas.

Part of the strong geographic effects on standards of living may be due to the fact that small rural and marginalized communities lack access to a wide range of public services. Table 5 provides statistics on the lack of access to public services in a sample of marginalized rural areas from the 1997 ENCASEH. In the group made up of the smallest communities with less than 20 households, only 40 percent of the villages have electricity. Forty percent of the smallest villages still do not have a primary school. Sewerage, public phones, and post offices are virtually nonexistent. A majority of the smallest villages are served by mobile health units, but 30 percent are not. Access to services improves with the size of the community, especially for schooling, but even in the larger communities there are gaps, for example, in healthcare. All this does not mean that a post office or a clinic should be placed in villages with less

Table 5. Lack of Access to Public Services (Percent)

| | Community Size (Number of Households) | | |
	Up to 20	21 to 60	61/more
Electricity	59	40	20
Sewerage	90	87	84
Public phone	97	90	52
Post office	98	98	95
Preschool	68	28	6
Primary school	40	13	2
Telesecondary school	99	95	69
Secondary school	100	100	95
SSA clinic	98	93	76
IMSS–Solidaridad	100	98	90
Local health auxiliaries	72	47	41
Health mobile unit	30	25	25

Source: World Bank staff estimates.

than 20 households, but it points to the lack of access to basic services on the part of the rural population.

Small communities also suffer from a lack of access to government programs. The smaller the community, the smaller the likelihood of benefiting from government programs as well (Table 6). DICONSA stores, which provide basic products at low prices, are not located in the smallest villages because they are not a sufficient market. The differences in access to DIF programs are smaller than those observed for DICONSA but nevertheless there are differences. Grants from various ministries

Table 6. Lack of Access to Programs (Percent)

| | Community Size (Number of Households) | | |
	Up to 20	21 to 60	61/more
Diconsa store	97	86	52
DIF school breakfasts	46	42	38
DIF community kitchen	96	93	89
Liconsa distribution	95	92	84
Subsidized tortilla	99	99	98
Grants (depensas)	70	59	53
Niños de Solidaridad	63	50	41
PROBECAT and Cimo	99	99	98
Empleo temporal	94	90	84

Source: World Bank staff estimates.

and *Niños de Solidaridad* also have a hard time making it to the smallest communities, as is the case of PET. Thus, those communities which are likely to be the poorest remain excluded from the programs implemented by the government for the reduction of extreme poverty. It should also be noted that PROGRESA is not reaching the smallest communities because the existence of a health center and a school are requirements for program participation at the community level. This is due to the fact that the program is based on co-responsibility for the parents to send their children to school and to visit the health center regularly. It would be worth investigating how to reach these communities (Ramo 33 gives the opportunity to states and localities to build schools and health centers, and this could provide an opportunity for the extension of PROGRESA).

Access to services and programs in poor rural areas helps build human capital. The impact of government services and programs on schooling and child labor in marginalized areas has been measured using the 1997 ENCASEH. Preliminary findings indicate that DIF's school breakfasts have some impact on child labor (reduced for boys) and schooling (increased for girls) in marginalized areas, while *Niños de Solidaridad* apparently does not have as much impact. Moreover, access to telesecondary school was found to increase the probability of going to school for both boys and girls between ages 8 and 14. Many children aged 12 to 14 who have completed primary school attend telesecondary school when it is available. It may also reflect a pulling effect from telesecondary to primary as the perspective of being able to attend telesecondary makes the expected benefits of completing the primary level more attractive.

Poor living conditions in rural areas have led to migration to urban areas and to the U.S. Today, 7 million Mexicans live in the U.S. The total value of remittances from international migration was estimated by the Central Bank at US$4.2 billion in 1997. Remittances are equivalent to the total agricultural output of Mexico, 57 percent of its available foreign exchange, and 5 percent of the income from total exports. Migration, both internal and international, can be seen as part of a portfolio of activities that households engage in not only to combat poverty, but also to alleviate risk. Migrant remittances protect rural households when they are confronted with declining economic conditions and inflation. Remittances also counteract seasonal cash-flow problems for farm households. Households with good incomes may also migrate when access to credit is limited in their place of origin. In some cases, remittances are used to invest in new business ventures or farming techniques. Yet while migration may lead to an influx of funds, in the long term the question arises as to whether it increases the options of migrant families or encourages a dependent relationship with little prospect for change.

Migration is not without social costs, and it poses a difficult infrastructure challenge in cities. While migration may appear to result in the reduction of poverty when measured through a standard index, it also generates high social costs. When a father migrates, the mother and the children often stay in their village of origin. Emphasis on the potential benefits from migration in economic terms may lead to the exclusion of migration issues at the policy level. Rural–urban migration within

Mexico is large, and during 1970–90 it contributed to an increase from 10 to 55 in the number of medium-sized cities of 100,000 to 1 million inhabitants. Many of these cities have problems providing sufficient employment and infrastructure for their population. The living conditions of some urban migrants are deplorable, and the cost of providing them with access to water, sewerage, and electricity is high. These issues are worth thoroughly examining in the context of the links between rural and urban poverty.

Good Institutions and Management are Needed for Decentralization to Be Pro-poor

Traditionally, in Mexico, budgets and allocation decisions were centralized at the federal level. Until recently, decisionmaking and social spending were centralized at the federal level. Apart from local needs, it has been argued that political negotiations and client-based relationships possibly played a role in budget allocations. For example, in President Salinas' (1988–94) PRONASOL, a large government program which provided money for local infrastructure, funds were delivered directly from the central government to local Solidarity committees, bypassing state and municipal governments. The allocation of PRONASOL funds was probably not as responsive to local needs as it could have been. The program favored urban areas over rural areas despite the fact that rural areas were poorer. Even if the allocation decisions were appropriate, however, a lack of transparency cast doubt on the program's management.

Recently, large funds including FAIS have been decentralized under *Ramo 33*. Things changed in 1995 when the government announced institutional reforms aimed at decentralizing public spending (*Nuevo Federalismo*). The aims of these reforms are threefold: (a) to improve both financial and political accountability at the local, regional, and national level; (b) to encourage the participation of local actors and strengthen state–civil society interactions; and (c) to ensure that service provision improves in poor and marginal areas. In 1996, as part of this plan, 60 percent of the funds available through *Ramo 26* were distributed to states through a public formula and went into a municipal development fund (*Fondo Del Desarollo Social Municipal,* FDSM). These funds were available for work in several areas: water and drainage, urbanization, electrification, basic health infrastructure, basic education infrastructure, housing improvement, rural roadways, and productive rural infrastructure. In 1998, decentralization went further with *Ramo 33*, through which 82 percent of all decentralized funds are now transferred. *Ramo 33* incorporates funds previously available from FDSM into FAIS, but its scope has been widened to also incorporate funds previously allocated through the Ministries of Health and Education. Apart from FAIS, *Ramo 33* consists of nine other funds: *Fondo de Aportaciones para la Educación Básica y Normal* (FAEB), *Fondo de Aportaciones para los Servicios de Salud* (FASSA), *Fondo de Aportaciones para la Infraestructura Social* (FAIS), *Fondo para la Infraestructura Social Esatal* (FISE), *Fondo para la Infraestructura Social Municipal* (FISM),

Fondo de Aportaciones para el Fortalecimiento Municipal (FAFM), *Fondo de Aportaciones Múltiples* (FAM), *Fondo de Aportaciones para la Educación Tecnológica y de Adultos* (FAETA), and *Fondo de Aportaciones para la Seguridad Pública* (FASP).

Because of the speed with which decentralization took place, some management issues remain. Mexico's decentralization took place in part to ensure a more equitable and transparent distribution of federal resources. It was also motivated, however, by negotiations between political parties. Because of deadlines for adopting the federal budget, decentralization was accelerated without giving much time to states and municipalities to get ready for the exercise of their new responsibilities. Other issues have not been resolved due to the speed with which decentralization took place. While decentralization has virtues, it is not a panacea, and in particular it need not be pro-poor, nor does it necessarily improve governance.

Allocations for existing social infrastructure continue to be based on past history rather than need. The allocations for basic education (FAEB) and 80 percent of health spending (FASSA), both of which account for three fourths of *Ramo 33's* budget, are based not on need, but on past expenditures and existing costs. The rest of FASSA (20 percent) is allocated through a formula that takes into account state deficits or surpluses in healthcare, but this still does not compensate fully for the unequal distribution of services. There is thus inequity because states that are well endowed continue to receive large portions of FAEB and FASSA funds. By contrast, the six states that account for 46 percent of the illiterate receive only 33 percent of FAEB (excluding the state of Mexico and the D.F.). Alternative formulas could provide more equity in the distribution of funds. In the case of education, this could include (a) a uniform per-student formula, (b) a per-student formula adjusted to the elasticity of enrollment by state (so that more money is given to lagging states whose elasticity of enrollment to public spending is higher); or (c) a formula that would include the above plus a provision to allocate supplementary funds to target children with special needs such as rural, indigenous, or poor children. It should be mentioned, though, that apart from FAEB and FASSA, there are other programs (such as CONAFE, INI, PROGRESA, INEA, and PAC) that directly aim at improving services to the poor.

Allocations for new infrastructure (FAIS) are based on need and rely on a publicly known formula. FAIS funds new social infrastructure projects mainly at the municipal level. The allocation of FAIS funds from the federal entity to the states is based on a weighted index of well-being called the *Masa Carencial Municipal* (MCM). MCM takes into account five indicators of well-being: the household per capita income (with a weight equal to 0.462), the average level of education per household (0.125 weight), a measure of the living space (0.239 weight), a measure of the availability of drainage (0.061 weight), and a measure of access to electricity–fuel combustion (0.114 weight). MCM is calculated first at the household level, then at the municipality level, and finally at the state level. The federal entity makes the transfers to the states on the basis of the state-level aggregate MCM, then the allocation is made from the state to the municipalities along similar lines. States which do not have the necessary information to apply the FAIS formula for their allocations to municipalities may use a simpler rule based on the arithmetic mean of the shares of the economically active population earning less than two minimum wages, the adult illiterate population, the population living in houses without drainage, and the population in houses without electricity. All but six states used this simpler formula in 1998. To cushion smaller and richer states from their reduction in infrastructure funding, 1 percent of FAIS was allocated to each state equally in 1998 (for a total of 31 percent of the budget). In 1999, each state received 0.5 percent of the FAIS budget. Thereafter, only the formula will rule (Table 7).

The FAIS formula has increased infrastructure funding for the poorest states. Figure 13 give the expected allocation of FAIS funding in 2000 as a function of a simplified measure of well-being at the state level. The use of need-based formulas to distribute the funds is clearly redistributive. The six poorest states have increased their share of these transfers from 29 percent in 1988 to 49 percent in 1999. In

Table 7. Allocation Rules for the Main Social Spending Funds in Ramo 33

Fund	Objective of the Fund	Allocation Criteria
FAEB	Covers the cost of basic education in states, including personnel salaries (88 percent of total costs), running costs, and general investments (except infrastructure).	The budget is allocated by the Ministry of Education (SEP) on the basis of past investments and costs, thereby showing inertia from year to year and little adaptation to local needs.
FASSA	Covers the cost of existing infrastructure for basic healthcare in states.	80 percent of the budget is allocated by the Ministry of Health to cover the costs of the existing infrastructure. The rest (20 percent) is allocated through a formula taking into account a minimal level of health expenditures per capita, and indicators such as the mortality rate, the uninsured population, and the state's marginalization index.
FAIS	Covers basic infrastructure, including clean water, sewerage, drainage, urbanization, electricity, basic education infrastructure, basic health infrastructure, rural roads, and rural productive infrastructure.	Funds are allocated according to needs as measured by a weighted index of five indicators of standards of living (illiteracy, drainage, electricity, water, and income). For the first two years, part of the funds are split equally between states to provide a cushion for richer states.

Source: Government of Mexico.

Figure 13. FAIS Allocations in 2000

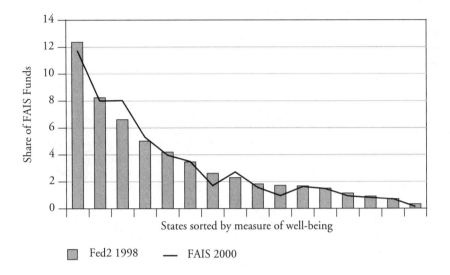

2000, with the elimination of the fixed 0.5 percent share provision, this share will further increase to 54 percent. While the FAIS formula could perhaps be improved by finding a better way to define the weights of the five indicators on the basis of their elasticities of substitution, the current formulas are probably good enough. Additional relevant household-level information (such as direct measures of access to education and health facilities) could be incorporated into the formula, but for policy purposes, the allocation between states would not be affected much because the various indicators are highly correlated with each other. What is more important is to find mechanisms to monitor the allocation of funds within municipalities.

The decision to apply similar formulas for the allocation within states is sound. The majority (90 percent) of FAIS funds are transferred to a municipal fund (FISM). The rest (10 percent of the FAIS budget) goes into a state municipal fund. This 90/10 repartition is intended to promote responsiveness to local needs and priorities. Moreover, as of 1998, the FAIS formula (or its simpler equivalent) must be used for the allocation of funds between municipalities to ensure redistribution within states and between states. The experience of 1997, during which states could allocate their funds to municipalities as they wished, shows that the imposition of federal rules for within-state allocations may be needed. In the states of Guerrero and Tlaxcala the allocations between municipalities in 1997 were almost uniform, without regard for the relative state of deprivation of the municipalities. The changes made to the law for fiscal coordination in 1999 should help ensure that FAIS resources go to poor communities.

VIII. Conclusion

The challenge ahead is to design appropriate institutional management and control mechanisms. Confusion between state and federal responsibilities for the control of the use of FAIS funds has led to problems of accountability. There have also been a number of other administrative issues that will need to be resolved. For example, originally, the calendar of distribution for the funds had been so uncertain that municipal governments had not been able to take full advantage of their new resources to start projects Moreover, while the allocation rules for the funds are clear, in principle, some municipalities still remain uninformed as to their new budget. Many of these problems have been solved, and the calendar for the distribution of funds is now officially published.

While some of these problems may be temporary, they are a warning to advocates of devolution who automatically cite its benefits. At the micro level, devolution may guarantee neither efficiency nor equity without appropriate institutions and control mechanisms. The problem is that many local governments lack the expertise and personnel to manage the FAIS funds, and resources have not yet been made available to help them increase their operating budgets, hire new staff or train existing staff, and modernize their administration. Another potential danger lies in the short-term assignments in the local political system. Municipal elections are held every three years and municipality presidents can serve for only one term, which may imperil the continuity of the municipal policy. On the other hand, while longer terms or reelection may improve stability, they can also create fiefdoms *(caciquismo)* when there is no voice from civil society. Civil society has a role to play here in ensuring that decentralization be pro-poor.

A Sustainable Future

26

Water

*This Chapter was written by Karin E. Kemper and Oscar E. Alvarado
with the contribution of John Briscoe, Jose Simas,
and Douglas C. Olson.*

Water is usually dealt with in subsectors such as irrigation, water supply and sanitation, hydropower, and navigation. It has both urban and rural dimensions, and in Mexico its characteristics vary considerably geographically, with the center-north being water scarce and the south relatively water rich. A further complexity of water is that it appears as both ground- and surface water, each requiring a different type of management.

This Chapter addresses the need for the effective and sustainable management of water, highlighting the overarching function of water resources management as it relates to the different subsectors. It also addresses subsector-specific issues in which the international community has provided assistance to Mexico in the past, and two issues—preventive drought and flood management—that have received little attention but are now growing in importance.

I. Current Situation: A Changing World

Background

Mexico's internal and external political and economic environment has undergone an amazing change in recent years. The decentralization of many aspects of decisionmaking in society, the country's entry into NAFTA, and accelerated economic growth in a number of sectors and regions have presented tremendous opportunities for development, but also challenges. What do these changes have to do with water?

In Mexico, the availability of water is inversely related to the demand for it. The country is slightly less than 2 million km² in size and the population has quadrupled from 25 million in 1950, to 100 million today. Population growth has occurred nationwide, but has been greater in the semi-arid and arid north, northwest, and central regions, which are precisely the regions with greater economic activity and where the major water shortage problems occur. Figure 1 shows the relationship between economic activity and water availability. It illustrates that northwestern, northern, and central Mexico account for 84 percent of GDP, 77 percent of the population, and 92 percent of irrigated areas. However, the same region has only 28 percent of the runoff.

During 1950–99, GDP increased from US$40 billion to slightly more than US$400 billion (constant US$ values in 1994), an increase of just over tenfold. Over the past five years, despite the severe financial crisis of 1995, Mexico's population and economy have continued to grow at annual rates exceeding 1.5 percent and 3.0 percent, respectively. These figures imply a growing demand for water for urban and industrial use in the arid and semi-arid zones.

Figure 2 gives an indication of what this means in terms of water availability for the different regions, showing that in the northwestern, northern, and central areas, total withdrawals come dangerously close to base natural availability, and that if current trends continue, a number of states, such as Aguascalientes, Baja California, Coahuila, the Federal District, Guanajuato, and Sonora will soon be facing severe water stress.

Figure 1. Economic Activity and Water Availability

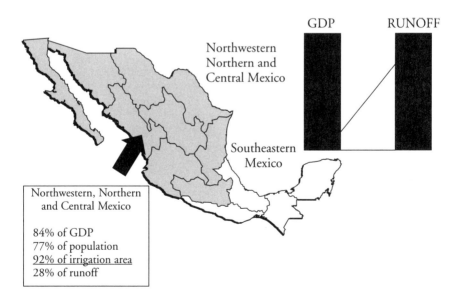

Source: CNA (1999).

Figure 2. Regional Water Availability and Withdrawals

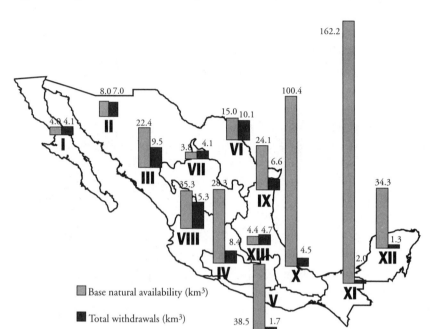

Source: CNA (1999).

Moreover, if current trends continue, they will have a negative impact on, among other things, (a) the possibility of attracting industries that are usually dependent on a secure water supply, thus hampering continued economic development; (b) the costs for supplying water to burgeoning urban populations; and (c) the financial sustainability of irrigation activities, especially in irrigation units depending on groundwater.

Groundwater is an especially challenging issue, because 100 out of Mexico's 647 aquifer systems are already being severely overexploited. These 100 aquifers where extraction exceeds recharge, stand for 50 percent of the country's groundwater supply and are—not surprisingly—also located in the semi-arid and arid northern, central, and northwestern regions. Figure 3 shows the overexploited aquifers.

Groundwater is one of Mexico's most valuable natural resources. Figure 4 shows the distribution of groundwater for different uses and illustrates the different sectors' dependence on this resource. In addition to the permanent types of uses shown, groundwater is also a strategic resource to complement waning surface water supplies in drought periods. Overexploitation and contamination of groundwater thus reduce response options towards drought.

Assuming continued population growth and a favorable climate for economic development, current water trends can be summarized as:

Figure 3. Overexploited Aquifers in Mexico and Relationship with Precipitation

☐ Límite Estatal

Acuiferos

⬜ No sobre-explotado

⬛ Sobre-explotado

Source: CNA (1998).

- Increasing water scarcity in Mexico's most-developed—and developing—regions.
- Increasing dependence on groundwater sources.
- Increasing water contamination due to agrochemical industrial activities and domestic wastewater.
- Increasing competition between sectors for sufficient water of adequate quality, at the right time.

It thus becomes clear that sustainable water resources management is of paramount importance for Mexico's continued development. The health of the water sector has a vital impact on all segments of society, including urban and rural populations, agriculture, industry, and the environment.

II. The Issues: What Are the Challenges for the Future?

The main challenges addressed in this Chapter relate to water resources management, irrigation, pollution control, water and sanitation, and flood and drought

Figure 4. Major Groundwater Uses

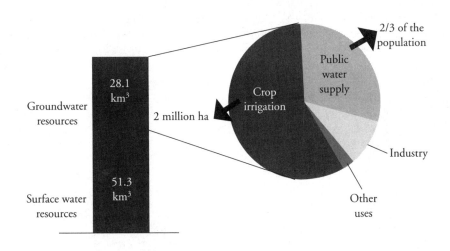

Source: CNA (1999).

management. While each part of the complex water sector has its own achievements, gaps, and challenges, there are also a number of common issues which relate to the institutional setup (decentralization, participation of stakeholders, including the private sector), and the legal and economic instruments that can be applied to improve performance (water use rights, pricing, contracts, financing, insurance).

The Good News: Results Achieved

Water Resources Management

The results of the government's efforts so far have been substantial. The overall objective has been to achieve sustainable water resources management and development at the river basin or aquifer level, with participation by major water users and other stakeholders. This objective involves, among other things, the maintenance of minimum flows and qualities in rivers and streams and the stabilization of the aquifers from both quantity and quality standpoints, while at the same time improving the efficiency and benefits of water usage. In pursuit of this long-term objective, the excellent modern National Water Law was passed in 1992 and regulations for its implementation were adopted in 1994. The National Water Commission (CNA) has been focusing its efforts on: (a) the legal registration and regularization of all water users (including dischargers); (b) developing mechanisms for approving new water rights and water right transfers; (c) establishing River Basin Councils (RBCs) and Aquifer Committees (ACs); (d) preparing master plans for river basins and aquifers; (e) improving groundwater and surface water (quantity and quality) monitoring, modeling, and assessment; (f) improving meteorological services; and (g) improving the operation of hydraulic infrastructure. Once these activities have been satisfactorily completed, the intention is to transfer more and more operational and executive responsibilities from CNA to the RBCs and ACs. Eventually, CNA's activities would focus mainly on the administration of the National Water Law and strategic planning and policymaking. Thus, the framework for overall management of water resources has been improved considerably.

Irrigation

Irrigated agriculture is crucial to both the agricultural sector as a whole and—because it consumes 80 percent of total water used—to water resources management. While over the past 20 years the value of Mexico's agricultural production has remained nearly constant, the participation of irrigated agriculture in the total value of production grew from 45 percent to 55 percent. In the early 1990s, the value of production and the physical yield per hectare of the irrigation zones were greater than those of rainfed zones (175 percent and 150 percent, respectively). Currently, irrigation production is the source of 70 percent of agricultural exports, contributing strongly to the trade balance of the agricultural sector. Irrigation is also very important to the NAFTA scenario (free of import-export barriers), and keeping its productivity and competitiveness is extremely strategic to the Mexican economy.

The economic crisis of the 1980s strongly affected irrigation infrastructure which became neglected and substandard. At the same time that the lack of funds drastically reduced the growth of areas under irrigation, the productivity of these areas was strongly affected by major reductions in maintenance. As part of an Irrigation Modernization program, the government then (a) invested in the rehabilitation of irrigation infrastructure that had been neglected; (b) created and developed (irrigation) users' organizations (WUOs); and (c) transferred to these organizations the functions of administration, operation, and maintenance. Currently, 92 percent of the surface area of irrigation districts (IDs), comprising about 55 out of the 82 IDs, has been transferred to the WUOs. Also, 70 percent of the IDs' surface area is completely transferred and sustainable (although there is still considerable need for rehabilitation and modernization); 20 percent is at an advanced stage of transfer and needs consolidation through rehabilitation, organization, and training; and 10 percent, the smallest but most problematic part, is in the process of being transferred and merits greater institutional attention and physical investments.

As a consequence of the above measures, farmer-financed investments in operation and maintenance have increased drastically, thus improving the lifetime of the infrastructure, and removing from the government the burden of continuous payments.

Water Supply and Sanitation

In the water supply and sanitation subsector, water supply service coverage continues to be high in spite of very low public investment. In the late 1980s, a promising reform process was initiated starting with decentralization of water and sanitation services to the municipalities. In accordance with the principles of integrated management of water resources, autonomous water utilities were created at the municipal level, and some at the state level to serve small localities and hence take advantage of economies of scale. Good professional capacity exists in many water and sanitation utilities, and a number of states are eager to improve management through institutional and legal change.

The Bad News: Gaps and New Challenges

Water Resources Management

Although the overall framework for water resources management has improved, a lot remains to be done. Until now, water resources development for consumptive purposes including irrigation, municipal, and industrial uses has been carried out without sufficient consideration of sustainable water resources availability and environmental needs. However, integrated water resources management at the river basin or aquifer level is necessary, with the participation of water users and other stakeholders. Because a portion of water diverted or extracted returns to the hydrologic system, water allocations and water rights transfers should be made in terms of consumptive use, and not according to diversion and extraction. Integrated water resources management should be carried out on a sound technical basis, considering appropriate consumptive use allocations. The RBCs and ACs need to play a central role in this management, including in the decisionmaking process for what investment options are most appropriate.

Following is a discussion of some of the most important areas that need to be addressed.

- Water rights, especially for groundwater, have been overallocated in several regions, which contributes to the continued overexploitation of aquifers.
- RBCs and ACs have been created, but they have not been granted legal authority. Furthermore, in the last few years, they have been created in a blanket approach all over the country, which would imply a very strong need for technical and financial assistance. Instead, however, the financing has been used to create additional councils and committees, and the already existing ones have largely been neglected. This approach has led to disillusionment on the part of water users. The strategic choice of some basins and some aquifers

would be far more effective and efficient, especially when resources are limited. Another missing ingredient in the RBC and AC approach is that independent financial resources are not provided for, again reducing incentives for stakeholders to participate, and making them perpetually dependent on CNA.

- Water fees are being applied only to industry because utilities generally do not pay, and farmers are exempt.
- The agricultural electricity subsidy *(Tarifa 09)* provides a strong disincentive to save water in irrigation, which is by far the largest water user.
- Monitoring and evaluation systems, operation of hydraulic infrastructure and aquifer management, meteorological and hydrological forecasting, and flood and drought management still need to be substantially improved. One of the major impacts on flood and drought management has been the lack of adequately trained personnel to perform these functions. Activities were planned based on an increase in trained personnel, but hiring has not taken place, thus leading to underuse of state-of-the art technologies and equipment.

In addition, water quality and pollution control need major attention and analysis. Much attention has been paid to water quantity issues without taking into account that deteriorating water quality also decreases the availability of water for different uses. It seems that data regarding water quality are considerably scarcer than for water quantity, but at the same time it is becoming obvious that both surface and groundwater sources are being increasingly polluted by both point and diffuse sources. Erosion and sedimentation due to deforestation and poor land use practices are widespread.

Especially in the case of groundwater, this type of pollution is reversible only at very high cost, if at all, and can thus pose permanent damage to human and environmental health and economic development. Thus, water quality management through monitoring and appropriate institutional and economic instruments is a very important issue and needs to be addressed not only within the sanitation and wastewater sector, but also within an integrated water resources management framework.

It is essential that water users participate in this process. This requires making available user-friendly data and providing ready access to appropriate decision support systems.

Irrigation

Of the 82 IDs, only 40 have been partially rehabilitated. The other 42 remain in a state of slow deterioration due to lack of financing. In addition, irrigation efficiency continues to be low, and distribution efficiency ranges from 24 to 34 percent, as compared, for example to 50 to 60 percent in Arizona and California. However, in Mexico, efficiency improvements are usually not carried out with proportional reductions in abstractions. Irrigation areas are consolidated and the agriculture frontier is often expanded, which results in major increases in agriculture consumptive use when compared to the existing condition. To make matters worse, water savings drastically reduce historic return flows which benefited the hydrologic system and therefore the net effect of efficiency improvements on the water resource bodies is often severely negative.

The water savings achieved through (quite costly) rehabilitation are not used for more productive uses, such as conversion from maize and grains to high-value production (as far as market demand permits), and to urban and industrial uses. The fact that this is not happening is related in part to a lack of incentives for farmers to adapt their cropping patterns to a changing market and increasing water resource scarcity, to insufficient training of farmers, and to a lack of consideration of water savings for environmental purposes, such as environmental stream flows. Given that incentives to producers and consumers are provided by price signals, the importance of *Tarifa 09*, the agricultural subsidized energy tariff, becomes clear. By subsidizing pumping costs, the government sends a signal to farmers that water (pumping) is cheap, thus encouraging wasteful use while spending an estimated annual US$300 million on these subsidies. A lump-sum subsidy for farmers to spend as they see fit could be a way to convert the energy subsidy without grave social consequences.

A major challenge is to decide what kinds of investments should be made in the irrigation subsector. An investment strategy of infrastructure rehabilitation needs to be formulated according to the type of production for which the infrastructure is rehabilitated. In addition, a closer and more technically sound relationship is needed between water use for irrigation and the sustainable availability of water resources.

It is clear that Mexican irrigated agriculture is undergoing a major change. Some 5.3 million hectares are under irrigation, about 50 percent of which are used for growing cereals, but only 10 percent for growing high-value crops such as fruits, vegetables, and oil seeds. At the same time that water scarcity is increasing, rendering water more valuable and expensive, market demand is not expected to be sufficient for all—or even the major part—of Mexico's irrigated area to be converted to high-value crops which could compete economically with the water demand from other uses.

At the same time, it is not feasible for the government to keep paying for the rehabilitation of unprofitable systems. In the past 10 years, agricultural prices have not kept pace with general food and commodity prices, leaving the poorer farmers especially, with less money for investments in better technologies. In addition, with the 15-year phaseout of tariffs and quotas on Canadian and U.S. agricultural exports, it can be expected that imports of cheap maize and wheat will increase, thus further threatening Mexican production. The competitiveness of irrigated corn and especially wheat production will be increasingly questionable in the future. In the long run the irrigated area within the IDs may be somewhat reduced to accommodate a different cropping pattern and its associated marketing potential, and to free up water for municipal and industrial, as well as environmental purposes. As stated earlier, the idea that efficiency improvements will result in much water availability for these purposes is somewhat of a misconception.

This dilemma calls for a comprehensive approach to irrigation, agriculture, and water policy that can identify (a) areas with high potential for change and market adaptability; (b) how to put in place a subsidy system without skewing water prices and the incentive to overexploit this vital resource base; and (c) how to design and implement regional comprehensive development approaches that allow farmers to make a transition from (irrigated) agriculture to other economic sectors.

The latter is of specific importance in groundwater areas, which constitute 2 million—or one-third—of the country's irrigated areas, most of which is in irrigation units (*unidades de riego*) and not irrigation districts. In these areas there are mainly poor subsistence farmers growing mostly grain for auto-consumption and local markets. It is shortsighted to continue to try to maintain these poor farmers in areas where their water usage is mining a vital national resource to grow low-value crops and maintain a marginal standard of living.

At the same time, there are significant groundwater areas where large farmers do grow high-value crops, but by depleting local aquifers for individual short-term economic gain. There are strong indications that in such areas (e.g., Hermosillo and Santo Domingo) small farmers are the first to be put out of the market when groundwater levels keep sinking and pumping becomes too expensive. In the current situation, due to the not-yet-functioning water rights system or water markets, they do not get any compensation for giving up their water rights and they cannot sell them to better-off farmers who still continue pumping. Thus, in the best case, they get jobs as day laborers in the newly created agribusinesses, but many end up going to the cities with no livelihood to speak of, increasing the ranks of the urban poor.

Mexico is slowly evolving from an agrarian society to an industrialized one and government programs should provide financial support to this transition with the objective of reaching sustainable use of resources and ensuring that the social well being of the people is preserved. In the irrigation unit areas, careful planning that considers significant reduction in irrigated areas, conversion to higher value crops, limiting water consumption to the safe yield and implementing safety valve programs to facilitate transitions from subsistence irrigated agriculture to other livelihoods are essential.

Water Supply and Sanitation

INCOMPLETE DECENTRALIZATION. While important decentralization advances have been achieved, including the creation of many local water utility companies (*Organismos Operadores,* OOs), reforms initiated in the late 1980s were incomplete, leading to an unclear and restrictive institutional framework, and ineffective decentralization. Hence results are well below development objectives. Unfortunately, most OOs in Mexico operate as municipal or state entities and not as free standing and commercially oriented public companies. For example, OOs perform only routine operation and maintenance (O&M), and billing and collection, but have little or no say in investments and long-term planning, or in undertaking investments. This framework does not provide sufficient incentives to the water user organizations to perform as commercially oriented companies. The OOs' financial statements reflect this fact, because the absence of assets depreciation, and the costs of water abstraction and pollution underestimate true operating costs and provisions for service expansions. This in turn, explains weak accountability and the poor financial performance of many utilities, which cover neither O&M costs nor depreciation, much less investments. Governance of OOs lacks continuity: the municipal president (there is a three-year political cycle) appoints OO's boards and general managers. CNA has estimated that the average duration of managers is 1.5 years. This environment has not been conducive to exercising integrated water resources policies because most OOs do not pay water abstraction fees or pollution taxes, and are unable to comply with environmental standards. In summary, most OOs are closer to a service company than to a utility. The transformation of OOs into autonomous utilities that can be audited by international standards has not met expectations.

INADEQUATE PRICING AND FINANCIAL POLICY MAKE OOs UNSUSTAINABLE. Since 1995 federal funding, which constituted the overwhelming majority of funds invested, has declined markedly due to the peso crisis and the fiscal priorities for other social sectors. In spite of innovative instruments to finance the sector with the strong leverage of federal grants (APAZU, FINFRA) and the introduction of sophisticated evaluation methodologies of investments, the sector still largely relies on direct federal transfers, with minimal contributions from subnational levels of government, utilities, and users. In addition, federal financial policy is beset with several problems including (a) transfers that usually respond more to emergencies and less to clear financial policies to stimulate reform, improve efficiency, and make investments feasible; (b) complex transfers with multiple sources, programs, and objectives; and (c) the difficulty of tracking the impact of investments because transfers do not include well-defined and monitorable indicators or selection criteria, and there is no follow-up system. Consequently, states and municipalities face weak incentives to generate new sources of revenues or to collect and operate more efficiently, since they are not linked to performance, have little control over how they spend their resources (which are tied as counterparts to federally funded projects), and the system provides ample scope for obtaining "free" resources through ad hoc and extraordinary transfers.

REGULATION REFORM AND PRIVATE SECTOR PARTICIPATION. A DISAPPOINTING STORY. Private sector participation (PSP) has been promoted since the early 1990s as a key sector to attract investments, primarily in wastewater treatment facilities. However, from the beginning, PSP took the wrong approach by emphasizing BOTs, especially for wastewater treatment plants. Given the current poor financial performance of most OOs, BOTs are difficult to finance and provide adequate guarantees thereto and do not address fundamental structural issues of the utility, like insolvency. Despite some positive results, including investment commitments totaling US$350 million, the effect of PSP has been limited and has experienced many failures, as evidenced by the fact that only 34 percent of contracts awarded are operating. Only 11 of the 50 wastewater treatment projects financed based on BOTs have reached the operating stage, and most have financial problems. This is because PSP through BOTs is not designed to address fundamental structural efficiency issues of water user organizations, and BOTs are treated more like construction contracts than like long-term service contracts. This in turn causes enormous problems in obtaining adequate guarantees from municipalities and governments. The issue of inadequacy of guarantees is related to the fact that most OOS generate revenue to barely cover basic O&M expenditures. The relative failure of PSP in Mexico has been exacerbated by a combination factors, including the absence of a clear regulatory framework for private participation, and design and procurement flaws resulting from ad hoc processes carried out by unprepared municipalities. Federal-level programs (FINFRA) to promote PSPs have fallen short of expectations because of their poor incentive structure, many bureaucratic hurdles, and limited funds.

As for water resources management, water supply systems have been developed and expanded without sufficient consideration of sustainable water resources availability, taking into account other uses and environmental needs. In addition, as previously mentioned, little attention has been paid to water quality and the integration of wastewater and pollution control policies in the context of river basin and aquifer management.

Drought and Flood Management

An aspect of water management that has traditionally been neglected by water sector professionals is the prevention of droughts and floods. While CNA is well known for its capacity to react to flood and drought emergencies, prevention of these disasters would yield far higher benefits in human, social, and economic terms. As mentioned in the Note on Disaster Management, the government has put into place the Fund for Natural Disasters (FONDEN), but so far it has addressed only the many emergencies occurring around the country, not their prevention.

Floods affect both urban–suburban and rural areas. Experience with damage levels due to floods along large rivers in Mexico suggests that floods not only cause losses in terms of material goods and a general deterioration of the quality of life, but also cause severe economic setbacks and social depression, especially among the poor.

For the urban population, the most serious impact of floods are damaged houses and the need to relocate. However, floods can cause lower income people (who are the largest proportion of urban residents affected) to lose their homes and belongings, because their homes are constructed with substandard materials. In intermediate social sectors, homes suffer major deterioration, resulting in high repair costs. Relocation conditions for the affected urban population (emergency relocation to shelters or homes of relatives and friends) create serious problems of overcrowding, promiscuity, health, and family disruption. In addition, the poor population suffers most from the disruption of labor and school activities due to flooding. In rural areas, the social strata affected are more diverse, and floods affect the productive bases of communities and have a negative impact on their capitalization and overall socioeconomic development.

The major risk of floods in Mexico exists in the riverine regions in the littoral of the Gulf, and in the southern and central parts of the Pacific Coast, where rivers flow into broad coastal flood plains. Another high risk area is located in the valleys of the Costa de Chiapas foothills, which are subject to rapid flood stages. In addition, widespread flash flooding in the major cities results in severe economic losses estimated at over US$150 million per year.

By any standard, Mexico is highly vulnerable to economic loss from flooding. Since insurance does not generally work for areas that flood more than once every 10 years, insurance is not a solution for the economic losses that might occur once in a decade. In addition, insurance is not a feasible solution for poor families because they cannot afford it and they have higher priorities for their limited resources.

Agricultural losses from floods are handled separately. Multiperil crop insurance had been available in Mexico since 1970, but was discontinued in 1990 due to poor management and corruption. Consequently, farmers—75 percent of whom are poor—absorb the losses from floods.

Some of the costs of general catastrophes are absorbed by urban and suburban disaster victims (who are predominantly poor). The primary resource for paying partial costs of catastrophes comes from the federal and state governments. However, no major preventive actions are foreseen for flood mitigation (see Chapter on Disaster Management).

In order to plan effectively for drought emergencies, it is necessary to understand the three main areas of impact. They are (a) economic (including income loss in agriculture, tourism and recreation, unemployment, capital shortfalls, and loss of tax revenues); (b) environmental (including damage to plant and animal species, wildlife habitat, and air and water quality; forest and range fires; degradation of landscape quality; loss of biodiversity; and soil erosion); and (c) social (involving public safety, health, conflicts between water users, reduced quality of life, and inequities in the distribution of impacts and disaster relief, and migration).

Mexico has a significant exposure to all four categories of droughts—meteorological, hydrological, agricultural, and socioeconomic. Among the world's developing countries, Mexico is one of the top 15 in drought risk as a percentage of GDP (over 0.5 percent). In Latin America, in terms of population affected, Mexico is the country second-most-exposed to droughts, following Brazil. Like the southeastern and southwestern United States, Mexico has a natural exposure to droughts. Drought exposure is related to climatic conditions and other natural resources endowments, but can be aggravated by other factors such as socio-economic conditions, economic development, land use, population growth, education, and poverty. The 11 most affected states are Baja California Sur, Chihuahua, Coahuila, Durango, Jalisco, Nuevo León, San Luis Potosi, Sinaloa, Sonora, Tamaulipas, and Zacatecas. Between 1980 and 1999, Mexico suffered 12 bouts with drought for a cost to the federal government of US$1 billion. The total impact of drought, which would include indirect effects and damage, would probably be 2.5 to 3 times this amount.

Although improvements were introduced in 1997, there is no comprehensive strategy, coherent policy, or coordinated action to deal with frequent drought disasters. The traditional strategy has been to provide emergency relief, and then to rechannel funds from the sectorial budgets (mostly from CNA and SAGAR) to provide minor local relief assistance to the poor. This is done through the creation of temporary, low-income jobs for rural workers, and the distribution of basic food kits. In addition, Mexico has established the FONDEN as a way to act in emergencies with less disruption to the normal budget.

III. Future Development: Policy Options and Recommendations

Although Mexico is an international example of best practices in irrigation reform (with regard to irrigation system transfer) and, to a certain extent, improved water management for water-stressed developing countries, the overall water situation in the country is critical, and there is still a lot to be done on its water policy agenda. Some core policy directions are suggested below.

Water Resources Management

The next administration will need to deepen the decentralization and regionalization process and strengthen the River Basin Councils (RBCs) and Aquifer Committees (ACs). The regional offices of CNA will need to be strengthened to provide the necessary technical backstopping to the RBCs and ACs in areas including monitoring, assessment and planning, as well as play a key role in water rights administration. This will involve (a) organizational, administrative, and procedural aspects; (b) technical aspects; and (c) financing.

Organizational, Administrative, and Procedural Aspects

These aspects address the institutionalization of RBCs and ACs so that the various water users and stakeholders develop a profound understanding of the limitations and potential for water use, development, and management. Functioning RBCs and ACs which give all stakeholders a voice and which work in partnership with the government, will also provide incentives for water users to preserve their resource base and, at times, make hard decisions.

It needs to be mentioned here that the ACs and RBCs are part of a common context, just as ground and surface water sources are connected, with many areas in Mexico practicing conjunctive use. At the same time, it needs to be recognized that stakeholders, including water users, have the most interest in managing the resource they are principally dependent on. Thus, even if, for example, an aquifer is part of a river basin, those users in the Council who live in an area far from the groundwater sources will pay little attention to factors such as management needs, development of aquifer management plans, and enforcing local water rights. In that sense, the ACs, as representatives of the local groundwater users, are the ones directly in charge of aquifer management, with representation in the pertinent Riverbasin Council for the management of the basin as a hydrological unit.

Technical Aspects

Water resources planning, water allocation, and water rights transfers need to be carried out in a technically sound way, with participation by water users and other stakeholders, and need to be in terms of consumptive use and not diversion and extraction. The technical underpinning for this dialogue is being created through CNA's monitoring of modeling and assessments, planning studies, activities related to the improvement of the operation of hydraulic infrastructure, and drought and flood management, and CNA's regional offices will need to play an important role in these activities during the next administration. Additionally, the water user identification, registry, and communication links being developed are expected to support wide dissemination. According to the plans, the technical dialogue will involve detailed programs of communication, education, feedback, and conflict resolution. The objective of this dialogue will be to reach consensus with the water users and stakeholders on (a) reduction in abstractions and discharges and their related water rights if necessary; (b) measurement and pricing; (c) monitoring and enforcement of agreed water rights (abstractions and discharges); and (d) investment needs (irrigation, water supply, treatment, flood control, etc.). Obviously, these goals can be achieved only if sufficient funds are allocated. This has been neglected in recent years.

The urgently required consensus (especially in overdrafted groundwater areas and overallocated rivers) will be reached only if the technical base is made available to the users through user-friendly decisionmaking support systems and a process that will not only consult about, but decentralize decisionmaking and management powers. In addition, priority basins and aquifers need to be tackled first to use scarce human and financial resources effectively and efficiently.

Financing

An important aspect of strengthening the RBCs and ACs will be securing financing for implementing the river basin and aquifer action plans on which consensus has been reached. While a considerable share of financial resources will need to come from external resources, a key element in the success of the RBCs and ACs will be establishing mechanisms for their self-financing. The government has a system of charging water fees for the use of the nation's water resources. This system is skewed and not conducive to good water management in that industrial users pay the lion's share of the fees, many municipal users fail to pay the much lower fees they are charged, and the agricultural users are exempt. Fees are paid into the federal treasury and there is an insufficient relationship between the fees collected and the water resources management and development activities of the government. One option would be to make the fees more uniform and to eventually collect them directly within the river basins or aquifer areas, with at least part of the resources used for water resources management and development activities in the same areas.

A potential conflict with this strategy is the decentralization goal of the government, which will transfer financial resource collection and application responsibilities to the states. In general the river basins and many of the aquifers cross state borders. Thus, the RBCs and ACs will need to play a principal role in defining the investments and use of the water fees. The states and municipalities could implement actions and invest resources on activities approved by the RBCs and ACs. The states are important members of the RBCs and ACs and can therefore be involved and reach consensus on financial resources allocations. However, the states may be reluctant to turn over these resources to the councils and committees once they have taken over these fiduciary responsibilities. This reluctance could be used as a window of opportunity to develop a truly river basin-based approach, provide the RBCs and ACs with legal authority, and let them take direct responsibility for resource allocations. This would certainly increase the incentives to implement and accept tariff schemes for more efficient use of the water resources.

Irrigation

Further investment in the irrigation subsector would ideally follow from the government's integrated approach to water resources management. Irrigation investments and projects should be designed within the overall water resources management context of the RBCs and ACs. Water user organizations in irrigation districts, modules, and units thus would have to be organized to have a key role in the RBCs and ACs.

Overall, there are two sets of complimentary and necessary policies, both involving institutional and structural components: (a) irrigation and water resources management policies (under the current government structure more linked to CNA and IMTA); and (b) agricultural policies and actions (linked to SAGAR and INIFAP).

Irrigation policy options linked to *water resources management* should include:

(i)   Decentralization of water management decisionmaking to levels closer to the water sources, uses and users, such as the regions, river basins, and aquifers.

(ii)   Creation of conditions for intersectorial reallocation of scarce water resources in terms of use, and recognition of the environment as a legitimate stakeholder.

(iii) Avoidance of public investments in "unbalanced" groundwater-fed areas and aquifers that are not linked to a relevant aquifer stabilization program

(iv)   Making the irrigation sector self-sustainable, and less reliant on public funds through the completion and consolidation of the transfer on a sustainable basis (this would imply the actual transfer of legal titles, which has been substantially delayed).

(v)   Making the irrigation sector more efficient and competitive through modernization of its management and key infrastructure; and improvement of irrigation technology, practices and institutional arrangements.

(vi) Strengthening the role of irrigation water user organizations' in RBCs and ACs.

(vii) Improving the empowerment of the WUOs through the selection of the priorities and cost sharing of investments related to modernization.

(viii) Prioritizing investments in improvements and modernization rather than expansion of new "green areas."

In the case of the *agricultural policies and actions* related to irrigated agriculture, the main actions to be contemplated are the improvement or provision of:

(i)   Analysis of the irrigated and nonirrigated agriculture sector as a whole, in light of the changes induced by NAFTA.

(ii) Identification of irrigated areas with high potential for change and adaptability to markets.

(iii) Development of integrated regional development approaches in regions where increasing groundwater scarcity or groundwater conservation programs can be expected to force poor farmers out of the market.

(iv) Review of subsidies that currently create perverse incentives for water use, especially the energy subsidy for groundwater pumping in the agricultural sector.

(v)   Adaptive research related to on-farm irrigation management best practices.

(vi) Mechanisms for technology transfer to smaller and worse-off farmers.

(vii) Agricultural research to improve or reconvert irrigated crops.

(viii) Marketing development for internal markets.

(ix) Marketing information and development for NAFTA and other external markets.

Water Supply and Sanitation

Estimates prepared by the World Bank, based on regional experience, indicate that in order to keep and increase water and sanitation coverage at reasonable service levels, Mexico will need to invest over US$1 billion per year over the next 10 years. This figure represents more than three times the reported amount invested in 1998. With federal funds for the sector declining, sector financing should come from tariffs, the private sector, and from public funds allocated to states and municipalities. This will require an increase in tariffs and big efficiency gains, along with renewed financing mechanisms and a much greater role of PSP.

Time is of the essence for the adoption of sector reforms in Mexico. Four policy recommendations are discussed below. They are interrelated and should be applied as part of an integrated plan to gain cohesive improvement in the sector. The suggested policy options aim at achieving an autonomous, financially self-sustained sector, with adequate and credible regulation and proper technical assistance. This vision will not become a reality overnight because of the obstacles to reform that exist, most notably in regard to tariff increases and, to a lesser extent, PSP. Thus, to have a long-lasting impact, the suggested policy recommendations need to become elements of a national Sector Consolidation Program managed at the federal level.

COMPLETE DECENTRALIZATION AND CREATING AUTONOMOUS UTILITIES. Autonomous utilities, with full responsibility for service provision, are key to sector performance. This matter should receive full support because it represents the policy with probably the most impact. The policy options considered are:

- Create or transform existing OOs into truly autonomous utilities. This would imply autonomous boards, which would elect their managers for periods independent of the municipal or state political cycle. The OOs would be fully responsible for true costs, including asset management and depreciation. Municipalities or states would make contractual arrangements with the utilities, related to performance. Municipalities would sign long-term "concession contracts" with the OOs delegating the system assets for the duration of the contract.
- Different institutional modalities would take place according to the specifics of each case, especially size of the operation. For example, large cities (>50,000 connections) should rely mostly on private operators with full responsibility for service provision, including investments; medium-size cities (5,000–50,000) could also expect PSP, perhaps with limited investment requirements in some cases. Public utilities should be designed autonomously and emulate private practices in governance structures, staffing, and budgeting, with full accountability. Various small towns could attract private operators (this is already happening in several LAC countries), and rural areas should rely mostly on community associations.
- Reduce transaction costs of PSP with model guidelines and standardized documentation, and more generally provide information that is currently lacking to policymakers and regulators.

ESTABLISH A CREDIBLE REGULATORY ENVIRONMENT TO REDUCE UNCERTAINTY. Credible and effective regulation needs to be established at the federal and state levels. In addition, it is necessary to establish an organization responsible for the water and sanitation sector in Mexico. The recommended policy options are:

- Reorient and strengthen general regulatory capacity at the federal level. General regulatory rules that require common application, such as general norms and standards, basic tariff structures, water quality and environmental standards, and PSP-related issues (concession terms and awards) might militate for specific federal-level regulations. General planning policy design would also reside at the federal level. This would promote better integration with water resource management in the areas of planning, financing, and supervision.

- Create credible and operative regulation at the state level. The state level would complement the general regulation and provide active and more detailed regulation, (for example, tariff regulations), and with some level of control. In addition, the states, prior to delegation from the municipalities, could supervise some of the service contracts with private operators. States could also establish technical assistance programs to support localities in delegating the services, and then supervising the corresponding contracts. In many cases, municipalities will directly supervise the water and sanitation contracts and promote informal benchmarking.

- Transform and concentrate existing water and sanitation areas within CNA into a water and sanitation leader area responsible for policies, norms, regulatory guidelines, knowledge and information management, training coordination, rural areas, and a technical assistance program. The area would also coordinate investment programs and sector-related agencies, but construction of systems would be decentralized to the state and local levels.

FIX THE FINANCES: ADJUST THE FINANCIAL POLICIES AND HARMONIZE PROGRAMS. Mexico needs a consistent and well-targeted financial policy for the sector. Key elements recommended are:

- Reorient federal financial assistance to provide incentives to local authorities to implement comprehensive reforms needed to improve service quality and sustainability. Federal and state financing should be made a powerful tool to better target federal financial assistance to the sector, and to push reform. For example, lending to municipalities should be tied to the municipal delegation and establishment of autonomous utilities. Significant amounts in federal grants should be made available to reforming states and localities on a transitional basis as tariffs are brought up and unit costs are brought down to levels sufficient to cover revenue requirements.

- Loans and subsidies should (a) help achieve financial viability, and (b) assist in covering externalities, including poverty and environment. Financing should focus on investments with large externalities, such as wastewater treatment, and target urban poverty and rural areas.

- Streamline lending and ensure that a fully consistent policy is applied.

- Develop financial services to private investors and operators to enhance PSP. In particular, a revitalized FINFRA, expecting commercial returns and with an active role in investments, could provide rollover bridge financing, subsovereign guarantees, and regulatory risk coverage.

- Adjust these types of financing instruments: lending to the public entities, and private guarantees available to operators, and grants. Improved financing instruments and programs need to be put in place, because it is not realistic to the assume private sector will mobilize all funds required.

- Devise a financing strategy for wastewater treatment that explicitly recognizes the partial public goods nature of this service and which balances the principle that the polluter pays with affordability and willingness to pay.
- Most important, fix the tariffs at adequate levels. The tariff system must be geared toward self-sustainability, and collection should cover depreciation.

Actively promote private sector participation. PSP should be promoted with renewed effort. To materialize, a more fertile environment needs to exist, along with a clearly defined technical assistance program. Making PSP a condition for receiving federal funds is one way to motivate participation.

- Create a federal incentives program using PSP as a tool to improve efficiency and sustainability of service.
- Technical assistance support is needed for drafting legislation, regulations, policy, and bid/contract design at the state and local levels.
- Stimulate local private providers with financial and technical assistance instruments.

Drought and Flood Management

The main issues related to drought and flood management are:

- The need for a change in perspective; away from emergency intervention toward prevention.
- A combination of structural and nonstructural investments, which implies a multisectoral approach spanning reforestation, watershed management, microzoning, and insurance, for flood management; and early alert systems, water demand management, crop insurance and adequate infrastructure for drought management.

To be effective, drought and flood management should be embedded within the overall management at the RBC and AC level. In addition, drought and flood management needs to focus on reaching a consensus with water users and other stakeholders on special water management arrangements during times of flood and droughts, then defining and implementing the necessary procedures and actions.

Institutions and Organizations: The Role of CNA

It is clear that the number of actions required, the linkages between the subsectors, and the dimensions of the needs of a growing population and economy are enormous. Meeting these demands will be possible only if incentives are provided for all stakeholders, including the different government agencies, water users, the private sector, and civil society, to participate in the management of their resources and in the provision of services.

At the same time it must be recognized that Mexico is one of the few countries with an explicit approach to integrated water resources management, as clearly demonstrated in the National Water Law. As yet, however, too little of this state-of-the-art framework has been implemented.

This implies the need to strengthen the administrative, regulatory, and strategy-setting functions at the central level, and decentralizing where possible, to take decisionmaking and enforcement more closely to those who will be affected by it. The track record of CNA, the institution hitherto in charge of promoting this change, has been mixed. While on the one hand RBCs and ACs have been created and some PSP in water supply and sanitation has taken place, the follow-up—for example, in terms of technical assistance to the OOs, RBCs and ACs—has been weak, and the sustainability of these institutional innovations is, therefore, questionable. In the case of the RBCs and ACs, for example, the blanket approach of creating scores of new entities in just a few years has been impossible to sustain, either institutionally, financially, or with regard to technical assistance. At the same time, the challenges in the water sector are so large that they cannot be met through the current structures.

In water and sanitation, an option would be for CNA to establish a specialized entity within the institution, with responsibility for leading the subsector in defining the regulatory framework, policy norms, information systems, training, and provision of technical assistance. While not itself being responsible for construction, this entity would coordinate investment programs for rural and urban areas and take a lead in coordination with other relevant agencies.

With regard to water resources management, CNA should accelerate its pace toward decentralization of administrative functions and regionalization of water resources management functions which can be carried out at lower levels, and just as in water and sanitation, focus on policy norms, the regulatory framework, information systems, and training, technical assistance and technical backstopping needs. This would also include communication and collaboration with other government entities such as SEMARNAP, SAGAR, and CFE, which is sorely needed, but as yet has hardly taken place.

Opening up to communication and collaboration with others would also need to include making data available to more actors, both at the national level (through the Internet, for example) and at the local level, where stakeholders need to take water management decisions. When trying to institute integrated water resources management, in addition to promoting regionalization, it is essential that the responsible agency also integrate its function to achieve better coherence in policy formulation and implementation.

Overall, devolving CNA's construction function to other government entities should be seriously considered so as not to interfere with policy, regulatory, and administrative tasks. Such a change could turn CNA into an effective sector agency responsible for development of the various subsectors. This would be in full accordance with the government's decentralization policies.

IV. Summary

Table 1 (next page) summarizes the institutional issues discussed for each subsector and issue, some of the legal and economic instruments recommended to improve performance, and the expected impact. The table is not exhaustive, but highlights the connections between the different subsectors and how the different pieces discussed in this Chapter fit together.

Table 1. Summary of Issues

Subsector/Issue	Institutional Issues	Legal and Economic Instruments	Expect Impact
Water Resources Management	• Complete decentralization to RBCs and ACs • Focus on priority basins and aquifers for effective improvements in water management • Grant financial autonomy and increased decisionmaking • Carry out technically sound integrated water resources management by making data widely available to stakeholders and creating an effective decisionmaking process	• Provide legal personality to RBCs and ACs • Introduce and enforce water resource fees (*derechos de agua*) for all users, not only industries • Finalize allocation of water use rights and facilitate water right trading	• Increased accountability and responsibility of water users • Improved decisionmaking about WRM and investments at the basin and aquifer level • Improved resource base, more productive use of water, avoidance of socially disruptive competition
Irrigation	• Complete transfer of Irrigation Districts to water user organizations • Better integrate IUs and IDs into RBCs and ACs, and define investment options in terms of water resources availability considering consumptive use and water quality • Integrate irrigation investments with access to agricultural product markets, especially in light of NAFTA	• Formalize recognition of Irrigation Districts as independent entities through titling • Increase participation in decisionmaking • Allocate funds to irrigation activities through RBCs and ACs • Cost-sharing arrangements • Increase financial autonomy through trust funds (*fideicomisos*)	• Give further incentives for WUOs to take on responsibilities for their systems, better selection of investment options, and incremental benefits, especially with regard to rehabilitation and modernization

Table 1. (Continued)

Subsector/Issue	Institutional Issues	Legal and Economic Instruments	Expect Impact
Water Supply and Sanitation	• Grant autonomy to OOs regarding contract; with municipalities • Increase private sector participation in large and medium towns • Improve regulatory function, with guidelines at federal level and operational at state level • Establish a water and sanitation area responsible for policy, norms, technical assistance, information. Exclude construction • Better integrate decisionmaking into RBCs and ACs, and define investment options in terms of water resources availability considering consumptive use and water quality	• Introduce cost-based pricing • Reorient financial policy to complement cash generation efforts of OOs and focus on environment, rural areas, and poverty. • Streamline lending • Improve financial services to operators and private investors • Enforce pricing • Integrate OOs into water rights system • Improve concession, BOT, etc. contracting	• Attract private-sector funds for Water and Sanitation services • Move toward sustainability of sector operations • Improve service to the population, especially the poor and rural areas
Flood Management	• Integrate flood management into the water sector as a *preventive* activity; • Work with other sectors e.g., watershed management, reforestation, soil management	• Explore options for insurance	• Create a culture of flood prevention • Reduce damaging impacts of floods, especially on the poor • Shift costs of flood damage from government to the private sector

Table 1. (Continued)

Subsector/Issue	Institutional Issues	Legal and Economic Instruments	Expect Impact
Drought Management	• Integrate drought management into the water sector as a *preventive* activity; • Work with other sectors building up early-alert systems, build up an incentive system for water savings and flexibility in water allocation during drought periods; build up drought resistant dryland agriculture outside of irrigation systems	• Explore options for insurance • Water pricing for demand management, especially for users of surface systems • Flexible temporary water use right reallocation, for example, through a Water Bank	• Create a culture of drought damage prevention

27

Biodiversity

*This Chapter was written by Raffaello Cervigni
with the valuable input of Adolfo Brizzi.*

Summary

Significant progress has been made in the last decade in promoting the conservation and sustainable use of Mexico's rich and endangered biodiversity, and in reversing a long-lasting trend of habitat loss and unsustainable exploitation of species.

Achievements in the areas of institutions, legislation, strategy, knowledge, and funding, although remarkable, remain inadequate to ensure long-term sustainability of biodiversity management, given mounting pressures to use biological resources as an outlet to unmet development needs, or as an avenue for tapping into market opportunities from trade in biological resources.

There are three key challenges for Mexico's biodiversity policy: (a) consolidating the protected areas system as the fundamental cornerstone of the conservation strategy; (b) reallocating existing development funds to activities consistent with the conservation and sustainable use of biodiversity; and (c) is turning existing or potential social benefits of biodiversity into tangible monetary values. Resources from domestic and foreign donors could be used in a selective and strategic manner to address the first challenge, but also, and perhaps more importantly, to facilitate progress (and ultimately self-sustainability) in the other two areas.

A diversified approach is therefore proposed to promote biodiversity mainstreaming, both in the social development and poverty alleviation agenda, and in the growth and market development agenda. To be effective, such an approach will need (a) convincing evidence on the need for change; (b) environmentally sensitive constituencies; (c) social and political leadership to broker agreements; and (d) human and institutional capacity to design and implement market creation and institutional reforms.

I. Current Developments

Facts and Figures

Estimates suggest that Mexico harbors more than 10 percent of the biological diversity of the planet,[1] making it one of the 12 megadiverse countries in the world. Together with Brazil, Colombia, and Indonesia, Mexico figures prominently in species richness.[2]

Because of its location at the transition zone between the neartic and the neotropical regions of the American continent, and because of the particular way prehistoric changes in global climate affected it, Mexico is the country with the highest ecological diversity in Latin America, featuring all of the five ecosystem types of the region, 9 of the 11 habitat types, and 51 of the total 151 ecoregions.[3] Recent technical reports indicate that Mexico is a key center of origin of agricultural crops.[4]

Detailed information on the conservation status of Mexico's biodiversity is available with varying degrees of geographical disaggregation and with different perio-

Table 1. Vegetation Types

Type of Vegetation Cover	Area (Hectares)	Percent of Vegetation	Percent of Total Territory
Temperate forest	30,433,893	21.5	15.8
Tropical forest	26,440,061	18.7	13.7
Arid zones vegetation	58,472,398	41.3	30.4
Hidrófile and halófile vegetation	4,163,343	2.9	2.2
Degraded areas	22,235,474	15.7	11.6
Total	141,745,169	100.0	73.7

Source: "Inventario Nacional Forestal Periódico, Memoria Nacional," (SARH 1994).

1. Toledo, V. M., and M. J. Ordóñez. 1993. "The Biodiversity Scenario of Mexico: A Review of Terrestrial Habitats." In: T. P. Ramamoorthy, R. Bye, A. Lot, and J. Fa, (eds.), *Biological Diversity of Mexico: Origins and Distribution.* Oxford University Press: New York.
2. Mittermeier, R., and C. Goettsch. 1992. "*La importancia de la biodiversidad en México.*" In: J. Sarukhán and R. Dirzo (comps.), *México ante los retos de la biodiversidad.* Comisión Nacional para el Conocimiento y Uso de la Biodiversidad. Mexico City, Mexico.
3. CONABIO. 1998. *La diversidad biológica de México: Estudio de País, 1998.* Comisión Nacional para el Conocimiento y Uso de la Biodiversidad. Mexico City, Mexico; and Dinerstein, E., D. M. Olson, D. J. Graham, A. L. Webster, S. A. Primm, M. P. Bookbinder and G. Ledec. 1995. "Conservation Assessment of the Terrestrial Ecoregions of Latin America and the Caribbean." World Bank/World Wildlife Fund. Washington, D.C.
4. Ramamoorthy, T. P., R. Bye, A. Lot, and J. Fa. 1993. *Biological Diversity of Mexico: Origins and Distribution.* New York: Oxford University Press.

dicity. The most comprehensive survey of vegetation cover is the forest inventory, undertaken by the government in 1994 (SARH 1994).[5] According to the inventory, some 70 percent of Mexico's territory is under some form of vegetation cover (including temperate and tropical forests, arid zone vegetation, aquatic vegetation, and degraded areas). Tropical forests (*selvas*) account for about 10 percent, and other forests and woodlands cover 14 percent of the national territory. The distribution of forested land is fairly uneven: the states of Chihuahua and Durango host about 40 percent of temperate forests, while 44 percent of tropical forests are concentrated primarily in the southern states of Campeche, Chiapas, Oaxaca, and Quintana Roo.

In addition to forests, other ecosystems and wilderness areas play a major role as havens of Mexico's biodiversity. Among aquatic ecosystems, wetlands are of particular significance: Mexico's 32 priority wetlands cover some 3 million hectares, with 6 of the wetlands declared of global importance under the Ramsar convention. Lagoons and estuary ecosystems cover wide areas of the coasts of several states such as Baja California Sur, Campeche, Sinaloa, and Tamaulipas (accounting for some 12 to 15 percent of the total coastline of these states). Important coral reefs exist in the Caribbean and Gulf regions on the Atlantic Coast, and in Baja California Sur on the Pacific side.

Mexico is also very rich in species diversity, with 24,000 species of flora and fauna identified, excluding invertebrates and nonvascular plants. Mexico ranks first in the world for diversity of reptile species, second in mammal diversity, and fourth in amphibian and plant diversity.

Value of Biodiversity

Assessing the economic value of biodiversity is important, and challenging in terms of both methodology and availability of data. To begin with, the object of valuation is itself difficult to define, given the multi-dimensional nature of biodiversity (commonly defined at the ecosystem, species, and genetic levels), and the lack of scientific agreement on which resource management options (apart from strict conservation) are compatible with biodiversity protection. In terms of data, while remarkable achievements have been made by the government (notably CONABIO), and by the academic and NGO sectors on the ecological and biological sides, socioeconomic information on the market and especially nonmarket benefits of biodiversity is still scant.

Several studies exist, which estimate various types of value of Mexico's natural resources; few of them (if any), however, focus solely on biodiversity or cover the entire country. In many cases values are estimated for selected ecosystems or resource types in specific locations or regions of the country. The forest sector, for example, has been studied on repeated occasions in the attempt to quantify the full range of

---

5. Periodic updates of the inventory are envisioned, with the first one being undertaken during 2000 for publication of the results in 2001.

values (including biodiversity) it generates. Broad countrywide estimates of the total economic value of Mexican forest nontimber benefits (including tourism, carbon sequestration, watershed protection, and option and existence values) point to lower bound estimates[6] of some US$80 per hectare per year (with about 80 percent of the value associated with carbon sequestration). These estimates do not include values of nontimber forest products; trade in medicinal and ornamental plants could be worth some US$1.5 billion per year (World Bank 1995). While there is considerable site- or situation-specific evidence on the importance of biodiversity for the traditional sector (food, shelter, fuel) and the modern sector (nature tourism, for example), generation of more systematic information on the economic value of biodiversity is a top priority to better assist decisionmaking processes and policy formulation in relevant sectors.

Pressures on Biodiversity

Over the last few decades a significant part of Mexico's biological wealth has been lost or put under growing strain. Between 1940 and 1990, the area under agriculture use increased from 5.9 million hectares to 18 million hectares: rainfed agriculture accounts for some 75 percent of cultivated land, with irrigation concentrated in the remaining 25 percent. Areas under pasture increased from 50 million hectares in 1950 to 130 million hectares in 1990 (or about two-thirds of the national territory) (CONABIO 1998).

Estimates of deforestation vary widely; annual estimates, for example, range from 0.3 hectares to 1 million hectares. FAO estimates that between 1980 and 1990 some 7 million hectares of forest were lost, while World Bank and IFPRI analysis, based on revised forest inventory data, suggest that 19 million hectares were lost.[7] Despite these variations in estimates, there is little controversy over the huge ecological impact of deforestation. According to CONABIO (1998), Mexico has lost about 95 percent of its humid tropical forests, more than 50 percent of its temperate forests, and around half of the original vegetation cover in arid zones. Several states in the humid tropic, such as Tabasco and Veracruz, have lost the vast majority of their primary forest, due primarily to conversion to pasture. Conversion to agriculture has been playing a complementary but no less important role; primarily through expansion of subsistence-oriented slash-and-burn systems in rainfed areas, and to a lesser degree, though growth of commercial, mechanized agriculture in irrigated areas.

In addition to threats to ecosystems, pressure on species is also quite high. There are over 130 species at risk of extinction, 336 are threatened, 433 are rare, and 49 are earmarked for special protection. Main sources of pressure on species include

---

6. Adger, Brown, Cervigni, and Moran. 1995. "Total Economic Value of forests in Mexico." *Ambio*, 24(5) :286–96.

7. Deininger, K., and B. Minten. 1997. "Poverty, Policies and Deforestation: The Case of Mexico," World Bank, IFPRI, Washington D.C.

illegal hunting for commercial, subsistence, and recreational purposes, and live capture for commercial use, both domestically and abroad.

Institutional and Policy Responses

Significant progress has been made in recent years on the institutional and policy front to address the challenges of biodiversity conservation and sustainable use. The creation of the National Commission for Biodiversity Knowledge and Use (CONABIO) in 1992 and SEMARNAP in 1995 have considerably strengthened the ability of Mexico to consolidate its biodiversity knowledge base and develop a wide range of policies and instruments to tackle the different dimensions of the biodiversity problem.

Several Mexican laws have relevance for biodiversity, and new laws include provisions on conservation and sustainable use. These include Article 27 of the Constitution, the General Law for Ecological Balance, the Forestry Law, the Federal Fishing Law, and the Federal Hunting Law.

The government's main analysis of and strategy on biodiversity include its Biodiversity Country Study, its Biodiversity Country Strategy, and SEMARNAP programs. Mexico's Biodiversity Country Study, *La Diversidad Biológica de México: Estudio de País,* identifies two overarching issues: (a) the loss of biodiversity, and the lack of systematized, reliable, readily available information about biodiversity; and (b) threats at four levels: global, ecosystem, species, and genetic.

Under the guidance of the Convention on Biological Diversity, Mexico (the government), academia, civil society organizations, the private sector, and other stakeholders) has been developing a Strategy for the Conservation, Use of, and Equitable Distribution of Benefits from Biodiversity. The Strategy, to have been finalized by May 2000, identifies four priority areas for action: (a) protection of biodiversity-rich ecosystems; (b) sustainable use of Mexico's biological resources; (c) expansion of the country's knowledge base related to its biodiversity; and (d) promotion of green market and valuation of biological resources. Rainforest, dry forest, and marine and coastal ecosystems are among the ecosystems identified as priorities for a federal protection status approach and for a major mainstreaming of biodiversity considerations in economic and public investment programs.

Since its creation in 1995, SEMARNAP has developed an array of sectoral and subsectoral programs directly or indirectly supporting the conservation and sustainable use of biodiversity. In addition to the overall Environmental Program 1995–2000, these include the Program for Natural Protected Areas 1995–2000, several forest-related initiatives under the Forestry and Soils Program 1995–2000 (forest development, forest frontier, forest fires, reforestation, plantations), the Program for Wildlife Management, Regional Sustainable Development (PRODERs), and initiatives for the protection of coastal and marine ecosystems.

The National System of Protected Natural Areas (SINAP) is a key element of Mexico's strategy for conservation of biological diversity. There are currently 117 protected areas, totaling 12.9 million hectares (9.8 million terrestrial, 3.1 million marine). After decades of weak or nonexistent enforcement of protection, notable progress has been made in recent times, in areas such as staffing, budget allocations, and the number and coverage of areas under active protection. In particular, the current fiscal budget for UCANP (INE's unit in charge of protected areas) of US$5 million per year represents more than a tenfold increase over the budget in 1994. Important advancements have also been made in terms of design and implementation of policy. In 1996 the broadly representative National Council for Protected Areas (CONANP) was established as the rational advisory body relative to protected area policy.

Despite these accomplishments, many challenges remain. The majority of land in the system is in the hands of private or communal owners rather than government—only 5 percent of the land is actually government owned. This means that a great deal of effort has been made and still needs to be made in terms of reorienting owners' land management toward sustainable practices. In many cases local residents have few options for subsistence other than reliance on the resources of the protected areas, and demographic and economic factors are increasing the pressures and tendencies toward unsustainable levels of use. Development projects in other sectors (roads, urban, and industrial development, etc.) sometimes proceed without sufficient attention to their impact on protected areas and their resources.

The Wildlife Management Program establishes the System of Units for the Conservation, Management and Sustainable Use of Wildlife (UMAs). The UMAs system purports to provide a regulatory framework for the commercial use of wildlife, reconciling socioeconomic development through wildlife use with biodiversity protection. The program issues permits to individuals or communities to harvest wild species subject to the preparation of a management plan, arrangements for habitat monitoring, controls on the use of wildlife, and certification of wildlife products. As of end of 1999, a total of 44 UMAs were registered, concentrated in the states of Baja California, Baja California Sur, and Sonora. Total area under certification was 2.8 million hectares, far below SEMARNAP's current targets for the program (see Table 2 for details).

The program for regional sustainable development (PRODERs) promotes an integral approach to natural resources management and social development in 25 regions throughout the country that are rich in biodiversity but have high levels of poverty and social exclusion. The program supports participatory, multidisciplinary diagnostic studies of each region's environmental and socioeconomic problems, and the establishment of multi-actor forums (regional councils) to generate consensus on strategies to address the problems identified. A particularly innovative aspect of the program is its integration in a broader effort undertaken by the federal government in 1997–98 to coordinate the rural development programs of eight ministries in a group of 36 priority regions, and to develop consensus on strategies and activities by means of participatory regional councils.

Such an integrated, multi-institutional approach has the potential of removing biodiversity from a specialized policy niche, and integrating it into broader (and better-funded) development initiatives. So far, regional councils have been established

Table 2. Vegetation Areas Under Management: Current Levels and Policy Objectives

	Total Area (forest inventory 1994)	Protected Areas		Wildlife Management Units (UMAS)ª			Sustainable Management^b under		Sustainable Forest Mgmt Area			Percent of Area under Mgmt (1999)	Percent of Mgmt (2005)	Percent of Area (long term)
		Now*	2005	Long-term	Now*	2005	2005	Long-term	Now*	2005	Area Long-term			
Temperate Forest	30.43	1.1	2.3	5.35	0.33	1.79		7.5	3.77	6.97	9	17.1	36.3	71.8
Tropical Forest	26.44	2.07	3.27	8.15	0.35	1.23		8	1.63	3.53	10	15.3	30.45	98.9
Arid Regions	58.47	3.93	5.73	9.5	9.01	14.26		33	1.05	1.2	3	23.9	36.2	77.8
Halophyte & Gypsophite	4.6	0.75	0.85	1.5	0.1	0.16		1.25				20.4	24.3	66.1
Other assicuatuibs	141.75	1.95	2.25	1.5	0.05	0.17		0.25	0.01	0.04				
Total	**261.25**	**9.8**	**14.4**	**26**	**9.84**	**17.61**		**50**	**6.46**	**5.28**	**22**			
Weighted Average												20.2	34.5	80.5

Notes: * Preliminary estimations/in PA only includes terrestrial coverage.
a. Does not include marine areas nor bodies of water.
b. Includes PRODEFOR.
Source: Non-published figures from the Undersecretary of Natural Resources and the National Ecology.

in most of the 36 priority regions, and the participating ministries have developed integrated packages of assistance (in 1999, according to preliminary estimates by SEMARNAP, the total package was worth some US$1 billion). After only two years of operation, however, it is difficult to determine the success of the initiative in promoting long-lasting regional development, or the degree to which environmental and biodiversity concern have been incorporated in the programs' design and execution.

The variety of programs undertaken attests to the breadth and integral nature of the policy approach to biodiversity. In an effort to consolidate its diversified approach into a synthetic programmatic framework, SEMARNAP has developed mid-term and long-term policy objectives for the management of biodiversity into the broad categories of conservation (protected areas), and sustainable use (both of forests and of wildlife through the UMAs). Table 2 (preceding page) summarizes the objectives, which call for an increase of total areas under different forms of management from the current 20 to 34 percent in 2005, to a long-term target of 80 percent.

In contrast with those ambitious objectives and with the diversified strategy to pursue them, the budgets of most of the programs are quite limited, especially when compared to the magnitude of the problems to be addressed.

Table 3 (next page) also summarizes available information on the budgets of bio-diversity-related programs for the years 1997–99. The average total budget was US$60m, or approximately 3 percent of SEMARNAP's total budget (not including CNA), between 1.8 and 3 percent of the budget of the agriculture ministry, and some 0.5 percent of the resources transferred to states and municipalities for local development programs under *Ramo 33*.

Clearly, there are a number of other policies and programs (reviewed in other Chapters) that have significant impacts on biodiversity conservation and sustainable use. The extent to which biodiversity is integrated into the design, funding, execution, and supervision of other sectors' activities varies from program to program. Anecdotal evidence exists on negative biodiversity impacts generated by programs such as PROCAMPO and PROCEDE through incentives for land use change. In general, it appears that significant further progress can be made to integrate biodivesity concerns into Mexico's economic and social development agenda in a systematic and strategic fashion (see Sections II and III below for further analysis). Many rural development initiatives can be turned from a potential biodiversity threat into an opportunity, provided there are adequate knowledge, seed funding, and political support.

II. Issues

Pressure on natural resources and biodiversity is likely to continue in the foreseeable future in Mexico. Figure 1 displays some of the key elements that will be characterizing the process, such as rate of population growth (based on comparison of 1990 and 1995 INEGI data), incidence of rural poverty, and geographical distribution of temperate and tropical forests throughout the country.

Table 3. Budgets of Selected Biodiversity-Related SEMARNAP Programs and of Other Sectors

Estrategia	Programa	Recursos Fiscales (1997)	Recursos Fiscales (1998)	Recursos Fiscales (1999)
			(Millones de pesos corrientes)	
Defensa de la biodiversidad y de los ecosistemas	Areas Naturales Protegidas	54.6	26.89	33.2
	Programa de Vida Silvestre		6.48	11.3
	Defensa de la frontera forestal/conservacion de los Suelos[1]		15.9	
	Prevención, detección y combate a incendios forstales			12.8
	Defensa de ecosistemas costeros y marinos		0.3	
Recuperación de Ecosistemas	Restauración de aeas afectadas por los incendios	14.8	258.1	302.6
	Programa Nacional de Reforestación			0.04
	Programa de reconversión productiva en el sureste			
	Restauración de Sistemas Lagunarios Costeros		75.58	52.5
Producción y fomento forestal	Programa de Desarrollo Forestal y Areas forestales bajo manejo	44.0	76.1	130.1
	Programa plantaciones forestales comerciales (PRODELAN)	201.2	149.7	52

Table 3. (Continued)

Estrategia / Programa	Recursos Fiscales (1997)	Recursos Fiscales (1998)	Recursos Fiscales (1999)
		(Millones de pesos corrientes)	
Programas regionales integrados			
Programas de Desarrollo Rural Sustentable			
Total (Million Mex Pesos)	36.5	32.2	29.8
Total (Million US$)	351.1	641.25	625.34
Exchange rate (Mex pesos per US$)	44.33	70.1	65.83
Average	7.92	9.14	9.5
			60.10
SEMARNAP total budget	9,198.80	12,297.10	13,315.97
CNA budget	7,778.90	9,478.20	NA
SEMARNAP total budget (not including CNA)	1,419.90	2,818.90	NA
Biodiversity-related program in % of SEMARNAP total budget (excluding CNA)	**3.12%**	**2.49%**	**NA**
Presupuestos de otros sectores			
08 Agricultura, Ganadería y Desarrollo Rural	19,803.20	22,905.49	21,117.15
20 Desarrollo Social	6,527.10	9,528.30	8,370.21
21 Turismo	922.10	1,103.31	642.39
26 Desarrollo Social y Productivo en Regiones de Pobreza	—	3,411.70	4,077.60
33 Aportaciones Federales para Entidades Federativas y Municipios	—	98,489.60	137,214.66

Sources: SEMARNAP; SHCP (http://www.semarnap.gob.mx/gestion/programas.htm; http://www.shcp.gob.mx/ieo/index.html).

Figure 1. Population Growth, Forest Cover, and Incidence of Rural Poverty

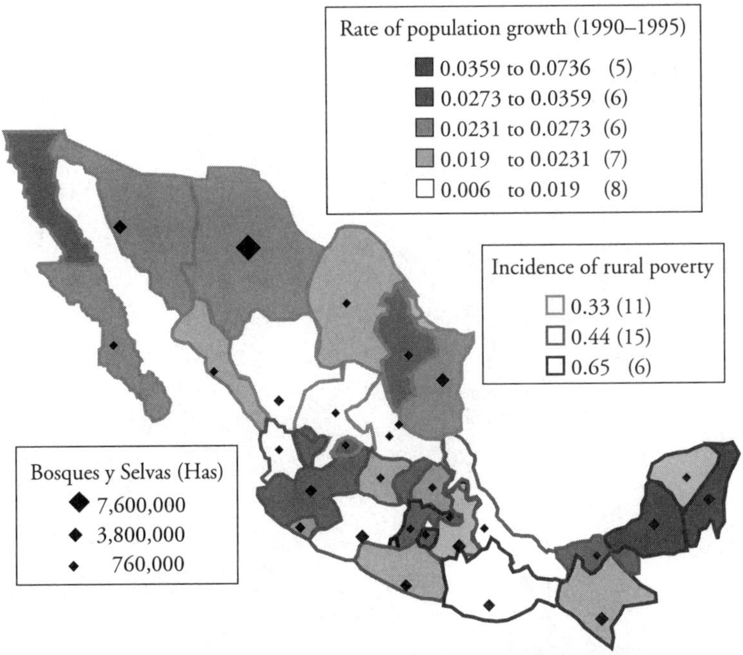

Source: Author analysis based on INEGI population data and SARH 1994 Forest Inventory.

In a number of states, increasing population pressure and large proportions of Mexico forests coexist. What is perhaps more important, however, is that several of those states, also feature high incidence of rural poverty (increasing incidence of rural poverty from 33 percent to 44 percent to 65 percent is indicated in the map by varying gray, state contours, respectively). In particular, poverty in southern states such as Campeche, Chiapas, Quintana Roo, and Yucatan strikes over two-thirds of the population in rural areas. Those states account for some 40 percent of tropical forests (*selvas*) and have among the highest rates of population growth.

Conceptual Issues

A simplified conceptual framework may assist in analyzing the salient issues related to biodiversity management, including both the features of past processes of loss and policy prospects for the future. Such a framework is illustrated in, and described in detail in Box 1 (next page).

The framework could be used to summarize in schematic terms historical patterns of biodiversity loss in Mexico. The social and economic processes that have

Box 1. Conceptual Framework for Biodiversity Management

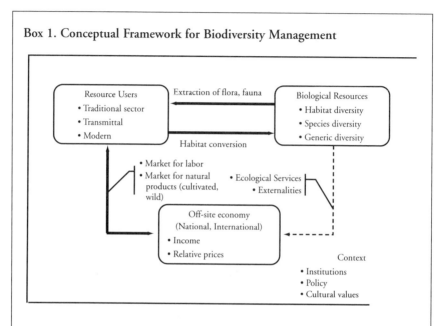

In an attempt to simplify relationships that are highly complex, the process of biodiversity loss (or conservation) can be analyzed as the result of interaction among three sets of agents:

- The natural system
- Local resource users
- The off-site economy (national and international)

Resource users affect the stock of biological resources through habitat modification or conversion, and extraction of flora and fauna from the wild. By undertaking those activities users impact the natural pattern of ecosystem, species, and genetic diversity.

Local resource users can be clustered in the three broad groups of the traditional, transitional, and modern sectors. The specific definition of the three groups would vary depending on the particular sector of economic activity under consideration, but in most cases they can be interpreted as situated along the spectrum of the various possible degrees of integration with the open market economy. Producers in the "modern" category are fully integrated into national and international markets for inputs and outputs, while "traditional" producers have a stronger subsistence orientation, constrained access to input markets such as land and credit, and access to output markets often only through long intermediation chains. The "transitional" group falls between the two extremes, and comprises producers that, as a result of policy interventions or of endogenous processes of socioeconomic transformation, are either moving from the traditional to the modern sector, or are shifting away from natural resource use, seeking employment and income sources in the urban economy.

Resource users make decisions on the location of their activities, output quantity and composition, and technology adopted, on the basis of signals received from local, national, and international markets (these include the limited, mediated, or distorted signals perceived by the "traditional" producers). The demand for three sets of goods or services is of particular importance for the present purposes: the demand for off-site labor (which generates alternatives to activities with direct impact on biodiversity); the demand for goods that entail the modification of natural habitats and the genetic homogenization of agricultural production (for example, cereals, livestock products, some citric fruit); and the demand for goods from the wild or for "biodiversity-friendly" agriculture products (for example, nontimber forest products, shaded coffee).

Biological resources provide ecological services (for example, watershed protection, climate regulation, scenic recreation) to local, national, and international consumers and residents. These services are typically not traded in readily available markets. Finally, institutions (including tenure systems and community structure), policies, and cultural values constitute the context in which the interaction between local resource users, markets, and biological resources takes place.

been leading to conversion of natural habitats to agriculture and pasture are complex and not entirely understood in their variability across latitudes, agroecological conditions, tenure arrangements, forms of social organization, and interaction with local political and institutional contexts. There are, however, a few recurring patterns that assist in establishing hypotheses for the purposes of policy analysis.

The expansion of cattle ranching in the past decades has benefited a relatively limited number of communities and individuals who took advantage of favorable conditions in the national and international markets, but especially who had access to generous public support (subsidies to credit, technology) for cattle development. Many of the fertile lowland areas have been converted to pasture, pushing slash-and-burn farmers unable to access large scale cattle development programs into the ecologically fragile, erosion-prone upper slopes of mountainous states such as Chiapas, Oaxaca, and Veracruz.

It appears that sustainable use of natural products has been confined to situations of low tenure conflicts and moderate population pressure, and to activities requiring low levels of physical and financial capital (for example, some types of nontimber forest products). Transfer of activities with higher requirements of physical capitalization and knowledge intensity (such as timber extraction) from private concessionaires to the social–community sector has been enhancing ecological sustainability, but has introduced new challenges of social and financial sustainability.

In summary, much of the process of habitat conversion and wildlife use of the recent past may be interpreted as determined by the response of the "transitional" and "modern" segments of the rural sector to policy and market signals, and partly by the reaction of the more "traditional" segments, who have been encroaching into wilderness areas in the absence of other viable livelihood strategies. Incentives for private or community investment into sustainable use of biological resources have been limited because of higher relative prices of more traditional outputs, high discount rates or risk premia attached to unclear market prospects, and thin or nonexisting markets for ecological services.

Recent empirical analysis of the *ejido* system (World Bank 1998) provides quantitative evidence on the current distribution of the rural population among the three producer groups identified above, and of the cross-group mobility during the 1990s. "Modernized" producers account for about half of the total surveyed in the study, concentrate in the Gulf and Pacific-North regions, have relatively larger land holding (in excess of 10 hectares per household), and tend to intensify production of corn, fruit, and vegetables. "Transitional" *ejido* members account for 10 to 15 percent of the total, tend to exit from corn and perishables, and are turning increasingly to migration and off-farm activities as livelihood strategies. Finally, "traditional" producers, which account for over 30 percent of the total, are scattered throughout the country, but with higher concentrations in the south. They own little land, on average, focus production on rainfed corn, and derive a significant part of their income (from 5 to 19 percent) from nonfarm, nonwage activities, several of which are related to natural resource use (for example, forest product sales).

Impacts on biodiversity from productive activities are likely to be different across these groups, as will be opportunities for conservation and improved management. Most of the "traditional" producers reside in marginal lands, many of which are remote and at the interface with pristine, biodiversity-rich wildlands. While promising in the long run, involvement of the traditional sector into "green markets" for biological resources is unlikely in the short term.

For the poorer producers, intensive (and possibly unsustainable) use of biological resources will remain the only option until basic development needs are met. The impact of poverty on natural resources has been analyzed in the context of recent World Bank–IFPRI studies[8] on deforestation in Mexico during 1980–90. Nationwide regression analysis based on *municipio*-level data confirms that poverty (as measured by the percentage of population earning one minimum wage or less) is statistically associated with deforestation. Furthermore, regression based on plot-level data in Chiapas and Oaxaca indicates that a 1 percent increase in poverty is associ-

8. Deininger, K., and B. Minten, (1997), "Poverty, Policies and Deforestation: The Case of Mexico," World Bank, IFPRI, Washington D.C.; Deininger, K., and B. Minten, (1996), "Determinants of Forest Cover and the Economics of Protection: an Application to Mexico," World Bank, Washington D.C.

ated with a 0.14 percent increase of deforestation probabilities. Based on this evidence and analysis, it seems that for this sector, integration of the biodiversity agenda with the poverty alleviation agenda seems unavoidable.

In the case of the "transition" sector, impacts on natural resources and biodiversity will depend on the timing and modality of the strategy of exit from the traditional sector. Enhanced income and employment opportunities outside the rural economy—presumably associated with development of urban growth poles—may reduce pressures from this sector on the natural resource base. At the same time, population growth (through migration) in urban areas will increase the demand for food in those areas and may increase the demand for products with potential impacts on natural resources, such as cattle products or fish.

Concerning the modern sector, impacts on natural resources and biodiversity are likely to be associated primarily not so much with further conversions of natural habitats into production (extensification), but rather with choices made on the output composition, input, and technology sides. On the output front, it is likely that increasing reliance on a narrow range of improved high-yielding varieties will continue, thereby displacing the broader range of indigenous cultivars traditionally adopted by smaller-scale farmers. On the input side, impacts on biodiversity, agro-biodiversity, and more generally ecosystem balance, will depend on the intensity and modality of use of agrochemicals (fertilizers and pesticides).

Inducing the modern sector to adopt more biodiversity-friendly production methods will therefore depend primarily on the existence of efficient and transparent "green markets," including both price rewards for certified green products, and the ability of consumers in Mexico and abroad to identify (and discriminate against) productions not meeting ecological standards.

III. Strategic Options for the Future

Recent achievements in the areas of institutions, legislation, strategy, knowledge, and funding have been remarkable. However, it appears that additional efforts will be necessary in the short and medium term to ensure long-term sustainability of biodiversity management, given mounting pressures to use biological resources as an outlet to unmet development needs, or as an avenue for tapping into market opportunities from trade in natural products and biological resources.

A Typology of Policy Options

A framework like the one presented in Section may be helpful in terms of policy analysis purposes for the following reasons:

- *Policy Objectives.* These objectives may address conservation of ecosystem, species, or genetic diversity. With respect to ecosystems in particular, an important element is choosing between targeting pristine and human-modified ecosystems (productive landscape). It is increasingly recognized that while human modified ecosystems typically host "less" biodiversity than pristine ecosystems, they still have an important role in an integral biodiversity strategy, as both a buffer from human pressure on pristine areas, and as a repository of biodiversity (especially agrobiodiversity) in their own right.

- *Policy Instruments.* To be successful, different policies will need to be considered for targeting different social and economic groupings of resource users, taking into account differences in livelihood strategies and objectives, property rights on land and other natural resources, and access to markets.

- *Policy Constraints.* The effectiveness of biodiversity policies and strategies may be hampered (or boosted), depending on prevailing macro conditions such as income growth and relative prices; and by other exogenous factors, such as cultural values and institutional context.

Different combinations of policy objectives, target social groups, policy instruments, and exogenous conditions may be constructed to analyze options available to decisionmakers and related likely outcomes. A simple grouping is proposed in Table 4 (next page), along the dimensions of target ecosystem types (pristine and modified) and of target social groups (traditional and modern–transitional sectors). The four cells identified by the matrix typify in a schematic fashion the variety of intermediate situations that can be found in reality. For that reason, no attempt is made to assign relative weights measuring the representativeness of each cell in terms of area or population.

The purpose of the matrix is to help establish simple trade-offs between biodiversity payoff (higher in cells A and C), complexity of intervention on the underlying social and economic sources of biodiversity pressure (higher in cells A and B), and limitations (possibly higher for cells C and D) imposed by external or exogenous factors, largely outside of the biodiversity policymakers' control (at least in the short to medium term).

Cells A and B represent the traditional domain of protected areas policies. These cells refer to those areas in temperate, tropical, and coastal–marine ecosystems with relatively lower degrees of human-induced habitat perturbation. Quite possibly, many of those areas are still pristine because of limited access and physical and economic distance from markets, and hence fall largely under category A. Nevertheless, there may well be a limited number of well-conserved areas owned or managed by private individuals or communities belonging to the modern or transitional sectors.

The ultimate policy objective for cells A and B is pretty much the same, namely conservation or minimization of impact from human use. Effective management of protected areas remains a fundamental instrument to achieve that objective. The consolidation of the protected area system is therefore essential, and is likely to require strong capacity to mobilize the necessary funding. Donor assistance may best be used

Table 4. A Framework for Biodiversity Policy Analysis

Resource Users Sector	Ecosystem Type	
	Pristine Ecosystems A	*Modified Ecosystems/Productive Landscape* B
Traditional	**Biodiversity Payoff:** High **Social Complexity:** High **Threats:** • *Habitat:* Encroachment for subsistence agriculture & pasture • *Individual Species:* Harvesting for direct consumption or cash supplement **Possible Strategies:** • Support to protected areas management • Coordination with local, national and international development programs to provide income opportunities away from ecologically sensitive areas • Support to low-impact sustainable use activities **Source of Financing:** Mainly reorientation of public spending **Context/Constraints:** Land tenure, social discrimination and other underlying factors resulting in persistent poverty	**Biodiversity Payoff:** Medium **Social Complexity:** High **Threats:** • *Habitat:* Increase habitat fragmentation for subsistence agriculture & cattle ranching • *Individual Species:* Harvesting for direct consumption or cash supplement **Possible Strategies:** • Support to community-level natural resource planning • Support to sustainable use activities compatible with maintenance of habitat ecological functions (e.g., agro-forestry) **Source of Financing:** Reorientation of public spending and to a lesser extent private capture of marketable biodiversity benefits **Context/Constraints:** Land tenure, social discrimination and other underlying factors resulting in persistent poverty

Table 4. (Continued)

Resource Users Sector	Ecosystem Type	
	Pristine Ecosystems	Modified Ecosystems/Productive Landscape
	C	D
	Biodiversity Payoff: High **Social Complexity:** Medium **Threats:** • *Habitat:* Conversion to low-diversity production system (e.g., monoculture agriculture, plantation); intensification through agrochemical use • *Individual Species:* Unsustainable harvesting for commercial purposes	**Biodiversity Payoff:** Medium **Social Complexity:** Medium **Threats:** • *Habitat:* Increase habitat fragmentation through conversion to low-diversity production system (e.g., monoculture agriculture, plantation) • *Individual Species:* Unsustainable harvesting for commercial purposes
Transitional/Modern	**Possible Strategies:** • Support to protected areas management • Develop mechanisms for trading development rights (e.g., easements) or for payment of environmental services • Facilitate access to market for certified green products; sustainable wildlife use schemes **Source of Financing:** Mainly private capture of marketable biodiversity benefits **Context/Constraints:** Cultural values, relative output, and input prices in national and international markets	**Possible Strategies:** • Develop mechanisms for trading development rights (e.g., easements) or for payment of environmental services • Facilitate access to market for certified green products; sustainable wildlife use schemes **Source of Financing:** Mainly private capture of marketable biodiversity benefits **Context/Constraints:** Cultural values, relative output, and input prices in national and international markets

to put in place self-sustaining mechanisms to raise resources for protected area management through user charges, entrance fees, trust funds, and associated interest income.

At the same time, it is important to note that protected areas by themselves may not be sufficient to ensure conservation, especially in the large number of cases where protected status (and related restrictions on resource use) is established not on national lands, but on land owned by individuals or communities. In those cases, complementary strategies to ensure conservation are needed; the more appropriate ones are likely to be quite different for cells A and B.

In the case of areas used by the traditional, subsistence-oriented, and poorer sector, the challenge is clearly the strategic integration with the rural development and poverty alleviation agenda. Over 50 percent of Mexico's rural population are below the extreme poverty line, and largely excluded from the provision of basic health, education, and infrastructure services; over 80 percent are below the moderate poverty line. For segments of these social groups residing in biodiversity-rich areas, encroachment on natural habitats and overexploitation of resources from the wild are often two of the few viable livelihood and survival strategies when off-farm or off-site employment opportunities are scarce, and access to agricultural markets is too limited to generate a sustainable flow of cash income. In these situations, strategic options would include:

- In coordination with regular development programs funded by federal or state agencies, promote income-generating opportunities away from ecologically sensitive areas.
- Ensure that provision of, and access to, basic infrastructure services are designed and executed in ways consistent with biodiversity conservation objectives, especially in and around protected areas.
- Promote selective programs of low-impact sustainable use of biological resources with financial sustainability potential, for direct consumption or, for those traditional groups closer to the "transition" sector, with a local or even export-market orientation.

Biodiversity-rich areas used primarily by the "modern" sector may be subject to different types of pressures, such as conversion to low-diversity production systems (for example, monocrop agriculture, and plantation forestry); or, in terms of pressure on individual species, there may be unsustainable harvesting of plant and animal species for larger-scale commercial purposes. Considering that this sector is likely to feature better-defined land tenure and property rights arrangements, and higher levels of human capital and better market access, strategic options for biodiversity conservation and sustainable use may include:

- Developing mechanisms for trading development rights (for example, easements) or for payment of environmental services.

- Facilitating access to market for certified green products, and promoting sustainable wild-life use schemes such as those under the UMA program.

Cells B and D in Table 4 refer to areas which have been more intensely modified by human intervention, but which still contain significant ecosystem, species and genetic diversity. While in general the biodiversity payoff per dollar invested may be lower than in cells A and C, the social complexity of designing and executing biodiversity programs may be lower. If, as a result, the area or number of beneficiaries covered by any given budget is larger than in the cases of more pristine areas, there may be an interesting trade-off between lower cost (but lower biodiversity payoff) per unit of area in modified ecosystems, and higher benefits (but higher cost) in pristine ecosystems.

The development of a technical and policy approach to managing biodiversity in the productive landscape is incipient, not only in Mexico but also in many other developing and developed countries. However, in the face of the growing social and economic pressures on protected areas (the more traditional realm of application of biodiversity conservation initiatives), and of the risk of ecological and genetic isolation faced by many of them, a broader "bioregional" approach appears to be a very promising avenue for the future. Mexico is experimenting with such an innovative approach through several initiatives, among which is the establishment of a network of biological corridors in the southeast (Campeche, Chiapas, Quintana Roo, and Yucatan), as part of the broader international effort of the Mesoamerican Biological Corridor project.

In modified ecosystems, the biodiversity management objective is unlikely to be outright conservation, but rather reduction or control of further habitat fragmentation, and more generally, the reorientation of development practices in ways that are compatible with maintenance of acceptable levels of ecosystem, landscape, species, and genetic diversity.

Strategies to support the conservation and sustainable use of biodiversity in the productive landscape would include, for the "traditional" sector:

- Support of community-level natural resource planning as a way to balance development priorities with the maintenance of ecological services of local relevance (such as water cycles and forest reserves for fuel and subsistence hunting).
- Support to sustainable-use activities compatible with maintenance of ecological and landscape diversity (for example, agroforestry).

In the case of more "modern" groups, the strategy could include options similar to those described above, but perhaps with territorial prioritization in areas of "strategic" ecological relevance to ensure maintenance or restoration of critical biological and genetic linkages among pristine areas.

Cross-Cutting Issues

Despite the existence of alternative biodiversity objectives, and the corresponding need to diversify policy responses, there are a few ingredients that are likely to be important across interventions in different ecological and socioeconomic settings. Several of the strategies outlined above entail reallocating public expenditures or establishing private rights on environmental commons. These actions require social and political consensus. Consensus, in turn, can be generated by convincing evidence on the need for change, by environmentally sensitive constituencies, by social and political leadership to broker agreements, and by technical capacity to design and implement reforms. Let us briefly review these elements in turn.

KNOWLEDGE ON BIODIVERSITY AND ITS VALUES. As recognized by the recently published national biodiversity strategy, the generation, organization, and diffusion of knowledge and information on biodiversity and its social and economic benefits are of paramount importance. Specific issues that may be considered in this area include:

- Refinement of existing biodiversity priority-setting exercises (such as those undertaken by CONABIO) to take more systematically into account trade-offs between pristine and human-modified habitats, and to better determine and predict degree of threat based on regional development models.
- Development of approaches to economic valuation that closely resemble *actual* decisionmaking processes of private and public decisionmakers. Several studies in the existing literature estimate aggregate values expressed in social terms. However, for any given biodiversity management option, politicians, entrepreneurs, and communities will be interested in the distribution of cost and benefits across *specific beneficiary groups*, and not in aggregate social values.
- Strengthening or updating ecological planning tools such as *Ordenamientos Ecologicos* to reflect economic values of alternative biodiversity management options, and to ensure their full integration with existing or upcoming state and municipal development plans and programs.

ENVIRONMENTAL CONSTITUENCIES. A large part of the biodiversity challenge for the foreseeable future is to mobilize the sectors of Mexico' society (government, private sector, and public opinion) that so far have been spectators (or opponents) in biodiversity protection efforts. The following options may be considered:

- Environmental education, through formal school curricula, or targeted to selected groups in the rural sector and the urban middle class, as a long-term investment especially in the young (tomorrow's voters and consumers).
- Targeted outreach campaigns to private sector leaders and high-level public sectors official to raise awareness of both the private and social costs of biodi-

versity loss, and of the private and social gains deriving from its sustainable use. Awareness raising would seem of particular importance for local government officials in light of increasing decentralization of decisions on public spending.

Capacity and institution building. Mexico possesses high levels of human capital in the academic and NGO sectors. One important challenge is to strengthen and broaden the skills of government officials (especially at the local level) in nonenvironmental agencies in order to improve processes of design and execution of development programs with potential biodiversity impacts. In terms of institutions, the process of consolidation of biodiversity-related agencies needs to continue. In particular, the forthcoming establishment of a deconcentrated, semi-autonomous Commission for Protected Areas has great potential for guaranteeing long-term institutional sustainability of the Protected Area System, through professionalization of the conservation career and establishment of innovative fundraising strategies.

References

Challenger, A. 1998. *Utilización y Conservación de los Ecosistemas Terrestres de México, Pasado, Presente y Futuro.* Comisión Nacional para el Conocimiento y Uso de la Biodiversidad. Mexico City, Mexico.

CONABIO. 1998. *La diversidad biológica de México: Estudio de País, 1998.* Comisión Nacional para el Conocimiento y Uso de la Biodiversidad. Mexico City, Mexico.

Deininger, K., and B. Minten. 1996. "Determinants of Forest Cover and the Economics of Protection: An Application to Mexico." World Bank, Washington, D.C.

Deininger, K., and B. Minten. 1997. "Poverty, Policies and Deforestation: The Case of Mexico." World Bank, and IFPRI, Washington D.C.

Dinerstein, E., D. M. Olson, D. J. Graham, A. L. Webster, S. A. Primm, M. P. Bookbinder, and G. Ledec. 1995. "Conservation Assessment of the Terrestrial Ecoregions of Latin America and the Caribbean." World Bank/World Wildlife Fund. Washington, D.C.

Dirzo, R. 1992. "Diversidad florística y estado de conservación de las selvas tropicales de México." In: J. Sarukhán, y R. Dirzo (comps.), *México ante los retos de la biodiversidad.* CONABIO. Mexico.

Instituto Nacional de Ecología. 1999. *Ordenamiento Ecológico General del Territorio.* Instituto Nacional de Ecología. Mexico City, Mexico.

Mittermeier, R., and C. Goettsch. 1992. "La importancia de la biodiversidad en México." In: J. Sarukhán, and R. Dirzo, (comps.), *México ante los retos de la biodiversidad.* Comisión Nacional para el Conocimiento y Uso de la Biodiversidad. Mexico City, Mexico.

Ramamoorthy, T. P., R. Bye, A. Lot, and J. Fa. 1993. *Biological Diversity of Mexico: Origins and Distribution*. New York: Oxford University Press.

SEMARNAP. 1996. "Programa de Áreas Naturales de México 1995–2000." SEMARNAP, INE. Mexico City, Mexico.

SEMARNAP. 1997. "Programa de Conservación de la Vida Silvestre y Diversificación Productiva en el Sector Rural: 1997–2000 México." SEMARNAP, INE. Mexico City, Mexico.

SEMARNAP. 1999. "Una experiencia en curso: la participación social en la SEMARNAP." Mexico City, Mexico. http://www.semarnap.gob.mx.

Toledo, V. M., and M. J. Ordóñez. 1993. "The Biodiversity Scenario of Mexico: A Review of Terrestrial Habitats." In: T. P. Ramamoorthy, R. Bye, A. Lot, and J. Fa, (eds.), *Biological Diversity of Mexico: Origins and Distribution*. New York: Oxford University Press.

World Bank. 1995. "Mexico Resource Conservation and Forest Sector Review." Washington D.C.

World Bank. 1997. "Mexico. Protected Areas Program: Proposed Restructuring Project." GEF. Report No. 16998–ME. Mexico Country Management Unit, Latin America and the Caribbean Regional Office. Global Environment Division, Environment Department, World Bank. Washington, D.C.

World Bank. 1998. "Mexico Ejido Reform." Washington, D.C.

28

Forestry and Land Management

*This Chapter was written by Augusta Molnar and
Thomas A. White (Forest Trends) with the contribution of
Luis F. Constantino and Adolfo Brizzi.*

I. Current Developments

Continued Resource Degradation Despite Reforms

Despite an enormous potential to provide economic, environmental, and social services, Mexico's land and forest base is threatened by land degradation and deforestation, reducing cultivable land area, increasing the impacts from natural disasters, limiting the potential of forest-based livelihoods, and threatening water supplies. Of Mexico's 197.3 million hectares, 72 percent is under some form of forest or natural vegetation. Temperate forests comprise 29 million hectares, and intact tropical forests, another 20 million, with 34 million hectares capable of permanently sustained timber production. Arid and desert ecozones include another 10 million hectares. A significant portion of this is degraded, however. Forest and land deforestation rates continue to be high despite the rural policy reforms of the 1990s. These policies were intended to encourage more intensive use of lands most appropriate for agriculture. These, in corollary, through the elimination of subsidies, price supports, and tariff barriers, would foster production of more competitive crops in irrigated areas and intensification in rainfed areas by aligning basic grain and other agricultural commodities to international prices. Lack of investment capital in rainfed areas where there is a persistence of subsistence crop production on marginal lands, combined with an unfavorable price for agricultural commodities, has limited changes in land-use patterns in forested areas, particularly the tropics.

Deforestation continues in the order of 600,000 hectares of standing forest lost per year. The bulk of deforestation took place over the past few decades due to policies that encouraged forest clearing for agriculture or livestock rearing, as part of frontier colonization programs or expansion of smallholders from their degraded agricultural lands to new plots. Between 1970 and 1990, for example, cultivated areas in Mexico grew 39 percent and livestock increased by 15 percent while the forested area shrunk by 13 percent, mainly in the southern states.

Soil erosion and salinization remain major problems in agriculture areas, with official estimates that up to 60 percent of the national lands are severely eroded, with a high incidence of salinization. In the north, for example, many of the severely eroded areas are common lands where there was not sufficient social capital to efficiently manage the common holding, and many ejidos opted to rent out their lands to a small number of large landowners. Without adequate regulations from *ejido* or local government authorities, these lands are severely overgrazed, leading to the degradation of native vegetation and soil erosion. Other areas are abandoned lands in marginal areas or areas under high population pressure that could not be left fallow for sufficient time periods, or which were poorly managed for lack of investment capital. Skewed water rights and ineffective controls in irrigation zones led to salinization in areas of over-irrigation and poor management in poorly served extensions. Soil erosion is a problem both because of the loss of fertile land for agriculture and pasture use—a significant problem where only 14 percent of the total national land area is arable—and because of the limited availability of affordable ground and surface water supplies. The heavy siltation downstream reduces the life of irrigation and drinking water reservoir systems and dramatically increases the cost of water supply, especially to urban areas.

Growing Recognition of the Multiple Social Values of Forests

Mexico's forests account for approximately 1 percent of the national GDP, over 100,000 permanent jobs, and are home to over 10 million citizens, most of who are disproportionately poor relative to national averages. In addition to the well-recognized benefits of jobs and the many commodities produced by Mexico's forests, there is growing recognition of the critical role of these forests in sustaining local livelihoods, enabling a strong and growing tourism market, and protecting the nation's critical water supplies.

Social use values of forests are high; about 2,000 species are identified by local people for distinct uses and 25 plant species are currently used in western medicines.. Important products include medicinals, fuelwood and fodder, wood and fibers for artesanal furniture, house building material, utensils, and foodstuffs, including meat and commercialized mushrooms, or seeds. Plant values are hard to estimate, but substantial. The value of medicinal plants traded in Mexico City alone could exceed US$1 million per year. A maize cultivar important in hybrid production in the US generates US$7 million per year in use permits, and the local market value of palm roofing in the Yucatan peninsula is equivalent to US$170 million. The extensive indigenous populations have maintained a broad ethno-botanical knowledge and agriculture and forest management practices that may be key to long-term sustainability of these resources. The many benefits of forest biodiversity are described in the Biodiversity Chapter.

Tourism and recreation activities in forest areas are increasing, both involving foreigners and the urbanized Mexican population. There are a growing number of forest communities with high-value enterprises or in areas of tourism that are beginning to set aside forest areas for conservation purposes as part of their overall management plan. This is an important opportunity to expand the national area under conservation status without the legal and institutional investment to declare areas as formally protected at the state or national level. In the frontier areas, community reserves are emerging as a strategy to secure land tenure and property rights, as evidenced in the positive movements in the Chimalapas, however still preliminary, and in the Selva Lacandona areas of the Montes Azules reserve.

Forests also play a critical role in protecting Mexico's 320 major watersheds in a situation in which many of the urban centers are located above their nearest water sources, requiring greater use of water flowing from higher elevations. The contribution of deforestation and land degradation to flooding is high; the recent event in the Gulf states during October 1999 affected more than 200,000 persons in 156 municipalities of Veracruz. Disaster refugees in this state comprised 91,610 people in 86 municipalities that experienced major damages in housing and infrastructure. Furthermore, the disaster damaged 898 km of roads and 18 bridges. The 1997 floods linked to Hurricane Pauline in Chiapas caused an estimated damage of US$447 million.

SEMARNAP has been implementing a multisectoral technical assistance program for land-use zoning at the local level, PRODERS, which is carried out in priority regions around high biodiversity sites/regions. Working with local communities to compare land use capacity and sustainable development options, PRODERS increases the capacity of local producers to develop their own strategy for increasing incomes and well-being and provides information to link them to available private and public resources for helping to implement that strategy.

Most encouraging is the growing interest in developing market-based approaches to compensate forest communities for the environmental services generated by their forests. As described above, these forests generate tremendous social benefits that are currently external to the market, meaning that forest holders do not have the incentive to continue to manage their lands in a manner that continues the production of these services. Reversing the trends of resource degradation will require devising new mechanisms and markets that recognize and reward landholders for protecting and managing their natural resources.

The Promise of Forestry-Based Community Development and Natural Forest Management

Mexico is unique in that 70 percent or more of its forest area is within the boundaries of social units—7,000–9,000 *ejidos* or indigenous communities have significant forested areas of which 65 percent may have commercial potential but only one quarter have any formal management plans (1,800 *ejidos*/communities). Given this unique forest tenure situation, and the fact that Mexico still has large natural productive forests that could be converted to real economic assets for rural development, it would appear that community and *ejido* forestry should be a major point of emphasis in the country's poverty alleviation and forest conservation strategies. As yet, there does not appear to be a clear vision of the potentials and constraints, or concerted attention to this sector.

Until the 1980s, Mexican forest policy focused on large-scale timber extraction and processing, providing minimal support to communal forest owners. With the passage of the 1992 forest law, there was a shift to privatized extension services, a more streamlined regulatory framework, and a continuation of the trend away from subsidizing large-scale operations and preparing for trade liberalization in the sector (NAFTA allowed a 15-year period of protection). This trend continued in the 1997 law revisions, but with increased regulation on forest management.

The current regulatory framework is based on command and control rather than incentives, and remains unnecessarily detailed and prescriptive. Compliance by landowners is difficult and extremely expensive, and given the limited capacity of regional government officer, these regulations are largely unenforceable. In addition, national lumber standards are biased in favor of the purchaser, and forest producers must over-dimension their products for the domestic market. In sum, the combination of an inflated regulatory burden for forestry and a pro-purchaser set of product standards not only discourages forestry, but puts forestry at a disadvantage to agriculture, where despite substantial environmental costs to poor management, remains relatively unregulated. A market for private extension services has emerged in the 1990s, but because of the high cost of management plansservice providers are under pressure to charge less for their services, requiring them to deliver a lower standard product. The total number of service providers in the country remained fairly small.

Remarkably, the market conditions for community forest products remain strong and promising, in part because of the peso devaluation, but also because of the proximity to domestic markets and the high relative quality of Mexican timber. International prospects for natural forest timber, both tropical and temperate, are positive. For these reasons, with the establishment of fair product standards and removal of remaining policy distortions, community forestry can become a much stronger contributor to poverty alleviation, as well as a greater source of domestic production. A limited number of these *ejidos* and communities have developed well-organized timber and multiproduct forest enterprises, but with greater efficiency, higher-valued products and access to new markets for certified products, more community enterprises could not only compete domestically, but globally.

The Emerging Need for Commercial Plantations

Mexico needs to develop its plantation sector, both to offset the rapidly growing pulp imports and to reduce pressure on its natural forests for low-valued commodity products. Forest plantation for commercial or environmental purposes has historically been limited—about 100 to 200 million trees planted per year according to official statistics, with estimated area currently covered under temperate forest plantations averaging 63,500 hectares overall. Plantations have been slow to develop, both because of the continued supply of products from natural forests, but also because of the difficulties in establishing plantations on commonly-held lands. Part of the problem seems to lie with the unclear strategy for reforestation in Mexico. On one hand, there is awareness that significant land area could be highly competitive for fast-growing commercial species—thereby bringing more area under forests. On the other, these projects have often chosen sites on the basis of environmental criteria rather than economic feasibility. At present, the government does not have a strategy for setting priorities between promoting plantations and managing its extensive native forests. It is clear that a key element of future government programs will be devising approaches to promote industry-community collaboration on plantations. It is likely that the government could contribute by establishing standard contracts, fiscal incentives as well as guarantees for investors. In this area Mexico could look to Brazil, China and South Africa for innovative examples.

Government Interventions in Land Management

Past agricultural sector reforms have caused a fundamental shift in the rural economy, with farmers in productive areas increasingly switching to new technologies and higher value crops. Both productive and marginal farmers have suffered from adverse price structures and limited access to rural finance, but for marginal farmers the hardship is greater, with increased outmigration and a search for any available (on or off-farm) employment. The situation is serious in poor, forest-rich mountain areas, where there has been no shift to higher value crops or sustainable intensification, and diversification of the rural economy has been limited. The intense outmigration from these areas provides an escape value, but most producers keep their roots and families *in situ*. Although the off-farm sources of income of rural *ejidatarios* and indigenous *comunitarios* supply an increasing share of family income, pressure on marginal lands remains high and forests at the agricultural frontier continue to be cleared for subsistence agriculture and animal husbandry. Seasonal and long-term migration has also had negative impacts on the availability of household male farm labor, limiting on-farm investments in soil and moisture conservation.

A shift has occurred in the strategies for maintaining soil fertility and reducing soil erosion, in recognition of the increasing land pressures and the limited availability of credit or investment capital for inputs on small farms. Agricultural programs have increased their emphasis on more sustainable land management in marginal areas, looking at adaptations of traditional practices to more sustainable, higher return options, and introducing rainfed crops and selective intensification more suited to the land capacity. New SAGAR programs emphasize integrated pest management technologies and low-cost soil and moisture conservation, in combination with higher-value crops, although quality extension coverage is still very limited.

PROCAMPO supports are important to support rural farm incomes in an adverse market environment, but do not allow the level of investment required for shifts in production, or for increased fallow cycles. Over-grazing of *ejidos* and common lands continues to be a problem, particularly in the north. Urban centers are increasingly taking interest in green areas as water catchment protection, a pollution sink, or recreational/biodiversity site, but there is still limited financing for management or restauration activities. Actions include better organization for fire control, promoting management of forests by surrounding communities and associations, and reforestation activities, some financed by the PRONARE (see below).

Government Interventions in the Forestry Sector

In anticipation of the new opportunities that would be presented by the reform of Article 27 of the Constitution and the lifting of restrictions on the lease of *ejido* lands, the government developed a program to promote establishment of commercial forest plantations on under-utilized lands in 1997, called PRODEPLAN. The program is targeted to areas with a comparative advantage in terms of availability of sufficient extensions of land and reasonable distance to a port or major marketing center.

PRONARE is a government financed reforestation program directed at degraded peri-urban areas and green spaces in urban areas under the *Solidaridad* social fund program. During the current administration, PRONARE was transferred to SEMARNAP's Subsecretariat of Natural Resources for restructuring to increase the technical oversight by professional foresters and thereby improve the quality of species selection, siting of species based on local ecology, and the production of viable nursery stock. To reduce labor costs of seedling production and plantation establishment, a sizable portion of the funds were made available to the armed forces in various states, so that they would supply the oversight and manpower. PRONARE, one source of funds for plantations, has had variable results due to the poor selection of species to match site conditions or provide local needs and the uneven commitment from producers and municipalities to protect the reforested areas after establishment.

Positive support from the government to communal owners is even more recent. Mexico began financing PROCYMAF in late 1997, a capacity-building and technical assistance pilot for forest communities in Oaxaca. This has already brought 165,000 hectares under improved management (including 76,000 hectares of new areas), created 13,000 hectares of conservation area, prepared land use plans in 117,000 hectares of non-commercial forests, and created 1,300 permanent forest-based jobs in community enterprises. This strategy works at both sides of the community/*ejido* forestry issue by stimulating the market for high-quality services through funding of management plans and complementary marketing and forestry studies, while offering training and capacity-building to forest owners and service providers on a range of technical and entrepreneurial topics. The quality of forest management plans improve, while the forest owners' returns from improved management go up, creating a stimulus for sustained resource management while generating rural income.PRODEFOR, a national forest management and development program modeled on the philosophy of PROCYMAF, was established in 1997 as a national trust fund which allocated technical assistance funds in up to 22 states with important forest resources through a matching fund scheme with participating states. Initially, 100 percent of PRODEFOR funds were to finance technical assistance study proposals from individual and community forest producers, with limited funds for promotion or monitoring, and no complementary financing of capacity-building activities targeted to forest producers. However, while there has been positive response to the program, the bulk of beneficiaries preparing proposals were the more advanced *ejidos* and private producers, rather than the broader range for which the program was designed. In addition, the number of service providers able to provide quality technical assistance to beneficiaries has been limited. The program has been adjusted to increase the counterpart contribution from the federal government, and to include a greater margin of resources for administration and promotional expenses. But, greater recognition is needed that without building the capacity and skills of both service providers and forest owners, quality proposals will not be presented or implemented, and targets will not be reached.

II. Issues for Sustainable Land and Forest Management

There are three main issues for sustainable land and forest management:

- Overregulation of the sector.
- Ensuring that poor communities capture the full market value of timber, non-timber and environmental services.
- Loss of productive land due to common land issues and skewed property rights.

OVERREGULATION OF THE SECTOR. Mexico is characterized by a comparative overregulation of the forestry sector, with strict requirements for preparation of management plans for any forest for which there is a planned, productive use, regardless of the size or relative environmental value of the forest. This has translated into a high cost to forest users and owners for having to have management plans and inventories to enable them to legally extract products from their forest. This is combined with a weak institutional capacity in SEMARNAP in budget and manpower, to technically apply and enforce norms and standards, and has resulted in a continued incentive for illegal extraction. It has not been cost-effective to disperse regulatory enforcement to all forest types and ownership patterns, when the risks of mismanagement are very different. For example, a standardized model of regulation does not make sense where there are small, dispersed forest-based enterprises with limited capital flows and fluctuating levels of returns (enterprises that burn fuel-wood, make packing cases, or that make furniture for national markets).

In the northern forests, regulation is also of variable value since the cost of trans-port provides an automatic disincentive for illegal extraction unless the extractor can reach a high economy of scale and has capital for investing in transport equipment. In addition, decentralization presents a challenge for effective forest regulation. As the political system decentralizes, the regulatory issue becomes more complicated, as more conflicts are likely to arise between federal and state entities. A related issue is the flexibility to be allowed by the regulations, to fit with variations at the local com-munity level. In some states, historical developments have led *ejidos* or communities to "parcel" forest areas into individual lots "assigned" to individual families. A for-mal management plan assumes a single extractive cut by a single entity, whether pri-vate contractor or community enterprise. In "parceled" forests, a more workable arrangement is an agreed allowable cut, but with the flexibility that each family can make their own selection within agreed standards. By the current law, this is con-sidered illegal logging, even if the total extraction is sustainable over time and pro-vides economic incentives for forest maintenance.

Compliance with the forestry law is a federal responsibility which few states have the desire to take over without adequate resource transfer and without the time frame to develop technical forestry units and infrastructure. There are also political issues in the forest-rich states, where powerful elites would make productive illegal activities more difficult to enforce, and the federal agencies have limited regulatory capacity. In response to these kinds of problems, other countries, such as Bolivia and Chile, have tried to create positive standards which are output oriented, and less costly for owners of less productive or non-commercial forests to apply. Voluntary programs like local or international certification are linked to preferential markets and can eventually link to management of forests for watershed protection services, tourism, or infrequently extracted, non-timber forest products.

Ensuring that poor communities capture the full market value of timber, non-timber and environmental services. There is a strong overlap between con-centration of forest resources and indigenous peoples, and a strong overlap between forests and concentrations of poverty. The regions where indigenous peoples pre-dominate include 45 percent of the forested areas of the country. Indigenous peo-ples make up more than 30 percent of the population of municipalities bordering protected areas in 51 out of 124 areas (excluding forest protection zones). Many of the ecological adaptations of indigenous cultural systems to their environment are still evident in farming practices, hunting, use of native plants, and reliance on for-est products for tools, building materials, food, and clothing. The continued prox-imity of indigenous peoples and forests stems in part from the positive relationship that has been established through cultural adaptation and economic choices. The challenge for such areas is how to build on the positive aspects of this relationship to allow communities to adapt to new economic livelihood strategies which allow them to exit poverty and generate higher income returns, while sustaining the natural resource base, including forest cover.

For many indigenous groups, marginal areas and forests have historically and continue to serve as a place of refuge from societal forces that undervalue indigenous ways of living or which directly threaten their land and resource access. This places an added value on maintaining the land and resource base, which can work in favor of sustainable forestry. The successful community-based forest enterprises are generating substantial income from timber extraction and processing, and diversifying into non-timber forest enterprises, while investing in social infrastructure and applying management practices aimed at environmental sustainability of their resource. There is still only limited support to capacity building of forest communities, particularly to complement the PRODEFOR technical assistance package, and limited policy work on how to help them reconcile social and environmental investments with demands of competitive timber markets.

Until now, it has not been possible to ensure that communities get the full value of their products, either timber and non-timber production or the environmental goods and services produced by the forests. The main economic product from native forests, even with the development of alternative markets and products, is timber. Due to its slow-growing nature, and the relatively higher cost of extracting from isolated sites, natural timber will only yield full value if processed for higher-value products, or in the absence of efficient industries, exported in log form. Finished products obviously provide the greatest return to private labor and communities in the form of employment created. At the same time, the historic exploitation of communities and *ejidos* by the timber industry makes it unlikely in most cases that there will be a model of joint ventures for some time to come, which could, in principle, give communities access to capital and create an economy of scale.

The alternative model that some communities are exploring is access to environmental markets—certified wood and carbon sink markets—and associations among *ejidos* and communities to create an economy of scale for marketing and investment. To date, sixteen communities have been certified to Forest Stewardship Council (FSC) standards. To expand this model, much more support is needed in capacity-building—technical and organizational—both for individual communities and for fostering of associations among *ejidos* and communities. Facilitating access to higher value markets may entail improved access to capital and expansion of private or publicly financed road infrastructure where transport costs are high.

Experiments with *non-timber options* are increasing in Mexico's forests. Communities exploit existing stocks of mushrooms, palm and other commercial non-timber products, and experiments with ecotourism enterprises, spring water bottling, and *exsitu* cultivation of orchids and bromelias are underway. Constraints are sustaining adequate production, raising quality, creating market linkages, and linking these activities to certification and environmental services such a water catchment protection. Both timber and non-timber options in community lands have the advantage of being able to seek differentiated markets that pay a premium for products with a known cultural or environmental value.

Plantation programs are also not designed to address the real limitations. On lands with a comparative advantage, it is not subsidies that are needed to promote commercial joint ventures, but a better framework for investments on lands owned by ejidos and communities.

LOSS OF PRODUCTIVE LAND DUE TO COMMON LAND ISSUES AND SKEWED PROPERTY RIGHTS. The agricultural reforms combined with the overall policy reforms in the 1990s should have created a more productive use of land and forests and encouraged investment in activities like commercial plantations, or higher-value, intensive agriculture, rather than let the agricultural frontier continue to expand. Also, the persistence of distortionary subsidies in the basic grains sector, has helped to maintain an incentive system skewed in favor of agriculture, including in those areas where land use has clearly a better vocation for forestry (see the Thematic Chapter on Sustainable Future and the chapter on Agriculture). Also, much of the market failure relates to the imperfect attention to land and property rights. The reforms to Article 27 and land regularization programs have made land markets more active for *ejido* lands and enabled contract arrangements for better use of idle *ejido* lands. The major obstacle for investors in commercial plantations on available tracts of land is the lack of secure rules of the game for initiating ventures between land owners and potential investors. Smallholders do not have the investment capital to make shifts from one type of production to another. Nor is there an active land market that enables communities and *ejidos* to buy land individually to reduce pressures on common pool resources, despite strong interest from indigenous communities to consolidate their territory.

This loss of productive land is also linked to negative impacts of natural disasters. The *El Niño*-induced forest fires in 1998 in Mexico concentrated their greatest damage in the southeastern areas with insecure land tenure and large numbers of landless or near landless rural families. Damage was greatest in the tropical areas of Chimalapas, between Oaxaca, Chiapas, and Veracruz where many of the fires were deliberately set. The flood-induced mudslides in 1999 in the Veracruz, Puebla, and Tabasco corridor were concentrated in areas of extreme rural poverty, where unsustainable agricultural practices on fragile lands are common, and government and private investment in services and infrastructure is limited. An issue for forest fire control is how to establish the appropriate balance between financing for fire fighting (costly and *ex-post*) with preventative action (intensifying agricultural practices and controlled burn information campaigns) or local level initiatives (equipping and training local community brigades).

III. Options for the Future

The key to sustainable forest and land management lies in a combination of an effective policy framework and positive incentive structure. There is no comprehensive forest strategy in place in Mexico. *A clear strategy is needed that prioritizes support to forest communities and ejidos who are the main owners of the nation's forests, including removing remaining distortions and developing markets for community products and market-based mechanisms to compensate forest owners for the environmental services they produce.* As a part of this strategy, an institutional analysis is needed to define optimal roles and responsibilities for government and other actors, recognizing the full range of values that forests bring economically, socially, and environmentally.

Policy Enhancements and Areas for Government Focus

These include: (a) revise the policy and regulatory framework for forestry to remove penalties against forestry, establish national product standards, and recognize the wide range of local management systems and focus increasingly on positive incentives, rather than coercive enforcement; (b) continue to build the capacity of forest-based communities and *ejidos* to manage their natural resources and develop diversified enterprises based on them, examining the need for minimum road infrastructure; (c) promoting certification efforts and the national framework for quality, independent certification (d) support community conservation initiatives to set aside forests for biodiversity conservation and environmental protection (e) promote on-farm soil and moisture conservation efforts as part of productive agricultural strategies; (f) promote watershed restoration efforts in the context of natural disaster prevention and water resource conservation; and (g) create a positive climate for commercial plantations near coastal access routes. Reforms to the Policy and Regulatory Framework should include:

- Revisit the whole set of agricultural, land tenure, and water policies with a view to assess whether the incidence of incentives and subsidies provided in these sectors causes a bias against forestry.
- Establish national forest product standards that conform to international norms and fairly represent producer and consumer interests.
- Eliminate the forest management plan requirement, replacing it with a requirement for communities to file detailed harvest plans, and observe simple set of regulations focused on mitigating critical environmental hazards.
- Establish a system of voluntary forest management practices and random audits in which forest managers are rewarded for adopting best management practices rather than penalized in a system of command and control.
- Review enforcement regulations and institutional responsibility to devolve responsibility to more local levels with realistic expectations in light of budget and technical capacity.
- Ensure that payments for environmental services accrue to local forest owners and managers, not to the government.

Capacity-Building of Communal Forestry Enterprises and Community Forest Managers

- Support community forest enterprises and community organizations for forest management in natural forest areas through capacity building and training.
- Provide formal technical training of young people from forest communities and technical assistance resources for improved management and market studies for wood and non-wood products and services.
- Improve the quality of private sector technical forestry services to communities, *ejidos,* through training and information.
- For indigenous communities and *ejidos* interested in conservation: support community conservation initiatives and complementary sustainable use activities; promote training and information flows on promising alternative livelihood activities; provide national recognition of communal statutes to facilitate community capture of external funds for conservation efforts and recognize community rights to environmental services provided by their ecosystems and their right to negotiate; match community investments in this area.

Market-based Approaches to Forest Conservation and Use

- Examining the context within which certification efforts are on-going at national level to ensure that sectoral development policies enable this activity and favor creating these markets.
- Promoting strategies of independent initiatives for certifying sustainable forest management (for example, FSC) which avoid distortions in the international markets and which provide more credibility for national producers to access certified markets; provide waivers for government regulation to forest producers who are certified internationally.
- Review the forest regulatory framework to identify more pragmatic strategies for ensuring compliance than relying fully upon a federal deconcentrated agency, by collaborating with NGO's and relying more upon independent, external audits. The government should focus more upon promoting certification schemes and regulating those entities responsible for providing certification to forest producers, than upon establishing forest management standard in isolation of types of end-uses and returns.

Support Community Conservation Initiatives on Community and Ejido lands

- Provide funds for land use zoning and identification of conservation areas within community and *ejido* lands.
- Match community investments in sustainable use activities that reduce pressures on conservation areas; assist in capitalization of local conservation funds.
- Support the creation of networks among communities engaged in complementary conservation efforts; recognize the validity of community customary

statutes that establish permanent conservation areas and incorporate these areas into the legally recognized areas under conservation within states and a national level.

Promote Company-Community Commercial Plantations

- For commercial plantation forestry, review the current PRODEPLAN scheme, which provides subsidies for plantation establishment costs to investors willing to establish commercial plantations, with an alternative model which focuses upon creating a more secure framework for investment, vis-à-vis joint ventures with local land owners (private or *ejidatarios*).
- A possible model could be to devise a minimum guarantee scheme that reduces the current risk in joint ventures, rather than subsidizing establishment cost.

Soil and Moisture Conservation on Farmlands and in Watersheds

- Expand programs such as those integrated into the Marginal Areas program of SAGAR which link land management and farming systems so that farmer incentives for adoption are increased productivity and ability to weather adverse climate cycles.
- For upland lands near urban centers and municipalities: link resources for disaster preparedness with municipal efforts for improved land and water management, including targeting of funds such as PRONARE to more active municipalities.
- Link erosion control and desertification initiatives to water management (including watershed protection where most effective) and incorporating the costs of watershed protection into water user costs to the extent possible; and third, promoting on-farm and micro-catchment soil and moisture conservation actions in the context of overall farm productivity enhancements.

29

Natural Disaster Management

This Chapter was written by Christopher J. Barham and Wendy S. Ayres with the valuable input of Alcira I. Kreimer.

I. Background

Natural Disaster Experience

In terms of geography and climate, Mexico is one of the most diverse countries in the world. It is susceptible to a wide range of natural disasters such as floods, droughts, volcanic eruptions, earthquakes, fires, and tropical cyclones. Natural disasters cause enormous economic, financial, and human losses each year. Disasters are recurrent events in Mexico, occurring an average of three times a year during 1980–98. Since 1980 direct damage from natural disasters totaled some US$11.1 billion, and some 8,000 people have lost their lives. Hydro-meteorological events accounted for about 30 percent of property damage, geological events for about 40 percent, and forest fires for about 35 percent. Table 1 provides details of deaths and property damage caused by natural disasters during 1980–98. Since the table is based only on estimates of verified financial costs, the related economic costs are most likely higher.

Impact of Disasters on the Country's Economy and Development Programs

Apart from the direct losses, disasters disrupt the development process because the need for emergency and reconstruction financing diverts budgetary resources from their originally intended uses, disrupting priority investment programs. For example, in recent years, an estimated 30 percent of funding for World Bank-assisted water projects in Mexico was rechanneled to respond to emergencies. Diversions have also occurred in road maintenance projects and others. The sudden unplanned reallocation can undermine, if not sacrifice altogether, the longer-term development objectives of the original projects.

Table 1. Natural Disasters, Deaths, and Economic Losses in Mexico, 1980–98

Year	Event	Deaths	Total Property Damage US$ Millions
1980	Floods	3	87
	Droughts		222.6
1982	Volcanic eruption	42	117.0
	Hurricane Paul	0	82.4
	Floods	8	114.6
1985	Earthquake Mexico City	6,000	4,104.0
	Floods	43	39.46
	Rains	0	16.4
1986	Forest fires		1.5
1987	Snowstorms	6	0.3
1988	Forest fires		1,250
	Droughts		168.4
	Hurricane Gilberto	225	76.0
	Other hurricanes	417	597.6
	Freezes	30	0.6
1989	Forest fire		684.0
1990	Freezes	52	1.3
	Hurricane Diana	139	90.7
	Floods	200	2.5
1991	Flood	5	0.7
	Winter storms		16.8
1992	Rain and snow		0.2
	Thunderstorms		11.8
	Hurricane Winifred		8.0
	Winter storms	64	78.0
	Hailstorms		2.5
	Freezes		27.0
1993	Volcano eruptions Popocatepetl 1993–98	5	12.0
	Hurricane Gert		18.1
	Winter storms	23	95.4
	Freezes		0.1
1994	Droughts		3.5
	Hailstorms		0.3
1995	Hurricane Ismael	56	26.0
	Hurricane Opal	14	124.7
	Earthquakes		21.1
	Forest fires		1.0
	Droughts		92.9
1996	Freezes	224	5.3
1997	Hurricane Pauline	228	447.8
1998	Forest fires		1,862.4
	Hailstorms		1.7
	Torrential rains	199	602.7
	Total	7,983	11,116.36

The need to respond to natural disasters may also undermine financial planning and budgeting as an instrument of economic and social development. If budgetary allocations are frequently disrupted to deal with natural disasters, confidence in the government and its commitment to long-term economic and social development and its ability to pursue such goals will be undermined.

Impact of Natural Disasters on the Poor

In Mexico, as in other developing countries, the poor are disproportionately affected by natural disasters. According to assessments by the National Center for Disaster Prevention (CENAPRED), 68 percent of people affected by natural disasters are the poor and extremely poor. Many lower-income people live in substandard housing that is less able to withstand natural forces than housing of the better-off. Some live in high-density settlements near cities, built on steep slopes vulnerable to landslides. Others live in low-lying areas and are at risk of flooding.

The poor also have less access than others to resources to help them recover from physical losses, and therefore can suffer permanent setbacks from natural disasters. They are less likely to have savings, insurance, or access to credit which could help them finance reconstruction costs. They are also more likely to lose their source of livelihood because they earn their living from small agricultural plots which are themselves damaged by the natural disasters. During crises, poor children may suffer malnutrition and health problems, and frequently drop out of school. These factors can lead to chronic poverty.

In turn, poverty, especially in rural areas, can contribute to natural disasters. In search of arable land, the rural poor sometimes clear frontier forest areas to create grazing or cropland. Mudslides following flooding in 1999 in the Veracruz, Puebla, and Tabasco corridor occurred in areas of extreme rural poverty, where unsustainable agricultural practices on fragile lands are common, and investment in infrastructure and services is limited. The 1998 forest fires, many of them deliberately set to clear land, were concentrated in areas of the Chimalapas, where large numbers of landless or near-landless families live.

Government Approach to Date

The government has taken important steps to reduce the impacts of natural disasters. These include:

- Establishment of the National Civil Defense System (SINAPROC) in 1986 as the main mechanism for interagency coordination of disaster preparedness and response. Responsibility for the system lies with the General Coordinating Body for Civil Protection in the Ministry of the Interior. The system coordinates the work of the Secretariat of Environment, Natural Resources and Fisheries (SEMARNAP), Secretariat of Social Development, Secretariat of

Trade and Industrial Development, and Secretariat of the Interior. SINAPROC has set up mechanisms for monitoring disasters including earthquakes, cyclones, and volcanoes.

- Establishment in 1996 of the Fund for Natural Disasters (FONDEN) as a last resort source of federal financing for reconstruction of public infrastructure, restoration of protected areas, purchase of emergency response equipment, and disaster relief. FONDEN is operated by the Secretariat of Finance and Public Credit (SHCP), acting on requests for assistance made through the Secretariat of Government (SEGOB). It provides incremental funding for disaster reconstruction directly to federal agencies and municipal governments through state trust funds (*fideicomisos mixtos estatales*). FONDEN has special provisions to assist poor and low-income households to rebuild their communities and reestablish their incomes in the event of a natural disaster. Since its establishment, FONDEN's budget has increased from about US$100 million in 1996, to US$250 million in 1997, to US$450 million in 1998, and to almost US$1 billion in 1999. Disasters varied over this time, with drought dominant in 1996, hurricanes in 1997, floods in 1998, and earthquakes and floods in 1999.
- Establishment of CENAPRED as a center for research and diffusion of mitigation technologies. CENAPRED bridges the gap between academic researchers and the government by channeling research applications developed by university researchers to the Secretariat of the Interior.
- Provision of support for university-based research on risk assessment and modeling (for example, at the National Autonomous University of Mexico).
- Adoption of risk-mitigation measures, such as establishment of scientific advisory committees; setting of standards for civil works; development of a Manual of Civil Works with engineering standards for earthquake, wind, and flood-resistant designs; retrofitting of schools to withstand earthquakes; and establishing a program for certifying hospitals that meet readiness standards.

II. Main Sector Issues

Mexico faces three main issues with regard to natural disaster management. The first is to establish an institutional structure with the mandate to coordinate disaster management programs across all levels of government. The second is to implement cost-effective measures to prevent natural disasters and mitigate their impacts. The third is to identify best ways to finance post-disaster reconstruction costs.

Institutional Coordination

In Mexico, state- and municipal-level authorities play a large role in responding to natural disasters. They also have an important part in preventing and mitigating impacts of natural disasters because of their intimate knowledge of local social and physical conditions, their ability to mobilize local authorities and organizations to respond to natural disasters, and their history of working with affected communities. Decentralization has enhanced the capabilities of municipal governments to perform critical functions by providing them with greater financial resources and more autonomy in decisionmaking. Decentralization has also led to better municipal-level administration and citizen participation in the political process. However, decentralization has made it more important to carefully define the roles of actors within various levels of government and to develop mechanisms to coordinate their disaster management activities. This will be an essential step for the development of integrated prevention investment programs, which may span administrative jurisdictions and require coordinated action by various sectoral agencies.

Prevention

The large rise in public expenditures for post-disaster reconstruction suggests the need for the government to find ways to reduce losses from natural disasters through adoption of prevention measures. States and municipalities need to adopt and enforce higher engineering and building standards, inform people of natural disaster risks and unsafe areas, prevent settlement in zones prone to natural disasters, and promote less-risky behaviors. Currently, individual sector agencies in Mexico and state and municipal governments implement prevention activities as part of their normal work programs. These activities are poorly integrated with one another, and do not necessarily include activities of high national priority.

According to the World Bank's *World Development Report 2000*, average natural disaster costs as a proportion of GDP are 20 percent higher in developing economies than in industrial economies. This suggests that developing countries may well be investing too little in prevention, and that Mexico could significantly reduce its human and economic losses from natural disasters through effective implementation of prevention measures.

Post-Disaster Financing

Countries with adequate use of insurance (both public and private sector) may not face lower financial costs from natural disasters than those without insurance, but they may recover economically from disasters much more quickly because they can readily mobilize the necessary resources for reconstruction. Currently, only about 10 percent of private property in Mexico is insured. This is too little to ensure rapid recovery from natural disasters. It also implies that the public sector is necessarily bearing a large share of natural disaster costs. Moreover, requiring insurance can also lead to more investment in prevention, because insurance providers often set rates based on customers' adoption of prevention measures. Finally, greater use of insurance for public assets would also enable the government to avoid diverting resources from development programs.

A 1998 study found that Mexico could significantly improve the quality of its insurance coverage of public sector property by more carefully targeting use of insurance and through better procurement practices for obtaining coverage. Currently, as required by law, federal agencies procure insurance for federal property. However, their use of insurance is often suboptimal, since they tend to purchase too much insurance against small risks and not enough against more significant risks.

III. Options for the Future

Institutional Coordination

The most pressing need is to the define roles of actors at various levels of government for natural disaster management and to develop mechanisms to coordinate them. Local governments also need to strengthen their administrative capacity, developing mechanisms of accountability and transparency. To underpin these reforms, analyses need to be carried out to assess the functioning of the municipal level civil defense system, identify effective prevention measures to be implemented by municipal authorities, and recommend changes in the natural disaster management operational structures, legal and institutional frameworks, financing schemes, and mechanisms for citizen participation in decisionmaking.

Prevention

Prevention measures may involve, among others:

- Changes in policies (such as building and construction codes, land-use planning, and provision of financial incentives to purchase insurance).
- Development of analytical techniques for assessing disaster risk and vulnerability.
- Development of information on natural phenomena and continuous monitoring of weather-related and geological data to provide early warning of natural events.
- Specific investments to reduce vulnerability of infrastructure and buildings from natural events (such as reinforcement of bridges, dams, and levies, and reforestation and other land-stabilization techniques).

The government should pursue a more systematic approach to prevention by developing and implementing a national prevention strategy. This strategy would identify the populations and properties at greatest risk from natural disasters, define the measures that could most cost-effectively reduce the risks, and outline a mechanism to finance them. This could include, for example, establishment of a "prevention window" in FONDEN. These steps would need to be supported by actions to improve risk mapping by municipalities, and by analytical work to assess risks and vulnerabilities in various regions and sectors, and identification of the activities that would provide the largest economic payoffs.

Post-Disaster Financing

Once a study on options for financing post-disaster reconstruction is completed, the government should take steps to implement its recommendations. These may require legal and regulatory steps to improve the functioning of insurance markets, refinement of practices for insurance purchase by the public sector, creation or strengthening of natural phenomenon monitoring systems (to generate risk information to support more accurate risk pricing), and better use of insurance instruments to finance post-disaster losses now covered by FONDEN. An important issue to be addressed in post-disaster financing schemes is how to limit moral hazard from subsidies to affected populations, so that they have incentives to reduce risky behavior.

30

Air Quality

*This Chapter was written by Jean-Jacques de St. Antoine and
James Cercone (Consultant), with the valuable input of
Patricio Marquez and Claudia Macias, and Carmen Hamann,
Thesis Consultores, and Dov Chernichovsky (Consultants).*

I. Background

Considerable progress has been achieved over the last 10 years in the improvement
of air quality, particularly in the Mexico City Metropolitan Area (MCMA). In the
MCMA, substantial reductions in the concentrations of critical pollutants (such as
lead, carbon monoxide, and sulfur dioxide) have been secured through the implementation of comprehensive air quality management programs.

The government has indeed focused its attention on addressing the air quality
problem in MCMA, which remains by far the most important, from the perspective
of both the seriousness of the issues and the size of the population affected (22 million inhabitants). Progress has also been achieved on air quality issues through
smaller programs, in, among other places, Ciudad Juárez, Guadalajara, and Monterrey. Most airborne pollution in Metropolitan areas is generated by fuel used in
transportation (almost 50 percent), by industry, services, and domestic sectors (25
percent),[1] and by land use changes (12 percent).[2]

Past efforts have included the development of air quality plans, improvements in
monitoring and evaluation of air pollution, implementation of specific measures
designed to abate major sources of pollution, and efforts to reform the regulatory
and policy framework and strengthen institutional capacity.

An example of past efforts is PROAIRE, the air quality management program
for the MCMA in effect since 1995. Under the PROAIRE, a number of priority
measures to reduce pollutants have been in implementation, as well as activities
leading to policy and regulatory reform actions. These include: wider coverage of

---

1. Pollutants considered here are SO_2, CO, NOx, HC, and suspended particulates (TSP).
2. PROAIRE reports for Mexico City and Ciudad Juarez.

the air monitoring network, strengthening and enforcement of the vehicle inspection and maintenance systems, a program to replace fuel oil by natural gas in industry and the power sector, specific actions to reduce emission of volatiles from gasoline stations and storage tanks in industry, and improved specifications for transport and industrial fuels. Still, some of the priority measures identified under PROAIRE have not been implemented (such as NOx reductions in power plants and reductions of leakages from the LPG distribution system) due to lack of resources, insufficient buyout by the agencies involved, lack of adequate information, and poor follow-up.

Recognition of the multisector nature of the issues involved, has led to the formation in the MCMA of an Environmental Commission (CAM), which in the area of air quality has tried to integrate the views and concerted actions of the related authorities (energy, transport, health, and urban planning). Efforts have also been undertaken to integrate air quality concerns with transport issues. The metropolitan governments adopted an integrated strategy published in 1998 that identifies the severity of the issues and the measures with the highest economic return and largest environmental impact. The strategy indicates that future demand for transport fuels is likely to grow at a faster rate than GDP, and that therefore it is critical that efforts be made to better understand the impacts of the sector on air quality and to further identify priority activities that could mitigate its effects.

On the issue of fuel quality, government authorities have taken the decision to improve fuel composition by gradually reducing sulfur in gasoline over the next 10 years, in concert with similar decisions taken in the large majority of industrial nations, including Mexico's NAFTA partners, U.S. and Canada. This measure has been characterized by leading international experts as being among the most cost-effective from an air quality and health perspectives since the efforts to reduce lead in gasoline were implemented. The specific regulations regarding the reduction in sulfur are being drafted. Similarly and in concert with international developments, consideration is being given to a specific program for reduction of sulfur in diesel. In order for these improvements to materialize, a fleet renovation program has been designed with the participation of industry that would yield an overwhelming renewal of the transport fleet by the time the new gasoline becomes available. These efforts should be continued and supported.

Likewise, Mexico has taken the strategic decision to increase the share of natural gas in its energy mix. Natural gas is a cleaner fuel that also produces somewhat lower greenhouse gas emissions. The intention of the government, as described in the *Prospectiva de Gas Natural*[3] is to increase market share in the power, industrial, and transport sectors while eliminating all fuel oil from power generation in urban areas with air quality concerns.

---

3. Prospectiva del Gas Natural (1995–2000); PEMEX, 1996.

There is increased recognition of the linkages (some reinforcing, others diverging) between local air quality problems and the nature of the global issue of climate change (global warming). Mexico has been an active party to the Convention on climate change. Recently, the Mexican Congress ratified the Kyoto Protocol (April 2000), thus confirming the intention of the country to be an active partner in efforts to mitigate climate change. Under the First Communication before the Convention, Mexico made an assessment of emissions of greenhouse gases (2.1 percent of world total, the largest in Latin America), conducted a vulnerability assessment, and initiated an impact assessment of climate change that shows the potential effect of projected reductions in rainfall for the central area of the country and increased exposure of coastal areas to weather events. Mexico has also produced a nonbinding plan for reduction of emissions. Under the provisions of the Kyoto Protocol, a Clean Development Mechanism is being designed that could be instrumental in the transfer of substantial financial resources for cost-effective abatement of emissions in the country. Mexico is currently in the process of developing its second communication which is due in November 2000.

II. Issues

Large and Unsustainable Impact on Health

Recent health studies done in Mexico and elsewhere confirm the negative and unsustainable impacts on health, welfare, and general quality of life resulting from exposure of urban populations and surrounding ecosystems to poor air quality. Despite considerable progress in abating key pollutants (lead, CO, Sulfur) in some urban air sheds, many urban centers (most notably the MCMA) remain exposed to unhealthy concentrations of airborne pollutants. Exposures to particulates and ozone have been proven to have direct links to health, and to impact productivity and the ecosystem. For both pollutants, the MCMA fails to meet standards 25 and 90 percent of the time, respectively. Unhealthy ozone levels are the result of the interaction of high levels of volatile organic compounds, mostly generated during the transport, storage, and use of fossil fuels, and of nitrogen oxides, themselves a result of combustion processes in vehicles and stationary sources (such as power plants). The large number of people concentrated in urban centers (56 percent of all Mexicans live in cities with 1 million or more) and the large percentage of children in the population make improvements in air quality a national priority.

There is also a need for better scientific knowledge of the problem, including a better understanding of current emissions and their sources, the mechanisms of diffusion in the atmosphere, and the exposure and impact functions in the population. This will enable the development of actions directed at reducing the root causes of the health impacts.

Weak Institutional Framework for Air Quality Management

Despite the existence of dedicated institutions, the CAM for example in the MCMA, their structures, mandates, and resources remain weak or insufficient. There is a need to secure institutional set-ups independent of political cycles, with stronger mandates and say over the adoption of sector policies (energy, transport, urban planning) and the resources required to implement them. There are literally millions of source contributions to the problem in the energy, transport, industry, and other sectors. This is truly a multisector issue and hence requires a multisector approach. There is also a need to ensure a large degree of continuity in the implementation of long-term action plans.

Indoor Pollution

Although there is no solid countrywide documentation on this issue, there are concerns regarding the level of exposure to indoor airborne pollutants in rural areas and poor neighborhoods in urban areas caused by the uncontrolled or inefficient burning of fuelwood. According to recent data, household use of fuelwood was second only to LPG, and more than twice that of electricity in 1996. This would have a significant adverse impact on public health because burning fuelwood gives off considerable fine particles. There is a need to better understand the level of exposure and the magnitude of the problem.

Weak (or Lack of) Internalization of Environmental and Health Costs in Policy Making

Traditionally, energy and transport policies have been formulated and implemented with limited internalization of environmental and health concerns. Fuel pricing, for example, does not reflect relative environmental costs and benefits, yet it has a substantial impact on rates of use, development of alternatives, costs of health impacts, and ultimately financial returns on air quality management programs. It is thus imperative to reflect full costs (including environmental costs) in fuel-pricing policies.

Limited Citizen Participation

Air quality is a "commons issue" (that is, it relates to a good, traditionally taken for free, on which a large population depends or is affected by). Yet, citizen involvement in decisionmaking has been limited. Progress has been achieved through the formalization of a citizen council at the CAM in the MCMA. However, ultimate success in the implementation of air quality management programs depend on specific sector action plans (energy, transport, urban planning) and on the degree of acceptance and involvement of the affected population at large and the availability of information.

Barriers to Gains in Energy Efficiency and the Promotion of Renewable Energy Resources

Energy is a key sector issue. Substantial gains remain to be achieved from improvements in the efficiency of energy use in end-use applications (domestic, industrial, and transport) that could drastically reduce the emission of airborne pollutants of local air quality and global concern. Obstacles that need to be addressed include lack of information, limited access to financing mechanisms, and the development of appropriate standards.

Barriers to Promotion of Cleaner Vehicles and Fuels

Barriers to the introduction of cleaner vehicles include obsolete and lax regulations, lack of operational and management experience in the private sector, limited access to credit, limited reach of emissions monitoring, and impediments to technology transfer. In the transport sector, the issues are fuel quality; emission standards for new vehicles and, equally important, in-use emission standards and their enforcement; and improved traffic engineering. Barriers to the introduction of cleaner fuels include lack of integration of full costs into the pricing of fuels (some fuels, like diesel, contribute comparatively more to local pollution); uneven application of taxes that prevent the introduction of cleaner fuels (for example, natural gas is taxed comparatively higher vis-à-vis diesel, and this has in the past reduced the financial incentives for gas use as a transport fuel even though it represents a cleaner option); and lack of infrastructure (distribution networks for natural gas are still limited).

Weak Incentives for Private Sector Participation

The role of the private sector in reducing emissions is essential. The government needs to provide the right signals and an appropriate institutional and regulatory framework to encourage the private sector to reduce emissions and to provide the necessary enforcement of these regulations.

III. Strategic Options and Policy Objectives

The key goals in air quality are:

- To promote cost-effective, continuous improvements in air quality over urban areas, thereby directly aiming at improvements in the quality of life and health of urban populations.
- To integrate air quality management strategies with transport, energy, and ultimately, urban planning concerns.

To achieve those two objectives, a series of strategic priorities and ensuring policy actions should be pursued. They are presented below.

1. Formulation of Long-Term, Multisector, Strategic Frameworks

Mexican authorities have been working on urban air quality improvements for several years, and the results have produced important, although not yet sufficient progress. In early 1999 Mexican authorities decided to continue the formulation, design, and implementation of the next stage of Air Quality Management in the MCMA (AQM-III: 2000–10). Multidisciplinary teams were organized that include some of the top government authorities in each field (Secretaries of Transport, Urban Development, and Environment). The thrust of the effort is very clear: "to improve health indicators through reductions in exposure of populations to airborne pollutants." AQM-III will be ready after the new Administration is in, and therefore it is critically important to ensure continuity in these efforts.

AQM-III would provide the strategic framework to guide necessary immediate interventions, and to further define the goals and priorities, while identifying barriers and required reforms. The plan will bring together a significant amount of disparate information on air quality issues in Mexico City. This valuable information will be integrated into a comprehensive assessment providing the basis for a long-term strategy to address air quality in the MCMA. Priority under AQM-III should be given to efforts to reduce particulates and ozone, both of which have been shown to have unsustainable impacts on health and the environment. The efforts being planned for the MCMA should kick off and support similar planning initiatives for other large urban centers in the country, particularly in cities like Monterrey, Guadalajara, and Ciudad Juarez, where there are emerging concerns regarding air quality.

2. Strengthening of the Institutional Framework for Air Quality Management

The actual implementation of Air Quality Management Plans greatly depends on the strengthen institutional framework. The regional and urban authorities need to take decisive steps toward improved coordination, diagnosis, and planning, and supervision capabilities. The driving force of all these is skill enhancement. Key priorities therefore are:

Strengthening of Air Quality Management Institutions

In the MCMA the CAM (Comisión Ambiental Metropolitana) is the lead institution for environmental policy in the city. It is made up of representatives from the government of the city, the Mexico State Government, the Health City Secretariat, and SEMARNAP. It is now necessary to reform the CAM and revitalize its stakeholding participation as a way to ensure wide participation and ownership of expert opinion from all relevant agencies. A strengthened CAM would provide the integration of environmental policies from different agencies, as well as environmental criteria to guide actions by different sectors. Similar institutional set-ups are required for other metropolitan areas.

Increased Citizen Participation and Communication

Community outreach and public participation complement expert opinion, and are necessary to improve public understanding of the issues and generate public support for difficult or costly decisions. There is a need to communicate risks and benefits from proposed actions. Likewise, it is important to provide an outlet to citizen participation in decisionmaking regarding environmental issues in sector policies, with particular emphasis on energy, transport, and urban planning.

Public education and consciousness raising on the costs and impact of air pollution is even more relevant than generating sympathetic public opinion on the technical or economic aspects of air pollution management. Public education should also include the raising of the metro's image among middle- and upper-class residents.

Achieving Sustainability in the Funding of Environmental Commissions for Air Quality Management

Long-term management of air quality requires the independence, continuity and support that a sustainable financial mechanism provides. Such a mechanism is currently missing and needs to be developed.

3. Focusing on the Transport Sector as the Most Important Source of Air Pollution in the Metropolitan Areas

Road transport is by far the most important source of air pollution in most metropolitan areas in Mexico. As part of the air quality efforts the MCMA, the COMETRAVI (Comisión Metropolitana de Transporte y Vialidad) produced a study on "Integrated Transport Air Quality Strategy." While the results of the strategy have yet to be validated, and concerns over methodologies used and the results produced have been raised, the Strategy does compare over 30 different measures on the basis of potential environmental impact and their cost. A summary of the results of this comparison reveals that improvements in the environmental performance of high-use vehicles (that is, the bus fleet and cargo transport) and passenger cars offer some of the highest economic benefits with the highest reductions in emission of airborne pollutants. This result coincides with similar assessments done elsewhere.[4] In addition, the INE has recently updated the emission inventories for mobile sources in the MCMA, illustrating the comparatively high contribution of these sources to the air quality problem in the region. Urban transport is the principal source of the pollutants (particulates and ozone precursors) which, as mentioned earlier, are of highest concern because of their health impact.

---

4. CARB, 1990; Harmonization Options for Local/Global Air Pollution. SAPAC, 1999.

The key environmental objective of transport strategies for cities is the reduction, or at least the containment, of traffic-generated air pollution through the promotion of low-emission public transport and nonmotorized transport, and the containment of pollution generated by cars and the movement of freight. Investment programs (such as rail lines or busways), regulatory measures (such as controls on emissions and traffic demand management), and pricing policies (such as charges on polluting fuels or on automobile access to congested areas) must be balanced against economic and social objectives and take account of the city's financial limitations.

One objective of urban transport strategies is to achieve integration between different modes of passenger transport. Integrating exclusive autobus routes serving the outer reaches of metropolitan areas with other modes of public transport (light rail, metros in the MCMA and Monterrey) will serve the twin objectives of reducing emissions from and improving the quality of the road-based public transport fleet

4. Improving the Integration Between Air Quality, Energy, and Transport

Despite some efforts already undertaken, there is a need to strengthen multisector strategies to tackle air pollution issues. Among these are:

Removing Barriers to Energy Efficiency and Energy Conservation

The adoption of energy-efficient demand side management practices and building technologies including regulations, design, space conditioning, and market applications, is required and would have a major impact on the reduction of airborne pollutants linked to fuel combustion and power generation. This includes the establishment of programs and incentives for efficient energy use, promotion of energy-efficient devices and practices, and increased public awareness of the benefits of efficient energy use. Through the *Comisión Nacional de Energía* (CONAE), the government has engaged in a national program for saving and conserving energy. This program, which is consistent with national efforts to diminish air pollution, could be enhanced by fostering deeper market penetration of energy-efficient devices that prevent leaks and minimize the energy intensity of current LPG use; through complementary regulations and standards; and through promotion of activities to help overcome existing barriers.

Promoting Parallel Track Efforts at Improving Fuel Quality and Vehicle Emission Standards

The Mexican Government is in the process of implementing further improvements in the quality of gasoline, following international adoption of stricter specifications for sulfur content. The adoption of these new standards is expected to be in place as the fleet is renovated to take advantage of improved availability of cleaner gasoline. It must also be supported by effective and strict emission and maintenance provisions and the adoption of durability requirements in the catalyst systems. Steps to cultivate a culture of proper and prompt vehicle maintenance are also required. Stricter enforcement will encourage new businesses in the area of vehicle repair and service, which is crucial for curbing vehicular emissions. Enforcement of catalyst durability requirements and other new standards will require specialized technical assistance that could be sought from partner environmental agencies in North America.

Cost-effectiveness of These and All Other Measures Should be a Primary Consideration in Their Adoption

While there is not yet an international consensus on the differentiated impact of particulates generated during combustion of diesel, improvements on diesel specifications should be further pursued. These improvements may represent increases in refining costs. Passing on the increases to the consumer is likely to be more difficult for diesel than for gasoline. Ultimately, fuel prices should reflect all costs, including those resulting from environmental and health damage, which until now have not been factored into fuel price policies. In this respect, reform of the tax regime for fuels is an important element (currently, CNG is taxed comparatively more heavily than diesel and LPG, while CNG is less polluting than diesel). Regulatory and pricing policies that could reduce traffic-generated air pollution need to be defined and agreed.

Promoting the Adoption of Renewable Energy by Removing Barriers and Reducing Implementation Costs

The government could also support measures aimed at promoting already commercially available renewable energy technologies (RETs) in urban areas. Mexico has a large potential for use of solar energy (high solar radiation levels), and there is a significant potential for use of solar energy in passive applications (water heating) and as a contributor to power generation in certain areas. Government strategies should aim at trying to overcome barriers to the use of renewable energy resources through provision of information services, design of innovative financing mechanisms to reduce perception of financial risks, support of legal and regulatory studies, and adoption of appropriate standards.

Removing Barriers for Market Penetration of Low-Emission, Energy-Efficient, and High Occupancy Vehicles

A main component of the government's strategy would be the removal of barriers for market penetration of low-emission, energy-efficient vehicles in metropolitan areas. Activities designed to overcome existing barriers, such as strategic urban planning, regulatory studies, development of standards, level playing-field tax regimes, and fuel specifications would be required to make these options viable.

Reducing Indoor Air Pollution

Options for moving people away from fuelwood to commercial fuels such as kerosene and LPG should be investigated. In some countries governments subsidize the cylinder deposit fees. Strictly from the point of view of economic benefits, this type of subsidy may have far greater (positive) impact than other existing energy subsidies in Mexico.

5. Harmonizing Efforts To Improve Air Quality with Global Air Quality Concerns

Improvements in local air quality will result not only in the abatement of local air pollutants, but would also yield reductions in the emission of global greenhouse gases, with relatively modest increases in cost to the country. Still, the incremental costs of these activities could be supported by the global community as better air quality in Mexico carries major positive externalities beyond its national frontiers.

6. Fostering Partnerships and Bringing Worldwide Expertise

The formulation of air quality plans represents a long-term, multisector, and ambitious effort, and requires considerable and highly specialized expertise. It is also a very visible venture. The nature of the air quality problem in the MCMA and its position as perhaps the largest urban area in the world, makes it a laboratory of worldwide relevance. As such, it has attracted the interest of air quality managers and scientists elsewhere. There is a need to continue to foster these partnerships and interests while pursuing the objectives outlined under the air quality management plans.

31

Solid Waste Management

This Chapter was written by Walter Vergara
with the valuable input of Richard Clifford and Carl R. Bartone.

I. Background

As is the case with many developing nations, Mexico faces serious difficulties in the management of urban refuse and solid waste. It is estimated that over 82,000 tons of solid waste is generated in the country every day. Yet, there is a general lack of proper treatment and disposal facilities, institutional capacities are weak, and financial support at local and municipal levels is frequently deficient. The problem is exacerbated by (a) the sustained growth of population, (b) the high rate of rural migration to urban settings, and (c) an increased degree of industrialization and associated local consumption patterns. For example, during the last several decades, Mexico has been urbanizing rapidly (currently, approximately 60 percent of the population of 92 million[1] live in cities with over 15,000 inhabitants).[2] Per capita generation of urban refuse has also increased. It is estimated that 0.7 kilograms to 1.3 kilogramsof solid waste is generated per person per day, with an average organic content of about 71 percent. Regrettably, of all the solid waste generated, only 77 percent is collected (62,000 tons), and less than 35 percent is disposed of under sanitary conditions (29,000 tons). Per capita solid waste generation is linked to household income and city size.

Mindful of the long-term costs of improper solid waste management, the government has been working on a program designed to address some of the underlying causes of improper solid waste management. The program, spearheaded by SEDESOL, supports efforts to strengthen regulations and institutions at the federal

---

1. Estimate of 1997 population size; annual growth rate of 2 percent.
2. National Communication of Mexico, available on the Climate Change Commission Homepage.

and local level conducive to more effective practices and incentives, and extend the provision of services in urban centers. This program is assisting specific communities committed to policy and institutional reform to develop, design, and operate long-term solid waste management programs. The government is also mapping a comprehensive recycling plan.

The Mexican authorities have been working on solid waste management issues for several years, and the results have produced important, but not yet sufficient, progress. Collection, transfer, and disposal of solid waste has improved in Mexico over the past few years, but still is short of providing service to close to 50 percent of the urban population. In its broadest form, the government's strategy for halting environmental degradation and remedying past problems is articulated in its *Plan Nacional de Desarollo: 1995–2000* and its *Programa Nacional para la Protección del Medio Ambiente*. More specifically, the authorities have established conditions to improve solid waste management through *La Norma Oficiál Mexicana* (NOM-083-ECOL–1996), and is now in the process of issuing of regulations for sanitary landfill construction, operation, and management (NOM-084-ECOL–2000). Overall, the federal framework for solid waste management and the existing regulations are modern and adequate.

II. Major Issues

LIMITED INFRASTRUCTURE (COVERAGE), AND LACK OF REGULATORY FRAMEWORK AT THE MUNICIPAL LEVEL. The key issue in solid waste management is the poor coverage of services as the result of limited and inadequate infrastructure; deficient municipal regulations; limited management capacity at a municipal level; and lack of proper equipment for collection, transfer, and disposal. While the seven largest urban centers have reasonable coverage for collection and disposal of some sort, the situation becomes progressively worse when the size of the urban center in question is reduced. In the 100 largest cities, other than the seven metropolitan areas, only 42 percent of solid waste is properly disposed of. In small cities only 4 percent of solid waste is properly disposed of. Although there has not been a survey on the issue, the environmental and health costs of this situation are large and unsustainable. Key barriers to improving expansion of service are poor financial management and cost recovery.

WEAK MUNICIPAL FINANCES, CAPACITY, AND GOVERNANCE. The delivery of municipal services in solid waste management is frequently affected by poor municipal finances and lack of a proper incentive framework to ensure that generators pay for the actual cost of disposal. The development of stable cost-recovery mechanisms has also been affected by limited managerial capacity that prevents sustained interest by private or autonomous entities in the provision of services. Other limitations at the municipal level include lack of planning, budgeting, and accounting procedures that would feed into a local management information system. Ideally, there should be accounting centers and segregated (autonomous) accounts for solid waste management.

Health and Environmental Impacts. Improper waste management practices contribute to serious health and safety problems in the affected communities through promotion of vector-borne diseases. It also reduces property values. Improper disposal of waste also contributes to the contamination of aquifers and surface waters caused by percolation and runoffs of leachates. Open or uncontrolled burning of solid waste that takes place in many open landfills in waste dumps also contributes to air pollution through the generation of particulates and smog.

Social Issues. The ad hoc character of disposal sites (open, poorly regulated dumps) has led to the exacerbation of the social problems associated with the *pepenadores*. These are indigents living off of the recovery of recyclable material at the dumps, often under poor hygienic and safety conditions and in some cases subject to organized crime rings. There are, however, some important and successful experiences that could be replicated nationwide. For example, in Monterrey, the municipality has been successful in eliminating all informal recycling and replacing it with a well-organized transfer and recycling center that has been able to employ many of the former pepenadores. A recycling cooperative has also been opened in Ciudad Juarez.

Greenhouse Gas Emissions. The waste that is deposited in landfills decomposes, producing LFG, usually composed of 50 percent methane. Methane emissions from landfills contribute about 10 percent of total methane emissions in Mexico.[3] The reduction of methane emissions is a critical part of the Mexican strategy to control emission of greenhouse gases. Methane is a powerful greenhouse gas. However, Mexican experience in LFG management is only now beginning, through preparation of a GEF project.

III. Strategic Options

The policy goal of solid waste management is to increase coverage of collection and disposal, extending it from the large metropolitan areas to the next largest 100 cities by 2006, thereby mitigating health and environmental impacts.

Strengthening of Regulations and Institutions at the Federal and Local Level

There is an urgent need to provide the regulatory and institutional base that would lead to better collection, transfer, and disposal of solid waste and the promotion of

---

3. *Avances en el desarrollo de indicadores para la evaluación del desempeño ambiental en México 1997*, Instituto Nacional de Ecológica, SEMARNAP.

cost recovery for solid waste collection and disposal. The key strategic actions in the regulatory and institutional reform process include:

(i) Formulation of a strengthened legal framework for solid waste management focusing on favoring the creation of decentralized operators,[4] to support the establishment of recovery quotas, and to reduce transaction costs to the private sector; there is also a need to continue with the program of enforcement of regulations at a local level.

(ii) Promotion and creation of institutional capacity at the local level for solid waste management.

There remains a major concern regarding the creditworthiness of municipalities (municipal finances), which is a generalized problem affecting many programs undertaken at the local level. This is an issue that will be resolved through continous improvements in governance and accountability, and is not exclusive of solid waste management programs.

Extending the Provision of Services to Medium- and Small-Size Localities

While sanitary landfills are now in operation in most large urban centers, there is a need to extend services to medium- and small-size localities, where indexes for collection and proper disposal are still very low. Strategically, the key priority is to promote the adoption of efforts to improve coverage of service through:

(i) Diagnosis of issues at the municipal level.

(ii) Adoption of cost-recovery programs for solid waste management that are tied to the demand for service quality (for example, frequency of collection and sidewalk service) and willingness to pay (assessed through proper survey tools), but that also meet federal and local environmental regulations.

(iii) Promotion of specific investments in collection, recycling, and proper disposal.

(iv) Promotion of private sector participation in provision of services, initially in collection but in the long term designed to improve private sector participation or involvement of autonomous entities in recycling and disposal.

(v) Adoption of action plans to continue the process of closure and rehabilitation of open dumps and their replacement by controlled sanitary landfills (as the size of cities involved decrease, there will be more and more opportunities for shared facilities to achieve the necessary economies of scale).

---

4. Decentralized operations are particularly suitable for collection services and could encompass even micro-enterprises serving small communities or low-income areas in larger cities. In the case of disposal, however, a centralized or shared facility serving several municipalities is frequently the best solution. This has been the case for example of Tampico-Altamira-Durango as well as municipalities in the urban area of Monterrey.

(vi) Adoption of clear strategic approaches (an integrated strategic framework) through the design and implementation of long-term plans that define the functional scope of the services, tend to the needs of the different stakeholders, and address the different strategic barriers preventing the delivery or improvement of services (political, institutional, social, financial, technical, economic, and environmental).

(vii) Design and adoption of a specific framework and instruments to promote higher private sector participation in the provision of services.

Reduction in Waste Generation (At-Source Reduction) and Promotion of Recycling

The most cost-effective waste disposal strategy is reduction at source (recycling of materials), thus reducing the need for ultimate disposal and promoting better use of resources. Recycling centers at the points of collection are a next-best option. There is a need to finalize efforts to formulate a national strategy for recovery and recycling of solid waste.

The long-term strategy for solid waste management in Mexico calls for a reduction in the amount of waste released on a per capita basis through efforts directed at promotion of recycling and reuse of solid residues. The key priority is to promote the assessment of the underlying causes behind the relative small volumes of recycling, and to promote the development of incentives for recovery of secondary materials (glass, metal, paper, and plastic) and organics. To promote this long-term strategy, there is a need to ensure that the proper incentive framework is in place to discourage waste generation through confronting generators with the true cost of managing the residues they produce. This is especially important in the case of large and institutional generators.

Addressing Social Issues (Pepenadores) through Involvement in Transfer Stations and Recycling Centers

The social dimensions of efforts to improve solid waste management should not be ignored. The development of sanitary landfills will bring about the elimination of *pepenadores*. Whenever feasible, these groups could be involved in the operation of transfer stations and recycling centers under much improved hygiene and safety conditions.

Harmonizing Efforts Seeking Solid Waste Management Improvements with Climate Change Concerns

The reduction of methane emissions from landfills is a critical part of the Mexican strategy to control emission of greenhouse gases. Methane is a powerful greenhouse gas and its emissions are targeted under the Kyoto Protocol. Its uncontrolled release represents an odor nuisance and a local risk of explosion, and contributes to about 10 percent of total methane emissions in Mexico.[5] The strategy should be to assist in efforts to integrate solid waste management with proper capture and use of land-fill gas, including its use as an alternative fuel.

Specific Actions

The agenda of specific actions include:

- Train, disseminate information to, and encourage participation of, municipal managers in modern solid waste management, using the efforts already completed in Monterrey and Tampico as examples of modern practices and for dissemination and training purposes.
- Facilitate adoption of cost-recovery mechanisms and sustainable financing that would encourage the private sector to participate in the delivery of services and encourage recycling.
- Encourage effective citizen consultation and participation in solid waste management decisions.
- Facilitate the identification and environmental assessment of suitable sites for sanitary disposal.
- Integrate land fill gas regulations into federal statutes for solid waste management.
- Facilitate the development and dissemination of programs for helping set up recycling cooperatives and transfer stations that address the social issue of the *pepenadores* and promote the reduction of waste ultimately destined for disposal.
- Improve the design of concession systems for collection and disposal services (reducing transaction costs but improving transparency and better-defining liabilities and responsibilities).

---

5. *Avances en el desarrollo de indicadores para la evaluacion del desempeño ambiental en Mexico 1997*, Institución Nacional de Ecologicá, SEMARNAP.

Accountability and the Demand for Quality Government

32

Decentralization

This Chapter was written by Steven B. Webb.

Although Mexico has been constitutionally a federation for decades, the fiscal system followed a path of increasing centralization until the early 1980s. Since then, however, and especially since the mid-1990s, spending and borrowing decisions have been rapidly decentralized. This change has many advantages and complements the increased political decentralization and competition at subnational and national levels. The change is not yet supported with adequate institutions, however, and there are imbalances in the pace of decentralizing different aspects of the fiscal system. For example, taxation is much more centralized than spending, and probably more than is necessary for efficient administration. This Chapter reviews the current situation, identifies the most important policy issues, discusses the policy options to address them.[1]

I. Mexico's Decentralization in International Perspective

The worldwide experience with decentralization provides three lessons relevant for Mexico. First, because decentralization has major effects on issues ranging from macroeconomic stability to poverty alleviation, the provision of social services, and the quality of governance, a country needs to develop a coherent strategy for decentralizing its public sector. Second, because decentralization is an ongoing, evolving activity, a successful strategy requires adequate institutional infrastructure to develop, monitor, and implement the decentralization policy. The necessary infra-

---

1. This Chapter is based on Giugale, Marcelo M. and Steven B. Webb, eds. 2000. *Achievements and Challenges of Fiscal Decentralization—Lessons from Mexico.* The World Bank. Washington, D.C.

structure includes legal and regulatory frameworks, agencies for coordination, dissemination of accurate and complete information, and capacity-building programs. Even the best-planned strategies do not sustain themselves without such institutional support. Third, the Latin American experience with decentralization shows that abrupt, across-the-board efforts generally fail. Countries have had to go back to incremental decentralization, with differentiated rules according to different management and financial capacity of the territorial units.

Mexico is progressing toward more autonomy, fiscal responsibility, and accountability at subnational levels of government. States now spend close to half as much as the federal government (see Table 1). The municipal share of public spending has also grown, although this trend is not as fully documented. This process is being driven by heightened political competition at all levels of government and by the desire of the federal government to include decentralization in its program for broadening political participation.

Each country must develop its own strategy of decentralization and institutional infrastructure in accordance with its history, its objectives, and the constraints it faces. The models of decentralization found in the world range along a wide spectrum. At one end is what might be called full legislative federalism, exemplified by Canada, in which the main source of funds for subnational governments is their own taxes, and they have almost complete autonomy as to how they spend them. At the other end of the spectrum is administrative federalism, found in Germany and Australia. In these countries transfers are the major source of states' revenues, and federal (or joint) policies guide most subnational expenditures. Regional equalization policies, largely implemented through transfers, are very strong, and subnational borrowing faces tight central controls. Varying combinations of the features mentioned—revenue independence, expenditure autonomy, debt autonomy, and equalization—may be found in other countries. Mexico could mix and match these

Table 1. Fiscal Magnitudes: Federal and State Governments, 1997

| | Percent of GDP | |
	Federal	States*
Own spending	11.5	4.9
1991	8.4	3.0
1996	7.7	4.9
Own revenue	15.8	1.0
Disposable revenue	13.2	5.4
Primary balance	-1.3	0.0
Overall balance	-4.9	-0.1
Debt service	18.4	0.3
Debt stock	31.0	1.5

Note: * Tabasco and Tamaulipas not included; no data.
Source: SHCP and World Bank estimates.

characteristics in a variety of ways in order to meet its own needs, subject to internal-consistency constraints.

II. Pending Policy Issues

Decentralization issues are divided here into spending, taxes, transfers, , and institution building. Most of the recent increases of decentralizing have been in spending, transfers, and borrowing. The taxation aspects of fiscal federalism have seen little change in the past 20 years.

Spending

Decentralization can provide many economic benefits in the areas of spending and service delivery, including the choice of the mix of public sector activities that best suit the taste and needs of citizens in a local area, provision of services in a more cost-effective way by adapting the method of delivery to local circumstances, and allowing citizens to express more directly their concerns about service provision. The benefits will also depend on strengthening the link between subnational spending choices and self-taxing decisions. This is not a matter of just changing rules, but also of creating a culture of devolution. It will take time.

The broad assignment of responsibilities by sectors in Mexico is reasonable: education and health to the states, local streets and sanitation to municipalities, and other sectors to the federal government. The problems are in the details. Four features dominate the current assignment of expenditure responsibilities as it evolved in the 1990s:

(i)   Obligations for important services such as education, health, or social assistance are concurrent at federal and state levels. Concurrent obligations often leave functions like maintenance, regulation, and inspection without any level taking adequate responsibility.

(ii)   The federal government earmarks most transfers and mandates how states fulfill their obligations.

(iii) Earmarked transfers are still based on historic costs and actual inputs, rather than on indicators of the magnitude of the spending obligation.

(iv)   Few responsibilities are assigned to the municipal level. Since 1998 smaller municipalities have received a large increase of resources from transfers, with no commensurate change in their responsibilities. Large municipalities, on the other hand, have faced popular political pressure to take on many critical tasks, often without the requisite financial resources.

Although more resources pass through their books than ever before, states in some ways have less fiscal autonomy now than they had a decade ago. With the exception of the new Fund for Strengthening the States, most of the resources they receive from the federal level (including from shared revenues) are effectively earmarked either for transfers to municipalities or social sector salaries, especially schoolteachers and university professors with federally mandated pay scales, or they are claimed by the terms of matching grant programs. This situation is inconsistent with the growing economic and political power of the states.

Transfers for education and health are allocated mainly on the basis of the number of staff and physical sites (schools, clinics, hospitals). Evidence from a number of countries indicates that formulas for sectoral transfers are more equitable and encourage efficiency better if they are based on a capitation formula, with adjustments made for population density, age, and gender. Moving toward such a system, as Mexico' social security system for health is starting to do, would improve the efficiency and equity of transfers.

Taxes

Tax revenues of the subnational governments in Mexico cover only a small fraction of what they spend. States typically have their own payroll taxes, annual taxes on automobiles, and fees. Currently they are legally prohibited from taxing interstate trade and some excises. Taxes represent only about 4.5 percent of total revenues of states (other than the Federal District). Payroll taxes are the most important, levied in 23 of the 32 states. States with strong economies are mostly pressing for more taxation authority. Municipal governments are on average only slightly less dependent than the states on revenue sharing and transfers. In the aggregate, they receive about two-thirds of total net revenues from these sources, but the pattern differs markedly across and within states. The perverse incentive structure in revenue-sharing arrangements partly accounts for low rates of tax collection. At least the larger municipal governments would benefit from having access to additional sources of revenue—beyond the property tax—and from improved incentives.

The subnational governments should raise more taxes for three reasons. First, the public sector needs more tax revenue for when revenues from oil decline, not only temporarily because of low oil prices but also permanently as a share of GDP because of economic growth and diversification. Second, to give citizens more control over the size of public spending within their jurisdictions, subnational governments need to have adequate taxing authority. If they want to spend more money in a program, they can raise taxes; if they decide to save money on a program, they can reduce taxes. This involves, primarily, having control over marginal (incremental) revenue—what a subnational government can affect by its own actions, especially by changing tax rates, but also by imposing new taxes or repealing old ones, by changing the tax base, and by varying administrative effort. Third, states that borrow need to control some source of funds with which to repay their debts. If they experience an unexpected adverse shock, relative to their fiscal plan at the time of borrowing, they need to be able to raise additional revenue (or cut costs) by enough to sustain their debt service.

Transfers

Intergovernmental transfers perform three key roles in federal systems. First, they balance the disparities between the expenditure needs and the revenue capacity of subnational governments. Second, they integrate fiscal federalism with the social and political dimensions of federations. For example, more conditionality for intergovernmental transfers signals an increase in the centralization of the federation and vice versa—less conditionality means more decentralization. Third, transfers are the main channel for implementing society's intentions regarding the equality of opportunity among citizens living in different states.

Mexico's two main categories of transfers today are *participaciones* and *aportaciones*. *Participaciones* were originally revenues of states and municipalities whose collection was delegated to the federal level in the Fiscal Pact for tax efficiency reasons. In practice, the federal government writes the formula for distribution of these funds and augments them from federal sources, like oil revenues, so they are different from tax sharing (where revenue collected in a state stays there) and are more like a transfer program of the general revenue-sharing type. Most of these transfers go out under *Ramo 28*. *Aportaciones* were conceived as federal money earmarked to pay for (formerly) federal commitments and transferred to the states and municipalities together with those commitments (for example, education and health). These funds, formerly under *Ramo 26*, now go out under *Ramo 33*.

In Mexico, as in many countries, society's intentions with regard to transfers are in flux and unclear. There were at least 11 major transfer programs in the 2000 budget, up from 3 in 1997. Each program addresses multiple objectives, and each objective is addressed in several programs. This makes it harder than necessary for subnational governments to calculate how much money they will receive and for the federal government to determine how well the transfer system is addressing its objectives. The constitution and the revenue-sharing law do not give explicit goals for the transfers, but their actual pattern reveals something about the intentions. The principal objectives of transfers in Mexico seem to be to (a) let states share in the federal government's greater potential to raise revenue; (b) subsidize subnational governments' provision of services with national externalities (basic health and education); (c) strengthen the autonomy of municipalities; and (d) provide additional resources to states with a high incidence of poverty. A fifth possible objective would be to compensate states with low per capita tax bases, as Canada does. Mexican transfers do not address this objective explicitly, although they address it partially through poverty-targeted transfers, because poverty is positively correlated with low tax base per capita.

When all the programs are added, state by state, the amount of per capita resources available to the states (total of their own revenues and all the various transfer programs) varies with a coefficient variation of 0.24 (in 1999), which is low by international standards for large federations. Furthermore, the variation does not correlate strongly with poverty. The resources per capita are about the same on average for states with middle and high levels of poverty, however, and the richer states (low levels of poverty) have only slightly higher-than-average resources. High per capita revenues in rich, low-poverty states are counterbalanced on average by poverty-targeted transfers to high-poverty states. This equality of per capita government resources across income levels may reflect a basic social value in Mexico.

The current transfer system has four main problems: First, it is too complex to achieve a coherent set of purposes. Consequently the federal government distributes more resources than necessary to achieve its objectives, and states are treated inequitably. The main beneficiaries of this complexity are states that get more than they would under a simple and transparent system. Second, basing many transfers on historical or current costs, rather than using per capita or per potential recipient costs, is inequitable and discourages efficiency. Third, at least up until 1999, the availability of ad hoc transfers for politically favored states undermined the incentives for managing spending well and for enhancing revenue. States had more incentive to curry political favor with the national government than to strengthen their own finances. Fourth, earmarking and matching grant requirements leave states with little autonomy for improving efficiency or adjusting allocation to meet local needs.

Debt and Borrowing

The past policies on subnational borrowing evolved when Mexico's intergovernmental fiscal relations could be kept on track by ad hoc transfers and negotiations between players in the same party hierarchy. Now that states and municipalities are more independent politically and are often governed by parties in the opposition at the national level, the challenge has been to develop a more strict and transparent system for managing subnational borrowing. Otherwise, debt problems could cripple the decentralization process and, in a worst-case scenario, eventually pose a macroeconomic hazard for the country as a whole (as in Brazil's Mina Gerais). The burden of debt has been a fiscal problem for some states (municipal debt is generally small, except for the Federal District, which is effectively a state).

The federal government debt bailouts in the past created inappropriate incentives. For states to have an incentive to control costs and increase their revenues—a stated goal of state and federal governments—it is important that neither states nor their lenders expect a bailout. Otherwise, borrowing becomes a means through which states can obtain extra federal resources, transferred to them or their creditors. All states received bailouts in the wake of the 1995 economic crisis. Since then borrowing has been low or zero by most states, but a few have borrowed heavily. Moving to a new practice of no bailouts will require not only changing the rules, but also assuring that challenges to the new rules are not overwhelming, especially during the transition, and that there is adequate political support for the rules.

Most borrowing by states and municipalities until 2000 was guaranteed with state *participaciones* as collateral. As a consequence, neither the states nor their creditors worried much about the repayment capacity. The federal government was the only stakeholder with a strong motive for concern about the state's true creditworthiness; sometimes it refused to register and collateralize state debt, but at other times politics or other considerations allowed excess borrowing. Following the 1995 series of bailouts, to prevent a recurrence, SHCP tried to end its involvement with the collateralization of state and local debt, but the states and commercial banks, still traumatized by the crisis, did not accept this. So SHCP agreed on a temporary basis to accept mandates from the states to act as disbursing agent for borrowing transactions of which they, SHCP, approved.

Aware of these problems in 2000, SHCP implemented a new and innovative regulatory regime for subnational borrowing.[2] The new borrowing framework has five key elements:

(i)   Eliminating discretionary transfers from the federal government.
(ii) Ending SHCP's role as *fideicomiso* for collateralizing debt with *participaciones*.
(iii) Giving banks ex ante signals about the riskiness of state debt, by making the debt subject to the same borrower concentration limits as other debt, and by requiring that capital risk weighting reflect riskiness, as indicated with international credit ratings.
(iv) Putting similar limits on lending by development banks.
(v)   Giving strong incentives for borrowers to publish their fiscal and financial information.

Of the many political problems with imposing a hard budget constraint on the states, the most difficult arises because the large share of spending for wages has created strong political pressure to use federal bailouts to avoid large cuts in spending rather than to service debt. Solving the problem will require not only firm resolve and coherent policy by the federal government to avoid bailouts, but also more fiscal authority and political responsibility by the states to control costs and raise additional revenue (to service debt or pay wages).

Making states creditworthy will require dealing with their contingent liabilities, which include pensions and health programs for their employees and guarantees on loans to their decentralized agencies and public enterprises. The experiences of Argentina and Brazil show the absolute necessity of dealing with state pensions.

Institution Building

The key institutional issues for Mexican decentralization are reinforcing confidence in decentralization among key stakeholders, improving intergovernmental coordination and conflict resolution, strengthening and democratizing the process for con-

---

2. For a detailed technical description of the new regime see Giugale, Marcelo M., Adam K. Korobow, and Steven B. Webb. 2000. "A New Model for Market-Based Regulation of Subnational Borrowing: The Mexican Approach." Policy Research Working Paper No. 2370. The World Bank, Washington, D.C.

trol and accountability, coordinating the multilevel budget process, regularizing the distinctions between municipalities with different administrative capacities, implementing cooperative capacity building, and dealing with the peculiarities of the Federal District's relationship with its neighbors and the federal government.

International experience shows the importance of, and difficulties with, collective institutions that steer the decentralization process and serve as forums for negotiations and preemptive conflict resolution. Thus far, Mexico has largely used top-down mechanisms, such as conditional transfers and federal monitoring, but these have not been able to create a consensus-building mechanism that is trusted by all parties to take care of the following tasks:

- Proposing a long-term view of decentralization with intermediate goals.
- Promoting forums for discussing and negotiating intergovernmental fiscal arrangements including reform of the fiscal pact.
- Producing annual progress reports on decentralization, keeping federal agencies and subnational governments alerted to their responsibilities within the decentralization process; and providing reliable information for public discussion of federal, state, and local fiscal and financial policy.

To help address these needs, in 2000 the Mexican federal government established a Decentralization Committee within the SHCP, with a Technical Secretariat. The work of the Committee barely began in the current administration, needs to be pressed ahead, and its participants should be broadened to include other Secretariats and representatives from states and Congress.

Sound intergovernmental coordination will require specific institutions for negotiations and conflict resolution, because no system can foresee and specify everything in advance and effective decentralization requires more than the design of revenues, transfers, borrowing, and spending responsibilities. Issues and disputes arise that need to be settled, and the method for doing this has important incentive effects for how the system actually works. Mostly Mexico relies on the courts for conflict resolution, but they are slow and expensive and lack the capacity to do the whole job. International experience has shown the benefits of alternative, nonjudicial means for resolving disputes. In the Mexican health sector, the National Health Council *(Consejo Nacional de Salud)* resolves many disputes, and this institution could be a model for other sectors with major decentralization issues, such as education, water, road transport, and the environment.

Effective controls and systematic public disclosure are both a prerequisite and an essential component of strengthening management capacity, autonomy, and democratic accountability at subnational levels. Although in principle each level of government should have its own independent controls, the federal level has organized arrangements that provide the basis for strengthening controls at all levels during the transition to a more decentralized system. Mexico has accumulated significant experience and technical expertise at SECODAM and some of the state comptrollers, and the congressional accounting offices, independent units of increasingly pluralist congresses, are emerging as some of the more trusted institutions in the country.

Mexico has over 2,400 municipalities, which range from cities with several million inhabitants, policymakers with high levels of formal education, and computerized fiscal accounts, to small towns with populations under 5,000, leaders with little formal education, and informal accounting practices at best. Less than half of the municipalities measure up to standard indicators of capacity: having a budget planning unit, an evaluation unit, and computerized accounts; having and using an internal administrative code; having regulations for the *cadastre*; and raising more than half of their own resources. It seems unrealistic to have the same rules for all municipalities. In practice, states often demand less than the legal requirement from small and poor municipalities. Large municipalities frequently need to do more than the legal minimum in order to satisfy the requirements of their own management or of their private sector creditors. The diversity of local governments needs to be matched with differentiated federal rules for them, and requires programs to build up their fiscal and administrative capacity so that they can take on more responsibilities.

The Federal District faces particular challenges in its relationship with the federal government and with neighboring states. For example, the Federal District has to have its budget and borrowing limits approved annually by the federal Congress, it does not get some of the *Ramo 33* funds, and it is not responsible for basic education. The Federal District believes that it subsidizes its neighbors through support for the metro train system, while its neighbors feel that they subsidize the Federal District through water allocation. The rapid transformation of the political and fiscal status of the Federal District, and the possible creation of municipalities within it, have made necessary a review and reform of its vertical and horizontal intergovernmental relations. International experience, such as that of the São Paulo metropolitan area in Brazil, may help to elucidate the range of options.

III. Policy Options

It is useful to think of the policy agenda for decentralization not only as a list of actions for the short, medium, and long term, but also as steps that could initiate various paths of reform. Given that Mexico has already made the major decisions about decentralization of spending responsibility and subnational borrowing, the next critical decision concerns the importance of transfers and the extent to which the tax system should be decentralized. This will go hand in hand with the decision about the degree to which federal transfers will compensate for the regional disparities that would otherwise follow from tax decentralization. Another important decision, which may require revision as the transfer system evolves, is the extent to which the center will guide, monitor, or control the details of expenditures (for example, through financial market regulations or conditions on transfers). The institutional structures mentioned earlier will be needed to attain consensus on these policy objectives and to implement and sustain them.

Continuing Current Reforms

Sustaining and completing the reforms introduced in 1999–2000 is an important part of the short-term agenda for Federal Government action. The three key elements are transparency, institution building, and the new regulatory environment for subnational borrowing.

From the federal perspective, the transparency reforms involve continuing and expanding the program of publishing (including in electronic form) information about how federal resources are distributed by program and territorial entity. This will make both the federal government (executive and legislature) more accountable for its distribution of resources, and the state governments more accountable for the resources they receive. For transparency in subnational fiscal activity, the federal regulatory treatment of bank lending to subnational government creates strong incentives for the states to publish good information and to get good credit ratings, for which the reports are published.

Institution building for decentralization also needs to continue at the federal and subnational levels. The Decentralization Committee within SHCP will need to promote reforms by disseminating information and forging links with other federal ministries and with state governments. Initially this could be done through the recruitment of personnel into the Technical Secretariat, and then through informal interagency contacts. At the subnational levels, various programs are promoting capacity building, including those from BANOBRAS and from the Monterrey Institute of Technology. These efforts need encouragement with resources and exchanges of information, and above all with continuation of an incentive framework, such as formula-driven transfers, that rewards states with good institutions.

The new regime for subnational borrowing exists clearly on paper in the laws and regulations. The most important and most difficult part will be consistent and timely application of the new regime in order to build its credibility. Borrowing and lending inherently depend on reputations—expectations of how people, including the government and regulators, will behave in the future. Therefore, strict application of the rules is essential, but states will also need assistance to implement the structural adjustments necessary to meet the new rules, because they will work only if a critical mass of states can and does follow them.

Reforming the Pacto Fiscal

The most important new area for reform of the decentralization process seems to be the joint revision of the allocation of tax authority and federal transfers. The current trend of increasing transfers at the expense of the rest of the federal budget cannot continue much longer, although rising oil prices might let it go on a little longer than otherwise. Sooner or later federal programmable spending cannot be cut further, and even an opposition-dominated Congress would not want to make further cuts. Furthermore, the deleterious effect of the states' excessive reliance on federal transfers will increase, impairing democratic accountability and the reliability of the states as debtors. (Unfortunately, this latter effect will not be a self-enforcing check on the increase of transfers.) In any case, some states with strong tax bases seem impatient with the dependence on transfers and anxious to take on taxing power as long as it will not lead to punitive cuts in their transfers. This is because politically dominant business interests in those places see a positive return to additional tax resources put into education and infrastructure that will support the local economies.

Accommodating the demands for local tax authority will challenge the unity of Mexican society, because many places are far from ready to take such a path. The challenge can be met. One way would be to help the areas wanting to do more with their own taxes by giving them more authority to use efficient taxes, such as excises or surcharges piggybacked on major federal taxes, like personal income or the value-added tax. In exchange for this help, the transfer system (especially *participaciones*) would be revised to have more emphasis on redistribution to the states with less-than-average tax bases per capita. The key message is that a variety of coherent reforms are possible and could make all parties better off. The alternative to a strategically coherent reform is not the status quo unchanged, but rather incoherent change—such as states with strong fiscal capacity coming to depend on inefficient taxes, and fiscally weak states falling farther behind the regional economic leaders.

Rationalizing Sectoral Decentralization

If the tax and transfer system is reformed to provide each state with a minimum level of unconditional resources per capita, then the sectoral decentralization programs—*aportaciones*—could be revised to focus on assuring that every Mexican has access to minimum levels of certain public services that are deemed rights of citizenship, such as basic education and health. For such a strategy, the formulas for these sectorally conditional programs would be shifted to a per-recipient basis. International experience indicates that this improves both efficiency and equity, because the money goes proportionately to where the most people are. Making such a change can be politically difficult and requires appropriate transitions, because of the political power of those groups such as teachers, who depend on and benefit from the historical allocation.

State-Level Reforms

Sustaining even the first phase of the Federal reforms and moving on to the phases will require the cooperation of the states: responding to the new in/ framework, dealing with a few cases of debt-overhang, and developing m/

agement capacity. Therefore, now that the federal reforms are underway, a second track of state-level reforms will need support. The States find themselves in very diverse situations. Virtually all states need sector reform and investment; a few are not only willing to reform but also have the management capacity and creditworthiness to proceed immediately with sector investment lending. Many states have the willingness to reform and not much debt at present, but lack financial and program management capacity; they will need to get substantial technical assistance prior to or perhaps along with investment lending, to assure that funds are well used and that borrowing is not excessive. Finally the fiscal situation in a few states is overburdened by rapid growth in needs for public services and remains deeply flawed by the inappropriate incentive framework of the past. The federal Government is rightly seeking to facilitate adjustment among such states. Such adjustment will be important to sustain public services in these states, mostly very populous, and to get them ready to participate in the next phases the Federal Government's decentralization reform. Adjustment of these States will also be important as a demonstration to encourage other sub-nationals to sustain fiscal restraint and as a way to build further national support (and avoid resistance) to its discipline-imposing reforms.

33

Governance

This Chapter was written by Robert Ayres.

"The greatest challenge we have in this country isn't the economy. It's public security and the fight against corruption."

> Francisco Labastida Ochoa, presidential candidate, Institutional Revolutionary Party (PRI), interview in *The Washington Post*, June 18, 2000, p. B5.

"For the first time, we will have rule of law. We're going to end corruption and live by the constitution."

> Vicente Fox Quesada, President-elect, National Action Party (PAN), interview in *The Washington Post*, June 18, 2000, p. B5.

I. The Components of Governance

Governance is fundamentally a question of transparency, accountability, and the rule of law. As such, it is closely related to corruption—the abuse of public office for private gain. Political systems and governmental decisionmaking processes characterized by transparency provide less fertile grounds for corruption than systems where openness and information about governmental activities are lacking. Systems in which there are institutionalized mechanisms through which citizens can hold public decisionmakers accountable for their actions are also less likely to be characterized by corruption than systems in which accountability is deficient or absent. Corruption also flourishes in the absence of the rule of law because impunity means that the corrupt go substantially or totally unpunished. In general, both the incidence and the nature of corruption are closely related to the mechanisms—or lack thereof—ensuring the transparency, accountability, and legality of the actions of public officials.

II. Governance in Mexico: Progress Made

Mexico has made undeniable advances in governance in recent years. The increasing democratization of the political system, especially the heightened political competition since 1997, has created a more supportive context for fighting corruption in its various manifestations. For example, the legislative branch of government has played a greater role in more substantive annual discussions of the federal budget and, more generally, in increasing oversight of the actions of the executive. The decentralization process (discussed previously and in another Chapter) has brought the delivery of public services closer to their beneficiaries and, thus, to their beneficiaries' scrutiny. At the level of the national administration, the work of *Secretaría de Contraloría y Desarrollo Administrativo* (SECODAM) has marked a considerable advance, especially in implementing important reforms in financial management and public procurement.

III. Corruption: Some Observations

Transparency International's Index

Despite these and other positive developments contributing to better governance, it is apparent that substantial deficiencies remain in transparency, accountability, and the rule of law. One consequence of these deficiencies is corruption. Analyzed from the perspective of Transparency International's Corruption Perceptions Index (the most widely cited international index of corruption), Mexico is in the middle tier of countries in Latin America and the Caribbean. Of 16 Latin American and Caribbean countries included in Transparency International's worldwide survey in 1999, six—Brazil, Chile, Costa Rica, El Salvador, Jamaica, and Peru—were rated as less corrupt than Mexico. However, nine countries in the region—Argentina, Bolivia, Colombia, Ecuador, Guatemala, Honduras, Nicaragua, Paraguay, and Venezuela—were rated as more corrupt (in some cases, substantially more corrupt). Mexico's ranking on this cross-national index is perhaps a reflection of a decline in systematic corruption in recent years, although such an alleged decline is difficult to verify with the limited data available. The ranking does not mean, however, that corruption is not a serious problem in today's Mexico. That it is, can be ascertained through an examination of what the Mexican people themselves think about corruption in their country.

Evidence from National Surveys

There is no comprehensive diagnostic of corruption such as those carried out by the World Bank Institute for other countries (most recently Ecuador). However, recent survey data provide some insights into public perceptions of the issue. These include the following:

- A national survey conducted for the newspaper *Reforma* on 8–9 April, 2000, found that 46 percent of respondents thought the government was "very corrupt" and another 36 percent thought it was "somewhat corrupt." Only 3 percent said it was "not corrupt."
- In a national survey conducted by a group of distinguished academics in late February 2000, respondents were asked whether they thought that corruption had increased, decreased, or remained the same in the previous 12 months. The responses were dramatic: 82 percent responded that corruption had increased either somewhat or substantially, and only 13 percent were of the opinion that it had declined (and only 1 percent said that it had declined substantially). Moreover, when asked to identify the three most important issues the next President of Mexico will face, 36 percent of the sample cited corruption as one of them.
- Another survey conducted on 11–14 February, 2000, found that only 8 percent of respondents thought the current Mexican administration was having "a lot of success" in combating corruption.
- In a survey on justice in Mexico City conducted by the newspaper *El Universal* on 20–21 October 1999, respondents were asked "whether there is justice in Mexico." Thirty-five percent answered yes, while 65 percent were of the opinion that "there is no justice in Mexico."

When combined with the voluminous amount of anecdotal and case study evidence regarding specific cases of corruption, it is apparent that corruption ranks as one of the most important issues that will confront any incoming Mexican Presidential Administration. Moreover, it is intimately related to the three issues that Mexicans, when asked in national surveys, tend to identify as the most salient items on their minds—public security, the state of the economy, and poverty. This is because, generally speaking, corruption reduces public security, impedes the growth of the economy, and worsens poverty.

IV. Recent Developments

Anti-Corruption Efforts in Mexico: Focus on SECODAM

The main focus of the anticorruption efforts of the Mexican authorities has been on the activities of SECODAM. Within the SECODAM domain, attention has been directed largely to issues of procurement (for example, the experience with COMPRANET, the open electronic bidding system for public purchases) and financial management (including audits and related topics). The principal focus has been on a relatively restricted number of activities within the executive branch of government (of which SECODAM itself is a part). The new Presidential administration should continue to work closely with SECODAM since it plays a key role in the monitoring and evaluation of the performance of other executive branch agencies of the Mexican public sector, and will likely be a key actor in any future efforts directed at administrative reform, improvements in service delivery by public agencies, and the reduction of corruption. However, the future work of SECODAM need not be restricted to issues of procurement and financial management.

While the authorities have interacted extensively with SECODAM on matters pertaining to procurement and financial management, they have given relatively little attention to SECODAM's role in ensuring the "voice" and participation of citizens in matters related to the delivery of services by public agencies (*atención ciudadana*). Two areas of SECODAM's activities appear of interest in this regard. One is the national system for dealing with citizen complaints and accusations. The second is that of social audits (*contralorías sociales*). Regarding the former, SECODAM reports that the number of citizens' complaints almost tripled between 1995 and 1999, in part because they were facilitated by the installation in the second half of 1997 of a telephone network for registering complaints. Regarding the latter, SECODAM reports having conducted 630 surveys involving 180,000 interviewees under its program of social audits.

However, the information made publicly available by SECODAM in its reports is very limited regarding both the citizen complaint process and the conduct of social audits. This suggests that there may be scope for expanding SECODAM's capacity for handling citizen complaints and monitoring service delivery by public agencies. For example, it could prove instructive to explore in greater depth the process by which citizen complaints and accusations are handled, the nature of the decisions taken, and the kinds of follow-up activities, if any, undertaken to correct deficiencies or avert any further abuses. Such an exercise could lead to an assessment of the strengths and weaknesses of the current system and proposals for strengthening it if deemed necessary. It could draw on the lessons of experience from such citizen complaint processes in other countries in the region and elsewhere. One possibility is to move from a highly individualistic system, in which individuals have to rely on their own means and initiative to file complaints, to one that provides for the more active participation of civil society groups and "citizen lobbies."

Regarding social audits, it would be useful to compile more systematic data on what they have revealed about corruption in service delivery—for example, whether there is any consistent pattern in particular sectors, public agencies, or areas of the country. As with the handling of citizen complaints, it would also be useful to explore what kinds of governmental actions have been taken in response to any findings of the social audits regarding systematic deficiencies in service delivery. There may be scope for instituting some variant of the "scorecard" approach adopted in other settings (for example, in Bangalore, India), in which survey techniques are employed in a systematic fashion over time to ascertain rising or declining levels of citizen satisfaction with the nature and modalities of the services provided.

Toward a More Comprehensive Anticorruption Agenda in Mexico

Research conducted for this Chapter, including an extensive consultation process with leading experts on Mexico both inside and outside the country, strongly pointed toward the need to go beyond SECODAM in efforts to address key governance issues. There was widespread agreement that work with SECODAM should constitute only a part—and perhaps only a small part—of any meaningful overall effort designed to bring greater transparency, accountability, and rule of law to government in Mexico. Some of the additional areas thought important to address are discussed in the remainder of this Chapter.

Strengthening Horizontal Accountability: The Role of Congress

Considerable importance attaches to strengthening horizontal accountability; that is, the accountability among the three branches of the Mexican government at the federal level. Of particular importance is the need for more effective legislative oversight of the executive branch. A key issue in this regard concerns the role of the congressional *Contaduría Mayor de Hacienda*, the external auditor of the executive branch (as opposed to SECODAM, which is its internal auditor). One study reviewed for this report estimated the budget for the congressional auditing office at about 15 percent of SECODAM's budget. The staff of the office is reportedly appointed by the Secretariat of Finance (SHCP) in the executive branch. Its role has been limited to verifying whether actual budgetary expenditures correspond to projected expenditures, and there has been a substantial time lag between the adoption of the budget and the subsequent rendering of the public expenditure account to the congressional auditing office. (For example, in 1998 the office was reported to be verifying the 1995 budget figures, by which time the statute of limitations on abuse of office in the period being analyzed had expired). A number of constitutional reforms due to take effect in January 2000 were designed to strengthen the work of the congressional auditing office. (Experts consulted for this study were unable to confirm whether such reforms had in fact been enacted.) It is unlikely, however, that these would sufficiently enhance the external auditing function, and it appears that further institutional strengthening would be required.

More generally, there are issues concerning the potential enhancement of congressional investigative powers, the adequacy of the congressional committee structure and committee staffs, and the ways in which emerging patterns of executive–legislative relations following the election of an opposition-controlled Congress in 1997 might facilitate greater accountability and transparency in the government.

Such issues, together with the need to address the future work of the *Contaduría Mayor de Hacienda*, would appear to provide the Mexican authorities with an ample agenda in the domain of strengthening the Congress. Depending on the evolution of such an agenda, it might prove useful to consider the possibility of creating a grant-based institutional development fund in support of various congressional activities, particularly those of the *Contaduría Mayor de Hacienda*.

Governance and the Changing Nature of Mexican Federalism

Another policy domain with a clear linkage to the governance agenda is that of the changing nature of federalism in Mexico. Various aspects of the political economy of fiscal federalism are crucial to the future of governance in the country.

The chapter on Decentralization discusses the various fiscal transfers occurring from the national government to the states in the Mexican federation. Scholarly work consulted during the preparation of this Chapter confirmed the importance of such transfers (including *participaciones, aportaciones federales,* etc.). In some states, especially poorer states, the reliance on indirect income in the form of *participaciones* is extremely high—in some cases as high as 80 percent of total state income. The mechanisms for the distribution of resources from the federal government to the states are formula-based and are considered by knowledgeable observers to be relatively transparent. More problematic, however, appear to be the mechanisms for distributing resources from the states to the municipalities within them (given that 20 percent of total *participaciones* are supposed to be passed on by the states to their municipalities).

The most thorough academic analysis of this issue concluded that the criteria for the allocation of resources from the states to the municipalities were unclear, and thus created a situation in which considerable state discretionary power continued to exist. In principle, each state arithmetically determines the formula for the distribution of funds to its municipalities based on certain standard indicators, including population, poverty, and amounts collected in taxes. In practice, however, the *participaciones* that a municipality receives appear to be largely or entirely determined at the state government level by both the state *Secretaría de Finanzas* and the state legislature. Because the federal Fiscal Coordination Law gives only rough guidelines about how states should allocate revenue sharing to municipalities, state legislatures are almost completely free to choose their own criteria—or to employ no precise criteria at all. Such a situation of minimal transparency obviously opens the door to the possibility of the political determination of revenue-sharing allocations between the states and municipalities, or the possibility of outright corruption in their distribution.

There appears, however, to be relatively little empirical analysis of the extent of abuse and corruption in the transfer processes (including those between the federal and state levels, which have not been emphasized here), or about the mechanisms that could potentially mitigate or prevent them. Some experts consulted for this study thought it important to strengthen the capabilities of the finance committees of the state legislatures (that is, the state-level analogues of the national *Contaduría Mayor de Hacienda*). Others thought that a systematic examination was required of the functioning of the state-level equivalents of SECODAM (that is, within the executive branches of the various state administrations) with a view toward ascertaining how a generally perceived pattern of ineffectiveness might be corrected. The aim in either case would be to increase the transparency of the mechanisms by which municipalities receive funds from their respective states, and thus reduce the potential for corrupt practices in this process. One possibility for launching this effort might be a comparative study of innovations in state financial management with a view toward ascertaining emerging "best practice."

Another recent study found similar issues and problems with regard to the two main categories of *aportaciones federales*, that is, the *Fondo de Aportaciones para la Infraestructura Social* (FAIS) and the *Fondo de Aportaciones para el Fortalecimiento de los Municipios* (FORTAMUN). In analyzing the states of Nuevo León and Yucatán, for example, it was found that a significant part of FAIS funds were used for purposes other than those specified by the *Ley de Coordinación Fiscal*; that many of the funds—up to 75 percent in some cases—obtained by municipalities were not disbursed at all, thereby contributing to the accumulation of a nontransparent pool of resources that could be employed at the discretion of the local authorities; that there was little transparency in the criteria for the distribution of resources within the states; that there was very little information about funded programs available to the citizens; and that, in general, the mechanisms for citizen participation in deciding how funds would be used were either nonexistent or defective.

Other studies involving other states and employing considerably more data would clearly need to be conducted before any definitive conclusions could be drawn regarding the possible misuse of *participaciones* and *aportaciones federales*. Studies would also appear to be required of other budgetary transfer categories that are in fact far more substantial than participaciones and *aportaciones federales* and that appear to be considerably more open to discretionary management. These include notably federal government investments in the states incorporated into the so-called *Programa Normal* of the federal budget. The point, however, is a more general one—that is, that the evolving nature of fiscal federalism in Mexico, while enormously positive in some respects, creates abundant opportunities for abuse and corruption. These need to be more thoroughly understood with a view toward designing and implementing strategies, including institutional strengthening at all levels of the federal system (but especially at the state level), for effectively combating them.

The Role of Civil Society

Enhanced work with Mexican civil society is another prominent theme on the governance agenda. Strengthening the role of civil society and incorporating it more in the fight against corruption could make a powerful contribution to greater transparency, accountability, and the rule of law in Mexico's democratic transition. For example, the recent founding of *Transparencia Mexicana* could provide a formidable partner in helping to stimulate and coordinate anticorruption initiatives. An example of the potential in this regard was the convening by *Transparencia Mexicana,* in the month before the July 2000 Presidential Elections, of a diverse group of members of the Mexican policy community with a view toward elaborating a set of priority anticorruption proposals to be presented to the candidates in the presidential campaign.

Interestingly, however, many experts consulted for this study were of the opinion that a "national anticorruption dialogue" or "national anticorruption action plan" involving civil society organizations was not a particularly fruitful way to proceed. Instead, a frequently voiced suggestion was that independent international financial institutions (such as the World Bank) work with selected civil society organizations to organize workshops and plan subsequent operational activities focused on quite specific problem areas—whether they be in specific sectors of service delivery, in specific parts of the country, or targeted on specific groups. This view implies that those institutions and Mexican civil society organizations working on governance issues should jointly aim at capacity- and institution-building centered around everyday problems encountered, especially by poor people, in performance monitoring and service delivery.

No effort was made in the research for this Chapter to conduct an overall assessment of the multitude of civil society organizations in Mexico with governance or governance-related agendas, nor to assess the effectiveness of their current activities. However, some highly interesting examples were nevertheless uncovered. One NGO, for example, is training groups of people in various aspects of budget monitoring and has initiated a pilot program in three states to train groups of women in monitoring social sector expenditures, including transfers from the federal government that are intended to be targeted to women. Other specific efforts included initiatives to enhance the access of groups to the justice system at the local level, to strengthen the capacities of indigenous women in making their demands heard to local authorities, and to facilitate the access of civil society organizations to mass communication media in order to provide more effective outlets for expressing their opinions and needs. The point is not to single out any one civil society organization for praise. It is simply to indicate the kinds of activities that are increasing and expanding throughout Mexico and that appear to be taking civil society involvement on behalf of better governance to a new, more precise, and potentially more effective level.

Crime, Violence, and Governance

Another key component of the governance agenda in Mexico is that of the linkages between crime, violence, and corruption. The issue of public security is at the top of the list of issues identified by the Mexican public as of immediate concern. The reasons are thoroughly understandable. From 1995 to 1997, violent crimes in, for example, the Federal District increased from about 1,700 per 100,000 inhabitants to 2,835 per 100,000 inhabitants. The astounding rise in the general crime rate has been due mainly to a pronounced increase in robberies. From 1975 to 1982, the annual average robbery rate was 422 per 100,000 inhabitants in the Federal District. However, from 1994 to 1997, robbery rates soared to an annual average of 1,567 per 100,000 inhabitants. Moreover between 1981 and 1995, the homicide rate increased from 10.2 to 19.6 per 100,000 inhabitants. In 1995, the social costs from violence in Mexico City were estimated to total 4.2 percent of the city's GDP in that year.

The determinants of violent crime have proven extremely difficult to establish both across and within countries. No effort is made here to discuss the many variables generally considered by analysts of violent crime. However, in the Mexican case, there are interesting linkages to some of the governance and corruption issues discussed throughout this Chapter. This was graphically illustrated by the results of a "victimization survey" carried out in the metropolitan area of Mexico City in May 1999, by the Mexican Health Foundation (FUNSALUD) and the World Bank. The study found that only 17 percent of the victims had reported the crimes to the police. The reasons for nonreporting are instructive: 70 percent of those interviewed thought it was either "pointless" or a "waste of time" to report the crime. (These findings are consistent with the results obtained in a survey on justice in Mexico City conducted on 20–21 October 1999. In that survey, 73 percent of the respondents stated that the police "cover up" or "protect" criminals "a lot or some of the time.") Moreover, of those who did report a crime, 45 percent of the victims said that "nothing had been done." Many victims said that they had to bribe the police in order to facilitate the investigation or to have their case followed up. Of the victims who reported crimes, 16 percent said that they had to pay between MXP$100 and MXP$5,000 in order to initiate a legal process (which is supposed to be free of charge), with an average disbursement of MXP$1,492. Victims were also asked whether they would be willing to pay money in order "not to feel insecure." Of the victims, 75 percent stated that they would be willing to pay varying amounts of pesos a month in order to "recover their previous quality of life" lost to crime and violence.

The nexus between crime, violence, and corruption may well be the central issue of governance in today's Mexico. However, it must be admitted that the connections are not well enough understood, and what precisely to do about the problems is not obvious. For example, the government of Mexico City initiated a new Law Enforcement Program for the Federal District for the period 1995 to 2000. The emphasis was on augmenting police resources and increasing the efficiency of the forces devoted to public security. By the first semester of 1997 the city government was spending about 20 percent of its total budget on law enforcement and safety. An assessment of these initiatives by FUNSALUD concluded, however, that they were largely ineffective because the crime rate continued to soar and the confidence of the public in the authorities appeared to continue to decline. It was suggested that new approaches to the many issues involved were now required.

This implies that, despite acknowledged political sensitivities, there could be a substantial value for the new Mexican authorities in the exploration of anticrime initiatives that have been undertaken with apparent success elsewhere in the world and that might have relevance to Mexico (for example, programs of community involvement in combating violent crime and programs targeted on "at-risk" youth). There might also be scope for looking more systematically into the issues of crime and violence within Mexico itself. In this connection, research conducted for this Chapter revealed at least two major ongoing academic studies of the relationships between crime, violence, and corruption in Mexico. Both involve leading Mexican and American scholars. One deals with governmental and societal responses to public insecurity in Mexico and the U.S.-Mexican borderlands. The second concerns organized crime and the links to democratic governance. An effort to bring together these and other leading experts on the rising crime wave throughout Mexico, to distill the lessons learned to date including the role that corruption plays in both fostering crime and preventing effective anticrime initiatives, and to suggest possible avenues for both governmental and non-governmental efforts to combat crime, could make an important contribution.

Governance and Public Sector Reform

The anticorruption agenda in Mexico is closely related to—indeed, may be virtually indistinguishable from—the overall public sector reform agenda. A World Bank report completed in early 1998[1] concluded that there existed an impressive array of proposals aimed at creating a more performance-oriented public administration in Mexico (including but not limited to the *Programa Nacional de Modernización de la Administración Publica*, PROMAP).

The same report, however, was far from optimistic regarding the likelihood that these various initiatives would be effectively implemented. It pointed to a "leadership challenge," in that the Executive appeared to be hesitant to proceed, and there appeared to be very little effort to work together among the various units pushing alternative reform initiatives (chiefly SECODAM and the SHCP). The report also pointed to an "implementation challenge," especially with regard to efforts to create a career civil service (something which is now confined to only a few Mexican public sector institutions). Fundamental changes in the political dynamics in Mexico, including the advent of an opposition-controlled Congress, were judged likely to create conflicting demands for exercising central controls over the public administration on the one hand and for enhancing delegation of authority and responsibility on the other.

The possibility arises, however, that the advent of a new Mexican Administration could provide a window of opportunity for readdressing some central questions of public sector reform, including key issues of the creation of a career civil service and the installation of performance-based and results-oriented administrative organization. In such an undertaking, however, it would be required to enhance significantly the knowledge base regarding the Mexican public sector. One possibility in this regard is a Mexican variant of a comprehensive Institutional and Governance Review, which could provide the analytical underpinnings for a renewed effort to assist the Mexican government, assuming the requisite political will in jump-starting the process of public sector reform. Such an effort, if undertaken, should involve the cadre of Mexican scholars now working in several institutions on both the theory and practice of public sector reform in Mexico. The linkages to an anticorruption agenda could be made explicit through a focus on service delivery as rendered by major public sector agencies.

---

1. See Mexico: Government Budget Reform and Performance Management—Final Report, unpublished report, World Bank 1998.

Access to Information

Finally, a number of experts consulted in the preparation of this Chapter argued that greater access to official information should be high on the governance agenda for Mexico. The legal framework governing access to information was felt to be in need of substantial overhaul and amplification. While there had been undeniable advances in press freedom and candor, it was felt by many that the scope for serious investigative journalism still required widening. Some felt that Mexico could learn from the experiences of other countries in expanding and facilitating access to official governmental records, accounts, and other information. This issue is obviously linked to some of the others previously discussed, including that of enhanced legislative oversight of the executive branch.

V. Conclusion

Several key determinants of the quality of governance have not been covered in this Chapter. For example, experts consulted were virtually unanimous in their identification of judicial reform as being at or near the top of the governance agenda in Mexico (such a reform is addressed in a separate chapter). Nor has mention been made of the funding of politicians and political parties and the associated issues of campaign finance reform, a factor seen by many observers as absolutely fundamental. The same could be said for the issue of police reform, which was also identified by many experts as an essential component of the governance agenda.

Despite these and other omissions, it is readily apparent from the foregoing discussion that the potential governance agenda in Mexico is substantial and diverse. A formidable task of selectivity and prioritization thus confronts the Mexican authorities. There are clearly extremely difficult questions of political sensitivity and comparative advantage. For these reasons, this Chapter has refrained from undue specificity or definitive proposals. The intent has simply been to present a highly preliminary itemization of what could constitute a strong agenda of activities for assisting Mexico to enhance governance through increased transparency, accountability, and the rule of law. Whether and to what extent the various elements of such a preliminary agenda might be acted upon is for the next Mexican Administration to decide.

34

Legal and Judicial Institutions

This Chapter was written by Linn Hammergren.

I. Background

Over the past few years, there has been growing attention to the role of legal and judicial institutions in advancing, or impeding, the realization of broader development goals. While the interest arose independently, it is consistent with the new concern for "second generation reforms" as the missing element in spurring economic growth, and the design and implementation of polices intended to promote such. The argument is that only a well-functioning legal and judicial system can promote the emergence of strong, market-based economic development. The statement is oversimplified and, as many have noted, a well-functioning judicial system may be as much the result as the cause of a modern economy.

Nonetheless, we have ample if partial evidence that legal and judicial weaknesses can have a negative impact on certain critical economic, social, and political transactions, and that even when compensatory informal mechanisms exist to take up the slack, the resulting distortions frequently pose excessive, and usually unequally shared costs. Furthermore, it is also evident that once an economy and polity have reached a certain level of development, citizens want improved legal and judicial systems for their own sakes. Few of them want to have their conflicts resolved by laws based on convoluted, outdated procedures and values, face lengthy delays, be charged irregular fees, or receive decisions seemingly made at random. In addition, most judges and court staff would prefer to receive transparent compensation for their services and be respected for their professional skills, not feared for their arbitrary power or their connections with the powerful.

In short, for a variety of reasons, legal and judicial reform and modernization are very much on the contemporary agenda. In recognition of this fact, the World Bank and other assistance agencies have responded with programs intended to help nations advance these efforts. In some cases, international assistance has been a major catalyst of reform, arriving before there was much domestic interest or a well-defined reform constituency. In other cases, the Bank's role has been to support developments already under way. Mexico will clearly be one of the latter; as discussed below, the country is well into a period of self-financed and self-directed reform. There is still plenty of room for external cooperation, but it is best advised to build on what is being done, helping participants find innovative ways to accelerate and improve the process.

II. Organization and Operations of the Legal-Judicial System

Three facts are essential for understanding Mexico's legal and judicial framework and its likely future evolution. Like the rest of Latin America, Mexico has a civil code tradition; unlike most countries, it has a federal organization; and because of its location and history, its legal–judicial system has been exposed to a unique set of influences. Civil code systems are a majority in the world; their particular approach to addressing certain universal challenges is widely understood and provides a series of alternative models of broader applicability. Federally organized judiciaries are a distinct minority, offering a surprisingly wide range of accommodations to the particular set of dilemmas they face. Much more than in unitary systems, the choices made seem influenced by historical and other contextual factors. Hence, they are less likely to provide models that can be generalized. Finally, for better or worse, Mexico's participation in regional judicial trends has been limited by its physical distance from those nations, which, by reason of their level of socioeconomic development or their federal organization, are its logical interlocutors. The evolution of its legal and judicial system has thus been more strongly shaped by domestic innovation, contact with European developments, and its economic and political relations with its neighbor to the north.

Despite these contextual variations, current concerns about the system's performance are not that unusual for the region (or for that matter, for judiciaries universally). They include an inability to keep pace with escalating demands for services, a failure to update substantive and procedural laws and internal administrative and functional processes, underfinancing, inadequate human resource management and deployment, insufficient independence (and varying degrees of political intervention), corrupt or biased decisions, and inaccessibility to the vast majority of poor or otherwise marginalized citizens. The concerns have been voiced for several decades, both as problems in their own right and as potential impediments to extrasectoral goals, and include sustainability and equitability, and ensuring market-based growth, citizen security, and the strengthening of effective institutions of governance and participatory politics.

Since the early 1990s, a series of measures has been adopted in Mexico to address system weaknesses and thus reduce the hypothesized negative impact on overall societal development. Changes in substantive and procedural laws are a continuous feature, although as critics have noted, they are overly shaped by doctrinal considerations with

little effort to predict likely results; consequently, their effect is frequently disappointing.[1] Constitutional reforms introduced since 1994 have a potentially greater impact;
they changed the composition and powers of the federal judiciary, and these and other
actions are being adopted across the 31 states and the Federal District.[2] Recent changes
have not been limited to the legal framework; at both the federal and state levels, governments have provided additional funding to judiciaries to allow implementation of
the reforms and an extensive program of court modernization.

Intersystem Relationships

Since the legal–judicial system is really 33 separate entities (the 31 states, the Federal District, and the federal system), further generalizations are difficult. Before
turning to separate discussions of the state and federal entities, a brief review of the
division of functions among them is in order. State courts and other sector agencies
(judicial councils, prosecution, defense, etc.) are organizationally independent of the
federal system, operating under their own organic (organizational), procedural, and
substantive laws. This basic legal framework closely resembles the comparable federal rules, varying only at the level of detail. States have superior, not supreme
courts, with largely appellate rather than judicial review functions. They usually
have a lower level of justices of the peace to handle minor infractions and small civil
claims. Procedural codes tend to be similar, but substantive ones cover different
issues, reflecting the basic jurisdictional divisions. As in all federal systems, national
law defines which level of courts will have unique or original jurisdiction in specific
kinds of cases, and where the responsibility lies with a state court (which see roughly
80 percent of the total caseload) it usually operates under the respective state law.
There is an area of shared jurisdiction, most notably in commercial cases, where federal law prevails; however, most cases originate in practice, but not by law, in the
state courts. This has been an source of increasing friction. State judiciaries claim
that the practice substantially expands their workload, subjects their operations to
an overly rigid legal framework, and in the end leads to further delays and arbitrary
reversals when the cases are reviewed by the federal courts.

A second major point of contact for the two systems is the role of the federal courts
in reviewing decisions by state judges. The usual vehicle for this review is the writ of
amparo, a device introduced to protest the violation of constitutional rights. While not
initially intended to be applicable to judicial decisions, it was ruled to be applicable
soon after its introduction in the mid 19th century on the basis of a "violation of due

---

1. Although law revision is a favorite and relatively easily accomplished element of reform
   efforts, it is increasingly recognized that it is an extremely ineffectual way to produce real
   change in behaviors. Change is even less likely if drafters do not recognize this fact, and
   thus look beyond the laws' content to the underlying sources of problematic performance.
   See Pistor, Frydman, for discussions.
2. Carbonell; Concha and Caballero.

process." *Amparos* now represent about 90 percent of the federal case load, and while not exclusively reserved for appeals of state judgments, this is a major use, contributing to the congestion of federal courts and additional delays in the resolution of issues first heard by the state judiciaries. Because placing an *amparo* is costly and requires specialized counsel, it is also argued that the device skews the system against the poor. Another source of complaints is the lack of uniform criteria among the federal courts in ruling on the *amparos*; the problem is augmented by the fact that cases from a single state court system may be distributed among several district and circuit courts.

A third point of contact, and a concern more to federal authorities, is that even cases reserved for federal courts may find their initial entry at the state level, where inadequate treatment may alter the eventual results. This is a particular problem in federal crimes (for example, drug trafficking) which may first be detected and investigated by state police and prosecutors. State authorities do not have jurisdiction over these cases, but can complicate matters with errors in the initial investigation or a misclassification of the issue. The new bankruptcy law, recently enacted by the Congress, diverts these cases from the state to federal courts and may represent another area where concerns about the abilities of state authorities have provoked a move to reassign responsibilities.

Federal Judiciary

The federal judiciary is composed of a Supreme Court (11 members, reduced from the 26 prior to 1994), and 23 judicial circuits, with a total of 346 courts and 560 judges. The judges are divided among 107 multijudge circuit courts, 49 unitary circuit courts, and 190 district courts. There are also special agrarian, labor, military, and tax courts, organizationally outside of the ordinary court system.[3] With the 1994 constitutional reforms, the Supreme Court's role as the administrative head of the system has been taken over by a Judicial Council, presided by the Supreme Court President, and composed of members chosen by the judiciary and other branches of government. The council is responsible for managing the judicial career (selection, training, evaluation, and placement of lower-level judges).[4] Constitutional amendments in 1988, 1994, and 1999 gave the Supreme Court constitutional review powers and relegated many of its former functions in hearing *amparos* to the circuit courts. Unlike most of Latin America, Mexico made an early transition from a strictly inquisitorial[5] criminal justice system; the responsibility for the investigation and prosecution of crimes thus lies not

---

3. With the 1994 reforms, the formerly separate electoral court was incorporated into the Judicial Branch.
4. See articles in Fernandez et al., Cossio (1996).
5. Mexicans continue to debate the extent of the transition. However, current problems are arguably less a result of remaining inquisitorial elements than of political intervention, inappropriate organization, and insufficient incentives for professional performance. Regional preferences to the contrary, an inquisitorial system is no more prone to these vices than is an accusatory system.

with investigative judges, but with a separate entity, the *Procuraduria General de la Republica*, composed of federal prosecutors with their own investigative police.

Although there are long-standing complaints about the percentage of the public budget used for the justice sector, the federal judiciary appears relatively well financed and offers salaries substantial enough to attract well-qualified candidates. Earlier complaints about the politicization of appointments are being addressed with the introduction of entry exams, training (under the *Instituto de la Judicatura Federal*), and a judicial career managed by the council. Clearly, the current Chief Justice's campaign to modernize the system will require additional investments in infrastructure and equipment, but even under their current budget, the federal courts have made strides in these areas. Additional needs, also being addressed, involve ways to reduce the massive caseload. Even after the recent reforms, the federal caseload remains overwhelming—the Supreme Court, the principal beneficiary of these changes, still makes over 6,000 annual rulings. The usual remedies—the addition of more courts and judges or the adoption of new technologies—will obviously be insufficient to resolve the underlying problems. Thus current discussions focus on simplifying procedures, eliminating or discouraging some types of filings and, most radically, finding ways to broaden the impact of decisions (by making them applicable beyond the specific case). The problem, as noted, affects more than the federal system, also delaying the resolution of cases originating at the state level.

The Supreme Court and the Judicial Council are in addition showing concern about other traditional complaints—a lack of transparency and independence, inadequate controls on allegedly incompetent or dishonest judges, and inaccessibility to the nonwealthy majority of citizens. However, as regards sheer malfeasance, the *Procuraduría* (Attorney General's Office) has been the more frequent target of criticism, and since the early 1990s has been attempting to screen and upgrade its human resources, improve its internal procedures, and develop more effective means for combating traditional and nonconventional criminal activity.

State Judiciaries

Although the basic organizational structure at the state level resembles the federal level, there is considerable variation in system resources and performance across states. One enormous difference is that between the Federal District and the 31 states. In sheer size the Federal District system dwarfs that of the states, but with proportionately far more cases and far more variation among them, it faces problems of an entirely different dimension as well. Its efforts to introduce improvements are partially frustrated by the burgeoning demand for services and by resource constraints. Thus, whereas it was among the early adopters of information technology, its current system appears less reliable than those introduced more recently in some state courts.[6]

---

6. For example, reports on court activities are collected manually and fed into a central database, whereas some state courts have introduced on-line submissions from outlying courts.

Among the 31 states, size, budget, organization, strengths and deficiencies vary widely. One indication is the amount per capita spent on the courts, ranging from MXP\$77 in Campeche to MXP\$16 in Tamaulipas.[7] Salaries are another indication, ranging from MXP\$372,000 annually for a First Instance judge in the state of Mexico to MXP\$53,000 in Baja California.[8] Total and per-judge caseload vary not only among states, but within them. A study in the early 1990s indicated that in the state of Jalisco, judges within the metropolitan area of Guadalajara had an average caseload of 4,500, while those in the rest of the state had about 1,600.[9] Resource constraints and the distribution of population may make further rationalization difficult, and in any case the state courts as a whole are overburdened by demands.

The quality of judicial and administrative staff varies as much as the quantity, but a general complaint is that state judiciaries have been excessively dependent on the executive branch (governor) and thus vulnerable to political interference. One positive sign is a general move to regularize appointments, introduce judicial careers (often under a newly created judicial council, following the federal example), and create or improve training programs. A recent study[10] reveals that a majority of states are undertaking additional reform programs, including the introduction of alternative dispute resolution, adoption of modern administrative and information technologies, and measures to improve service to the public and increase transparency. Not surprisingly, wealthier more economically developed states have tended to take the lead here, but not without exception. For example, the state of Chiapas recently introduced an innovative program to provide a bridge between traditional community dispute resolution systems and the formal courts. Developments in other sector organizations (*Procuradurias*, police, and private bar) have been slower, and these remain targets of complaints in their own right.

It is generally agreed that state courts, even more than the federal system, require additional funding to introduce improved infrastructure and equipment and attract and keep higher-quality personnel. However, here too there are limits to the improvements that can be achieved through these means. There are additional needs for less financially costly but more politically difficult changes, including strengthening of the judiciaries as independent institutions (and thus distancing them from political intervention); creation of real career systems (and an eventual reduction of the often arbitrary powers of superior courts and chief judges); modification and updating of basic legislation (including that set by the federal legislature); rationali-

---

7. Carbonell, p. 16.
8. Carbonell, p. 18. Carbonell also indicates an interesting variation within each judiciary. Whereas a Superior Court Justice in the state of Mexico makes about twice the salary (MXP\$613,000) of a First Instance judge, in Baja California the salaries are about equal—MXP\$57,000 and MXP\$53,000.
9. Zepeda.
10. Conducted by the Autonomous University's *Instituto de Investigaciones Juridicas* (UNAM/IIJ). Concha et al.

zation of relations with the federal system (in terms of what cases are handled, possibility of appeals, and initial handling of cases that will go to federal courts); improved legal education for judges, lawyers, and the public; development of specialized formal and alternative services, particularly those expanding access for the poor; and the involvement of a greater variety of stakeholders and potential beneficiaries, as opposed to the current trend of efficient but top-down imposition of change, often by a progressive chief judge and governor.

One advantage of a federal system is the possibility for decentralized experimentation and the development of a variety of alternative models. To a large extent, this is already occurring in Mexico. However, the relative lack of contact among states, despite the presence of an association of state court presidents, makes for less-than-optimal use of the lessons being learned. This is especially critical for the poorer states, where resource constraints and a less-welcoming political environment may impede local experimentation. It is also a concern for the wealthier states to avoid reinventing programs that have already been developed and tested by their neighbors. Although the federal judiciary may play an important role here, it is also likely that neither the federal example nor that of the most-developed states will suit the poorer regions, which face exceptional obstacles and also may require different practices to meet the needs of their more marginalized, larger, rural populations. It goes almost without saying that in poorer states, there are complaints of massive underfunding, corruption, political dependence, lack of access for the poor, an undefined role for community tradition, and a lack of political will for change.

Overview of Other Legal Framework and Ancillary Institutions

Although the focus of this Chapter is the justice sector and the legal framework directly shaping its operations, it is obviously difficult to draw precise boundaries.[11] Mexico, like much of Latin America or civil code countries as a whole, can be criticized for having placed excessive reliance on legal change as a means to improve system performance. Nonetheless, it is generally agreed that while they are in better shape than much of the region, the basic organizational, substantive, and procedural codes and a number of more specific laws could be updated, simplified, and modified to bring them into consistency with contemporary reality. Given the massive task that implies, it would probably be wiser to identify particularly inefficient legally mandated practices for immediate change rather than attempting to take on entire codes at once. Experience with wholesale code reform in other countries suggests that the exercise is not only lengthy, but also often creates as many problems as it resolves when new practices are introduced without

---

11. Issues of substantive legal reform (for example, drafting of new laws and regulations, enforcement of existing laws, modernization of procedural codes), particularly with regard to bankruptcy, secured lending, and other financial and commercial laws, will be covered in the Banking Chapter.

adequate consideration of their intended and unintended results.[12] Experience also suggests that adequate time must be allowed for preparing legal staff and users for the changed practices, and for creating or modifying institutions required for their implementation. When laws go into effect immediately, without such preparation, their effect is often nil.[13] In some cases, this has produced a backlash and the undoing of the attempted changes.

Anecdotal evidence, which is all we have for the most part, also suggests that a part of poor judicial performance is less the responsibility of the judiciary per se than of a series of related organizations and actors. These range from private and state litigators to the police, prosecutors, court administrative staff, registries and the staff maintaining them, and officials charged with enforcing judgments. The shortcomings or absence of additional formal and informal mechanisms found in other countries may also force recourse to courts for conflicts which could be resolved in another manner or might never arise at all. An example common in the literature is the enforcement of contracts and debt collection, where insufficient social controls or inadequate access to basic information (as might be provided by credit bureaus) may force excessive reliance on judicial remedies. Thus before assuming problems in these areas are essentially judicial and looking to judicial reform as the solution, further study will be necessary on their broader nature and causes.[14]

III. Issues

Mexico's past few years of accelerating attention to its justice sector and resulting modernization and reform programs have already resulted in significant change in how the system operates. It is not evident, however, that what has been done or what is contemplated for the near future is making any dent in three major problems:

- Continuing citizen distrust of the judiciary and in fact of the seriousness of efforts to improve the quality and quantity of services it offers.
- Specific weaknesses in internal operations and output (timeliness, relevance, and predictability of decisions, access, transparency, independence, and fair-

---

12. This lesson is especially evident in the adoption of more accusatory criminal procedures codes throughout Latin America. In their haste to make things different, drafters often adopted legislation from other countries without considering its actual impact, or the additional factors (that is, the presence of new organizations, specially trained personnel, different cultural settings) which determine its success.

13. Here there are potent lessons from Eastern Europe and the former Soviet Union, where following several years of massive legal change to create the conditions for a market economy, participants have been vastly disappointed in the consequences. See Pistor, Frydman.

14. See Stone, for a sample of writings on this theme.

ness) which have been the targets of most complaints, and presumably of the reforms.
- The judiciary's reputedly negative impact on extra-system goals—things like economic development, equity, poverty reduction, and political legitimacy.

The three problems are interrelated; their respective solutions are different as is the ease of their execution. Conventional reforms usually address the first two problems, assuming that to the extent they are successful, the third will also be resolved. Unfortunately, the state of the art in judicial reform forces a continuing reliance on that assumption. As noted earlier, while there is every reason to believe that poor judicial performance has broader negative consequences, we are not yet in a position to define the structural characteristics of a "well-functioning" judiciary, nor to identify the causal links between structure, function, and the rate, for example, of economic growth. For the time being, most reforms in Mexico will have to address more immediate complaints about internal operations and output; if these complaints are what genuinely bother citizens (not what reformers assume they want), then the program should also improve their confidence in both the judicial system and the seriousness of reform. As explained below, downstream impacts may be addressed on a very limited, case-by-case basis, or as part of a more widely focused attack (in which the judiciary is only one element) on a series of social ills.

This said, there is still significant room for improvement in ongoing programs. The improvement is essential from the standpoint of optimizing the use of the considerable funds being invested, satisfying citizen demand for change, and ensuring that, however poorly we understand its dimensions, the negative impact of poor performance does not become worse. For the most part, the necessary adjustments have to do with improving the strategy for introducing and implementing change and refining the criteria for selecting and prioritizing reform goals.

Better Information to Support Reform Planning

One critical need, which is just beginning to be addressed, is for more information on system operations, output deficiencies, and the results of purported remedies. Many of the measures introduced early on were based on conventional wisdom and anecdotal evidence as to the nature of performance weaknesses and their proximate causes. Most of them would probably be required eventually, but it is not evident that they have resulted in any visible improvements or that the improvements intended or achieved are those that most matter to current clients or the public at large. Whether from the standpoint of effecting significant change in performance or of increasing citizen confidence, the reforms clearly must be guided by a better understanding of what was wrong in the first place. Experience elsewhere suggests that conventional wisdom is frequently in error in this regard.

Monitoring and Evaluating Results

Whether based on conventional beliefs, theory, or past experience, reform strategies are essentially working hypotheses; thus, their results must be subject to frequent monitoring and evaluation. Little if any of this has been done in Mexico, and more casual observation suggests it is urgently needed. In some instances, programs have already generated negative consequences, suggesting readjustment is in order. Mexican researchers for example argue that an emphasis on moving caseload at the federal level has led to an increase in the percentage of rejected filings, as judges struggle to make their quotas.[15] Measures intended to increase transparency (for example, the elimination of the judges' private offices in some state courts) may have costs in terms of the quality of resolutions, since they also reduce the opportunity for uninterrupted intellectual work. Changes in judicial governance (introduction of judicial councils), appointment systems, and terms of service have, as in other countries, brought mixed results, and in some cases charges that they have merely put a new face on old vices.

Getting the Right Mix of Reform and Modernization

A related issue is the necessity of distinguishing between judicial modernization (where most of the expenditures have been directed) and judicial reform. Where the underlying problem is inefficiencies in an essentially acceptable system, modernization (the introduction of simplified procedures, updating of antiquated codes, new technologies, or upgraded equipment and infrastructure) may be the appropriate solution. However, where the system itself is flawed, more basic changes in the underlying rules of the game are in order. The nature of the complaints about Mexico's judiciary suggests that reform is a necessary part of the equation; unless the rules and incentives behind judicial operations change, no amount of computers, training, or new buildings is going to affect the quality, and even the quantity, of output in the desired directions. What is known about the institutional setting suggests that two kinds of changes will be required: (a) those affecting the relationship between the judiciary and external, especially political, actors; and (b) those defining how individual actors (judges and staff) relate to their roles and organization. There is no simple recipe for designing these changes. They are usually difficult (because they directly affect interests vested in the status quo); can be easily subverted (when adopted in form but not spirit—that is, a "merit" appointment system with many subjective elements, a change in governance mechanisms which merely allows the old forces to reconvene in a new setting); and require a delicate balance between values like independence and accountability, access and efficiency, and predictability and fairness. In addition to the diagnostic information mentioned above, the design of these strategic reform elements can be improved through a review of

---

15. Magaloni.

international experience, comparison of different in-country programs, and expanded consultations with a variety of stakeholders.

Ways to Address Extrasectoral Impacts of Reform

Better information and a focus on reform and modernization needs should improve the chances of producing desired changes in judicial operations—in the direction of such goals as greater transparency, access, efficiency, quality of judgments, and an ability to cope with new levels and types of demands for services. There will obviously be trade-offs among these goals, but here consultations with judges, users, and the broader public will help make wise choices while also increasing confidence in both the judicial system and the reforms. The third problem area, that of system impacts on downstream policy goals, is more difficult—because it is the one about which we know least, either in Mexico or in general. That situation will not soon change, but over the short to medium term there are two practical responses. Although not mutually exclusive, they work at opposite ends of the spectrum.

In the first alternative, reformers focus on very specific complaints—a legal provision which impedes a certain kind of commercial operation, a practice which obstructs the investigation or prosecution of some kind of crime, a procedural rule which causes additional delays in the handling of some kind of case—and make very targeted modifications to address them. Whether over the longer run this will significantly impact the larger value (lower crime rate, higher economic growth) is at best a guess. Still, these targeted remedies, combined with a longer-term reform and modernization strategy, have more chance of satisfying needs than the current recourse to an arbitrary mix of modernizing inputs.

The second option, which attempts to address the downstream impacts more globally, must also define the problems in a global context. The issue here is not to use the judiciary to resolve a nonjudicial situation, but to address that situation through its multiple causes. The problems are big ones—encouraging investment and new forms of economic activity, inequity, poverty, crime, corruption, and so on—and the judiciary's role in impeding their solution is often marginal or highly contingent on the performance of other institutions. Some of these institutions are in the justice sector—for example, a program to reduce crime requires improvements in the performance of police, prosecutors, the private bar, and completely extrasectoral measures such as job creation, education, and expanded social services. Similarly, in the area of contract enforcement, as studies elsewhere have suggested,[16] the judiciary's role is complemented by that of other sectoral institutions, and also by numerous extrasectoral organizations and formal and informal practices. In these and many other cases, if one really wants to resolve the problem, one must first understand how it is currently addressed, and look to changes in a variety of judicial and nonjudicial activities. Working only on the judiciary or on any other single institution is not likely to be effective.

---

16. See Stone.

IV. Policy Options

Mexico has begun its own program of judicial modernization and reform. At the moment there are a number of directions in which it can proceed. The options discussed here are far fewer than the universe of possibilities because they begin with the assumption that the three key problems—citizen mistrust, specific complaints about operations and output, and potentially negative impact on developmental goals—must be addressed more effectively. If this is the case, then such alternatives as dropping the initiative or continuing it in its current form cannot be recommended.

This also means that the issues raised above must be part of any improved policy, and that the acceptable alternative approaches are distinguished by other details. Before proceeding to a discussion of these differences it thus bears emphasizing that the following changes are assumed:

- Support for empirical studies to increase understanding of how the present system operates, the specific nature and dimensions of the operational and output weaknesses assumed to exist, and the internal and external traits and pressures accounting for their presence.
- An inventory of ongoing programs, an evaluation of their consequences, and the adoption of systematic monitoring and evaluation programs for all further work.
- Review of international trends and experience to further inform planning.
- Specification and prioritization of the operational and output changes being sought, on the basis of the diagnostics, stakeholder consultations, and further analysis of feasibility, costs, benefits, and risks.
- Clarification and adoption of the reform ("rule" change) elements that will be needed, in addition to simple modernization, to achieve these revised objectives.
- Efforts to explain and publicize what is being attempted, what is expected as a result and how it will be recognized, and why this course of action is being taken. Most reforms take time, and one way to enhance their chances of success to build a supportive constituency which can survive the inevitable changes of administrations and leaders.

With these as constants, the major differences in the viable options have to do with the entry point, the scope of change attempted, and the extent of coordination among the various state and federal programs.

Entry Point

While Mexico is a federal system, we are assuming a national policy. That policy will vary as to what level of systemic change it pursues first. There are four obvious if not mutually exclusive alternatives:

(i)   A systemic focus which looks at overall operations (state and federal) and tries to rationalize the division of labor among the levels as a first step to improving each one.

(ii) An emphasis on the federal courts first.

(iii) An emphasis on state courts.

(iv) A program of simultaneous change at both levels.

The current program tends toward the latter choice. One concern is that it or alternatives two or three might introduce changes that would later be negated by an eventual redistribution of labor. For this reason, option one should probably be a part of any strategy, although not the major focus. Like an exclusive focus on federal courts, it appears to offer fewer immediate concrete benefits. It may be the planner's ideal, but from the standpoint of citizens who want to see results, either a largely state or combined state and federal emphasis seems best.

One other consideration in selecting an entry point is the likelihood of leveraging further change. This is especially relevant as regards the choice between the federal and state courts. In a unitary system, there are more advantages in using the topmost court—which also heads the entire system. In a federal system this advantage is less obvious. Mexican state courts have followed the federal lead in adopting the recent constitutional changes. However, given differences in resources, needs, and contextual variables between the state and federal levels and among the states, there are limits to the problems a federally generated model can resolve. Thirty-three different change laboratories offer an enviable opportunity for experimentation, but the question remains as to how successes in one will affect trends in the others. The real dilemma may be less where to start, than how to ensure that, at both the federal and state level, the successful models are more widely adopted. This question is addressed below.

Scope of Change Attempted

Most programs attempt to do everything, but a narrower focus may produce results more quickly—and so enhance the chances of a second round of reform. This is more an issue of sequencing than of overall goals—which problems one addresses first to optimize impact, leveraging, and client satisfaction. There are tactical and strategic or technical concerns here, and the tactics must address issues of political support, broader constituencies, and how both can be mobilized over the short and long run. Somehow a balance must be struck between satisfying the immediate and often very limited interests of supporters, and maintaining their involvement in a longer-term effort. Judges and economic leaders are two important constituencies, but once judges get higher salaries and stable tenure, or businessmen get an expedited procedure or a special court to deal with their cases, they could easily defect from the reform alliance. Hence if scope can be too broad, it can also be too narrow. Because the options here are virtually infinite, they are best presented as a series of broad alternatives, ranging from the most widely targeted to the most specific:

(i)   Arming the program as part of an attack on a broader policy issue (for example, crime prevention, improving the investment climate, affording advantages to small entrepreneurs, and conflict reduction) or as a justice reform strategy (and so including other sector institutions). In the former case, the judiciary and even the justice sector would be just one element of the larger program, but reforms in its operations would focus on impacts on the larger issue.

(ii) Focusing on one aspect of sectorwide performance (for example, criminal justice or handling of commercial, social, or administrative issues) or on the judiciary alone.

(iii) Focusing on generic aspects of judicial performance (overall institutional strengthening) or first selecting a more limited number of problem areas (for example, access, corruption, efficiency, delays, or predictability of decisions).

(iv) Focusing on problem areas as they affect all issues and clients or narrowing the emphasis to a limited number of specific concerns and complaints (for example, more efficient handling of child support or debt collection cases, or broadening access for poor rural populations or indigent defendants).

(v)   From the standpoint of tactics, feasibility, and longer-term impact, the two extremes—the broad policy issue or the very targeted remedies—seem less advisable as overall strategy. Both are too diffuse, while the first is also too abstract, and the last excessively concrete. Mexico needs policies for crime control, encouragement of investment, and conflict reduction, but efforts to improve judicial performance will suffer if predicated on those larger programs. Conversely, although any strategy should include remedies for concrete problems, it also has to rise above that level of detail.

The choice among the medium-range alternatives is less clear cut. Depending on the national circumstances there may be advantages to focusing on sector performance in one area (crime and corruption are obvious ones) or on emphasizing one or two areas of specifically judicial weakness. None of the choices is exclusive, but a strategy will attract more support if defined around a few major themes. Institutional strengthening, while implicit in all the alternatives, is thus less useful as a theme than discussions of broadening access, reducing delays, or increasing transparency of decisions. Finally, because we are talking about 33 judicial or justice systems, there is room for considerable variation among them. Goals at the federal and state levels or among states need not be the same—in fact, they probably should be different. However, as discussed in the final section, a national policy may be used to support a more limited number of options, assuming a consensus can be developed as to which ones are most important.

Types of Horizontal and Vertical Coordination

In a federal system there are limits to what national policy can do. Nonetheless, there is the potential for accelerating or consolidating progress, and four principal options for how the overall reform might be orchestrated. They are:

(i) Completely decentralized planning and implementation of reforms—this is the current practice; the federal courts and each state court proceeds according to the priorities set within its respective political system.

(ii) A program sponsored by the national government, the federal judiciary, or by a state courts association to encourage the exchange of information, activities of common interest, or jointly funded studies and pilot projects.

(iii) A centralized program providing funding to state (and federal) courts to carry out reforms or incorporating certain common elements or emphases.

(iv) A centralized program which through funding or some other mechanism provides a reform template for all judiciaries.

Once again the two extremes, absolute decentralization or absolute centralization, seem least desirable. The current absence of any coordination incurs losses due to redundant efforts and the lesser possibility of learning from others successes and mistakes. It also provides no means for encouraging reform in areas where political will is lacking—those areas where reform is most needed. On the other hand, a completely centralized program, which may not be politically feasible, loses the benefits of decentralized experimentation, and violates the principle of the independence of jurisdictions. The two middle-range options deserve further consideration. If judicial reform is a priority of the nation as a whole, then it makes sense to find ways to coordinate efforts.

References

Carbonell, Miguel. (n.d.). "Poder Judicial y Reforma del Estado de México." Unpublished draft. Universidad Nacional Autonoma de Mexico, Instituto de Investigaciones Juridicas.

Concha, Hugo and Antonio Caballero. 2000. Unpublished report on state court systems. Prepared for USAID. UNAM/IIJ.

Cossio Diaz, and Jose Ramon. 1998. *Constitucion, Tribunales y Democracia*. Mexico: Editorial Thesis.

_____. 1996. *Jurisdiccion Federal y Carrera Judicial en México*. Mexico: Universidad Nacional Autonoma de Mexico.

Fernandez Aguirre, Ferman, Fernando Ortiz Arana, and Jose Luis Soberanes. 1997. *La Justicia Mexicana: Hacia el siglo XXI*. Mexico: Universidad Nacional Autonoma de México.

Fix-Fierro, Hector. 1995. *La eficiencia de la Justicia*. Mexico: Universidad Autonoma de México.

Fix-Zamudio, Hector, and Jose Ramon Cossio Diaz. 1996. *El Poder Judicial en el ordenamiento mexicano*. Mexico: Fondo de Cultura Economica.

Frydman, Roman, Cheryl Gray, and Andrzej Rapaczynski, (eds.). 1996. *Corporate Governance in Central Europe and Russia*. Budapest: CEU University Press.

Magaloni, Ana Laura, and Layda Negrete. (n.d.). "El Poder Judicial Federal y su politica de decidir sin resolver." Unpublished draft, Mexico. Centro de Investigacion y Docencia Economicas.

Pistor, Katarina. 1995. "Law Meets the Market: Matches and Mismatches in Transition Economies." Background paper prepared for the *World Development Report*, World Bank, 1996.

Stone, Andrew, Brian Levy, and Ricardo Paredes. 1996. "Public Institutions and Private Transactions: A Comparative Analysis of the Legal and Regulatory Environment for Business Transactions in Brazil and Chile." In Lee J. Alston, Thrainn Eggertsson, and Douglass North, (eds.), *Empirical Studies in Institutional Change*. Cambridge: Cambridge University Press.

Zepeda Lecuona, Guillermo R. 1995. "Analisis economico de los costos de acceso a la justicia en los ambitos federal y local (Estado de Jalisco)." *Revista de la Facultad de Derecho de México*, XLV, 201–202, May–August, pp. 41–78.

05/30/2001   11:47 AM
Receipt# 21036034   Sales ID 204167
            B - Bank Staff

SKU Title/Description	List	Quan @ Price Ext Amount
14914	65.00	45.50
Mexico		45.50

Gross Sale	1	65.00
Less Discount		-19.50
Total		45.50

Master/Visa - 543643000001XXX   45.50